SOCIAL THEORY
AND
SOCIAL STRUCTURE

Revised and Enlarged Edition

Social Theory and

ROBERT K. MERTON

Social Structure

REVISED
AND ENLARGED EDITION

THE FREE PRESS OF GLENCOE
Collier-Macmillan Limited, London

Designed by Sidney Solomon

ROBERT K. MERTON

Social Structure

REVISED
AND ENLARGED EDITION

THE FREE PRESS OF GLENCOE

Collier-Macmillan Limited, London

Designed by Sidney Solomon

To the Memory of Charles H. Hopkins,
Friend, Teacher and Kin

PREFACE TO
THE REVISED EDITION

Somewhat more than a third of its contents is new to this edition. The principal changes consist of four new chapters and of two bibliographic postscripts reviewing recent developments in the subject dealt with in the chapters to which they are appended. I have also tried to improve the exposition at various places in the book by rewriting paragraphs which were not as clear as they ought to have been and I have eliminated several insipid errors which should never have been made.

Of the four chapters, added to this edition, two come from published symposia, one of which is out of print and the other of which, I am told, is nearing that same state of exhaustion. "Patterns of Influence," which first appeared in *Communications Research, 1948-49* (P. F. Lazarsfeld and F. N. Stanton, editors), is part of a continuing series of studies by the Columbia University Bureau of Applied Social Research dealing with the role of personal influence in society. This chapter sets forth the concept of 'the influential,' identifies two distinctive types of influentials, the 'local' and the 'cosmopolitan,' and relates these types to the structure of influence in the local community. The second of these chapters, "Contributions to the Theory of Reference Group Behavior," was written in collaboration with Mrs. Alice S. Rossi and was originally published in *Continuities in Social Research* (R. K. Merton and P. F. Lazarsfeld, editors). It draws upon the ample evidence provided by *The American Soldier* to formulate certain conditions under which people orient themselves to the norms of various groups, in particular the groups with which they are not affiliated.

The other two chapters added to this edition have not been published before. The first of these, "Continuities in the Theory of Social Structure and Anomie," tries to consolidate recent empirical and theoretical analyses of the sources and consequences of that breakdown of social norms which is described as anomie. The second, "Continuities in the Theory of Reference Groups and Social Structure," tries to bring out some of the specifically sociological, as distinct from the socio-

psychological, implications of current inquiries into reference-group behavior. The intent is to examine some of the theoretical problems of
social structure which must be solved before certain further advances
can be made in the sociological analysis of reference groups.

The bibliographical postscripts are concerned briefly with functional
analysis in sociology and, at some length, with the role of Puritanism in
the development of modern science.

I owe special thanks to Dr. Elinor Barber and Mrs. Marie Klink
for help in reading proofs and to Mrs. Bernice Zelditch for preparing
the index. In revising this book, I have benefitted from a small grant-in-
aid provided by the Behavioral Sciences Program of the Ford Foundation as part of its roster of grants without prior restrictions to a specified
'project.'

R. K. M.

Hastings-on-Hudson, New York
Thanksgiving Day, 1956

ACKNOWLEDGMENTS

No MAN KNOWS fully what has shaped his own thinking. It is difficult for me to trace in detail the provenience of the conceptions set forth in this book, and to track down the reasons for their progressive modifications as I have worked with them over the years. Many social scientists have contributed to the development of these conceptions and whenever the source is known, reference is made in the numerous notes to the separate chapters. But among these, there are six to whom I owe an especial debt, though of varying degree and kind, and to them I want to pay tribute.

The earliest and greatest of these debts is slightly and too late acknowledged in the dedication of this book to Charles H. Hopkins. Because this man, the husband of my sister, lived, many lives were deepened in human dignity. As long as any of us whose lives touched his still live, he will live. It is with love and respect and gratitude that I dedicate this book to Hop, who learned for himself that he might teach others.

To my good friend, George Eaton Simpson, now of Oberlin College, I am grateful for having taken a brash sophomore in hand to make him *see* the intellectual excitement of studying the operation of systems of social relations. I could not easily have had a more propitious introduction to sociology.

Before he became absorbed in the study of historical movements on the grand scale as represented in his *Social and Cultural Dynamics*, Pitirim A. Sorokin helped me escape from the provincialism of thinking that effective studies of society were confined within American borders and from the slum-encouraged provincialism of thinking that the primary subject-matter of sociology was centered in such peripheral problems of social life as divorce and juvenile delinquency. I gladly acknowledge this honest debt, still not discharged.

To George Sarton, most esteemed among historians of science, I am thankful for friendship as well as guidance, and for the privilege of having been allowed to work the greater part of two years in his famed workshop at Harvard Library 189. Some small sign of his stimulus will be found in Part IV of this book, devoted to studies in the sociology of science.

Those who read the following pages will soon recognize the great debt I owe to my teacher and friend, Talcott Parsons, who so early in his teaching career conveyed his enthusiasm for analytical theory to so many. The measure of his calibre as a teacher is found in his having stirred up intellectual enthusiasm, rather than creating obedient disciples. In the intellectual intimacy afforded by the *small* graduate department of sociology at Harvard in the early 1930's, it was possible for a graduate student, like myself, to have close and continued working relations with an instructor, like Dr. Parsons. It was indeed a collegium, today not easily found in departments numbering many score of graduate students and a small, hard-driven group of professors.

In recent years, while we have worked in double harness in the Columbia University Bureau of Applied Social Research, I have learned most from Paul F. Lazarsfeld. Since it is evident from our countless conversations that he has no conception of the full extent of my intellectual debt to him, I am especially happy to have this occasion for forcing it upon his attention in public. Not least valuable to me has been his sceptical curiosity which has compelled me to articulate more fully than I might otherwise have done my reasons for considering functional analysis the presently most promising, though not the only, theoretical orientation to a wide range of problems of human society. And above all, he has, through his own example, reinforced in myself the conviction that the great difference between social science and social dilettantism resides in the systematic and *serious,* that is to say, the intellectually responsible and austere, pursuit of what is first entertained as an interesting idea. This, I take it, is what Whitehead also means by the closing lines of the passage in the epigraph to this book.

There are four others who need little acknowledgment: one, because all who know me know my great obligation to her; the other three, because they will in due course discover for themselves the precise nature of my considerable obligation to them.

CONTENTS
— AN OVERVIEW

TABLE OF CONTENTS

SOCIAL THEORY
AND
SOCIAL STRUCTURE

Revised and Enlarged Edition

INTRODUCTION

"A science which hesitates to forget its founders is lost."
"It is characteristic of a science in its earlier stages
. . . to be both ambitiously profound in its aims and
trivial in its handling of details."
"But to come very near to a true theory, and to grasp
its precise application, are two very different things,
as the history of science teaches us. Everything of
importance has been said before by somebody who
did not discover it."

ALFRED NORTH WHITEHEAD,
The Organisation of Thought.

A T THEIR FIRST WRITING, the papers which make up this book
were not intended as consecutive chapters of a single volume. It would
be idle to suggest, therefore, that the papers as now arranged exhibit a
natural progression, leading with stern inevitability from one to the next.
Yet I am reluctant to believe that the book lacks altogether the logical,
and not merely literary, graces of coherence, unity and emphasis.

To make the coherence easily visible, the book is divided into four
major parts—the first setting out a theoretical orientation in terms of
which three types of sociological problems are thereafter examined. Brief
introductions to each of the major sections are intended to make it unnecessary for the reader to find for himself a means of intellectual passage
from one part to the next.

In the interest of unity, the papers have been assembled with an eye
to the gradual unfolding and developing of two sociological concerns
which pervade the whole of the book, concerns more fully expressed in
the perspective found in all chapters than in the particular subject-matter
under discussion. These are, first, the concern with the interplay of social
theory and social research and, second, the concern with progressively
codifying both substantive theory and the procedures of sociological
analysis, most particularly of qualitative analysis.

It will be granted that these two interests do not suffer from excessive
modesty of dimensions. In fact, were I to hint that the essays do more
than skirt the edges of these large and imperfectly charted territories,
the very excess of the claim would only emphasize the smallness of the
yield. But since the consolidation of theory and research and the codification of theory and method are the two concerns threaded through the
chapters of this book, it may be useful to discuss each by way of general
introduction.

CONSOLIDATION OF SOCIAL THEORY AND RESEARCH

This announced interest in consolidating the reciprocal relations between social theory and social research is suspiciously irreproachable. Where will one find a social scientist disclaiming the desirability of the "integration" of theory and empirical research? Unless it is given some special force, this position will possess the same measure of trivial truth as the position held by Calvin Coolidge's preacher who was unexceptionably "against sin."

If it is to be more than another announcement of conventional faith, this interest in consolidation must be made *specific* and must be *concretely exemplified.* The three chapters in Part I are designed toward this end. Implicit in these programmatic chapters is a point of view found repeatedly throughout the book which it may be useful to summarize briefly.[1]

History of Theory and Systematics of Theory

Despite their many references to the writings of sociologists of the last few generations, these chapters deal not with the *history* of sociological theory but with the *systematics* of certain theories with which sociologists now provisionally work. The attractive but fatal confusion of utilizable sociological theory with the history of sociological theory— who said what by way of speculation or hypothesis?—should long since have been dispelled by recognizing their very different functions. After all, schools of medicine do not confuse the history of medicine with current medical knowledge, nor do departments of biology identify the history of biology with the viable theory now employed in guiding and interpreting biological research. Once said, this seems obvious enough to be embarrassing. Yet the extraordinary fact is that in sociology, this plain distinction between the history of theory and currently operating theory has in many places not caught hold—at least, if we may judge from curricula and publications.

---

1. The next few pages are a paraphrase and extension of my paper discussing "the position of sociological theory" as published in *American Sociological Review*, 1948, 13, 164-168. For apposite observations on the role of the *history* of social thought as distinct from that of currently viable sociological theory, see Howard Becker, "Vitalizing sociological theory," *ibid.*, 1954, 19, 377-388, esp. 379-81. A somewhat different view of the nature and functions of social theory will be found in Theodore Abel, "The present status of social theory," *ibid.*, 1952, 17, 156-164, in the discussion of this paper by Kenneth E. Bock and Stephen W. Reed, 164-67; and in Herbert Blumer, "What is wrong with social theory," *ibid.*, 1954, 19, 3-10. An overview of current sociology in the light of sustained theory is provided by Kingsley Davis, *Human Society* (New York: Macmillan, 1949), and an overview of the history of sociological thought in the recent work of N. S. Timasheff, *Sociological Theory: Its Nature and Growth* (New York: Random House, Inc., 1954), and in E. F. Borgatta and H. J. Meyer (editors), *Sociological Theory* (New York: A. A. Knopf, 1956).

The assumption underlying the opening chapters of this book is to the contrary: although the history and the systematics of sociological theory should both be of concern in training sociologists, this is no reason for merging and confusing the two. Systematic sociological theory, as characterized in Chapters II and III, represents the highly selective accumulation of those small parts of earlier theory which have thus far survived the tests of empirical research. But the history of theory includes also the far greater mass of conceptions which fell to bits when confronted with empirical test. It includes also the false starts, the archaic doctrines and the fruitless errors of the past. Though acquaintance with all this may be a useful adjunct to the sociologist's training, it is no substitute for training in the actual use of theory in research. We can with profit study much of what the forefathers of sociology wrote as exercises in the conduct of intellectual inquiry, but this is quite another matter.

The clearly visible fact is that the early history of sociology—as represented, for example, in the speculations of a Comte or a Spencer, a Hobhouse or a Ratzenhofer—is very far from cumulative. The conceptions of each seldom build upon the work of those who have gone before. They are typically laid out as alternative and competing conceptions rather than consolidated and extended into a cumulative product. Consequently, little of what these early forerunners wrote remains pertinent to sociology today. Their works testify to the large merits of talented men, but they do not often provide guidelines to the current analysis of sociological problems. They were grand achievements for their day, but that day is not ours. We sociologists of today may be only intellectual pigmies but, unlike the overly-modest Newton, we are not pigmies standing on the shoulders of giants. The accumulative tradition is still so slight that the shoulders of the giants of sociological science do not provide a very solid base on which to stand. Whitehead's apothegm, affixed to the masthead of this introduction, is therefore all the more binding on sociology than on those physical sciences which have a larger measure of selectively accumulative advance: "a science which hesitates to forget its founders is lost."

Theories of the Middle Range

Like so many words which are bandied about, the word *theory* threatens to become emptied of meaning. The very diversity of items to which the word is applied leads to the result that it often obscures rather than creates understanding. Throughout this book, and quite explicitly in Part I, the term *sociological theory* refers to logically interconnected conceptions which are limited and modest in scope, rather than all-embracing and grandiose. Throughout I attempt to focus attention on what might be called *theories of the middle range*: theories intermediate to the minor working hypotheses evolved in abundance during the day-by-day routines of research, and the all-inclusive speculations comprising a master conceptual scheme from which it is hoped to derive a very large number of empirically observed uniformities of social behavior.

In these essays, it must be admitted, I assume that the search for a total system of sociological theory, in which all manner of observations promptly find their preordained place, has the same large challenge and the same small promise as those all-encompassing philosophical systems which have fallen into deserved disuse. There are some who talk as though they expect, here and now, formulation of *the* sociological theory adequate to encompass vast ranges of precisely observed details of social behavior and fruitful enough to direct the attention of thousands of research workers to pertinent problems of empirical research. This I take to be a premature and apocalyptic belief. We are not ready. The preparatory work has not yet been done.

A sense of historical development may be sufficiently humbling to liberate these extravagant optimists from this clearly premature hope. Even they would not have expected Einstein to follow hard on the heels of Kepler. This could not be. Intervening centuries of research and systematic thought about the results of research were first needed to prepare the terrain. By all this I do not mean that sociology must uncritically adopt modest expectations simply because their elder and more experienced siblings among the sciences have done so with profit. Here, as elsewhere, unthinking imitation has little to commend it. But there are some pertinent features of the history of physical science which, properly understood, can be both instructive and encouraging. A proper appreciation of these would keep social scientists from permitting the very existence of the highly developed physical sciences to evoke these large and excessively optimistic hopes. We social scientists happen to live at a time in which some of the physical sciences have achieved comparatively great precision of theory and experiment, a great aggregate of instruments and tools, and an abundance of technological by-products. Looking about them, many social scientists take this as the standard for self-appraisal. Understandably, they want to compare biceps with their bigger brothers. They, too, want to *count*. And when it becomes evident to all who would look that they neither have the rugged physique nor pack the murderous wallop of their big brothers, the youngsters become afflicted with despair. They begin to ask: is a science of society *really* possible?

Not only would it be more modest and more realistic but also, perhaps, psychologically more rewarding to note the difference in age and hard-won experience. To perceive difference here would be to achieve proportion. It would be to avoid the error of assuming that *all cultural products existing at the same moment of history must have the same degree of intellectual maturity*. Because a discipline called physics and a discipline called sociology are both identifiable in the mid-twentieth century, it is gratuitously assumed that the achievements of the one must be the measure of the other. But this is to ignore the distinctive fore-history of each: between twentieth-century physics and twentieth-century sociology stand billions of man-hours of sustained, disciplined, and cumulative research. Perhaps sociology is not yet ready for its Einstein because it has not yet found its Kepler. Even the nonpareil Newton had, in his day, acknowledged the indispensable contribution of cumulative research, saying: "If I have seen farther, it is by standing on the shoulders of giants."

Nor is the comparison with the physical sciences the only source of this conviction among some sociologists that we must, here and now, achieve theoretical schemes on the grand scale. This belief, as premature as it is challenging, is, I believe, in part a response to the ambiguous status of sociology in contemporary West-European and American societies. (The present status of sociology in other societies is an altogether different matter: there, it is more difficult to identify the existence of sociology at all than to determine the functions of what little sociology does exist.) The very uncertainty of having accumulated knowledge adequate to the large demands now being laid upon sociology—by policy-makers, reformers and reactionaries, by business men and government men, by college presidents and college sophomores—this uncertainty provokes an overly-zealous and defensive conviction among sociologists that they must somehow be equal to these demands, however premature and extravagant they may be.

Despite its psychological functions for the social scientist, this conviction involves the error of supposing that competence means adequacy to *any and all* demands, just or unjust, wise or stupid, which are made of him. Implicitly, it is the sacrilegious and masochistic error of assuming oneself to be omniscient. In effect, this belief holds that to admit less than universal knowledge is to admit failure. So it often happens in the early phases of a fledgling discipline that its exponents typically make extravagant claims to having evolved total systems of theory, adequate to the entire range of problems encompassed by the discipline. As White-head has observed in the passage I have taken as an epigraph for this book, "It is characteristic of a science in its earlier stages . . . to be both ambitiously profound in its aims and trivial in its handling of details."

Complete sociological systems today, as in their day complete systems of medical theory or of chemical theory, must give way to less imposing but better grounded theories of the middle range. We cannot expect any individual to create an architectonic system of theory providing a manual for the solution of problems, social and sociological. Science, even socio-logical science, isn't that simple.

Like the social scientist who errs in thoughtlessly comparing himself with the *contemporary* physical scientist because of the accident that they both happen to be alive at the same instant of history, so the informed public, and strategic decision-makers in that public, often err in appraising social science, once and for all, on the basis of its present capacity to solve the large and urgent problems of society which press in on all of us. The misplaced masochism of the social scientist and the inadvertent sadism of the public both result from the same fault: failure to see that social science, like all civilization, is continually in the process of development and that there is no providential dispensation providing that, at any given moment, science must be adequate to the entire array of problems confronting men at that moment. Historical perspective might enable scientist and layman alike to see these facts of repeated experience in their fitting proportion. Otherwise it is as though the status and promise of medicine in the seventeenth century had been forever judged by its ability to produce, then and there, a preventive or cure for cardiac diseases. Suppose that the problem had been widely acknowledged to be urgent—look at the growing rate of death from coronary thrombosis!—and it might well have been that the very importance of the problem would have obscured the *entirely independent question* of the adequacy of the medical science of 1600 (or 1800 or 1900) for solving that particular problem. Yet it is precisely this illogic which lies behind so much of practical demands currently made of sociology (and the other social sciences). Because war and exploitation and poverty and discrimination and psychological insecurity are plaguing men in modern society, social science, if it is worth its salt, must provide solutions for each and all of them. It is possible, of course, that social scientists are as well equipped to solve these urgent problems *in 1955* as were Harvey or Sydenham to identify, study and cure coronary thrombosis *in 1655.* Yet, as history shows, the inadequacy of seventeenth century medicine in coping with this particular problem scarcely meant that it had no powers of development. If everyone were to back the sure thing, who would support the colt yet to come into his own?

This emphasis on the disproportion between the practical problems sometimes assigned the sociologist and the state of his accumulated skills and knowledge does not at all mean, of course, that the sociologist *should not* work on researches relevant for urgent practical problems, that he should deliberately seek out the pragmatically trivial problem. The emphasis is intended only to re-establish a historical sense of proportion. The urgency or immensity of a practical social problem does not entail the assurance of its solution. At any given moment, men are variously equipped to solve various problems. It should be remembered that, even by repeated popular testimony, necessity is only the mother of invention; socially accumulated knowledge is its father. Unless the two are brought together, necessity remains infertile. Yet present infertility does not mean that she may not conceive at some future time when she is properly mated. But the mate requires time (and sustenance) if he is to grow to the size and vigor needed for the demands which will be laid upon him.

From all this it would seem reasonable to suppose that sociology will advance in the degree that its major concern is with developing theories of the middle range and will be frustrated if attention centers on theory in the large. I believe that our major task *today* is to develop special theories applicable to limited ranges of data—theories, for example, of class dynamics, of conflicting group pressures, of the flow of power and the exercise of interpersonal influence—rather than to seek at once the "integrated" conceptual structure adequate to derive all these and other theories. The sociological theorist *exclusively* committed to the exploration of high abstractions runs the risk that, as with modern *décor*, the furniture of his mind will be sparse, bare, and uncomfortable. To say that both the general and the special theories are needed is to be correct and banal: the problem is one of allocating our scant resources. I am suggesting that the road to effective conceptual schemes in sociology will be the more effectively built through work on special theories, and that it will remain a largely unfulfilled plan, if one seeks to build it directly at this time. So it is that in his inaugural address at the University of London, T. H. Marshall has lately put in a plea for "sociological stepping stones in the middle distance."

That this emphasis may be needed can be seen from a review of books on sociological theory. Note how few, how scattered and, it must be said, how unimpressive the instances of specific sociological hypotheses which are *derived* from a master conceptual scheme. The basic theory (or speculation) runs so far ahead of confirmed special theories as to remain an unrealized program rather than a *consolidation* of apparently discrete theories. This is no dirge. As Talcott Parsons has indicated, much progress has lately been made. The gradual convergence of some streams of theory in social psychology, social anthropology and sociology promises large theoretic gains. Yet, having said this, one must admit that a large part of what is now called sociological theory consists of *general orientations toward data, suggesting types of variables which need somehow to be taken into account, rather than clear, verifiable statements of relationships between specified variables.*[2] We have many concepts but few confirmed theories; many points of view, but few theorems; many "approaches," but few arrivals. Perhaps a shift in emphasis would be all to the good.

Sociological theory must advance on these interconnected planes:

---

2. This observation is somewhat amplified in Chapter II. For a recent suggestion that convergence rather than continued division has characterized recent developments in sociological theory, see George A. Lundberg, "The natural science trend in sociology," *American Journal of Sociology*, 1955, 61, 191-202. It must be acknowledged, however, that in substantial measure the convergence is that of general orientation rather than that of sociological theory. But manifestly, not everything can happen at once; the gain in convergence is real even though it is partial rather than complete.

through special theories adequate to limited ranges of social data, and through the evolution of a more general conceptual scheme adequate to *consolidate* groups of special theories.

To concentrate entirely on special theories is to run the risk of emerging with unconnected *ad hoc* speculations consistent with a limited range of observations and inconsistent among themselves.

To concentrate entirely on the master conceptual scheme for deriving all subsidiary theories is to run the risk of producing twentieth-century sociological equivalents of the large philosophical systems of the past, with all their varied suggestiveness, all their architectonic splendor and all their scientific sterility.

Men allocate their scant resources somehow, whether they know it or not, and this allocation reflects their workaday policies. This holds as much for the men concerned with the production of sociological theory as for the men concerned with the production of plumbing supplies. These observations, elicited by Parsons' paper on the position of sociological theory,[3] are intended to bring out one such policy decision faced by the men who practice sociological theory. Which shall have the greater share of our immediate energies and resources: the search for confirmed theories of the middle range or the search for all-inclusive conceptual schemes? I believe, and beliefs are of course notoriously subject to error, that for some time to come, it is the theories of the middle range which hold the largest promise,[4] *provided that,* underlying this modest search for social uniformities, there is an enduring and pervasive concern with *consolidating* the special theories into a more general set of concepts and mutually consistent propositions. Even so, we must adopt the provisional outlook of our big brothers, remembering with them, as with Tennyson, that

> Our little systems have their day;
> They have their day and cease to be.

---

3. This refers to the paper later re-printed as Chapter I of Talcott Parsons, *Essays in Sociological Theory: Pure and Applied* (Glencoe, The Free Press, 1949); for further discussion, see Chapter XVII of the revised edition, 1954.

4. For a careful formulation of logical requirements of theories of the middle range, see Hans L. Zetterberg, *On Theory and Verification in Sociology* (Stockholm: Almqvist & Wiksell; New York: The Tressler Press, 1954); for observations on the distinctive characteristics of theories of the middle range, see Frank H. Hankins, "A forty-year perspective," *Sociology and Social Research,* 1956, 40, 391-98; Jiri Nehnevajsa, "Reflections on theories and sociometric systems," *International Journal of Sociometry,* 1956, 1, 8-15; Peter H. Rossi, "Methods of social research, 1945-55," in *Sociology in the United States of America: A Trend Report,* edited by Hans L. Zetterberg (Unesco, 1956), 21-34, esp. at 23 ff. It should be noted, however, that the empirical testability of theories of the middle range is not their only or their major attribute. Rather, it is the double fact that the concepts in such theories involve a middling level of generality: that they are specific enough to be effectively utilized in organizing the evidence bearing upon determinate ranges of social phenomena and general enough to be consolidated into increasingly broader sets of generalizations.

The Theoretic Orientation

Though impeccable in purpose, the objective of consolidating sociological theory and research remains sterile in performance until it is brought down to cases. This requires us to attend to questions of this order: Which theoretic orientation is provisionally adopted as a point of departure? And on what grounds is the choice made? How has this theoretic orientation served to guide and to illuminate empirical research? How, indeed, has sociological theory of whatever kind shaped empirical research and, reciprocally, how has empirical research affected sociological theory? Having first indicated the character of my theoretic orientation, then, I want to examine its actual workings, and to set out the varied interrelations between it and research. This is in substance the further assignment for Part I of this book.

Chapter I, one of the three essays in the book which have not been published before, attempts to lay out the foundations and framework of the kind of social theory called functional analysis. A fragment from a larger work which will take more years for maturation, this brief discussion is centered in a paradigm of functional analysis, codifying the assumptions, concepts and procedures which have been implicit (and, at some points, explicit) in functional interpretations in the fields of sociology, social psychology and social anthropology. If the large connotations of the word *discovery* are abandoned, then it can be said that, in large part, the elements of the paradigm have been *discovered*, not *invented*. In part, they have been found by critically scrutinizing the researches and theoretic discussions of those who cultivate the functional approach to the behavior of men in society. For the rest, they have grown out of my own studies of social structure.

It is this framework of functional analysis which has variously guided the writing of all papers in this volume.

The two chapters following, the one dealing with the functions of theory for research and the other, with the functions of research for theory, are intended to summarize the types of reciprocal relations between theory and research presently obtaining in sociological inquiry.

Chapter II distinguishes the related but distinct types of inquiry which are caught up in the vague term *sociological theory:* methodology or the logic of procedure, general orientations, analysis of concepts, *ex post facto* interpretations, empirical generalizations, and theory proper. In describing the interconnections between these—the fact that they are interconnected implies that they are also distinct—I seek to emphasize the limitations as well as the functions of general theoretic orientations, with which sociology is more abundantly endowed than it is with theoretically derived and empirically confirmed specific propositions. So, too, the importance as well as the halfway character of the empirical generalization in sociology is stressed throughout. It is there suggested that through theoretical *codification,* these disparate empirical generalizations must be revamped, collated and consolidated. They then become special cases of a general rule.

Chapter III examines the other direction of this reciprocal relation between theory and research: the diverse kinds of impact of research data upon the development of social theory. Only those who merely *read about* rather than *engage* in the activities of empirical research can continue to believe that the exclusive, or even primary, function of research is to test pre-established hypotheses. This represents an obvious and essential but narrow function of empirical research. Research plays a far more active role than is implied by this essentially passive function. As this chapter states at some length, empirical research also *initiates, reformulates, re-focusses, and clarifies* the theories and conceptions of sociology. And in the measure that observation thus directs and fructifies the development of theory, it is evident that the theorist who is remote from all research, of which he learns only by hearsay as it were, runs the risk of being insulated from the very experiences most likely to turn his attention in fruitful directions. His mind has not been prepared by experience. He is, above all, removed from the type of disciplined empirical observation which sometimes leads to *serendipity,* the discovery through chance by a theoretically prepared mind of valid findings which were not sought for. Weber was probably right in subscribing to the view that one need not be Caesar, in order to understand Caesar. But there is a temptation for sociological theorists to act sometimes as though in order to understand Caesar, it is not necessary even to study Caesar.

The three chapters comprising Part I, then, are together devoted to an overview of some methods employed by the sociological theorist in the course of his theorizing, in the course, that is, of his provisionally adopting concepts and hypotheses which emerge from and are re-subjected to confrontation with the empirical data of disciplined observation.

CODIFICATION OF SOCIOLOGICAL THEORY

The second major concern permeating the whole of this volume is that of codification, particularly the codification of substantive theory and of procedures of qualitative analysis in sociology. (Though there is no inherent reason why this should be the case, functional analysis in sociology has to this point been almost entirely qualitative in character.)

Codification involves orderly, disciplined reflection. As noted earlier in this introduction, it entails the *discovery* of what has in fact been the strategic experience of scientific investigators, rather than the *invention* of new strategies of research. But the discovery of the one may facilitate the invention of the other. As here construed, codification is the orderly and compact arrangement of systematized fruitful experience with procedures of inquiry and with the substantive findings which result from the use of these procedures.

At periodic points in the book, I use the device of the *analytical paradigm* for presenting codified materials: in the first chapter, dealing with functional analysis; in Chapter IV, presenting an analysis of deviant social behavior; and in Chapter XII, critically reviewing research and theory in the sociology of knowledge.[5]

Something should be said by way of explanation about the repeated use of formal paradigms such as these. I believe them to have great propaedeutic value. For one thing, they bring out into the open air for all to see the array of assumptions, concepts and basic propositions employed in a sociological analysis. They thus minimize the inadvertent tendency to hide the hard core of analysis behind a veil of random and logically unconnected thoughts, ruminations and comments. Sociology has few formulae, in the sense of highly abbreviated symbolic expressions of relationships between sociological variables. Consequently, sociological interpretations come to be highly discursive. The logic of procedure, the key concepts, and the relationships between variables not uncommonly become lost in an avalanche of words. They are then obscured from the reader and, at times, from the author as well, and in these instances, the critical reader must laboriously search out for himself the implicit assumptions of the author. The paradigm minimizes this tendency of the sociological theorist to deceive himself and others by the careless and unwitting employment of tacit concepts and assumptions.

Contributing to this tendency of sociological exposition to become lengthy rather than lucid is the received tradition—inherited slightly from philosophy, substantially from history, and greatly from literature—which holds that sociological accounts should be written vividly and intensely, conveying all the rich fullness of the human scene with which they deal. The sociologist who does not disavow this handsome but alien heritage becomes more intent on expressing the full individuality of his *response* to the sociological case in hand than on seeking out the generalizable, objective and readily transmissible concepts and relationships pertinent to that case. In place of using objective concepts—the very core of a science as distinct from the arts—the sociologist who depends on his heritage from the humanities searches for the exceptional constellation of words which will best express the particularity of his experience. Too

---

5. I have set forth analytic paradigms in papers not re-printed in this volume: "Intermarriage and the social structure: fact and theory," *Psychiatry,* 1941, 4, 361-374; and "Discrimination and the American Creed," in *Discrimination and National Welfare,* edited by R. M. MacIver (New York, Harper & Brothers, 1948).

often, he is confirmed in this misplaced use of his genuine artistic skills by the plaudits of a lay public, gratefully assuring him that he writes like a novelist and not like an overly-domesticated and academically hen-pecked Ph.D. Not infrequently, and of course not always, he pays for this popular applause, for the closer he approaches eloquence, the farther he retreats from sense. It must be acknowledged, however, as St. Augustine suggested in mild rebuttal long ago, that ". . . a thing is not necessarily true because badly uttered, nor false because spoken magnificently."

Thus it is that ostensibly scientific reports become obscured by inclusion of the irrelevant. In extreme cases, the hard skeleton of fact, inference and theoretic conclusion becomes overlaid with the soft flesh of stylistic ornamentation. Yet other disciplines—physics and chemistry are here in company with biology, geology and statistics—have escaped this misplaced concern with the literary graces. Anchored to the purposes of science, these disciplines prefer brevity, precision and objectivity to exquisitely rhythmic patterns of language, richness of connotation and deep-felt verbal imagery. Because one does not subscribe to the unthinking doctrine that sociology must in all respects hew to the line laid down by chemistry, physics, or biology, one need not subscribe to the contrary doctrine that it must emulate history, discursive philosophy or literature. Each to his last, and the last of the sociologist is that of lucidly presenting claims to logically interconnected and empirically confirmed propositions about the behavior of man in his relations with other men, and the social consequences of that behavior. Paradigms for sociological analysis are intended to help the sociologist work at his trade.

Since sound sociological interpretation inevitably *implies* some theoretic paradigm, it seems the better part of wisdom to bring it out into the open. If true art consists in concealing all signs of art, true science consists in revealing its scaffolding as well as its finished structure.

Without pretending that this tells the whole story, I suggest that paradigms for qualitative analysis in sociology have at least five closely related functions.[6]

First, paradigms have a notational function. They provide a compact parsimonious arrangement of the central concepts and their interrelations as these are utilized for description and analysis. Having one's concepts set out in sufficiently brief compass to permit their *simultaneous* inspection is an important aid to self-correction of one's successive interpretations, a result difficult to achieve when one's concepts are scattered and hidden in page after page of discursive exposition. (As may be seen from

---

6. The next few pages are a paraphrase and extension of the appendix to the paper on "Discrimination and the American creed," *op. cit.* For other discussions of the use of qualitative paradigms in sociology, see P. F. Lazarsfeld, "Some remarks on the typological procedure in social research," *Zeitschrift für Sozialforschung*, 1937, 6, 119-139; C. G. Hempel and P. Oppenheim, *Der Typusbegriff im Lichte der neuen Logik* (Leiden, A. W. Sijthoff, 1936), esp. 44-101.

the work of Cajori on their history, this appears to be one of the major reasons for the importance of mathematical symbols: they permit the simultaneous inspection of all terms entering into the analysis.)

Second, the explicit statement of analytic paradigms lessens the likelihood of inadvertently importing hidden assumptions and concepts, since each new assumption and each new concept must be either logically *derivable* from the previous terms of the paradigm or explicitly *incorporated* in it. The paradigm thus supplies a pragmatic and logical guide for the avoidance of *ad hoc* (*i.e.,* logically irresponsible) hypotheses.

Third, paradigms advance the *cumulation* of theoretical interpretation. In this connection, we can regard the paradigm as the foundation upon which the house of interpretations is built. If a new story cannot be built directly upon the paradigmatic foundations, if it cannot be derived from the foundations, then it must be considered a new wing of the total structure, and the foundations (of concepts and assumptions) must be extended to support the new wing. Moreover, each new story which *can* be built upon the original foundations strengthens our confidence in their substantial quality just as every new extension, precisely because it requires additional foundations, leads us to suspect the soundness of the original substructure. To pursue the figure further: a paradigm in which we can justifiably repose great confidence will in due course support an interpretative structure of skyscraper dimensions, with each successive story testifying to the substantial and well-laid quality of the original foundations, whereas a defective paradigm will support only a rambling one-story structure, in which each new set of observations requires a new foundation to be laid, since the original cannot bear the weight of additional stories.

Fourth, paradigms, by their very arrangement, suggest the *systematic* cross-tabulation of presumably significant concepts and may thus sensitize the analyst to types of empirical and theoretic problems which might otherwise be overlooked. They promote *analysis* rather than concrete description. They direct our attention, for example, to the components of social behavior, to possible strains and tensions among these components, and thereby to sources of departure from the behavior which is socially expectable.

Fifth, and in this accounting, finally, paradigms make for the codification of methods of *qualitative* analysis in a manner approximating the logical, if not the empirical, rigor of *quantitative* analysis. The procedures for computing a standard deviation and the mathematical bases of these procedures are expressly codified as a matter of course: they are open to inspection by all, and the assumptions and procedures can be critically scrutinized by all who care to read. In frequent contrast to this public character of codified quantitative analysis, the sociological analysis of qualitative data is assumed to reside in a private world inhabited exclusively by penetrating but unfathomable insights and by ineffable understandings. Indeed, discursive expositions not based upon an explicit paradigm often involve perceptive interpretations; as the cant phrase has it, they are rich in "illuminating insights." But it is not always clear just which operations with analytic concepts were involved in these insights. There consequently results an aggregate of discrete insights rather than a codified body of knowledge, subject to reproducible research. In some quarters, the very suggestion that these intensely private experiences must be reshaped into publicly certifiable procedures if they are to be scientifically relevant is itself taken as a sign of blind impiety. Now, it is true that not all sociologists are blessed with the same degree of perceptiveness, any more than all cabbage heads are blessed with the same degree of succulence as Brussels sprouts. Yet the procedures of even the most perceptive of sociologists must be standardizable and the results of their insights testable by others. Science, and this includes sociological science, is public, not private. It is not that we average sociologists wish to cut all talents to our own small stature; it is only, we suggest, that the contributions of the great and small alike must be codified if they are to advance the development of sociology.

Since all virtues can readily become vices merely by being carried to excess, the sociological paradigm can be abused almost as easily as it can be used. It is a temptation to mental indolence. Equipped with his paradigm, the sociologist may shut his eyes to strategic data not expressly called for in the paradigm. He may turn the paradigm from a sociological field-glass into a sociological blinker. Misuse results from absolutizing the paradigm rather than using it tentatively, as a point of departure.

The paradigms in this book are, without exception, provisional, undoubtedly destined to be modified in the immediate future as they have been in the recent past. But for the time being, these explicit paradigms seem preferable to tacit assumptions.

Part I

SOCIOLOGICAL THEORY

I   MANIFEST AND LATENT FUNCTIONS

TOWARD THE CODIFICATION OF FUNCTIONAL ANALYSIS IN SOCIOLOGY

UNCTIONAL ANALYSIS is at once the most promising and possibly the least codified of contemporary orientations to problems of sociological interpretation. Having developed on many intellectual fronts at the same time, it has grown in shreds and patches rather than in depth. The accomplishments of functional analysis are sufficient to suggest that its large promise will progressively be fulfilled, just as its current deficiencies testify to the need for periodically overhauling the past the better to build for the future. At the very least, occasional re-assessments bring into open discussion many of the difficulties which otherwise remain tacit and unspoken.

Like all interpretative schemes, functional analysis depends upon a triple alliance between theory, method and data. Of the three allies, method is by all odds the weakest. Many of the major practitioners of functional analysis have been devoted to theoretic formulations and to the clearing up of concepts; some have steeped themselves in data directly relevant to a functional frame of reference; but few have broken the prevailing silence regarding how one goes about the business of functional analysis. Yet the plenty and variety of functional analyses force the conclusion that *some* methods have been employed and awaken the hope that much may be learned from their inspection.

Although methods can be profitably examined without reference to theory or substantive data—methodology or the logic of procedure of course has precisely that as its assignment—empirically oriented disciplines are more fully served by inquiry into procedures if this takes due account of their theoretic problems and substantive findings. For the use of "method" involves not only logic but, unfortunately perhaps for those who must struggle with the difficulties of research, also the practical problems of aligning data with the requirements of theory. At least, that is our premise. Accordingly, we shall interweave our account with a systematic review of some of the chief conceptions of functional theory.

THE VOCABULARIES OF FUNCTIONAL ANALYSIS

From its very beginnings, the functional approach in sociology has been caught up in terminological confusion. *Too often, a single term has been used to symbolize different concepts, just as the same concept has been symbolized by different terms.* Clarity of analysis and adequacy of communication are both victims of this frivolous use of words. At times, the analysis suffers from the unwitting shift in the conceptual content of a given term, and communication with others breaks down when the essentially same content is obscured by a battery of diverse terms. We have only to follow, for a short distance, the vagaries of the concept of 'function' to discover how conceptual clarity is effectively marred and communication defeated by competing vocabularies of functional analysis.

Single Term, Diverse Concepts

The word "function" has been pre-empted by several disciplines and by popular speech with the not unexpected result that its connotation often becomes obscure in sociology proper. By confining ourselves to only five connotations commonly assigned to this one word, we neglect numerous others. There is first, popular usage, according to which function refers to some public gathering or festive occasion, usually conducted with ceremonial overtones. It is in this connection, one must assume, that a newspaper headline asserts: "Mayor Tobin Not Backing Social Function," for the news account goes on to explain that "Mayor Tobin announced today that he is not interested in any social function, nor has he authorized anyone to sell tickets or sell advertising for any affair." Common as this usage is, it enters into the academic literature too seldom to contribute any great share to the prevailing chaos of terminology. Clearly, *this* connotation of the word is wholly alien to functional analysis in sociology.

A second usage makes the term function virtually equivalent to the term occupation. Max Weber, for example, defines occupation as "the mode of specialization, specification and combination of the functions of an individual so far as it constitutes for him the basis of a continual opportunity for income or for profit."[1] This is a frequent, indeed almost a typical, usage of the term by some economists who refer to the "functional analysis of a group" when they report the distribution of occupations in that group. Since this is the case, it may be expedient to follow the suggestion of Sargant Florence,[2] that the more nearly descriptive phrase "occupational analysis" be adopted for such inquiries.

---

1. Max Weber, *Theory of Social and Economic Organization* (edited by Talcott Parsons), (London: William Hodge and Co., 1947), 230.

2. P. Sargent Florence, *Statistical Method in Economics,* (New York: Harcourt, Brace and Co., 1929), 357-58n.

A third usage, representing a special instance of the preceding one, is found both in popular speech and in political science. Function is often used to refer to the activities assigned to the incumbent of a social status, and more particularly, to the occupant of an office or political position. This gives rise to the term functionary, or official. Although function in this sense overlaps the broader meaning assigned the term in sociology and anthropology, it had best be excluded since it diverts attention from the fact that functions are performed not only by the occupants of designated positions, but by a wide range of standardized activities, social processes, culture patterns and belief-systems found in a society.

Since it was first introduced by Leibniz, the word function has its most precise significance in mathematics, where it refers to a variable considered in relation to one or more other variables in terms of which it may be expressed or on the value of which its own value depends. This conception, in a more extended (and often more imprecise) sense, is expressed by such phrases as "functional interdependence" and "functional relations," so often adopted by social scientists.[3] When Mannheim observes that "every social fact is a function of the time and place in which it occurs," or when a demographer states that "birth-rates are a function of economic status," they are manifestly making use of the mathematical connotation, though the first is not reported in the form of equations and the second is. The context generally makes it clear that the term function is being used in this mathematical sense, but social scientists not infrequently shuttle back and forth between this and another related, though distinct, connotation, which also involves the notion of "interdependence," "reciprocal relation" or "mutually dependent variations."

It is this fifth connotation which is central to functional analysis as this has been practiced in sociology and social anthropology. Stemming in part from the native mathematical sense of the term, this usage is more often explicitly adopted from the biological sciences, where the term function is understood to refer to the "vital or organic processes considered in the respects in which they contribute to the maintenance of the organism."[4] With modifications appropriate to the study of human

3. Thus, Alexander Lesser: "In its logical essentials, what is a functional relation? Is it any different in kind from functional relations in other fields of science? I think not. A genuinely functional relation is one which is established between two or more terms or variables such that it can be asserted that under certain defined conditions (which form one term of the relation) certain determined expressions of those conditions (which is the other term of the relation) are observed. The functional relation or relations asserted of any delimited aspect of culture must be such as to explain the nature and character of the delimited aspect under defined conditions." "Functionalism in social anthropology," *American Anthropologist*, N.S. 37 (1935), 386-93, at 392.

4. See for example, Ludwig von Bertalanffy, *Modern Theories of Development*, (New York: Oxford University Press, 1933), 9 ff., 184 ff.; W. M. Bayliss, *Principles of General Physiology* (London, 1915), 706, where he reports his researches on the functions of the hormone discovered by Starling and himself; W. B. Cannon, *Bodily Changes in Pain, Hunger, Fear and Rage* (New York: Appleton & Co., 1929), 222, describing the "emergency functions of the sympathetico-adrenal system."

society, this corresponds rather closely to the key concept of function as adopted by the anthropological functionalists, pure or tempered.[5]

Radcliffe-Brown is the most often explicit in tracing his working conception of social function to the analogical model found in the biological sciences. After the fashion of Durkheim, he asserts that "the function of a recurrent physiological process is thus a correspondence between it and the needs (*i.e.*, the necessary conditions of existence) of the organism." And in the social sphere where individual human beings, "the essential units," are connected by networks of social relations into an integrated whole, "the function of any recurrent activity, such as the punishment of a crime, or a funeral ceremony, is the part it plays in the social life as a whole and therefore the contribution it makes to the maintenance of the structural continuity."[6]

Though Malinowski differs in several respects from the formulations of Radcliffe-Brown, he joins him in making the core of functional analysis the study of "the part which [social or cultural items] play in the society." "This type of theory," Malinowski explains in one of his early declarations of purpose, "aims at the explanation of anthropological facts at all levels of development by *their function, by the part which they play within the integral system of culture, by the manner in which they are related to each other within the system. . . .*"[7]

As we shall presently see in some detail, such recurrent phrases as "the part played in the social or cultural system" tend to blur the important distinction between the concept of function as "interdependence" and as "process." Nor need we pause here to observe that the postulate which holds that every item of culture has *some* enduring relations with other items, that it has *some* distinctive place in the total culture scarcely equips the field-observer or the analyst with a specific guide to procedure. All this had better wait. At the moment, we need only recognize that more recent formulations have clarified and extended this concept of function through progressive specifications. Thus, Kluckhohn: ". . . a given bit of culture is 'functional' insofar as it defines a mode of response

---

5. Lowie makes a distinction between the "pure functionalism" of a Malinowski and the "tempered functionalism" of a Thurnwald. Sound as the distinction is, it will soon become apparent that it is not pertinent for our purposes. R. H. Lowie, *The History of Ethnological Theory* (New York: Farrar & Rinehart, 1937), Chapter 13.

6. A. R. Radcliffe-Brown, "On the concept of function in social science," *American Anthropologist*, 1935, 37, 395-6. See also his later presidential address before the Royal Anthropological Institute, where he states: ". . . I would define the social function of a socially standardized mode of activity, or mode of thought, as its relation to the social structure to the existence and continuity of which it makes some contribution. Analogously, in a living organism, the physiological function of the beating of the heart, or the secretion of gastric juices, is its relation to the organic structure. . . ." "On social structure," *The Journal of the Royal Anthropological Institute of Great Britain and Ireland*, 1940, 70, Pt. I, 9-10.

7. B. Malinowski, "Anthropology," *Encyclopaedia Britannica*, First Supplementary Volume, (London and New York, 1926), 132-133 [italics supplied].

which is adaptive from the standpoint of the society and adjustive from the standpoint of the individual."[8]

From these connotations of the term "function," and we have touched upon only a few drawn from a more varied array, it is plain that many concepts are caught up in the same word. This invites confusion. And when many different words are held to express the same concept, there develops confusion worse confounded.

Single Concept, Diverse Terms

The large assembly of terms used indifferently and almost syn. onymously with "function" presently includes use, utility, purpose, mo. tive, intention, aim, consequences. Were these and similar terms put tu use to refer to the same strictly defined concept, there would of course be little point in noticing their numerous variety. But the fact is that the undisciplined use of these terms, with their ostensibly similar conceptual reference, leads to successively greater departures from tight-knit and rigorous functional analysis. The connotations of each term which differ from rather than agree with the connotation that they have in common are made the (unwitting) basis for inferences which become increasingly dubious as they become progressively remote from the central concept of function. One or two illustrations will bear out the point that a shifting vocabulary makes for the multiplication of misunderstandings.

In the following passage drawn from one of the most sensible of treatises on the sociology of crime, one can detect the shifts in meaning of nominally synonymous terms and the questionable inferences which depend upon these shifts. (The key terms are italicized to help in picking one's way through the argument.)

Purpose of Punishment. Attempts are being made to determine the *purpose or function* of punishment in different groups at different times. Many investigators have insisted that some one *motive* was *the motive* in punishment. On the other hand, the *function* of punishment in restoring the solidarity of the group which has been weakened by the crime is emphasized. Thomas and Znaniecki have indicated that among the Polish peasants the punishment of crime is *designed primarily* to restore the situation which existed before the crime and renew the solidarity of the group, and that revenge is *a secondary consideration.* From this point of view punishment *is concerned primarily* with the group and only *secondarily* with the offender. On the other hand, expiation, deterrence, retribution, reformation, income for the state, and other things have been posited as *the function* of punishment. In the past as at present it is not clear that any one of these is *the motive;* punishments seem to grow from *many motives* and to perform *many functions.* This is true both of the individual victims of crimes and of the state. Certainly the laws of the present

---

8. Clyde Kluckhohn, *Navaho Witchcraft,* Papers of the Peabody Museum of American Archaeology and Ethnology, Harvard University, (Cambridge: Peabody Museum. 1944). XXII. No. 2, 47a.

day are not consistent in *aims or motives;* probably the same condition existed in earlier societies.[9]

We should attend first to the list of terms ostensibly referring to the same concept: purpose, function, motive, designed, secondary consideration, primary concern, aim. Through inspection, it becomes clear that *these terms group into quite distinct conceptual frames of reference.* At times, some of these terms—motive, design, aim and purpose—clearly refer to the *explicit ends-in-view of the representatives of the state.* Others —motive, secondary consideration—refer to the *ends-in-view of the victim of the crime.* And both of these sets of terms are alike in referring to the *subjective anticipations of the results of punishment.* But the concept of function involves the standpoint of *the observer,* not necessarily that of the participant. Social function refers to *observable objective consequences,* and not to *subjective dispositions* (aims, motives, purposes). And the failure to distinguish between the objective sociological consequences and the subjective dispositions inevitably leads to confusion of functional analysis, as can be seen from the following excerpt (in which the key terms are again italicized):

> The extreme of unreality is attained in the discussion of the so-called "functions" of the family. The family, we hear, performs important *functions* in society; it provides for the perpetuation of the species and the training of the young; it performs economic and religious functions, and so on. Almost we are encouraged to believe that *people marry and have children because* they are eager to perform these needed societal functions. In fact, people marry *because* they are in love, or for other less romantic but no less personal reasons. The *function* of the family, *from the viewpoint of individuals,* is to satisfy their wishes. The *function* of the family or any other social institution is *merely what people use it for.* Social *"functions"* are mostly *rationalizations of established practices; we* act first, explain afterwards; *we* act for *personal reasons,* and justify *our* behavior by social and ethical *principles.* Insofar as these *functions* of institutions have any real basis, it must be stated in terms of the social processes in which people engage *in the attempt* to satisfy their wishes. Functions arise from the inter-action of concrete human beings and concrete *purposes.*[10]

This passage is an interesting medley of small islets of clarity in the midst of vast confusion. Whenever it mistakenly identifies (subjective) motives with (objective) functions, it abandons a lucid functional approach. For it need not be assumed, as we shall presently see, that the *motives* for entering into marriage ("love," "personal reasons") are identical with the *functions* served by families (socialization of the child). Again, it need not be assumed that the *reasons* advanced by people for their behavior (*"we* act for personal reasons") are one and

---

9. Edwin H. Sutherland, *Principles of Criminology,* third edition, (Philadelphia: J. B. Lippincott, 1939), 349-350.

10. Willard Waller, *The Family,* (New York: Cordon Company, 1938), 26.

the same as the observed consequences of these patterns of behavior. The subjective disposition may coincide with the objective consequence, but again, it may not. The two vary independently. When, however, it is said that people are motivated to engage in behavior which may give rise to (not necessarily intended) functions, there is offered escape from the troubled sea of confusion.[11]

This brief review of competing terminologies and their unfortunate consequences may be something of a guide to later efforts at codification of the concepts of functional analysis. There will plainly be occasion to limit the use of the sociological concept of function, and there will be need to distinguish clearly between subjective categories of disposition and objective categories of observed consequences. Else the substance of the functional orientation may become lost in a cloud of hazy definitions.

PREVAILING POSTULATES IN FUNCTIONAL ANALYSIS

Chiefly but not solely in anthropology, functional analysts have commonly adopted three interconnected postulates which, it will now be suggested, have proved to be debatable and unnecessary to the functional orientation.

Substantially, these postulates hold first, that standardized social activities or cultural items are functional for the *entire* social or cultural system; second, that *all* such social and cultural items fulfill sociological functions; and third, that these items are consequently *indispensable*. Although these three articles of faith are ordinarily seen only in one another's company, they had best be examined separately, since each gives rise to its own distinctive difficulties.

Postulate of the Functional Unity of Society

It is Radcliffe-Brown who characteristically puts this postulate in explicit terms:

The function of a particular social usage is the contribution it makes to the *total social life* as the functioning of the *total social system*. Such a view implies that a social system (*the total social structure* of a society together with the totality of social usages, in which that structure appears and on which it depends for its continued existence) has a certain kind of unity, which we

---

11. These two instances of confusion between motive and function are drawn from an easily available storehouse of additional materials of the same kind. Even Radcliffe-Brown, who ordinarily avoids this practice, occasionally fails to make the distinction. For example: ". . . the exchange of presents did not serve the same *purpose* as trade and barter in more developed communities. The *purpose* that it did serve is a moral one. The *object* of the exchange was to produce a friendly feeling between the two persons concerned, and unless it did this it failed of its *purpose*." Is the "object" of the transaction seen from the standpoint of the observer, the participant, or both? See A. R. Radcliffe-Brown, *The Andaman Islanders*, (Glencoe, Illinois: The Free Press, 1948), 84 [italics supplied].

may speak of as a functional unity. We may define it as a condition in which all parts of the social system work together with a sufficient degree of harmony or internal consistency, *i.e.*, without producing persistent conflicts which can neither be resolved nor regulated.[12]

It is important to note, however, that he goes on to describe this notion of functional unity as a hypothesis which requires further test.

It would at first appear that Malinowski was questioning the empirical acceptability of this postulate when he notes that "the sociological school" (into which he thrusts Radcliffe-Brown) "exaggerated the social solidarity of primitive man" and "neglected the individual."[13] But it is soon apparent that Malinowski does not so much abandon this dubious assumption as he succeeds in adding another to it. He continues to speak of standardized practices and beliefs as functional "for culture as a whole," and goes on to assume that they are *also* functional for every member of the society. Thus, referring to primitive beliefs in the supernatural, he writes:

> Here the functional view is put to its acid test. . . . It is bound to show in what way belief and ritual work for social integration, technical and economic efficiency, for *culture as a whole*—indirectly therefore for the biological and mental welfare *of each individual member*.[14]

If the one unqualified assumption is questionable, this twin assumption is doubly so. Whether cultural items do uniformly fulfill functions for the society viewed as a system and for all members of the society is presumably an empirical question of fact, rather than an axiom.

Kluckhohn evidently perceives the problem inasmuch as he extends the alternatives to include the possibility that cultural forms "are adjustive or adaptive . . . for the members of the society *or* for the society considered as a perduring unit."[15] This is a necessary first step in allowing for variation in the *unit* which is subserved by the imputed function. Compelled by the force of empirical observation, we shall have occasion to widen the range of variation in this unit even further.

It seems reasonably clear that the notion of functional unity is *not* a postulate beyond the reach of empirical test; quite the contrary. The

---

12. Radcliffe-Brown, "On the concept of function," *op. cit.*, 397 [italics supplied].

13. See Malinowski, "Anthropology," *op. cit.*, 132 and "The group and the individual in functional analysis," *American Journal of Sociology*, 1939, 44, 938-64, at 939.

14. Malinowski, "Anthropology," *op. cit.*, 135, Malinowski maintained this view, without essential change, in his later writings. Among these, consult, for example, "The group and the individual in functional analysis," *op. cit.*, at 962-3: ". . . we see that every institution contributes, on the one hand, toward the integral working of *the community as a whole*, but it also satisfies the derived and basic needs of the individual . . . everyone of the benefits just listed is enjoyed *by every individual member*." [italics supplied].

15. Kluckhohn, *Navaho Witchcraft*, 46b [italics supplied].

degree of integration is an empirical variable,[16] changing for the same society from time to time and differing among various societies. That all human societies must have *some* degree of integration is a matter of definition—and begs the question. But not all societies have that *high* degree of integration in which *every* culturally standardized activity or belief is functional for the society as a whole and uniformly functional for the people living in it. Radcliffe-Brown need in fact have looked no further than to his favored realm of analogy in order to suspect the adequacy of his assumption of functional unity. For we find significant variations in the degree of integration even among individual biological organisms, although the commonsense assumption would tell us that here, surely, all the parts of the organism work toward a "unified" end. Consider only this:

One can readily see that there are *highly integrated organisms* under close control of the nervous system or of hormones, the loss of any major part of which will strongly affect the whole system, and frequently will cause death, but, on the other hand, there are the lower *organisms much more loosely correlated,* where the loss of even a major part of the body causes only temporary inconvenience pending the regeneration of replacement tissues. Many of these more loosely organized animals are *so poorly integrated that different parts may be in active opposition to each other.* Thus, when an ordinary starfish is placed on its back, part of the arms may attempt to turn the animal in one direction, while others work to turn it in the opposite way. . . . On account of its *loose integration,* the sea anemone may move off and leave a portion of its foot clinging tightly to a rock, so that the animal suffers serious rupture.[17]

If this is true of single organisms, it would seem *a fortiori* the case with complex social systems.

One need not go far afield to show that the assumption of the complete functional unity of human society is repeatedly contrary to fact. Social usages or sentiments may be functional for some groups and dysfunctional for others in the same society. Anthropologists often cite "increased solidarity of the community" and "increased family pride" as instances of functionally adaptive sentiments. Yet, as Bateson[18] among others has indicated, an increase of pride among individual families may often serve to disrupt the solidarity of a small local community. Not only is the postulate of functional unity often contrary to fact, but it has little heuristic value, since it diverts the analyst's attention from possible disparate consequences of a given social or cultural item (usage, belief,

----

16. It is the merit of Sorokin's early review of theories of social integration that he did not lose sight of this important fact. *Cf.* P. A. Sorokin, "Forms and problems of culture-integration," *Rural Sociology,* 1936, 1, 121-41; 344-74.

17. G. H. Parker, *The Elementary Nervous System,* quoted by W. C. Allee, *Animal Aggregation,* (University of Chicago Prses, 1931), 81-82.

18. Gregory Bateson, *Naven,* (Cambridge [England] University Press, 1936), 31-32.

behavior pattern, institution) for diverse social groups and for the individual members of these groups.

If the body of observation and fact which negates the assumption of functional unity is as large and easily accessible as we have suggested, it is interesting to ask how it happens that Radcliffe-Brown and others who follow his lead have continued to abide by this assumption. A possible clue is provided by the fact that this conception, in its recent formulations, was developed by social *anthropologists,* that is, by men primarily concerned with the study of non-literate societies. In view of what Radin has described as "the highly integrated nature of the majority of aboriginal civilizations," this assumption may be tolerably suitable for some, if not all, non-literate societies. But one pays an excessive intellectual penalty for moving this possibly useful assumption from the realm of small non-literate societies to the realm of large, complex and highly differentiated literate societies. In no field, perhaps, do the dangers of such a transfer of assumption become more visible than in the functional analysis of religion. This deserves brief review, if only because it exhibits in bold relief the fallacies one falls heir to by sympathetically adopting this assumption without a thorough screening.

The Functional Interpretation of Religion. In examining the price paid for the transfer of this tacit assumption of functional unity from the field of relatively small and relatively tightknit non-literate groups to the field of more highly differentiated and perhaps more loosely integrated societies, it is useful to consider the work of sociologists, particularly of sociologists who are ordinarily sensitized to the assumptions on which they work. This has passing interest for its bearing on the more general question of seeking, without appropriate modification, to apply to the study of literate societies conceptions developed and matured in the study of non-literate societies. (Much the same question holds for the transfer of research procedures and techniques, but this is not at issue here.)

The large, spaceless and timeless generalizations about "the integrative functions of religion" are largely, though not of course wholly, derived from observations in non-literate societies. Not infrequently, the social scientist implicitly adopts the findings regarding such societies and goes on to expatiate upon the integrative functions of religion *generally.* From this, it is a short step to statements such as the following:

> *The reason why religion is necessary* is apparently to be found in the fact that human society *achieves its unity* primarily through the possession by its members of certain ultimate values and ends in common. Although these values and ends are subjective, they influence behavior, and their integration enables this society to operate as a system.[19]

---

19. Kingsley Davis and Wilbert E. Moore, "Some principles of stratification," *American Sociological Review,* April 1945, 10, 242-49, at 244. [italics supplied].

In an extremely advanced society built on scientific technology, the priest-hood tends to lose status, because sacred tradition and supernaturalism drop into the background . . . [but] *No society* has become so completely secularized as to liquidate *entirely* the belief in transcendental ends and supernatural entities. Even in a secularized society *some system* must exist for the integration of ultimate values, for their ritualistic expression, and for the emotional adjustments required by disappointment, death, and disaster.[20]

Deriving from the Durkheim orientation which was based largely upon the study of non-literate societies, these authors tend to single out *only* the apparently integrative consequences of religion and to neglect its possibly disintegrative consequences *in certain types of social structure.* Yet consider the following very well-known facts and queries. (1) When different religions co-exist in the same society, there often occurs deep conflict between the several religious groups (consider only the enormous literature on inter-religious conflict in European societies). In what sense, then, does religion make for integration of "the" society in the numerous multi-religion societies? (2) It is clearly the case that "human society achieves its unity [insofar as it exhibits such unity] primarily through the possession by its members of certain ultimate values and ends in common." But what is the evidence indicating that "non-religious" people, say, in our own society less often subscribe to certain common "values and ends" than those devoted to religious doctrines? (3) In what sense does religion make for integration of the larger society, if the content of its doctrine and values is at odds with the content of other, non-religious values held by many people in the same society? (Consider, for example, the conflict between the opposition of the Catholic Church to child-labor legislation and the secular values of preventing "exploitation of youthful dependents." Or the contrasting evaluations of birth control by diverse religious groups in our society.)

This list of commonplace facts regarding the role of religion in contemporary literate societies could be greatly extended, and they are of course very well known to those functional anthropologists and sociologists who describe religion as integrative, without limiting the range of social structures in which this is indeed the case. It is at least conceivable that a theoretic orientation derived from research on non-literate societies has served to obscure otherwise conspicuous data on the functional role of religion in multi-religion societies. Perhaps it is the transfer of the assumption of functional unity which results in blotting out the entire history of religious wars, of the Inquisition (which drove a wedge into society after society), of internecine conflicts among religious groups. For the fact remains that all this abundantly known material is ignored in favor of illustrations drawn from the study of religion in non-literate society. And it is a further striking fact that the same paper, cited above,

---

20. *Ibid.*, 246. [italics supplied].

that goes on to speak of "religion, which provides integration in terms of sentiments, beliefs and rituals," does not make a single reference to the possibly divisive role of religion.

Such functional analyses may, of course, mean that religion provides integration of those who believe in the *same* religious values, but it is unlikely that this is meant, since it would merely assert that integration is provided by any consensus on any set of values.

Moreover, this again illustrates the danger of taking the assumption of functional unity, which *may* be a reasonable approximation for some non-literate societies, as part of an implicit model for *generalized* functional analysis. Typically, in non-literate societies, there is but one prevailing religious system so that, apart from individual deviants, the membership of the total society and the membership of the religious community are virtually co-extensive. Obviously, in this type of social structure, a common set of religious values may have as *one* of its consequences the reinforcement of common sentiments and of social integration. But this does not easily lend itself to defensible generalization about other types of society.

We shall have occasion to return to other theoretic implications of current functional analyses of religion but, for the moment, this may illustrate the dangers which one inherits in adopting the unqualified postulate of functional unity. This unity of the total society cannot be usefully posited in advance of observation. It is a question of fact, and not a matter of opinion. The theoretic framework of functional analysis must expressly require that there be *specification* of the *units* for which a given social or cultural item is functional. It must expressly allow for a given item having diverse consequences, functional and dysfunctional, for individuals, for subgroups, and for the more inclusive social structure and culture.

Postulate of Universal Functionalism

Most succinctly, this postulate holds that all standardized social or cultural forms have positive functions. As with other aspects of the functional conception, Malinowski advances this in its most extreme form:

> The functional view of culture *insists* therefore upon the principle that in *every type of civilization, every custom, material object, idea and belief fulfills some vital function. . . .*[21]

Although, as we have seen, Kluckhohn allows for variation in the unit subserved by a cultural form, he joins with Malinowski in postulating functional value for all surviving forms of culture. ("My basic postulate . . . is that *no* culture forms survive unless they constitute responses which

---

21. Malinowski, "Anthropology," *op. cit.*, 132 [The italics, though supplied, are perhaps superfluous in view of the forceful language of the original.]

are adjustive or adaptive, in some sense . . ."[22]) This universal functional-ism may or may not be a heuristic postulate; that remains to be seen. But one should be prepared to find that it too diverts critical attention from a range of non-functional consequences of existing cultural forms.

In fact, when Kluckhohn seeks to illustrate his point by ascribing "functions" to seemingly functionless items, he falls back upon a type of function which would be found, *by definition* rather than by inquiry, served by all persisting items of culture. Thus, he suggests that

> The at present mechanically useless buttons on the sleeve of a European man's suit subserve the "function" of preserving the familiar, of maintaining a tradition. People are, in general, more comfortable if they feel a continuity of behavior, if they feel themselves as following out the orthodox and socially approved forms of behavior.[23]

This would appear to represent the marginal case in which the im-putation of function adds little or nothing to the direct description of the culture pattern or behavior form. It may well be assumed that all *estab-lished* elements of culture (which are loosely describable as 'tradition') have the minimum, though not exclusive, function of "preserving the familiar, of maintaining a tradition." This is equivalent to saying that the 'function' of conformity to *any* established practice is to enable the con-formist to avoid the sanctions otherwise incurred by deviating from the established practice. This is no doubt true but hardly illuminating. It serves, however, to remind us that we shall want to explore the *types of functions* which the sociologist imputes. At the moment, it suggests the provisional assumption that, although any item of culture or social struc-ture *may* have functions, it is premature to hold unequivocally that every such item *must* be functional.

The postulate of universal functionalism is of course the historical product of the fierce, barren and protracted controversy over "survivals" which raged among the anthropologists during the early part of the century. The notion of a social survival, that is, in the words of Rivers, of "a custom . . . [which] cannot be explained by its present utility but only becomes intelligible through its past history,"[24] dates back at least to Thucydides. But when the evolutionary theories of culture became prominent, the concept of survival seemed all the more strategically important for reconstructing "stages of development" of cultures, par-ticularly for non-literate societies which possessed no written record. For

---

22. Kluckhohn, *Navaho Witchcraft*, 46. [italics supplied].

23. *Ibid.*, 47.

24. W. H. R. Rivers, "Survival in sociology," *The Sociological Review*, 1913, 6, 293-305. See also E. B. Tylor, *Primitive Culture*, (New York, 1874), esp. I, 70-159; and for a more recent review of the matter, Lowie, *The History of Ethnological Theory*, 44 ff., 81 f. For a sensible and restrained account of the problem, see Emile Durkheim, *Rules of Sociological Method*, Chapter 5, esp. at 91.

the functionalists who wished to turn away from what they regarded as the usually fragmentary and often conjectural "history" of non-literate societies, the attack on the notion of survival took on all the symbolism of an attack on the entire and intellectually repugnant system of evolutionary thought. In consequence, perhaps, they over-reacted against this concept central to evolutionary theory and advanced an equally exaggerated "postulate" to the effect that "every custom [everywhere] . . . fulfills some vital function."

It would seem a pity to allow the polemics of the anthropological forefathers to create splendid exaggerations in the present. Once discovered, ticketed and studied, social survivals cannot be exorcized by a postulate. And if no specimens of these survivals can be produced, then the quarrel dwindles of its own accord. It can be said, furthermore, that even when such survivals are identified in contemporary literate societies, they seem to add little to our understanding of human behavior or the dynamics of social change. Not requiring their dubious role as poor substitutes for recorded history, the sociologist of literate societies may neglect survivals with no apparent loss. But he need not be driven, by an archaic and irrelevant controversy, to adopt the unqualified postulate that all culture items fulfill vital functions. For this, too, is a problem for investigation, not a conclusion in advance of investigation. Far more useful as a directive for research would seem the provisional assumption that persisting cultural forms have a *net balance of functional consequences* either for the society considered as a unit or for subgroups sufficiently powerful to retain these forms intact, by means of direct coercion or indirect persuasion. This formulation at once avoids the tendency of functional analysis to concentrate on positive functions and directs the attention of the research worker to other types of consequences as well.

Postulate of Indispensability

The last of this trio of postulates common among functional social scientists is, in some respects, the most ambiguous. The ambiguity becomes evident in the aforementioned manifesto by Malinowski to the effect that

in every type of civilization, every custom, material object, idea and belief fulfills some *vital* function, has some task to accomplish, represents an *indispensable part* within a working whole.[25]

From this passage, it is not at all clear whether he asserts the indispensability of the *function,* or of the *item* (custom, object, idea, belief) fulfilling the function, or *both.*

This ambiguity is quite common in the literature. Thus, the previously cited Davis and Moore account of the role of religion seems at

---

25. Malinowski, "Anthropology," *op. cit.,* 132 [italics supplied].

first to maintain that it is the *institution* which is indispensable: "The reason why religion is necessary . . ."; ". . . religion . . . plays a unique and indispensable part in society."[26] But it soon appears that it is not so much the institution of religion which is regarded as indispensable but rather the functions which religion is taken typically to perform. For Davis and Moore regard religion as indispensable only insofar as it functions to make the members of a society adopt "certain ultimate values and ends in common." These values and ends, it is said,

must . . . appear to the members of the society to have some reality, and it is the role of religious belief and ritual to supply and reinforce this appearance of reality. Through ritual and belief the common ends and values are connected with an imaginary world symbolized by concrete sacred objects, which world in turn is related in a meaningful way to the facts and trials of the individual's life. Through the worship of the sacred objects and the beings they symbolize, and the acceptance of *supernatural prescriptions* that are at the same time codes of behavior, a powerful control over human conduct is exercised, guiding it along lines sustaining the institutional structure and conforming to the ultimate ends and values.[27]

The alleged indispensability of religion, then, is based on the assumption of fact that it is through "worship" and "supernatural prescriptions" *alone* that the necessary minimum of "control over human conduct" and "integration in terms of sentiments and beliefs" can be achieved.

In short, the postulate of indispensability as it is ordinarily stated contains two related, but distinguishable, assertions. First, it is assumed that there are certain *functions* which are indispensable in the sense that, unless they are performed, the society (or group or individual) will not persist. This, then, sets forth a concept of *functional prerequisites,* or *preconditions functionally necessary* for a society, and we shall have occasion to examine this concept in some detail. Second, and this is quite another matter, it is assumed that *certain cultural or social forms* are indispensable for fulfilling each of these functions. This involves a concept of specialized and irreplaceable structures, and gives rise to all manner of theoretic difficulties. For not only can this be shown to be manifestly contrary to fact, but it entails several subsidiary assumptions which have plagued functional analysis from the very outset. It diverts attention from the fact that alternative social structures (and cultural forms) have served, under conditions to be examined, the functions necessary for the persistence of groups. Proceeding further, we must set forth a major theorem of functional analysis; *just as the same item may have multiple functions, so may the same function be diversely fulfilled*

26. Kingsley Davis and Wilbert E. Moore, *op. cit.,* 244, 246. See the more recent review of this matter by Davis in his Introduction to W. J. Goode, *Religion Among the Primitives* (Glencoe, Illinois: The Free Press, 1951) and the instructive functional interpretations of religion in that volume.

27. Ibid., 244-245. [italics supplied].

by alternative items. Functional needs are here taken to be permissive, rather than determinant, of specific social structures. Or, in other words, there is a range of variation in the structures which fulfill the function in question. (The limits upon this range of variation involve the concept of structural constraint, of which more presently).

In contrast to this implied concept of indispensable cultural forms (institutions, standardized practices, belief-systems, etc.), there is, then, the concept of *functional alternatives,* or *functional equivalents,* or *functional substitutes.* This concept is widely recognized and used, but it should be noted that it cannot rest comfortably in the same theoretical system which entails the postulate of indispensability of particular cultural forms. Thus, after reviewing Malinowski's theory of "the functional necessity for such mechanisms as magic," Parsons is careful to make the following statement:

. . . wherever such uncertainty elements enter into the pursuit of emotionally important goals, if not magic, at least *functionally equivalent* phenomena could be expected to appear.[28]

This is a far cry from Malinowski's own insistence that

Thus magic fulfills *an indispensable function* within culture. It satisfies a definite need *which cannot be satisfied by any other factors of primitive civilization.*[29]

This twin concept of the indispensable function and the irreplaceable belief-and-action pattern flatly excludes the concept of functional alternatives.

In point of fact, the concept of functional alternatives or equivalents has repeatedly emerged in every discipline which has adopted a functional framework of analysis. It is, for example, widely utilized in the psychological sciences, as a paper by English admirably indicates.[30] And in neurology, Lashley has pointed out on the basis of experimental and clinical evidence, the inadequacy of the "assumption that individual neurons are specialized for particular functions," maintaining instead that a particular function may be fulfilled by a range of alternative structures.[31]

Sociology and social anthropology have all the more occasion for avoiding the postulate of indispensability of given structures, and for systematically operating with the concept of functional alternatives and functional substitutes. For just as laymen have long erred in assuming

28. Talcott Parsons, *Essays in Sociological Theory, Pure and Applied,* (Glencoe, Illinois: The Free Press, 1949), 58.

29. Malinowski, "Anthropology," *op. cit.,* 136. [italics supplied].

30. Horace B. English, "Symbolic versus functional equivalents in the neuroses of deprivation," *Journal of Abnormal and Social Psychology,* 1937, 32, 392-94.

31. K. S. Lashley, "Basic neural mechanisms in behavior," *Psychological Review,* 1930, 37, 1-24.

that the "strange" customs and beliefs of other societies were "mere superstitions," so functional social scientists run the risk of erring in the other extreme, first, by being quick to find functional oɪ adaptive value in these practices and beliefs, and second, by failing to see which alternative modes of action are ruled out by cleaving to these ostensibly functional practices. Thus, there is not seldom a readiness among some functionalists to conclude that magic or certain religious rites and beliefs are functional, because of their effect upon the state of mind or self-confidence of the believer. Yet it may well be in some instances, that these magical practices obscure and take the place of accessible secular and more adaptive practices. As F. L. Wells has observed,

> To nail a horseshoe over the door in a smallpox epidemic may bolster the morale of the household but it will not keep out the smallpox; such beliefs and practices will not stand the secular tests to which they are susceptible, and the sense of security they give is preserved only while the real tests are evaded.[32]

Those functionalists who are constrained by their theory to attend to the effects of such symbolic practices *only* upon the individual's state of mind and who therefore conclude that the magical practice is functional, neglect the fact that these very practices may on occasion take the place of more effective alternatives.[33] And those theorists who refer to the indispensability of standardized practices or prevailing institutions because of their observed function in reinforcing common sentiments must look

---

32. F. L. Wells, "Social maladjustments: adaptive regression," in Carl A. Murchison, ed., *Handbook of Social Psychology*, (Clark University Press, 1935), 880. Wells's observation is far from being antiquarian. As late as the 1930's, smallpox was not "being kept out" in such states as Idaho, Wyoming, and Montana which, lacking compulsory vaccination laws, could boast some 4,300 cases of smallpox in a five-year period at the same time that the more populous states of Massachusetts, Pennsylvania and Rhode Island, states with compulsory vaccination laws, had no cases of smallpox at all. On the shortcomings of 'common sense' in such matters, see Hugh Cabot, *The Patient's Dilemma* (New York: Reynal & Hitchcock, 1940), 166-167.

33. It should perhaps be noted that this statement is made with full cognizance of Malinowski's observation that the Trobrianders did not *substitute* their magical beliefs and practices for the application of rational technology. The problem remains of assessing the degree to which technological development is slackened by the semi-dependence on magic for dealing with the "range of uncertainty." This area of uncertainty is presumably not fixed, but is itself related to the available technology. Rituals designed to regulate the weather, for example, might readily absorb the energies of men who might otherwise be reducing that "area of uncertainty" by attending to the advancement of meteorological knowledge. Each case must be judged on its merits. We refer here only to the increasing tendency among social anthropologists and sociologists to confine themselves to the observed "morale" effects of rationally and empirically ungrounded practices, and to forego analysis of the alternatives which would be available in a given situation, did not the orientation toward "the transcendental" and "the symbolic" focus attention on other matters. Finally, it is to be hoped that all this will not be mistaken for a re-statement of the sometimes naive rationalism of the Age of Enlightenment.

first to functional substitutes before arriving at a conclusion, more often premature than confirmed.

Upon review of this trinity of functional postulates, several basic considerations emerge which must be caught up in our effort to codify this mode of analysis. In scrutinizing, first, *the postulate of functional unity,* we found that one cannot assume full integration of all societies, but that this is an empirical question of fact in which we should be prepared to find a range of degrees of integration. And in examining the special case of functional interpretations of religion, we were alerted to the possibility that, though human nature may be of a piece, it does not follow that the structure of non-literate societies is uniformly like that of highly differentiated, "literate" societies. A difference in degree between the two—say, the existence of several disparate religions in the one and not in the other—may make hazardous the passage between them. From critical scrutiny of this postulate, it developed that a theory of functional analysis must call for *specification* of the social units subserved by given social functions, and that items of culture must be recognized to have multiple consequences, some of them functional and others, perhaps, dysfunctional.

Review of the second *postulate of universal functionalism,* which holds that all persisting forms of culture are inevitably functional, resulted in other considerations which must be met by a codified approach to functional interpretation. It appeared not only that we must be prepared to find dysfunctional as well as functional consequences of these forms but that the theorist will ultimately be confronted with the difficult problem of developing an organon for assessing the net balance of consequences if his research is to have bearing on social technology. Clearly, expert advice based only on the appraisal of a limited, and perhaps arbitrarily selected, range of consequences to be expected as a result of contemplated action, will be subject to frequent error and will be properly judged as having small merit.

The postulate of indispensability, we found, entailed two distinct propositions: the one alleging the indispensability of certain functions, and this gives rise to the concept of *functional necessity* or *functional prerequisites;* the other alleging the indispensability of existing social institutions, culture forms, or the like, and this when suitably questioned, gives rise to the concept of *functional alternatives, equivalents or substitutes.*

Moreover, the currency of these three postulates, singly and in concert, is the source of the common charge that functional analysis inevitably involves certain ideological commitments. Since this is a question which will repeatedly come to mind as one examines the further conceptions of functional analysis, it had best be considered now, if our attention is not to be repeatedly drawn away from the analytical problems in hand by the spectre of a social science tainted with ideology.

FUNCTIONAL ANALYSIS AS IDEOLOGY

Functional Analysis as Conservative

In many quarters and with rising insistence, it has been charged that, whatever the intellectual worth of functional analysis, it is inevitably committed to a "conservative" (even a "reactionary") perspective. For some of these critics, functional analysis is little more than a latter-day version of the eighteenth century doctrine of a basic and invariable identity of public and private interests. It is viewed as a secularized version of the doctrine set forth by Adam Smith, for example, when in his *Theory of Moral Sentiments,* he wrote of the "harmonious order of nature, under divine guidance, which promotes the welfare of man through the operation of his individual propensities."[34] Thus, say these critics, functional theory is merely the orientation of the conservative social scientist who would defend the present order of things, just as it is, and who would attack the advisability of change, however moderate. On this view, the functional analyst systematically ignores Tocqueville's warning not to confound the familiar with the necessary: ". . . what we call necessary institutions are often no more than institutions to which we have grown accustomed. . . ." It remains yet to be shown that functional analysis inevitably falls prey to this engaging fallacy but, having reviewed the postulate of indispensability, we can well appreciate that *this* postulate, if adopted, might easily give rise to this ideological charge. Myrdal is one of the most recent and not the least typical among the critics who argue the inevitability of a conservative bias in functional analysis:

. . . if a thing has a "function" it is good or at least essential.* The term "function" can have a meaning *only* in terms of an assumed *purpose***; if that purpose is left undefined or implied to be the "interest of society" which is not further defined,*** a considerable leeway for arbitrariness in practical implication is allowed but the main direction is given: *a description of social institutions in terms of their functions must lead to a conservative teleology.*[35]

Myrdal's remarks are instructive less for their conclusion than for their premises. For, as we have noted, he draws upon two of the postu-

---

34. Jacob Viner, "Adam Smith and Laissez Faire," *Journal of Political Economy,* 1937, 35, 206.

35. Gunnar Myrdal, *An American Dilemma* (New York: Harper and Brothers, 1944) II, 1056 [italics and parenthetical remarks supplied].

* Here, be it noted, Myrdal gratuitously *accepts* the doctrine of indispensability as intrinsic to any functional analysis.

** This, as we have seen, is not only gratuitous, but false.

*** Here, Myrdal properly notes the dubious and vague postulate of functional unity.

lates so often adopted by functional analysts to reach the unqualified charge that he who describes institutions in terms of functions is unavoidably committed to "a conservative teleology." But nowhere does Myrdal challenge the inevitability of the postulates themselves. It will be interesting to ask how ineluctable the commitment when one has escaped from the premises.

In point of fact, if functional analysis in sociology were committed to teleology, let alone a conservative teleology, it would soon be subjected, and properly so, to even more harsh indictments than these. As has so often happened with teleology in the history of human thought, it would be subjected to a *reductio ad absurdum.* The functional analyst might then meet the fate of Socrates (though not for the same reason) who suggested that God put our mouth just under our nose so that we might enjoy the smell of our food.[36] Or, like the Christian theologians devoted to the argument from design, he might be cozened by a Ben Franklin who demonstrated that God clearly "wants us to tipple, because He has made the joints of the arm just the right length to carry a glass to the mouth, without falling short of or overshooting the mark: 'Let us adore, then, glass in hand, this benevolent wisdom; let us adore and drink.' "[37] Or, he might find himself given to more serious utterances, like Michelet who remarked "how beautifully everything is arranged by nature. As soon as the child comes into the world, it finds a mother who is ready to care for it."[38] Like any other system of thought which borders on teleology, though it seeks to avoid crossing the frontier into that alien and unproductive territory, functional analysis in sociology is threatened with a reduction to absurdity, once it adopts the postulate of all existing social structures as indispensable for the fulfillment of salient functional needs.

Functional Analysis as Radical

Interestingly enough, others have reached a conclusion precisely opposed to this charge that functional analysis is intrinsically committed to the view that whatever is, is right or that this is, indeed, the best of all possible worlds. These observers, LaPiere for example, suggest that functional analysis is an approach inherently critical in outlook and pragmatic in judgment:

There is . . . a deeper significance than might at first appear in the shift from structural description to functional analysis in the social sciences. This shift represents a break with the social absolutism and moralism of Christian

36. Farrington has some further interesting observations on pseudo-teleology in his *Science in Antiquity* (London: T. Butterworth, 1936), 160.

37. This, in a letter by Franklin to the Abbé Morellet, quoted from the latter's *mémoires* by Dixon Wecter, *The Hero in America,* (New York: Scribner, 1941), 53-54.

38. It is Sigmund Freud who picked up this remark in Michelet's *The Woman.*

theology. If the important aspect of any social structure is its functions, it follows that no structure can be judged in terms of structure alone. In practice this means, for example, that the patriarchal family system is collectively valuable *only if and to the extent that* it functions to the satisfaction of collective ends. As a social structure, *it has no inherent value*, since its functional value will vary from time to time and from place to place.

The functional approach to collective behavior will, undoubtedly, *affront all those who believe that specific sociopsychological structures have inherent values.* Thus, to those who believe that a church service is good because it is a church service, the statement that some church services are formal motions which are devoid of religious significance, that others are functionally comparable to theatrical performances, and that still others are a form of revelry and are therefore comparable to a drunken spree will be an affront to common sense, an attack upon the integrity of decent people, or, at the least, the ravings of a poor fool.[39]

The fact that functional analysis can be seen by some as inherently conservative and by others as inherently radical suggests that it may be *inherently* neither one nor the other. It suggests that functional analysis may involve no *intrinsic* ideological commitment although, like other forms of sociological analysis, it can be infused with any one of a wide range of ideological values. Now, this is not the first time that a theoretic orientation in social science or social philosophy has been assigned diametrically opposed ideological implications. It may be helpful, therefore, to examine one of the most notable prior instances in which a sociological and methodological conception has been the object of the most varied ideological imputations, and to compare this instance, so far as possible, with the case of functional analysis. The comparable case is that of dialectical materialism; the spokesmen for dialectical materialism are the nineteenth century economic historian, social philosopher and professional revolutionary, Karl Marx, and his close aide and collaborator, Friedrich Engels.

The Ideological Orientations of Dialectical Materialism

1. "The mystification which dialectic suffers at Hegel's hands by no means prevents him from being the first to present *its general form* of working in a comprehensive and conscious manner. With him it is standing on its head. It must be turned right side up again if you would discover the *rational kernel* within the *mystical shell.*

2. "*In its mystified form* dialectic became the fashion in Germany, *because it seemed to transfigure and to glorify the existing state of things.*

Comparative Ideological Orientations of Functional Analysis

1. *Some* functional analysts have gratuitously *assumed* that *all* existing social structures fulfill indispensable social functions. This is sheer faith, mysticism, if you will, rather than the final product of sustained and systematic inquiry. The postulate must be earned, not inherited, if it is to gain the acceptance of men of social science.

2. The three postulates of functional unity, universality and indispensability comprise a system of premises which must inevitably lead to a glorification of the existing state of things.

---

39. Richard LaPiere, *Collective Behavior*, (New York: McGraw-Hill, 1938), 55-56 [italics supplied].

*The Ideological Orientations of
Dialectical Materialism*

*Comparative Ideological Orientations
of Functional Analysis*

3. *"In its rational form* it is a scandal and an abomination to bourgeoisdom and its doctrinaire professors, because *it includes in its comprehensive and affirmative recognition of the existing state of things,* at the same time also, *the recognition of the negation of* that state [of affairs], of its inevitable breaking up;

3. In its more empirically oriented and analytically precise forms, functional analysis is often regarded with suspicion by those who consider an existing social structure as eternally fixed and beyond change. This more exacting form of functional analysis includes, not only a study of the *functions* of existing social structures, but also a study of their *dysfunctions* for diversely situated individuals, subgroups or social strata, and the more inclusive society. It provisionally assumes, as we shall see, that when *the net balance of the aggregate of consequences* of an existing social structure is clearly dysfunctional, there develops a strong and insistent pressure for change. It is possible, though this remains to be established, that beyond a given point, this pressure will inevitably result in more or less predetermined directions of social change.

4. *"because it regards every historically developed form* as in fluid movement, and therefore takes into account *its transient nature* not less than *its momentary existence;* because it lets nothing impose upon it, and is *in its essence* critical and revolutionary."[40]

4. Though functional analysis has often focused on the *statics* of social structure rather than the *dynamics* of social change, this is not intrinsic to that system of analysis. By focusing on dysfunctions as well as on functions, this mode of analysis can assess not only the bases of social stability but the potential sources of social change. The phrase "historically developed forms" may be a useful reminder that social structures are typically undergoing discernible change. It remains to discover the pressures making for various types of change. To the extent that functional analysis focuses wholly on functional consequences, it leans toward an ultraconservative ideology; to the extent that it focuses wholly on dysfunctional consequences, it leans toward an ultra-radical utopia. "In its essence," it is neither one nor the other.

5. *"*. . . all successive historical situations are *only transitory stages* in the endless course of development of human society from the lower to the higher. *Each stage is necessary, therefore justi-*

5. Recognizing, as they must, that social structures are forever changing, functional analysts must nevertheless explore the interdependent and often mutually supporting elements of social

---

40. The passage to this point is quoted, without deletion or addition but only with the introduction of italics for appropriate emphasis, from that fount of dialectical materialism, Karl Marx, *Capital,* (Chicago: C. H. Kerr, 1906), I, 25-26.

The Ideological Orientations of Dialectical Materialism	*Comparative Ideological Orientations of Functional Analysis*

fied for the time and conditions to which it owes its origin.

structure. In general, it seems that most societies are integrated to the extent that many, if not all, of their several elements are reciprocally adjusted. Social structures do not have a random assortment of attributes, but these are variously interconnected and often mutually sustaining. To recognize this, is not to adopt an uncritical affirmation of every *status quo;* to fail to recognize this, is to succumb to the temptations of radical utopianism.

6. "But in the newer and higher conditions which *gradually develop in its own bosom, each loses its validity and justification.* It must give way to a higher form which will also in its turn decay and perish . . .

6. The strains and stresses in a social structure which accumulate as dysfunctional consequences of existing elements are not cabin'd, cribb'd and confined by appropriate social planning and will in due course lead to institutional breakdown and basic social change. When this change has passed beyond a given and not easily identifiable point, it is customary to say that a new social system has emerged.

7. "It [dialectical materialism] reveals the transitory character of everything and in everything; nothing can endure before it except the uninterrupted process of becoming and of passing away . . . *It* [dialectic] *has, of course, also a conservative side: it recognizes that definite stages of knowledge and society are justified for their time and circumstances; but only so far. The conservatism of this mode of outlook is relative; its revolutionary character is absolute—the only absolute it admits.*"[41]

7. But again, it must be reiterated: neither change alone nor fixity alone can be the proper object of study by the functional analyst. As we survey the course of history, it seems reasonably clear that all major social structures have in due course been cumulatively modified or abruptly terminated. In either event, they have not been eternally fixed and unyielding to change. But, at a given moment of observation, any such social structure may be tolerably well accommodated both to the subjective values of many or most of the population, and to the objective conditions with which it is confronted. To recognize this is to be true to the facts, not faithful to a preestablished ideology. And by the same token, when the structure is observed to be out of joint with the wants of the people or with the equally solid conditions of action, this too must be recognized. Who dares do all that, may become a functional analyst, who dares do less is none.[42]

---

41. Similarly, the subsequent passage is quoted, with deletion only of irrelevant material and again with italics supplied, from Friedrich Engels, in *Karl Marx, Selected Works,* (Moscow: Cooperative Publishing Society, 1935), I, 422.

42. It is recognized that this paraphrase does violence to the original intent of the bard, but it is hoped that the occasion justifies the offense.

This systematic comparison may be enough to suggest that functional analysis does not, any more than the dialectic, *necessarily* entail a specific ideological commitment. This is not to say that such commitments are not often implicit in the works of functional analysts. But this seems extraneous rather than intrinsic to functional theory. Here, as in other departments of intellectual activity, abuse does not gainsay the possibility of use. *Critically* revised, functional analysis is neutral to the major ideological systems. To this extent, and only in this limited sense,[43] it is like those theories or instruments of the physical sciences which lend themselves indifferently to use by opposed groups for purposes which are often no part of the scientists' intent.

Ideology and the Functional Analysis of Religion

Again, it is instructive to turn, however briefly, to discussions of the functions of religion to show how the *logic* of functional analysis is adopted by people otherwise opposed in their ideological stance.

The social role of religion has of course been repeatedly observed and interpreted over the long span of many centuries. The hard core of continuity in these observations consists in an emphasis on religion as an institutional means of social control, whether this be in Plato's concept of "noble lies," or in Aristotle's opinion that it operates "with a view to the persuasion of the multitude" or in the comparable judgment by Polybius that "the masses . . . can be controlled only by mysterious terrors and tragic fears." If Montesquieu remarks of the Roman lawmakers that they sought "to inspire a people that feared nothing with fear of the gods, and to use that fear to lead it whithersoever they pleased," then Jawaharlal Nehru observes, on the basis of his own experience, that "the only books that British officials heartily recommended [to political prisoners in India] were religious books or novels. It is wonderful how dear to the heart of the British Government is the subject of religion and how impartially it encourages all brands of it."[44] It would appear that there is an ancient and abiding tradition holding, in one form or another, that religion has served to control the masses. It appears, also, that the language in which this proposition is couched usually gives a clue to the ideological commitment of the author.

How is it, then, with some of the current functional analyses of religion? In his critical consolidation of several major theories in the sociology of religion, Parsons summarizes some of the basic conclusions

43. This should not be taken to deny the important fact that the values, implicit and openly acknowledged, of the social scientist may help fix his choice of problems for investigation, his formulation of these problems and, consequently, the utility of his findings for certain purposes, and not for others. The statement intends only what it affirms: functional analysis had no *intrinsic* commitment to any ideological camp, as the foregoing discussion at least illustrates.

44. Jawaharlal Nehru, *Toward Freedom,* (New York: John Day, 1941), 7.

which have emerged regarding the "functional significance of religion":

. . . if moral norms and the sentiments supporting them are of such primary importance, what are the mechanisms by which they are maintained *other than external processes of enforcement?* It was Durkheim's view that religious ritual was of primary significance as a mechanism for *expressing and reinforcing* the *sentiments* most essential to the *institutional integration* of the society. It can readily be seen that this is clearly linked to Malinowski's views of the significance of funeral ceremonies as *a mechanism for reasserting the solidarity of the group* on the occasion of severe emotional strain. Thus Durkheim worked out certain aspects of the specific relations between *religion and social structure* more sharply than did Malinowski, and in addition put the problem in a different functional perspective in that he applied it to the society as a whole in abstraction from particular situations of tension and strain for the individual.[45]

And again, summarizing an essential finding of the major comparative study in the sociology of religion, Parsons observes that "perhaps the most striking feature of Weber's analysis is the demonstration of the extent to which precisely the variations in socially sanctioned values and goals in secular life correspond to the variations in the dominant religious philosophy of the great civilizations."[46]

Similarly, in exploring the role of religion among racial and ethnic subgroups in the United States, Donald Young in effect remarks the close correspondence between their "socially sanctioned values and goals in secular life" and their "dominant religious philosophy":

One function which a minority religion may serve is that of *reconciliation with inferior status and its discriminatory consequences.* Evidence of religious service of this function may be found among all American minority peoples. On the other hand, religious institutions may also develop in such a way as to be *an incitement and support of revolt against inferior status.* Thus, the Christianized Indian, with due allowance for exceptions, has tended to be *more submissive* than the pagan. Special cults such as those associated with the use of peyote, the Indian Shaker Church, and the Ghost Dance, all three containing both Christian and native elements, were foredoomed attempts to develop *modes of religious expression adapted to individual and group circumstances.* The latter, with its emphasis on an assured millennium of freedom from the white man, encouraged forceful revolt. The Christianity of the Negro, in spite of appreciable encouragement of verbal criticism of the existing order, *has emphasized acceptance of present troubles in the knowledge of better times to come in the life hereafter.* The numerous varieties of Christianity and the Judaism brought by immigrants from Europe and Mexico, in spite of common nationalistic elements, also *stressed later rewards rather than immediate direct action.*[47]

---

45. Talcott Parsons, *Essays in Sociological Theory,* 61 [italics supplied].

46. *Ibid.,* 63.

47. Donald Young, *American Minority Peoples,* (New York: Harper, 1937), 204 [italics supplied]. For a functional analysis of the Negro church in the United States, see George Eaton Simpson and J. Milton Yinger, *Racial and Cultural Minorities* (New York: Harper & Brothers, 1953), 522-530.

These diverse and scattered observations, with their notably varied ideological provenience, exhibit some basic similarities. First, they are all given over to the consequences of specific religious systems for prevailing sentiments, definitions of situations and action. These consequences are rather consistently observed to be those of reinforcement of prevailing moral norms, docile acceptance of these norms, postponement of ambitions and gratifications (if the religious doctrine so demands), and the like. However, as Young observes, religions have also served, under determinate conditions, to provoke rebellion, or as Weber has shown, religions have served to motivate or to canalize the behavior of great numbers of men and women toward the modification of social structures. It would seem premature, therefore, to conclude that all religion everywhere has only the one consequence of making for mass apathy.

Second, the Marxist view implicitly and the functionalist view explicitly affirm the central point that systems of religion *do affect behavior,* that they are *not merely* epiphenomena but partially independent determinants of behavior. For presumably, it makes a difference if "the masses" do or do not accept a particular religion just as it makes a difference if an individual does or does not take opium.

Third, the more ancient as well as the Marxist theories deal with the *differential* consequences of religious beliefs and rituals for various subgroups and strata in the society—*e.g.,* "the masses"—as, for that matter, does the non-Marxist Donald Young. The functionalist is not confined, as we have seen, to exploring the consequences of religion for "society as a whole."

Fourth, the suspicion begins to emerge that the functionalists, with their emphasis on religion as a *social mechanism* for "reinforcing the sentiments most essential to the institutional integration of the society," may not differ materially in their *analytical framework* from the Marxists who, if their metaphor of "opium of the masses" is converted into a neutral statement of social fact, also assert that religion operates as a social mechanism for reinforcing certain secular as well as sacred sentiments among its believers.

The point of difference appears only when *evaluations* of this commonly accepted fact come into question. Insofar as the functionalists refer only to "institutional integration" without exploring the diverse consequences of integration about very different types of values and interests, they confine themselves to purely *formal* interpretation. For integration is a plainly formal concept. A society may be integrated around norms of strict caste, regimentation, and docility of subordinated social strata, just as it may be integrated around norms of open mobility, wide areas of self-expression and independence of judgment among temporarily lower strata. And insofar as the Marxists assert, without qualification, that all religion everywhere, whatever its doctrinal content and its organizational form, involves "an opiate" for the masses, they too shift to purely formal interpretations, without allowing, as the excerpt from Young shows to be the case, for particular religions in particular social structures serving to activate rather than to lethargize mass action. It is in the *evaluation* of these functions of religion, rather than in the logic of analysis, then, that the functionalists and the Marxists part company. And it is the *evaluations* which permit the pouring of ideological content into the bottles of *functionalism*.[48] The bottles themselves are

---

48. This type of talking-past-each-other is perhaps more common than one is wont to suspect. Often, the basic agreement in the *analysis* of a situation is plentifully obscured by the basic disagreement in the *evaluation* of that situation. As a result, it is erroneously assumed that the opponents differ in their cognitive procedures and findings, whereas they differ only in their sets of values. Consider, for example, the recent striking case of the public debates and conflicts between Winston Churchill and Harold Laski, where it was generally assumed, among others by Churchill himself, that the two disagreed on the substantive premise that social change is more readily accepted in time of war than in time of peace. Yet compare the following excerpts from the writings of the two men.

"The former peace-time structure of society had for more than four years been superseded and life had been raised to a strange intensity by the war spell. Under that mysterious influence, men and women had been appreciably exalted above death and pain and toil. *Unities and comradeships had become possible* between men and classes and nations and grown stronger *while the hostile pressure and the common cause endured.* But now the spell was broken: too late for some purposes, too soon for others, and too suddenly for all! *Every victorious country subsided to its old levels and its previous arrangements;* but these latter were found to have fallen into much disrepair, their fabric was weakened and disjointed, they seemed narrow and out of date."

"*With the passing of the spell there passed also,* just as the new difficulties were at their height, *much of the exceptional powers of guidance and control.* . . . To the faithful, toil-burdened masses the victory was so complete that no further effort seemed required. . . . *A vast fatigue dominated collective action.* Though every subversive element endeavored to assert itself, *revolutionary rage like every other form of psychic energy burnt low.*"

"The atmosphere of war permits, and even compels, innovations and experiments that are not possible when peace returns. The invasion of our wonted routine of life accustoms us to what William James called the vital habit of breaking habits. . . . *We find ourselves stimulated to exertions, even sacrifices,* we did not know we had it in us to make. *Common danger builds a basis for a new fellowship* the future of which is dependent wholly upon whether its foundations are temporary or permanent. If they are temporary, then the end of the war sees the resumption of all our previous differences exacerbated tenfold by the grave problems it will have left." "I am, therefore, arguing that the changes which we require we can make by consent in a period in which, as now, conditions make men remember their identities and not their differences."

"We can begin those changes now because the atmosphere is prepared for their reception. It is highly *doubtful whether we can make them by consent when that atmosphere is absent.* It is the more doubtful because the effort the war requires will induce in many, above all in those who have agreed to the suspension of privilege, *a fatigue, a hunger for the ancient ways, which it will be difficult to resist.*"

neutral to their contents, and may serve equally well as containers for ideological poison or for ideological nectar.

THE LOGIC OF PROCEDURE

Prevalence of the Functional Orientation

The functional orientation is of course neither new nor confined to the social sciences. It came, in fact, relatively late on the sociological scene, if one may judge by its earlier and extended use in a great variety of other disciplines.[49] The central orientation of functionalism—expressed

---

"The intensity of the exertions evoked by the national danger far exceeded the ordinary capacities of human beings. All were geared up to an abnormal pitch. *Once the supreme incentive had disappeared, everyone became conscious of the severity of the strain. A vast and general relaxation and descent to the standards of ordinary life was imminent.* No community could have gone on using up treasure and life energy at such a pace. *Most of all was the strain apparent in the higher ranks of the brain workers.* They had carried on uplifted by the psychological stimulus which was now to be removed. 'I can work until I drop' was sufficient while the cannon thundered and armies marched. *But now it was peace: and on every side exhaustion,* nervous and physical, unfelt or unheeded before, became evident."

"In all revolutions there comes a period of inertia when *the fatigue of the effort compels a pause in the process of innovation.* That period is bound to come with the cessation of hostilities. *After a life on the heights the human constitution seems to demand tranquility and relaxation.* To insist, in the period of pause, that we gird up our loins for a new and difficult journey, above all for a journey into the unknown, is to ask the impossible. . . . When hostilities against Nazism cease, *men will want, more than anything, a routine of thought and habit which does not compel the painful adaptation of their minds to disturbing excitement.*"

The Gibbonesque passages in the first column are, of course, by Churchill, the Winston Churchill between the Great Wars, writing in retrospect about the aftermath of the first of these: *The World Crisis:* Volume 4, *The Aftermath,* (London: Thornton Butterworth, 1928), 30, 31, 33. The observations in the second column are those of Harold Laski, writing during the Second Great War to say that it is the policy of Mr. Churchill to make "the conscious postponement of any issue deemed 'controversial' until the victory is won [and] this means . . . that the relations of production are to remain unchanged until peace comes, and that, accordingly, none of the instruments for social change on a large scale, will be at the national disposal for agreed purposes." *Revolution of Our Time,* (New York: Viking Press, 1943), 185, 187, 193, 227-8, 309. Unless Churchill had forgotten his analysis of the aftermath of the first war, it is plain that he and Laski were *agreed on the diagnosis* that significant and deliberately enacted social change was unlikely in the immediate postwar era. The difference clearly lay in the appraisal of the desirability of instituting designated changes at all. (The italics in both columns were by neither author.)

It may be noted, in passing, that the very expectation on which both Churchill and Laski were *agreed—i.e.* that the post-war period in England would be one of mass lethargy and indifference to planned institutional change—was not altogether borne out by the actual course of events. England after the second great war did not exactly repudiate the notion of planned change.

---

49. The currency of a functionalist outlook has been repeatedly noted. For example: "The fact that in all fields of thinking the same tendency is noticeable, proves that there is now a general trend toward interpreting the world in terms of interconnection of operation rather than in terms of separate substantial units. Albert

in the practice of interpreting data by establishing their consequences for larger structures in which they are implicated—has been found in virtually all the sciences of man—biology and physiology, psychology, economics and law, anthropology and sociology.[50] The prevalence of the

---

Einstein in physics, Claude Bernard in physiology, Alexis Carrel in biology, Frank Lloyd Wright in architecture, A. N. Whitehead in philosophy, W. Koehler in psychology, Theodor Litt in sociology, Hermann Heller in political science, B. Cardozo in law: these are men representing different cultures, different countries, different aspects of human life and the human spirit, and yet all approaching their problems with a sense of 'reality' which is looking not to material substance but to functional interaction for a comprehension of phenomena." G. Niemeyer, *Law Without Force*, (Princeton University Press, 1941), 300. This motley company suggests anew that agreement on the functional outlook need not imply identity of political or social philosophy.

50. The literature commenting on the trend toward functionalism is almost as large and considerably more sprawling than the diverse scientific literatures exemplifying the trend. Limitations of space and concern for immediate relevance limit the number of such references which must here take the place of an extended review and discussion of these collateral developments in scientific thought.

For *biology*, a general, now classical, source is J. H. Woodger, *Biological Principles: A Critical Study*, (New York: Harcourt Brace and Co., 1929), esp. 327 ff. For correlative materials, at least the following are indicated: Bertalanffy, *Modern Theories of Development, op. cit.*, particularly 1-46, 64 ff., 179 ff.; E. S. Russell, *The Interpretation of Development and Heredity: A Study in Biological Method*, (Oxford: Clarendon Press, 1930), esp. 166-280. Foreshadowing discussions will be found in the less instructive writings of W. E. Ritter, E. B. Wilson, E. Ungerer, J. Schaxel, J. von Uexküll, etc. The papers of J. Needham—*e.g.*, "Thoughts on the problem of biological organization," *Scientia*, August 1932, 84-92—can be consulted with profit.

For *physiology*, consider the writings of C. S. Sherrington, W. B. Cannon, G. E. Coghill, Joseph Barcroft, and especially the following: C. S. Sherrington, *The Integrative Action of the Nervous System*, (New Haven: Yale University Press, 1923); W. B. Cannon, *Bodily Changes in Pain, Hunger, Fear and Rage*, chapter 12, and *The Wisdom of the Body*, (New York: W. W. Norton, 1932), all but the unhappy epilogue on "social homeostasis"; G. E. Coghill, *Anatomy and the Problem of Behavior*, (Cambridge University Press, 1929); Joseph Barcroft, *Features in the Architecture of Physiological Function*, (Cambridge University Press, 1934).

For *psychology*, virtually any of the basic contributions to dynamic psychology are in point. It would not only be low wit but entirely true to say that Freudian conceptions are instinct with functionalism, since the major concepts are invariably referred to a functional (or dysfunctional) framework. For a different order of conception, see Harvey Carr, "Functionalism," in Carl Murchison, ed. *Psychologies of 1930*, (Clark University Press, 1930); and as one among many articles dealing with substantially this set of conceptions, see J. M. Fletcher, "Homeostasis as an explanatory principle in psychology," *Psychological Review*, 1942, 49, 80-87. For a statement of application of the functional approach to personality, see chapter I in Clyde Kluckhohn and Henry A. Murray, ed. *Personality in Nature, Society and Culture*, (New York: A. A. Knopf, 1948), 3-32. The important respects in which the Lewin group is oriented toward functionalism have been widely recognized.

For *law*, see the critical paper by Felix S. Cohen, "Transcendental nonsense and the functional approach," *Columbia Law Review*, 1935, XXXV, 809-849, and the numerous annotated references therein.

For *sociology and anthropology*, see the brief sampling of references throughout this chapter. The volume edited by Robert Redfield provides a useful bridge across the chasm too often separating the biological from the social sciences. Levels of Integration in Biological and Social Systems, *Biological Symposia*, 1943, VIII. For an important effort to set out the conceptual framework of functional analysis, see Talcott Parsons, *The Social System*, (Glencoe, Illinois: Free Press, 1951).

functional outlook is in itself no warrant for its scientific value, but it does suggest that cumulative experience has forced this orientation upon the disciplined observers of man as biological organism, psychological actor, member of society and bearer of culture.

More immediately relevant is the possibility that prior experience in other disciplines may provide useful methodological models for functional analysis in sociology. To learn from the canons of analytical procedure in these often more exacting disciplines is not, however, to adopt their specific conceptions and techniques, lock, stock and barrel. To profit from the logic of procedure successfully employed in the biological sciences, for example, is not to backslide into accepting the largely irrelevant analogies and homologies which have so long fascinated the devotees of organismic sociology. To examine the *methodological* framework of biological researches is not to adopt their *substantive* concepts.

The *logical structure* of experiment, for example, does not differ in physics, or chemistry or psychology, although the substantive hypotheses, the technical tools, the basic concepts and the practical difficulties may differ enormously. Nor do the near-substitutes for experiment—controlled observation, comparative study and the method of 'discerning'—differ in their *logical structure* in anthropology, sociology or biology.

In turning briefly to Cannon's logic of procedure in physiology, then, we are looking for a methodological model which might possibly be derived for sociology, without adopting Cannon's unfortunate homologies between the structure of biological organisms and of society.[51] His procedures shape up somewhat as follows. Adopting the orientatior of Claude Bernard, Cannon first indicates that the organism *requires* a relatively constant and stable state. One task of the physiologist, then, is to provide "a concrete and detailed account of the modes of assuring steady states." In reviewing the numerous "concrete and detailed" accounts provided by Cannon, we find that the *general mode of formulation* is invariable, irrespective of the specific problem in hand. A typical formulation is as follows: *"In order that* the blood shall . . . serve as a circulating medium, fulfilling the various *functions* of a common carrier of nutriment and waste . . ., *there must be* provision for holding it back whenever there is danger of escape." Or, to take another statement: *"If* the life of the cell is to continue . . ., the blood . . . *must* flow with sufficient speed to deliver to the living cells the (necessary) supply of oxygen."

---

51. As previously implied, Cannon's epilogue to his *Wisdom of the Body* remains unexcelled as an example of the fruitless extremes to which even a distinguished mind is driven once he sets about to draw *substantive* analogies and homologies between biological organisms and social systems. Consider, for example, his comparison between the fluid matrix of the body and the canals, rivers and railroads on which "the products of farm and factory, of mine and forest, are borne to and fro." This kind of analogy, earlier developed in copious volumes by René Worms, Schaeffle, Vincent, Small, and Spencer among others, does *not* represent the distinctive value of Cannon's writings for the sociologist.

Having established the *requirements* of the organic system, Cannon then proceeds to describe *in detail* the various *mechanisms* which operate to meet these requirements (*e.g.*, the complicated changes which lead to clotting, the local contraction of injured blood vessels that lessen the severity of bleeding; accelerated clot formation through the secretion of adrenin and the action of adrenin upon the liver, *etc.*). Or again, he describes the various biochemical arrangements which ensure a proper supply of oxygen to the normal organism and the compensating changes which occur when some of these arrangements do not operate adequately.

If the logic of this approach is stated in its more general terms, the following interrelated sequence of steps becomes evident. First of all, certain functional requirements of the organisms are established, requirements which must be satisfied if the organism is to survive, or to operate with some degree of effectiveness. Second, there is a concrete and detailed description of the arrangements (structures and processes) through which these requirements are typically met in "normal" cases. Third, if some of the typical mechanisms for meeting these requirements are destroyed, or are found to be functioning inadequately, the observer is sensitized to the need for detecting compensating mechanisms (if any) which fulfill the necessary function. Fourth, and implicit in all that precedes, there is a detailed account of the structure *for which* the functional requirements hold, as well as a detailed account of the arrangements *through which* the function is fulfilled.

So well established is the logic of functional analysis in the biological sciences that these requirements for an adequate analysis come to be met almost as a matter of course. Not so with sociology. Here, we find extraordinarily varied conceptions of the appropriate design of studies in functional analysis. For some, it consists largely (or even exclusively) in establishing empirical interrelations between "parts" of a social system; for others, it consists in showing the "value for society" of a socially standardized practice or a social organization; for still others, it consists in elaborate accounts of the purposes of formal social organizations.

As one examines the varied array of functional analyses in sociology, it becomes evident that sociologists in contrast, say, to physiologists, do not typically carry through operationally intelligible procedures, do not systematically assemble needed types of data, do not employ a common body of concepts and do not utilize the same criteria of validity. In other words, we find in physiology, a body of standard concepts, procedures and design of analysis and in sociology, a variegated selection of concepts, procedures and designs, depending, it would seem, on the interests and tastes of the individual sociologist. To be sure, this difference between the two disciplines has *something*—perhaps, a good deal—to do with differences in the character of the data examined by the physiologist and the sociologist. The relatively large opportunities for experimental work in physiology are, to be trite about it, scarcely matched in sociology. But this scarcely accounts for the systematic ordering of procedure and concepts in the one instance and the disparate, often uncoordinated and not infrequently defective character of procedure and concepts in functional sociology.

A PARADIGM FOR FUNCTIONAL ANALYSIS IN SOCIOLOGY

As an initial and admittedly tentative step in the direction of codifying functional analysis in sociology, we set forth a paradigm of the concepts and problems central to this approach. It will soon become evident that the chief components of this paradigm have progressively emerged in the foregoing pages as we have critically examined the vocabularies, postulates, concepts and ideological imputations now current in the field. The paradigm brings these together in compact form, thus permitting simultaneous inspection of the major requirements of functional analysis and serving as an aid to self-correction of provisional interpretations, a result difficult to achieve when concepts are scattered and hidden in page after page of discursive exposition.[52] The paradigm presents the hard core of concept, procedure and inference in functional analysis.

Above all, it should be noted that the paradigm does not represent a set of categories introduced *de novo,* but rather a *codification* of those concepts and problems which have been forced upon our attention by critical scrutiny of current research and theory in functional analysis. (Reference to the preceding sections of this chapter will show that the groundwork has been prepared for every one of the categories embodied in the paradigm.)

1. *The item(s) to which functions are imputed*
    The entire range of sociological data can be, and much of it has been, subjected to functional analysis. The basic requirement is that the object of analysis represent a *standardized* (*i.e.* patterned and repetitive) item, such as social roles, institutional patterns, social processes, cultural pattern, culturally patterned emotions, social norms, group organization, social structure, devices for social control, *etc.*

    BASIC QUERY: What must enter into the protocol of observation of the given item if it is to be amenable to systematic functional analysis?

2. *Concepts of subjective dispositions (motives, purposes)*
    At some point, functional analysis invariably assumes or explicitly operates with some conception of the motivation of individuals involved in a social system. As the foregoing discussion has shown, these concepts of subjective disposition are often and erroneously merged with the related, but different, concepts of objective consequences of attitude, belief and behavior.

---

52. For a brief statement of the purpose of analytical paradigms such as this, see the note on paradigms elsewhere in this volume.

BASIC QUERY: In which types of analysis is it sufficient to take observed motivations as *data*, as given, and in which are they properly considered as *problematical*, as derivable from other data?

3. Concepts of objective consequences (functions, dysfunctions)

We have observed two prevailing types of confusion enveloping the several current conceptions of "function":

(1) The tendency to confine sociological observations to the *positive* contributions of a sociological item to the social or cultural system in which it is implicated; and

(2) The tendency to confuse the subjective category of *motive* with the objective category of *function*.

Appropriate conceptual distinctions are required to eliminate these confusions.

The first problem calls for a concept of *multiple consequences* and *a net balance of an aggregate of consequences.*

Functions are those observed consequences which make for the adaptation or adjustment of a given system; and *dysfunctions*, those observed consequences which lessen the adaptation or adjustment of the system. There is also the empirical possibility of *nonfunctional* consequences, which are simply irrelevant to the system under consideration.

In any given instance, an item may have both functional and dysfunctional consequences, giving rise to the difficult and important problem of evolving canons for assessing the net balance of the aggregate of consequences. (This is, of course, most important in the use of functional analysis for guiding the formation and enactment of policy.)

The second problem (arising from the easy confusion of motives and functions) requires us to introduce a conceptual distinction between the cases in which the subjective aim-in-view coincides with the objective consequence, and the cases in which they diverge.

Manifest functions are those objective consequences contributing to the adjustment or adaptation of the system which are intended and recognized by participants in the system;

Latent functions, correlatively, being those which are neither intended nor recognized.*

BASIC QUERY: What are the effects of the transformation of a previously latent function into a manifest function (involving the problem of the role of knowledge in human behavior and the problems of "manipulation" of human behavior)?

---

* The relations between the "unanticipated consequences" of action and "latent functions" can be clearly defined, since they are implicit in the foregoing section of the paradigm. The unintended consequences of action are of three types:

    (1) those which are functional for a designated system, and these comprise the latent functions;

    (2) those which are dysfunctional for a designated system, and these comprise the latent dysfunctions; and

    (3) those which are irrelevant to the system which they affect neither functionally nor dysfunctionally, *i.e.*, the pragmatically unimportant class of non-functional consequences.

For a preliminary statement, see R. K. Merton, "The unanticipated consequences of purposive social action," *American Sociological Review* 1936, 1, 894-904; for a tabulation of these types of consequences see Goode, *Religion Among the Primitives,* 32-33.

4. *Concepts of the unit subserved by the function*

We have observed the difficulties entailed in *confining* analysis to functions fulfilled for "the society," since items may be functional for some individuals and subgroups and dysfunctional for others. It is necessary, therefore, to consider a *range* of units for which the item has designated consequences: individuals in diverse statuses, subgroups, the larger social system and culture systems. (Terminologically, this implies the concepts of psychological function, group function, societal function, cultural function, *etc.*)

5. *Concepts of functional requirements (needs, prerequisites)*

Embedded in every functional analysis is some conception, tacit or expressed, of the functional requirements of the system under observation. As noted elsewhere,[53] this remains one of the cloudiest and empirically most debatable concepts in functional theory. As utilized by sociologists, the concept of functional requirement tends to be tautological or *ex post facto;* it tends to be confined to the conditions of "survival" of a given system; it tends, as in the work of Malinowski, to include biological as well as social "needs."

This involves the difficult problem of establishing *types* of functional requirements (universal vs. specific); procedures for validating the assumption of these requirements; *etc.*

BASIC QUERY: What is required to establish the validity of such a variable as "functional requirement" in situations where rigorous experimentation is impracticable?

6. *Concepts of the mechanisms through which functions are fulfilled*

Functional analysis in sociology, as in other disciplines like physiology and psychology, calls for a "concrete and detailed" account of the mechanisms which operate to perform a designated function. This refers, not to psychological, but to social, mechanisms (*e.g.*, role-segmentation, insulation of institutional demands, hierarchic ordering of values, social division of labor, ritual and ceremonial enactments, *etc.*).

BASIC QUERY: What is the presently available inventory of social mechanisms corresponding, say, to the large inventory of psychological mechanisms? What methodological problems are entailed in discerning the operation of these social mechanisms?

7. *Concepts of functional alternatives (functional equivalents or substitutes)*

As we have seen, once we abandon the gratuitous assumption of the functional indispensability of particular social structures, we immediately require some concept of functional alternatives, equivalents, or substitutes. This focuses attention on the *range of possible variation* in the items which can, in the case under examination, subserve a functional requirement. It unfreezes the identity of the existent and the inevitable.

BASIC QUERY: Since scientific proof of the equivalence of an alleged functional alternative ideally requires rigorous experimentation, and since this is not often practicable in large-scale sociological situations, which practicable procedures of inquiry most nearly approximate the logic of experiment?

8. *Concepts of structural context (or structural constraint)*

The range of variation in the items which *can* fulfill designated functions in a social structure is not unlimited (and this has been repeatedly noted in our foregoing discussion). The interdependence of the elements of a social structure limits the effective possibilities of change or functional alternatives.

---

53. R. K. Merton, "Discussion of Parsons' 'Position of sociological theory,'" *American Sociological Review,* 1949, *13,* 164-168.

The concept of structural constraint corresponds, in the area of social structure, to Goldenweiser's "principle of limited possibilities" in a broader sphere. Failure to recognize the relevance of interdependence and attendant structural restraints leads to utopian thought in which it is tacitly assumed that certain elements of a social system can be eliminated without affecting the rest of that system. This consideration is recognized by both Marxist social scientists (e.g. Karl Marx) and by non-Marxists (e.g. Malinowski).[54]

BASIC QUERY: How narrowly does a given structural context limit the range of variation in the items which can effectively satisfy functional requirements? Do we find, under conditions yet to be determined, an area of indifference, in which any one of a wide range of alternatives may fulfill the function?

9. Concepts of dynamics and change

We have noted that functional analysts *tend* to focus on the statics of social structure and to neglect the study of structural change.

This emphasis upon statics is not, however, *inherent* in the theory of functional analysis. It is, rather, an adventitious emphasis stemming from the concern of early anthropological functionalists to counteract preceding tendencies to write conjectural histories of non-literate societies. This practice, useful at the time it was first introduced into anthropology, has disadvantageously persisted in the work of some functional sociologists.

The concept of dysfunction, which implies the concept of strain, stress and tension on the structural level, provides an analytical approach to the study of dynamics and change. How are observed dysfunctions contained within a particular structure, so that they do not produce instability? Does the accumulation of stresses and strains produce pressure for change in such directions as are likely to lead to their reduction?

BASIC QUERY: Does the prevailing concern among functional analysts

---

54. Previously cited excerpts from Marx document this statement, but these are, of course, only a few out of many places in which Marx in effect stresses the importance of taking account of the structural context. In *A Contribution to the Critique of Political Economy* (appearing in 1859 and republished in Karl Marx, *Selected Works, op. cit.,* I, 354-371), he observes for example: "No social order ever disappears before all the productive forces for which there is room in it have been developed; and new higher relations of production never appear before the material conditions of their existence have matured in the womb of the old society itself. Therefore, mankind always sets itself only such tasks as it can solve; since, looking at the matter more closely, we will always find that the task itself arises only when the material conditions necessary for its solution already exist or are at least in the process of formation." (p. 357) Perhaps the most famous of his many references to the constraining influence of a given social structure is found in the second paragraph of *The Eighteenth Brumaire of Louis Napoleon:* "Man makes his own history, but he does not make it out of whole cloth: he does not make it out of conditions chosen by himself, but out of such conditions as he finds close at hand." (From the paraphrase of the original as published in Marx, *Selected Works,* II, 315.) To my knowledge, A. D. Lindsay is the most perceptive among the commentators who have noted the theoretic implications of statements such as these. See his little book, *Karl Marx's Capital: An Introductory Essay,* (Oxford University Press, 1931), esp. at 27-52.

And for other language with quite different ideological import and essentially similar theoretic implications, see B. Malinowski, "Given a definite cultural need, the means of its satisfaction are small in number, and therefore the cultural arrangement which comes into being in response to the need is determined within narrow limits." "Culture," *Encyclopedia of the Social Sciences, op. cit.,* 626.

with the concept of *social equilibrium* divert attention from the phenomena of *social disequilibrium?* Which available procedures will permit the sociologist most adequately to gauge the accumulation of stresses and strains in a social system? To what extent does knowledge of the structural context permit the sociologist to anticipate the most probable directions of social change?

10. *Problems of validation of functional analysis*

Throughout the paradigm, attention has been called repeatedly to the *specific* points at which assumptions, imputations and observations must be validated.[55] This requires, above all, a rigorous statement of the sociological procedures of analysis which most nearly approximate the *logic* of experimentation. It requires a systematic review of the possibilities and limitations of *comparative* (cross-cultural and cross-group) *analysis*.

BASIC QUERY: To what extent is functional analysis limited by the difficulty of locating adequate *samples of social systems* which can be subjected to comparative (quasi-experimental) study?[56]

11. *Problems of the ideological implications of functional analysis*

It has been emphasized in a preceding section that functional analysis has no intrinsic commitment to an ideological position. This does not gainsay the fact that *particular* functional analyses and *particular* hypotheses advanced by functionalists may have an identifiable ideological role. This, then, becomes a specific problem for the sociology of knowledge: to what extent does the social position of the functional sociologist (*e.g., vis-a-vis* a particular "client" who has authorized a given research) evoke one rather than another formulation of a problem, affect his assumptions and concepts, and limit the range of inferences drawn from his data?

BASIC QUERY: How does one detect the ideological tinge of a functional analysis and to what degree does a particular ideology stem from the basic assumptions adopted by the sociologist? Is the incidence of these assumptions related to the status and research role of the sociologist?

Before proceeding to a more intensive study of some parts of this paradigm, let us be clear about the uses to which it is supposed the paradigm can be put. After all, taxonomies of concepts may be multiplied endlessly without materially advancing the tasks of sociological analysis. What, then, are the purposes of the paradigm and how might it be used?

---

55. By this point, it is evident that we are considering functional analysis as a method for the *interpretation* of sociological data. This is not to gainsay the important role of the functional orientation in sensitizing sociologists to the *collection* of types of data which might otherwise be neglected. It is perhaps unnecessary to reiterate the axiom that one's concepts *do* determine the inclusion or exclusion of data, that, despite the etymology of the term, *data* are not "given" but are "contrived" with the inevitable help of concepts. In the process of evolving a functional interpretation, the sociological analyst invariably finds it necessary to obtain data other than those initially contemplated. Interpretation and the collection of data are thus inextricably bound up in the array of concepts and propositions relating these concepts. For an extension of these remarks, see Chapter II.

56. George P. Murdock's *Social Structure*, (New York: Macmillan, 1949), is enough to show that procedures such as those involved in the cross-cultural survey hold large promise for dealing with certain methodological problems of functional analysis. See also the procedures of functional analysis in George C. Homans and David M. Schneider, *Marriage, Authority, and Final Causes* (Glencoe: The Free Press, 1955).

Purposes of the Paradigm

The first and foremost purpose is to supply a provisional codified guide for adequate and fruitful functional analyses. This objective evidently implies that the paradigm contains the minimum set of concepts with which the sociologist must operate in order to carry through an adequate functional analysis and, as a corollary, that it can be used here and now as a guide for the critical study of existing analyses. It is thus intended as an all-too-compact and elliptical guide to the formulation of researches in functional analysis and as an aid in locating the distinctive contributions and deficiencies of earlier researches. Limitations of space will permit us to apply only limited sections of the paradigm to a critical appraisal of a selected list of cases in point.

Secondly, the paradigm is intended to lead directly to the postulates and (often tacit) assumptions underlying functional analysis. As we have found in earlier parts of this chapter, some of these assumptions are of central importance, others insignificant and dispensable, and still others, dubious and even misleading.

In the third place, the paradigm seeks to sensitize the sociologist not only to the narrowly scientific implications of various types of functional analysis, but also to their political and sometimes ideological implications. The points at which a functional analysis presupposes an implicit political outlook and the points at which it has bearing on "social engineering" are concerns which find an integral place in the paradigm.

It is obviously beyond the limits of this chapter to explore in detail the large and inclusive problems involved in the paradigm. This must await fuller exposition in a volume devoted to this purpose. We shall, therefore, confine the remainder of the present discussion to brief applications of only the first parts of the paradigm to a severely limited number of cases of functional analysis in sociology. And, from time to time, these few cases will be used as a springboard for discussion of special problems which are only imperfectly illustrated by the cases in hand.

ITEMS SUBJECTED TO FUNCTIONAL ANALYSIS

At first glance, it would appear that the sheer *description* of the item to be analyzed functionally entails few, if any, problems. Presumably, one should describe the item "as fully and as accurately" as possible. Yet, at second thought, it is evident that this maxim provides next to no guidance for the observer. Consider the plight of a functionally oriented neophyte armed only with this dictum as an aid to answering the question: *what* am I to observe, *what* am I to incorporate into my field notes, and *what* may I safely omit?

Without assuming that a detailed and circumstantial answer can now be supplied to the field worker, we can nevertheless note that the question itself is legitimate and that *implicit* answers have been partly developed. To tease out these implicit answers and to codify them, it is necessary to approach cases of functional analysis with the query: *what kinds of data have been consistently included, no matter what the item undergoing analysis, and why have these rather than other data been included?*

It soon becomes apparent that the functionalist orientation largely determines what is included in the description of the item to be interpreted. Thus, the description of a magical performance or a ceremonial is not confined to an account of the spell or formula, the rite and the performers. It includes a systematic account of the people participating and the onlookers, of the types and rates of interaction among performers and audience, of changes in these patterns of interaction in the course of the ceremonial. Thus, the description of Hopi rain ceremonials, for example, entails more than the actions seemingly oriented toward the intervention of the gods in meteorological phenomena. It involves a report of the persons *who* are variously involved in the pattern of behavior. And the description of the participants (and on-lookers) is in *structural terms,* that is, in terms of locating these people in their inter-connected social statuses.

Brief excerpts will illustrate how functional analyses begin with a systematic inclusion (and, preferably, charting) of the statuses and social interrelations of those engaging in the behavior under scrutiny.

> *Chiricahua puberty ceremonial for girls: the extended domestic family* (parents and relatives financially able to help) bear the expense of this four-day ceremony. The parents select the time and place for the ceremonial. "All the members of the *girl's encampment* attend and nearly all the *members of the local group.* A goodly sprinkling of visitors from *other local groups* and some *travelers from outside bands* are to be seen, and their numbers increase as the day wears on." The *leader of the local group* to which the girl's family belongs speaks, welcoming all visitors. In short, this account explicitly calls attention to the following statuses and groups variously involved in the ceremonial: the girl; her parents and immediate family; the local group, especially through its leader; the band represented by members of outside local groups, and the "tribe by members of other bands."[57]

As we shall see in due course, although it bears stating at this point, *the sheer description* of the ceremony in terms of the statuses and group affiliations of those variously involved *provides a major clue to the functions* performed by this ceremonial. In a word, we suggest that the structural description of participants in the activity under analysis provides hypotheses for subsequent functional interpretations.

---

57. Morris E. Opler, "An outline of Chiricahua Apache social organization," in Fred Eggan ed. *Social Anthropology of North American Tribes,* (Chicago: University of Chicago Press, 1937), 173-239, esp. at 226-230 [italics supplied].

Another illustration will again indicate the nature of such descriptions in terms of role, status, group affiliation and the interrelations among these.

Patterned responses to mirriri (hearing obscenity directed at one's sister) among the Australian Murngin. The standardized pattern must be all too briefly described: when a husband swears at his wife in the presence of her brother, the brother engages in the seemingly anomalous behavior of throwing spears at the wife (not the husband) and her sisters. The description of this pattern goes on to include status descriptions of the participants. The *sisters* are members of the brother's *clan;* the husband comes from another clan.

Note again that participants are *located* within social structures and this location is basic to the subsequent functional analysis of this behavior.[58]

Since these are cases drawn from non-literate society, it might be assumed that these requirements for description are peculiar to non-literate materials. Turning to other instances of functional analyses of patterns found in modern Western society, however, we can identify this same requirement as well as additional guides to "needed descriptive data."

The "romantic love complex" in American society: although all societies recognize "occasional violent emotional attachments," contemporary American society is among the few societies which capitalize upon romantic attachments and in popular belief, at least, make these the basis for choice of a marriage partner. This characteristic pattern of choice minimizes or eliminates the selection of one's mate by parents or the wider kinship group.[59]

Note that the emphasis upon one pattern of choice of mates thereby excludes alternative patterns of choice known to occur elsewhere.

This case suggests a *second* desideratum for a type of data to be included in the account of the item subjected to functional analysis. In describing the characteristic (modal) pattern for handling a standardized problem (choice of marriage-partner), the observer, wherever possible, indicates the principal alternatives which are thereby excluded. This, as we shall see, provides direct clues to the structural context of the pattern and, by suggesting pertinent comparative materials, points toward the validation of the functional analysis.

A *third* integral element of the description of the problematical item

---

58. W. L. Warner, *A Black Civilization—A Social Study of an Australian Tribe,* (New York: Harper & Bros., 1937), 112-113.

59. For various approaches to a functional analysis of the "romantic love complex," see Ralph Linton, *Study of Man,* (New York: D. Appleton-Century Co., 1936), 174-5; T. Parsons, "Age and sex in the social structure of the United States," *American Sociological Review,* Oct. 1942, 7, 604-616, esp. at 614-15; T. Parsons, "The kinship system of the contemporary United States," *American Anthropologist,* 1943, 45, 22-38, esp. at 31-32, 36-37, both reprinted in his *Essays in Sociological Theory, op. cit.;* T. Parsons, "The social structure of the family," in Ruth N. Anshen ed., *The Family: Its Function and Destiny,* (New York: Harper, 1949), 173-201; R. K. Merton, "Intermarriage and the social structure," *Psychiatry,* 1941, 4, 361-74, esp. at 367-8; and Isidor Thorner, "Sociological aspects of affectional frustration," *Psychiatry,* 1943, 6, 157-173, esp. at 169-172.

preparatory to the actual functional analysis—a further requirement for preparing the specimen for analysis, so to speak—is to include the *"meanings"* (or cognitive and affective significance) of the activity or pattern for members of the group. In fact, as will become evident, a fully circumstantial account of the meanings attached to the item goes far toward suggesting appropriate lines of functional analysis. A case drawn from Veblen's many functional analyses serves to illustrate the general thesis:

> *The cultural pattern of conspicuous consumption:* the conspicuous consumption of relatively expensive commodities "means" (symbolizes) the possession of sufficient wealth to "afford" such expenditures. Wealth, in turn, is honorific. Persons engaging in conspicuous consumption not only derive gratification from the direct consumption but also from the heightened status reflected in the attitudes and opinions of others who observe their consumption. This pattern is most notable among the leisure class, *i.e.,* those who can and largely do refrain from productive labor [this is the status or role component of the description]. However, it diffuses to other strata who seek to emulate the pattern and who likewise experience pride in "wasteful" expenditures. Finally, consumption in conspicuous terms tends to crowd out other criteria for consumption (*e.g.* "efficient" expenditure of funds). [This is an explicit reference to alternative modes of consumption obscured from view by the cultural emphasis on the pattern under scrutiny.][60]

As is well known, Veblen goes on to impute a variety of functions to the pattern of conspicuous consumption—functions of aggrandizement of status, of validation of status, of "good repute," of display of pecuniary strength (p. 84). These consequences, as experienced by participants in the patterned activity, are gratifying and go far toward explaining the continuance of the pattern. *The clues to the imputed functions are provided almost wholly by the description of the pattern itself* which includes explicit references to (1) the status of those differentially exhibiting the pattern, (2) known alternatives to the pattern of consuming in terms of display and "wastefulness" rather than in terms of private and "intrinsic" enjoyment of the item of consumption; and (3) the divers meanings culturally ascribed to the behavior of conspicuous consumption by participants in and observers of the pattern.

These three components of the description of the specimen to be analyzed are by no means exhaustive. A full descriptive protocol, adequate for subsequent functional analysis, will inevitably spill over into a range of immediate psychological and social consequences of the behavior. But these may be more profitably examined in connection with the concepts of function. It is here only necessary to repeat that the description of the item does not proceed according to whim or intuition, but must include at least these three characteristics of the item, if the descriptive protocol is to be of optimum value for functional analysis. Although much remains to be learned concerning desiderata for the de-

---

60. Thorstein Veblen, *The Theory of the Leisure Class,* (New York: Vanguard Press, 1928), esp. chapters 2-4.

scriptive phase of the total analysis, this brief presentation of models for descriptive content may serve to indicate that procedures for functional analysis *can* be codified—ultimately to the point where the sociological field worker will have a chart guiding observation.

Another case illustrates a further desideratum for the description of the item to be analyzed.

> *Taboo on out-marriage:* the greater the degree of group solidarity, the more marked the sentiment adverse to marriage with people outside the group. "It makes no difference what is the cause of the desire for group solidarity. . . ." Outmarriage *means* either losing one's group-member to another group or incorporation into one's own group of persons who have not been thoroughly socialized in the values, sentiments and practices of the in-group.[61]

This suggests a *fourth* type of datum to be included in the description of the social or cultural specimen, prior to functional analysis. Inevitably, participants in the practice under scrutiny have *some* array of motives for conformity or for deviation. *The descriptive account should, so far as possible, include an account of these motivations, but these motives must not be confused, as we have seen, with (a) the objective pattern of behavior or (b) with the social functions of that pattern.* Inclusion of motives in the descriptive account helps explain the *psychological* functions subserved by the pattern and often proves suggestive with respect to the social functions.

Thus far, we have been considering items which are clearly patterned practices or beliefs, patterns recognized as such by participants in the society. Thus, members of the given society can, in varying degrees, describe the contours of the Chiricahua puberty ceremony, the Murngin mirriri pattern, the choice of mates on the basis of romantic attachments, the concern with consuming conspicuously and the taboos on out-marriage. These are all parts of the overt culture and, as such, are more or less fully known to those who share in this culture. The social scientist, however, does not confine himself to these overt patterns. From time to time, he uncovers a covert cultural pattern, a set of practices or beliefs which is as consistently patterned as overt patterns, but which is not regarded as a normatively regulated pattern by the participants. Examples of this are plentiful. Thus, statistics show that in a quasi-caste situation such as that governing Negro-white relations in this country, the prevailing pattern of interracial marriage (when it occurs) is between white females and Negro males (rather than between Negro females and white males). Although this pattern, which we may call caste hypogamy, is not institutionalized, it is persistent and remarkably stable.[62]

61. Romanzo Adams, *Interracial Marriage in Hawaii,* esp. at 197-204; Merton, "Intermarriage . . .," *op. cit.,* esp. at 368-9; K. Davis "Intermarriage in caste societies," *American Anthropologist,* 1941, 43, 376-395.

62. *Cf.* Merton, "Intermarriage . . .," *op. cit.;* Otto Klineberg ed., *Characteristics of the American Negro,* (New York: Harper, 1943).

Or consider another instance of a fixed but apparently unrecognized pattern. Malinowski reports that Trobrianders cooperatively engaged in the technological task of building a canoe are engaged not only in that explicit technical task but also in establishing and reinforcing inter-personal relations among themselves in the process. Much of the recent data on those primary groups called "informal organizations" deals with these patterns of relations which are observed by the social scientist but are unrecognized, at least in their full implications, by the participants.[63]

All this points to a *fifth* desideratum for the descriptive protocol: regularities of behavior *associated* with the nominally central activity (although not part of the explicit culture pattern) should be included in the protocols of the field worker, since these *unwitting regularities* often provide basic clues to distinctive functions of the total pattern. As we shall see, the inclusion of these "unwitting" regularities in the descriptive protocol directs the investigator almost at once to analysis of the pattern in terms of what we have called latent functions.

In summary, then, the descriptive protocol should, so far as possible, include:

1) location of participants in the pattern within the social structure—dif-ferential participation;

2) consideration of alternative modes of behavior excluded by emphasis on the observed pattern (*i.e.* attention not only to what occurs but also to what is neglected by virtue of the existing pattern);

3) the emotive and cognitive meanings attached by participants to the pattern;

4) a distinction between the motivations for participating in the pattern and the objective behavior involved in the pattern;

5) regularities of behavior not recognized by participants but which are nonetheless associated with the central pattern of behavior.

That these desiderata for the observer's protocol are far from com-plete is altogether likely. But they do provide a tentative step in the direction of *specifying* points of observation which facilitate subsequent functional analysis. They are intended to be somewhat more specific than the suggestions ordinarily found in general statements of procedure, such as those advising the observer to be sensitive to the "context of situation."

MANIFEST AND LATENT FUNCTIONS

As has been implied in earlier sections, the distinction between mani-fest and latent functions was devised to preclude the inadvertent con-fusion, often found in the sociological literature, between conscious *motivations* for social behavior and its *objective consequences*. Our

---

63. The rediscovery of the primary group by those engaged in sociological studies of industry has been one of the chief fillips to the functional approach in recent sociological research. Reference is had here to the work of Elton Mayo, Roethlisberger and Dickson, William Whyte, and Burleigh Gardner, among many others. There remain, of course, the interesting differences in *interpretation* to which these data lend themselves.

scrutiny of current vocabularies of functional analysis has shown how easily, and how unfortunately, the sociologist may identify *motives* with *functions*. It was further indicated that the motive and the function vary independently and that the failure to register this fact in an established terminology has contributed to the unwitting tendency among sociologists to confuse the subjective categories of motivation with the objective categories of function. This, then, is the central purpose of our succumbing to the not-always-commendable practice of introducing new terms into the rapidly growing tehnical vocabulary of sociology, a practice regarded by many laymen as an affront to their intelligence and an offense against common intelligibility.

As will be readily recognized, I have adapted the terms "manifest" and "latent" from their use in another context by Freud (although Francis Bacon had long ago spoken of "latent process" and "latent configuration" in connection with processes which are below the threshold of superficial observation).

The distinction itself has been repeatedly drawn by observers of human behavior at irregular intervals over a span of many centuries.[64] Indeed, it would be disconcerting to find that a distinction which we have come to regard as central to functional analysis had not been made by any of that numerous company who have in effect adopted a functional orientation. We need mention only a few of those who have, in recent decades, found it necessary to distinguish in their specific interpretations of behavior between the end-in-view and the functional consequences of action.

George H. Mead[65]: ". . . that attitude of hostility toward the law-breaker has the unique advantage [read: latent function] of uniting all members of the community in the emotional solidarity of aggression. While the most admirable of humanitarian efforts are sure to run counter to the individual interests of very many in the community, or fail to touch the interest and imagination of the multitude and to leave the community divided or indifferent, the cry of thief or murderer is attuned to profound complexes, lying below the surface of competing individual efforts, and citizens who have [been] separated by divergent interests stand together against the common enemy."

Emile Durkheim's[66] similar analysis of the social functions of punishment is also focused on its latent functions (consequences for the community) rather than confined to manifest functions (consequences for the criminal).

---

64. References to some of the more significant among these earlier appearances of the distinction will be found in Merton, "Unanticipated consequences . . .," *op. cit.*

65. George H. Mead, "The psychology of punitive justice," *American Journal of Sociology*, 1918, 23, 577-602, esp. 591.

66. As suggested earlier in this chapter, Durkheim adopted a functional orientation throughout his work, and he operates, albeit often without explicit notice, with concepts equivalent to that of latent function in all of his researches. The reference in the text at this point is to his "Deux lois de l'évolution penale," *L'année sociologique*, 1899-1900, 4, 55-95, as well as to his *Division of Labor in Society* (Glencoe, Illinois: The Free Press, 1947).

W. G. Sumner[67]: ". . . from the first acts by which men try to satisfy needs, each act stands by itself, and looks no further than the immediate satisfaction. From recurrent needs arise habits for the individual and customs for the group, but these results are consequences which were never conscious, and never foreseen or intended. They are not noticed until they have long existed, and it is still longer before they are appreciated." Although this fails to locate the latent functions of standardized social actions for a designated social structure, it plainly makes the basic distinction between ends-in-view and objective consequences.

R. M. MacIver[68]: In addition to the direct effects of institutions, "there are further effects by way of control which lie outside the direct purposes of men . . . this type of reactive form of control . . . may, though unintended, be of profound service to society."

W. I. Thomas and F. Znaniecki[69]: "Although all the new [Polish peasant cooperative] institutions are thus formed with the definite purpose of satisfying certain specific needs, their social function is by no means limited to their explicit and conscious purpose . . . every one of these institutions—commune or agricultural circle, loan and savings bank, or theater—is not merely a mechanism for the management of certain values but also an association of people, each member of which is supposed to participate in the common activities as a living, concrete individual. Whatever is the predominant, official common interest upon which the institution is founded, the association as a concrete group of human personalities unofficially involves many other interests; the social contacts between its members are not limited to their common pursuit, though the latter, of course, constitutes both the main reason for which the association is formed and the most permanent bond which holds it together. Owing to this combination of an abstract political, economic, or rather rational mechanism for the satisfaction of specific needs with the concrete unity of a social group, the new institution is also the best intermediary link between the peasant primary-group and the secondary national system."

These and numerous other sociological observers have, then, from time to time distinguished between categories of subjective disposition ("needs, interests, purposes") and categories of generally unrecognized but objective functional consequences ("unique advantages," "never conscious" consequences, "unintended . . . service to society," "function not limited to conscious and explicit purpose").

---

67. This one of his many such observations is of course from W. G. Sumner's *Folkways*, (Boston: Ginn & Co., 1906), 3. His collaborator, Albert G. Keller retained the distinction in his own writings; see, for example, his *Social Evolution*, (New York: Macmillan, 1927), at 93-95.

68. This is advisedly drawn from one of MacIver's earlier works, *Community*, (London: Macmillan, 1915). The distinction takes on greater importance in his later writings, becoming a major element in his *Social Causation*, (Boston: Ginn & Co., 1942), esp. at 314-321, and informs the greater part of his *The More Perfect Union*, (New York: Macmillan, 1948).

69. The single excerpt quoted in the text is one of scores which have led to *The Polish Peasant in Europe and America* being deservedly described as a "sociological classic." See pages 1426-7 and 1523 ff. As will be noted later in this chapter, the insights and conceptual distinctions contained in this one passage, and there are many others like it in point of richness of content, were forgotten or never noticed by those industrial sociologists who recently came to develop the notion of "informal organization" in industry.

Since the occasion for making the distinction arises with great frequency, and since the purpose of a conceptual scheme is to direct observations toward salient elements of a situation and to prevent the inadvertent oversight of these elements, it would seem justifiable to designate this distinction by an appropriate set of terms. This is the rationale for the distinction between manifest functions and latent functions; the first referring to those objective consequences for a specified unit (person, subgroup, social or cultural system) which contribute to its adjustment or adaptation and were so intended; the second referring to unintended and unrecognized consequences of the same order.

There are some indications that the christening of this distinction may serve a heuristic purpose by becoming incorporated into an explicit conceptual apparatus, thus aiding both systematic observation and later analysis. In recent years, for example, the distinction between manifest and latent functions has been utilized in analyses of racial intermarriage,[70] social stratification,[71] affective frustration,[72] Veblen's sociological theories,[73] prevailing American orientations toward Russia,[74] propaganda as a means of social control,[75] Malinowski's anthropological theory,[76] Navajo witchcraft,[77] problems in the sociology of knowledge,[78] fashion,[79] the dynamics of personality,[80] national security measures,[81] the internal social dynamics of bureaucracy,[82] and a great variety of other sociological problems.

The very diversity of these subject-matters suggests that the theoretic

---

70. Merton, "Intermarriage and the social structure," *op. cit.*

71. Kingsley Davis, "A conceptual analysis of stratification," *American Sociological Review*, 1942, 7, 309-321.

72. Thorner, *op. cit.*, esp. at 165.

73. A. K. Davis, *Thorstein Veblen's Social Theory*, Harvard Ph.D. dissertation, 1941 and "Veblen on the decline of the Protestant Ethic," *Social Forces*, 1944, 22, 282-86; Louis Schneider, *The Freudian Psychology and Veblen's Social Theory*, New York: King's Crown Press, 1948), esp. Chapter 2.

74. A. K. Davis, "Some sources of American hostility to Russia," *American Journal of Sociology*, 1947, 53, 174-183.

75. Talcott Parsons, "Propaganda and social control," in his *Essays in Sociological Theory*.

76. Clyde Kluckhohn, "Bronislaw Malinowski, 1884-1942," *Journal of American Folklore*, 1943, 56, 208-219.

77. Clyde Kluckhohn, *Navaho Witchcraft, op. cit.*, esp. at 46-47 and ff.

78. Merton, Chapter XII of this volume.

79. Bernard Barber and L. S. Lobel, " 'Fashion' in women's clothes and the American social system," *Social Forces*, 1952, 31, 124-131.

80. O. H. Mowrer and C. Kluckhohn, "Dynamic theory of personality," in J. M. Hunt, ed., *Personality and the Behavior Disorders*, (New York: Ronald Press, 1944), 1, 69-135, esp. at 72.

81. Marie Jahoda and S. W. Cook, "Security measures and freedom of thought: an exploratory study of the impact of loyalty and security programs," *Yale Law Journal*, 1952, 61, 296-333.

82. Philip Selznick, *TVA and the Grass Roots* (University of California Press, 1949); A. W. Gouldner, *Patterns of Industrial Bureaucracy* (Glencoe, Illinois: The Free Press, 1954); P. M. Blau, *The Dynamics of Bureaucracy* (University of Chicago Press, 1955); A. K. Davis, "Bureaucratic patterns in Navy officer corps," *Social Forces* 1948, 27, 142-153.

distinction between manifest and latent functions is not bound up with a limited and particular range of human behavior. But there still remains the large task of ferreting out the specific uses to which this distinction can be put, and it is to this large task that we devote the remaining pages of this chapter.

Heuristic Purposes of the Distinction

Clarifies the analysis of seemingly irrational social patterns. In the first place, the distinction aids the sociological interpretation of many social practices which persist even though their manifest purpose is clearly not achieved. The time-worn procedure in such instances has been for diverse, particularly lay, observers to refer to these practices as "superstitions," irrationalities," "mere inertia of tradition," *etc.* In other words, when group behavior does not—and, indeed, often cannot—attain its ostensible purpose there is an inclination to attribute its occurrence to lack of intelligence, sheer ignorance, survivals, or so-called inertia. Thus, the Hopi ceremonials designed to produce abundant rainfall may be labelled a superstitious practice of primitive folk and that is assumed to conclude the matter. It should be noted that this in no sense accounts for the group behavior. It is simply a case of name-calling; it substitutes the epithet "superstition" for an analysis of the actual role of this behavior in the life of the group. Given the concept of latent function, however, we are reminded that this behavior *may* perform a function for the group, although this function may be quite remote from the avowed purpose of the behavior.

The concept of latent function extends the observer's attention beyond the question of whether or not the behavior attains its avowed purpose. Temporarily ignoring these explicit purposes, it directs attention *toward* another range of consequences: those bearing, for example, upon the individual personalities of Hopi involved in the ceremony and upon the persistence and continuity of the larger group. Were one to confine himself to the problem of whether a manifest (purposed) function occurs, it becomes a problem, not for the sociologist, but for the meteorologist. And to be sure, our meteorologists agree that the rain ceremonial does not produce rain; but this is hardly to the point. It is merely to say that the ceremony does not have this technological use; that this purpose of the ceremony and its actual consequences do not coincide. But with the concept of latent function, we continue our inquiry, examining the consequences of the ceremony not for the rain gods or for meteorological phenomena, but for the groups which conduct the ceremony. And here it may be found, as many observers indicate, that the ceremonial does indeed have functions—but functions which are non-purposed or latent.

Ceremonials may fulfill the latent function of reinforcing the group identity by providing a periodic occasion on which the scattered members of a group assemble to engage in a common activity. As Durkheim among others long since indicated, such ceremonials are a means by which collective expression is afforded the sentiments which, in a further analysis, are found to be a basic source of group unity. Through the systematic application of the concept of latent function, therefore, *apparently* irrational behavior may *at times* be found to be positively functional for the group. Operating with the concept of latent function, we are not too quick to conclude that if an activity of a group does not achieve its nominal purpose, then its persistence can be described only as an instance of "inertia," "survival," or "manipulation by powerful sub-groups in the society."

In point of fact, some conception like that of latent function has very often, almost invariably, been employed by social scientists observing *a standardized practice designed to achieve an objective which one knows from accredited physical science cannot be thus achieved.* This would plainly be the case, for example, with Pueblo rituals dealing with rain or fertility. *But with behavior which is not directed toward a clearly unattainable objective, sociological observers are less likely to examine the collateral or latent functions of the behavior.*

Directs attention to theoretically fruitful fields of inquiry. The distinction between manifest and latent functions serves further to direct the attention of the sociologist to precisely those realms of behavior, attitude and belief where he can most fruitfully apply his special skills. For what is his task if he confines himself to the study of manifest functions? He is then concerned very largely with determining whether a practice instituted for a particular purpose does, in fact, achieve this purpose. He will then inquire, for example, whether a new system of wage-payment achieves its avowed purpose of reducing labor turnover or of increasing output. He will ask whether a propaganda campaign has indeed gained its objective of increasing "willingness to fight" or "willingness to buy war bonds," or "tolerance toward other ethnic groups." Now, these are important, and complex, types of inquiry. But, so long as sociologists *confine* themselves to the study of manifest functions, their inquiry is set for them by practical men of affairs (whether a captain of industry, a trade union leader, or, conceivably, a Navaho chieftain, is for the moment immaterial), rather than by the theoretic problems which are at the core of the discipline. By dealing primarily with the realm of manifest functions, with the key problem of whether deliberately instituted practices or organizations succeed in achieving their objectives, the sociologist becomes converted into an industrious and skilled recorder of the altogether familiar pattern of behavior. *The terms of appraisal are fixed and limited by the question put to him by the non-theoretic men of affairs, e.g.,* has the new wage-payment program achieved such-and-such purposes?

But armed with the concept of latent function, the sociologist extends his inquiry in those very directions which promise most for the theoretic development of the discipline. He examines the familiar (or planned) social practice to ascertain the latent, and hence generally unrecognized, functions (as well, of course, as the manifest functions). He considers, for example, the consequences of the new wage plan for, say, the trade union in which the workers are organized or the consequences of a propaganda program, not only for increasing its avowed purpose of stirring up patriotic fervor, but also for making large numbers of people reluctant to speak their minds when they differ with official policies, *etc.* In short, it is suggested that the *distinctive* intellectual contributions of the sociologist are found primarily in the study of unintended consequences (among which are latent functions) of social practices, as well as in the study of anticipated consequences (among which are manifest functions).[83]

There is some evidence that it is precisely at the point where the research attention of sociologists has shifted from the plane of manifest to the plane of latent functions that they have made their *distinctive* and major contributions. This can be extensively documented but a few passing illustrations must suffice.

THE HAWTHORNE WESTERN ELECTRIC STUDIES:[84] As is well known, the early stages of this inquiry were concerned with the problem of the relations of "illumination to efficiency" of industrial workers. For some two and a half years, attention was focused on problems such as this: do variations in the intensity of lighting affect production? The initial results showed that within wide limits there was no uniform relation between illumination and output. Production output increased *both* in the experimental group where illumination was increased (or *decreased*) *and* in the control group where no changes in illumination were introduced. In short, the investigators confined themselves wholly to a search for the manifest functions. Lacking a concept of latent social function, no attention whatever was initially paid to the social consequences *of the experiment* for relations among members of the test and control groups or for relations between workers and the test room authorities. In other words, the investigators lacked a sociological frame of reference and

---

83. For a brief illustration of this general proposition, see Robert K. Merton, Marjorie Fiske and Alberta Curtis, *Mass Persuasion,* (New York: Harper, 1946), 185-189; Jahoda and Cook, *op. cit.*

84. This is cited as a case study of how *an elaborate research was wholly changed in theoretic orientation and in the character of its research findings by the introduction of a concept approximating the concept of latent function.* Selection of the case for this purpose does not, of course, imply full acceptance of the *interpretations* which the authors give their findings. Among the several volumes reporting the Western Electric research, see particularly F. J. Roethlisberger and W. J. Dickson, *Management and the Worker,* (Harvard University Press, 1939).

operated merely as "engineers" (just as a group of meteorologists might have explored the "effects" upon rainfall of the Hopi ceremonial).

Only after continued investigation, did it occur to the research group to explore the consequences of the new "experimental situation" for the self-images and self-conceptions of the workers taking part in the experiment, for the interpersonal relations among members of the group, for the coherence and unity of the group. As Elton Mayo reports it, "the illumination fiasco had made them alert to the need that very careful records should be kept of everything that happened in the room in addition to the obvious engineering and industrial devices. Their observations therefore included not only records of industrial and engineering changes but also records of physiological or medical changes, and, *in a sense,* of social and anthropological. This last took the form of a 'log' that gave as full an account as possible of the actual events of every day. . . ."[85] In short, it was only after a long series of experiments which wholly neglected the latent social functions of the experiment (as a contrived social situation) that this distinctly sociological framework was introduced. "With this realization," the authors write, "the inquiry changed its character. No longer were the investigators interested in testing for the effects of single variables. In the place of a controlled experiment, they substituted the notion of a social situation which needed to be described and understood as a system of interdependent elements." Thereafter, as is now widely known, inquiry was directed very largely toward ferreting out the latent functions of standardized practices among the workers, of informal organization developing among workers, of workers' games instituted by "wise administrators," of large programs of worker counselling and interviewing, *etc.* The new conceptual scheme entirely altered the range and types of data gathered in the ensuing research.

One has only to return to the previously quoted excerpt from Thomas and Znaniecki in their classical work of some thirty years ago, to recognize the correctness of Shils' remark:

. . . indeed the history of the study of primary groups in American sociology is a supreme instance of the *discontinuities of the development of this discipline:* a problem is stressed by one who is an acknowledged founder of the discipline, the problem is left unstudied, then, some years later, it is taken up with enthusiasm as if no one had ever thought of it before.[86]

For Thomas and Znaniecki had repeatedly emphasized the sociological view that, whatever its major purpose, "the association as a concrete group of human personalities unofficially involves many other interests;

---

85. Elton Mayo, *The Social Problems of an Industrial Civilization,* (Harvard University Press, 1945), 70.

86. Edward Shils, *The Present State of American Sociology,* (Glencoe, Illinois: The Free Press, 1948), 42 [italics supplied].

the social contacts between its members are not limited to their common pursuit. . . ." In effect, then, it had taken years of experimentation to turn the attention of the Western Electric research team to the latent social functions of primary groups emerging in industrial organizations. It should be made clear that this case is not cited here as an instance of defective experimental design; that is not our immediate concern. It is considered only as an illustration of the pertinence for *sociological* inquiry of the concept of latent function, and the associated concepts of functional analysis. It illustrates how the inclusion of this concept (whether the term is used or not is inconsequential) can sensitize sociological investigators to a range of significant social variables which are otherwise easily overlooked. The explicit ticketing of the concept may perhaps lessen the frequency of such occasions of discontinuity in future sociological research.

The discovery of latent functions represents significant increments in sociological knowledge. There is another respect in which inquiry into latent functions represents a distinctive contribution of the social scientist. It is precisely the latent functions of a practice or belief which are *not* common knowledge, for these are unintended and generally unrecognized social and psychological consequences. As a result, findings concerning latent functions represent a greater increment in knowledge than findings concerning manifest functions. They represent, also, greater departures from "common-sense" knowledge about social life. Inasmuch as the latent functions depart, more or less, from the avowed manifest functions, the research which uncovers latent functions very often produces "paradoxical" results. The seeming paradox arises from the sharp modification of a familiar popular preconception which regards a standardized practice or belief *only* in terms of its manifest functions by indicating some of its subsidiary or collateral latent functions. The introduction of the concept of latent function in social research leads to conclusions which show that "social life is not as simple as it first seems." For as long as people confine themselves to *certain* consequences (*e.g.* manifest consequences), it is comparatively simple for them to pass moral judgments upon the practice or belief in question. Moral evaluations, generally based on these manifest consequences, tend to be polarized in terms of black or white. But the perception of further (latent) consequences often complicates the picture. Problems of moral evaluation (which are not our immediate concern) and problems of social engineering (which are our concern[87]) both take on the additional complexities usually involved in responsible social decisions.

---

87. This is not to deny that social engineering has direct moral implications or that technique and morality are inescapably intertwined, but I do not intend to deal with this range of problems in the present chapter. For some discussion of these problems see chapters VI, XV and XVII; also Merton, Fiske and Curtis, *Mass Persuasion,* chapter 7.

An example of inquiry which implicitly uses the notion of latent function will illustrate the sense in which "paradox"—discrepancy between the apparent, merely manifest, function and the actual, which also includes latent functions—tends to occur as a result of including this concept. Thus, to revert to Veblen's well-known analysis of conspicuous consumption, it is no accident that he has been recognized as a social analyst gifted with an eye for the paradoxical, the ironic, the satiric. For these are frequent, if not inevitable, outcomes of applying the concept of latent function (or its equivalent).

THE PATTERN OF CONSPICUOUS CONSUMPTION. The manifest purpose of buying consumption goods is, of course, the satisfaction of the needs for which these goods are explicitly designed. Thus, automobiles are obviously intended to provide a certain kind of transportation; candles, to provide light; choice articles of food to provide sustenance; rare art products to provide aesthetic pleasure. Since these products *do* have these uses, it was largely assumed that these encompass the range of socially significant functions. Veblen indeed suggests that this was ordinarily the prevailing view (in the pre-Veblenian era, of course): "The end of acquisition and accumulation is conventionally held to be the consumption of the goods accumulated. . . . This is at least felt to be the economically legitimate end of acquisition, *which alone it is incumbent on the theory to take account of.*"[88]

However, says Veblen in effect, as sociologists we must go on to consider the latent functions of acquisition, accumulation and consumption, and these latent functions are remote indeed from the manifest functions. "But, it is only when taken in a sense far removed from its naive meaning [*i.e.* manifest function] that the consumption of goods can be said to afford the incentive from which accumulation invariably proceeds." And among these latent functions, which help explain the persistence and the social location of the pattern of conspicuous consumption, is its symbolization of "pecuniary strength and so of gaining or retaining a good name." The exercise of "punctilious discrimination" in the excellence of "food, drink, shelter, service, ornaments, apparel, amusements" results not merely in direct gratifications derived from the consumption of "superior" to "inferior" articles, but also, and Veblen argues, more importantly, it results in a *heightening or reaffirmation of social status.*

The Veblenian paradox is that people buy expensive goods not so much because they are superior but because they are expensive. For it is the latent equation ("costliness = mark of higher social status") which he singles out in his functional analysis, rather than the manifest equation ("costliness = excellence of the goods"). Not that he denies manifest functions *any* place in buttressing the pattern of conspicuous

---

88. Veblen, *Theory of Leisure Class, op. cit.*, p. 25.

consumption. These, too, are operative. "What has just been said must not be taken to mean that there are no other incentives to acquisition and accumulation than this desire to excel in pecuniary standing and so gain the esteem and envy of one's fellowmen. The desire for added comfort and security from want is present as a motive at every stage. . . ." Or again: "It would be hazardous to assert that a useful purpose is ever absent from the utility of any article or of any service, however obviously its prime purpose and chief element is conspicuous waste" and derived social esteem.[89] It is only that *these direct, manifest functions do not fully account for the prevailing patterns of consumption. Otherwise put, if the latent functions of status-enhancement or status-reaffirmation were removed from the patterns of conspicuous consumption, these patterns would undergo severe changes of a sort which the "conventional" economist could not foresee.*

In these respects, Veblen's analysis of latent functions departs from the common-sense notion that the end-product of consumption is "of course, the direct satisfaction which it provides": "People eat caviar because they're hungry; buy Cadillacs because they want the best car they can get; have dinner by candlelight because they like the peaceful atmosphere." The common-sense interpretation in terms of selected manifest motives gives way, in Veblen's analysis, to the collateral latent functions which are also, and perhaps more significantly, fulfilled by these practices. To be sure, the Veblenian analysis has, in the last decades, entered so fully into popular thought, that these latent functions are now widely recognized. [This raises the interesting problem of the changes occurring in a prevailing pattern of behavior when its *latent* functions become generally recognized (and are thus no longer latent). There will be no occasion for discussing this important problem in the present publication.]

The discovery of latent functions does not merely render conceptions of the functions served by certain social patterns more precise (as is the case also with studies of manifest functions), but introduces a *qualitatively different increment in the previous state of knowledge.*

Precludes the substitution of naive moral judgments for sociological

---

89. *Ibid.*, 32, 101. It will be noted throughout that Veblen is given to loose terminology. In the marked passages (and repeatedly elsewhere) he uses "incentive," "desire," "purpose," and "function" interchangeably. Since the context usually makes clear the denotation of these terms, no great harm is done. But it is clear that the expressed purposes of conformity to a culture pattern are by no means identical with the latent functions of the conformity. Veblen occasionally recognizes this. For example, "In strict accuracy nothing should be included under the head of conspicuous waste but such expenditure as is incurred on the ground of an invidious pecuniary comparison. But in order to bring any given item or element in under this head *it is not necessary that it should be recognized as waste in this sense by the person incurring the expenditure.*" (*Ibid.* 99; italics supplied). *Cf.* A. K. Davis, "Veblen on the decline of the Protestant Ethic," *op. cit.*

analysis. Since moral evaluations in a society tend to be largely in terms of the manifest consequences of a practice or code, we should be prepared to find that analysis in terms of latent functions at times runs counter to prevailing moral evaluations. For it does not follow that the latent functions will operate in the same fashion as the manifest consequences which are ordinarily the basis of these judgments. Thus, in large sectors of the American population, the political machine or the "political racket" are judged as unequivocally "bad" and "undesirable." The grounds for such moral judgment vary somewhat, but they consist substantially in pointing out that political machines violate moral codes: political patronage violates the code of selecting personnel on the basis of impersonal qualifications rather than on grounds of party loyalty or contributions to the party war-chest; bossism violates the code that votes should be based on individual appraisal of the qualifications of candidates and of political issues, and not on abiding loyalty to a feudal leader; bribery, and "honest graft" obviously offend the proprieties of property; "protection" for crime clearly violates the law and the mores; and so on.

In view of the manifold respects in which political machines, in varying degrees, run counter to the mores and at times to the law, it becomes pertinent to inquire how they manage to continue in operation. The familiar "explanations" for the continuance of the political machine are not here in point. To be sure, it may well be that if "respectable citizenry" would live up to their political obligations, if the electorate were to be alert and enlightened; if the number of elective officers were substantially reduced from the dozens, even hundreds, which the average voter is now expected to appraise in the course of town, county, state and national elections; if the electorate were activated by the "wealthy and educated classes without whose participation," as the not-always democratically oriented Bryce put it, "the best-framed government must speedily degenerate";—if these and a plethora of similar changes in political structure were introduced, perhaps the "evils" of the political machine would indeed be exorcized.[90] But it should be noted that these changes are often not introduced, that political machines have had the phoenix-like quality of arising strong and unspoiled from their ashes, that, in short, this structure has exhibited a notable vitality in many areas of American political life.

Proceeding from the functional view, therefore, that we should

---

90. These "explanations" are "causal" in design. They profess to indicate the social conditions under which political machines come into being. In so far as they are empirically confirmed, these explanations of course add to our knowledge concerning the problem: how is it that political machines operate in certain areas and not in others? How do they manage to continue? *But these causal accounts are not sufficient.* The functional consequences of the machine, as we shall see, go far toward supplementing the causal interpretation.

ordinarily (not invariably) expect persistent social patterns and social structures to perform positive functions *which are at the time not adequately fulfilled by other existing patterns and structures,* the thought occurs that perhaps this publicly maligned organization is, *under present conditions,* satisfying basic latent functions.[91] A brief examination of current analyses of this type of structure may also serve to illustrate additional problems of functional analysis.

SOME FUNCTIONS OF THE POLITICAL MACHINE. Without presuming to enter into the variations of detail marking different political machines—a Tweed, Vare, Crump, Flynn, Hague are by no means identical types of bosses—we can briefly examine the functions more or less common to the political machine, as a generic type of social organization. We neither attempt to itemize all the diverse functions of the political machine nor imply that all these functions are similarly fulfilled by each and every machine.

The key structural function of the Boss is to organize, centralize and maintain in good working condition "the scattered fragments of power" which are at present dispersed through our political organization. By this centralized organization of political power, the boss and his apparatus can satisfy the needs of diverse subgroups in the larger community which are not adequately satisfied by legally devised and culturally approved social structures.

To understand the role of bossism and the machine, therefore, we must look at two types of sociological variables: (1) the *structural context* which makes it difficult, if not impossible, for morally approved structures to fulfill essential social functions, thus leaving the door open for political machines (or their structural equivalents) to fulfill these functions and (2) the subgroups whose distinctive needs are left unsatisfied, except for the latent functions which the machine in fact fulfills.[92]

Structural Context: The constitutional framework of American political organization specifically precludes the legal possibility of highly centralized power and, it has been noted, thus "discourages the growth

----

91. I trust it is superfluous to add that this hypothesis is not "in support of the political machine." The question whether the dysfunctions of the machine outweigh its functions, the question whether alternative structures are not available which may fulfill its functions without necessarily entailing its social dysfunctions, still remain to be considered at an appropriate point. We are here concerned with documenting the statement that moral judgments based *entirely* on an appraisal of manifest functions of a social structure are "unrealistic" in the strict sense, *i.e.,* they do not take into account other actual consequences of that structure, consequences which may provide basic social support for the structure. As will be indicated later, "social reforms" or "social engineering" which ignore latent functions do so on pain of suffering acute disappointments and boomerang effects.

92. Again, as with preceding cases, we shall not consider the possible dysfunctions of the political machine.

of effective and responsible leadership. The framers of the Constitution, as Woodrow Wilson observed, set up the check and balance system 'to keep government at a sort of mechanical equipoise by means of a standing amicable contest among its several organic parts.' They distrusted power as dangerous to liberty: and therefore they spread it thin and erected barriers against its concentration." This dispersion of power is found not only at the national level but in local areas as well. "As a consequence," Sait goes on to observe, "when *the people or particular groups* among them demanded positive action, no one had adequate authority to act. The machine provided an antidote."[93]

The constitutional dispersion of power not only makes for difficulty of effective decision and action but when action does occur it is defined and hemmed in by legalistic considerations. In consequence, there developed "a much *more human system* of partisan government, whose chief object soon became the circumvention of government by law. . . . The lawlessness of the extra-official democracy was merely the counterpoise of the legalism of the official democracy. The lawyer having been permitted to subordinate democracy to the Law, the Boss had to be called in to extricate the victim, which he did after a fashion and for a consideration."[94]

Officially, political power is dispersed. Various well-known expedients were devised for this manifest objective. Not only was there the familiar separation of powers among the several branches of the government but, in some measure, tenure in each office was limited, rotation in office approved. And the scope of power inherent in each office was severely circumscribed. Yet, observes Sait in rigorously functional terms, "Leadership is necessary; and *since* it does not develop readily within the constitutional framework, the Boss provides it in a crude and irresponsible form from the outside."[95]

Put in more generalized terms, *the functional deficiencies of the official structure generate an alternative (unofficial) structure to fulfill existing needs somewhat more effectively.* Whatever its specific historical origins, the political machine persists as an apparatus for satisfying otherwise unfulfilled needs of diverse groups in the population. By turning to a few of these subgroups and their characteristic needs, we shall be led at once to a range of latent functions of the political machine.

Functions of the Political Machine for Diverse Subgroups. It is well known that one source of strength of the political machine derives from

---

93. Edward M. Sait, "Machine, Political," *Encyclopedia of the Social Sciences,* IX, 658 b [italics supplied]; *cf.* A. F. Bentley, *The Process of Government* (Chicago, 1908), Chap. 2.

94. Herbert Croly, *Progressive Democracy,* (New York, 1914), p. 254, cited by Sait, *op. cit.,* 658 b.

95. Sait, *op. cit.,* 659 a. [italics supplied].

its roots in the local community and the neighborhood. The political machine does not regard the electorate as an amorphous, undifferentiated mass of voters. With a keen sociological intuition, the machine recognizes that the voter is a person living in a specific neighborhood, with specific personal problems and personal wants. Public issues are abstract and remote; private problems are extremely concrete and immediate. It is not through the generalized appeal to large public concerns that the machine operates, but through the direct, quasi-feudal relationships between local representatives of the machine and voters in their neighborhood. Elections are won in the precinct.

The machine welds its link with ordinary men and women by elaborate networks of personal relations. Politics is transformed into personal ties. The precinct captain "must be a friend to every man, assuming if he does not feel sympathy with the unfortunate, and utilizing in his good works the resources which the boss puts at his disposal."[96] The precinct captain is forever a friend in need. In our prevailingly impersonal society, the machine, through its local agents, fulfills the important social *function of humanizing and personalizing all manner of assistance* to those in need. Foodbaskets and jobs, legal and extra-legal advice, setting to rights minor scrapes with the law, helping the bright poor boy to a political scholarship in a local college, looking after the bereaved—the whole range of crises when a feller needs a friend, and, above all, a friend who knows the score and who can do something about it,—all these find the ever-helpful precinct captain available in the pinch.

To assess this function of the political machine adequately, it is important to note not only that aid *is* provided but *the manner in which it is provided.* After all, other agencies do exist for dispensing such assistance. Welfare agencies, settlement houses, legal aid clinics, medical aid in free hospitals, public relief departments, immigration authorities—these and a multitude of other organizations are available to provide the most varied types of assistance. But in contrast to the professional techniques of the welfare worker which may typically represent in the mind of the recipient the cold, bureaucratic dispensation of limited aid following upon detailed investigation of *legal* claims to aid of the "client" are the unprofessional techniques of the precinct captain who asks no questions, exacts no compliance with legal rules of eligibility and does not "snoop" into private affairs.[97]

---

96. *Ibid.,* 659 a.

97. Much the same contrast with official welfare policy is found in Harry Hopkins' open-handed and non-political distribution of unemployment relief in New York State under the governorship of Franklin Delano Roosevelt. As Sherwood reports: "Hopkins was harshly criticized for these irregular activities by the established welfare agencies, which claimed it was 'unprofessional conduct' to hand out work tickets without thorough investigation of each applicant, his own or his family's financial resources and probably his religious affiliations. 'Harry told the agency to go to hell,' said [Hopkins' associate, Dr. Jacob A.] Goldberg." Robert E. Sherwood, *Roosevelt and Hopkins, An Intimate History,* (New York: Harper, 1948), 30.

For many, the loss of "self-respect" is too high a price for legalized assistance. In contrast to the gulf between the settlement house workers who so often come from a different social class, educational background and ethnic group, the precinct worker is "just one of us," who understands what it's all about. The condescending lady bountiful can hardly compete with the understanding friend in need. In *this struggle between alternative structures for fulfilling the nominally same function* of providing aid and support to those who need it, it is clearly the machine politician who is better integrated with the groups which he serves than the impersonal, professionalized, socially distant and legally constrained welfare worker. And since the politician can at times influence and manipulate the official organizations for the dispensation of assistance, whereas the welfare worker has practically no influence on the political machine, this only adds to his greater effectiveness. More colloquially and also, perhaps, more incisively, it was the Boston ward-leader, Martin Lomasny, who described this essential function to the curious Lincoln Steffens: "I think," said Lomasny, "that there's got to be in every ward somebody that any bloke can come to—no matter what he's done—and get help. *Help, you understand; none of your law and justice, but help.*"[98]

The "deprived classes," then, constitute one subgroup for whom the political machine satisfies wants not adequately satisfied in the same fashion by the legitimate social structure.

For a second subgroup, that of business (primarily "big" business but also "small"), the political boss serves the function of providing those political privileges which entail immediate economic gains. Business corporations, among which the public utilities (railroads, local transportation and electric light companies, communications corporations) are simply the most conspicuous in this regard, seek special political dispensations which will enable them to stabilize their situation and to near their objective of maximizing profits. Interestingly enough, corporations often want to avoid a chaos of uncontrolled competition. They want the greater security of an economic czar who controls, regulates and organizes competition, providing that this czar is not a public official with his decisions subject to public scrutiny and public control. (The latter would be "government control," and hence taboo.) The political boss fulfills these requirements admirably.

Examined for a moment apart from any moral considerations, the political apparatus operated by the Boss is effectively designed to perform these functions with a minimum of inefficiency. Holding the strings of diverse governmental divisions, bureaus and agencies in his competent hands, the Boss rationalizes the relations between public and

---

98. *The Autobiography of Lincoln Steffens*, (Chautauqua, New York: Chautauqua Press, 1931), 618. Deriving largely from Steffens, as he says, F. Stuart Chapin sets forth these functions of the political machine with great clarity. See his *Contemporary American Institutions*, (New York: Harper, 1934), 40-54.

private business. He serves as the business community's ambassador in the otherwise alien (and sometimes unfriendly) realm of government. And, in strict business-like terms, he is well-paid for his economic services to his respectable business clients. In an article entitled, "An Apology to Graft," Lincoln Steffens suggested that "Our economic system, which held up riches, power and acclaim as prizes to men bold enough and able enough to buy corruptly timber, mines, oil fields and franchises and 'get away with it,' was at fault."[99] And, in a conference with a hundred or so of Los Angeles business leaders, he described a fact well known to all of them: the Boss and his machine were an *integral part* of the organization of the economy. "You cannot build or operate a railroad, or a street railway, gas, water, or power company, develop and operate a mine, or get forests and cut timber on a large scale, or run any privileged business, without corrupting or joining in the corruption of the government. You tell me privately that you must, and here I am telling you semi-publicly that you must. And that is so all over the country. And that means that we have an organization of society in which, *for some reason,* you and your kind, the ablest, most intelligent, most imaginative, daring, and resourceful leaders of society, are and must be against society and its laws and its all-around growth."[100]

Since the demand for the services of special privileges are built into the structure of the society, the Boss fulfills diverse functions for this second subgroup of business-seeking-privilege. These "needs" of business, as presently constituted, are not adequately provided for by conventional and culturally approved social structures; consequently, the extra-legal but more-or-less efficient organization of the political machine comes to provide these services. To adopt an *exclusively* moral attitude toward the "corrupt political machine" is to lose sight of the very structural conditions which generate the "evil" that is so bitterly attacked. To adopt a functional outlook is to provide not an apologia for the political machine but a more solid basis for modifying or eliminating the machine, *providing* specific structural arrangements are introduced either for eliminating these effective demands of the business community or, if that is the objective, of satisfying these demands through alternative means.

A third set of distinctive functions fulfilled by the political machine for a special subgroup is that of providing alternative channels of social mobility for those otherwise excluded from the more conventional avenues for personal "advancement." Both the sources of this special

---

99. *Autobiography of Lincoln Steffens,* 570.

100. *Ibid.,* 572-3 [italics supplied]. This helps explain, as Steffens noted after Police Commissioner Theodore Roosevelt, "the prominence and respectability of the men and women who intercede for crooks" when these have been apprehended in a periodic effort to "clean up the political machine." *Cf.* Steffens, 371, and *passim.*

"need" (for social mobility) and the respect in which the political machine comes to help satisfy this need can be understood by examining the structure of the larger culture and society. As is well known, the American culture lays enormous emphasis on money and power as a "success" goal legitimate for all members of the society. By no means alone in our inventory of cultural goals, it still remains among the most heavily endowed with positive affect and value. However, certain sub-groups and certain ecological areas are notable for the relative absence of opportunity for achieving these (monetary and power) types of success. They constitute, in short, sub-populations where "the cultural emphasis upon pecuniary success has been absorbed, but where there is *little access to conventional and legitimate* means for attaining such success. The conventional occupational opportunities of persons in (such areas) are almost completely limited to manual labor. Given our cultural stigmatization of manual labor,[101] and its correlate, the prestige of white-collar work, it is clear that the result is a tendency to achieve these culturally approved objectives *through whatever means are possible.* These people are on the one hand, "asked to orient their conduct toward the prospect of accumulating wealth [and power] and, on the other, they are largely denied effective opportunities to do so institutionally."

It is within this context of social structure that the political machine fulfills the basic function of providing avenues of social mobility for the otherwise disadvantaged. Within this context, even the corrupt political machine and the racket "represent the triumph of amoral intelligence over morally prescribed 'failure' when the channels of vertical mobility are closed or narrowed *in a society which places a high premium on economic affluence, [power] and social ascent for all its members.*"[102] As one sociologist has noted on the basis of several years of close observation in a slum area:

---

101. See the National Opinion Research Center survey of evaluation of occupations which firmly documents the general impression that the manual occupations rate very low indeed in the social scale of values, *even among those who are themselves engaged in manual labor.* Consider this latter point in its full implications. In effect, the cultural and social structure exacts the values of pecuniary and power success even among those who find themselves confined to the stigmatized manual occupations. Against this background, consider the powerful motivation for achieving this type of "success" by any means whatsoever. A garbage-collector who joins with other Americans in the view that the garbage-collector is "the lowest of the low" occupations can scarcely have a self-image which is pleasing to him; he is in a "pariah" occupation in the very society where he is assured that "all who have genuine merit can get ahead." Add to this, his occasional recognition that "he didn't have the same chance as others, no matter what they say," and one perceives the enormous psychological pressure upon him for "evening up the score" by finding some means, whether strictly legal or not, for moving ahead. All this provides the structural and derivatively psychological background for the "socially induced need" in *some* groups to find some accessible avenue for social mobility.

102. Merton, "Social structure and anomie," chapter IV of this volume.

The sociologist who dismisses racket and political organizations as deviations from desirable standards thereby neglects some of the major elements of slum life. . . . *He does not discover the functions they perform for the members* [of the groupings in the slum]. The Irish and later immigrant peoples have had the greatest difficulty in finding places for themselves in our urban social and economic structure. Does anyone believe that the immigrants and their children could have achieved their present degree of social mobility without gaining control of the political organization of some of our largest cities? The same is true of the racket organization. *Politics and the rackets have furnished an important means of social mobility for individuals, who, because of ethnic background and low class position,* are blocked from advancement in the "respectable" channels.[103]

This, then, represents a third type of function performed for a distinctive subgroup. This function, it may be noted in passing, is fulfilled by the *sheer* existence and operation of the political machine, for it is in the machine itself that these individuals and subgroups find their culturally induced needs more or less satisfied. It refers to the services which the political apparatus provides for its own personnel. But seen in the wider social context we have set forth, it no longer appears as *merely* a means of self-aggrandizement for profit-hungry and power-hungry *individuals,* but as an organized provision for *subgroups* otherwise excluded from or handicapped in the race for "getting ahead."

Just as the political machine performs services for "legitimate" business, so it operates to perform not dissimilar services for "illegitimate" business: vice, crime and rackets. Once again, the basic sociological role of the machine in this respect can be more fully appreciated only if one temporarily abandons attitudes of moral indignation, to examine in all moral innocence the actual workings of the organization. In this light, it at once appears that the subgroup of the professional criminal, racketeer or gambler has basic similarities of organization, demands and operation to the subgroup of the industrialist, man of business or speculator. If there is a Lumber King or an Oil King, there is also a Vice King or a Racket King. If expansive legitimate business organizes administra-

103. William F. Whyte, "Social organization in the slums," *American Sociological Review,* Feb. 1943, 8, 34-39 (italics supplied). Thus, the political machine and the racket represent a special case of the type of organizational adjustment to the conditions described in chapter IV. It represents, note, an *organizational* adjustment: definite structures arise and operate to reduce somewhat the acute tensions and problems of individuals caught up in the described conflict between the "cultural accent on success-for-all" and the "socially structured fact of unequal opportunities for success." As chapter IV indicates, other types of *individual* "adjustment" are possible: lone-wolf crime, psychopathological states, rebellion, retreat by abandoning the culturally approved goals, etc. Likewise, other types of *organizational adjustment* sometimes occur; the racket or the political machine are not *alone* available as organized means for meeting this socially induced problem. Participation in revolutionary organizations, for example, can be seen within this context, as an alternative mode of organizational adjustment. All this bears theoretic notice here, since we might otherwise overlook the basic functional concepts of functional substitutes and functional equivalents, which are to be discussed at length in a subsequent publication.

tive and financial syndicates to "rationalize" and to "integrate" diverse areas of production and business enterprise, so expansive rackets and crime organize syndicates to bring order to the otherwise chaotic areas of production of illicit goods and services. If legitimate business regards the proliferation of small business enterprises as wasteful and inefficient, substituting, for example, the giant chain stores for hundreds of corner groceries, so illegitimate business adopts the same businesslike attitude and syndicates crime and vice.

Finally, and in many respects, most important, is the basic similarity, if not near-identity, of the economic role of "legitimate" business and of "illegitimate" business. *Both are in some degree concerned with the provision of goods and services for which there is an economic demand.* Morals aside, they are both business, industrial and professional enterprises, dispensing goods and services which some people want, for which there is a market in which goods and services are transformed into commodities. And, in a prevalently market society, we should expect appropriate enterprises to arise whenever there is a market demand for certain goods or services.

As is well known, vice, crime and the rackets *are* "big business." Consider only that there have been estimated to be about 500,000 professional prostitutes in the United States of 1950, and compare this with the approximately 200,000 physicians and 350,000 professional registered nurses. It is difficult to estimate which have the larger clientele: the professional men and women of medicine or the professional men and women of vice. It is, of course, difficult to estimate the economic assets, income, profits and dividends of illicit gambling in this country and to compare it with the economic assets, income, profits and dividends of, say, the shoe industry, but it is altogether possible that the two industries are about on a par. No precise figures exist on the annual expenditures on illicit narcotics, and it is probable that these are less than the expenditures on candy, but it is also probable that they are larger than the expenditure on books.

It takes but a moment's thought to recognize that, *in strictly economic terms,* there is no relevant difference between the provision of licit and of illicit goods and services. The liquor traffic illustrates this perfectly. It would be peculiar to argue that prior to 1920 (when the 18th amendment became effective), the provision of liquor constituted an economic service, that from 1920 to 1933, its production and sale no longer constituted an economic service dispensed in a market, and that from 1934 to the present, it once again took on a serviceable aspect. Or, it would be *economically* (not morally) absurd to suggest that the sale of bootlegged liquor in the dry state of Kansas is less a response to a market demand than the sale of publicly manufactured liquor in the neighboring wet state of Missouri. Examples of this sort can of course be multiplied many times over. Can it be held that in European countries, with registered and legalized prostitution, the prostitute contributes an economic service, whereas in this country, lacking legal sanction, the prostitute provides no such service? Or that the professional abortionist is in the economic market where he has approved legal status and that he is out of the economic market where he is legally taboo? Or that gambling satisfies a specific demand for entertainment in Nevada, where it constitutes the largest business enterprise of the larger cities in the state, but that it differs essentially in this respect from motion pictures in the neighboring state of California?[104]

The failure to recognize that these businesses are only *morally* and not *economically* distinguishable from "legitimate" businesses has led to badly scrambled analysis. Once the economic identity of the two is recognized, we may anticipate that if the political machine performs functions for "legitimate big business" it will be all the more likely to perform not dissimilar functions for "illegitimate big business." And, of course, such is often the case.

The distinctive function of the political machine for their criminal, vice and racket clientele is to enable them to operate in satisfying the economic demands of a large market without due interference from the government. Just as big business may contribute funds to the political party war-chest to ensure a minimum of governmental interference, so with big rackets and big crime. In both instances, the political machine can, in varying degrees, provide "protection." In both instances, many features of the structural context are identical: (1) market demands for goods and services; (2) the operators' concern with maximizing gains from their enterprises; (3) the need for partial control of government which might otherwise interfere with these activities of businessmen; (4) the need for an efficient, powerful and centralized agency to provide an effective liaison of "business" with government.

Without assuming that the foregoing pages exhaust either the range of functions or the range of subgroups served by the political machine, we can at least see that *it presently fulfills some functions for these diverse subgroups which are not adequately fulfilled by culturally approved or more conventional structures.*

Several additional implications of the functional analysis of the political machine can be mentioned here only in passing, although they

104. Perhaps the most perceptive statement of this view has been made by Hawkins and Waller. "The prostitute, the pimp, the peddler of dope, the operator of the gambling hall, the vendor of obscene pictures, the bootlegger, the abortionist, all are productive, all produce services or goods which people desire and for which they are willing to pay. It happens that society has put these goods and services under the ban, but people go on producing them and people go on consuming them, and an act of the legislature does not make them any less a part of the economic system." "Critical notes on the cost of crime," *Journal of Criminal Law and Criminology,* 1936, 26, 679-94, at 684.

obviously require to be developed at length. First, the foregoing analysis has direct implications for *social engineering*. It helps explain why the periodic efforts at "political reform," "turning the rascals out" and "cleaning political house" are typically (though not necessarily) short-lived and ineffectual. It exemplifies a basic theorem: *any attempt to eliminate an existing social structure without providing adequate alternative structures for fulfilling the functions previously fulfilled by the abolished organization is doomed to failure.* (Needless to say, this theorem has much wider bearing than the one instance of the political machine.) When "political reform" confines itself to the manifest task of "turning the rascals out," it is engaging in little more than sociological magic. The reform may for a time bring new figures into the political limelight; it may serve the casual social function of re-assuring the electorate that the moral virtues remain intact and will ultimately triumph; it may actually effect a turnover in the personnel of the political machine; it may even, for a time, so curb the activities of the machine as to leave unsatisfied the many needs it has previously fulfilled. But, inevitably, unless the reform also involves a "re-forming" of the social and political structure such that the existing needs are satisfied by alternative structures or unless it involves a change which eliminates these needs altogether, the political machine will return to its integral place in the social scheme of things. *To seek social change, without due recognition of the manifest and latent functions performed by the social organization undergoing change, is to indulge in social ritual rather than social engineering.* The concepts of manifest and latent functions (or their equivalents) are indispensable elements in the theoretic repertoire of the social engineer. In this crucial sense, these concepts are not "merely" theoretical (in the abusive sense of the term), but are eminently practical. In the deliberate enactment of social change, they can be ignored only at the price of considerably heightening the risk of failure.

A second implication of this analysis of the political machine also has a bearing upon areas wider than the one we have considered. The paradox has often been noted that the supporters of the political machine include both the "respectable" business class elements who are, of course, opposed to the criminal or racketeer and the distinctly "unrespectable" elements of the underworld. And, at first appearance, this is cited as an instance of very strange bedfellows. The learned judge is not infrequently called upon to sentence the very racketeer beside whom he sat the night before at an informal dinner of the political bigwigs. The district attorney jostles the exonerated convict on his way to the back room where the Boss has called a meeting. The big business man may complain almost as bitterly as the big racketeer about the "extortionate" contributions to the party fund demanded by the Boss. Social opposites meet—in the smoke-filled room of the successful politician.

In the light of a functional analysis all this of course no longer seems paradoxical. Since the machine serves both the businessman and the criminal man, the two seemingly antipodal groups intersect. This points to a more general theorem: *the social functions of an organization help determine the structure (including the recruitment of personnel involved in the structure), just as the structure helps determine the effectiveness with which the functions are fulfilled.* In terms of social status, the business group and the criminal group are indeed poles apart. But status does not fully determine behavior and the inter-relations between groups. Functions modify these relations. Given their distinctive needs, the several subgroups in the large society are "integrated," whatever their personal desires or intentions, by the centralizing structure which serves these several needs. In a phrase with many implications which require further study, *structure affects function and function affects structure.*

CONCLUDING REMARKS

This review of some salient considerations in structural and functional analysis has done little more than indicate some of the principal problems and potentialities of this mode of sociological interpretation. Each of the items codified in the paradigm require sustained theoretic clarification and cumulative empirical research. But it is clear that in functional theory, stripped of those traditional postulates which have fenced it in and often made it little more than a latter-day rationalization of existing practices, sociology has one beginning of a systematic and empirically relevant mode of analysis. It is hoped that the direction here indicated will suggest the feasibility and the desirability of further codification of functional analysis. In due course each section of the paradigm will be elaborated into a documented, analyzed and codified chapter in the history of functional analysis.

BIBLIOGRAPHICAL POSTSCRIPT

When first written in 1948, the preceding paper constituted an effort to systematize the principal assumptions and conceptions of the then slowly evolving theory of functional analysis in sociology. The development of this sociological theory has since gained marked momentum. In preparing this edition, I have incorporated some of the intervening extensions and emendations of theory, but have postponed a detailed and extended formulation for a volume now in preparation. It might therefore be useful to list, at this juncture, some, though manifestly far from all, recent theoretical contributions to functional analysis in sociology.

The major contribution in recent years is, of course, that by Talcott Parsons in *The Social System* (Glencoe, Illinois: The Free Press, 1951), supplemented by further works by Parsons and his associates: T. Parsons, R. F. Bales and E. A. Shils, *Working Papers in the Theory of Action*

(Glencoe, Illinois: The Free Press, 1953); T. Parsons and E. A. Shils (editors), *Toward a General Theory of Action* (Cambridge: Harvard University Press, 1951). The salient contributions of so comprehensive and logically complex a work as *The Social System* cannot be readily distinguished from its more provisional and at times debatable conceptual developments; sociologists are only now engaged in working out the needed discriminations. But on the evidence, both of research stemming from Parsons' formulations and of critical theoretical review, it is plain that this represents a decisive step toward a methodical statement of current sociological theory.

M. J. Levy, Jr., *The Structure of Society* (Princeton University Press, 1953) derives largely, as the author says, from Parsons' conceptual scheme, and presents a logical multiplication of numerous categories and concepts. It remains to be seen whether such taxonomies of concepts will prove appropriate and useful in the analysis of sociological problems.

Less extensive but more incisive analyses of selected theoretical problems of functional analyses have been provided in a number of papers stemming from diverse 'cultural areas' of sociological theory, as can be seen from the following short bibliography. Perhaps the most penetrating and productive among these is the pair of related papers by Ralf Dahrendorf, "Struktur und Funktion," *Kölner Zeitschrift für Soziologie und Sozialpsychologie,* 1955, 7, 492-519 and by David Lockwood, "Some remarks on 'The Social System,'" *The British Journal of Sociology,* 1956, 7, 134-146. Both papers are exemplary instances of *systematic* theorizing, designed to indicate specific gaps in the present state of functional theory. A considered and unpolemical statement of the status of functional theory and of some of its key unsolved problems will be found in Bernard Barber, "Structural-functional analysis: some problems and misunderstandings," *American Sociological Review,* 1956, 21, 129-135. An effort to clarify the important problem of the logic of analysis involved in that part of functional sociology which is designed to interpret observed structural patterns in society has been made by Harry C. Bredemeier, "The methodology of functionalism," *American Sociological Review,* 1955, 20, 173-180. Although this paper questionably attributes certain assumptions to several functional analyses under review, it has the distinct merit of raising the important question of the appropriate logic of functional analysis.

For anthropologists' ordering of functional analysis in contemporary sociology (not in anthropology, merely), see the instructive paper by Melford E. Spiro, "A typology of functional analysis," *Explorations,* 1953, 1, 84-95 and the thorough-going critical examination by Raymond Firth, "Function," in *Current Anthropology,* (edited by William L. Thomas, Jr.) University of Chicago Press, 1956, 237-258.

The diffusion of functional theory as recently developed in the United States is manifested in a series of critical examinations of that theory in

Belgium, France, Italy and Brazil. Among the most significant of these are: Henri Janne, "Fonction et finalité en sociologie," *Cahiers Internationaux de Sociologie*, 1954, 16, 50-67 which attempts to link up current functional theory with the antecedent and contemporary theory of French and Belgian sociologists. A thorough-going critique of functional analysis in sociology is undertaken by Georges Gurvitch, "Le concept de structure sociale," *Cahiers Internationaux de Sociologie*, 1955, 19, 3-44. A comprehensive examination of functional theory in its bearings upon selected problems of sociological research will be found in Filippo Barbano, *Teoria e Ricerca nella Sociologia Contemporanea* (Milano: Dott. A. Giuffrè, 1955). Florestan Fernandes, *Ensaio sôbre o Método de Interpretação Funcionalista na Sociologia* (São Paulo: Universidade de São Paulo, Boletim No. 170, 1953) is an informative and systematic monograph which rewards even a plodding and fallible reading such as mine.

The paradigm developed in the preceding pages has been formalized in terms of an abstract set of notations designed to make explicit how its various parts are related to elements of the functional approach in biology. See "A formalization of functionalism, with special reference to its application in the social sciences," in the forthcoming collection of papers by Ernest Nagel, *Logic Without Metaphysics* (Glencoe: The Free Press, 1957). For detailed application of the paradigm, see Warren Breed, "Social control in the newsroom: a functional analysis," *Social Forces*, 1955, 33, 326-335; A. H. Leighton and C. C. Hughes, "Notes on Eskimo patterns of suicide," *Southwestern Journal of Anthropology*, 1955, 11, 327-338; Joan Chapman and Michael Eckstein, "A social-psychological study of the alleged visitation of the Virgin Mary in Puerto Rico," *Year Book of the American Philosophical Society*, 1954, 203-206; Dennis Chapman, *The Home and Social Status* (London: Routledge & Kegan Paul, 1955); Christian Bay, *The Freedom of Expression: A Study in Political Ideals and Socio-Psychological Realities* (forthcoming); Michael Eckstein, "Diverse action and response to crime," (forthcoming); Y. B. Damle, *Communication of Modern Ideas and Knowledge in Indian Villages* (Cambridge: Massachusetts Institute of Technology, Center for International Studies, 1955).

For an interesting discussion of manifest and latent consequences of action in relation to self-justifying and self-defeating images, see Chapter 8 of Kenneth Boulding, *The Image* (Ann Arbor: University of Michigan Press, 1956).

II THE BEARING OF SOCIOLOGICAL THEORY ON EMPIRICAL RESEARCH

THE RECENT HISTORY of sociological theory can in large measure be written in terms of an alternation between two contrasting emphases. On the one hand, we observe those sociologists who seek above all to generalize, to find their way as rapidly as possible to the formulation of sociological laws. Tending to assess the significance of sociological work in terms of scope rather than the demonstrability of generalizations, they eschew the "triviality" of detailed, small-scale observation and seek the grandeur of global summaries. At the other extreme stands a hardy band who do not hunt too closely the implications of their research but who remain confident and assured that what they report is so. To be sure, their reports of facts are verifiable and often verified, but they are somewhat at a loss to relate these facts to one another or even to explain why these, rather than other, observations have been made. For the first group the identifying motto would at times seem to be: "We do not know whether what we say is true, but it is at least significant." And for the radical empiricist the motto may read: "This is demonstrably so, but we cannot indicate its significance."

Whatever the bases of adherence to the one or the other of these camps—different but not necessarily contradictory accountings would be provided by psychologists, sociologists of knowledge, and historians of science—it is abundantly clear that there is no logical basis for their being ranged *against* each other. Generalizations can be tempered, if not with mercy, at least with disciplined observation; close, detailed observations need not be rendered trivial by avoidance of their theoretical pertinence and implications.

With all this there will doubtless be widespread if, indeed, not unanimous agreement. But this very unanimity suggests that these remarks are platitudinous. If, however, one function of theory is to explore the implications of the seemingly self-evident, it may not be amiss to look into what is entailed by such programmatic statements about the relations of sociological theory and empirical research. In doing so, every effort should be made to avoid dwelling upon illustrations drawn from the "more mature" sciences—such as physics and biology—not because these do not exhibit the logical problems involved but because their very maturity permits these disciplines to deal *fruitfully* with abstractions of a high order to a degree which, it is submitted, is not yet the case with sociology. An indefinitely large number of discussions of scientific method have set forth the logical prerequisites of scientific theory, but, it would seem, they have often done so on such a high level of abstraction that the prospect of translating these precepts into current sociological research becomes utopian. Ultimately, sociological research must meet the canons of scientific method; immediately, the task is so to express these requirements that they may have more direct bearing on the analytical work which is at present feasible.

The term "sociological theory" has been widely used to refer to the products of several related but distinct activities carried on by members of a professional group called sociologists. But since these several types of activity have significantly different bearings upon empirical social research—since they differ in their scientific functions—they should be distinguished for purposes of discussion. Moreover, such discriminations provide a basis for assessing the contributions and limitations characteristic of each of the following six types of work which are often lumped together as comprising sociological theory: (1) methodology; (2) general sociological orientations; (3) analysis of sociological concepts; (4) *post factum* sociological interpretations; (5) empirical generalizations in sociology and (6) sociological theory.

METHODOLOGY

At the outset we should distinguish clearly between sociological theory, which has for its subject matter certain aspects and results of the interaction of men and is therefore substantive, and methodology, or the logic of scientific procedure. The problems of methodology transcend those found in any one discipline, dealing either with those common to groups of disciplines[1] or, in more generalized form, with those common to all scientific inquiry. Methodology is not peculiarly bound up with sociological problems, and, though there is a plenitude of methodological discussions in books and journals of sociology, they are not thereby rendered sociological in character. Sociologists, in company with all others who essay scientific work, must be methodologically wise; they must be

---

1. Consider several volumes which set forth methodological as distinct from procedural concerns of sociology: Florian Znaniecki, *The Method of Sociology* (New York: Farrar & Rinehart, 1934); R. M. MacIver, *Social Causation* (Boston: Ginn & Co., 1942); G. A. Lundberg, *Foundations of Sociology* (New York: Macmillan Co., 1939); Felix Kaufmann, *Methodology of the Social Sciences* (New York: Oxford University Press, 1944); P. F. Lazarsfeld and M. Rosenberg, (eds.) *The Language of Social Research*, (Glencoe: The Free Press, 1955), esp. the Introductions to sections.

aware of the design of investigation, the nature of inference, the requirements of a theoretic system. But such knowledge does not contain or
imply the particular *content* of sociological theory. There is, in short, a
clear and decisive difference between *knowing how to test* a battery of
hypotheses and *knowing the theory* from which to derive hypotheses to
be tested.[2] It is my impression that current sociological training is more
largely designed to make students understand the first than the second.

As Poincaré observed a half-century ago, sociologists have long been
hierophants of methodology, thus, perhaps, diverting talents and energies
from the task of building substantive theory. This focus of attention upon
the logics of procedure has its patent scientific function, since such in-
ventories serve a critical purpose in guiding and assessing theoretical and
empirical inquiries. It also reflects the growing-pains of an immature
discipline. Just as the apprentice who acquires new skills self-consciously
examines each element of these skills in contrast to the master who
habitually practices them with seeming indifference to their explicit
formulation, so the exponents of a discipline haltingly moving toward
scientific status laboriously spell out the logical grounds of their procedure. The slim books on methodology which proliferate in the fields
of sociology, economics, and psychology do not find many counterparts
among the technical works in the sciences which have long since come of
age. Whatever their intellectual function, these methodological writings
imply the perspectives of a fledgling discipline, anxiously presenting its
credentials for full status in the fraternity of the sciences. But, significantly enough, the instances of adequate scientific method utilized by
sociologists for illustrative or expository purposes are usually drawn from
disciplines other than sociology itself. Twentieth-century, not sixteenth-
century, physics and chemistry are taken as methodological prototypes
or exemplars for twentieth-century sociology, with little explicit recognition that between sociology and these other sciences is a difference of
centuries of cumulating scientific research. These comparisons are inevitably programmatic rather than realistic. More appropriate methodological demands would result in a gap between methodological
aspiration and actual sociological attainment at once less conspicuous
and less invidious.

GENERAL SOCIOLOGICAL ORIENTATIONS

Much of what is described in textbooks as sociological theory consists of general orientations toward substantive materials. Such orienta-

---

2. However, it should be noted not only that instruments and procedures used in
sociological (or other scientific) inquiry must meet methodological criteria but that
they also logically presuppose substantive theories. As Pierre Duhem observed in this
connection, the instrument as well as the experimental results obtained in science are
shot through with specific assumptions and theories of a substantive order. *La théorie
physique* (Paris: Chevalier et Rivière, 1906), 278.

tions involve broad postulates which indicate *types* of variables which are somehow to be taken into account rather than specifying determinate relationships between particular variables. Indispensable though these orientations are, they provide only the broadest framework for empirical inquiry. This is the case with Durkheim's generic hypothesis, which holds that the "determining cause of a social fact should be sought among the social facts preceding it" and identifies the "social" factor as institutional norms toward which behavior is oriented.[3] Or, again, it is said that "to a certain approximation it is useful to regard society as an integrated system of mutually interrelated and functionally interdependent parts."[4] So, too, the importance of the "humanistic coefficient" in cultural data as expounded by Znaniecki and Sorokin, among others, belongs to this category. Such general orientations may be paraphrased as saying in effect that the investigator ignores this *order of fact* at his peril. They do not set forth specific hypotheses.

The chief function of these orientations is to provide a general context for inquiry; they facilitate the process of arriving at determinate hypotheses. To take a case in point: Malinowski was led to re-examine the Freudian notion of the Oedipus complex on the basis of a general sociological orientation, which viewed sentiment formation as patterned by social structure. This generic view clearly underlay his exploration of a specific "psychological" complex in its relation to a system of status relationships in a society differing in structure from that of western Europe. The *specific* hypotheses which he utilized in this inquiry were all congruent with the generic orientation but were not prescribed by it. Otherwise put, the general orientation indicated the relevance of *some* structural variables, but there still remained the task of ferreting out the particular variables to be included.

Though such general theoretic outlooks have a more inclusive and profound effect on the development of scientific inquiry than do specific hypotheses—they constitute the matrix from which, in the words of Maurice Arthus, "new hypotheses follow one another in breathless succession and a harvest of facts follow closely the blossoming of these hypotheses"—though this is the case, they constitute only the point of departure for the theorist. It is his task to develop specific, interrelated hypotheses by reformulating empirical generalizations in the light of these generic orientations.

It should be noted, furthermore, that the growing contributions of sociological theory to its sister-disciplines lie more in the realm of general sociological orientations than in that of specific confirmed hypotheses.

3. Durkheim, *The Rules of Sociological Method,* 110; *L'Education morale* (Paris: Félix Alcan, 1925), 9-45, *passim.*

4. Conrad M. Arensberg and Solon Kimball, *Family and Community in Ireland* (Cambridge: Harvard University Press, 1940). xxvi.

The development of social history, of institutional economics, and the importation of sociological perspectives into psychoanalytic theory involve recognition of the sociological dimensions of the data rather than incorporation of specific confirmed theories. Social scientists have been led to detect sociological gaps in the application of their theory to concrete social behavior. They do not so often exhibit sociological naiveté in their interpretations. The economist, the political scientist, and the psychologist have increasingly come to recognize that what they have systematically taken as given, as data, may be sociologically problematical. But this receptivity to a sociological outlook is often dissipated by the paucity of adequately *tested specific theories* of, say, the determinants of human wants or of the social processes involved in the distribution and exercise of social power. Pressures deriving from the respective theoretic gaps of the several social sciences may serve, in time, to bring about an increasing formulation of specific and systematic sociological theories appropriate to the problems implied by these gaps. General orientations do not suffice. Presumably this is the context for the complaint voiced by an economist:

[The economist always seeks to refer his analysis of a problem] back to some "datum," that is to say, to something which is extra-economic. This something may be apparently very remote from the problem which was first taken up, for the chains of economic causation are often very long. But he always wants to hand over the problem in the end to some sociologist or other—*if there is a sociologist waiting for him. Very often there isn't.*[5]

ANALYSIS OF SOCIOLOGICAL CONCEPTS

It is at times held that theory is comprised of concepts, an assertion which, being incomplete, is neither true nor false but vague. To be sure, conceptual analysis, which is confined to the specification and clarification of key concepts, is an indispensable phase of theoretic work. But an array of concepts—status, role, *Gemeinschaft*, social interaction, social distance, *anomie*—does not constitute theory, though it may enter into a theoretic system. It may be conjectured that, in so far as an antitheoretic bias occurs among sociologists, it is in protest against those who identify theory with clarification of definitions, who mistakenly take the part for the whole of theoretic analysis. It is only when such concepts are interrelated in the form of a scheme that a theory begins to emerge. Concepts, then, constitute the definitions (or prescriptions) of what is to be observed; they are the variables between which empirical relationships are to be sought. When propositions are logically interrelated, a theory has been instituted.

5. J. R. Hicks, "Economic theory and the social sciences," *The Social Sciences: Their Relations in Theory and in Teaching* (London: Le Play Press, 1936), p. 135. (Italics mine.)

The choice of concepts guiding the collection and analysis of data is, of course, crucial to empirical inquiry. For, to state an important truism, if concepts are selected such that no relationships between them obtain, the research will be sterile, no matter how meticulous the subsequent observations and inferences. The importance of this truism lies in its implication that truly trial-and-error procedures in empirical inquiry are likely to be comparatively unfruitful, since the number of variables which are not significantly connected is indefinitely large.

It is, then, one function of conceptual clarification to make explicit the character of data subsumed under a concept.[6] It thus serves to reduce the likelihood that spurious empirical findings will be couched in terms of given concepts. Thus, Sutherland's re-examination of the received concept of "crime" provides an instructive instance of how such clarification induces a revision of hypotheses concerning the data organized in terms of the concept.[7] He demonstrates an equivocation implicit in criminological theories which seek to account for the fact that there is a much higher rate of crime, as "officially measured," in the lower than in the upper social classes. These crime "data" (organized in terms of a particular operational concept or measure of crime) have led to a series of hypotheses which view poverty, slum conditions, feeble-mindedness, and other characteristics held to be highly associated with low-class status as the "causes" of criminal behavior. Once the concept of crime is clarified to refer to the violation of criminal law and is thus extended to include "white-collar criminality" in business and professions—violations which are less often reflected in official crime statistics than are lower-class violations—the presumptive high association between low social status and crime may no longer obtain. We need not pursue Sutherland's analysis further to detect the function of conceptual clarification in this instance. It provides for a *reconstruction of data* by indicating more precisely just what they include and what they exclude. In doing so, it leads to a liquidation of hypotheses set up to account for spurious data by questioning the assumptions on which the initial statistical data were based. By hanging a question mark on an implicit assumption under-

---

6. As Schumpeter remarks about the role of "analytic apparatus": "If we are to speak about price levels and to devise methods of measuring them, we must know what a price level is. If we are to observe demand, we must have a precise concept of its elasticity. If we speak about productivity of labor, we must know what propositions hold true about total product per man-hour and what other propositions hold true about the partial differential coefficient of total product with respect to man-hours. No hypotheses enter into such concepts, which simply embody methods of description and measurement, nor into the propositions defining their relation (so-called theorems), and yet their framing is the chief task of theory, in economics as elsewhere. This is what we mean by *tools of analysis*." Joseph A. Schumpeter, *Business Cycles* (New York: McGraw-Hill Book Co., 1939), I, 31.

7. Edwin H. Sutherland, "White-collar criminality," *American Sociological Review*, 1940, 5, 1-12.

lying the research definition of crime—the assumption that violations of the criminal code by members of the several social classes are representatively registered in the official statistics—this conceptual clarification had direct implications for a nucleus of theories.

In similar fashion, conceptual analysis may often resolve apparent antinomies in empirical findings by indicating that such contradictions are more apparent than real. This familiar phrase refers, in part, to the fact that initially crudely defined concepts have tacitly included significantly different elements so that data organized in terms of these concepts differ materially and thus exhibit apparently contradictory tendencies.[8] The function of conceptual analysis in this instance is to maximize the likelihood of the comparability, in significant respects, of data which are to be included in a research.

The instance drawn from Sutherland merely illustrates the more general fact that in research, as in less disciplined activities, our conceptual language tends to fix our perceptions and, derivatively, our thought and behavior. The concept defines the situation, and the research worker responds accordingly. Explicit conceptual analysis helps him recognize to what he is responding and which (possibly significant) elements he is ignoring. The findings of Whorf on this matter are, with appropriate modifications, applicable to empirical research.[9] He found that behavior was oriented toward linguistic or conceptual meanings connoted by the terms applied to a situation. Thus, in the presence of objects which are conceptually described as "gasoline drums," behavior will tend modally toward a particular type: great care will be exercised. But when people are confronted with what are called *"empty* gasoline drums," behavior is different: it is careless, with little control over smoking and the disposition of cigarette stubs. Yet the "empty" drums are the more hazardous, since they contain explosive vapor. Response is not to the physical but to the conceptualized situation. The concept "empty" is here used equivocally: as a synonym for "null and void, negative, inert," and as a term applied to physical situations without regard to such "irrelevancies" as vapor and liquid vestiges in the container. The situation is conceptualized in the second sense, and the concept is then responded to in the first sense, with the result that "empty" gasoline drums become the occasion for fires. Clarification of just what "empty" means in the universe of discourse would have a profound effect on behavior. This case may serve as a paradigm of the functional effect of conceptual

---

8. Elaborate formulations of this type of analysis are to be found in Corrado Gini, *Prime linee di patologia economica* (Milan: Giuffre, 1935); for a brief discussion see C. Gini, "Un tentativo di armonizzarre teorie disparate e osservazioni contrastanti nel campo dei fenomeni sociali," *Rivista di politica economica*, 1935, 12, 1-24.

9. B. L. Whorf, "Relation of habitual thought and behavior to language," in L. Spier, A. I. Hallowell, and S. S. Newman (eds.), *Language, Culture, and Personality* (Menasha: Sapir Memorial Fund Publication, 1941), 75-93.

clarification upon research behavior: it makes clear just what the research worker is doing when he deals with conceptualized data. He draws different consequences for empirical research as his conceptual apparatus changes.

This is not to say, however, that the vocabulary of concepts fixes perceptions, thought and associated behavior once and for all. Even less is it to say that such instances of misleading terminology are embedded in one or another language (as Whorf tended to imply in this theory of linguistic behaviorism). Men are not permanently imprisoned in the framework of the (often inherited) concepts they use; they can not only break out of this framework but can create a new one, better suited to the needs of the occasion. Yet, at any particular time, one should be prepared to find that the governing concepts can, and often do, lag behind the behavioral requirements of the case. During these sometimes prolonged periods of lag, misapplied concepts do their damage. However, this very inaptness of concept to situation, recognized through painful experience, will often evoke self-correcting and more appropriate formulations. The job is to identify conceptual lag and to liberate ourselves from the patterns of cognitive misbehavior which it tends to produce.[9a]

A further task of conceptual analysis is to institute observable indices of the social data with which empirical research is concerned. Early efforts in this direction were manifest in the works of Durkheim (and constitute one of his most significant contributions to sociology). Though his formalized conceptions along these lines do not approach the sophistication of more recent formulations, he was patently utilizing "intervening variables," as lately described by Tolman and Hull, and seeking to establish indices for these variables.[10] The problem, as far as it need be stated

---

9a. For an extended discussion, see the posthumously published volume of selected writings by B. L. Whorf, *Language, Thought and Reality* (Cambridge: Technology Press of M.I.T., 1956). It is the extreme Whorfian position which Joshua Whatmough attacks in his *Language: A Modern Synthesis* (New York: St Martin's Press, 1956), 85, 186-7, 227-34. Yet Whatmough's well-placed salvoes do not entirely destroy Whorf's position but only compel a retreat to a more limited and defensible position. Socially entrenched concepts do affect perception, thought and behavior but the structure of language provides sufficient scope for inappropriate concepts to be replaced by more suitable concepts. An appreciative review of Whorf's ideas will be found in Franklin Fearing, "An examination of the conceptions of Benjamin Whorf in the light of theories of perception and cognition," Harry Hoijer, ed. *Language in Culture* (University of Chicago Press, 1954), 47-81.

10. Durkheim's basic formulation, variously repeated in each of his monographs, reads as follows: "It is necessary . . . to substitute for the internal fact which escapes us an external fact that symbolizes it and to study the former through the latter." See his *Rules of Sociological Method*, chap. ii; *Le Suicide* (Paris: F. Alcan, 1930), 22 ff. Most detailed consideration of Durkheim's views on social indices is provided by Harry Alpert, *Emile Durkheim and His Sociology* (New York: Columbia University Press, 1939), 120 ff. On the general problem see C. L. Hull, "The problem of Intervening Variables in molar behavior theory," *Psychological Review*, 1943, 50, 273-91.

for our immediate purposes, consists in devising indices of unobservables or symbolic constructs (e.g., social cohesion)—indices which are theoretically supportable. Conceptual analysis thus enters as one basis for an initial and periodic critical appraisal of the extent to which assumed signs and symbols are an adequate index of the social substratum. Such analysis suggests clues for determining whether in fact the index (or measuring instrument) proves adequate to the occasion.[11]

POST FACTUM SOCIOLOGICAL INTERPRETATIONS

It is often the case in empirical social research that data are collected and only then subjected to interpretative comment. This procedure in which the observations are at hand and the interpretations are subsequently applied to the data has the logical structure of clinical inquiry. The observations may be case-history or statistical in character. The defining characteristic of this procedure is the introduction of an interpretation *after* the observations have been made rather than the empirical testing of a predesignated hypothesis. The implicit assumption is that a body of generalized propositions has been so fully established that it can be approximately applied to the data in hand.

Such *post factum* explanations, designed to "explain" observations, differ in logical function from speciously similar procedures where the observational materials are utilized in order to *derive* fresh hypotheses to be confirmed by *new* observations.

A disarming characteristic of the procedure is that the explanations are indeed consistent with the given set of observations. This is scarcely surprising, in as much as only those *post factum* hypotheses are selected which do accord with these observations. If the basic assumption holds—namely, that the *post factum* interpretation utilizes abundantly confirmed theories—then this type of explanation indeed "shoots arrowy light into the dark chaos of materials." But if, as is more often the case in sociological interpretation, the *post factum* hypotheses are also *ad hoc* or, at the least, have but a slight degree of prior confirmation, then such "precocious explanations," as H. S. Sullivan called them, produce a spurious sense of adequacy at the expense of instigating further inquiry.

Post factum explanations remain at the level of *plausibility* (low evidential value) rather than leading to "compelling evidence" (a high degree of confirmation). Plausibility, in distinction to compelling evi-

---

11. Among the many functions of conceptual analysis at this point is that of instituting inquiry into the question of whether or not the index is "neutral" to its environment. By searching out the assumptions underlying the selection (and validation for a given population) of observables as indices (e.g., religious affiliation, an attitude scale), conceptual analysis initiates appropriate tests of the possibility that the index has become dissociated from its substratum. For a clear statement of this point see Louis Guttman, "A basis for scaling qualitative data," *American Sociological Review*, 1944, 9, 139-50, esp. 149-50.

dence, is found when an interpretation is consistent with one set of data (which typically has, indeed, given rise to the decision to utilize one, rather than another, interpretation). It also implies that alternative interpretations equally consistent with these data have not been systematically explored and that inferences drawn from the interpretation have not been tested by new observations.

The logical fallacy underlying the *post factum* explanation rests in the fact that there is available a variety of crude hypotheses, each with some measure of confirmation but designed to account for quite contradictory sets of affairs. The method of *post factum* explanation does not lend itself to nullifiability, if only because it is so completely flexible. For example, it may be reported that "the unemployed tend to read fewer books than they did previously." This is "explained" by the hypothesis that anxiety increases as a consequence of unemployment and, therefore, that any activity requiring concentration, such as reading, becomes difficult. This type of accounting is plausible, since there is some evidence that increased anxiety *may* occur in such situations and since a state of morbid preoccupation does interfere with organized activity. If, however, it is now reported that the original data were erroneous and it is a fact that "the unemployed read more than previously" a new *post factum* explanation can at once be invoked. The explanation now holds that the unemployed have more leisure or that they engage in activity intended to increase their personal skills. Consequently, they read more than before. Thus, whatever the observations, a new interpretation can be found to "fit the facts."[12] This example may be sufficient to indicate that such reconstructions serve only as illustrations and not as tests. It is this logical inadequacy of the *post factum* construction that led Peirce to observe:

> It is of the essence of induction that the consequence of the theory should be drawn first in regard to the unknown, or virtually unknown, result of experiment; and that this should virtually be only ascertained afterward. For if we look over the phenomena to find agreements with the theory, it is a mere question of ingenuity and industry how many we shall find.[13]

These reconstructions typically by-pass an explicit formulation of the conditions under which the hypotheses will be found to hold true. In order to meet this logical requirement, such interpretations would necessarily be predictive rather than postdictive.

As a case in point, we may quote the frequency with which Blumer asserts that the Thomas-Znaniecki analyses of documents "merely seem

---

12. The pertinent data have not been assembled. But, on the plausibility of the second interpretation, see Douglas Waples, *People and Print: Social Aspects of Reading in the Depression* (Chicago: University of Chicago Press, 1937), 198.

13. Charles Sanders Peirce, *Collected Papers*, ed. Charles Hartshorne and Paul Weiss (Cambridge: Harvard University Press, 1932), II, 496.

to be plausible."[14] The basis for plausibility rests in the consistency between the interpretation and the data; the absence of compelling evidence stems from the failure to provide distinctive tests of the interpretations apart from their consistency with the initial observations. The analysis is fitted to the facts, and there is no indication of just which data would be taken to contravene the interpretations. As a consequence, the documentary evidence merely illustrates rather than tests the theory.[15]

EMPIRICAL GENERALIZATIONS IN SOCIOLOGY

Not infrequently it is said that the object of sociological theory is to arrive at statements of social uniformities. This is an elliptical assertion and hence requires clarification. For there are two types of statements of sociological uniformities which differ significantly in their bearing on theory. The first of these is the empirical generalization: an isolated proposition summarizing observed uniformities of relationships between two or more variables.[16] The sociological literature abounds with such generalizations which have not been assimilated to sociological theory. Thus, Engel's "laws" of consumption may be cited as examples. So, too, the Halbwachs finding that laborers spend more per adult unit for food than white-collar employees of the same income class.[17] Such generalizations may be of greater or less precision, but this does not affect their logical place in the structure of inquiry. The Groves-Ogburn finding, for a sample of American cities, that "cities with a larger percentage engaged in manufacturing also have, on the average, slightly larger percentages of young persons married" has been expressed in an equation indicating the degree of this relationship. Although propositions of this order are essential in empirical research, a miscellany of such propositions only provides the raw materials for sociology as a discipline. The theoretic task, and the orientation of empirical research toward theory, first begins when the bearing of such uniformities on a set of interrelated propositions is tentatively established. The notion of directed research implies

14. Herbert Blumer, *An Appraisal of Thomas and Znaniecki's "The Polish Peasant in Europe and America"* (New York: Social Science Research Council, 1939), 38, see also *ibid.,* 39, 44, 46, 49, 50, 75.

15. It is difficult to see on what grounds Blumer asserts that these interpretations cannot be mere cases of illustration of a theory. His comment that the materials "acquire significance and understanding that they did not have" would apply to *post factum* explanations generally.

16. This usage of the term "empirical" is common, as Dewey notes. In this context, *"empirical* means that the subject-matter of a given proposition which has existential inference, represents merely a set of uniform conjunctions of traits repeatedly observed to exist, without any understanding of *why* the conjunction occurs; without a theory which states its rationale." John Dewey, *Logic: The Theory of Inquiry* (New York: Henry Holt & Co., 1938), 305.

17. See a considerable collection of such uniformities summarized by C. C. Zimmerman, *Consumption and Standards of Living* (New York: D. Van Nostrand Co., 1936), 51 ff.

that, in part,[18] empirical inquiry is so organized that if and when empirical uniformities are discovered, they have direct consequences for a theoretic system. In so far as the research is directed, the rationale of findings is set forth before the findings are obtained.

SOCIOLOGICAL THEORY

The second type of sociological generalization, the so-called scientific law, differs from the foregoing in as much as it is a statement of invariance *derivable* from a theory. The paucity of such laws in the sociological field perhaps reflects the prevailing bifurcation of theory and empirical research. Despite the many volumes dealing with the history of sociological theory and despite the plethora of empirical investigations, sociologists (including the writer) may discuss the logical criteria of sociological laws without citing a single instance which fully satisfies these criteria.[19]

Approximations to these criteria are not entirely wanting. To exhibit the relations of empirical generalizations to theory and to set forth the functions of theory, it may be useful to examine a familiar case in which such generalizations were incorporated into a body of substantive theory. Thus, it has long been established as a statistical uniformity that in a variety of populations, Catholics have a lower suicide rate than Protestants.[20] In this form the uniformity posed a theoretical problem. It merely constituted an empirical regularity which would become significant for theory only if it could be derived from a set of other propositions, a task

---

18. "In part," if only because it stultifies the possibilities of obtaining fertile new findings to confine researches *wholly* to the test of predetermined hypotheses. Hunches originating in the course of the inquiry which may not have immediately obvious implications for a broader theoretic system may eventuate in the discovery of empirical uniformities which can later be incorporated into a theory. For example, in the sociology of political behavior, it has been recently established that the larger the number of social cross-pressures to which voters are subjected, the less interest they exhibit in a presidential election (P. F. Lazarsfeld, Bernard Berelson, and Hazel Gaudet, *The People's Choice* [New York: Duell, Sloan & Pearce, 1944], 56-64). This finding, which was wholly unanticipated when the research was first formulated, may well initiate new lines of systematic inquiry into political behavior, even though it is not yet integrated into a generalized theory. Fruitful empirical research not only tests theoretically derived hypotheses; it also originates new hypotheses. This might be termed the "serendipity" component of research, i.e., the discovery, by chance or sagacity, of valid results which were not sought for.

19. E.g., see the discussion by George A. Lundberg, "The concept of law in the social sciences," *Philosophy of Science*, 1938, 5, 189-203, which affirms the possibility of such laws without including any case in point. The book by K. D. Har, *Social Laws* (Chapel Hill: University of North Carolina Press, 1930), does not fulfil the promise implicit in the title. A panel of social scientists discussing the possibility of obtaining social laws finds it difficult to instance cases (Blumer, *op. cit.*, 142-50).

20. It need hardly be said that this statement assumes that education, income, nationality, rural-urban residence, and other factors which might render this finding spurious have been held constant.

which Durkheim set himself. If we restate his theoretic assumptions in formal fashion, the paradigm of his theoretic analysis becomes clear:

1. Social cohesion provides psychic support to group members subjected to acute stresses and anxieties.
2. Suicide rates are functions of *unrelieved* anxieties and stresses to which persons are subjected.
3. Catholics have greater social cohesion than Protestants.
4. Therefore, lower suicide rates should be anticipated among Catholics than among Protestants.[21]

This case serves to locate the place of empirical generalizations in relation to theory and to illustrate the several functions of theory.

1. It indicates that theoretic pertinence is not inherently present or absent in empirical generalizations but appears when the generalization is conceptualized in abstractions of higher order (Catholicism—social cohesion—relieved anxieties—suicide rate) which are embodied in more general statements of relationships.[22] What was initially taken as an isolated uniformity is restated as a relation, not between religious affiliation and behavior, but between groups with certain conceptualized attributes (social cohesion) and the behavior. The *scope* of the original empirical finding is considerably extended, and several seemingly disparate uniformities are seen to be interrelated (thus differentials in suicide rates between married and single persons can be derived from the same theory).

2. Once having established the theoretic pertinence of a uniformity by deriving it from a set of interrelated propositions, we provide for the *cumulation* both of theory and of research findings. The differentials-in-suicide-rate uniformities add confirmation to the set of propositions from which they—and other uniformities—have been derived. This is a major function of *systematic theory*.

3. Whereas the empirical uniformity did not lend itself to the drawing of diverse consequences, the reformulation gives rise to various consequences in fields of conduct quite remote from that of suicidal behavior. For example, inquiries into obsessive behavior, morbid pre-

---

21. We need not examine further aspects of this illustration, e.g., (1) the extent to which we have adequately stated the premises implicit in Durkheim's interpretation; (2) the supplementary theoretic analysis which would take these premises not as given but as problematic; (3) the grounds on which the potentially infinite regression of theoretic interpretations is halted at one rather than another point; (4) the problems involved in the introduction of such intervening variables as social cohesion which are not directly measured; (5) the extent to which the premises have been empirically confirmed; (6) the comparatively low order of abstraction represented by this illustration and (7) the fact that Durkheim derived several empirical generalizations from this same set of hypotheses.

22. Thorstein Veblen has put this with typical cogency: "All this may seem like taking pains about trivialities. But the data with which any scientific inquiry has to do are trivialities in some other bearing than that one in which they are of account." *The Place of Science in Modern Civilization* (New York: Viking Press, 1932), 42.

occupations, and other maladaptive behavior have found these also to be related to inadequacies of group cohesion.[23] The conversion of empirical uniformities into theoretic statements thus increases the *fruitfulness* of research through the successive exploration of implications.

4. By providing a rationale, the theory introduces a *ground for prediction* which is more secure than mere empirical extrapolation from previously observed trends. Thus, should independent measures indicate a decrease of social cohesion among Catholics, the theorist would predict a tendency toward increased rates of suicide in this group. The atheoretic empiricist would have no alternative, however, but to predict on the basis of extrapolation.

5. The foregoing list of functions presupposes one further attribute of theory which is not altogether true of the Durkheim formulation and which gives rise to a general problem that has peculiarly beset sociological theory, at least, up to the present. If theory is to be productive, it must be sufficiently *precise* to be *determinate*. Precision is an integral element of the criterion of *testability*. The prevailing pressure toward the utilization of statistical data in sociology, whenever possible, to control and test theoretic inferences has a justifiable basis, when we consider the logical place of precision in disciplined inquiry.

The more precise the inferences (predictions) which can be drawn from a theory, the less the likelihood of *alternative* hypotheses which will be adequate to these predictions. In other words, precise predictions and data serve to reduce the *empirical* bearing upon research of the *logical* fallacy of affirming the consequent.[24] It is well known that verified predictions derived from a theory do not prove or demonstrate that theory; they merely supply a measure of confirmation, for it is always possible that alternative hypotheses drawn from different theoretic systems can also account for the predicted phenomena.[25] But those theories which

---

23. See, e.g., Elton Mayo, *Human Problems of an Industrial Civilization* (New York: Macmillan Co., 1933), 113 *et passim*. The theoretical framework utilized in the studies of industrial morale by Whitehead, Roethlisberger, and Dickson stemmed appreciably from the Durkheim formulations, as the authors testify.

24. The paradigm of "proof through prediction" is, of course, logically fallacious:
If A (hypothesis), then B (prediction).
B is observed.
Therefore, A is true.
This is not overdisturbing for scientific research, in as much as other than formal criteria are involved.

25. As a case in point, consider that different theorists had predicted war and internecine conflict on a large scale at midcentury. Sorokin and some Marxists, for example, set forth this prediction on the basis of quite distinct theoretic systems. The actual outbreak of large-scale conflicts does not in itself enable us to choose between these schemes of analysis, if only because the observed fact is consistent with both. Only if the predictions had been so *specified*, had been so precise, that the actual occurrences coincided with the one prediction and not with the other, would a determinate test have been instituted.

admit of precise predictions confirmed by observation take on strategic importance since they provide an initial basis for choice between competing hypotheses. In other words, precision enhances the likelihood of approximating a "crucial" observation or experiment.

The internal coherence of a theory has much the same function, for if a variety of empirically confirmed consequences are drawn from one theoretic system, this reduces the likelihood that competing theories can adequately account for the same data. The integrated theory sustains a larger measure of confirmation than is the case with distinct and unrelated hypotheses, thus accumulating a greater weight of evidence.

Both pressures—toward precision and logical coherence—can lead to unproductive activity, particularly in the social scienes. Any procedure can be abused as well as used. A premature insistence on precision at all costs may sterilize imaginative hypotheses. It may lead to a reformulation of the scientific problem in order to permit measurement with, at times, the result that the subsequent materials do not bear on the initial problem in hand.[26] In the search for precision, care must be taken to see that significant problems are not thus inadvertently blotted from view. Similarly, the pressure for logical consistency has at times invited logomachy and sterile theorizing, in as much as the assumptions contained in the system of analysis are so far removed from empirical referents or involve such high abstractions as not to permit of empirical inquiry.[27] But the warrant for these criteria of inquiry is not vitiated by such abuses.

FORMAL DERIVATIONS AND CODIFICATION

This limited account has, at the very least, pointed to the need for a closer connection between theory and empirical research. The prevailing division of the two is manifested in marked *discontinuities* of empirical research, on the one hand, and systematic theorizing unsustained by empirical test, on the other.[27a] There are conspicuously few instances of consecutive research which have cumulatively investigated a succession of hypotheses derived from a given theory. Rather, there tends to be a marked dispersion of empirical inquiries, oriented toward a concrete field of human behavior, but lacking a central theoretic orientation. The plethora of discrete empirical generalizations and of *post factum* inter-

---

26. Stuart A. Rice comments on this tendency in public opinion research; see *Eleven Twenty-six: A Decade of Social Science Research*, ed. Louis Wirth (Chicago: University of Chicago Press, 1940), 167.

27. It is this practice to which E. Ronald Walker refers, in the field of economics, as "theoretic blight." *From Economic Theory to Policy* (Chicago: University of Chicago Press, 1943), chap. iv.

27a. See in this connection the dramatic example of such *discontinuity* cited in Chapter I (*i.e.*, the recent rediscovery of the primary group within formal associations some decades after this had been elaborately treated by Thomas and Znaniecki).

pretations reflect this pattern of research. The large bulk of general orientations and conceptual analyses, as distinct from sets of inter-related hypotheses, in turn reflect the tendency to separate theoretic activity from empirical research. It is a commonplace that continuity, rather than dispersion, can be achieved only if empirical studies are theory-oriented and if theory is empirically confirmable. However, it is possible to go beyond such affirmations and to suggest certain conventions for sociological research which might well facilitate this process. These conventions may be termed "formalized derivation" and "codification."[28]

Both in the design and in the reporting of empirical research, it might be made a definite convention that hypotheses and, whenever possible, the theoretic grounds (assumptions and postulates) of these hypotheses be explicitly set forth. The report of data would be in terms of their immediate pertinence for the hypotheses and, derivatively, the underlying theory. Attention should be called specifically to the introduction of interpretative variables other than those entailed in the original formulation of hypotheses and the bearing of these upon the theory should be indicated. *Post factum* interpretations which will inevitably arise when new and unexpected relationships are discovered should be so stated that the direction of further probative research becomes evident. The conclusions of the research might well include not only a statement of the findings with respect to the initial hypotheses but, when this is in point, an indication of the order of observations needed to test anew the further implications of the investigation. Formal derivation of this character has had a salutary effect in psychology and economics, leading, in the one case, to sequential experiments[29] and, in the other, to an articulated series of investigations. One consequence of such formalization is that it serves as a control over the introduction of un-related, undisciplined, and diffuse interpretations. It does not impose upon the reader the task of ferreting out the relations between the inter-pretations embodied in the text.[30] Above all, it prepares the way for consecutive and cumulative research rather than a buckshot array of dispersed investigations.

---

28. To be sure, these conventions are deduction and induction, respectively. Our sole interest at this point is to translate these logical procedures into terms appropriate to current sociological theory and research.

29. The work of Clark Hull and associates is preeminent in this respect. See, e.g., Hull, *Principles of Behavior* (New York: D. Appleton-Century Co., 1943); also comparable efforts toward formalization in the writings of Kurt Lewin (e.g., Kurt Lewin, Ronald Lippitt, and S. K. Escalona, *Studies in Topological and Vector Psychology I* ["University of Iowa Studies in Child Welfare," Vol. XVI (Iowa City, 1940)], 9-42).

30. A book such as John Dollard's *Caste and Class in a Southern Town* teems with suggestiveness, but it is an enormous task for the reader to work out explicitly the theoretic problems which are being attacked, the interpretative variables, and the implicit assumptions of the interpretations. Yet all this needs to be done if a sequence of studies building upon Dollard's work is proposed.

The correlative process which seems called for is that which Lazarsfeld terms "codification." Whereas formal derivation focuses our attention upon the implications of a theory, codification seeks to systematize available empirical generalizations in *apparently different* spheres of behavior. Rather than permitting such separate empirical findings to lie fallow or to be referred to distinctive areas of behavior, the deliberate attempt to institute relevant provisional hypotheses promises to extend existing theory, subject to further empirical inquiry. Thus, an abundance of empirical findings in such fields as propaganda and public opinion, reactions to unemployment, and family responses to crises suggest that when persons are confronted with an "objective stimulus-pattern" which would be expected to elicit responses counter to their "initial predispositions," their actual behavior can be more successfully predicted on the basis of predispositions than of the stimulus-pattern. This is implied by "boomerang effects" in propaganda,[31] by findings on adjustive and maladjustive responses to unemployment,[32] and by research on the stability of families confronted with severe reductions in income.[33] A codified formulation, even as crude as this, gives rise to theoretic problems which would be readily overlooked if the several empirical findings were not re-examined within a single context. It is submitted that codification, as a procedure complementing the formal derivation of hypotheses to be tested, will facilitate the codevelopment of viable sociological theory and pertinent empirical research.

31. Paul F. Lazarsfeld and Robert K. Merton, "Studies in radio and film propaganda," *Transactions of the New York Academy of Sciences, Series II,* 1943, 6, 58-79.

32. O. M. Hall, "Attitudes and unemployment," *Archives of Psychology,* No. 165 (March, 1934); E. W. Bakke, *The Unemployed Worker* (New Haven: Yale University Press, 1940).

33. Mirra Komarovsky, *The Unemployed Man and His Family* (New York: Dryden Press, 1940); R. C. Angell, *The Family Encounters the Depression* (New York: Charles Scribner's Sons, 1936); E. W. Burgess, R. K. Merton, *et al., Restudy of the Documents Analyzed by Angell in The Family Encounters the Depression* (New York: Social Science Research Council, 1942).

III   THE BEARING OF EMPIRICAL RESEARCH ON SOCIOLOGICAL THEORY

H ISTORY HAS A CERTAIN GIFT for outmoding stereotypes. This can be seen, for example, in the historical development of sociology. The steretotype of the social theorist high in the empyrean of pure ideas uncontaminated by mundane facts is fast becoming no less outmoded than the stereotype of the social researcher equipped with questionnaire and pencil and hot on the chase of the isolated and meaningless statistic. For in building the mansion of sociology during the last decades, theorist and empiricist have learned to work together. What is more, they have learned to talk to one another in the process. At times, this means only that a sociologist has learned to talk to himself since increasingly the same man has taken up both theory and research. Specialization and integration have developed hand in hand. All this has led not only to the realization that theory and empirical research *should* interact but to the result that they *do* interact.

As a consequence, there is decreasing need for accounts of the relations between theory and research to be wholly programmatic in character. A growing body of theoretically oriented research makes it progressively possible to discuss with profit the actual relations between the two. And, as we all know, there has been no scarcity of such discussions. Journals abound with them. They generally center on the role of theory in research, setting forth, often with admirable lucidity, the functions of theory in the initiation, design and prosecution of empirical inquiry. But since this is not a one-way relationship, since the two *interact*, it may be useful to examine the other direction of the relationship: the role of empirical research in the development of social theory. That is the purpose of this chapter.

THE THEORETIC FUNCTIONS OF RESEARCH

With a few conspicuous exceptions, recent sociological discussions have assigned but one major function to empirical research: the testing or verification of hypotheses. The model for the proper way of performing this function is as familiar as it is clear. The investigator begins with a hunch or hypothesis, from this he draws various inferences and these, in turn, are subjected to empirical test which confirms or refutes the hypothesis.[1] But this is a logical model, and so fails, of course, to describe much of what actually occurs in fruitful investigation. It presents a set of logical norms, not a description of the research experience. And, as logicians are well aware, in purifying the experience, the logical model may also distort it. Like other models, it abstracts from the temporal sequence of events. It exaggerates the creative role of explicit theory just as it minimizes the creative role of observation. For research is not merely logic tempered with observation. It has its psychological as well as its logical dimensions, although one would scarcely suspect this from the logically rigorous sequence in which research is usually reported.[2] It is both the psychological and logical pressures of research upon social theory which we seek to trace.

It is my central thesis that empirical research goes far beyond the passive role of verifying and testing theory: it does more than confirm or refute hypotheses. Research plays an active role: it performs at least four major functions which help shape the development of theory. It *initiates,* it *reformulates,* it *deflects* and it *clarifies* theory.[3]

1. THE SERENDIPITY PATTERN

(THE UNANTICIPATED, ANOMALOUS AND STRATEGIC DATUM EXERTS PRESSURE FOR INITIATING THEORY)

Under certain conditions, a research finding gives rise to social theory. In a previous paper, this was all too briefly expressed as follows: "Fruitful empirical research not only tests theoretically derived hypotheses; it also originates new hypotheses. This might be termed the 'serendipity' component of research, *i.e.,* the discovery, by chance or sagacity, of valid results which were not sought for."[4]

---

1. See, for example, the procedural review of Stouffer's "Theory of intervening opportunities" by G. A. Lundberg, "What are sociological problems?", *American Sociological Review,* 1941, 6, 357-369.

2. See R. K. Merton, "Science, population and society," *The Scientific Monthly,* 1937, 44, 170-171; the apposite discussion by Jean Piaget, *Judgment and Reasoning in the Child,* (London, 1929), Chaps. V, IX, and the comment by William H. George, *The Scientist in Action,* (London, 1936), 153. "A piece of research does not progress in the way it is 'written up' for publication."

3. The fourth function, clarification, has been elaborated in publications by Paul F. Lazarsfeld.

4. R. K. Merton, "Sociological Theory," *American Journal of Sociology,* 1945, 50, 469n. Interestingly enough, the same outlandish term 'serendipity' which has had little currency since it was coined by Horace Walpole in 1754 has also been used to refer to this component of research by the physiologist Walter B. Cannon. See his *The Way of an Investigator,* (New York: W. W. Norton, 1945), Chap. VI, in which he sets forth numerous instances of serendipity in several fields of science.

The serendipity[4a] pattern refers to the fairly common experience of observing an *unanticipated, anomalous and strategic* datum which becomes the occasion for developing a new theory or for extending an existing theory. Each of these elements of the pattern can be readily described. The datum is, first of all, unanticipated. A research directed toward the test of one hypothesis yields a fortuitous by-product, an unexpected observation which bears upon theories not in question when the research was begun.

Secondly, the observation is anomalous, surprising,[5] either because it seems inconsistent with prevailing theory or with other established facts. In either case, the seeming inconsistency provokes curiosity; it stimulates the investigator to "make sense of the datum," to fit it into a

---

4a. Since the foregoing note was first written in 1946, the word *serendipity*, fox all its etymological oddity, has diffused far beyond the limits of the academic community. The marked speed of its diffusion can be illustrated by its most recent movement among the pages of the *New York Times*. On May 22, 1949, Waldemar Kaempffert, science editor of the *Times*, had occasion to refer to serendipity in summarizing an article by the research scientist, Ellice McDonald—this, in an innermost page devoted to recent developments in science. Some three weeks later, on June 14, Orville Prescott, book reviewer of the daily *Times*, has evidently become captivated by the word, for in a review of a book in which the hero has a love of outlandish words, Prescott wonders if the hero knew the word serendipity. On Independence Day of 1949, serendipity wins full social acceptance. Stripped of qualifying inverted commas and no longer needing an appositive defining phrase, serendipity appears, without apology or adornment, on the front page of the *Times*. It achieves this prominence in a news dispatch from Oklahoma City, reporting an address by Sir Alexander Fleming, the discoverer of penicillin, at the dedication of the Oklahoma Medical Research Foundation. ("Sir Alexander's experience, which led to the development of modern disease-killing drugs," says the dispatch under the by-line of Robert K. Plumb, "is frequently cited as an outstanding example of the importance of serendipity in science. He found penicillin by chance, but had been trained to look for significance in scientific accidents.") In these travels from the esoteric page devoted to science to the less restricted columns of the book-review to the popular front-page, serendipity had become naturalized. Perhaps it would soon find its way into American abridged dictionaries.

This, then, is yet another instance in which a term, long unmet in common usage, has been recovered and put to fairly frequent use. (Compare note 6 in Chapter IV, referring to the similar history of the term, *anomie.*) And here again, one might ask: what accounts for the cultural resonance in recent years of this contrived, odd-sounding and useful word?

Questions of this order are being explored in a monographic study, by Elinor G. Barber and myself, of the sociological semantics involved in the cultural diffusion of the word *serendipity*. The study examines the social and cultural contexts of the coinage of the word in the eighteenth century; the climate of relevant opinion in which it first saw print in the nineteenth century; the patterned responses to the neologism when it was first encountered; the diverse social circles of littérateurs, physical and social scientists, engineers, lexicographers and historians in which it has diffused; the changes of meaning it has undergone in the course of diffusion and the ideological uses to which it has been variously put.

5. Charles Sanders Peirce had long before noticed the strategic role of the "surprising fact" in his account of what he called "abduction," that is, the initiation and entertaining of a hypothesis as a step in inference. See his *Collected Papers*, VI, 522-528.

broader frame of knowledge. He explores further. He makes fresh observations. He draws inferences from the observations, inferences depending largely, of course, upon his general theoretic orientation. The more he is steeped in the data, the greater the likelihood that he will hit upon a fruitful direction of inquiry. In the fortunate circumstance that his new hunch proves justified, the anomalous datum leads ultimately to a new or extended theory. The curiosity stimulated by the anomalous datum is temporarily appeased.

And thirdly, in noting that the unexpected fact must be strategic, *i.e.*, that it must permit of implications which bear upon generalized theory, we are, of course, referring rather to what the observer brings to the datum than to the datum itself. For it obviously requires a theoretically sensitized observer to detect the universal in the particular. After all, men had for centuries noticed such "trivial" occurrences as slips of the tongue, slips of the pen, typographical errors, and lapses of memory, but it required the theoretic sensitivity of a Freud to see these as strategic data through which he could extend his theory of repression and symptomatic acts.

The serendipity pattern, then, involves the unanticipated, anomalous and strategic datum which exerts pressure upon the investigator for a new direction of inquiry which extends theory. Instances of serendipity have occurred in many disciplines, but I should like to draw upon a recent sociological research for illustration. In the course of our research into the social organization of Craftown,[6] a suburban housing community of some 700 families, largely of working class status, we observed that a large proportion of residents were affiliated with more civic, political and other voluntary organizations than had been the case in their previous places of residence. Quite incidentally, we noted further that this increase in group participation had occurred also among the parents of infants and young children. This finding was rather inconsistent with common-sense knowledge. For it is well known that, particularly on the lower economic levels, youngsters usually tie parents down and preclude their taking active part in organized group life outside the home. But Craftown parents themselves readily explained their behavior. "Oh, there's no real problem about getting out in the evenings," said one mother who belonged to several organizations. "It's easy to find teen-agers around here to take care of the kids. There are so many more teen-agers around here than where I used to live."

The explanation appears adequate enough and would have quieted the investigator's curiosity, had it not been for one disturbing datum: like most new housing communities, Craftown actually has a very small proportion of adolescents—only 3.7 per cent for example, in the 15-19

6. Drawn from continuing studies in the Sociology and Social Psychology of Housing, under a grant from the Lavanburg Foundation.

year age group. What is more, the majority of the adults, 63 per cent, are under 34 years of age, so that their children include an exceptionally large proportion of infants and youngsters. Thus, far from their being many adolescents to look after the younger children in Craftown, quite the contrary is true: the ratio of adolescents to children under ten years of age is 1:10, whereas in the communities of origin, the ratio hovers about 1:1.5.[7]

We were at once confronted, then, by an anomalous fact which was certainly no part of our original program of observation. We manifestly did not enter and indeed could not have entered the field of research in Craftown with a hypothesis bearing upon an illusory belief in the abundance of teen-age supervisors of children. Here was an observation both unanticipated and anomalous. Was it also strategic? We did not prejudge its "intrinsic" importance. It seemed no more and no less trivial than Freud's observation during the last war (in which he had two sons at the front) that he had mis-read a newspaper headline, "Die *Feinde* vor Görz" (The *Enemy* before Görz), as "Der *Friede* von Görz" (The *Peace* of Görz). Freud took a trivial incident and converted it into a strategic fact. Unless the observed discrepancy between the subjective impressions of Craftown residents and the objective facts could undergo a somewhat similar transformation it had best be ignored, for it plainly had little "social significance."

What first made this illusion a peculiarly intriguing instance of a general theoretic problem was the difficulty of explaining it as merely the calculated handiwork of vested-interests engaged in spreading a contrary-to-fact belief. Generally, when the sociologist with a conceptual scheme stemming from utilitarian theory observes a patently untrue social belief, he will look for special groups in whose interest it is to invent and spread this belief. The cry of "propaganda!" is often mistaken for a theoretically sound analysis.[8] But this is clearly out of the question in the present instance: there are plainly no special-interest groups seeking to misrepresent the age-distribution of Craftown. What, then, was the source of this social illusion?

Various other theories suggested points of departure. There was Marx's postulate that it is men's "social existence which determines their consciousness." There was Durkheim's theorem that social images ("col-

---

7. Essentially the same discrepancies in age distribution between Craftown and communities of origin are found if we compare proportions of children under ten with those between 10 and 19. If we make children under five the basis of comparison, the disproportions are even more marked.

8. To be sure, vested-interests often do spread untrue propaganda and this may reinforce mass illusions. But the vested-interest or priestly-lie theories of fallacious folk beliefs do not always constitute the most productive point of departure nor do they go far toward explaining the bases of acceptance or rejection of the beliefs. The present case in point, trivial though it is in any practical sense, is theoretically significant in showing anew the limitations of a utilitarian scheme of analysis.

lective representations") in some fashion reflect a social reality although "it does not follow that the reality which is its foundation conforms objectively to the idea which believers have of it." There was Sherif's thesis that "social factors" provide a framework for selective perceptions and judgments in relatively unstructured situations. There was the prevailing view in the sociology of knowledge that social location determines the perspectives entering into perception, beliefs and ideas. But suggestive as these general orientations[9] were, they did not directly suggest *which* features of social existence, *which* aspects of the social reality, *which* social factors, *which* social location may have determined this seemingly fallacious belief.

The clue was inadvertently provided by further interviews with residents. In the words of an active participant in Craftown affairs, herself the mother of two children under six years of age:

My husband and I get out together much more. You see, there are more people around to mind the children. *You feel more confident about having some thirteen-or-fourteen-year-old in here when you know most of the people. If you're in a big city, you don't feel so easy about having someone who's almost a stranger come in.*

This clearly suggests that the sociological roots of the "illusion" are to be found in the structure of community relations in which Craftown residents are enmeshed. The belief is an unwitting reflection, not of the statistical reality, but of the community cohesion. It is not that there are objectively more adolescents in Craftown, but more who are *intimately known* and who, therefore, *exist socially* for parents seeking aid in child supervision. Most Craftown residents having lately come from an urban setting now find themselves in a community in which proximity has developed into reciprocal intimacies. The illusion expresses the perspective of people for whom adolescents as potential child-care aides "exist" only if they are well-known and therefore merit confidence. In short, perception was a function of confidence and confidence, in turn, was a function of social cohesion.[10]

From the sociological viewpoint, then, this unanticipated finding fits

---

9. As the differences between theory and general orientations have been considered in Chapter II.

10. Schedule data from the study provide corroborative evidence. In view of the exceptionally high proportion of young children, it is striking that 54 per cent of their parents affirm that it is "easier in Craftown to get people to look after our children when we want to go out" than it was in other places where they have lived; only 21 per cent say it is harder and the remaining 25 per cent feel there is no difference. Those who come from the larger urban communities are more likely to report greater ease in obtaining assistance in Craftown. Moreover, as we would expect from the hypothesis, those residents who are more closely geared in with Craftown, who identify themselves most fully with it, are more likely to believe it easier to find such aid; 61 per cent of these do so as against 50 per cent of those who identify with other communities, whereas only 12 per cent find it more difficult in comparison with 26 per cent of the latter group.

into and extends the theory that social perception is the product of a social framework. It develops further the "psychology of social norms,"[11] for it is not merely an instance of individuals assimilating particular norms, judgments, and standards from other members of the community. The social perception is, rather, a by-product, a derivative, of the structure of human relations.

This is perhaps sufficient to illustrate the operation of the serendipity pattern: an unexpected and anomalous finding elicited the investigator's curiosity, and conducted him along an unpremeditated by-path which led to a fresh hypothesis.

2. THE RECASTING OF THEORY
(New Data Exert Pressure for the Elaboration of a Conceptual Scheme)

But it is not only through the anomalous fact that empirical research invites the extension of theory. It does so also through the repeated observation of hitherto neglected facts. When an existing conceptual scheme commonly applied to a subject-matter does not adequately take these facts into account, research presses insistently for its reformulation. It leads to the introduction of variables which have not been systematically included in the scheme of analysis. Here, be it noted, it is not that the data are anomalous or unexpected or incompatible with existing theory; it is merely that they had not been considered pertinent. Whereas the serendipity pattern centers in an apparent inconsistency which presses for resolution, the reformulation pattern centers in the hitherto neglected but relevant fact which presses for an extension of the conceptual scheme.

Examples of this in the history of social science are far from limited. Thus it was a series of fresh empirical facts which led Malinowski to incorporate new elements into a theory of magic. It was his Trobrianders, of course, who gave him the clue to the distinctive feature of his theory. When these islanders fished in the inner lagoon by the reliable method of poisoning, an abundant catch was assured and danger was absent. Neither uncertainty nor uncontrollable hazards were involved. And here, Malinowski noted, magic was not practiced. But in the open-sea fishing, with the uncertain yield and its often grave dangers, the rituals of magic flourished. Stemming from these pregnant observations was his theory that magical belief arises to bridge the uncertainties in man's practical pursuits, to fortify confidence, to reduce anxieties, to open up avenues of escape from the seeming impasse. Magic was construed as a supple-

---

11. Muzafer Sherif's book by this title should be cited as basic in the field, although it tends to have a somewhat limited conception of "social factors," *The Psychology of Social Norms* (New York, 1936).

mentary technique for reaching practical objectives. It was these empirical facts which suggested the incorporation of new dimensions into earlier theories of magic—particularly the relations of magic to the fortuitous, the dangerous and the uncontrollable. It was not that these facts were *inconsistent* with previous theories; it was simply that these conceptual schemes had not taken them adequately into account. Nor was Malinowski testing a preconceived hypothesis—he was developing an enlarged and improved theory on the basis of suggestive empirical data.

For another example of this pressure of empirical data for the recasting of a specific theory we turn closer home. The investigation dealt with a single dramatic instance of mass persuasion: broadcasting at repeated intervals over a span of eighteen hours, Kate Smith, a radio star, sold large quantities of war-bonds in the course of a day. It is not my intention to report fully on the dynamics of this case of mass persuasion;[12] for present purposes, we are concerned only with the implications of two facts which emerged from the study.

First of all, in the course of intensive interviews many of our informants—New Yorkers who had pledged a bond to Smith—expressed a thorough disenchantment with the world of advertising, commercials and propaganda. They felt themselves the object of manipulation—and resented it. They objected to being the target for advertising which cajoles, insists and terrorizes. They objected to being engulfed in waves of propaganda proposing opinions and actions not in their own best interests. They expressed dismay over what is in effect a pattern of *pseudo-Gemeinschaft*—subtle methods of salesmanship in which there is the feigning of personal concern with the client in order to manipulate him the better. As one small businessman phrased it, "In my own business, I can see how a lot of people in their business deals will make some kind of gesture of friendliness, sincerity and so forth, most of which is phony." Drawn from a highly competitive, segmented metropolitan society, our informants were describing a climate of reciprocal distrust, of *anomie*, in which common values have been submerged in the welter of private interests. Society was experienced as an arena for rival frauds. There was small belief in the disinterestedness of conduct.

In contrast to all this was the second fact: we found that the persuasiveness of the Smith bond-drive among these same informants largely rested upon their firm belief in the integrity and sincerity of Smith. And much the same was found to be true in a polling interview with a larger cross-section sample of almost a thousand New Yorkers. Fully 80% asserted that in her all-day marathon drive, Smith was *exclusively* concerned with promoting the sale of war bonds, whereas only 17% felt that she was *also* interested in publicity for herself, and a negligible 3% believed she was *primarily* concerned with the resulting publicity.

---

12. Merton, Fiske and Curtis, *Mass Persuasion.*

This emphasis on her sincerity is all the more striking as a problem for research in the molding of reputations because she herself appeared on at least six commercially sponsored radio programs each week. But although she is engaged in apparently the same promotional activities as others, she was viewed by the majority of our informants as the direct antithesis of all that these other announcers and stars represent. In the words of one devotee, "She's sincere and *she really means anything* she ever says. It isn't just sittin' up there and talkin' and gettin' paid for it. She's different from what other people are."

Why this overwhelming belief in Smith's sincerity? To be sure, the same society which produces a sense of alienation and estrangement generates in many a craving for reassurance, an acute will to believe, a flight into faith. But why does Smith become the object of this faith for so many otherwise distrustful people? Why is she seen as genuine by those who seek redemption from the spurious? Why are her motives believed to rise above avarice and ambition and pride of class? What are the social-psychological sources of this image of Smith as sincerity incarnate?

Among the several sources, we wish to examine here the one which bears most directly upon a theory of mass persuasion. The clue is provided by the fact that a larger proportion of those who heard the Smith marathon war-bond drive are convinced of her disinterested patriotism than of those who did not. This appears to indicate that the marathon bond-drive enhanced public belief in her sincerity. But we must recognize the possibility that her devoted fans, for whom her sincerity was unquestioned, would be more likely to have heard the marathon broadcasts. Therefore, to determine whether the marathon did in fact extend this belief, we must compare regular listeners to her programs with those who are not her fans. Within each group, a significantly larger proportion of people who heard the marathon are convinced of Smith's exclusive concern with patriotic purposes.[12a] This is as true for her devoted fans as for those who did not listen to her regular programs at all. In other words, we have caught for a moment, as with a candid camera, a snapshot of Smith's reputation of sincerity in the process of being even further enhanced. We have frozen in mid-course the process of building a reputation.

But if the marathon increased the belief in Smith's sincerity, how did this come about? It is at this point that our intensive interviews, with their often ingenuous and revealing details, permit us to interpret the statistical results of the poll. The marathon had all the atmosphere of determined, resolute endeavor under tremendous difficulties. Some could detect signs of strain—and courageous persistence. "Her voice was not quite so strong later, but she stuck it out like a good soldier," says a dis-

---

12a. The statistical data will be found in *ibid.*, pp. 87-88.

cerning housewife. Others projected themselves into the vividly imagined situation of fatigue and brave exertion. Solicitous reports by her co-adjutor, Ted Collins, reinforced the emphatic concern for the strain to which Smith was subjecting herself. "I felt, I can't stand this any longer," recalls one informant. "Mr. Collins' statement about her being exhausted affected me so much that I just couldn't bear it." The marathon took on the attributes of a sacrificial ritual.

In short, it was not so much what Smith *said* as what she *did* which served to validate her sincerity. It was the presumed stress and strain of an eighteen-hour series of broadcasts, it was the deed not the word which furnished the indubitable proof. Listeners might question whether she were not unduly dramatizing herself, but they could not escape the in-controvertible evidence that she was devoting the entire day to the task. Appraising the direct testimony of Smith's behavior, another informant explains that "she was on all day and the others weren't. So it seemed that she was sacrificing more and was more sincere." Viewed as a process of persuasion, the marathon converted initial feelings of scepticism and distrust among listeners into at first a reluctant, and later, a full-fledged acceptance of Smith's integrity. The successive broadcasts served as a fulfillment in action of a promise in words. The words were reinforced by things she had actually done. The currency of talk was accepted be-cause it was backed by the gold of conduct. The gold reserve, moreover, need not even approximate the amount of currency it can support.

This empirical study suggests that propaganda-of-the-deed may be effective among the very people who are distrustful of propaganda-of-the-word. Where there is social disorganization, *anomie,* conflicting values, we find propaganditis reaching epidemic proportions. Any state-ment of values is likely to be discounted as "mere propaganda." Ex-hortations are suspect. But the propaganda of the deed elicits more con-fidence. Members of the audience are largely permitted to draw their conclusions from the action—they are less likely to feel manipulated. When the propagandist's deed and his words symbolically coincide, it stimulates belief in his sincerity. Further research must determine whether this propaganda pattern is significantly more effective in so-cieties suffering from anomie than in those which are more fully in-tegrated. But not unlike the Malinowski case-in-point, this may illustrate the role of research in suggesting new variables to be incorporated into a specific theory.

3. THE RE-FOCUSING OF THEORETIC INTEREST
(New Methods of Empirical Research Exert Pressure for New Foci of Theoretic Interest.)

To this point we have considered the impact of research upon the development of particular theories. But empirical research also affects more general trends in the development of theory. This occurs chiefly through the invention of research procedures which tend to shift the foci of theoretic interest to the growing points of research.

The reasons for this are on the whole evident. After all, sound theory thrives only on a rich diet of pertinent facts and newly invented procedures help provide the ingredients of this diet. The new, and often previously unavailable, data stimulate fresh hypotheses. Moreover, theorists find that their hypotheses can be put to immediate test in those spheres where appropriate research techniques have been designed. It is no longer necessary for them to wait upon data as they happen to turn up—researches directed to the verification of hypotheses can be instituted at once. The flow of relevant data thus increases the tempo of advance in certain spheres of theory whereas in others, theory stagnates for want of adequate observations. Attention shifts accordingly.

In noting that new centers of theoretic interest have followed upon the invention of research procedures, we do not imply that these alone played a decisive role.[13] The growing interest in the theory of propaganda as an instrument of social control, for example, is in large part a response to the changing historical situation, with its conflict of major ideological systems, new technologies of mass communication which have opened up new avenues for propaganda and the rich research treasuries provided by business and government interested in this new weapon of war, both declared and undeclared. But this shift is also a by-product of accumulated facts made available through such newly developed, and confessedly crude, procedures as content-analysis, the panel technique and the focused interview.

Examples of this impact in the recent history of social theory are numerous but we have time to mention only a few. Thus, the increasing concern with the theory of character and personality formation in relation to social structure became marked after the introduction of new projective methods; the Rorschach test, the thematic apperception test, play techniques and story completions being among the most familiar. So, too, the sociometric techniques of Moreno and others, and fresh advances in the technique of the "passive interview" have revived interest in the theory of interpersonal relations. Stemming from such techniques as well is the trend toward what might be called the "rediscovery of the primary group," particularly in the shape of theoretic concern with informal social structures as mediating between the individual and large formal organizations. This interest has found expression in an entire literature on the role and structure of the informal group, for example, in factory social systems, bureaucracy and political organizations. Similarly, we may anticipate that the recent introduction of the panel tech-

---

13. It is perhaps needless to add that these procedures, instruments and apparatus are in turn dependent upon prior theory. But this does not alter their stimulating effect upon the further development of theory.

nique—the repeated interviewing of the same group of informants—will in due course more sharply focus the attention of social psychologists upon the theory of attitude formation, decisions among alternative choices, factors in political participation and determinants of behavior in cases of conflicting role demands, to mention a few types of problems to which this technique is especially adapted.

Perhaps the most direct impact of research procedures upon theory has resulted from the *creation* of sociological statistics organized in terms of theoretically pertinent categories. Talcott Parsons has observed that numerical data are scientifically important only when they can be fitted into analytical categories and that "a great deal of current research is producing facts in a form which cannot be utilized by any current generalized analytical scheme."[14] These well-deserved strictures of a short while ago are proving progressively less applicable. In the past, the sociologist has largely had to deal with *pre-collected series* of statistics usually assembled for nonsociological purposes and, therefore, not set forth in categories directly pertinent to any theoretical system. As a result, at least so far as quantitative facts are concerned, the theorist was compelled to work with makeshift data bearing only a tangential relevance to his problems. This not only left a wide margin for error—consider the crude indexes of social cohesion upon which Durkheim had to rely—but it also meant that theory had to wait upon the incidental and, at times, almost accidental availability of relevant data. It could not march rapidly ahead. This picture has now begun to change.

No longer does the theorist depend almost exclusively upon the consensus of administrative boards or social welfare agencies for his quantitative data. Tarde's programmatic sketch[15] a half century ago of the need for statistics in social psychology, particularly those dealing with attitudes, opinions and sentiments, has become a half-fulfilled promise. So, too, investigators of community organization are creating statistics on class structure, associational behavior, and clique formations, and this has left its mark on theoretic interests. Ethnic studies are beginning to provide quantitative data which are re-orienting the theorist. It is safe to suppose that the enormous accumulation of sociological materials during the war—notably by the Research Branch of the Information and Education Division of the War Department—materials which are in part the result of new research techniques, will intensify interest in the theory of group morale, propaganda and leadership.[15a] But it is perhaps needless to multiply examples.

---

14. Talcott Parsons, "The role of theory in social research," *American Sociological Review*, III (1938), 19; *cf.* his *The Structure of Social Action*, (New York, 1937), 328-329n. ". . . in the social field most available statistical information is on a level which cannot be made to fit directly into the categories of analytical theory."

15. Gabriel Tarde, *Essais et mélanges sociologiques*, (Paris, 1895), 230-270.

15a. As appears to be the case now that it has been published: S. A. Stouffer *et al.*, *The American Soldier*.

What we have said does not mean that the piling up of statistics in itself advances theory; it does mean that theoretic interest tends to shift to those areas in which there is an abundance of *pertinent* statistical data.[15b] Moreover, we are merely calling attention to this shift of focus, not evaluating it. It may very well be that it sometimes deflects attention to problems which, in a theoretic or humanistic sense, are "unimportant"; it may divert attention from problems with larger implications onto those for which there is the promise of immediate solutions. Failing a detailed study, it is difficult to come to any overall assessment of this point. But the pattern itself seems clear enough in sociology as in other disciplines; as new and previously unobtainable data become available through the use of new techniques, theorists turn their analytical eye upon the implications of these data and bring about new directions of inquiry.

4. THE CLARIFICATION OF CONCEPTS

(EMPIRICAL RESEARCH EXERTS PRESSURE FOR CLEAR CONCEPTS)

A good part of the work called "theorizing" is taken up with the clarification of concepts—and rightly so. It is in this matter of clearly defined concepts that social science research is not infrequently defective. Research activated by a major interest in methodology may be centered on the *design* of establishing causal relations without due regard for analyzing the variables involved in the inquiry. This methodological empiricism, as the design of inquiry without correlative concern with the clarification of substantive variables may be called, characterizes a large part of current research. Thus, in a series of effectively designed experiments Chapin finds that "the rehousing of slum families in a public housing project results in improvement of the living conditions and the social life of these families."[16] Or through controlled experiments, psychologists search out the effects of foster home placement upon children's performances in intelligence tests.[17] Or, again through experimental inquiry, researchers seek to determine whether a propaganda film has achieved its purpose of improving attitudes toward the British. These several cases, and they are representative of a large amount of research which has advanced social science method, have in common the fact that the empirical variables are not analyzed in terms of their

---

15b. The statistical data also facilitate sufficient *precision* in research to put theory to determinate tests; see the discussion of the functions of precision in Chapter II.

16. F. S. Chapin, "The effects of slum clearance and rehousing on family and community relationships in Minneapolis," *American Journal of Sociology*, 1938, 43, 744-763.

17. R. R. Sears, "Child Psychology," in Wayne Dennis, ed., *Current Trends in Psychology*, (University of Pittsburgh Press, 1947), 55-56. Sears' comments on this type of research state the general problem admirably.

conceptual elements.[18] As Rebecca West, with her characteristic lucidity, put this general problem of methodological empiricism, one might "know that A and B and C were linked by certain causal connexions, but he would never apprehend with any exactitude the nature of A or B or C." In consequence, these researches advance the procedures of inquiry, but their findings do not enter into the repository of cumulative social science theory.

But in general, the clarification of concepts, commonly considered a province peculiar to the theorist, is a frequent result of empirical research. Research sensitive to its own needs cannot easily escape this pressure for conceptual clarification. *For a basic requirement of research is that the concepts, the variables, be defined with sufficient clarity to enable the research to proceed,* a requirement easily and unwittingly not met in the kind of discursive exposition which is often miscalled sociological theory.

The clarification of concepts ordinarily enters into empirical research in the shape of establishing *indices* of the variables under consideration. In non-research speculations, it is possible to talk loosely about "morale" or "social cohesion" without any clear conceptions of what is entailed by these terms, but they *must* be clarified if the researcher is to go about his business of systematically observing instances of low and high morale, of social cohesion or social cleavage. If he is not to be blocked at the outset, he must devise indices which are observable, fairly precise and meticulously clear. The entire movement of thought which was christened "operationalism" is only one conspicuous case of the researcher demanding that concepts be defined clearly enough for him to go to work.

This has been typically recognized by those sociologists who combine a theoretic orientation with systematic empirical research. Durkheim, for example, despite the fact that his terminology and indices now appear crude and debatable, clearly perceived the need for devising indices of his concepts. Repeatedly, he asserted that "it is necessary . . . to substitute for the internal fact which escapes us an external fact that symbolizes it and to study the former through the latter."[19] The index, or sign of the conceptualized item, stands ideally in a one-to-one correlation with what it signifies (and the difficulty of establishing this relation is of course one of the critical problems of research). Since the

---

18. However crude they may be, procedures such as the focused interview are expressly designed as aids for detecting possibly relevant variables in an initially undifferentiated situation. See R. K. Merton, M. Fiske and P. L. Kendall, *The Focused Interview,* (Glencoe, Illinois: The Free Press, 1956).

19. Emile Durkheim, *Division of Labor in Society,* (New York: Macmillan, 1933), 66; also his *Les règles de la méthode sociologique,* (Paris, 1895), 55-58; *Le Suicide,* (Paris, 1930), 356 and *passim. Cf.* R. K. Merton, "Durkheim's *Division of Labor in Society,"* American Journal of Sociology, 1934, 40, esp. 326-7 which touches on the problem of indices; for a greatly developed analysis, see Lazarsfeld and Rosenberg, eds., *The Language of Social Research,* Intro. to Section I.

index and its object are so related, one may ask for the grounds on which one is taken as the index and the other as the indexed variable. As Durkheim implied and as Suzanne Langer has indicated anew, the index is that one of the correlated pair which is perceptible and the other, harder or impossible to perceive, is theoretically relevant.[20] Thus, attitude scales make available indices of otherwise not discriminable attitudes, just as ecological statistics represent indices of diverse social structures in different areas.

What often appears as a tendency in research for quantification (through the development of scales) can thus be seen as a special case of attempting to clarify concepts sufficiently to permit the conduct of empirical investigation. The development of valid and observable indices becomes central to the use of concepts in the prosecution of research. A final illustration will indicate how research presses for the clarification of ancient sociological concepts which, on the plane of discursive exposition, have remained ill-defined and unclarified.

A conception basic to sociology holds that individuals have multiple social roles and tend to organize their behavior in terms of the structurally defined expectations assigned to each role. Further, it is said, the less integrated the society, the more often will individuals be subject to the strain of incompatible social roles. Type-cases are numerous and familiar: the Catholic Communist subjected to conflicting pressures from party and church, the marginal man suffering the pulls of conflicting societies, the professional woman torn between the demands of family and career. Every sociological textbook abounds with illustrations of incompatible demands made of the multiselved person.

Perhaps because it has been largely confined to discursive interpretations and has seldom been made the focus of systematic research, this central problem of conflicting roles has yet to be materially clarified and advanced beyond the point reached decades ago. Thomas and Znaniecki long since indicated that conflicts between social roles *can* be reduced by conventionalization and by role-segmentation (by assigning each set of role-demands to different situations).[21] And others have noted that frequent conflict between roles is dysfunctional for the society as well as for the individual. But all this leaves many salient problems untouched: on which grounds does one predict the behavior of persons subject to conflicting roles? And when a decision must be made, which role (or which group solidarity) takes precedence? Under which conditions does one or another prove controlling? On the plane of discursive thought, it has been suggested that the role with which the individual

---

20. Suzanne K. Langer, *Philosophy in a New Key,* (New York: Penguin Books, 1948), 46-47.

21. W. I. Thomas and F. Znaniecki, *The Polish Peasant,* (New York: Knopf, 1927), 1866-70, 1888, 1899 ff.

identifies most fully will prove dominant, thus banishing the problem through a tautological pseudo-solution. Or, the problem of seeking to predict behavior consequent to incompatibility of roles, a research problem requiring operational clarification of the concepts of solidarity, conflict, role-demands and situation, has been evaded by observing that conflicts of roles typically ensue in frustration.

More recently, empirical research has pressed for clarification of the key concepts involved in this problem. Indices of conflicting group pressures have been devised and the resultant behavior observed in specified situations. Thus, as a beginning in this direction, it has been shown that in a concrete decision-situation, such as voting, individuals subject to these cross-pressures respond by delaying their vote-decision. And, under conditions yet to be determined, they seek to reduce the conflict by escaping from the field of conflict: they lose interest in the political campaign. Finally, there is the intimation in these data that in cases of cross-pressures upon the voter, it is socio-economic position which is typically controlling.[22]

However this may be, the essential point is that, in this instance, as in others, the very requirements of empirical research have been instrumental in clarifying received concepts. The process of empirical inquiry raises conceptual issues which may long go undetected in theoretic inquiry.

There remain, then, a few concluding remarks. My discussion has been devoted exclusively to four impacts of research upon the development of social theory: the initiation, reformulation, refocusing and clarification of theory. Doubtless there are others. Doubtless, too, the emphasis of this chapter lends itself to misunderstanding. It may be inferred that some invidious distinction has been drawn at the expense of theory and the theorist. That has not been my intention. I have suggested only that an explicitly formulated theory does not invariably precede empirical inquiry, that as a matter of plain fact the theorist is not inevitably the lamp lighting the way to new observations. The sequence is often reversed. Nor is it enough to say that research and theory must be married if sociology is to bear legitimate fruit. They must not only exchange solemn vows—they must know how to carry on from there. Their reciprocal roles must be clearly defined. This chapter is a short essay toward that definition.

---

22. Lazarsfeld, Berelson and Gaudet, *The People's Choice*, Chapter VI and the subsequent study by B. Berelson, P. F. Lazarsfeld and W. N. McPhee, *Voting*, (University of Chicago Press, 1954).

Part II

STUDIES IN SOCIAL AND
CULTURAL STUCTURE

INTRODUCTION

T HE EIGHT CHAPTERS comprising Part II deal with selected problems of social structure from the theoretic standpoint of functional
analysis.

Chapter IV, "Social Structure and Anomie," was first published in
1938, but has been more recently extended and revised. It exemplifies the
theoretic orientation of the functional analyst who considers *socially
deviant behavior* just as much a product of social structure as *conformist
behavior.* This orientation is directed sharply against the fallacious
premise, strongly entrenched in Freudian theory and found also in the
writings of such Freudian revisionists as Fromm, that the structure of
society primarily restrains the free expression of man's fixed native impulses and that, accordingly, man periodically breaks into open rebellion
against these restraints to achieve freedom. Occasionally, this freedom is
of a character not highly regarded by the conventional representatives of
the society, and it is promptly tagged as criminal, or pathological, or
socially dangerous. The political philosophy implied by such a doctrine
is, of course, crude anarchism; benevolent anarchism, as in the case of
Fromm, or sometimes, as in the case of Freud and Hobbes, a conception
of anarchism as malevolent, in which man is seen as entering into a social
compact aimed to protect himself from this malevolence. In either case,
the social structure is seen as an evil necessity, first springing from and
later restraining the free expression of hostile impulses.

In contrast to such anarchistic doctrines, functional analysis conceives
of the social structure as active, as producing fresh motivations which
cannot be predicted on the basis of knowledge about man's native drives.
If the social structure restrains some dispositions to act, it creates others.
The functional approach therefore abandons the position, held by various
individualistic theories, that different rates of deviant behavior in diverse
groups and social strata are the accidental result of varying proportions
of pathological personalities found in these groups and strata. It attempts
instead to determine how the social and cultural structure generates

pressure for socially deviant behavior upon people variously located in that structure.

In Chapter IV, this general orientation gives rise to some specific hypotheses on the structural sources of deviant behavior. High rates of departure from institutional requirements are seen as the result of culturally induced, deep motivations which cannot be satisfied among those social strata with limited access to opportunity. The culture and the social structure operate at cross-purposes.

In referring to departures from institutional requirements, I have attempted to make it clear that *some* deviations may also be regarded as a *new* pattern of behavior, possibly emerging among subgroups at odds with *those* institutional patterns supported by groups other than themselves and by the law. It is not enough to refer to "the institutions" as though they were all uniformly supported by all groups and strata in the society. Unless systematic consideration is given the *degree* of support of particular "institutions" by *specific* groups, we shall overlook the important place of power in society. To speak of "legitimate power" or authority is often to use an elliptical and misleading phrase. Power may be legitimized for *some* without being legitimized for *all* groups in a society. It may, therefore, be misleading to describe non-conformity with *particular* social institutions merely as deviant behavior; it may represent the beginning of a new alternative pattern, with its own distinctive claims to moral validity.

In this chapter, then, I am concerned primarily with extending the theory of functional analysis to deal with problems of social and cultural *change*. As I have noted elsewhere, the great concern of functional sociologists and anthropologists with problems of "social order" and with the "maintenance" of social systems has generally focused their scientific attention on the study of processes whereby a social system is preserved largely intact. In general, they have not devoted much attention to the processes utilizable for determinate basic changes in social structure. If the analysis in Chapter IV does not materially advance toward its solution, at the very least it recognizes this as a significant problem. It is oriented toward problems of social dynamics and change.

The key concept bridging the gap between statics and dynamics in functional theory is that of strain, tension, contradiction, or discrepancy between the component elements of social and cultural structure. Such strains may be dysfunctional for the social system in its then existing form; they may also be instrumental in leading to changes in that system. In any case, they exert pressure for change. When social mechanisms for controlling them are operating effectively, these strains are kept within such bounds as to limit change of the social structure. (In some systems of political theory and ideology, the workings of these control mechanisms are called 'concessions' and 'compromises,' inhibiting the process of basic structural change.)

All this is not to say, of course, that these strains are alone in making for change in a social structure, but they do represent a theoretically strategic source of change which has yet to be the object of sufficiently sustained and cumulative sociological research. Among the problems calling for further research are the following: the extent to which Americans in different social strata have in fact assimilated the *same* culturally induced goals and values;* the operation of social mechanisms, such as social differentiation, which minimize the strains resulting from these seeming contradictions between cultural goals and socially restricted access to these goals; the operation of psychological mechanisms whereby discrepancies between culturally induced aspirations and socially feasible attainments are made tolerable; the functional significance for the stability of a social system of having diverse occupations which provide distinctive nonpecuniary rewards, perhaps thus curbing otherwise intolerable strains; the extent to which these strains exert pressure for change upon the culture (substituting 'security' for 'ambition' as a primary value) and upon the social structure (changing the rules of the game to enlarge the area of economic and political opportunity for the previously dispossessed).

Some of these problems have been accorded systematic study since the first edition of this book. To bring out the essential importance of continuity of research and conception for the development of a discipline such as sociology, I have examined these studies at some length in a newly-prepared Chapter (V), rather than incorporating their findings in a revision of the earlier paper. In this way, I believe, one may give fitting emphasis to the importance of theoretical and empirical continuities in inquiry which extend, modify and correct earlier formulations, and thereby constitute the hallmark of systematic inquiry.

As in the analysis of deviant behavior in the two preceding chapters, functional theory is utilized in the analysis of bureaucratic structure and personality in Chapter VI. Again, I assume that the structure constrains individuals variously situated within it to develop cultural emphases, social behavior patterns and psychological bents. And once again, I assume that this holds true for social deviations and dysfunctions as it does for social conformity and functions. Deviations are not necessarily dysfunctional for a social system, as we have seen, any more than conformity is necessarily functional.

From the functional analysis of bureaucratic structure, it is clear that, under determinate conditions, conformity to regulations can be dysfunctional both for realizing the objectives of the structure and for various groups in the society which the bureaucracy is intended to serve. Regu-

---

* A step in this direction has been taken by Herbert H. Hyman, "The value systems of different classes," in Reinhard Bendix and Seymour Martin Lipset (editors), *Class, Status and Power: A Reader in Social Stratification,* (Glencoe: The Free Press, 1953), 426-442.

lations are in such cases applied even when the circumstances which initially made them functional and effective have so materially changed that conformity to the rule defeats its purpose. If only in the light of biblical distinctions between the letter and the spirit, it is obvious that this is anything but a new observation. Through the centuries, many have noticed that rules, once sanctified by cultural values, often continue to be binding even when changed conditions render them obsolete. Indeed, this is another of those old, repeated observations, grown so familiar and hackneyed that its very familiarity has been mistaken for solid intelligibility. As a result, the large sociological implications of this important commonplace have not yet been *seriously* studied, that is to say, studied systematically and with technical skill. How does this inflexibility come to be, in bureaucratic organization? Is it because the regulations have become too effectively rooted among bureaucratic personnel, because the regulations have been overly-imbued with affect and sentiment, that they remain ruthlessly fixed and inexorable even when they are no longer appropriate to their functions? Duty, honor, loyalty, decency—these are but a few of the eulogistic terms ostensibly describing conformance with certain social norms. Do these norms become absolutized and hence more resistant to change than norms regarded as wholly instrumental in character? It is with questions such as these that Chapter VI deals.

In this chapter, bureaucratic dysfunctions are regarded as stemming not only from an overly-close and static adjustment to a set of conditions which no longer obtain, but also from the breakdown of ordinarily self-regulating social mechanisms (*e.g.*, the orientation of bureaucratic officials toward a well-ordered career may in due course make for excessive caution and not merely for the technically most efficient measure of conformity to regulations). In view of the recently growing interest in mechanisms of self-regulation in social systems—social homeostasis, social equilibrium, feedback mechanisms are among the varied terms registering this interest—, there is all the more need for studying empirically the conditions under which such mechanisms, once identified, cease to be self-regulating and become dysfunctional for the social system. As lately exemplified in Philip Selznick's study, *TVA and the Grass Roots*, this theoretical problem can be empirically investigated to good purpose in bureaucratic organization since there, the interconnections of structure and mechanisms are more readily observable than in less highly organized social systems.

Just as Chapter VI addresses itself to the bearing of bureaucratic structure upon the development of an occupational personality, so Chapter VII addresses itself to the hazards, limitations and potentialities of the social science expert in public bureaucracies. Both chapters explore general structural problems of bureaucracy, on the one hand, and problems in the sociology of occupations, on the other. Manifestly, both these fields require much more cumulative empirical research than they have been accorded.

Sociological studies of bureaucracy are plainly needed to provide a broader and firmer base for the understanding of administration, both public and private. Thus far, sociological discussions have tended to be speculative, bare and abstract, or if informed with concrete materials, these have generally been altogether impressionistic. This conspicuous gap has belatedly attracted notice and, accordingly, a series of empirical monographs on sociological problems of bureaucracy has been initiated in the Department of Sociology of Columbia University, some of these studies with the aid of fellowships granted by the Social Science Research Council. The previously cited study by Selznick (1949) centers its analysis on the unanticipated consequences of organized action for bureaucratic policy; Seymour Martin Lipset's *Agrarian Socialism* (1950) examines the interplay between bureaucratic personnel and policy-makers; two monographs by Alvin W. Gouldner—*Patterns of Industrial Bureaucracy* (1954) and *Wildcat Strike* (1954)—trace out the functions and dysfunctions, both latent and manifest, of bureaucratic rules in an industrial plant; and *The Dynamics of Bureaucracy* (1955) by Peter M. Blau analyzes the conditions under which changes in the structure of two governmental bureaucracies come about. Still unpublished is Donald D. Stewart's study of local draft boards (1950) which examines the role of volunteer participation in a bureaucratic organization. Together, these studies provide observational data on the workings of bureaucracy of a kind not obtainable from documentary sources alone and begin to clarify some of the principal issues in the study of bureaucracy.[1]

---

1. Additional materials on the structure and workings of bureaucracy are assembled in two collections of papers: R. K. Merton, A. P. Gray, B. Hockey and H. C. Selvin, eds., *Reader in Bureaucracy* (Glencoe, Illinois: The Free Press, 1952), and Robert Dubin, *Human Relations in Administration*, (New York: Prentice-Hall, Inc., 1951). An excellent guide to reading and research on bureaucratic structure is provided by Harold L. Wilensky, *Syllabus of Industrial Relations*, (Chicago: The University of Chicago Press, 1954), and an over-view of recent theoretical developments by Peter M. Blau, *Bureaucracy in Modern Society*, (New York: Random House, 1956).

Most recently, there has appeared an independent study of bureaucracy, described by the authors as running largely parallel to the studies by Gouldner and Blau, and coming to much the same conclusions—Roy G. Francis and Robert C Stone, *Service and Procedure in Bureaucracy* (Minneapolis: University of Minnesota Press, 1956). As the authors remark, "This convergence of research is particularly interesting because the various studies were, to the best of our knowledge, conducted quite independently. It would appear that the theory of bureaucracy has led to common problems, and to common empirical investigations." Page v. The Columbia studies and this Tulane study do indeed come to similar conclusions and the time is perhaps not far off when the theoretic force of these conclusions can be brought into single focus. Here, it can only be asserted, not demonstrated, that these studies make for an extension and specification of the sociological theory of bureaucracy rather than for a scrapping of antecedent theory.

The other major field of study touched on in Chapter VII is the socio-logical analysis of occupations, in this instance, the occupation of the social science expert. Here the need for cumulative research is even more evident. A good many scattered studies of occupations have been pub-lished during the past thirty years and references to a sampling of these will be found in the notes appended to several chapters in this book. (Among these, the series of books on professions and semi-professions by Esther Brown has been the most useful for practical purposes.) But until recently, these studies have ordinarily not been oriented to a body of consistent sociological theory. However interesting or practically useful these studies have been, they have consequently achieved little by way of advancing sociological theory or by way of applying that theory to the understanding of this important sector of man's activity.

And assuredly, by the most diverse criteria and among the most diverse groups, occupations *are* widely recognized as an important nucleus of the organization of society. The great part of most men's waking hours is devoted to their occupational activities; the economic supports for group survival are provided through the pooled work of socially connected occupations; men's personal aspirations, interests, and sentiments are largely organized and stamped with the mark of their occupational outlook. So we know impressionistically and, on the basis of some studies, with occasional reliability, that people in the various occupations tend to take different parts in the society, to have different shares in the exercise of power, both acknowledged and unacknowledged, and to *see* the world differently. All this is widely felt but little investi-gated. Thus W. H. Auden, seeking to put current ideas into the poetic mould, has seen how the possibility of occupationally conditioned out-looks trails off into questions in the sociology of knowledge:

> Malinowski, Rivers,
> Benedict and others
> Show how common culture
>   Shapes the separate lives:
> Matrilineal races
> Kill their mothers' brothers
> In their dreams and turn their
>   Sisters into wives.
>
> Who when looking over
> Faces in the subway,
> Each with its uniqueness
>   Would not, did he dare,
> Ask what forms exactly
> Suited to their weakness
> Love and desperation
>   Take to govern there.

Would not like to know what
Influence occupation
Has on human vision
  Of the human fate:
Do all the clerks for instance
Pigeon-hole creation,
Brokers see the Ding-an-
  -sich as Real Estate?

When a politician
Dreams about his sweetheart,
Does he multiply her
  Face into a crowd,
Are her fond responses
All-or-none reactions,
Does he try to buy her,
  Is the kissing loud?

Perhaps this is indeed truth the poet sings; perhaps, it is not. In any event, it is distinctly worth investigation. Partly as a result of the altogether preliminary efforts represented by such discussions as Chapters V and VI, I have become impressed by the potential value of a systematic and, above all, *cumulative* series of empirical studies of occupations and professions guided by and in turn extending a body of sociological theory. The first steps in the direction of such a program of consolidated research on the sociology of occupations have been taken. Surely, in this large and significant field of sociological inquiry,[2] it may be supposed that what's past is only prologue.

Chapters VIII and IX, both written since the first edition of this book, are efforts to utilize functional analysis in the study of an important component of social structure: the reference group. Written in collaboration with Alice S. Rossi, Chapter VIII examines and organizes the contributions of *The American Soldier* to the theory of reference group behavior and relates these to kindred conceptions which have gone before. Throughout, reference groups are considered not only from the standpoint of social psychology but also from the standpoint of their patterning by the social structure in which they emerge. Later continuities in reference group theory are traced in Chapter IX, now published for the first time. It is directed toward clarifying some basic concepts of the theory in the light of recent research and toward working out its *problematics*, i.e., the principal problems (conceptual, substantive, and procedural) which must be solved in order to advance this theory of the middle range.

Chapter X, also new to this edition, introduces the concept of 'in-

2. William J. Goode, Robert K. Merton and Mary Jean Huntington, *The Professions in American Society: A Sociological Analysis and Casebook* (forthcoming) is an intensive examination of the field and a theoretic framework for further research.

fluentials'; identifies and characterizes two types of influentials—the local and the cosmopolitan—and examines their patterns of action in the influence-structure of a community. It finds that the extent of the influence individuals exert upon others is not wholly determined by their social class position and, therefore, that substantial numbers of influentials can be found in each stratum of the class structure. In this respect, the study reported in Chapter X is part of a developing tradition of sociological research on the exercise of influence in local communities.[3]

Although Chapter XI, "The Self-Fulfilling Prophecy," was written originally for a lay audience, I have included it in this volume because it deals with that much neglected sector of functional analysis in sociology, the study of dynamic social mechanisms.

The reader will soon observe that the mechanism of the self-fulfilling social belief, in which confident error generates its own spurious confirmation, bears a close theoretical connection with the concept of latent function. Both are types of unanticipated consequences of action or decision or belief, the one producing the very circumstance erroneously assumed to exist, the other producing results which were not intended at all. Both mechanisms, implicitly considered in my early paper on "unanticipated consequences of purposive social action," are yet another instance of sociological patterns which are often noticed, but little studied. (This is, in the present instance, in strong contrast with individual psychology which has given great and cumulating attention to the pattern of the self-fulfilling belief, as one type of psychological vicious circle.)

A third pattern of unanticipated consequences, that of the self-destroying belief, is briefly mentioned but not developed at any length in this chapter. This mechanism, picturesquely termed the "suicidal prophecy" by the nineteenth century logician John Venn, involves beliefs which prevent fulfillment of the very circumstance which would otherwise come to pass. Examples of this are plentiful and familiar. Confident that they will win a game or a war or a cherished prize, groups become complacent, their complacency leads to lethargy, and lethargy to eventual defeat. Many men, particularly men experienced in the management of public affairs, have of course long noticed and sometimes taken into account the pattern of the suicidal belief. Lincoln, for example, was acutely conscious of the pattern. In the dark days of 1862, when McClellan was stalemated and the armies in the west immobilized, Lincoln did not issue a public call for the desperately needed thousands of new troops, explaining, "I would publicly appeal to the country for this new force were it not that I fear a general panic and stampede would follow, so hard it is to have a thing understood as it really is."

---

3. For a circumstantial account of the origins and development of this line of continuity in sociological inquiry, see Elihu Katz and P. F. Lazarsfeld, *Personal Influence* (Glencoe, Illinois: The Free Press, 1955) Introduction and Part I.

But from the standpoint of research, the investigation of these distinctive and important dynamic mechanisms is only in its bare beginnings. Cases of each have been abundantly identified, and used for casual illustrative purposes (as they are here), but little research has been devoted to digging below the surface. Again, as I have suggested repeatedly in these pages, the very human tendency to want to fight shy of platitudes leads us to ignore the occasionally important truths which these platitudes conceal. The pattern of the self-destroying belief is familiar, almost as familiar to us today as were the oscillations of a pendulum to the people of Galileo's day. And because it is familiar, it is conscientiously neglected, not systematically followed up in its implications. Consequently, it remains a detached empirical observation, an alien thing, cut off from a body of empirically attested sociological theory.

Here, then, is another area for research into basic processes of social dynamics and change: determination of the conditions under which the three kinds of typically unanticipated consequences occur: the self-fulfilling belief (prediction, prophecy), the self-defeating or suicidal belief, and the latent function or social windfall.

The self-fulfilling prediction and the suicidal prediction hold double interest for the social scientist. They represent not only patterns which he wishes to investigate in the behavior of others, but also patterns which create acute and very special methodological problems in his own research. It makes most difficult the empirical testing of social science predictions. For since these predictions can be taken into account by the very people to whom they refer, the social scientist everlastingly faces the possibility that his prediction will enter into the situation as a *new and dynamic* factor, changing the very conditions under which the prediction initially held true. This characteristic of predictions is peculiar to human affairs. It is not found among predictions about the world of nature (except as natural phenomena are technologically shaped by men).[4] So far as we know, the meteorologist's prediction of continued rainfall has until now not perversely led to the occurrence of a drought. But the government economist's distant forecast of an oversupply of

---

4. That the parenthetical qualification is required has been shown by Adolf Grünbaum, who observes: ". . . consider the goal-directed behavior of a servo-mechanism like a homing device which employs feedback and is subject to automatic fire control. Clearly, every phase of the operation of such a device constitutes an exemplification of one or more purely *physical* principles. Yet the following situation is *allowed* by these very principles: a computer predicts that, in its present course, the missile will miss its target, and the communication of this information to the missile in the form of a new set of instructions induces it to alter its course and thereby to reach its target, contrary to the computer's original prediction. How does this differ, in principle, from the case in which the government economist's forecast of an oversupply of wheat has the effect of instructing the wheat growers to alter their original planting intentions?" See Grünbaum's instructive note, "Historical determinism, social activism, and predictions in the social sciences," to appear in *The British Journal for the Philosophy of Science.*

wheat may possibly lead individual producers of wheat so to curtail their planned production as to invalidate the forecast.

All this suggests that an extensive and as yet imperfectly identified type of social science prediction is confronted with a paradox: if it is made public, the prediction becomes seemingly invalidated, and if it is not made public, it is generally regarded not as a prediction but as a postdiction. It is considered knowledge after the fact. (This represents a kind of difficulty in social science kindred but not equivalent to what I roughly understand to be the difficulty in some limited ranges of physical science represented by the Heisenberg principle of uncertainty.) To be sure, in misanthropic mood, or in excessive devotion to the values of social science above all other human values, or in the self-defined role of a scientific samurai, the social scientist might write out, seal and safely deposit his prediction of impending unemployment or war or internecine conflict, bringing it to light only after the predicted events had come to pass. But this would be almost as reckless of the body politic as of his own corporeal self. When one considers the profound objection of many individuals to being regarded as psychological guinea pigs, one can roughly imagine the aggregated fury of an entire population upon discovering itself transmogrified into one immense sociological guinea pig. Perhaps this Circean experiment had better be reconsidered.

In addition to his general interest in the mechanism of the self-destroying belief, therefore, the social scientist has considerable incentive for systematic and painstaking inquiry into the conditions under which this self-destroying prediction or forecast operates in the social realm. Through such serious research, perhaps, he will learn what is needed to convert the potentially suicidal prediction into a socially beneficent and objectively sound prediction.

Part II, then, is devoted primarily to the interplay between social structures and occupations within a context of dynamic social mechanisms. It is intended to present some theoretically relevant, empirically tractable, and socially useful lines of sociological investigation. In any case, the large blanks in these fields have persuaded this one sociologist to put his immediate research efforts into the sociological study of bureaucracy and the functional analysis of occupations.

IV   SOCIAL STRUCTURE AND ANOMIE

U<small>NTIL RECENTLY</small>, and all the more so before then, one could speak of a marked tendency in psychological and sociological theory to attribute the faulty operation of social structures to failures of social control over man's imperious biological drives. The imagery of the relations between man and society implied by this doctrine is as clear as it is questionable. In the beginning, there are man's biological impulses which seek full expression. And then, there is the social order, essentially an apparatus for the management of impulses, for the social processing of tensions, for the "renunciation of instinctual gratifications," in the words of Freud. Nonconformity with the demands of a social structure is thus assumed to be anchored in original nature.[1] It is the biologically rooted impulses which from time to time break through social control. And by implication, conformity is the result of an utilitarian calculus or of unreasoned conditioning.

With the more recent advancement of social science, this set of conceptions has undergone basic modification. For one thing, it no longer appears so obvious that man is set against society in an unceasing war between biological impulse and social restraint. The image of man as an untamed bundle of impulses begins to look more like a caricature than a portrait. For another, sociological perspectives have increasingly entered into the analysis of behavior deviating from prescribed patterns of conduct. For whatever the role of biological impulses, there still remains the further question of why it is that the frequency of deviant behavior varies within different social structures and how it happens that the deviations have different shapes and patterns in different social structures. Today, as then, we have still much to learn about the processes through which social structures generate the circumstances in which infringement of social codes constitutes a "normal" (that is to say, an expectable) re-

---

1. See, for example, S. Freud, *Civilization and Its Discontents* (*passim*, and esp. at 63); Ernest Jones, *Social Aspects of Psychoanalysis* (London, 1924) 28. If the Freudian notion is a variety of the "original sin" doctrine, then the interpretation advanced in this paper is a doctrine of "socially derived sin."

sponse.[2] This chapter is an essay seeking clarification of the problem.

The framework set out in this essay is designed to provide one systematic approach to the analysis of social and cultural sources of deviant behavior. Our primary aim is to discover how some *social structures exert a definite pressure upon certain persons in the society to engage in nonconforming rather than conforming conduct.* If we can locate groups peculiarly subject to such pressures, we should expect to find fairly high rates of deviant behavior in these groups, not because the human beings comprising them are compounded of distinctive biological tendencies but because they are responding normally to the social situation in which they find themselves. Our perspective is sociological. We look at variations in the *rates* of deviant behavior, not at its incidence.[3] Should our quest be at all successful, some forms of deviant behavior will be found to be as psychologically normal as conformist behavior, and the equation of deviation and psychological abnormality will be put in question.

PATTERNS OF CULTURAL GOALS AND INSTITUTIONAL NORMS

Among the several elements of social and cultural structures, two are of immediate importance. These are analytically separable although they merge in concrete situations. The first consists of culturally defined goals, purposes and interests, held out as legitimate objectives for all or for diversely located members of the society. The goals are more or less integrated—the degree is a question of empirical fact—and roughly ordered in some hierarchy of value. Involving various degrees of sentiment and significance, the prevailing goals comprise a frame of aspira-

---

2. "Normal" in the sense of the psychologically expectable, if not culturally approved, response to determinate social conditions. This statement does not, of course, deny the role of biological and personality differences in fixing the *incidence* of deviant behavior. It is simply that *this* is not the problem considered here. It is in this same sense, I take it, that James S. Plant speaks of the "normal reaction of normal people to abnormal conditions." See his *Personality and the Cultural Pattern* (New York, 1937), 248.

3. The position taken here has been perceptively described by Edward Sapir. ". . . problems of social science differ from problems of individual behavior in degree of specificity, not in kind. Every statement about behavior which throws the emphasis, explicitly or implicitly, on the actual, integral experiences of defined personalities or types of personalities is a datum of psychology or psychiatry rather than of social science. Every statement about behavior which aims, not to be accurate about the behavior of an actual individual or individuals or about the expected behavior of a physically and psychologically defined type of individual, but which abstracts from such behavior in order to bring out in clear relief certain expectancies with regard to those aspects of individual behavior which various people share, as an interpersonal or 'social' pattern, is a datum, however crudely expressed, of social science." I have here chosen the second perspective; although I shall have occasion to speak of attitudes, values and function, it will be from the standpoint of how the social structure promotes or inhibits their appearance in specified types of situations. See Sapir, "Why cultural anthropology needs the psychiatrist," *Psychiatry*, 1938, 1, 7-12.

tional reference. They are the things "worth striving for." They are a basic, though not the exclusive, component of what Linton has called "designs for group living." And though some, not all, of these cultural goals are directly related to the biological drives of man, they are not determined by them.

A second element of the cultural structure defines, regulates and controls the acceptable modes of reaching out for these goals. Every social group invariably couples its cultural objectives with regulations, rooted in the mores or institutions, of allowable procedures for moving toward these objectives. These regulatory norms are not necessarily identical with technical or efficiency norms. Many procedures which from the standpoint of particular individuals would be most efficient in securing desired values—the exercise of force, fraud, power—are ruled out of the institutional area of permitted conduct. At times, the disallowed procedures include some which would be efficient for the group itself—*e.g.*, historic taboos on vivisection, on medical experimentation, on the sociological analysis of "sacred" norms—since the criterion of acceptability is not technical efficiency but value-laden sentiments (supported by most members of the group or by those able to promote these sentiments through the composite use of power and propaganda). In all instances, the choice of expedients for striving toward cultural goals is limited by institutionalized norms.

Sociologists often speak of these controls as being "in the mores" or as operating through social institutions. Such elliptical statements are true enough, but they obscure the fact that culturally standardized practices are not all of a piece. They are subject to a wide gamut of control. They may represent definitely prescribed or preferential or permissive or proscribed patterns of behavior. In assessing the operation of social controls, these variations—roughly indicated by the terms *prescription, preference, permission* and *proscription*—must of course be taken into account.

To say, moreover, that cultural goals and institutionalized norms operate jointly to shape prevailing practices is not to say that they bear a constant relation to one another. The cultural emphasis placed upon certain goals varies independently of the degree of emphasis upon institutionalized means. There may develop a very heavy, at times a virtually exclusive, stress upon the value of particular goals, involving comparatively little concern with the institutionally prescribed means of striving toward these goals. The limiting case of this type is reached when the range of alternative procedures is governed only by technical rather than by institutional norms. Any and all procedures which promise attainment of the all-important goal would be permitted in this hypothetical polar case. This constitutes one type of malintegrated culture. A second polar type is found in groups where activities originally conceived as instrumental are transmuted into self-contained practices, lacking further objectives. The original purposes are forgotten and close adherence to institutionally prescribed conduct becomes a matter of ritual.[4] Sheer conformity becomes a central value. For a time, social stability is ensured—at the expense of flexibility. Since the range of alternative behaviors permitted by the culture is severely limited, there is little basis for adapting to new conditions. There develops a tradition-bound, 'sacred' society marked by neophobia. Between these extreme types are societies which maintain a rough balance between emphases upon cultural goals and institutionalized practices, and these constitute the integrated and relatively stable, though changing, societies.

An effective equilibrium between these two phases of the social structure is maintained so long as satisfactions accrue to individuals conforming to both cultural constraints, *viz.*, satisfactions from the achievement of goals and satisfactions emerging directly from the institutionally canalized modes of striving to attain them. It is reckoned in terms of the product and in terms of the process, in terms of the outcome and in terms of the activities. Thus continuing satisfactions must derive from sheer participation in a competitive order as well as from eclipsing one's competitors if the order itself is to be sustained. If concern shifts exclusively to the outcome of competition, then those who perenially suffer defeat may, understandably enough, work for a change in the rules of the game. The sacrifices occasionally—not, as Freud assumed, invariably—entailed by conformity to institutional norms must be compensated by socialized rewards. The distribution of statuses through competition must be so organized that positive incentives for adherence to status obligations are provided *for every position* within the distributive order. Otherwise, as will soon become plain, aberrant behavior ensues. It is, indeed, my central hypothesis that aberrant behavior may be regarded sociologically as a symptom of dissociation between culturally prescribed aspirations and socially structured avenues for realizing these aspirations.

Of the types of societies which result from independent variation of cultural goals and institutionalized means, we shall be primarily concerned with the first—a society in which there is an exceptionally strong emphasis upon specific goals without a corresponding emphasis upon institutional procedures. If it is not to be misunderstood, this statement must be elaborated. No society lacks norms governing conduct. But societies do differ in the degree to which the folkways, mores and institutional controls are effectively integrated with the goals which stand high in the hierarchy of cultural values. The culture may be such as to

---

4. This ritualism may be associated with a mythology which rationalizes these practices so that they appear to retain their status as means, but the dominant pressure is toward strict ritualistic conformity, irrespective of the mythology. Ritualism is thus most complete when such rationalizations are not even called forth.

lead individuals to center their emotional convictions upon the complex of culturally acclaimed ends, with far less emotional support for pre-scribed methods of reaching out for these ends. With such differential emphases upon goals and institutional procedures, the latter may be so vitiated by the stress on goals as to have the behavior of many individuals limited only by considerations of technical expediency. In this context, the sole significant question becomes: Which of the available procedures is most efficient in netting the culturally approved value?[5] The technically most effective procedure, whether culturally legitimate or not, becomes typically preferred to institutionally prescribed conduct. As this process of attenuation continues, the society becomes unstable and there de-velops what Durkheim called "anomie" (or normlessness).[6]

The working of this process eventuating in anomie can be easily glimpsed in a series of familiar and instructive, though perhaps trivial, episodes. Thus, in competitive athletics, when the aim of victory is shorn of its institutional trappings and success becomes construed as "winning the game" rather than "winning under the rules of the game," a premium is implicitly set upon the use of illegitimate but technically efficient means. The star of the opposing football team is surreptitiously slugged; the wrestler incapacitates his opponent through ingenious but illicit techniques; university alumni covertly subsidize "students" whose talents are confined to the athletic field. The emphasis on the goal has so at-tenuated the satisfactions deriving from sheer participation in the com-petitive activity that only a successful outcome provides gratification. Through the same process, tension generated by the desire to win in a poker game is relieved by successfully dealing one's self four aces or, when the cult of success has truly flowered, by sagaciously shuffling the cards in a game of solitaire. The faint twinge of uneasiness in the last instance and the surreptitious nature of public delicts indicate clearly

---

5. In this connection, one sees the relevance of Elton Mayo's paraphrase of the title of Tawney's well-known book. "Actually the problem is *not that of the sickness of an acquisitive society; it is that of the acquisitiveness of a sick society.*" *Human Problems of an Industrial Civilization,* 153. Mayo deals with the process through which wealth comes to be the basic symbol of social achievement and sees this as arising from a state of anomie. My major concern here is with the social conse-quences of a heavy emphasis upon monetary success as a goal in a society which has not adapted its structure to the implications of this emphasis. A complete analysis would require the simultaneous examination of both processes.

6. Durkheim's resurrection of the term "anomie" which, so far as I know, first appears in approximately the same sense in the late sixteenth century, might well become the object of an investigation by a student interested in the historical filiation of ideas. Like the term "climate of opinion" brought into academic and political popularity by A. N. Whitehead three centuries after it was coined by Joseph Glanvill, the word "anomie" (or anomy or anomia) has lately come into frequent use, once it was re-introduced by Durkheim. Why the resonance in contemporary society? For a magnificent model of the type of research required by questions of this order, see Leo Spitzer, "*Milieu* and *Ambiance:* an essay in historical semantics," *Philosophy and Phenomenological Research,* 1942, 3, 1-42, 169-218.

that the institutional rules of the game are *known* to those who evade them. But cultural (or idiosyncratic) exaggeration of the success-goal leads men to withdraw emotional support from the rules.[7]

This process is of course not restricted to the realm of competitive sport, which has simply provided us with microcosmic images of the social macrocosm. The process whereby exaltation of the end generates a literal *demoralization, i.e.*, a de-institutionalization, of the means occurs in many[8] groups where the two components of the social structure are not highly integrated.

Contemporary American culture appears to approximate the polar type in which great emphasis upon certain success-goals occurs without equivalent emphasis upon institutional means. It would of course be fanciful to assert that accumulated wealth stands alone as a symbol of success just as it would be fanciful to deny that Americans assign it a place high in their scale of values. In some large measure, money has been consecrated as a value in itself, over and above its expenditure for articles of consumption or its use for the enhancement of power. "Money" is peculiarly well adapted to become a symbol of prestige. As Simmel emphasized, money is highly abstract and impersonal. However acquired, fraudulently or institutionally, it can be used to purchase the same goods and services. The anonymity of an urban society, in conjunction with these peculiarities of money, permits wealth, the sources of which may be unknown to the community in which the plutocrat lives or, if known, to become purified in the course of time, to serve as a symbol of high status. Moreover, in the American Dream there is no final stopping point. The measure of "monetary success" is conveniently indefinite and relative. At each income level, as H. F. Clark found, Americans want just about twenty-five per cent more (but of course this "just a bit more" continues to operate once it is obtained). In this flux of shifting standards, there is no stable resting point, or rather, it is the point which manages always to be "just ahead." An observer of a community in which annual salaries in six figures are not uncommon, reports the anguished words of one victim of the American Dream: "In this town, I'm snubbed socially because I only get a thousand a week. That hurts."[9]

To say that the goal of monetary success is entrenched in American

---

7. It appears unlikely that cultural norms, once interiorized, are wholly eliminated. Whatever residuum persists will induce personality tensions and conflict, with some measure of ambivalence. A manifest rejection of the once-incorporated institutional norms will be coupled with some latent retention of their emotional correlates. Guilt feelings, a sense of sin, pangs of conscience are diverse terms referring to this unrelieved tension. Symbolic adherence to the nominally repudiated values or rationalizations for the rejection of these values constitute a more subtle expression of these tensions.

8. "Many," not all, unintegrated groups, for the reason mentioned earlier. In groups where the primary emphasis shifts to institutional means, the outcome is normally a type of ritualism rather than anomie.

9. Leo C. Rosten, *Hollywood* (New York, 1940), 40.

culture is only to say that Americans are bombarded on every side by precepts which affirm the right or, often, the duty of retaining the goal even in the face of repeated frustration. Prestigeful representatives of the society reinforce the cultural emphasis. The family, the school and the workplace—the major agencies shaping the personality structure and goal formation of Americans—join to provide the intensive disciplining required if an individual is to retain intact a goal that remains elusively beyond reach, if he is to be motivated by the promise of a gratification which is not redeemed. As we shall presently see, parents serve as a transmission belt for the values and goals of the groups of which they are a part—above all, of their social class or of the class with which they identify themselves. And the schools are of course the official agency for the passing on of the prevailing values, with a large proportion of the textbooks used in city schools implying or stating explicitly "that education leads to intelligence and consequently to job and money success."[10] Central to this process of disciplining people to maintain their unfulfilled aspirations are the cultural prototypes of success, the living documents testifying that the American Dream can be realized if one but has the requisite abilities. Consider in this connection the following excerpts from the business journal, *Nation's Business,* drawn from a large amount of comparable materials found in mass communications setting forth the values of business class culture.

The Document	*Its Sociological Implications*
(Nation's Business, Vol. 27, No. 8, p. 7)	
'You have to be born to those jobs, buddy, or else have a good pull.'	Here is a heretical opinion, possibly born of continued frustration, which rejects the worth of retaining an apparently unrealizable goal and, moreover, questions the legitimacy of a social structure which provides differential access to this goal.
That's an old sedative to ambition.	The counter-attack, explicitly asserting the cultural value of retaining one's aspirations intact, of not losing "ambition."
Before listening to its seduction, ask these men:	A clear statement of the function to be served by the ensuing list of "successes." These men are living testimony that the social structure is such as to permit these aspirations to be achieved, *if one is worthy.* And correlatively, failure to reach these goals testifies only to one's own personal shortcomings. Aggression provoked by failure should therefore be directed inward and not outward, against oneself and not against a social structure which provides free and equal access to opportunity.

10. Malcolm S. MacLean, *Scholars, Workers and Gentlemen* (Harvard University Press, 1938), 29.

The Document	*Its Sociological Implications*
Elmer R. Jones, president of Wells-Fargo and Co., who began life as a poor boy and left school at the fifth grade to take his first job.	Success prototype I: *All* may properly have the *same* lofty ambitions, for however lowly the starting-point, true talent can reach the very heights. Aspirations must be retained intact.
Frank C. Ball, the Mason fruit jar king of America, who rode from Buffalo to Muncie, Indiana, in a boxcar along with his brother George's horse, to start a little business in Muncie that became the biggest of its kind.	Success prototype II: Whatever the present results of one's strivings, the future is large with promise; for the common man may yet become a king. Gratifications may seem forever deferred, but they will finally be realized as one's enterprise becomes "the biggest of its kind."
J. L. Bevan, president of the Illinois Central Railroad, who at twelve was a messenger boy in the freight office at New Orleans.	Success prototype III: If the secular trends of our economy seem to give little scope to small business, then one may rise within the giant bureaucracies of private enterprise. If one can no longer be a king in a realm of his own creation, he may at least become a president in one of the economic democracies. No matter what one's present station, messenger boy or clerk, one's gaze should be fixed at the top.

From divers sources there flows a continuing pressure to retain high ambition. The exhortational literature is immense, and one can choose only at the risk of seeming invidious. Consider only these: The Reverend Russell H. Conwell, with his *Acres of Diamonds* address heard and read by hundreds of thousands and his subsequent book, *The New Day,* or *Fresh Opportunities: A Book for Young Men;* Elbert Hubbard, who delivered the famous *Message to Garcia* at Chautauqua forums throughout the land; Orison Swett Marden, who, in a stream of books, first set forth *The Secret of Achievement,* praised by college presidents, then explained the process of *Pushing to the Front,* eulogized by President McKinley and finally, these democratic testimonials notwithstanding, mapped the road to make *Every Man a King.* The symbolism of a commoner rising to the estate of economic royalty is woven deep in the texture of the American culture pattern, finding what is perhaps its ultimate expression in the words of one who knew whereof he spoke, Andrew Carnegie: "Be a king in your dreams. Say to yourself, 'My place is at the top.'"[11]

Coupled with this positive emphasis upon the obligation to maintain lofty goals is a correlative emphasis upon the penalizing of those who draw in their ambitions. Americans are admonished "not to be a quitter" for in the dictionary of American culture, as in the lexicon of youth,

---

11. *Cf.* A. W. Griswold, *The American Cult of Success* (Yale University doctoral dissertation, 1933); R. O. Carlson, *"Personality Schools": A Sociological Analysis,* (Columbia University Master's Essay, 1948).

"there is no such word as 'fail.'" The cultural manifesto is clear: one must not quit, must not cease striving, must not lessen his goals, for "not failure, but low aim, is crime."

Thus the culture enjoins the acceptance of three cultural axioms: First, all should strive for the same lofty goals since these are open to all; second, present seeming failure is but a way-station to ultimate success; and third, genuine failure consists only in the lessening or withdrawal of ambition.

In rough psychological paraphrase, these axioms represent, first, a symbolic secondary reinforcement of incentive; second, curbing the threatened extinction of a response through an associated stimulus; third, increasing the motive-strength to evoke continued responses despite the continued absence of reward.

In sociological paraphrase, these axioms represent, first, the deflection of criticism of the social structure onto one's self among those so situated in the society that they do not have full and equal access to opportunity; second, the preservation of a structure of social power by having individuals in the lower social strata identify themselves, not with their compeers, but with those at the top (whom they will ultimately join); and third, providing pressures for conformity with the cultural dictates of unslackened ambition by the threat of less than full membership in the society for those who fail to conform.

It is in these terms and through these processes that contemporary American culture continues to be characterized by a heavy emphasis on wealth as a basic symbol of success, without a corresponding emphasis upon the legitimate avenues on which to march toward this goal. How do individuals living in this cultural context respond? And how do our observations bear upon the doctrine that deviant behavior typically derives from biological impulses breaking through the restraints imposed by culture? What, in short, are the consequences for the behavior of people variously situated in a social structure of a culture in which the emphasis on dominant success-goals has become increasingly separated from an equivalent emphasis on institutionalized procedures for seeking these goals?

TYPES OF INDIVIDUAL ADAPTATION

Turning from these culture patterns, we now examine types of adaptation by individuals within the culture-bearing society. Though our focus is still the cultural and social genesis of varying rates and types of deviant behavior, our perspective shifts from the plane of patterns of cultural values to the plane of types of adaptation to these values among those occupying different positions in the social structure.

We here consider five types of adaptation, as these are schematically set out in the following table, where $(+)$ signifies "acceptance," $(-)$ signifies "rejection," and $(\pm)$ signifies "rejection of prevailing values and substitution of new values."

A TYPOLOGY OF MODES OF INDIVIDUAL ADAPTATION[12]

Modes of Adaptation	*Culture Goals*	*Institutionalized Means*
I. Conformity	$+$	$+$
II. Innovation	$+$	$-$
III. Ritualism	$-$	$+$
IV. Retreatism	$-$	$-$
V. Rebellion[13]	$\pm$	$\pm$

Examination of how the social structure operates to exert pressure upon individuals for one or another of these alternative modes of behavior must be prefaced by the observation that people may shift from one alternative to another as they engage in different spheres of social activities. These categories refer to role behavior in specific types of situations, not to personality. They are types of more or less enduring response, not types of personality organization. To consider these types of adaptation in several spheres of conduct would introduce a complexity unmanageable within the confines of this chapter. For this reason, we shall be primarily concerned with economic activity in the broad sense of "the production, exchange, distribution and consumption of goods

---

12. There is no lack of typologies of alternative modes of response to frustrating conditions. Freud, in his *Civilization and Its Discontents* (p. 30 ff.) supplies one; derivative typologies, often differing in basic details, will be found in Karen Horney, *Neurotic Personality of Our Time* (New York, 1937); S. Rosenzweig, "The experimental measurement of types of reaction to frustration," in H. A. Murray *et al.*, *Explorations in Personality* (New York, 1938), 585-99; and in the work of John Dollard, Harold Lasswell, Abram Kardiner, Erich Fromm. But particularly in the strictly Freudian typology, the perspective is that of types of individual responses, quite apart from the place of the individual within the social structure. Despite her consistent concern with "culture," for example, Horney does not explore differences in the impact of this culture upon farmer, worker and businessman, upon lower-, middle-, and upper-class individuals, upon members of various ethnic and racial groups, *etc.* As a result, the role of "inconsistencies in culture" is *not* located in its differential impact upon diversely situated groups. Culture becomes a kind of blanket covering all members of the society equally, apart from their idiosyncratic differences of life-history. It is a primary assumption of our typology that these responses occur with different frequency within various sub-groups in our society precisely because members of these groups or strata are differentially subject to cultural stimulation and social restraints. This sociological orientation will be found in the writings of Dollard and, less systematically, in the work of Fromm, Kardiner and Lasswell. On the general point, see note 3 of this chapter.

13. This fifth alternative is on a plane clearly different from that of the others. It represents a transitional response seeking to *institutionalize* new goals and new procedures to be shared by other members of the society. It thus refers to efforts to *change* the existing cultural and social structure rather than to accommodate efforts *within* this structure.

and services" in our competitive society, where wealth has taken on a highly symbolic cast.

I. CONFORMITY

To the extent that a society is stable, adaptation type I—conformity to both cultural goals and institutionalized means—is the most common and widely diffused. Were this not so, the stability and continuity of the society could not be maintained. The mesh of expectancies constituting every social order is sustained by the modal behavior of its members representing conformity to the established, though perhaps secularly changing, culture patterns. It is, in fact, only because behavior is typically oriented toward the basic values of the society that we may speak of a human aggregate as comprising a society. Unless there is a deposit of values shared by interacting individuals, there exist social relations, if the disorderly interactions may be so called, but no society. It is thus that, at mid-century, one may refer to a Society of Nations primarily as a figure of speech or as an imagined objective, but not as a sociological reality.

Since our primary interest centers on the sources of *deviant* behavior, and since we have briefly examined the mechanisms making for conformity as the modal response in American society, little more need be said regarding this type of adaptation, at this point.

II. INNOVATION

Great cultural emphasis upon the success-goal invites this mode of adaptation through the use of institutionally proscribed but often effective means of attaining at least the simulacrum of success—wealth and power. This response occurs when the individual has assimilated the cultural emphasis upon the goal without equally internalizing the institutional norms governing ways and means for its attainment.

From the standpoint of psychology, great emotional investment in an objective may be expected to produce a readiness to take risks, and this attitude may be adopted by people in all social strata. From the standpoint of sociology, the question arises, which features of our social structure predispose toward this type of adaptation, thus producing greater frequencies of deviant behavior in one social stratum than in another?

On the top economic levels, the pressure toward innovation not infrequently erases the distinction between business-like strivings this side of the mores and sharp practices beyond the mores. As Veblen observed, "It is not easy in any given case—indeed it is at times impossible until the courts have spoken—to say whether it is an instance of praiseworthy salesmanship or a penitentiary offense." The history of the great American fortunes is threaded with strains toward institutionally dubious innovation as is attested by many tributes to the Robber Barons. The reluctant admiration often expressed privately, and not seldom publicly, of these "shrewd, smart and successful" men is a product of a cultural structure in which the sacrosanct goal virtually consecrates the means. This is no new phenomenon. Without assuming that Charles Dickens was a wholly accurate observer of the American scene and with full knowledge that he was anything but impartial, we cite his perceptive remarks on the American

love of "smart" dealing: which gilds over many a swindle and gross breach of trust; many a defalcation, public and private; and enables many a knave to hold his head up with the best, who well deserves a halter. . . . The merits of a broken speculation, or a bankruptcy, or of a successful scoundrel, are not gauged by its or his observance of the golden rule, "Do as you would be done by," but are considered with reference to their smartness. . . . The following dialogue I have held a hundred times: "Is it not a very disgraceful circumstance that such a man as So-and-so should be acquiring a large property by the most infamous and odious means, and notwithstanding all the crimes of which he has been guilty, should be tolerated and abetted by your Citizens? He is a public nuisance, is he not?" "Yes, sir." "A convicted liar?" "Yes, sir." "He has been kicked and cuffed, and caned?" "Yes, sir." "And he is utterly dishonorable, debased, and profligate?" "Yes, sir." "In the name of wonder, then, what is his merit?" "Well, sir, he is a smart man."

In this caricature of conflicting cultural values, Dickens was of course only one of many wits who mercilessly probed the consequences of the heavy emphasis on financial success. Native wits continued where alien wits left off. Artemus Ward satirized the commonplaces of American life until they seemed strangely incongruous. The "crackerbox philosophers," Bill Arp and Petroleum Volcano [later Vesuvius] Nasby, put wit in the service of iconoclasm, breaking the images of public figures with unconcealed pleasure. Josh Billings and his alter ego, Uncle Esek, made plain what many could not freely acknowledge, when he observed that satisfaction is relative since "most of the happiness in this world konsists in possessing what others kant git." All were engaged in exhibiting the social functions of tendentious wit, as this was later to be analyzed by Freud, in his monograph on *Wit and Its Relation to the Unconscious*, using it as "a weapon of attack upon what is great, dignified and mighty, [upon] that which is shielded by internal hindrances or external circumstance against direct disparagement. . . ." But perhaps most in point here was the deployment of wit by Ambrose Bierce in a form which made it evident that *wit* had not cut away from its etymological origins and still meant the power by which one knows, learns, or thinks. In his characteristically ironical and deep-seeing essay on "crime and its correctives," Bierce begins with the observation that "Sociologists have long been debating the theory that the impulse to commit crime is a disease, and the ayes appear to have it—the disease." After this prelude, he describes the ways in which the successful rogue achieves social legitimacy, and proceeds to anatomize the discrepancies between cultural values and social relations.

The good American is, as a rule, pretty hard on roguery, but he atones for his austerity by an amiable toleration of rogues. His only requirement is that he must personally know the rogues. We all "denounce" thieves loudly enough if we have not the honor of their acquaintance. If we have, why, that is different—unless they have the actual odor of the slum or the prison about them. We may know them guilty, but we meet them, shake hands with them, drink with them and, if they happen to be wealthy, or otherwise great, invite them to our houses, and deem it an honor to frequent theirs. We do not "approve their methods"—let that be understood; and thereby they are suf-ficiently punished. The notion that a knave cares a pin what is thought of his ways by one who is civil and friendly to himself appears to have been invented by a humorist. On the vaudeville stage of Mars it would probably have made his fortune.

[And again:] If social recognition were denied to rogues they would be fewer by many. Some would only the more diligently cover their tracks along the devious paths of unrighteousness, but others would do so much violence to their consciences as to renounce the disadvantages of rascality for those of an honest life. An unworthy person dreads nothing so much as the with-holding of an honest hand, the slow, inevitable stroke of an ignoring eye.

We have rich rogues because we have "respectable" persons who are not ashamed to take them by the hand, to be seen with them, to say that they know them. In such it is treachery to censure them; to cry out when robbed by them is to turn state's evidence.

One may smile upon a rascal (most of us do many times a day) if one does not know him to be a rascal, and has not said he is; but knowing him to be, or having said he is, to smile upon him is to be a hypocrite—just a plain hypocrite or a sycophantic hypocrite, according to the station in life of the rascal smiled upon. There are more plain hypocrites than sycophantic ones, for there are more rascals of no consequence than rich and distinguished ones, though they get fewer smiles each. The American people will be plundered as long as the American character is what it is; as long as it is tolerant of successful knaves; as long as American ingenuity draws an imaginary dis-tinction between a man's public character and his private—his commercial and his personal. In brief, the American people will be plundered as long as they deserve to be plundered. No human law can stop, none ought to stop it, for that would abrogate a higher and more salutary law: "As ye sow, ye shall reap."[14]

---

14. The observations by Dickens are from his *American Notes* (in the edition, for example, published in Boston: Books, Inc., 1940), 218. A sociological analysis which would be the formal, albeit inevitably lesser, counterpart of Freud's psycho-logical analysis of the functions of tendentious wit and of tendentious wits is long overdue. The doctoral dissertation by Jeannette Tandy, though not sociological in character, affords one point of departure: *Crackerbox Philosophers: American Humor and Satire* (New York: Columbia University Press, 1925). In Chapter V of *Intel-lectual America* (New York: Macmillan, 1941), appropriately entitled "The In-telligentsia," Oscar Cargill has some compact observations on the role of the nineteenth century masters of American wit, but this naturally has only a small place in this large book on the "march of American ideas." The essay by Bierce from which I have quoted at such length will be found in *The Collected Works of Ambrose Bierce* (New York and Washington: The Neale Publishing Company.

Living in the age in which the American robber barons flourished, Bierce could not easily fail to observe what became later known as "white-collar crime." Nevertheless, he was aware that not all of these large and dramatic departures from institutional norms in the top economic strata are known, and possibly fewer deviations among the lesser middle classes come to light. Sutherland has repeatedly documented the prevalence of "white-collar criminality" among business men. He notes, further, that many of these crimes were not prosecuted because they were not detected or, if detected, because of "the status of the business man, the trend away from punishment, and the relatively unorganized resentment of the public against white-collar criminals."[15] A study of some 1,700 prevalently middle-class individuals found that "off the record crimes" were common among wholly "respectable" members of society. Ninety-nine per cent of those questioned confessed to having committed one or more of 49 offenses under the penal law of the State of New York, each of these offenses being sufficiently serious to draw a maximum sentence of not less than one year. The mean number of offenses in adult years—this excludes all offenses committed before the age of sixteen—was 18 for men and 11 for women. Fully 64% of the men and 29% of the women acknowledged their guilt on one or more counts of felony which, under the laws of New York is ground for depriving them of all rights of citizenship. One keynote of these findings is expressed by a minister, referring to false statements he made about a commodity he sold, "I tried truth first, but it's not always successful." On the basis of these results, the authors modestly conclude that "the number of acts legally constituting crimes are far in excess of those officially reported. Unlawful behavior, far from being an abnormal social or psychological manifestation, is in truth a very common phenomenon."[16]

But whatever the differential rates of deviant behavior in the several social strata, and we know from many sources that the official crime statistics uniformly showing higher rates in the lower strata are far from complete or reliable, it appears from our analysis that the greatest pressures toward deviation are exerted upon the lower strata. Cases in point permit us to detect the sociological mechanisms involved in producing

---

1912), volume XI, 187-198. For what it is worth, I must differ with the harsh and far from justified judgment of Cargill on Bierce. It seems to be less a judgment than the expression of a prejudice which, in Bierce's own understanding of "prejudice," is only "a vagrant opinion without visible means of support."

15. E. H. Sutherland, "White collar criminality," *op. cit.;* "Crime and business," *Annals, American Academy of Political and Social Science,* 1941, 217, 112-118; "Is 'white collar crime' crime?", *American Sociological Review,* 1945, 10, 132-139; Marshall B. Clinard, *The Black Market: A Study of White Collar Crime* (New York: Rinehart & Co., 1952); Donald R. Cressey, *Other People's Money: A Study in the Social Psychology of Embezzlement* (Glencoe: The Free Press, 1953).

16. James S. Wallerstein and Clement J. Wyle, "Our law-abiding law-breakers," *Probation,* April, 1947.

these pressures. Several researches have shown that specialized areas of vice and crime constitute a "normal" response to a situation where the cultural emphasis upon pecuniary success has been absorbed, but where there is little access to conventional and legitimate means for becoming successful. The occupational opportunities of people in these areas are largely confined to manual labor and the lesser white-collar jobs. Given the American stigmatization of manual labor *which has been found to hold rather uniformly in all social classes,*[17] and the absence of realistic opportunities for advancement beyond this level, the result is a marked tendency toward deviant behavior. The status of unskilled labor and the consequent low income cannot readily compete *in terms of established standards of worth* with the promises of power and high income from organized vice, rackets and crime.[18]

For our purposes, these situations exhibit two salient features. First, incentives for success are provided by the established values of the culture *and* second, the avenues available for moving toward this goal are largely limited by the class structure to those of deviant behavior. It is the *combination* of the cultural emphasis and the social structure which produces intense pressure for deviation. Recourse to legitimate channels for "getting in the money" is limited by a class structure which is not fully open at each level to men of good capacity.[19] Despite our persisting open-class-ideology,[20] advance toward the success-goal is relatively rare and notably difficult for those armed with little formal education and

---

17. National Opinion Research Center, *National Opinion on Occupations,* April, 1947. This research on the ranking and evaluation of ninety occupations by a nation-wide sample presents a series of important empirical data. Of great significance is their finding that, despite a slight tendency for people to rank their own and related occupations higher than do other groups, there is a substantial agreement in ranking of occupations among all occupational strata. More researches of this kind are needed to map the cultural topography of contemporary societies. (See the comparative study of prestige accorded major occupations in six industrialized countries: Alex Inkeles and Peter H. Rossi, "National comparisons of occupational prestige," *American Journal of Sociology,* 1956, 61, 329-339.)

18. See Joseph D. Lohman, "The participant observer in community studies," *American Sociological Review,* 1937, 2, 890-98 and William F. Whyte, *Street Corner Society* (Chicago, 1943). Note Whyte's conclusions: "It is difficult for the Cornerville man to get onto the ladder [of success], even on the bottom rung. . . . He is an Italian, and the Italians are looked upon by upper-class people as among the least desirable of the immigrant peoples . . . the society holds out attractive rewards in terms of money and material possessions to the 'successful' man. For most Cornerville people these rewards are available only through advancement in the world of rackets and politics." (273-74.)

19. Numerous studies have found that the educational pyramid operates to keep a large proportion of unquestionably able but economically disadvantaged youth from obtaining higher formal education. This fact about our class structure has been noted with dismay, for example, by Vannevar Bush in his governmental report, *Science: The Endless Frontier.* Also, see W. L. Warner, R. J. Havighurst and M. B. Loeb, *Who Shall Be Educated?* (New York, 1944).

20. The shifting historical role of this ideology is a profitable subject for exploration.

few economic resources. The dominant pressure leads toward the gradual attenuation of legitimate, but by and large ineffectual, strivings and the increasing use of illegitimate, but more or less effective, expedients.

Of those located in the lower reaches of the social structure, the culture makes incompatible demands. On the one hand, they are asked to orient their conduct toward the prospect of large wealth—"Every man a king," said Marden and Carnegie and Long—and on the other, they are largely denied effective opportunities to do so institutionally. The consequence of this structural inconsistency is a high rate of deviant behavior. The equilibrium between culturally designated ends and means becomes highly unstable with progressive emphasis on attaining the prestige-laden ends by any means whatsoever. Within this context, Al Capone represents the triumph of amoral intelligence over morally prescribed "failure," when the channels of vertical mobility are closed or narrowed *in a society which places a high premium on economic affluence and social ascent for all its members.*[21]

This last qualification is of central importance. It implies that other aspects of the social structure, besides the extreme emphasis on pecuniary success, must be considered if we are to understand the social sources of deviant behavior. A high frequency of deviant behavior is not generated merely by lack of opportunity or by this exaggerated pecuniary emphasis. A comparatively rigidified class structure, a caste order, may limit opportunities far beyond the point which obtains in American society today. It is only when a system of cultural values extols, virtually above all else, certain *common* success-goals *for the population at large* while the social structure rigorously restricts or completely closes access to approved modes of reaching these goals *for a considerable part of the same population,* that deviant behavior ensues on a large scale. Otherwise said, our egalitarian ideology denies by implication the existence of non-competing individuals and groups in the pursuit of pecuniary success. Instead, the same body of success-symbols is held to apply for all. Goals are held to transcend class lines, not to be bounded by them, yet the actual social organization is such that there exist class differentials in accessibility of the goals. In this setting, a cardinal American virtue, "ambition," promotes a cardinal American vice, "deviant behavior."

This theoretical analysis may help explain the varying correlations

---

21. The role of the Negro in this connection raises almost as many theoretical as practical questions. It has been reported that large segments of the Negro population have assimilated the dominant caste's values of pecuniary success and social advancement, but have "realistically adjusted" themselves to the "fact" that social ascent is presently confined almost entirely to movement within the caste. See Dollard, *Caste and Class in a Southern Town,* 66 ff.; Donald Young, *American Minority Peoples,* 581; Robert A. Warner, *New Haven Negroes* (New Haven, 1940), 234. See also the subsequent discussion in this chapter.

between crime and poverty.[22] "Poverty" is not an isolated variable which operates in precisely the same fashion wherever found; it is only one in a complex of identifiably interdependent social and cultural variables. Poverty as such and consequent limitation of opportunity are not enough to produce a conspicuously high rate of criminal behavior. Even the notorious "poverty in the midst of plenty" will not necessarily lead to this result. But when poverty and associated disadvantages in competing for the culture values approved for *all* members of the society are linked with a cultural emphasis on pecuniary success as a dominant goal, high rates of criminal behavior are the normal outcome. Thus, crude (and not necessarily reliable) crime statistics suggest that poverty is less highly correlated with crime in southeastern Europe than in the United States. The economic life-chances of the poor in these European areas would seem to be even less promising than in this country, so that neither poverty nor its association with limited opportunity is sufficient to account for the varying correlations. However, when we consider the full configuration—poverty, limited opportunity and the assignment of cultural goals—there appears some basis for explaining the higher correlation between poverty and crime in our society than in others where rigidified class structure is coupled with *differential class symbols of success.*

The victims of this contradiction between the cultural emphasis on pecuniary ambition and the social bars to full opportunity are not always aware of the structural sources of their thwarted aspirations. To be sure, they are often aware of a discrepancy between individual worth and social rewards. But they do not necessarily see how this comes about. Those who do find its source in the social structure may become alienated from that structure and become ready candidates for Adaptation V (rebellion). But others, and this appears to include the great majority, may attribute their difficulties to more mystical and less sociological sources. For as the distinguished classicist and sociologist-in-spite-of-himself, Gilbert Murray, has remarked in this general connection, "The best seed-ground for superstition is a society in which the fortunes of men seem to bear practically no relation to their merits and efforts. A stable and well-governed society does tend, speaking roughly, to ensure that the Virtuous and Industrious Apprentice shall succeed in life, while

---

22. This analytical scheme may serve to resolve some of the apparent inconsistencies in the relation between crime and economic status mentioned by P. A. Sorokin. For example, he notes that "not everywhere nor always do the poor show a greater proportion of crime . . . many poorer countries have had less crime than the richer countries. . . . The economic improvement in the second half of the nineteenth century, and the beginning of the twentieth, has not been followed by a decrease of crime." See his *Contemporary Sociological Theories,* (New York, 1928), 560-61. The crucial point is, however, that low economic status plays a different dynamic role in different social and cultural structures, as is set out in the text. One should not, therefore, expect a linear correlation between crime and poverty.

the Wicked and Idle Apprentice fails. And in such a society people tend
to lay stress on the reasonable or visible chains of causation. But in [a
society suffering from anomie] . . ., the ordinary virtues of diligence,
honesty, and kindliness seem to be of little avail."[23] And in such a society
people tend to put stress on mysticism: the workings of Fortune, Chance,
Luck.

In point of fact, both the eminently "successful" and the eminently
"unsuccessful" in our society not infrequently attribute the outcome to
"luck." Thus, the prosperous man of business, Julius Rosenwald, declared
that 95% of the great fortunes were "due to luck."[24] And a leading business journal, in an editorial explaining the social benefits of great individual wealth, finds it necessary to supplement wisdom with luck as
the factors accounting for great fortunes: "When one man through wise
investments—aided, we'll grant, by good luck in many cases—accumulates
a few millions, he doesn't thereby take something from the rest of us."[25]
In much the same fashion, the worker often explains economic status in
terms of chance. "The worker sees all about him experienced and skilled
men with no work to do. If he is in work, he feels lucky. If he is out of
work, he is the victim of hard luck. *He can see little relation between
worth and consequences.*"[26]

But these references to the workings of chance and luck serve distinctive functions according to whether they are made by those who have
reached or those who have not reached the culturally emphasized goals.
For the successful, it is in psychological terms, a disarming expression
of modesty. It is far removed from any semblance of conceit to say, in
effect, that one was lucky rather than altogether deserving of one's good
fortune. In sociological terms, the doctrine of luck as expounded by the
successful serves the dual function of explaining the frequent discrepancy between merit and reward while keeping immune from criticism a social structure which allows this discrepancy to become frequent.

---

23. Gilbert Murray, *Five Stages of Greek Religion* (New York, 1925), 164-5.
Professor Murray's chapter on "The Failure of Nerve," from which I have taken this
excerpt, must surely be ranked among the most civilized and perceptive sociological
analyses in our time.

24. See the quotation from an interview cited in Gustavus Meyers, *History of the
Great American Fortunes* (New York, 1937), 706.

25. *Nation's Business*, Vol. 27, No. 9, pp. 8-9.

26. E. W. Bakke, *The Unemployed Man* (New York, 1934), p. 14 (I have
supplied the emphasis.) Bakke hints at the structural sources making for a belief in
luck among workers. "There is a measure of hopelessness in the situation when a
man knows that *most of his good or ill fortune is out of his own control and depends
on luck.*" (Emphasis supplied) In so far as he is forced to accommodate himself to
occasionally unpredictable decisions of management, the worker is subject to job
insecurities and anxieties: another "seed-ground" for belief in destiny, fate, chance.
It would be instructive to learn if such beliefs become lessened where workers'
organizations reduce the probability that their occupational fate will be out of their
own hands.

For if success is primarily a matter of luck, if it is just in the blind nature of things, if it bloweth where it listeth and thou canst not tell whence it cometh or whither it goeth, then surely it is beyond control and will occur in the same measure *whatever the social structure.*

For the unsuccessful and particularly for those among the unsuccessful who find little reward for their merit and their effort, the doctrine of luck serves the psychological function of enabling them to preserve their self-esteem in the face of failure. It may also entail the dysfunction of curbing motivation for sustained endeavor.[27] Sociologically, as implied by Bakke,[28] the doctrine may reflect a failure to comprehend the workings of the social and economic system, and may be dysfunctional inasmuch as it eliminates the rationale of working for structural changes making for greater equities in opportunity and reward.

This orientation toward chance and risk-taking, accentuated by the strain of frustrated aspirations, may help explain the marked interest in gambling—an institutionally proscribed or at best permitted rather than preferred or prescribed mode of activity—within certain social strata.[29]

Among those who do not apply the doctrine of luck to the gulf between merit, effort and reward there may develop an individuated and cynical attitude toward the social structure, best exemplified in the cultural cliché that "it's not what you know, but who you know, that counts."

In societies such as our own, then, the great cultural emphasis on pecuniary success for all and a social structure which unduly limits practical recourse to approved means for many set up a tension toward innovative practices which depart from institutional norms. But this form of adaptation presupposes that individuals have been imperfectly socialized so that they abandon institutional means while retaining the success-aspiration. Among those who have fully internalized the institutional values, however, a comparable situation is more likely to lead to an alternative response in which the goal is abandoned but conformity to the mores persists. This type of response calls for further examination.

III. RITUALISM

The ritualistic type of adaptation can be readily identified. It involves the abandoning or scaling down of the lofty cultural goals of great pecuniary success and rapid social mobility to the point where one's

---

27. At its extreme, it may invite resignation and routinized activity (Adaptation III) or a fatalistic passivism (Adaptation IV), of which more presently.

28. Bakke, *op. cit.*, 14, where he suggests that "the worker knows less about the processes which cause him to succeed or have no chance to succeed than business or professional people. There are more points, therefore, at which events appear to have their incidence in good or ill luck."

29. *Cf.* R. A. Warner, *New Haven Negroes* and Harold F. Gosnell, *Negro Politicians* (Chicago, 1935), 123-5, both of whom comment in this general connection on the great interest in "playing the numbers" among less-advantaged Negroes.

aspirations can be satisfied. But though one rejects the cultural obligation to attempt "to get ahead in the world," though one draws in one's horizons, one continues to abide almost compulsively by institutional norms.

It is something of a terminological quibble to ask whether this represents genuinely deviant behavior. Since the adaptation is, in effect, an internal decision and since the overt behavior is institutionally permitted, though not culturally preferred, it is not generally considered to represent a social problem. Intimates of individuals making this adaptation may pass judgment in terms of prevailing cultural emphases and may "feel sorry for them," they may, in the individual case, feel that "old Jonesy is certainly in a rut." Whether this is described as deviant behavior or no, it clearly represents a departure from the cultural model in which men are obliged to strive actively, preferably through institutionalized procedures, to move onward and upward in the social hierarchy.

We should expect this type of adaptation to be fairly frequent in a society which makes one's social status largely dependent upon one's achievements. For, as has so often been observed,[30] this ceaseless competitive struggle produces acute status anxiety. One device for allaying these anxieties is to lower one's level of aspiration—permanently. Fear produces inaction, or more accurately, routinized action.[31]

The syndrome of the social ritualist is both familiar and instructive. His implicit life-philosophy finds expression in a series of cultural clichés: "I'm not sticking *my* neck out," "I'm playing safe," "I'm satisfied with what I've got," "Don't aim high and you won't be disappointed." The theme threaded through these attitudes is that high ambitions invite frustration and danger whereas lower aspirations produce satisfaction and security. It is a response to a situation which appears threatening and excites distrust. It is the attitude implicit among workers who carefully regulate their output to a constant quota in an industrial organization where they have occasion to fear that they will "be noticed" by managerial personnel and "something will happen" if their output rises and falls.[32] It is the perspective of the frightened employee, the zealously conformist bureaucrat in the teller's cage of the private banking enter-

---

30. See, for example, H. S. Sullivan, "Modern conceptions of psychiatry," *Psychiatry*, 1940, 3, 111-12; Margaret Mead. *And Keep Your Powder Dry* (New York, 1942), Chapter VII; Merton, Fiske and Curtis, *Mass Persuasion*, 59-60.

31. P. Janet, "The fear of action," *Journal of Abnormal Psychology*, 1921, 16, 150-60, and the extraordinary discussion by F. L. Wells, "Social maladjustments: adaptive regression," *op. cit.*, which bears closely on the type of adaptation examined here.

32. F. J. Roethlisberger and W. J. Dickson, *Management and the Worker*, Chapter 18 and 531 ff.; and on the more general theme, the typically perspicacious remarks of Gilbert Murray, *op. cit.*, 138-39.

prise or in the front office of the public works enterprise.[33] It is, in short, the mode of adaptation of individually seeking a *private* escape from the dangers and frustrations which seem to them inherent in the competition for major cultural goals by abandoning these goals and clinging all the more closely to the safe routines and the institutional norms.

If we should expect *lower-class* Americans to exhibit Adaptation II— "innovation"—to the frustrations enjoined by the prevailing emphasis on large cultural goals and the fact of small social opportunities, we should expect *lower-middle class* Americans to be heavily represented among those making Adaptation III, "ritualism." For it is in the lower middle class that parents typically exert continuous pressure upon children to abide by the moral mandates of the society, and where the social climb upward is less likely to meet with success than among the upper middle class. The strong disciplining for conformity with mores reduces the likelihood of Adaptation II and promotes the likelihood of Adaptation III. The severe training leads many to carry a heavy burden of anxiety. The socialization patterns of the lower middle class thus promote the very character structure most predisposed toward ritualism,[34] and it is in this stratum, accordingly, that the adaptive pattern III should most often occur.[35]

---

33. See the three following chapters.

34. See, for example, Allison Davis and John Dollard, *Children of Bondage* (Washington, 1940), Chapter 12 ("Child Training and Class"), which, though it deals with the lower- and lower-middle class patterns of socialization among Negroes in the Far South, appears applicable, with slight modification, to the white population as well. On this, see further M. C. Erickson, "Child-rearing and social status," *American Journal of Sociology,* 1946, 53, 190-92; Allison Davis and R. J. Havighurst, "Social class and color differences in child-rearing," *American Sociological Review,* 1946, 11, 698-710: ". . . *the pivotal meaning of social class* to students of human development is that it defines and systematizes different learning environments for children of different classes." "Generalizing from the evidence presented in the tables, we would say that middle-class children [the authors do not distinguish between lower-middle and upper-middle strata] are subjected earlier and more consistently to the influences which make a child an orderly, conscientious, responsible, and tame person. In the course of this training middle-class children probably suffer more frustration of their impulses."

35. This hypothesis still awaits empirical test. Beginnings in this direction have been made with the "level of aspiration" experiments which explore the determinants of goal-formation and modification in specific, experimentally devised activities. There is, however, a major obstacle, not yet surmounted, in drawing inferences from the laboratory situation, with its relatively slight ego-involvement with the casual task—pencil-and-paper mazes, ring-throwing, arithmetical problems, *etc.*—which will be applicable to the strong emotional investment with success-goals in the routines of everyday life. Nor have these experiments, with their *ad hoc* group formations, been able to reproduce the acute social pressures obtaining in daily life. (What laboratory experiment reproduces, for example, the querulous nagging of a modern Xantippe: "The trouble with you is, you've got no ambition; a real man would go out and do things"?) Among studies with a definite though limited relevance, see especially R. Gould, "Some sociological determinants of goal strivings," *Journal of Social Psychology,* 1941, 13, 461-73; L. Festinger, "Wish, expectation and group standards as factors influencing level of aspiration," *Journal of Abnormal and Social*

But we should note again, as at the outset of this chapter, that we are here examining *modes of adaptation* to contradictions in the cultural and social structure: we are not focusing on character or personality types. Individuals caught up in these contradictions can and do move from one type of adaptation to another. Thus it may be conjectured that some ritualists, conforming meticulously to the institutional rules, are so steeped in the regulations that they become bureaucratic virtuosos, that they over-conform precisely because they are subject to guilt engendered by previous nonconformity with the rules (*i.e.*, Adaptation II). And the occasional passage from ritualistic adaptation to dramatic kinds of illicit adaptation is well-documented in clinical case-histories and often set forth in insightful fiction. Defiant outbreaks not infrequently follow upon prolonged periods of over-compliance.[36] But though the psychodynamic mechanisms of this type of adaptation have been fairly well identified and linked with patterns of discipline and socialization in the family,

---

Psychology, 1942, 37, 184-200. For a resume of researches, see Kurt Lewin *et al.*, "Level of Aspiration," in J. McV. Hunt, ed., *Personality and the Behavior Disorders* (New York, 1944), I, Chap. 10.

The conception of "success" as a ratio between aspiration and achievement pursued systematically in the level-of-aspiration experiments has, of course, a long history. Gilbert Murray (*op. cit.*, 138-9) notes the prevalence of this conception among the thinkers of fourth century Greece. And in *Sartor Resartus*, Carlyle observes that "happiness" (gratification) can be represented by a fraction in which the numerator represents achievement and the denominator, aspiration. Much the same notion is examined by William James (*The Principles of Psychology* [New York, 1902], I, 310). See also F. L. Wells, *op. cit.*, 879, and P. A. Sorokin, *Social and Cultural Dynamics* (New York, 1937), III, 161-164. The critical question is whether this familiar insight can be subjected to rigorous experimentation in which the contrived laboratory situation adequately reproduces the salient aspects of the real-life situation or whether disciplined observation of routines of behavior in everyday life will prove the more productive method of inquiry.

36. In her novel, *The Bitter Box* (New York, 1946), Eleanor Clark has portrayed this process with great sensitivity. The discussion by Erich Fromm, *Escape from Freedom* (New York, 1941), 185-206, may be cited, without implying acceptance of his concept of "spontaneity" and "man's inherent tendency toward self-development." For an example of a sound sociological formulation: "As long as we assume . . . that the anal character, as it is typical of the European lower middle class, is caused by certain early experiences in connection with defecation, we have hardly any data that lead us to understand why a specific class should have an anal social character. However, if we understand it as one form of relatedness to others, rooted in the character structure and resulting from the experiences with the outside world, we have a key for understanding why the whole mode of life of the lower middle class, its narrowness, isolation, and hostility, made for the development of this kind of character structure." (293-4) For an example of a formulation stemming from a kind of latter-day benevolent anarchism here judged as dubious: ". . . there are also certain psychological qualities inherent in man that need to be satisfied. . . . The most important seems to be the tendency to grow, to develop and realize potentialities which man has developed in the course of history—as, for instance, the faculty of creative and critical thinking. . . . It also seems that this general tendency to grow—which is the psychological equivalent of the identical biological tendency—results in such specific tendencies as the desire for freedom and the hatred against oppression, since freedom is the fundamental condition for any growth." (287-88)

much sociological research is still required to explain why these patterns are presumably more frequent in certain social strata and groups than in others. Our own discussion has merely set out one analytical framework for sociological research focused on this problem.

IV. RETREATISM

Just as Adaptation I (conformity) remains the most frequent, Adaptation IV (the rejection of cultural goals and institutional means) is probably the least common. People who adapt (or maladapt) in this fashion are, strictly speaking, *in* the society but not *of* it. Sociologically, these constitute the true aliens. Not sharing the common frame of values, they can be included as members of the *society* (in distinction from the *population*) only in a fictional sense.

In this category fall some of the adaptive activities of psychotics, autists, pariahs, outcasts, vagrants, vagabonds, tramps, chronic drunkards and drug addicts.[37] They have relinquished culturally prescribed goals and their behavior does not accord with institutional norms. This is not to say that in some cases the source of their mode of adaptation is not the very social structure which they have in effect repudiated nor that their very existence within an area does not constitute a problem for members of the society.

From the standpoint of its sources in the social structure, this mode of adaptation is most likely to occur when *both* the culture goals and the institutional practices have been thoroughly assimilated by the individual and imbued with affect and high value, but accessible institutional avenues are not productive of success. There results a twofold conflict: the interiorized moral obligation for adopting institutional means conflicts with pressures to resort to illicit means (which may attain the goal) and the individual is shut off from means which are both legitimate and effective. The competitive order is maintained but the frustrated and handicapped individual who cannot cope with this order drops out. Defeatism, quietism and resignation are manifested in escape mechanisms which ultimately lead him to "escape" from the requirements of the society. It is thus an expedient which arises from continued failure to near the goal by legitimate measures and from an inability to use the illegitimate route because of internalized prohibitions, *this process occurring while the supreme value of the success-goal has not yet been renounced.* The conflict is resolved by abandoning *both* precipitating

---

37. Obviously, this is an elliptical statement. These individuals may retain some orientation to the values of their own groupings within the larger society or, occasionally, to the values of the conventional society itself. They may, in other words, shift to other modes of adaptation. But Adaptation IV can be easily detected. Nels Anderson's account of the behavior and attitudes of the bum, for example, can readily be recast in terms of our analytical scheme. See *The Hobo* (Chicago, 1923), 93-98, *et passim.*

elements, the goals and the means. The escape is complete, the conflict is eliminated and the individual is asocialized.

In public and ceremonial life, this type of deviant behavior is most heartily condemned by conventional representatives of the society. In contrast to the conformist, who keeps the wheels of society running, this deviant is a non-productive liability; in contrast to the innovator who is at least "smart" and actively striving, he sees no value in the success-goal which the culture prizes so highly; in contrast to the ritualist who conforms at least to the mores, he pays scant attention to the institutional practices.

Nor does the society lightly accept these repudiations of its values. To do so would be to put these values into question. Those who have abandoned the quest for success are relentlessly pursued to their haunts by a society insistent upon having all its members orient themselves to success-striving. Thus, in the heart of Chicago's Hobohemia are the book stalls filled with wares designed to revitalize dead aspirations.

The Gold Coast Book Store is in the basement of an old residence, built back from the street, and now sandwiched between two business blocks. The space in front is filled with stalls, and striking placards and posters.

These posters advertise such books as will arrest the attention of the down-and-out. One reads: ". . . Men in thousands pass this spot daily, but the majority of them are not financially successful. They are never more than two jumps ahead of the rent men. Instead of that, they should be more bold and daring," "Getting Ahead of the Game," before old age withers them and casts them on the junk heap of human wrecks. If you want to escape this evil fate—the fate of the vast majority of men—come in and get a copy of *The Law of Financial Success*. It will put some new ideas in your head, and put you on the highroad to success. 35 cents.

There are always men loitering before its stalls. But they seldom buy. Success comes high, even at thirty-five cents, to the hobo.[38]

But if this deviant is condemned in real life, he may become a source of gratification in fantasy-life. Thus Kardiner has advanced the speculation that such figures in contemporary folklore and popular culture bolster "morale and self-esteem by the spectacle of man rejecting current ideals and expressing contempt for them." The prototype in the films is of course Charlie Chaplin's bum.

He is Mr. Nobody and is very much aware of his own insignificance. He is always the butt of a crazy and bewildering world in which he has no place and from which he constantly runs away into a contented do-nothingness. *He is free from conflict because he has abandoned the quest for security and prestige, and is resigned to the lack of any claim to virtue or distinction.* [A precise characterological portrait of Adaptation IV.] He always becomes involved in the world by accident. There he encounters evil and aggression against the weak and helpless which he has no power to combat. Yet always, in spite of himself, he becomes the champion of the wronged and oppressed,

38. H. W. Zorbaugh, *The Gold Coast and the Slum* (Chicago, 1929), 108.

not by virtue of his great organizing ability but by virtue of homely and insolent trickiness by which he seeks out the weakness of the wrongdoer. He always remains humble, poor, and lonely, but is contemptuous of the incomprehensible world and its values. He therefore represents the character of our time who is *perplexed by the dilemma either of being crushed in the struggle to achieve the socially approved goals of success and power* (he achieves it only once—in *The Gold Rush*) *or of succumbing to a hopeless resignation and flight from them.* Charlie's bum is a great comfort in that he gloats in his ability to outwit the pernicious forces aligned against him if he chooses to do so and affords every man the satisfaction of feeling that the ultimate flight from social goals to loneliness is an act of *choice* and not a symptom of his defeat. Mickey Mouse is a continuation of the Chaplin saga.[39]

This fourth mode of adaptation, then, is that of the socially disinherited who if they have none of the rewards held out by society also have few of the frustrations attendant upon continuing to seek these rewards. It is, moreover, a privatized rather than a collective mode of adaptation. Although people exhibiting this deviant behavior may gravitate toward centers where they come into contact with other deviants and although they may come to share in the subculture of these deviant groups, their adaptations are largely private and isolated rather than unified under the aegis of a new cultural code. The type of collective adaptation remains to be considered.

V. REBELLION

This adaptation leads men outside the environing social structure to envisage and seek to bring into being a new, that is to say, a greatly modified social structure. It presupposes alienation from reigning goals and standards. These come to be regarded as purely arbitrary. And the arbitrary is precisely that which can neither exact allegiance nor possess legitimacy, for it might as well be otherwise. In our society, organized movements for rebellion apparently aim to introduce a social structure in which the cultural standards of success would be sharply modified and provision would be made for a closer correspondence between merit, effort and reward.

But before examining "rebellion" as a mode of adaptation, we must distinguish it from a superficially similar but essentially different type, *ressentiment.* Introduced in a special technical sense, by Nietzsche, the concept of *ressentiment* was taken up and developed sociologically by Max Scheler.[40] This complex sentiment has three interlocking elements.

---

39. Abram Kardiner, *The Psychological Frontiers of Society* (New York, 1945), 369-70. (Emphases supplied.)

40. Max Scheler, *L'homme du ressentiment* (Paris, n. d.). This essay first appeared in 1912; revised and completed, it was included in Scheler's *Abhandlungen und Aufsätze,* appearing thereafter in his *Vom Umsturz der Werte* (1919). The last text was used for the French translation. It has had considerable influence in varied intellectual circles. For an excellent and well-balanced discussion of Scheler's essay,

First, diffuse feelings of hate, envy and hostility; second, a sense of being powerless to express these feelings actively against the person or social stratum evoking them; and third, a continual re-experiencing of this impotent hostility.[41] The essential point distinguishing *ressentiment* from rebellion is that the former does not involve a genuine change in values. *Ressentiment* involves a sour-grapes pattern which asserts merely that desired but unattainable objectives do not actually embody the prized values—after all, the fox in the fable does not say that he abandons all taste for sweet grapes; he says only that these particular grapes are not sweet. Rebellion, on the other hand, involves a genuine transvaluation, where the direct or vicarious experience of frustration leads to full denunciation of previously prized values—the rebellious fox simply renounces the prevailing taste for sweet grapes. In *ressentiment,* one condemns what one secretly craves; in rebellion, one condemns the craving itself. But though the two are distinct, organized rebellion may draw upon a vast reservoir of the resentful and discontented as institutional dislocations become acute.

When the institutional system is regarded as the barrier to the satisfaction of legitimized goals, the stage is set for rebellion as an adaptive response. To pass into organized political action, allegiance must not only be withdrawn from the prevailing social structure but must be transferred to new groups possessed of a new myth.[42] The dual function of the myth is to locate the source of large-scale frustrations in the social structure and to portray an alternative structure which would not, presumably, give rise to frustration of the deserving. It is a charter for action. In this context, the functions of the counter-myth of the conservatives—briefly sketched in an earlier section of this chapter—become further clarified: whatever the source of mass frustration, it is not to be found in the basic structure of the society. The conservative myth may thus assert that these frustrations are in the nature of things and would occur in *any* social system: "Periodic mass unemployment and business depressions can't be legislated out of existence; it's just like a person who feels good one day and bad the next."[43] Or, if not the doctrine of

---

indicating some of its limitations and biasses, the respects in which it prefigured Nazi conceptions, its anti-democratic orientation and, withal, its occasionally brilliant insights, see V. J. McGill, "Scheler's theory of sympathy and love," *Philosophy and Phenomenological Research*, 1942, 2, 273-91. For another critical account which properly criticizes Scheler's view that social structure plays only a secondary role in *ressentiment,* see Svend Ranulf, *Moral Indignation and Middle-Class Psychology: A Sociological Study* (Copenhagen, 1938), 199-204.

41. Scheler, *op. cit.,* 55-56. No English word fully reproduces the complex of elements implied by the word *ressentiment;* its nearest approximation in German would appear to be *Groll.*

42. George S. Pettee, *The Process of Revolution* (New York, 1938), 8-24; see particularly his account of "monopoly of the imagination."

43. R. S. and H. M. Lynd, *Middletown in Transition* (New York, 1937), 408, for a series of cultural clichés exemplifying the conservative myth.

inevitability, then the doctrine of gradual and slight adjustment: "A few changes here and there, and we'll have things running as ship-shape as they can possibly be." Or, the doctrine which deflects hostility from the social structure onto the individual who is a "failure" since "every man really gets what's coming to him in this country."

The myths of rebellion and of conservatism both work toward a "monopoly of the imagination" seeking to define the situation in such terms as to move the frustrate toward or away from Adaptation V. It is above all the renegade who, though himself successful, renounces the prevailing values that becomes the target of greatest hostility among those in rebellion. For he not only puts the values in question, as does the out-group, but he signifies that the unity of the group is broken.[44] Yet, as has so often been noted, it is typically members of a rising class rather than the most depressed strata who organize the resentful and the rebellious into a revolutionary group.

THE STRAIN TOWARD ANOMIE

The social structure we have examined produces a strain toward anomie and deviant behavior. The pressure of such a social order is upon outdoing one's competitors. So long as the sentiments supporting this competitive system are distributed throughout the entire range of activities and are not confined to the final result of "success," the choice of means will remain largely within the ambit of institutional control. When, however, the cultural emphasis shifts from the satisfactions deriving from competition itself to almost exclusive concern with the outcome, the resultant stress makes for the breakdown of the regulatory structure. With this attenuation of institutional controls, there occurs an approximation to the situation erroneously held by the utilitarian philosophers to be typical of society, a situation in which calculations of personal advantage and fear of punishment are the only regulating agencies.

This strain toward anomie does not operate evenly throughout the society. Some effort has been made in the present analysis to suggest the strata most vulnerable to the pressures for deviant behavior and to set forth some of the mechanisms operating to produce those pressures. For purposes of simplifying the problem, monetary success was taken as the major cultural goal, although there are, of course, alternative goals in the repository of common values. The realms of intellectual and artistic achievement, for example, provide alternative career patterns which may not entail large pecuniary rewards. To the extent that the cultural structure attaches prestige to these alternatives and the social structure permits access to them, the system is somewhat stabilized. Potential deviants may still conform in terms of these auxiliary sets of values.

---

44. See the acute observations by Georg Simmel, *Soziologie* (Leipzig, 1908), 276-77.

But the central tendencies toward anomie remain, and it is to these that the analytical scheme here set forth calls particular attention.

THE ROLE OF THE FAMILY

A final word should be said drawing together the implications scattered throughout the foregoing discussion concerning the role played by the family in these patterns of deviant behavior.

It is the family, of course, which is a major transmission belt for the diffusion of cultural standards to the oncoming generation. But what has until lately been overlooked is that the family largely transmits that portion of the culture accessible to the social stratum and groups in which the parents find themselves. It is, therefore, a mechanism for disciplining the child in terms of the cultural goals and mores characteristic of this narrow range of groups. Nor is the socialization confined to direct training and disciplining. The process is, at least in part, inadvertent. Quite apart from direct admonitions, rewards and punishments, the child is exposed to social prototypes in the witnessed daily behavior and casual conversations of parents. Not infrequently, *children detect and incorporate cultural uniformities even when these remain implicit and have not been reduced to rules.*

Language patterns provide the most impressive evidence, readily observable in clinical fashion, that children, in the process of socialization, detect uniformities which have not been explicitly formulated for them by elders or contemporaries and which are not formulated by the children themselves. Persistent errors of language among children are most instructive. Thus, the child will spontaneously use such words as "mouses" or "moneys," *even though he has never heard such terms or been taught "the rule for forming plurals."* Or he will create such words as "falled," "runned," "singed," "hitted," though he has not been taught, at the age of three, "rules" of conjugation. Or, he will refer to a choice morsel as "gooder" than another less favored, or perhaps through a logical extension, he may describe it as "goodest" of all. Obviously, he has detected the implicit paradigms for the expression of plurality, for the conjugation of verbs, and the inflection of adjectives. The very nature of his error and misapplication of the paradigm testifies to this.[45]

It may be tentatively inferred, therefore, that he is also busily engaged in *detecting and acting upon the implicit paradigms of cultural evaluation, and categorization of people and things, and the formation of estimable goals* as well as assimilating the explicit cultural orientation

---

45. W. Stern, *Psychology of Early Childhood* (New York, 1924), 166, notes the *fact* of such errors (*e.g.*, "drinked" for "drank"), but does not draw the inferences regarding the detection of implicit paradigms.

set forth in an endless stream of commands, explanations and exhortations by parents. It would appear that in addition to the important researches of the depth psychologies on the socialization process, there is need for supplementary types of direct observation of culture diffusion within the family. It may well be that the child retains the implicit paradigm of cultural values detected in the day-by-day behavior of his parents even when this conflicts with their explicit advice and exhortations.

The projection of parental ambitions onto the child is also centrally relevant to the subject in hand. As is well known, many parents confronted with personal "failure" or limited "success" may mute their original goal-emphasis and may defer further efforts to reach the goal, attempting to reach it vicariously through their children. "The influence may come through the mother or the father. Often it is the case of a parent who hopes that the child will attain heights that he or she failed to attain."[46] In a recent research on the social organization of public housing developments, we have found among both Negroes and Whites on lower occupational levels, a substantial proportion having aspirations for a professional career for their children.[47] Should this finding be confirmed by further research it will have large bearing upon the problem in hand. For if compensatory projection of parental ambition onto children is widespread, then it is precisely those parents least able to provide free access to opportunity for their children—the "failures" and "frustrates"—who exert great pressure upon their children for high achievement. And this syndrome of lofty aspirations and limited realistic opportunities, as we have seen, is precisely the pattern which invites deviant behavior. This clearly points to the need for investigation focused upon occupational goal-formation in the several social strata if the inadvertent role of family disciplining in deviant behavior is to be understood from the perspectives of our analytical scheme.

CONCLUDING REMARKS

It should be apparent that the foregoing discussion is not pitched on a moralistic plane. Whatever the sentiments of the reader concerning the moral desirability of coördinating the goals-and-means phases of the social structure, it is clear that imperfect coördination of the two leads to anomie. In so far as one of the most general functions of social structure is to provide a basis for predictability and regularity of social behavior, it becomes increasingly limited in effectiveness as these elements of the social structure become dissociated. At the extreme, predictability is mini-

---

46. H. A. Murray *et al.*, *Explorations in Personality*, 307.
47. From a study of the social organization of planned communities by R. K. Merton, Patricia S. West and M. Jahoda, *Patterns of Social Life*.

mized and what may be properly called anomie or cultural chaos supervenes.

This essay on the structural sources of deviant behavior remains but a prelude. It has not included a detailed treatment of the structural elements which predispose toward one rather than another of the alternative responses open to individuals living in an ill-balanced social structure; it has largely neglected but not denied the relevance of the social-psychological processes determining the specific incidence of these responses; it has only briefly considered the social functions fulfilled by deviant behavior; it has not put the explanatory power of the analytical scheme to full empirical test by determining group variations in deviant and conformist behavior; it has only touched upon rebellious behavior which seeks to refashion the social framework.

It is suggested that these and related problems may be advantageously analyzed by use of this scheme.

CONTINUITIES IN THE THEORY OF SOCIAL STRUCTURE AND ANOMIE

R̲ECENT YEARS have seen the appearance of a sizable sociologi-cal literature which bears upon one or another aspect of anomie. This provides an enlarged basis for clarifying and extending the formulations set out in the preceding paper. Interest in the concept of anomie has indeed grown rapidly enough for it to become (almost inevitably) vulgarized as it diffuses to wider and wider social circles. As one ex-ample of vulgarization, consider the case of the news-weekly which seizes upon a sober and careful inquiry by Gerhart Niemeyer into the social consequences of anomie and promptly imbues the account with 'reader appeal' by beginning in these folksy and shrill terms: " 'Boy, that's what I call acute anomie,' whistled Bleecker Totten, one of 225 students at Oglethorpe University."[1] Less sibilant but more instructive are the theoretical, substantive, and procedural studies of anomie now to be examined.

THE EXTENDED CONCEPT OF ANOMIE

As initially developed by Durkheim, the concept of anomie referred to a condition of relative normlessness in a society or group. Durkheim made it clear that this concept referred to a property of the social and cultural structure, not to a property of individuals confronting that struc-ture. Nevertheless, as the utility of the concept for understanding diverse forms of deviant behavior became evident, it was extended to refer to a condition of individuals rather than of their environment.

This psychological conception of anomie has been simultaneously formulated by R. M. MacIver and by David Riesman. Since their formulations are substantially alike, what is said of one may be said of both.

"Anomy"—MacIver is resurrecting the sixteenth-century and long obsolete spelling of the word—"signifies the *state of mind* of one who has been pulled

---

1. *Pathfinder*, May 17, 1950, 55.

up by his moral roots, who has no longer any standards but only disconnected urges, who has no longer any sense of continuity, of folk, of obligation. The anomic man has become spiritually sterile, responsive only to himself, responsible to no one. He derides the values of other men. His only faith is the philosophy of denial. He lives on the thin line of sensation between no future and no past." And again: "Anomy is a *state of mind* in which the individual's sense of social cohesion—the mainspring of his morale—is broken or fatally weakened."[2]

As has been noted, "MacIver's approach is thus psychological (i.e. anomie is for him a state of *mind,* not a state of society—though the state of mind may reflect social tensions), and his psychological types [of anomie] correspond to the elements (anxiety-isolation-purposeless) which form the subjective aspect of Durkheim's concept."[3] That the psychological concept of anomie has a definite referent, that it refers to identifiable 'states of mind' of particular individuals, is beyond question, as the crowded casebooks of psychiatrists attest. But the psychological concept is nevertheless a counterpart of the sociological concept of anomie, and not a substitute for it.

The sociological concept of anomie, as developed in the preceding pages, presupposes that the salient environment of individuals can be usefully thought of as involving the cultural structure, on the one hand, and the social structure, on the other. It assumes that, however intimately connected these in fact are, they must be kept separate for purposes of analysis before they are brought together again. In this connection, cultural structure may be defined as that organized set of normative values governing behavior which is common to members of a designated society or group. And by social structure is meant that organized set of social relationships in which members of the society or group are variously implicated. Anomie is then conceived as a breakdown in the cultural structure, occurring particularly when there is an acute disjunction between the cultural norms and goals and the socially structured capacities of members of the group to act in accord with them. In this conception, cultural values may help to produce behavior which is at odds with the mandates of the values themselves.

On this view, the social structure strains the cultural values, making action in accord with them readily possible for those occupying certain statuses within the society and difficult or impossible for others. The

---

2. R. M. MacIver, *The Ramparts We Guard* (New York: The Macmillan Company, 1950), 84, 85, and the whole of Chapter Ten; italics supplied. Compare the independently conceived but equivalent description of 'the anomics' by David Riesman, in collaboration with Reuel Denney and Nathan Glazer, *The Lonely Crowd* (New Haven: Yale University Press, 1950), 287 ff.

3. R. H. Brookes, "The anatomy of anomie," *Political Science,* 1951, 3, 44-51; 1952, 4, 38-49—a review-article examining recent conceptual extensions of anomie. H. L. Ansbacher undertakes to relate anomie to the Adlerian notion of "lack of social interest" in a note appearing in *Individual Psychology News Letter: Organ of the International Association of Individual Psychology,* London, June-July 1956.

social structure acts as a barrier or as an open door to the acting out of cultural mandates. When the cultural and the social structure are mal-integrated, the first calling for behavior and attitudes which the second precludes, there is a strain toward the breakdown of the norms, toward normlessness. It does not follow, of course, that this is the sole process making for the social condition of anomie; further theory and research are directed toward searching out other patterned sources of a high degree of anomie.

An effort has been made to catch up the psychological and socio-logical concepts in a distinction between 'simple' and 'acute' anomie.[4] Simple anomie refers to the state of confusion in a group or society which is subject to conflict between value-systems, resulting in some degree of uneasiness and a sense of separation from the group; acute anomie, to the deterioration and, at the extreme, the disintegration of value-systems, which results in marked anxieties. This has the merit of terminologically ear-marking the often stated but sometimes neglected fact that, like other conditions of society, anomie varies in degree and perhaps in kind.

Having identified some of the processes conducing to anomie, the preceding chapter sets out a typology of adaptive responses to this con-dition and the structural pressures making for a greater or less frequency of each of these responses among the several strata of the class struc-ture. The underlying premise here is that class strata are not only differentially subject to anomie but are differentially subject to one or another type of response to it. Talcott Parsons has taken up this typology and has derived it, in motivational terms, from his conceptual scheme of social interaction.[5] This analysis proceeds from the assumption that neither tendencies toward deviant behavior nor tendencies toward re-equilibration of a system of social interaction can develop at random; instead, they work out in one or more of a limited number of identifiable directions. This is to say, that deviant behavior is itself patterned.

In the words of Parsons and Bales, "Deviance was shown to involve four basic directions, according to whether the need to express aliena-tion from the normative pattern—including the repudiation of attach-ment to alter as an object—or to maintain compulsive conformity with the normative pattern and attachment to alter, and according to whether the mode of action was actively or passively inclined. This yielded four directional types, those of aggressiveness and withdrawal on the aliena-tive side, and of compulsive performance and compulsive acceptance, on the side of compulsive conformity. It was furthermore shown that

4. Sebastian De Grazia, *The Political Community* (University of Chicago Press, 1948), 72-74, *passim; cf.* Brookes, *op. cit.,* 46.

5. Parsons, *The Social System,* 256-267, 321-325; Talcott Parsons, Robert F. Bales and Edward A. Shils, *Working Papers in the Theory of Action* (Glencoe: The Free Press, 1953), 67-78.

this paradigm, independently derived, is essentially the same as that previously put forward by Merton for the analysis of social structure and anomie."[6]

This first extension of the typology of response, it will be noted, continues to take account of *both* the cultural structure—"the normative pattern"—and the social structure—patterned attachments to other people or alienation from them. It goes on, however, to characterize the types of response in terms of their being either active or passive, meaning by this that the deviant behavior can involve either actively " 'taking the situation in hand,' doing more in attempting to control it than the [institutionalized] expectations" call for, or passively "falling short of asserting the degree of active control" required by these expectations. The types of deviant behavior can be further subdivided by distinguishing between cases in which the strains are primarily in the social relations with others or in the cultural norms with which conformity is expected.[7] Such concrete manifestations of reaction to anomic strains as delinquency, crime, and suicide, as well as such conceptually intermediate types of responses as innovation, ritualism, retreatism and rebellion thus become classifiable as resultants of certain abstract properties of interaction systems identified by Parsons. Having been developed so recently, this more complex classification of types of deviant behavior has yet to be extensively utilized in empirical investigations.

INDICATORS OF ANOMIE

Like many of us who have tried to follow in his large footsteps and consequently wobble a bit in these excessively spacious areas, Durkheim did not afford explicit and methodical guidance to the various signs of anomie, to the observables of normlessness and deteriorated social relationships. Yet it is plain that indicators must be developed if the concept of anomie is to be utilized in empirical research.

A step in this direction has been taken by Leo Srole in developing a preliminary 'scale of anomie.'[8] In part, the scale incorporates items referring to the individual's perception of his social environment; in part, to his perception of his own place within that environment. More specifically, the five items comprising this preliminary scale refer to (1) the perception that community-leaders are indifferent to one's needs; (2) the perception that little can be accomplished in the society which is seen as basically unpredictable and lacking order; (3) the perception that life-goals are receding rather than being realized; (4) a sense of futility; and (5) the conviction that one cannot count on personal asso-

---

6. Parsons et al., *Working Papers*, 68.

7. *Ibid.*, 74.

8. In a paper read before the American Sociological Society, 1951, entitled "Social dysfunction, personality, and social distance attitudes"; and again, in an extended but still unpublished version, entitled "Social integration and certain corollaries."

ciates for social and psychological support.[9] As Srole indicates in some detail, this effort to develop a scale of anomie has various limitations and some inadequacies, but it does furnish a beginning toward a standardized measure of anomie, as perceived and experienced by individuals in a group or community.

This scale can be taken to measure anomie as *subjectively* experienced; manifestly needed is a further measure of anomie, as an *objective* condition of group life. A symptomatic advance toward this latter type of measure has been made by Bernard Lander.[10] Through factor analysis of eight properties of census tracts in an American city, he has identified two clusters of variables, one of which he designates as "an *anomic* factor." By this he means that this cluster of variables—having the values of a high delinquency rate, a large percentage of non-white residents in the area and a small percentage of dwellings occupied by the owner—seems, on inspection, to characterize areas of relative normlessness and social instability. As Lander is the first to recognize, the anomic factor is at best only roughly measured by this particular cluster of variables. Its decisive limitation derives from a circumstance which regularly confronts sociologists seeking to devise measures of theoretical concepts by drawing upon the array of social data which *happen* to be recorded in the statistical series established by agencies of the society—namely, the circumstance that these data of social bookkeeping which happen to be on hand are not necessarily the data which best measure the concept. That is why I have described Lander's ingenious effort as a 'symptomatic' rather than a decisive advance. For just as the mere availability of official statistics constrained Durkheim to employ such rough, indirect and highly provisional measures of anomie as occupational status, marital status and family disintegration (divorce), so the fortuity that census tract records in Baltimore include data on delinquency, racial composition and house-ownership led Lander to use these as a rough, indirect and highly provisional measure of anomie. Pragmatic considerations of this sort are of course no suitable alternative to theoretically derived indicators of the concept. Turnover in residence may be an indirect measure of the rate of breakdown in established social relationships, but it is evident that the measure would be substantially improved if provision were made to obtain data directly on rates of disrupted social relationships. And so with the other objective components of anomie, conceived as both normative and relational

---

9. The specific wording of these items is reported in Alan H. Roberts and Milton Rokeach, "Anomie, authoritarianism, and prejudice: a replication," *American Journal of Sociology*, 1956, 61, 355-358, at note 14. In a published comment on this paper, Srole questions that his study has in fact been replicated; *Ibid.*, 1956, 62, 63-67.

10. *Towards an Understanding of Juvenile Delinquency* (New York: Columbia University Press, 1954), esp. Chapters V-VI. See also the instructive review-article based on this book by Ernest Greenwood, "New directions in delinquency research," *The Social Service Review*, 1956, 30, 147-157.

breakdown. This is no mere counsel of unattainable perfection. It merely states, what is abundantly evident, that just as scales of the subjective aspects of anomie must be further improved, so must scales of its objective aspects. The utilization of available social-bookkeeping data is only a pragmatically enforced and interim substitute.

Growing out of the conception of both subjective and objective components of anomie is the further evident requirement that research on the sources and consequences of anomie deal *simultaneously* with the interaction of the two types of components. Concretely and illustratively, this means that the behavior of 'anomic' and 'eunomic' *individuals* within groups having a designated degree of objective anomie could be systematically compared, just as the behavior of individuals of the same type could be examined in groups with varying degrees of anomie. This kind of research plainly constitutes the next step forward in the study of anomie.[11]

Recent theoretical and procedural contributions have thus somewhat clarified the concept of anomie and have begun to fashion the tools needed for its systematic study. Other substantive contributions have lately appeared which have direct bearing on one or another part of the structural and functional analysis of anomie set forth in the preceding paper.

THE SUCCESS-THEME IN AMERICAN CULTURE

It will be remembered that we have considered the emphasis on monetary success as *one* dominant theme in American culture, and have traced the strains which it differentially imposes upon those variously located in the social structure. This was not to say, of course,— as was repeatedly indicated— that the disjunction between cultural goals and institutionally legitimate means derives only from *this* extreme goal-emphasis. The theory holds that *any* extreme emphasis upon achievement —whether this be scientific productivity, accumulation of personal wealth or, by a small stretch of the imagination, the conquests of a Don Juan— will attenuate conformity to the institutional norms governing behavior designed to achieve the particular form of 'success,' especially among those who are socially disadvantaged in the competitive race. It is the conflict between cultural goals and the availability of using institutional means—whatever the character of the goals—which produces a strain toward anomie.[12]

---

11. For the general logic of this kind of analysis, see the section on "statistical indices of social structure," 260-262 of this volume, and Paul F. Lazarsfeld and Morris Rosenberg, *The Language of Social Research* (Glencoe: The Free Press, 1955).

12. W. J. H. Sprott has expressed this with enviable clarity in the Josiah Mason lectures delivered at the University of Birmingham. *Science and Social Action* (London: Watts & Co., 1954), 113.

The goal of monetary success was selected for illustrative analysis on the assumption that it, in particular, has been firmly entrenched in American culture. An array of studies in history and historical sociology has recently lent further support to that widely-held assumption. In his detailed monograph on the American gospel of economic success through self-help—the achievement motif—Irvin Gordon Wyllie has shown that, although 'success' has of course been diversely defined in American culture (and variously among the several social strata), no other definition "enjoys such universal favor in America as that which equates success with making money."[13]

This heavy accent on financial success is of course not peculiar to Americans. Max Weber's analytical and long-standing observation is still much in point: "The impulse to acquisition, pursuit of gain, of money, of the greatest possible amount of money, has in itself nothing to do with capitalism [and, in the present instance, with the specifically American culture]. This impulse exists and has existed among waiters, physicians, coachmen, artists, prostitutes, dishonest officials, soldiers, nobles, crusaders, gamblers and beggars. One may say that it has been common to all sorts and conditions of men at all times and in all countries of the earth, wherever the objective possibility of it is or has been given."[14]

But what makes American culture relatively distinctive in this regard and what was taken as central to the analysis of this case in the foregoing chapter is that this is "a society which places a high premium on economic affluence and social ascent for *all* its members." As a success-primer of the late nineteenth century admirably pictured this cultural belief: "The road to fortune, like the public turnpike, is open alike to the children of the beggar, and the descendant of kings. There are tolls to be paid by all, yet all have rights, and it only remains for us to avail ourselves of these."[15] The distinctive nature of this cultural doctrine is twofold: first, striving for success is not a matter of individuals *happening* to have acquisitive impulses, rooted in human nature, but is a socially-defined expectation, and second, this patterned expectation is regarded as appropriate for everyone, irrespective of his initial lot or station in life. Not, of course, that identical standards of achievement are concretely exacted of everyone in the society; the nature and extent of this movement up the economic ladder can become differently defined among the several social strata. But the prevailing cultural orientations assign great emphasis to this form of success and hold it appropriate that all should strive for it. (As we shall soon see, this is far removed

13. Irvin Gordon Wyllie, *The Self-Made Man in America* (New Brunswick: Rutgers University Press, 1954), 3-4 and throughout the book.

14. Max Weber, *The Protestant Ethic and the Spirit of Capitalism* (New York: Charles Scribner's Sons, 1930), 17.

15. A. C. McCurdy, *Win Who Will* (Philadelphia, 1872), 19, as cited by Wyllie, *op. cit.*, 22.

from the empirical proposition that the same proportions of people in all social classes in fact accept this cultural emphasis and assimilate it into their personal value-structure.) It is only that in pulpit and in press, in fiction and in motion pictures, in the course of formal education and of informal socialization, in the various public and private communications which come to the attention of Americans, there is a comparatively marked emphasis on the moral obligation as well as the factual possibility of striving for monetary success, and of achieving it.

As Wyllie shows, inspirational lectures in lyceums, mercantile library associations and business colleges and a large library of success-manuals insistently propagated this theme. (123 ff.) This is further documented by what amounts to a series of content-analyses of widely-read novels, of endlessly reprinted primers used in grammar schools throughout the land, and of the values reaffirmed in the obituaries of some of America's most famous men of business. Kenneth S. Lynn traces the pervasive theme of rags-to-riches in the novels of Theodore Dreiser, Jack London, David Graham Phillips, Frank Norris and Robert Herrick. The enduring presence of the same theme in the seemingly inexhaustible series of McGuffey readers is demonstrated by Richard D. Mosier.[16] And in *The Reputation of the American Businessman*,[17] Sigmund Diamond analyzes a large array of obituaries, those depositories of moral sentiment, published after the death of Stephen Girard, John Jacob Astor, Cornelius Vanderbilt, J. P. Morgan, John D. Rockefeller, and Henry Ford and detects the theme that as long as a man "has the requisite qualities, success will be his at any time, in any place, under any circumstances."

This cultural theme not only holds that monetary success is possible for all, irrespective of station, and that striving for success is incumbent on all, but, on occasion, that the seeming disadvantages of poverty are actually advantages for, in the words of Henry Ward Beecher, it is " 'the hard but kind bosom of Poverty, who says to them, 'Work!' and, working, makes them men.' "[18]

This leads naturally to the subsidiary theme that success or failure are results wholly of personal qualities; that he who fails has only himself to blame, for the corollary to the concept of the self-made man is the self-unmade man. To the extent that this cultural definition is assimilated by those who have not made their mark, failure represents a double defeat: the manifest defeat of remaining far behind in the race for success and the implicit defeat of not having the capacities and moral stamina needed for success. Whatever the objective truth or falsity of the doctrine in any particular instance, and it is important that this can-

---

16. Kenneth S. Lynn, *The Dream of Success* (Boston: Little Brown, 1955); Richard D. Mosier, *Making the American Mind* (New York: King's Crown Press, 1947). See also Marshall W. Fishwick, *American Heroes: Myth and Reality* (Washington, D.C.: Public Affairs Press, 1954).
17. Cambridge: Harvard University Press, 1955.
18. Quoted by Wyllie, 22-23.

not be readily discovered, the prevailing definition exacts a psychic toll of those who do not measure up. It is in this cultural setting that, in a significant proportion of cases, the threat of defeat motivates men to the use of those tactics, beyond the law or the mores, which promise 'success.'

The moral mandate to achieve success thus exerts pressure to succeed, by fair means if possible and by foul means if necessary. The moral norms of course continue to reiterate the rules of the game and to call for 'fair play,' even while behavior departs from the norm. On occasion, however, even success-manuals urge men "to 'go in and win' by making use of all available means of scrambling ahead of competitors," as in the understandably anonymous tract of 1878, *How to Become Rich*. And, "in the period between 1880 and 1914, Populists, single-taxers, muckrakers, and Socialists looked behind the moral façade of business to examine the practice. What they found scarcely squared with the wealth-through-virtue theme. Their findings were not entirely new, for skeptics had long suspected that something other than virtue might be involved in the making of money. What was new was the documentation—concrete evidence that the greatest barons were robber barons, men who made their way by corrupting legislatures, appropriating resources, organizing monopolies, and crushing competitors."[19]

These recent studies thus confirm what has often been noticed before: that an extreme cultural emphasis on the goal of success attenuates conformity to institutionally prescribed methods of moving toward this goal. "Ambition" comes to approximate the meaning of its etymological origins: "to run around" and not only in the form practiced by the little politicians of ancient Rome who solicited votes from one and all in their 'precincts' and used all manner of devices to ensure a plenty of appropriate votes. It is in this way that the culturally established goal moves toward sanctifying all those means which enable one to attain it. This is what was meant in the foregoing essay by the process of 'de-moralization,' in which norms are robbed of their power to regulate behavior, and the 'normlessness' component of anomie ensues.

This process making for anomie need not, however, continue unimpeded. Under conditions still to be identified, countervailing tendencies may develop. To some degree, to judge from the historical record, this may have occurred in American society. The cultural emphasis on success-open-to-all has become qualified, partly, it may be, in response to cumulative recognition of the actual structure of opportunity and partly in response to the occasionally observed demoralizing consequences of the unqualified theme. This is to say that, although the original theme persists, it is occasionally hedged in by qualifications advising some to lower their aspirations. That popular missionary of the gospel of success, Orison Swett Marden, advises his readers: "The fact

---

19. Wyllie, 84-85, 146.

is that most of us can never hope to be rich.'" A handbook of success, published at the turn of the century, offers a philosophy of consolation which re-defines success: "It is just as much to be a common soldier in the ranks as to be a general that leads. We cannot all be generals. If you are a good soldier in a select crowd, and have a good reputation, that is success in itself." Even such a journal as the *American Banker* finds it possible to assert that "only a few of us that share the common lot are destined to accumulate great wealth, or achieve conspicuous stations. The number of such stations and the chances for such accumulations never did correspond, and never will, to the number of energetic, ambitious and capable men which is hopeful of achieving them. This unpalatable truth the literature of success abhors."[20]

But though these doctrines, accommodating to the visible facts of the case, find periodic expression and provide a rationale for slow and limited ascent in the economic hierarchy, Wyllie and other recent students of the subject indicate that they are still only secondary emphases in the culture of the time. To a considerable extent, the success-theme still dominates in the public communications of American culture.

But if the communications addressed to generations of Americans continue to reiterate the gospel of success, it does not follow that Americans in all groups, regions and class strata have uniformly assimilated this set of values. There is no swift and unbroken passage from the values expressed in the popular culture to the values by which men actually live. It would be equally mistaken, however, to assume that the two are wholly unrelated simply because they are not identical. It is a matter for inquiry, not a matter of supposition, to find out how widely the values under examination have been assimilated. That is why, in the introduction to Part II of this book, it was said that "among the problems calling for further research [is] the following: the extent to which Americans in different social strata have in fact assimilated the *same* culturally induced goals and values. . . ." (123) This problem can be further clarified by examining research which has been focused on it.

DIFFERENTIALS IN ASSIMILATION
OF SUCCESS-VALUES

In a recent paper, Herbert H. Hyman has addressed himself to the problem by collating and re-analyzing data available in public opinion surveys which bear directly or tangentially on the distribution of success-values among economic and social strata.[21] As he first puts the

---

20. For these and comparable observations, see Wyllie, 144 ff.

21. Herbert H. Hyman, "The value systems of different classes," in Bendix and Lipset, editors, *Class, Status and Power*, 426-442. Apposite evidence on the aspirations and achievements of religious and racial minorities is also presented by Gerhart Saenger and Norma S. Gordon, "The influence of discrimination on minority group members in its relation to attempts to combat discrimination," *Journal of Social Psychology*, 1950, 31, 95-120, esp. 113 ff.

general issue, "It is clear that Merton's analysis assumes that the cultural goal is in actuality internalized by lower class individuals." (427) In view of the data which are subsequently presented, it becomes essential to state this assumption more clearly by qualifying it: the analysis assumes that *some* individuals in the lower economic and social strata actually adopt the success-goal. For, after all, the analysis holds not that *all* or *most* members of the lower strata are subject to pressure toward nonconformist behavior of the various kinds set out in the typology of adaptation, but only that *more* of them are subject to this pressure than of those in the higher strata. On the hypothesis under review, deviant behavior is still the subsidiary pattern and conformity the modal pattern. It is therefore sufficient that a *sizable minority* of the lower strata assimilate this goal for them to be differentially subject to this pressure as a result of their relatively smaller opportunities to achieve monetary success.

Hyman further prefaces his paper by observing that "what is obviously required is empirical evidence on *the degree to which individuals in different strata* value the culturally prescribed goal of success, believe that opportunity is available to them, and hold other values which would aid or hinder them in their attempts to move towards their goal. This paper, in a preliminary way, is thus complementary to Merton's theoretical analysis."[22] Here again, if the data in hand are to be appropriately connected with the hypothesis, the statement must be qualified. It is true that the analysis calls for empirical evidence on "the degree to which individuals in different strata" set store by the success-goal; patently, the success-value will provide little by way of motivation unless they are significantly committed to it. As it happens, the survey data available to Hyman do not discriminate between the *degrees* of commitment to the goal but indicate only the relative *frequency* with which individuals in the samples drawn from the several social strata express some unknown degree of acceptance of the success-goal and of related values. From the outset, then, it appears that subsequent inquiry might be usefully directed toward studying the intensity as well as the extent to which these values are held in diverse groups, social strata, and communities.

---

22. *Ibid.*, 427-8 [italics inserted]. Empirical inquiries into the comparative frequency of the success-motif in different social groups have been begun. For one such study, see R. W. Mack, R. J. Murphy and S. Yellin, "The Protestant ethic, level of aspiration, and social mobility: an empirical test," *American Sociological Review*, 1956, 21, 295-300. This study intimates, although it was not directed to demonstrate, that the American ethos of success may be pervasive enough to override differences in cultural emphasis found among Protestants and Catholics in the United States.

Another study finds that "the Horatio Alger myth is a middle class myth which percolates down to some, but not all, members of the common man class." Joseph A. Kahl, "Educational and occupational aspirations of 'common man' boys," *Harvard Educational Review*, 1953, 23, 186-203.

We should take note, then, that the hypothesis of the foregoing chapter requires that an appreciable minority, not all or most, of those in the lower social strata will have assimilated the cultural mandate for monetary success, and that it presupposes affectively significant assimilation of this value rather than merely verbal acquiescence with it. These two qualifications provide a context for locating the theoretical implications of the empirical evidence brought together in Hyman's germane and compact paper.

By and large, the array of evidence, which is not reviewed here in full detail since it is readily accessible, uniformly shows *differentials* in the *proportions* of both adults and youth in the lower, middle and upper social strata who are positively oriented toward occupational success and toward established means for aiding the achievement of such success. For example: one national survey of opinion in the late nineteen-thirties found class differentials in the belief in occupational opportunity as registered by responses to the question: "Do you think that today any young man with thrift, ability and ambition has the opportunity to rise in the world, own his own home, and earn $5000 a year?" Among "the prosperous," 53% affirmed the belief that this was so, compared with what Hyman describes as "only" 31% among "the poor."[23] Another national survey found 63% of professional and executive employees expressing their belief that the years ahead held a good chance for advancing beyond their present position, in comparison with 48% of factory workers; furthermore, 58% of the first aggregate of more highly placed employees maintained that harder work would net them a promotion, while 40% of the second aggregate of manual workers held this optimistic view.

To these data, cited by Hyman, can be added others, drawn from a sociological study of white and Negro residents in a low-rent housing development.[24] These 500 residents, at different levels within the lower reaches of the occupational hierarchy, set out their appraisals of opportunity for advancement, in their occupation at large, and in their own workplace in particular.[25] Three significant patterns of appraisal emerge.

---

23. *Ibid.*, 437. Belief in the realistic prospects of opportunity for occupational advancement seems to be fairly widespread among workers, at least as recently as the late forties. For example, Roper reports that among a sample of workers, 70 per cent said that their chances of getting ahead were better than those their fathers had had and 62 per cent said that the chances for their sons would be even better than their own. This *relative* appraisal of occupational opportunity involving comparisons between consecutive generations may be more pertinent, in terms of an image of opportunity, than *absolute* appraisals for one's own generation. See Elmo Roper, "A self portrait of the American people—1947," *Fortune*, 1947, 35, 5-16.

24. R. K. Merton, P. S. West and M. Jahoda, *Patterns of Social Life*, Chapter 3, unpublished.

25. The questions eliciting the appraisals were these: "What are the chances for a person in your occupation to get ahead if he really sets his mind to it?" "How about the place where you work now—what are the chances for getting ahead there?"

First, there is a pattern of mounting optimism about the chances for "getting ahead" in the occupation at large at each successively higher level in this modest hierarchy of jobs. It is as though the sheer existence of others in occupational strata lower than one's own supports the conviction that ascent up the ladder is possible, for one *is*, after all, in a relatively higher stratum. Among Negroes in white-collar or skilled jobs, 63% believe that the chances for advancement in their occupation are good or fair, compared with 44% of those in semi-skilled jobs and 31% in unskilled or domestic service jobs. Though not as pronounced, the same pattern obtains among whites.

Second, much the same pattern, though with a significantly narrower range of variation, occurs in the estimates of chances prevailing in *their own* place of employment. The higher the job-level, the larger the proportion believing that chances for advancement in their place of work are good or fair. Among the Negroes, the percentages recording their optimism are respectively 43, 32 and 27; among the whites, 58, 47 and 44.

The third pattern in the appraisal of opportunity, however, definitely distinguishes the outlook of Negro and white workers as aggregates. White workers tend to see little difference between prospects in the occupation at large and in their own workplace: what they take to hold true in general they assume to hold true in their immediate surroundings. Among the Negro workers, particularly among those in the somewhat higher-status jobs, all this changes. However they estimate the opportunities in their occupation in general, they tend to be decidedly more pessimistic in appraising the opportunities where they themselves work. What these statistics of occupational expectation appear to show is the frequent conviction among Negro workers on each occupational level that they are barred from equitable access to advancement.

To this evidence on class and racial differentials in the belief in occupational opportunities can be added evidence, cited by Hyman, on class differentials in the value placed upon formal education as a means for enlarging the prospect of occupational success. For example: substantially larger proportions of the higher than of the lower social strata express the belief that "some college training" is required "to get along well in the world"; again, 91% of the "prosperous" individuals interviewed in one national survey, compared with 68% of the "poor" individuals expressed a preference that their children go on to college rather than take a job immediately after having been graduated from high school; further, 74% of a sample of teen-age boys from "wealthy and prosperous" families compared with 42% of those from "the lower class" preferred college education to a job as the sequel to graduation from high school; and finally, in this selection from the numerous data summarized by Hyman, 14% of high school youths from "poor" families stated a preference for a job that provided high income but great risk as compared with 31% of those from families of business executives or professional people.[26]

The available though still scanty evidence, then, consistently exhibits *differentials in the proportions* of the several social strata (and perhaps, of Negroes and whites) affirming the culturally patterned belief in opportunities for occupational success, aspiring to high-paying though risk-laden jobs and placing value upon higher education as a means for occupational advancement. But what Hyman fails to note, in his otherwise instructive and useful collation of the evidence, is that from the standpoint of the hypothesis advanced in the preceding paper, *it is not the relative proportions of the several social classes adopting the cultural goal of success that matter, but their absolute numbers.* To say that a larger *percentage* of the upper social and economic strata hold fast to the cultural goal of success is not to say that larger *numbers* of them than of lower-class people do so. Indeed, since the number of people in the topmost stratum identified in these studies is substantially smaller than the number in the lowest stratum, it is sometimes the case that *more* lower-class than upper-class people abide by this goal.

By centering almost exclusively[27] on the *comparative proportions* in the several social strata having one or another value-orientation—a matter which of course holds interest in its own right—Hyman fails to consider the facts most directly germane to the hypothesis under review. For, as has been repeatedly said, the hypothesis does not require that larger proportions or even larger numbers in the lower social strata be oriented toward the success-goal, but only that a *substantial number* be so oriented. For it is the *disjunction* between culturally induced high aspirations and socially structured obstacles to realization of these aspirations which is held to exert distinct pressure for deviant behavior. By a 'substantial number,' then, is meant a number sufficiently large to result in a more frequent *disjunction* between goals and opportunity among the lower-class strata than among the more advantaged upper-class strata. It may even be, though adequate empirical data on this are still wanting, that this disjunction is more frequent in the lower strata than in the middle strata, since the evidently larger number of middle-class Americans adopting the success-goal may include a sufficiently smaller

---

26. Hyman, *op. cit.*, 430-434.

27. At one point toward the close of his paper, Hyman clearly notes the distinction between comparative proportions and absolute proportions (and absolute numbers). But he does so in connection with a special problem of reference-group theory and does not draw the implications basic to the hypothesis in hand. His observation is as follows: "While the evidence thus far presented provides consistent and strong evidence that lower class individuals *as a group* have a value system that reduces the likelihood of individual advancement, it is also clear from the data that there is a sizable proportion of the lower group who do not incorporate this value system. [With regard to some items Hyman has reported, this 'sizable proportion' represents a substantial majority.] Similarly, there are individuals in the upper classes who do not show the modal tendency of their group." *Ibid.*, 441.

proportion who are seriously impeded in their efforts to reach out toward this goal.

In any event, the fundamental analytical requirement is to distinguish systematically between the findings on relative proportions and on absolute numbers[28] in the several social classes accepting the cultural goal and to recognize that it is the frequency of disjunction between the goal and socially structured access to it which is of theoretical moment. Further research will have to solve the difficult problem of obtaining systematic data on *both* goals and on patterned access to opportunity and of analyzing these *jointly* to see whether the combination of lofty aspirations and small opportunity occurs with substantially different frequency in various social strata, groups, and communities and whether, in turn, these differentials are related to differing rates of deviant behavior. Schematically, this would call for data on *socially patterned differentials in*

1. *exposure* to the cultural goal and norms regulating behavior oriented toward that goal;

2. *acceptance* of the goal and norms as moral mandates and internalized values;

3. *relative accessibility to the goal:* life-chances in the opportunity-structure;

4. *the extent of discrepancy* between the accepted goal and its accessibility;

5. *the degree of anomie;* and

6. *the rates of deviant behavior* of the various kinds set out in the typology of modes of adaptation.

It is plainly no easy matter to assemble adequate data on all these distinct though related items. Until now, sociologists have had to work with avowedly rough and imperfect measures of almost all these variables—using the extent of formal education, for example, as an indicator of access to opportunity. But it is increasingly the case in sociology that once theoretically strategic variables have been identified, improved measures of them have been devised. There is a growing interplay between theory, which states the case for the significance of certain variables; methodology, which works out the logic of empirical inquiry involving these variables; and technique, which develops the tools and procedures for measuring the variables. As we have seen, definite beginnings have lately been made in developing measures of both the subjective and the objective components of anomie. It may not be too

---

28. It should be noted, at least in passing, that the requirement for making this distinction has wide bearing on the analysis of social life. Important as it is in its own right, the *relative* proportions of those in various social strata and groups exhibiting particular attitudes, talents, wealth or any behavior-pattern should not be allowed to obscure, as they often do in sociological studies, the equally important fact of the *absolute numbers* manifesting these items in different strata and groups. From the standpoint of effects upon the society, it is often the absolute numbers and not the relative proportions that matter. For other instances of this same general consideration, see Chapter X of this book, at n. 16.

much to assume that these measures will continue to be improved, and that suitable measures of the other variables will be developed—in particular, improved measures of the still loosely-utilized but important concept of what Weber called 'life-chances' in the opportunity-structure.

In this way, it will become possible to discover the social topography of anomie. It will become possible to locate the structural places in American society, for example, where the disjunction between the cultural values enjoining people to aim for certain goals and the patterned possibilities of living up to these values is at a maximum. Such inquiry would counter any unthinking tendency to assume that American society is uniformly riddled with anomie. It would search out, on the contrary, the statuses in the structure of American society which entail the greatest difficulty for people to live up to the normative requirements, for this is what is meant by saying that the disjunction between accepted norms and opportunities for socially rewarded conformity to these norms 'exerts pressure' for deviant behavior and produces anomie.

Just as it is in point to identify the sources of differing degrees of anomie in different sectors of society, so it is in point to examine the varying adaptations to anomie and the forces making for one rather than another type of adaptation. A number of recent studies bear on this general problem.

ANOMIE AND FORMS OF DEVIANT BEHAVIOR

Innovation

The first form of deviant behavior identified in the typology set out in the preceding chapter was described as innovation. This, it may be remembered, refers to the rejection of institutional practices but the retention of cultural goals. This would seem to characterize a substantial part of the deviant behavior which has been accorded the greatest share of research attention—namely that which is loosely caught up in the blanket-concepts of 'crime' and 'delinquency.' Since the law provides formal criteria of this form of deviance, it is relatively visible and readily becomes a focus for study. In contrast, other forms of behavior which are sociologically though not legally departures from accepted norms— what we have called 'retreatism,' for example—are less visible and receive little attention.

Several studies have lately indicated that the received concepts of 'crime' and 'delinquency' may serve to obscure rather than to clarify our understanding of the numerous variety of deviant behavior to which they refer. Aubert, for example, observes that "the legal definition of crime . . . probably [represents] little in common between all the phenomena covered by the concept. And the same seems to be true of white-collar crime. This type can also differ very much in its nature, and may need quite different causal explanations."[29]

In the course of assigning a term such as crime or delinquency to a class of behavior, there develops a tendency to attend primarily to the similarities—consequential or not—between the items of behavior encompassed in that class. Sociologically quite distinct forms of behavior by youngsters, for example, come to be designated by the generic term, 'juvenile delinquency.' This often carries with it the assumption that the wide diversity of behavior or the individuals engaging in one or another form of this behavior are of theoretically like kind. Yet, it is questionable that the behavior of the youngster who has purloined some baseball equipment is significantly similar to that of the youngster who periodically assults members of an out-group.

Furthermore, the decision to encompass a wide array of behavior in the one rubric of crime or delinquency tends to lead to the assumption that a single theory will account for the entire range of behavior placed in this category. This is not too remote, in logical structure, from the assumption of a Benjamin Rush or a John Brown that there must be *a* theory of disease, rather than distinct theories of disease—of tuberculosis and arthritis, of Mèniere's syndrome and syphilis. Just as classifying enormously varied conditions and processes under the one heading of disease led some zealous medical systematists to believe that is was their task to evolve a single over-arching theory of disease, so, it seems, the established idiom, both vernacular and scientific, of referring to 'juvenile delinquency' as though it were a single entity, leads some to believe that there must be *a* basic theory of 'its' causation. Perhaps this is enough to suggest what is meant by referring to crime or juvenile delinquency as a blanket-concept which may get in the way of theoretical formulations of the problem.

Once it is recognized that the behavior ordinarily described as criminal or delinquent is, from the sociological standpoint, quite varied and disparate, it becomes evident that the theory under review does not purport to account for all such forms of deviant behavior. In his theoretically sensitive book, Albert K. Cohen suggests that this theory is "highly plausible as an explanation for adult professional crime and for the property delinquency of some older and semi-professional juvenile thieves. Unfortunately," he goes on to say, "it fails to account for

---

29. Vilhelm Aubert, "White-collar crime and social structure," *American Journal of Sociology*, 1952, 58, 263-271, at 270; *cf.* also, R. K. Merton, "The social-cultural environment and anomie," in Helen L. Witmer and Ruth Kotinsky, editors, *New Perspectives for Research on Juvenile Delinquency* (Washington, D. C.: U. S. Department of Health, Education, and Welfare, Children's Bureau, 1956), 24-50, including discussion by members of the conference; Daniel Glaser, "Criminality theories and behavioral images," *American Journal of Sociology* 1956, 61, 433-443, at 434.

the non-utilitarian quality of the subculture. . . . Were the participant in the delinquent subculture merely employing illicit means to the end of acquiring economic goods, he would show more respect for the goods he has thus acquired. Furthermore, the destructiveness, the versatility, the zest and the wholesale negativism which characterizes the delinquent subculture are beyond the purview of this theory."[30]

The first and major point made by Cohen commands assent and deserves reiteration. The foregoing theory of anomie is designed to account for some, not all, forms of deviant behavior customarily described as criminal or delinquent. The second point is important if it turns out to be true and, in any case, has the merit of focusing future inquiry on its implications. This is the point that the theory of social structure and anomie does not account for the "non-utilitarian" character of much of the behavior occurring in the delinquency-groups. But in exploring this matter further, it should be remembered, for purposes of theoretical clarity, that this theory does *not* maintain that the resulting deviant behavior is rationally calculated and utilitarian. Instead, it centers on the *acute* pressures created by the discrepancy between culturally induced goals and socially structured opportunities. The responses to these pressures with the consequent strains upon individuals subject to them may involve a considerable degree of frustration and of non-rational or of irrational behavior.[31] 'Destructiveness' has often been psychologically identified as one form of response to continued frustration. So, too, it would appear that 'wholesale negativism' can be construed, without enlarging the theory to incorporate new *ad hoc* variables, as a sustained repudiation of the authorities which exemplify the contradiction between legitimized cultural aspirations and socially restricted opportunities.

It seems to be the case, however, that the 'versatility' and the 'zest' with which some boys are observed to pursue their group-supported deviations are not directly accounted for by the theory of social structure and anomie. For the sources of these properties of the deviant

---

30. Albert K. Cohen, *Delinquent Boys* (Glencoe: The Free Press, 1955), 36. Since some of the principal theoretical issues are being examined in connection with Cohen's book, the following discussions which bear upon the paradigm of social structure and anomie as a basis for analyzing criminal and delinquent behavior are only cited. Milton L. Barron, "Juvenile delinquency and American values," *American Sociological Review* 1951, 16, 208-214; Solomon Kobrin, "The conflict of values in delinquency areas," *American Sociological Review*, 1951, 16, 653-662; Ralph H. Turner, "Value conflict in social disorganization," *Sociology and Social Research* 1954, 38, 301-308; W. J. H. Sprott, *The Social Background of Delinquency* (University of Nottingham, 1954), as reviewed by John C. Spencer, *The Howard Journal* 1955, 9, 163-165; Hermann Mannheim, "Juvenile delinquency," *British Journal of Sociology* 1956, 7, 147-152; Aubert, *op. cit.*; Glaser, *op. cit.*

31. In his comment on precisely this point, Hermann Mannheim indicates that the theory "may be quite capable of explaining much more than merely the utilitarian form of expressing frustrated aspirations." *Op. cit.*, 149.

behavior, one must presumably look to the social interaction among these likeminded deviants who mutually reinforce their deviant attitudes and behavior which, in the theory, result from the more or less common situation in which they find themselves. It is to this phase of the total process of gang-supported deviant behavior that Cohen primarily applies his instructive analysis. But, as he indicates later in his book (54), before proceeding to analyze the types of 'solutions' to the difficulties which the 'delinquent boys' encounter in their immediate social milieu, one must account for the varying frequencies with which these difficulties turn up. In this part of his analysis, Cohen does, in fact, examine the social and cultural sources of these pressures in much the same terms as those we have been considering. His thoroughly sociological analysis considerably advances our understanding of certain forms of deviant behavior commonly found in delinquency-groups and does so by extending the type of structural and functional theory now under review.

In examining the delinquency subculture, Cohen is of course in a direct line of continuity with the earlier studies by Shaw, McKay, and, particularly, Thrasher.[32] However, he goes on to observe that these studies were principally concerned with the problem of how the delinquency subculture is *transmitted* to youngsters, and that the correlative problem, to which he addresses himself, concerns the *origin* of these cultural patterns. In much the same way, it is possible to distinguish between a theory which deals only with the responses of individuals to culturally-induced stresses, like that advanced by Karen Horney, for example, and a theory which deals also with *the effects of the aggregated and sometimes socially organized responses upon the normative structure itself.*

The social process linking anomie and deviant behavior. To put this problem in its appropriate theoretical context requires us to see the emergence and growth of anomie as a resultant of ongoing social process and not simply as a condition which happens to obtain.[33] Within this context, the process can be provisionally pictured in the following way. Owing to their objectively disadvantaged position in the group as well as to distinctive personality configurations,[34] some individuals are sub-

---

32. Among the many well-known publications by this group of sociologists, see Clifford R. Shaw and Henry D. McKay, *Juvenile Delinquency and Urban Areas* (University of Chicago Press, 1942); Frederic M. Thrasher, *The Gang* (University of Chicago Press, 1936), 2nd edition.

33. See Merton, "The social and cultural environment and *anomie*," *op. cit.*

34. It is consistent with the theory under review to recognize that distinctive family constellations can promote vulnerability to anomic pressures. For example, Franz Alexander writes of his patients drawn "from second-generation Americans, members of immigrant families, and . . . a racial minority group" that the father's role goes far toward imbuing the son with a driving concern with success. As he puts it, "one common outcome is that the son, usurping father's place in mother's

jected more than others to the strains arising from the discrepancy between cultural goals and effective access to their realization. They are consequently more vulnerable to deviant behavior. In some proportion of cases, again dependent upon the control-structure of the group, these departures from institutional norms are socially rewarded by 'successful' achievement of goals. But these deviant ways of achieving the goals occur within social systems. The deviant behavior consequently affects not only the individuals who first engage in it but, in some measure, it also affects other individuals with whom they are inter-related in the system.

A mounting frequency of deviant but 'successful' behavior tends to lessen and, as an extreme potentiality, to eliminate the legitimacy of the institutional norms for others in the system. The process thus enlarges the extent of anomie within the system so that others, who did not respond in the form of deviant behavior to the relatively slight anomie which first obtained, come to do so as anomie spreads and is intensified. This, in turn, creates a more acutely anomic situation for still other and initially less vulnerable individuals in the social system. In this way, anomie and mounting rates of deviant behavior can be conceived as interacting in a process of social and cultural dynamics, with cumulatively disruptive consequences for the normative structure, unless counteracting mechanisms of control are called into play. In each specific case under examination, then, it is essential, as we have said before, to identify the control mechanisms which "minimize the strains

---

affections as well as in many material respects, develops tremendous ambition. He wants to justify all the hopes and sacrifices of the mother and thus appease his guilty conscience toward the father. There is only one way to accomplish this end. He must become successful, whatever the cost. In the hierarchy of values, success becomes supreme, overshadowing everything else, and failure becomes equivalent to sin. . . . Consequently all other vices, such as insincerity in human relationships, unfairness in competition, disloyalty, disregard for everyone else, appear comparatively as nothing; and there emerges the formidable phenomenon of the ruthless careerist, obsessed by the single idea of self-promotion, a caricature of the self-made man, a threat to Western civilization, the principles of which he reduces to an absurdity." Franz Alexander, "Educative influence of personality factors in the environment," re-printed in Clyde Kluckhohn, Henry A. Murray and David M. Schneider, editors, *Personality in Nature, Society, and Culture* (New York: A. A. Knopf, 1953, 2d ed.), 421-435, at 431-433.

This essentially psychological analysis of the formation of unqualified and therefore normatively disruptive success-goals must, however, be connected with a sociological analysis, if it is to do justice to the facts of the case. For even though these strivings for success may develop anew and more or less independently in *each* of the families being described, the deviant behavior occurs in a social system which variously links up these diversely initiated patterns of behavior. In this way, whatever the initial situation for each individual, the deviant behavior of individuals *outside the family* tends to become mutually supporting and disruptive of established norms. Anomie becomes a social phenomenon, well beyond the confines of an aggregate of separate and distinct families. For a related analysis, see Ralph Pieris, "Ideological momentum and social equilibrium," *American Journal of Sociology* 1952, 57, 339-346.

resulting from seeming [or actual] contradictions between cultural goals and socially restricted access" to them. (123)

Further Assumptions of the Theory

A preceding section of this chapter examines evidence bearing upon forms of response to anomie encompassed in the affectively and ethically neutral concept of 'innovation': the use of institutionally proscribed means for attaining a culturally valued goal. Before turning to evidence on other major types of response—ritualism, retreatism, and rebellion— we must emphasize again that the general theory of social structure and anomie is *not* confined to the specific goal of monetary success and of social restrictions upon access to it. The theory has been found applicable, for example, to a case of interdisciplinary research in science, and to cases of mass communications behavior,[35] to a case of deviations from religious orthodoxy,[36] and to a case of conformity with and deviation from social norms in a military prison[37]—cases which, at least, on the face of them, would otherwise seem to have little in common and that little, assuredly not the dominant goal of monetary success. As was said in the initial exposition of the theory, "monetary success was taken as the major cultural goal" only "for purposes of simplifying the problem . . . although there are, of course, alternative goals in the repository of common values." (157) In terms of the general conception, *any* cultural goals which receive extreme and only negligibly qualified emphasis in the culture of a group will serve to attenuate the emphasis on institutionalized practices and make for anomie.

In the same way, it is necessary to reiterate that the typology of deviant behavior is far from being confined to the behavior which is ordinarily described as criminal or delinquent. From the standpoint of sociology, other forms of departure from regulatory norms may have little or nothing to do with violation of the established law of the land. Merely to identify some types of deviation is itself a difficult problem

---

35. Warren G. Bennis, "Some barriers to teamwork in social research," *Social Problems* 1956, 3, 223-235; Matilda White Riley and Samuel H. Flowerman, "Group relations as a variable in communications research," *American Sociological Review* 1951, 16, 174-180; Leonard I. Pearlin, *The Social and Psychological Setting of Communications Behavior* (Columbia University, unpublished doctoral dissertation in sociology, 1957). Pearlin finds strong tendencies toward using television as "escape" among those who are both highly motivated to achieve social mobility and placed in an occupation which does not readily allow this motive to be satisfied. One of the principal conclusions of this empirical study is that "television is well established as one instrument by which people can withdraw from conflicts and stresses which have their etiology in the social system."

36. Celia Stopnicka Rosenthal, "Deviation and social change in the Jewish community of a small Polish town," *American Journal of Sociology* 1954, 60, 177-181.

37. Richard Cloward, *The Culture of a Military Prison: A Case Study of Anomie* (Glencoe: The Free Press, to be published); and Cloward's partial summary of this study in Witmer and Kotinsky, *op. cit.*, 80-91.

of sociological theory which is being progressively clarified. For example, a distinct theoretical advance was effected by Parsons's conception that *illness* is, in one of its principal aspects, "to be defined as a form of deviant behavior, and that the elements of motivation to deviance which are expressed in the sick role are continuous with those expressed in a variety of other channels, including types of compulsive conformity which are not socially defined as deviant."[38]

As another example, the behavior describable as "over-conformity" or "over-compliance" with institutional norms has been sociologically analyzed as deviant even though it too may at first glance appear to represent overt conformity.[39] As the *typology* of responses to anomie is intended to make clear, these are distinct kinds of behavior which, in contrast to their manifest appearance of conformity to institutionalized expectations, can be shown upon further sociological analysis to represent departures from these expectations.

Finally, by way of preamble to this review of other types of deviant behavior, it should be noted once again that, from the standpoint of sociology, not all such deviation from the dominant norms of the group is necessarily dysfunctional to the basic values and adaptation of the group. Correlatively, strict and unquestioned adherence to all prevailing norms would be functional only in a group that never was: a group which is completely static and unchanging in a social and cultural environment which is static and unchanging. Some (unknown) degree of deviation from current norms is probably functional for the basic goals of all groups. A certain degree of 'innovation,' for example, may result in the formation of new institutionalized patterns of behavior which are more adaptive than the old in making for realization of primary goals.

It would be a shortsighted view and a concealed ethical judgment, moreover, to assume that even the deviant behavior which is dysfunctional to the current values of the group is also ethically deficient. For, as we have had frequent occasion to note in this book, the concept of social dysfunction is not a latter-day terminological substitute for 'immorality' or 'unethical practice.' A particular pattern of behavior which departs from the dominant norms of the group may be dysfunctional in lessening the stability of the group or in reducing its prospect of achieving the goals it values. But, judged by one or another set of ethical standards, it may be the norms of the group which are at fault, not the innovator who rejects them. This has been put with characteristic insight and eloquence by one of the truly great men of our time:

> In the primitive tribe every class has its appointed *Moira* or portion, its *Ergon* or function, and things go right if each class and each individual fulfills his *Moira* and performs his *Ergon*, and does not transgress or trespass on

---

38. Parsons, *The Social System*, 476-477, and the whole of Chapter X.

39. See the further discussion of this in the following section devoted to the retreatist pattern of response to anomie.

those of others. In modern language each has his social service to perform and his consequent rights. It is the old *Themis* [law or justice personified, the things which 'are done']; but a *Themis* vastly extended by the imagination and made more positive. A *Themis* in which you may be called upon not merely to die for your country—the oldest tribal laws involved that—but to die for the truth, or, as he explains in a wonderful passage in the second book, to defy the whole conventional law of your society for the sake of the true law which it has forsaken or forgotten. No one who has read it can easily forget the account of the righteous man in the evil or mistaken society, how he is to be scourged and blinded and at last impaled or crucified by the society that misunderstands him, because he is righteous and seems the reverse, and how after all it is better for him so to suffer than to follow the multitude in doing wrong.[40]

All this would require no repetition were it not for the occasional and, it seems, increasingly frequent, assumption that deviant behavior is necessarily equivalent to social dysfunction, and social dysfunction, in turn, to violation of an ethical code. In the history of every society, presumably, some of its culture heroes have been regarded as heroic precisely because they have had the courage and the vision to depart from norms then obtaining in the group. As we all know, the rebel, revolutionary, nonconformist, individualist, heretic or renegade of an earlier time is often the culture hero of today.

It should also be said again, since it is so easily forgotten, that to center this theory upon the cultural and structural sources of deviant behavior is *not* to imply that such behavior is the characteristic, let alone the exclusive, response to the pressures we have been examining. This is an analysis of varying *rates and types* of deviant behavior, not an empirical generalization to the effect that *all* those subject to these pressures respond by deviation. The theory only holds that those located in places in the social structure which are particularly exposed to such stresses are more likely than others to exhibit deviant behavior. Yet, as a result of countervailing social mechanisms, most even of these stressful positions do not *typically* induce deviation; conformity tends to remain the modal response. Among the countervailing mechanisms, as has been suggested in the preceding chapter, is access to "alternative goals in the repository of common values. . . . To the extent that the cultural structure attaches prestige to these alternatives and the social structure permits access to them, the system is somewhat stabilized. Potential deviants may still conform in terms of these auxiliary sets of values." (157) Inquiry has been begun into the workings of such alternatives as curbs upon deviant behavior.[40a]

---

40. Gilbert Murray, *Greek Studies* (Oxford: Clarendon Press, 1946), 75. The allusion is to the second book of Plato's *Republic;* it is a nice question of judgment whether the original formulation by Plato does justice to the paraphrase by Gilbert Murray.

40a. See the forthcoming paper by Ruth B. Granick, "Biographies of popular Negro 'heroes.'" Following the procedures established by Leo Lowenthal in his study

In quick summary, then, it should be evident that (1) the theory under review deals with culturally emphasized goals of diverse kinds and not only with the goal of monetary success which was examined for the purpose of illustration; (2) that it distinguishes forms of deviant behavior which may be far removed from those which represent violations of the law; (3) that the deviant behavior is not *necessarily* dysfunctional to the effective operation and development of the group; (4) that the concepts of social deviation and social dysfunction do not harbor concealed ethical premises; and (5) that alternative cultural goals provide a basis for stabilizing the social and cultural systems.

Ritualism

As located in the typology, ritualism refers to a pattern of response in which culturally defined aspirations are abandoned while "one continues to abide almost compulsively by institutional norms." As was said when this concept was introduced, "it is something of a terminological quibble to ask whether this represents 'genuinely deviant behavior.' Since the adaptation is, in effect, an internal decision and since the overt behavior is institutionally permitted, though not culturally preferred, it is not generally considered to represent a 'social problem.' Intimates of individuals making this adaptation may pass judgment in terms of prevailing cultural emphases and may 'feel sorry for them'; they may, in the individual case, feel that 'old Jonesy is certainly in a rut.' Whether this is described as deviant behavior or no, it clearly represents a departure from the cultural model in which men are obliged to strive actively, preferably through institutionalized procedures, to move onward and upward in the social hierarchy." (150)

In this way, it was suggested, the acute status-anxiety in a society which emphasizes the achievement-motif may induce the deviant be-

---

of popular biographies, Granick has analyzed the social composition of "Negro heroes" in two popular magazines designed primarily for Negro readers, within the context supplied by the theory of deviant behavior here under review. She finds different routes to success in the world of entertainment for Negroes and whites, although the apparently valued statuses seem much the same for these two subgroups. What is more in point is her provisional finding that access to alternative goals of success provides ample room for conformist, rather than deviant, behavior. The well-known study by Lowenthal is his "Biographies in popular magazines," in P. F. Lazarsfeld and F. N. Stanton (editors), *Radio Research, 1942-1943* (New York: Duell, Sloan and Pearce, 1944).

It has been pointed out also that patterns of consumption behavior—for example, the trickling-down of styles and fashion in the stratification system—serve the latent function of making the system gratifying even for those who do not rise appreciably within it. See Bernard Barber and Lyle S. Lobel, " 'Fashion' in women's clothes and the American social system," *Social Forces*, 1952, 31, 124-131 and a correlative paper by Lloyd A. Fallers, "A note on the 'trickle effect,' " *Public Opinion Quarterly*, 1954, 18, 314-321.

For pertinent observations on differential symbols of accomplishment which serve to mitigate a sense of personal failure, see Margaret M. Wood, *Paths of Loneliness* (New York: Columbia University Press, 1953), 212 ff.

havior of 'over-conformity' and 'over-compliance.' For example, such over-compliance may be found among 'bureaucratic virtuosos,' some of whom may "over-conform precisely because they are subject to guilt engendered by previous nonconformity with the rules."[41] There is still little by way of systematic evidence on this particular hypothesis, apart from a psychoanalytic study of twenty "bureaucrats" which did find that they tended to be "compulsive neurotics."[42] Even this scanty evidence, however, does not bear directly on the present theory which has to do, not with types of *personality,* important as this is for other purposes, but with types of *role-performance* in response to socially structured situations.

Of more direct relevance is the study of the behavior of bureaucrats by Peter M. Blau.[43] He suggests that observed cases of overconformity are "not due to the fact that ritualistic adherence to existing operating procedure had become an inescapable habit" and that "ritualism results not so much from overidentification with rules and strong habituation to established practices as from lack of security in important social relationships in the organization." It is, in short, when the structure of the situation does not allay the status-anxiety and anxiety over the capacity to measure up to institutionalized expectations that individuals in these organizations respond with over-compliance.

The situations patterned by the social structure which invite the ritualist response of overconformity to normative expectations have been experimentally and, of course, only homologously reproduced among sheep and goats. (The reader will surely resist the temptation of concluding that no more symbolically appropriate animals could possibly have been selected for the purpose.) The situation inviting ritualism, it will be recalled, involves either the repeated frustration of strongly-held goals or the continued experience of finding that reward is not proportioned to conformity. The psychobiologist, Howard S. Liddell, has in effect reproduced both these conditions in his series of experiments.[44] As one among many examples,

A goat . . . is brought to the laboratory every day and subjected to a simple test: every two minutes a telegraph sounder clicks once a second for ten seconds followed by a shock to the foreleg. After twenty signal-shock combinations the goat returns to the pasture. It soon acquires a satisfactory

41. Page 152, see also the discussion of "structural sources of overconformity" in Chapter VI and of the "renegade" and "convert" in Chapters VIII and IX of this book; and the observation by Parsons and Bales that "the first important insight in this connection [of relating their independently developed theories] was that 'over-conformity' should be defined as deviance." Parsons *et al., Working Papers,* 75.

42. Otto Sperling, "Psychoanalytic aspects of bureaucracy," *Psychoanalytic Quarterly,* 1950, 19, 88-100.

43. P. M. Blau, *The Dynamics of Bureaucracy,* Chapter XII, esp. 184-193.

44. Conveniently summarized in Howard S. Liddell, "Adaptation on the threshold of intelligence," *Adaptation,* edited by John Romano, (Ithaca: Cornell University Press, 1949), 55-75.

level of motor skill and seemingly adapts well to this assembly-line procedure. Within six or seven weeks, however, the observer notes that a change in the animal's deportment has insidiously developed. It comes willingly to the laboratory but, upon entering, it exhibits a certain mannered deliberation and its conditioned responses are exceedingly precise. It seems to be trying 'to do just the right thing.' Some years ago our group began calling such animals 'perfectionists.' . . . We discovered that in Pavlov's laboratory the expression 'formal behavior' was used to characterize such conduct in the dog.

This does seem to bear more than a passing resemblance to what we have described as "the syndrome of the social ritualist" who "responds to a situation which appears threatening and excites distrust" by "clinging all the more closely to the safe routines and the institutional norms."[45] And indeed, Liddell goes on to report that "what we may infer to be similar behavior in man under threatening circumstances is to be found in Mira's portrayal of the six stages of human fear [the first of which is described as follows]:

Prudence and Self Restraint: Observed from without, the subject appears modest, prudent, and unpretending. By means of voluntary self-restraint he limits his aims and ambitions, and renounces all those pleasures which entail risk or exposure. The individual in this stage is already under the inhibitory influence of fear. He reacts with a prophylactic avoidance of the approaching situation. *Introspectively*, the subject is not yet conscious of being afraid. On the contrary, he is rather self-satisfied and proud because he considers himself endowed with greater foresight than other human beings.[46]

This characterological portrait of the compulsive conformist who thanks God that he is not as other men limns the essential elements of a kind of ritualist response to threatening situations. It is the office of sociological theory to identify the structural and cultural processes which produce high rates of such conditions of threat in certain sectors of the society and negligible rates in others, and it is that type of problem to which the theory of social structure and anomie addresses itself. In this way, there develops a consolidation of 'psychological' and 'sociological' interpretations of observed patterns of behavior, such as that exemplified by ritualism.

Further apposite data and ideas, focused on personality rather than on role-performance in designated types of situations, are found in the studies centered on "intolerance of ambiguity."[47] What these studies lack by way of systematic incorporation of variables and dynamics of social structure is largely compensated by their detailed characterization of the components which presumably enter into ritualist responses to pat-

---

45. Chapter IV of this book, at 150-151.
46. Emilio Mira y López, *Psychiatry in War* (New York: Academy of Medicine, 1943), as quoted by Liddell, *op. cit.*, 70.
47. Else Frenkel-Brunswik, "Intolerance of ambiguity as an emotional and perceptual personality variable," *Journal of Personality*, 1949, 18, 108-143; also T. W. Adorno et al., *The Authoritarian Personality* (New York: Harper & Brothers, 1950); Richard Christie and Marie Jahoda, editors, *Studies in the Scope and Method of 'The Authoritarian Personality'* (Glencoe: The Free Press, 1954).

terned situations and not only into the structure of the rigid personality. As set forth in a recent rapid inventory, the components of intolerance of ambiguity include: "undue preference for symmetry, familiarity, definiteness, and regularity; tendency toward black-white solutions, over-simplified dichotomizing, unqualified either-or solutions, premature closure, perseveration and stereotypy; a tendency toward excessively 'good' form (that is, excessive *Prägnanz* of *Gestalt* organization), achieved either by diffuse globality or by over-emphasis on concrete detail; compartmentalization, stimulus-boundness; avoidance of uncertainty as accomplished by the narrowing of meanings, by inaccessibility to experience, by mechanical repetition of sets, or by a segmentary randomness and an absolutizing of those aspects of reality which have been preserved."[48]

The substantive significance of each of these components cannot be apparent from this compact listing; the details are set forth in numerous publications. But what is evident, even from the list, is that the concept of intolerance of ambiguity refers to 'an excess' of designated kinds of perception, attitudes and behavior (as indicated by such terms as "undue preference," "over-simplified," "unqualified," "over-emphasis," and the like). The norms in terms of which these are judged to be 'excessive,' however, need not be confined to the statistical norms observed in an aggregate of personalities under observation or to norms of 'functional appropriateness' established by considering individuals *seriatim* in abstraction from their social environments. The norms can also be derived from the standardized normative expectations which obtain in various groups so that behavior which, by the first set of standards, may be regarded as 'psychological over-rigidity' can, on occasion, be regarded by the second set of standards, as adaptive social conformity. This is only to say that although there is probably a linkage between the concept of overly-rigid personalities and the concept of socially induced ritualistic behavior, the two are far from being identical.

Retreatism

The retreatist pattern consists of the substantial abandoning both of the once-esteemed cultural goals and of institutionalized practices directed toward those goals. Approximations to this pattern have recently been identified among what has been described as "problem families"—roughly, those families who do not measure up to the normative expectations prevailing in their social environment.[49] Further evidence of

48. Else Frenkel-Brunswik, in Christie and Jahoda, *op. cit.*, 247.

49. W. Baldamus and Noel Timms, "The problem family: a sociological approach," *British Journal of Sociology*, 1955, 6, 318-327. The authors conclude by saying that "although individual traits of personality structure appeared to have a more powerful effect . . . than was expected, the evidence of deviant beliefs and orientations as a separate determinant is still sufficient to warrant a more elaborate inquiry into the nature and the importance of this factor. Thus it appeared that,

this mode of response is found among workers who develop a state of psychic passivity in response to some discernible extent of anomie.[50]

Generally, however, retreatism seems to occur in response to acute anomie, involving an abrupt break in the familiar and accepted normative framework and in established social relations, particularly when it appears to individuals subjected to it that the condition will continue indefinitely. As Durkheim noted with characteristic insight,[51] such disruptions may be found in the 'anomie of prosperity,' when Fortune smiles and many experience radical upward shifts from their accustomed status, and not only in the 'anomie of depression,' when Fortune frowns and apparently exits for good. Much the same anomic condition often obtains in those patterned situations which 'exempt' individuals from a wide array of role-obligations, as, for example, in the case of 'retirement' from the job being imposed upon people without their consent and in the case of widowhood.[52]

In a study of the widowed and those retired from their job, Zena S. Blau examines in detail the circumstances making for retreatism, as one

---

with certain qualifications, the more extreme cases of disorganization and inefficiency in problem families approach a situation of retreatism . . .: conformity to established values is virtually relinquished especially in respect of standards of behaviour." From all indications, retreatism seems to be marked among those in the lower-lower social stratum, as this has been described by W. Lloyd Warner and Paul S. Lunt, *The Social Life of a Modern Community* (New Haven: Yale University Press, 1941).

50. Ely Chinoy, *Automobile Workers and the American Dream* (New York: Doubleday & Company, 1955); and see on this point, the review of the book by Paul Meadows, *American Sociological Review*, 1955, 20, 624.

As we noted in first presenting the types of adaptation, these refer "to role behavior . . . not to personality." It does not follow, of course, that the adaptations remain fixed throughout the life-cycle of individuals; on the contrary, there is room for systematic inquiry into patterns of *role-sequence* which develop under deter minate conditions. Conformist striving, for example, may be followed by a ritualist adaptation and this, in turn, by retreatism; other types of role-sequence can also be identified. For an interesting study which begins to deal with sequences of role-adaptation, see Leonard Reissman, "Levels of aspiration and social class," *American Sociological Review*, 1953, 18, 233-242.

51. As with most insights into the behavior of men, this one had of course been 'anticipated.' In *The Way of All Flesh*, for example, Samuel Butler remarks: 'Adversity, if a man is set down to it by degrees, is more supportable with equanimity by most people than any great prosperity arrived at in a single lifetime." (Chapter V) The difference is, of course, that Durkheim went on to incorporate his insight into an orderly set of theoretical ideas which he followed out in their implications; this was not Butler's *métier* and he went on, instead, to numerous other unconnected insights into man and his society.

52. Here again, the man of letters perceives what the social scientist goes on to examine, in its details and implications. Charles Lamb's classic essay on *The Superannuated Man* describes the syndrome of disorientation experienced by those who are removed from the role-obligation of being tethered to a desk, with all the possibly dull but thoroughly comfortable routines which gave order to daily existence. And he goes on to "caution persons grown old in active business, not lightly, nor without weighing their own resources, to forego their customary employment *all at once*, for there may be danger in it." The italics are supplied to direct attention to what Durkheim and Butler and Lamb take as the nub of the matter: the suddenness of change of status and role.

of several patterns of response.[53] As she points out, both the widowed and the 'retirants' have lost a major role and, in some measure, experience a sense of isolation. She finds that retreatism tends to occur more often among isolated widows and widowers, and goes on to account for its even greater frequency among widowed women than widowed men. Retreatism is manifested in nostalgia for the past and apathy in the present. Retreatists are even more reluctant to enter into new social relations with others than are those described as 'alienated,' with the result that they tend to continue in their apathetic condition.

Possibly because retreatism represents a form of deviant behavior which is not publicly registered in social bookkeeping statistics, as is decidedly the case for such deviant behavior as crime and delinquency, and because it has not the same dramatic and highly visible effect upon the functioning of groups as violations of law, it has tended to be neglected as a subject for study by sociologists, if not by psychiatrists. Yet the syndrome of retreatism has been identified for centuries and under the label of accidie (or variously, acedy, acedia, and accidia) was regarded by the Roman Catholic Church as one of the deadly sins. As the sloth and torpor in which the 'wells of the spirit run dry,' accidie has interested theologians from the Middle Ages onward. It has engaged the attention of men and women of letters from at least the time of Langland and Chaucer, down through Burton, to Aldous Huxley and Rebecca West. Psychiatrists without number have dealt with it in the form of apathy, melancholy, or anhedonia.[54] But sociologists have accorded the syndrome singularly little attention. Yet it would seem that this form of deviant behavior has its social antecedents as well as its manifest social consequences, and we may look for more sociological inquiry into it of the kind represented by Zena Blau's recent study.

It remains to be seen whether the kinds of political and organizational apathy now being investigated by social scientists can be theoretically related to the social forces which, on this theory, make for retreatist behavior.[55] This possibility has been stated in the following terms:

. . . rejection of norms and goals includes the phenomenon of cultural apathy with respect to standards of conduct. Qualitatively different aspects

---

53. Zena Smith Blau, *Old Age: A Study of Change in Status,* Unpublished doctoral dissertation in sociology, Columbia University, 1956.

54. For a few among the many accounts of accidie: Langland's *Piers Plowman* and Chaucer's "Parson's Tale"; Burton's *Anatomy of Melancholy;* the essay by Aldous Huxley in *On The Margin;* Rebecca West, *The Thinking Reed.* Further, F. L. Wells, "Social maladjustments: adaptive regression," in Carl A. Murchison, ed., *Handbook of Social Psychology,* 869 ff. and the cited paper by A. Meyerson, "Anhedonia," *American Journal of Psychiatry,* 1922, 2, 97-103.

55. *Cf.* Bernard Barber, *'Mass Apathy' and Voluntary Social Participation in the United States,* unpublished doctoral dissertation in sociology, Harvard University, 1949; B. Zawadski and Paul F. Lazarsfeld, "The psychological consequences of unemployment," *Journal of Social Psychology,* 1935, 6.

of the latter condition are variously connoted by terms such as indifference, cynicism, moral fatigue, disenchantment, withdrawal of affect, opportunism. One prominent type of apathy is the loss of involvement in a previously sought cultural goal, such as occurs when continued striving results in persistent and seemingly unavoidable frustration. The loss of central life-goals leaves the individual in a social vacuum, without focal direction or meaning. But another crucial kind of apathy seems to emerge from conditions of great normative complexity and/or rapid change, when individuals are pulled this way and that by numerous conflicting norms and goals, until the person is literally dis-oriented and de-moralized, unable to secure a firm commitment to a set of norms that he can feel as self-consistent. Under certain conditions, not yet understood, the result is a kind of 'resignation from responsibility': a discounting of principled conduct, a lack of concern for the maintenance of a moral community. It seems that this lostness is *one* of the basic conditions out of which some types of political totalitarianism emerge. The individual renounces moral autonomy, and is subjected to an external discipline.[56]

Rebellion

It should be plain by now that the theory under review sees the conflict between culturally defined goals and institutional norms as one *source* of anomie; it does not *equate* value-conflict and anomie.[57] Quite

---

56. Robin M. Williams, Jr. *American Society* (New York: A. A. Knopf, 1951), 534-535.

57. As first formulated, the theory is evidently more than usually obscure on this point. At least, this conclusion would seem indicated by the fact that two perceptive discussions have suggested that a conflict between norms has been equated with normlessness (the cultural aspect of anomie). Ralph H. Turner, "Value conflict in social disorganization," *Sociology and Social Research*, 1954, 38, 301-308; Christian Bay, *The Freedom of Expression*, unpublished ms., Chapter III.

An historical sociologist has identified the outlines of a process of disenchantment with both cultural goals and institutional means in the later 1930's in the United States, as this was registered, for example, in journals of opinion upon the death of John D. Rockefeller. He observes: "Clearly the dissenters did not see eye to eye regarding the measures to be taken to reform society, but from the point of view of the defenders of Rockefeller and of business enterprise that disagreement was perhaps of less importance than was the evidence of distrust in the regime of enterprise and of alienation—particularly in the lower ranks of the social order—from the goals and standards which provided its ideological security. For these critics, such goals and standards no longer possessed legitimacy, no longer could serve to exact allegiance; and with allegiance broken, how then could business enterprisers confidently expect the routine of actions and responses that characterized industrial discipline to be maintained? But more than dissent and dissatisfaction lurked in the diatribes of the critics. If the activities of an entrepreneur like Rockefeller were functions of a social organization which was itself the cause of discontent—of poverty and unemployment—then no longer, its critics maintained, did that social organization deserve to be supported and no longer would 'young men' fall into rank behind its cultural standards. With sufficient change—and it was at this point that the critics themselves differed—a new and better social organization could be achieved. This was—or could become—more than merely discussion; it was a charter for action. And because the action contemplated restricting the scope and freedom of action of enterprise, its journalistic defenders had to meet the challenge. Loyalties in jeopardy needed reaffirmation, and every new evidence that they were in jeopardy—from sitdown strikes in Flint to New Deal legislation in Washington—added urgency to the task." Sigmund Diamond, *The Reputation of the American Businessman*, 116-117.

the contrary: conflicts between the norms held by distinct subgroups in a society of course often result in an increased adherence to the norms prevailing in each subgroup. It is the conflict between culturally accepted values and the socially structured difficulties in living up to these values which exerts pressure toward deviant behavior and disruption of the normative system. This outcome of anomie, however, may be only a prelude to the development of new norms, and it is this response which we have described as 'rebellion' in the typology of adaptation.

When rebellion is confined to relatively small and relatively powerless elements in a community, it provides a potential for the formation of subgroups, alienated from the rest of the community but unified within themselves. This pattern is exemplified by alienated adolescents teaming up in gangs or becoming part of a youth movement with a distinctive subculture of its own.[58] This response to anomie tends, however, to be unstable unless the new groups and norms are sufficiently insulated from the rest of the society which rejects them.

When rebellion becomes endemic in a substantial part of the society, it provides a potential for revolution, which reshapes both the normative and the social structure. It is in this connection that a recent study of the changing role of the bourgeoisie in eighteenth century France significantly extends the present theory of anomie. This extension is compactly stated as follows:[59]

It has been suggested that . . . too great a discrepancy between the expectation of mobility and actual fulfillment results in a state of *anomie*, that is, a partial social disintegration reflecting the weakening of moral norms. The same demoralization will very likely also arise when there is *de facto* mobility without the accompanying moral approval, and it was with discrepancies of both these kinds that the 18th century French bourgeoisie was faced to an increasing extent as the century progressed.

Quite apart from the particular historical case in point, this directs theoretical attention to the general conception that anomie may result from two kinds of discrepancy between objective rates of social mobility and cultural definitions of the moral right (and obligation) to move up in a hierarchical social system. Throughout, we have been considering only the one type of discrepancy in which culturally valued ascent is objectively restricted, and it may turn out that this is historically the more frequent type of instance. But the correlative discrepancy, as Dr. Barber observes, also introduces severe strains upon the system. In general terms, this can be identified as the familiar pattern, increasingly

58. See the highly instructive study by Howard Becker, *German Youth: Bond or Free* (London: Routledge & Kegan Paul, 1946); S. N. Eisenstadt, *From Generation to Generation: Age Groups and Social Structure* (Glencoe: The Free Press, 1956), esp. Chapter VI.

59. Elinor G. Barber, *The Bourgeoisie in 18th Century France* (Princeton: Princeton University Press, 1955), 56.

familiar to Americans, in which both caste and open-class norms obtain in a society, with a resulting widespread ambivalence toward the *de facto* class *and* caste mobility of those assigned by many to a lower caste. The phase of demoralization which results from a structural situation of this kind is exemplified not only in the relations between the races in various parts of the United States but in a large number of societies once colonized by the West. These familiar facts would seem to be of a piece, in terms of sociological theory, with the facts regarding the bourgeoisie of the *ancien régime* which Dr. Barber has put in this theoretical setting.[60]

CHANGING SOCIAL STRUCTURE AND DEVIANT BEHAVIOR

In terms of the theory under review, it is plain that differential pressures for deviant behavior will continue to be exerted upon certain groups and strata only as long as the structure of opportunity and the cultural goals remain substantially unchanged. Correlatively, as significant changes in the structure or goals occur, we should expect corresponding changes in the sectors of the population most severely exposed to these pressures.

We have had frequent occasion to note that criminal 'rackets' and sometimes associated political machines persist by virtue of the social functions they perform for various parts of the underlying population who constitute their acknowledged and unacknowledged clientele.[61] It should be expected, therefore, that as legitimate structural alternatives for performing these functions develop, this would result in substantial changes in the social distribution of deviant behavior. It is precisely this thesis which is developed by Daniel Bell in an analytically perceptive paper.[62]

Bell observes that "the mobsters, by and large, had immigrant roots, and crime, as the pattern showed, was a route of social ascent and place in American life." (142) And as sociological students of the subject have often observed, each new immigrant group found itself occupying the

---

60. Since it is the theoretical contribution, rather than the specific empirical findings, which is of immediate interest, I do not summarize the substantive materials set forth by Dr. Barber. These are summed up in her tentative conclusion that "it was the rigidification of the class system that precipitated the alienation of this [middle] segment of the bourgeoisie from the existing class structure to which it had, up to the Revolution, given its predominant allegiance. When he was denied the right to improve his social position, the bourgeois found the strain of conflicting moralities intolerable, so that he rejected altogether the disapproval of social mobility." *Ibid.*, 144.

61. See the observation by William F. Whyte quoted in Chapter I of this book (78) and see the further discussion of crime as a means of social mobility in Chapter IV.

62. Daniel Bell, "Crime as an American way of life," *The Antioch Review,* Summer 1953, 131-154.

lowermost social stratum lately quitted by an immigrant group which had come before. For example, by the time the Italians had experienced a generation or two of American life, they found the "more obvious big city paths from rags to riches pre-empted" by the Jews and Irish. And as Bell goes on to say,

Excluded from the political ladder—in the early '30's there were almost no Italians on the city payroll in top jobs, nor in books of the period can one find discussion of Italian political leaders—[and] finding few open routes to wealth, some turned to illicit ways. In the children's court statistics of the 1930's, the largest group of delinquents were the Italian. . . . (146)

It was the one-time racketeer, seeking respectability, says Bell, who "provided one of the major supports for the drive to win a political voice for Italians in the power structure of the urban political machines." And a decisive change in the sources of funds for the urban political machines provided the context facilitating this alliance of the racketeer and the political organization. For the substantial funds which formerly came from big business were now being diverted from municipal to national political organizations. One of the substitute sources for financing these machines was ready to hand in "the new, and often illegally earned, Italian wealth. This is well illustrated by the career of Costello and his emergence as a political power in New York. Here the ruling motive has been the search for an entrée—for oneself and one's ethnic group—into the ruling circles of the big city." (147) In due course, Italians came to achieve a substantial degree of political influence for the first time.

In abbreviated summary, these are the terms in which Bell traces a "distinct ethnic sequence in the modes of obtaining illicit wealth." Although the evidence is still far from adequate, there is some basis for concluding, as Bell does, that "men of Italian origin appeared in most of the leading roles in the high drama of gambling and mobs, just as twenty years ago the children of East European Jews were the most prominent figures in organized crime, and before that individuals of Irish descent were similarly prominent." (150-151)

But with changes in the structure of opportunity, a "growing number of Italians with professional training and legitimate business success . . . both prompts and permits the Italian group to wield increasing political influence; and increasingly it is the professionals and businessmen who provide models for Italian youth today, models that hardly existed twenty years ago." (152-153)

Finally, and ironically, in view of the close connection of Roosevelt with the large urban political machines, it is a basic structural change in the form of providing services, through the rationalized procedures of what some call 'the welfare state,' that largely spelled the decline of the political machine. It would be figurative but essentially true to say that it was the system of 'social security' and the growth of more-or-less bureaucratically administered scholarships which, more than direct assaults of reformers, have so greatly reduced the power of the political machine. As Bell concludes,

with the rationalization and absorption of some illicit activities into the structure of the economy, the passing of an older generation that had established a hegemony over crime, the rise of minority groups to social position, and the breakup of the urban boss system, the pattern of crime we have discussed is passing as well. Crime, of course, remains as long as passion and the desire for gain remain. But big, organized city crime, as we have known it for the past seventy-five years, was based on more than these universal motives. It was based on characteristics of the American economy, American ethnic groups, and American politics. The changes in all these areas means that it too, in the form we have known it, is at an end. (154)

We need seek no more fitting close, in terms of an essentially structural and functional analysis, to this review of continuities in the analysis of the relation of social structure to anomie.

VI   BUREAUCRATIC STRUCTURE
AND PERSONALITY

A FORMAL, RATIONALLY ORGANIZED social structure involves clearly defined patterns of activity in which, ideally, every series of actions is functionally related to the purposes of the organization.[1] In such an organization there is integrated a series of offices, of hierarchized statuses, in which inhere a number of obligations and privileges closely defined by limited and specific rules. Each of these offices contains an area of imputed competence and responsibility. Authority, the power of control which derives from an acknowledged status, inheres in the office and not in the particular person who performs the official role. Official action ordinarily occurs within the framework of preexisting rules of the organization. The system of prescribed relations between the various offices involves a considerable degree of formality and clearly defined social distance between the occupants of these positions. Formality is manifested by means of a more or less complicated social ritual which symbolizes and supports the pecking order of the various offices. Such formality, which is integrated with the distribution of authority within the system, serves to minimize friction by largely restricting (official) contact to modes which are previously defined by the rules of the organization. Ready calculability of others' behavior and a stable set of mutual expectations is thus built up. Moreover, formality facilitates the interaction of the occupants of offices despite their (possibly hostile) private attitudes toward one another. In this way, the subordinate is protected from the arbitrary action of his superior, since the actions of both are constrained by a mutually recognized set of rules. Specific procedural devices foster objectivity and restrain the "quick passage of impulse into action."[2]

THE STRUCTURE OF BUREAUCRACY

The ideal type of such formal organization is bureaucracy and, in

---

1. For a development of the concept of "rational organization," see Karl Mannheim, *Mensch und Gesellschaft im Zeitalter des Umbaus* (Leiden: A. W. Sijthoff, 1935), esp. 28 ff.

2. H. D. Lasswell, *Politics* (New York: McGraw-Hill, 1936), 120-21.

many respects, the classical analysis of bureaucracy is that by Max Weber.[3] As Weber indicates, bureaucracy involves a clear-cut division of integrated activities which are regarded as duties inherent in the office. A system of differentiated controls and sanctions is stated in the regulations. The assignment of roles occurs on the basis of technical qualifications which are ascertained through formalized, impersonal procedures (*e.g.*, examinations). Within the structure of hierarchically arranged authority, the activities of "trained and salaried experts" are governed by general, abstract, and clearly defined rules which preclude the necessity for the issuance of specific instructions for each specific case. The generality of the rules requires the constant use of *categorization*, whereby individual problems and cases are classified on the basis of designated criteria and are treated accordingly. The pure type of bureaucratic official is appointed, either by a superior or through the exercise of impersonal competition; he is not elected. A measure of flexibility in the bureaucracy is attained by electing higher functionaries who presumably express the will of the electorate (*e.g.*, a body of citizens or a board of directors). The election of higher officials is designed to affect the purposes of the organization, but the technical procedures for attaining these ends are carried out by continuing bureaucratic personnel.[4]

Most bureaucratic offices involve the expectation of life-long tenure, in the absence of disturbing factors which may decrease the size of the organization. Bureaucracy maximizes vocational security.[5] The function of security of tenure, pensions, incremental salaries and regularized procedures for promotion is to ensure the devoted performance of official duties, without regard for extraneous pressures.[6] The chief merit of bureaucracy is its technical efficiency, with a premium placed on precision, speed, expert control, continuity, discretion, and optimal returns on input. The structure is one which approaches the complete elimination of personalized relationships and nonrational considerations (hostility, anxiety, affectual involvements, etc.).

With increasing bureaucratization, it becomes plain to all who would see that man is to a very important degree controlled by his social rela-

---

3. Max Weber, *Wirtschaft und Gesellschaft* (Tübingen: J. C. B. Mohr, 1922), Pt. III, chap. 6; 650-678. For a brief summary of Weber's discussion, see Talcott Parsons, *The Structure of Social Action*, esp. 506 ff. For a description, which is not a caricature, of the bureaucrat as a personality type, see C. Rabany, "Les types sociaux: le fonctionnaire," *Revue générale d'administration*, 1907, 88, 5-28.

4. Karl Mannheim, *Ideology and Utopia* (New York: Harcourt, Brace, 1936), 18n., 105 ff. See also Ramsay Muir, *Peers and Bureaucrats* (London: Constable, 1910), 12-13.

5. E. G. Cahen-Salvador suggests that the personnel of bureaucracies is largely constituted by those who value security above all else. See his "La situation matérielle et morale des fonctionnaires," *Revue politique et parlementaire* (1926), 319.

6. H. J. Laski, "Bureaucracy," *Encyclopedia of the Social Sciences*. This article is written primarily from the standpoint of the political scientist rather than that of the sociologist.

tions to the instruments of production. This can no longer seem only a tenet of Marxism, but a stubborn fact to be acknowledged by all, quite apart from their ideological persuasion. Bureaucratization makes readily visible what was previously dim and obscure. More and more people discover that to work, they must be employed. For to work, one must have tools and equipment. And the tools and equipment are increasingly available only in bureaucracies, private or public. Consequently, one must be employed by the bureaucracies in order to have access to tools in order to work in order to live. It is in this sense that bureaucratization entails separation of individuals from the instruments of production, as in modern capitalistic enterprise or in state communistic enterprise (of the midcentury variety), just as in the post-feudal army, bureaucratization entailed complete separation from the instruments of destruction. Typically, the worker no longer owns his tools nor the soldier, his weapons. And in this special sense, more and more people become workers, either blue collar or white collar or stiff shirt. So develops, for example, the new type of scientific worker, as the scientist is "separated" from his technical equipment—after all, the physicist does not ordinarily own his cyclotron. To work at his research, he must be employed by a bureaucracy with laboratory resources.

Bureaucracy is administration which almost completely avoids public discussion of its techniques, although there may occur public discussion of its policies.[7] This secrecy is confined neither to public nor to private bureaucracies. It is held to be necessary to keep valuable information from private economic competitors or from foreign and potentially hostile political groups. And though it is not often so called, espionage among competitors is perhaps as common, if not as intricately organized, in systems of private economic enterprise as in systems of national states. Cost figures, lists of clients, new technical processes, plans for production—all these are typically regarded as essential secrets of private economic bureaucracies which might be revealed if the bases of all decisions and policies had to be publicly defended.

THE DYSFUNCTIONS OF BUREAUCRACY

In these bold outlines, the positive attainments and functions of bureaucratic organization are emphasized and the internal stresses and strains of such structures are almost wholly neglected. The community at large, however, evidently emphasizes the imperfections of bureaucracy, as is suggested by the fact that the "horrid hybrid," bureaucrat, has become an epithet, a *Schimpfwort*.

The transition to a study of the negative aspects of bureaucracy is afforded by the application of Veblen's concept of "trained incapacity,"

---

7. Weber, *op. cit.,* 671.

Dewey's notion of "occupational psychosis" or Warnotte's view of "professional deformation." Trained incapacity refers to that state of affairs in which one's abilities function as inadequacies or blind spots. Actions based upon training and skills which have been successfully applied in the past may result in inappropriate responses *under changed conditions.* An inadequate flexibility in the application of skills, will, in a changing milieu, result in more or less serious maladjustments.[8] Thus, to adopt a barnyard illustration used in this connection by Burke, chickens may be readily conditioned to interpret the sound of a bell as a signal for food. The same bell may now be used to summon the trained chickens to their doom as they are assembled to suffer decapitation. In general, one adopts measures in keeping with one's past training and, under new conditions which are not recognized as *significantly* different, the very soundness of this training may lead to the adoption of the wrong procedures. Again, in Burke's almost echolalic phrase, "people may be unfitted by being fit in an unfit fitness"; their training may become an incapacity.

Dewey's concept of occupational psychosis rests upon much the same observations. As a result of their day to day routines, people develop special preferences, antipathies, discriminations and emphases.[9] (The term psychosis is used by Dewey to denote a "pronounced character of the mind.") These psychoses develop through demands put upon the individual by the particular organization of his occupational role.

The concepts of both Veblen and Dewey refer to a fundamental ambivalence. Any action can be considered in terms of what it attains or what it fails to attain. "A way of seeing is also a way of not seeing—a focus upon object A involves a neglect of object B."[10] In his discussion, Weber is almost exclusively concerned with what the bureaucratic structure attains: precision, reliability, efficiency. This same structure may be examined from another perspective provided by the ambivalence. What are the limitations of the organizations designed to attain these goals?

For reasons which we have already noted, the bureaucratic structure exerts a constant pressure upon the official to be "methodical, prudent, disciplined." If the bureaucracy is to operate successfully, it must attain a high degree of reliability of behavior, an unusual degree of conformity with prescribed patterns of action. Hence, the fundamental importance of discipline which may be as highly developed in a religious or economic bureaucracy as in the army. Discipline can be effective only if the ideal patterns are buttressed by strong sentiments which entail devotion to one's duties, a keen sense of the limitation of one's authority and competence, and methodical performance of routine activities. The efficacy

---

8. For a stimulating discussion and application of these concepts, see Kenneth Burke, *Permanence and Change* (New York: New Republic, 1935), pp. 50 ff.; Daniel Warnotte, "Bureaucratie et Fonctionnarisme," *Revue de l'Institut de Sociologie,* 1937, 17, 245.

9. *Ibid.,* 58-59.

10. *Ibid.,* 70.

of social structure depends ultimately upon infusing group participants with appropriate attitudes and sentiments. As we shall see, there are definite arrangements in the bureaucracy for inculcating and reinforcing these sentiments.

At the moment, it suffices to observe that in order to ensure discipline (the necessary reliability of response), these sentiments are often more intense than is technically necessary. There is a margin of safety, so to speak, in the pressure exerted by these sentiments upon the bureaucrat to conform to his patterned obligations, in much the same sense that added allowances (precautionary overestimations) are made by the engineer in designing the supports for a bridge. But this very emphasis leads to a transference of the sentiments from the *aims* of the organization onto the particular details of behavior required by the rules. Adherence to the rules, originally conceived as a means, becomes transformed into an end-in-itself; there occurs the familiar process of *displacement of goals* whereby "an instrumental value becomes a terminal value."[11] Discipline, readily interpreted as conformance with regulations, whatever the situation, is seen not as a measure designed for specific purposes but becomes an immediate value in the life-organization of the bureaucrat. This emphasis, resulting from the displacement of the original goals, develops into rigidities and an inability to adjust readily. Formalism, even ritualism, ensues with an unchallenged insistence upon punctilious adherence to formalized procedures.[12] This may be exaggerated to the point where primary concern with conformity to the rules interferes with the achievement of the purposes of the organization, in which case we have the familiar phenonenon of the technicism or red tape of the official. An extreme product of this process of displacement of goals is the bureaucratic virtuoso, who never forgets a single rule

---

11. This process has often been observed in various connections. Wundt's *heterogony of ends* is a case in point; Max Weber's *Paradoxie der Folgen* is another. See also MacIver's observations on the transformation of civilization into culture and Lasswell's remark that "the human animal distinguishes himself by his infinite capacity for making ends of his means." See Merton, "The unanticipated consequences of purposive social action," *American Sociological Review*, 1936, 1, 894-904. In terms of the psychological mechanisms involved, this process has been analyzed most fully by Gordon W. Allport, in his discussion of what he calls "the functional autonomy of motives." Allport emends the earlier formulations of Woodworth, Tolman, and William Stern, and arrives at a statement of the process from the standpoint of individual motivation. He does not consider those phases of the social structure which conduce toward the "transformation of motives." The formulation adopted in this paper is thus complementary to Allport's analysis; the one stressing the psychological mechanisms involved, the other considering the constraints of the social structure. The convergence of psychology and sociology toward this central concept suggests that it may well constitute one of the conceptual bridges between the two disciplines. See Gordon W. Allport, *Personality* (New York: Henry Holt & Co., 1937), chap. 7.

12. See E. C. Hughes, "Institutional office and the person," *American Journal of Sociology*, 1937, 43, 404-413; E. T. Hiller, "Social structure in relation to the person," *Social Forces*, 1937, 16, 34-4.

binding his action and hence is unable to assist many of his clients.[13] A case in point, where strict recognition of the limits of authority and literal adherence to rules produced this result, is the pathetic plight of Bernt Balchen, Admiral Byrd's pilot in the flight over the South Pole.

> According to a ruling of the department of labor Bernt Balchen . . . cannot receive his citizenship papers. Balchen, a native of Norway, declared his intention in 1927. It is held that he has failed to meet the condition of five years' continuous residence in the United States. The Byrd antarctic voyage took him out of the country, although he was on a ship carrying the American flag, was an invaluable member of the American expedition, and in a region to which there is an American claim because of the exploration and occupation of it by Americans, this region being Little America.
>
> The bureau of naturalization explains that it cannot proceed on the assumption that Little America is American soil. That would be *trespass on international questions* where it has no sanction. So far as the bureau is concerned, Balchen was out of the country and *technically* has not complied with the law of naturalization.[14]

STRUCTURAL SOURCES OF OVERCONFORMITY

Such inadequacies in orientation which involve trained incapacity clearly derive from structural sources. The process may be briefly recapitulated. (1) An effective bureaucracy demands reliability of response and strict devotion to regulations. (2) Such devotion to the rules leads to their transformation into absolutes; they are no longer conceived as relative to a set of purposes. (3) This interferes with ready adaptation under special conditions not clearly envisaged by those who drew up the general rules. (4) Thus, the very elements which conduce toward efficiency in general produce inefficiency in specific instances. Full realization of the inadequacy is seldom attained by members of the group who have not divorced themselves from the meanings which the rules have for them. These rules in time become symbolic in cast, rather than strictly utilitarian.

Thus far, we have treated the ingrained sentiments making for rigorous discipline simply as data, as given. However, definite features of the bureaucratic structure may be seen to conduce to these sentiments. The bureaucrat's official life is planned for him in terms of a graded career, through the organizational devices of promotion by seniority, pensions, incremental salaries, *etc.*, all of which are designed to provide incentives for disciplined action and conformity to the official regulations.[15] The

---

13. Mannheim, *Ideology and Utopia,* 106.

14. Quoted from the *Chicago Tribune* (June 24, 1931, p. 10) by Thurman Arnold, *The Symbols of Government* (New Haven: Yale University Press, 1935), 201-2. (My italics.)

15. Mannheim, *Mensch und Gesellschaft,* 32-33. Mannheim stresses the importance of the "Lebensplan" and the "Amtskarriere." See the comments by Hughes, *op. cit.,* 413.

official is tacitly expected to and largely does adapt his thoughts, feelings and actions to the prospect of this career. But *these very devices* which increase the probability of conformance also lead to an over-concern with strict adherence to regulations which induces timidity, conservatism, and technicism. Displacement of sentiments from goals onto means is fostered by the tremendous symbolic significance of the means (rules).

Another feature of the bureaucratic structure tends to produce much the same result. Functionaries have the sense of a common destiny for all those who work together. They share the same interests, especially since there is relatively little competition in so far as promotion is in terms of senjority. In-group aggression is thus minimized and this arrangement is therefore conceived to be positively functional for the bureaucracy. However, the *esprit de corps* and informal social organization which typically develops in such situations often leads the personnel to defend their entrenched interests rather than to assist their clientele and elected higher officials. As President Lowell reports, if the bureaucrats believe that their status is not adequately recognized by an incoming elected official, detailed information will be withheld from him, leading him to errors for which he is held responsible. Or, if he seeks to dominate fully, and thus violates the sentiment of self-integrity of the bureaucrats, he may have documents brought to him in such numbers that he cannot manage to sign them all, let alone read them.[16] This illustrates the defensive informal organization which tends to arise whenever there is an apparent threat to the integrity of the group.[17]

It would be much too facile and partly erroneous to attribute such resistance by bureaucrats simply to vested interests. Vested interests oppose any new order which either eliminates or at least makes uncertain their differential advantage deriving from the current arrangements. This is undoubtedly involved in part in bureaucratic resistance to change but another process is perhaps more significant. As we have seen, bureaucratic officials affectively identify themselves with their way of life. They have a pride of craft which leads them to resist change in established routines; at least, those changes which are felt to be imposed by others. This nonlogical pride of craft is a familiar pattern found even, to judge from Sutherland's *Professional Thief*, among pickpockets who, despite the risk, delight in mastering the prestige-bearing feat of "beating a left breech" (picking the left front trousers pocket).

In a stimulating paper, Hughes has applied the concepts of "secular" and "sacred" to various types of division of labor; "the sacredness" of

---

16. A. L. Lowell, *The Government of England* (New York, 1908), I, 189 ff.

17. For an instructive description of the development of such a defensive organization in a group of workers, see F. J. Roethlisberger and W. J. Dickson, *Management and the Worker* (Boston: Harvard School of Business Administration, 1934).

caste and *Stände* prerogatives contrasts sharply with the increasing secularism of occupational differentiation in our society.[18] However, as our discussion suggests, there may ensue, in particular vocations and in particular types of organization, the *process of sanctification* (viewed as the counterpart of the process of secularization). This is to say that through sentiment-formation, emotional dependence upon bureaucratic symbols and status, and affective involvement in spheres of competence and authority, there develop prerogatives involving attitudes of moral legitimacy which are established as values in their own right, and are no longer viewed as merely technical means for expediting administration. One may note a tendency for certain bureaucratic norms, originally introduced for technical reasons, to become rigidified and sacred, although, as Durkheim would say, they are *laïque en apparence*.[19] Durkheim has touched on this general process in his description of the attitudes and values which persist in the organic solidarity of a highly differentiated society.

PRIMARY VS. SECONDARY RELATIONS

Another feature of the bureaucratic structure, the stress on depersonalization of relationships, also plays its part in the bureaucrat's trained incapacity. The personality pattern of the bureaucrat is nucleated about this norm of impersonality. Both this and the categorizing tendency, which develops from the dominant role of general, abstract rules, tend to produce conflict in the bureaucrat's contacts with the public or clientele. Since functionaries minimize personal relations and resort to categorization, the peculiarities of individual cases are often ignored. But the client who, quite understandably, is convinced of the special features of *his* own problem often objects to such categorical treatment. Stereotyped behavior is not adapted to the exigencies of individual problems. The impersonal treatment of affairs which are at times of great personal significance to the client gives rise to the charge of "arrogance" and "haughtiness" of the bureaucrat. Thus, at the Greenwich Employment Exchange, the unemployed worker who is securing his insurance

---

18. E. C. Hughes, "Personality types and the division of labor," *American Journal of Sociology*, 1928, 33, 754-768. Much the same distinction is drawn by Leopold von Wiese and Howard Becker, *Systematic Sociology* (New York: John Wiley & Sons, 1932), 222-25 *et passim*.

19. Hughes recognizes one phase of this process of sanctification when he writes that professional training "carries with it as a by-product assimilation of the candidate to a set of professional attitudes and controls, *a professional conscience and solidarity. The profession claims and aims to become a moral unit.*" Hughes, *op. cit.*, 762, (italics inserted). In this same connection, Sumner's concept of *pathos*, as the halo of sentiment which protects a social value from criticism, is particularly relevant, inasmuch as it affords a clue to the mechanism involved in the process of sanctification. See his *Folkways*, 180-181.

payment resents what he deems to be "the impersonality and, at times, the apparent abruptness and even harshness of his treatment by the clerks. . . . Some men complain of the superior attitude which the clerks have."[20]

Still another source of conflict with the public derives from the bureaucratic structure. The bureaucrat, in part irrespective of his position within the hierachy, acts as a representative of the power and prestige of the entire structure. In his official role he is vested with definite authority. This often leads to an actually or apparently domineering attitude, which may only be exaggerated by a discrepancy between his position within the hierarchy and his position with reference to the public.[21] Protest and recourse to other officials on the part of the client are often ineffective or largely precluded by the previously mentioned *esprit de corps* which joins the officials into a more or less solidary in-group. This source of conflict *may* be minimized in private enterprise since the client can register an effective protest by transferring his trade to another organization within the competitive system. But with the monopolistic nature of the public organization, no such alternative is possible. Moreover, in this case, tension is increased because of a discrepancy between ideology and fact: the governmental personnel are held to be "servants of the people," but in fact they are often superordinate, and release of tension can seldom be afforded by turning to

---

20. " 'They treat you like a lump of dirt they do. I see a navvy reach across the counter and shake one of them by the collar the other day. The rest of us felt like cheering. Of course he lost his benefit over it. . . . But the clerk deserved it for his sassy way.' " (E. W. Bakke, *The Unemployed Man*, 79-80). Note that the domineering attitude was *imputed* by the unemployed client who is in a state of tension due to his loss of status and self-esteem in a society where the ideology is still current that an "able man" can always find a job. That the imputation of arrogance stems largely from the client's state of mind is seen from Bakke's own observation that "the clerks were rushed, and had no time for pleasantries, but there was little sign of harshness or a superiority feeling in their treatment of the men." In so far as there is an objective basis for the imputation of arrogant behavior to bureaucrats, it may possibly be explained by the following juxtaposed statements. "Auch der moderne, sei es öffentliche, sei es private, Beamte erstrebt immer und geniesst meist den Beherrschten gegenüber eine spezifisch gehobene, 'ständische' soziale Schätzung." (Weber, *op. cit.*, 652.) "In persons in whom the craving for prestige is uppermost, hostility usually takes the form of a desire to humiliate others." K. Horney, *The Neurotic Personality of Our Time*, 178-79.

21. In this connection, note the relevance of Koffka's comments on certain features of the pecking-order of birds. "If one compares the behavior of the bird at the top of the pecking list, the despot, with that of one very far down, the second or third from the last, then one finds the latter much more cruel to the few others over whom he lords it than the former in his treatment of all members. As soon as one removes from the group all members above the penultimate, his behavior becomes milder and may even become very friendly. . . . It is not difficult to find analogies to this in human societies, and therefore one side of such behavior must be primarily the effects of the social groupings, and not of individual characteristics." K. Koffka, *Principles of Gestalt Psychology* (New York: Harcourt, Brace, 1935), 668-9.

other agencies for the necessary service.[22] This tension is in part attributable to the confusion of the status of bureaucrat and client; the client may consider himself socially superior to the official who is at the moment dominant.[23]

Thus, with respect to the relations between officials and clientele, one structural source of conflict is the pressure for formal and impersonal treatment when individual, personalized consideration is desired by the client. The conflict may be viewed, then, as deriving from the introduction of inappropriate attitudes and relationships. Conflict *within* the bureaucratic structure arises from the converse situation, namely, when personalized relationships are substituted for the structurally required impersonal relationships. This type of conflict may be characterized as follows.

The bureaucracy, as we have seen, is organized as a secondary, formal group. The normal responses involved in this organized network of social expectations are supported by affective attitudes of members of the group. Since the group is oriented toward secondary norms of impersonality, any failure to conform to these norms will arouse antagonism from those who have identified themselves with the legitimacy of these rules. Hence, the substitution of personal for impersonal treatment within the structure is met with widespread disapproval and is characterized by such epithets as graft, favoritism, nepotism, apple-polishing, etc. These epithets are clearly manifestations of injured sentiments.[24] The function of such virtually automatic resentment can be clearly seen in terms of the requirements of bureaucratic structure.

Bureaucracy is a secondary group structure designed to carry on certain activities which cannot be satisfactorily performed on the basis

---

22. At this point the political machine often becomes functionally significant. As Steffens and others have shown, highly personalized relations and the abrogation of formal rules (red tape) by the machine often satisfy the needs of individual "clients" more fully than the formalized mechanism of governmental bureaucracy. See the slight elaboration of this as set forth in Chapter I.

23. As one of the unemployed men remarked about the clerks at the Greenwich Employment Exchange: " 'And the bloody blokes wouldn't have their jobs if it wasn't for us men out of a job either. That's what gets me about their holding their noses up.' " Bakke, *op. cit.,* 80. See also H. D. Lasswell and G. Almond, "Aggressive behavior by clients towards public relief administrators," *American Political Science Review,* 1934, 28, 643-55.

24. The diagnostic significance of such linguistic indices as epithets has scarcely been explored by the sociologist. Sumner properly observes that epithets produce "summary criticisms" and definitions of social situations. Dollard also notes that "epithets frequently define the central issues in a society," and Sapir has rightly emphasized the importance of context of situations in appraising the significance of epithets. Of equal relevance is Linton's observation that "in case histories the way in which the community felt about a particular episode is, if anything, more important to our study than the actual behavior. . . ." A sociological study of "vocabularies of encomium and opprobrium" should lead to valuable findings.

of primary group criteria.[25] Hence behavior which runs counter to these formalized norms becomes the object of emotionalized disapproval. This constitutes a functionally significant defence set up against tendencies which jeopardize the performance of socially necessary activities. To be sure, these reactions are not rationally determined practices explicitly designed for the fulfillment of this function. Rather, viewed in terms of the individual's interpretation of the situation, such resentment is simply an immediate response opposing the "dishonesty" of those who violate the rules of the game. However, this subjective frame of reference notwithstanding, these reactions serve the latent function of maintaining the essential structural elements of bureaucracy by reaffirming the necessity for formalized, secondary relations and by helping to prevent the disintegration of the bureaucratic structure which would occur should these be supplanted by personalized relations. This type of conflict may be generically described as the intrusion of primary group attitudes when secondary group attitudes are institutionally demanded, just as the bureaucrat-client conflict often derives from interaction on impersonal terms when personal treatment is individually demanded.[26]

PROBLEMS FOR RESEARCH

The trend towards increasing bureaucratization in Western Society, which Weber had long since foreseen, is not the sole reason for sociologists to turn their attention to this field. Empirical studies of the interaction of bureaucracy and personality should especially increase our understanding of social structure. A large number of specific questions invite our attention. To what extent are particular personality types selected and modified by the various bureaucracies (private enterprise, public service, the quasi-legal political machine, religious orders)? Inasmuch as ascendancy and submission are held to be traits of personality, despite their variability in different stimulus-situations, do bureaucracies select personalities of particularly submissive or ascendant tendencies? And since various studies have shown that these traits can be modified, does participation in bureaucratic office tend to increase ascendant tendencies? Do various systems of recruitment (*e.g.*, patronage, open competition involving specialized knowledge or general mental capacity,

25. *Cf.* Ellsworth Faris, *The Nature of Human Nature* (New York: McGraw-Hill, 1937), 41 ff.

26. Community disapproval of many forms of behavior may be analyzed in terms of one or the other of these patterns of substitution of culturally inappropriate types of relationship. Thus, prostitution constitutes a type-case where coitus, a form of intimacy which is institutionally defined as symbolic of the most "sacred" primary group relationship, is placed within a contractual context, symbolized by the exchange of that most impersonal of all symbols, money. See Kingsley Davis, "The sociology of prostitution," *American Sociological Review*, 1937, 2, 744-55.

practical experience) select different personality types?[27] Does promotion through seniority lessen competitive anxieties and enhance administrative efficiency? A detailed examination of mechanisms for imbuing the bureaucratic codes with affect would be instructive both sociologically and psychologically. Does the general anonymity of civil service decisions tend to restrict the area of prestige-symbols to a narrowly defined inner circle? Is there a tendency for differential association to be especially marked among bureaucrats?

The range of theoretically significant and practically important questions would seem to be limited only by the accessibility of the concrete data. Studies of religious, educational, military, economic, and political bureaucracies dealing with the interdependence of social organization and personality formation should constitute an avenue for fruitful research. On that avenue, the functional analysis of concrete structures may yet build a Solomon's House for sociologists.

---

27. Among recent studies of recruitment to bureaucracy are: Reinhard Bendix, *Higher Civil Servants in American Society* (Boulder: University of Colorado Press, 1949); Dwaine Marwick, *Career Perspectives in a Bureaucratic Setting* (Ann Arbor: University of Michigan Press, 1954); R. K. Kelsall, *Higher Civil Servants in Britain* (London: Routledge and Kegan Paul, 1955); W. L. Warner and J. C. Abegglen, *Occupational Mobility in American Business and Industry* (Minneapolis: University of Minnesota Press, 1955).

VII ROLE OF THE INTELLECTUAL IN PUBLIC BUREAUCRACY

MERICAN SOCIOLOGISTS have long devoted themselves to the study of functional and occupational groups in society. They have also enlarged current knowledge of social problems and social deviations. Much is known, for example, about the sources of juvenile delinquency and crime. But perhaps the past of sociology is too much with us; perhaps we have not moved far enough from our early moorings in the study of such social problems to examine as well other ranges of problems which are likewise rooted in social structure and which have a more direct bearing on the development of that structure.[1] As a case in point, intellectuals devoted to social science have been so busy examining the behavior of others that they have largely neglected to study their own problems, situation, and behavior. The hobo and the saleslady have been singled out for close study but we seem reluctant to analyze the social scientist as an occupational type. We have empirical monographs concerning the professional thief and the professional beggar, but, until recently, none which deals with the role of the professional intellectual in our society.[2] Yet it would seem that clarity might well begin at home.

---

1. For a suggestive interpretation of the different orientations of sociology in Europe and America, see Karl Mannheim, "German Sociology (1918-1933)" *Politica*, 1934, 29-33.

2. This is not to ignore several recent studies which are moving in this direction. However, the work of Florian Znaniecki, *The Social Role of the Man of Knowledge* (New York, 1940) is devoted to a theoretical outline rather than to an empirical study. Logan Wilson, *The Academic Man,* (New York, 1941), confines itself, as the title indicates, to the academic context. Claude Bowman's study of *The College Professor* (Phila., 1938), is concerned with the images of the professor presented in 19 magazines within the past half-century. And Willard Waller's *Sociology of Teaching* is largely devoted to the elementary and high school teacher. Karl Mannheim refers to an unpublished monograph on the intellectual and there are, of course, numerous brief studies in the (chiefly European) literature. These, however, are generally not based on detailed empirical data concerning the actual roles of intellectuals with respect to social policies and decisions. General bibliographies on the intellectual are to be found in the works of Mannheim and in Roberto Michel's article on "Intellectuals" in the *Encyclopedia of the Social Sciences*.

THE INTELLECTUAL AS OCCUPATIONAL TYPE

Indicative of this gap in our current research is the absence of much of the necessary detailed data. Intellectuals have to be converted to the notion that they, too, are human and so, to follow the Terentian phrase, not alien to study by themselves. And indeed, the crisis decades have directed the attention of intellectuals toward their place in society.[3] Many, having experienced status-insecurities, have begun to re-examine the more general sources of these insecurities, not only for other strata in the population but for themselves as well. They have begun to assess the connections between their place in the social structure and their concepts, theories, and perspectives. Some have come to believe that their wants cannot be satisfied within the existing institutional structure and have begun to ask why. It is now almost respectable to recognize the existence of class conflict; so much so that a writer in the big-business journal, Fortune, rejects "hypocritical vague verbiage" and "mealy-mouthed phrases" in favor of "the more realistic terminology and analytical methods employed in Europe, where the existence of classes and the conflict of their interests are as clearly recognized by non-Marxian political analysts as by the Marxists who first pointed them out."[4]

It may be that, once having recognized these problems, American intellectuals will assemble the data needed to appraise the actualities and potentialities of their role in relation to broad social policy. Perhaps they can be persuaded to record their experiences in close detail. What roles are they called upon to perform? What conflicts and frustrations are experienced in their efforts to perform these roles? What institutional pressures are exerted upon them? Who, for example, defines their intellectual problems? Under what conditions do they initiate problems for

---

3. See, for example, H. D. Lasswell, "The relation of ideological intelligence to public policy," Ethics, 1942, 53, 25-34; H. D. Lasswell and M. S. McDougal, "Legal education and public policy: professional training in the public interest," Yale Law Journal, 1943, 52, 203-295. Journals of law have lately come to devote considerable attention to such problems.

4. Sherry Mangan, "State of the Nation," Fortune, 28 (1943), 138. Mangan's further comments emphasize the relation between open avowal of class conflict and current economic development. "The prime maxim of American political writing has long appeared to be: 'Don't name it and you can have it.' In perhaps no other nation are political definitions, trends and events swathed in such hypocritically vague verbiage. This imprecision stems from no mere literary idiosyncrasy. It reflects rather the comparative political backwardness of the American people, for whom even such tremendous crises as that of 1929-39 have not yet, as in Europe, sufficiently shattered the economic fabric as to bring the social regime into serious question. An excellent precedent in cutting through this terminological porridge was recently established by Mr. Eric Johnston, President of the U. S. Chamber of Commerce, in calling for the supplanting of such mealymouthed phrases as the 'free-enterprise system' and the 'American way of life' by the precise scientific term 'capitalism.'" Do such acknowledgments of class conflict signify that social crises are beginning to corrode the screen of false consciousness?

inquiry? What is the effect upon policy of such inquiries? What are the effects of bureaucratization upon the outlook of intellectuals? Do they find that, even when originating problems for analysis, they tend to think in terms of narrowly restricted alternatives? What are the characteristic problems of maintaining lines of communication between policymakers and intellectuals? An extended list of guide-lines for participant-observation by intellectuals both in and out of bureaucracies can be developed. Only such detailed information will enable us to move from the plane of broad approximations to intensive and well-grounded analyses of intellectuals' relations to social policy. Only when we have these data in bulk, will the sociology of knowledge no longer be so largely concerned with wide-sweeping generalizations which have not been strained through the sieve of adequate empirical test.

But since the available data are scarce, our discussion must be based on scattered published materials and on informal interviews with intellectuals concerning their experiences in connection with public policy. Therefore, we can only sketch out some aspects of the intellectual's role: its possibilities and limitations, its futilities and rewards. Our discussion is little more than a reconnaissance which may suggest promising lines for further inquiry. It deals with selected aspects of the intellectual's role, particularly within governmental bureaucracies.[5]

INTELLECTUALS' STATUS AND SOCIAL POLICY

For our purposes, the term "intellectual" need not be defined very precisely. We shall consider persons as intellectuals *in so far as* they devote themselves to cultivating and formulating knowledge. They have access to and advance a cultural fund of knowledge which does not derive solely from their direct personal experience.[6] Their activities may be vocational or avocational; this is not decisive. The fact that John Stuart Mill spent many years in the India Office does not rule him out as an intellectual.

It should be noted that "the intellectual" refers to a social role and not to a total person. Although this role overlaps various occupational roles, it need not coincide with these. Thus, we normally include teachers and professors among the intellectuals. As a rough approximation, this may be adequate, but it does not follow that every teacher or professor is an intellectual. He may or may not be, depending on the actual nature of his activities. The limiting case occurs when a teacher *merely* communicates the content of a textbook, without further interpretations or applications. In such cases, the teacher is no more an intellectual than a

---

5. As read at the meeting of the American Sociological Society, this paper included an extensive analysis of intellectuals' activities in helping to define and implement policy during the Paris Peace Conference.

6. Znaniecki, *op. cit.*, pp. 37-38.

radio announcer who merely reads a script prepared for him by others. He is then merely a cog in the transmission belt of communicating ideas forged by others.

We shall be concerned with a certain class of intellectuals: those who are specialists in the field of social, economic, and political knowledge. Roughly speaking, this includes social scientists and lawyers. In many respects, their role, particularly with relation to public policy, is sociologically distinct from that of specialists in the physical and biological sciences.

In the first place, there is a considerable degree of *indeterminacy* in the social scientist's findings, in so far as they bear upon projected action. He is confronted with far greater contingencies than, say, the electrical engineer. The latter can predict, for example, how a vacuum tube designed for a particular purpose will work under the very conditions in which it will be used; "pre-testing" in social affairs is only a rough approximation and even so, there is a large measure of contingency in determining the conditions under which the suggested plan will have to operate. The alternatives developed by the social scientist, then, often do not and sometimes cannot have the authority of reliable forecasts adequate for the purpose in hand. Expert knowledge here consists rather in reducing palpable errors of judgment. Such indeterminacy possibly underlies the ambivalence of distrust and hopeful expectation directed toward the social scientist in his capacity as advisor.

Secondly, this element of indeterminacy contributes also toward undermining the relation which exists between experts and clients. In evaluating the expert's competence, the client cannot always rely on results, for the judgment is always comparative. Perhaps the problem could have been solved more effectively by another specialist; perhaps it could not. There is a large area of indeterminacy in appraising the expert's performance. And consequently, there is an important fiduciary component in the expert's role. There must be a social organization— *e.g.,* a professional society, a university which affixes a label of competence—which makes it likely that the client's confidence in experts is, *in general,* merited. But the more indefinite the objective standards of appraisal the greater the possibility of interpersonal relations, sentiments, and other nonobjective factors determining the degree of the client's confidence in the expert. Against this background, we can understand one source of discontent among experts who observe a colleague, in terms of technical criteria less competent than themselves, sitting at the right hand of a policy-maker. Indeterminacy of appraisal opens the way for discrepancies between the position of the expert and his competence. It is suggested that such discrepancies are more likely in the case of social scientists who serve as advisors than of technologists operating in fields where the comparative efficiency of their work can be more accurately assessed.

Thirdly, this indeterminacy of appraising achievement in the field of human affairs increases the need for policy-makers to rely on the judgment of experts in recruiting new expert personnel. It is in this way, quite apart from deliberate nepotism, that *cliques* of advisors tend to develop. For those experts who are in an organization are quite likely to call upon other experts *whom they know* and concerning whom they can pass grounded judgment on the basis of this direct familiarity. Networks of personal relations among intellectuals serve often as agencies for establishing self-contained cliques, at least among the more important advisors.

Fourth, the intellectual concerned with human affairs deals with data and problems about which policy-makers are often convinced they have considerable knowledge. It is by no means evident to the policy-maker that the expert has more competence in dealing with these problems than the policy-maker himself. When the social scientist is virtually certain of the validity of his advice, he is, very often, dealing with picayune affairs. When he deals with the larger issues, his relevant knowledge may not be as great as that acquired by the policy-maker through years of firsthand experience. This is, perhaps, a reason for the unenviable plight of the social science intellectual who is consigned to purgatory, never quite clear whether he is destined for heaven or hell. He is on call, but is seldom regarded as indispensable. If his advice does not bear out the views of the "men of action," he may be returned to his private purgatory. When there is high indeterminacy in forecasting the consequences of alternative policies, the social scientist's advice can be readily ignored.

Finally, the intellectual dealing with human conduct and culture is concerned with alternatives which have immediate and obvious value-implications. He is peculiarly subject to attack by those whose interests and sentiments are violated by his findings. This aspect of his work coupled with the relatively low order of probability of his predictions concerning the effects of alternative policies renders him especially vulnerable to that rapid turnover of experts which we have come to expect in certain bureaucracies.

For these reasons, and doubtless others, intellectuals concerned with human affairs in general find themselves in a less secure status than the physical and biological scientists who affect public policy.

BUREAUCRATIC AND UNATTACHED INTELLECTUALS

We can conveniently classify these intellectuals into two major types:

those who exercise advisory and technical functions within a bureaucracy and those intellectuals who are not attached to a bureaucracy.

The distinction is pointed up by recognizing a difference in the "client" of the two kinds of intellectuals: for the bureaucratic intellectual, it is those policy-makers in the organization for whom he is, directly or remotely, performing a staff function; for the unattached intellectual,[7] the clientele is a public.

We shall be primarily concerned with the relations to policy of the intellectual in public bureaucracies with some consideration of the un-attached intellectual in this same connection. The unattached intellectual who, during periods of social crisis, temporarily enters a public bureau-cracy constitutes an intermediate type.

RECRUITMENT OF INTELLECTUALS BY PUBLIC BUREAUCRACY

Bureaucratization involves an accent on rationality of procedure (within limited contexts) which requires intellectually specialized per-sonnel. In increasing numbers, young intellectuals in the United States have been recruited by public bureaucracies for at least the last gen-eration. Two aspects of this development deserve attention: (1) its im-plications for a change in the values of younger intellectuals and (2) the ways in which the bureaucracy converts politically-minded intellectuals into technicians.

Many intellectuals have become *alienated* from the assumptions, ob-jectives and rewards of private enterprise. Such estrangement from business class values is a reflection of the institutional dislocations which breed insecurity and uncertainties. The experience of recurrent economic depressions makes itself felt in a withdrawal of allegiance from the pre-vailing power structure. Intellectuals become imbued with values and standards which, they believe, are not consistent with a place in the business world. Some turn to teaching, particularly university teaching, which presumably provides a possibility for them to exercise their in-tellectual interests and to avoid direct subjection to "business control." For many alienated intellectuals, however, the profession of teaching means standing on the sidelines looking on, rather than participating in, the historical movements which are in process. Rather than be on the edge of history, they prefer to have a sense of helping to make history,

---

7. The term "unattached intellectual" is not here used in Mannheim's or Alfred Weber's sense. It refers merely to those intellectuals who do not perform a staff function in helping to formulate or to implement policies of a bureaucracy. Academic men are included among the unattached intellectuals, despite their connection with an "academic bureaucracy." Their role differs from that of bureaucratic intellectuals since they typically are not expected to utilize their specialized knowledge for shaping the policies of the bureaucracy.

by taking a place within public bureaucracies which presumably puts them closer to the actual locus of important decisions.

There is, in the lure of Washington for the intellectual, a symptom, perhaps, of the belief that the locus of effective control in our society is shifting; shifting, let us say, from Wall Street to Constitution Avenue. That this may not be the case, that, as Walton Hamilton has suggested, it may be rather a case of Wall Street having transferred its headquarters to the capital, is not here in question. But alienated intellectuals working in governmental bureaucracy do not generally conceive their career as an indirect contribution to the business class. They are more likely to view the government and their role, great or small, in it as an instrument for modifying the business power system from which they have become alienated. For these persons, government service represents a frontal attack on the interest groups who have hitherto made the significant decisions.

Intellectuals who may have previously pledged their allegiance to political movements seeking to modify our economic and political structure have now in increasing numbers, it would seem, adopted the alternative of seeking to work these changes through constituted governmental authority. In so far as the intellectual thus conceives the present place of government, he is likely to find himself thinking in terms of supplying the expert knowledge upon which are based executive decisions which move in new directions.

This type of motivation is of course not assumed to be *characteristic* of intellectuals in our public bureaucracies. Its frequency is a question of fact, but that it occurs to some extent is manifest to those who have examined the flow of intellectuals into the state bureaucracy, particularly before the war. In contrast to these alienated intellectuals stands the doubtlessly far larger aggregate of recruits to public bureaucracies: the technicians who are professedly indifferent to any given social policies but whose sentiments and values are broadly those of prevailing power groups. The technicians conceive their role as merely that of implementing whichever policies are defined by policy-makers. The occupational code of the technician constrains him to accept a dependency-relation to the executive. This sense of dependency, which is hedged about with sentiment, is expressed in the formula: the policy-maker supplies the goals (ends, objectives) and we technicians, on the basis of expert knowledge, indicate alternative means for reaching these ends. So controlling and pervasive is this occupational code that it has led technicians to abide by this sharp distinction of means and ends, without recognizing that the verbal distinction itself can support the technician's flight from social responsibility. He regards an end or goal as the terminus of action. He may not see it as the occasion for further consequences. He may not see that the action includes its consequences.

There are, finally, the unattached intellectuals who, in time of acute social crisis such as war or depression, swarm temporarily into public bureaucracies. These *ad hoc* bureaucrats may or may not have been alienated from prevalent power groups. But not having identified their careers with service in bureaucracy, they are probably less constrained by bureaucratic pressures. For them, there is the ready alternative of return to private life.

All this suggests lines of research concerning the recruitment of intellectuals by public bureaucracies. Data concerning the objective criteria for selection are readily available, but these are of secondary interest. We should like to know the class location of intellectuals who find their way into these bureaucracies. Concretely, at what points do alternatives emerge in the intellectual's career line? What pressures lead him to prefer public to private bureaucracies? To what extent does alienation from and repudiation of business-class values play a part in such choices? What are the sources of such estrangement? Can we thus throw light on the common pattern of intellectuals divorcing themselves from the nominally sovereign values to identify themselves with the fate of potential power-centers? Does the flow of intellectuals into public bureaucracy serve as a barometric reading of actual or impending shifts in power? What anticipations are common among intellectuals who expect to find their spiritual home in a state bureaucracy? Data on questions such as these constitute a first step in determining the later effects of bureaucratic life upon the intellectual. Only when this information is assembled can we test the hypothesis that bureaucracies provoke gradual transformations of the alienated intellectual into the a-political technician, whose role is to serve whatever strata happen to be in power.

BUREAUCRATIC POSITION AND PERSPECTIVES

Although we have drawn a contrast between the alienated (policy-minded) intellectual and the technician at the time they enter upon bureaucratic life, this distinction may become increasingly attenuated in the course of their service within the bureaucracy. It appears that the state bureaucracy exerts a pressure upon the alienated intellectual to accommodate himself to the policies of those who make the strategic decisions, with the result that, in time, the role of the one-time alienated intellectual may become indistinguishable from that of the technician.

In describing the process whereby the intellectual in a bureaucracy is converted into a technician, we proceed on the assumption that perspectives and outlook are largely a product of social position. Intellectuals are oriented toward more or less defined social circles and accommodate their interests, attitudes, and objectives to these circles. The demands and expectations inherent in a social position tend to shape the behavior of occupants of that position. As Mead has so well indicated, the social self arises through taking over the organized set of attitudes of significant others. Moreover, this progressive importation of other's evaluations and expectations is cumulative and commonly occurs without the process entering into awareness, except at occasional points of conflict.[8] This view of the formation of role personalities at once directs our attention to differences in the "significant others" for the bureaucratic and un-attached intellectual: in short, it requires us to examine the different clientele of the two types of intellectual and the part they play in shaping the intellectual's role.

Remotely or directly, the client of the bureaucratic intellectual is a policy-maker who is concerned with translating certain vague or well-defined purposes into programs of action. The client's demands of the intellectual may vary, but in essentials they can probably all be subsumed under a limited number of types.

The *specificity* of the client's demands upon the bureaucratic intellectual goes far toward determining the nature of the latter's activities. At one extreme, the policy-maker may simply indicate a general area with no indication of the nature of decisions which are contemplated. This is a vaguely defined area in which there will presumably be need for action at some future date (*e.g.* ethnic relations in Europe or the state of morale in the army). The intellectual is asked to assemble pertinent facts upon the basis of which later decisions may be "intelligently" made. At this point of low specificity of the client's demands, the intellectual has the largest possible scope—at times, an uncomfortably broad scope leading to anxieties as an outcome of imperfect orientation—for defining problems, deciding what are pertinent data and recommending alternative policies. Or a somewhat more definite formulation by the client may be made in the form of indicating a specific area in which policies are to be blocked out and a request made for information bearing on this more clearly defined area (*e.g.* Serb-Croat relations in Europe or production by small industrial concerns during the war). This delimitation of the field reduces the scope of the intellectual in deciding both the nature of the practical problems and the character of pertinent information. Or the problem may be presented to the intellectual at progressively advanced points in the *continuum of decision:* at the point where alternative policies are being considered or when a specific policy has been adopted and there is need for information on means of implementing this policy through a definite program of action or finally, after a given program has been put into practice and there is a demand for assessing the effectiveness of the program. These intervals in the continuum of decision set different types of problems for the intellectual.

---

8. See G. H. Mead, *Mind, Self and Society* (Chicago, 1934), Part III.

In general, there appears to be an inverse relation between the specificity of the problem as defined by the client and scope for initiating policy proposals by the intellectual.

The earlier in the continuum of decision that the bureaucratic intellectual operates, the greater his potential influence in guiding the decision. When the area of inquiry is vaguely indicated by the policy-maker, the intellectual's research can, within limits, focus attention on certain alternative lines of action by ascribing greater weight to certain types of evidence. This seems to have been the case, for example, with Wilson's Fourteen Points which were, in large part, the outgrowth of an appraisal of the total situation by intellectuals "whose brains he borrowed," to use the President's own phrase. In helping to establish such general frameworks of policy, the intellectual can initiate some control from below. In rare situations of this sort, the policy-maker may find himself in the notorious position of the Frenchman in 1848 who, when urged not to join the mob storming the barricades, answered: "I must follow them; I am their leader."

More typically, however, the bureaucratic intellectual finds himself in a position where he is called upon to provide information for alternative or specific policies which have already been formulated by policy-makers. As an expert he is requested to indicate what needs to be taken into account in selecting one or the other of proposed alternatives or in implementing a particular policy. When problems reach the intellectual at this late stage in the continuum of decision, he comes to think largely in instrumental terms and to accept the prevailing definitions of objectives. His perspectives are fixed accordingly. He gets to see only those aspects of the total situation which are directly related to the proposed policy. He may or may not be aware that he is ignoring possible alternatives in his research, by focusing on the consequences or modes of implementing limited alternatives which have been presented to him. He may overlook the fact that a way of seeing also implies a way of not-seeing: that limiting one's purview to alternatives A and B means ignoring alternatives C and D.

This problem of relation to the policy-maker takes on an entirely different cast for the unattached intellectual. *His perspectives may be directed by his position within the class structure* but they are somewhat less subject to the immediate control of a *specific* clientele. He characteristically approaches the problem area quite apart from the prior assumptions and interests of a bureaucratic client. He may feel free to consider the consequences of alternative policies which may have been ignored or rejected by the bureaucracy. His limitations are not so much a matter of by-passing alternatives without adequate inquiry. But, not being subjected to the constraints of impending decisions based on his work, the unattached intellectual may dwell in the realm of good intentions and bad programs for action. Even when he formulates both policy and program in realistic terms, it is difficult for his views to *gain access to responsible policy-makers.* So far as affecting public policy is concerned, he who is not in the bureaucracy becomes a small and often a still voice.

From all this arises the dilemma facing the intellectual who is actively concerned with furthering social innovations. Not too inaccurately, this may be expressed in a slogan: he who innovates is not heard; he who is heard does not innovate. If the intellectual is to play an effective role in putting his knowledge to work, it is increasingly necessary that he become a part of a bureaucratic power-structure. This, however, often requires him to abdicate his privilege of exploring policy-possibilities which he regards as significant. If, on the other hand, he remains unattached in order to preserve full opportunity of choice, he characteristically has neither the resources to carry through his investigations on an appropriate scale nor any strong likelihood of having his findings accepted by policy-makers as a basis for action.

Needless to say, full integrity may be found among both the bureaucratic and unattached intellectuals: the essential differences lie in the relationship to a client and the attendant pressures which play a part in defining the problems which are regarded as significant. Both types of intellectual may have full integrity within the limits of their *definition of problems.* But they have each made an important and, often, a different value decision in accepting or rejecting the definition of a problem. To take a case in point. Both bureaucratic and unattached intellectuals may find themselves dealing with the same problem-area: racial segregation in a northern industrial center. On the fact-finding level, both intellectuals may emerge with much the same conclusions: that a large proportion of Negro workers have low morale and low industrial output, apparently as a result of experiencing continued discrimination. The investigators may also agree that a considerable number of white workers object to any proposal for eliminating segregation. The difference between the outlook and research of the bureaucratic and unattached intellectuals may well become manifest on the next level: that of establishing a policy and converting it into a program. The policy may be defined *for* the bureaucratic intellectual in these terms: how can we make segregation tolerable if not palatable to the Negro worker? Accordingly, the bureaucratic adviser may indicate that certain types of propaganda directed toward the Negro population may serve to heighten morale, without eliminating segregation. The research of the bureaucratic intellectual has thus served to implement a pre-defined policy. The unattached intellectual, however, need not confine his investigation in this way but may study means of eliminating racial segregation without appreciably lowering morale of white workers. He may, in other words, question the prevailing policy by exploring its consequences and by examining ways of implementing an alternative policy. It should be noted that the *validity* of the two sets of findings is not in question but the respective researches will be of use for one purpose and not for the other. *The crucial point is to recognize the value-implications entailed by the very choice and definition of the problem itself and that the choice will be in part fixed by the intellectual's position within the social structure.* The bureaucratic intellectual who must permit the policy-maker to define the scope of his research problem is implicitly lending his skills and knowledge to the preservation of a particular institutional arrangement. The unattached intellectual may not directly affect the prevailing policy but he does bring forward knowledge which would presumably be of service in modifying the current arrangement. Thus, the intellectual makes his most significant value decision in selecting both his clientele and derivatively, the type of problem with which he shall be concerned.[9]

There is another way in which the orientation of intellectuals entering a bureaucracy tends to change, and this derives from the pressure for action. They tend to become, as the loose phrase has it, "less theoretical and more practical." To what does this refer? The closer to the actual locus of decision, the more necessary it is for broad policy to be translated into programs of action and the larger the number of considerations which must be taken into account, over and above the original formulation of policy. This "taking into account" of additional variables generally means a partial change of the original policy; it means, "compromise with the realities of the case." Thus, the closer to the point of actual decision that the intellectual is located, the more he experiences a pressure to temper the wind to the shorn lamb, that is, to fit his original abstract formulations to the exigencies of the situation. This pressure, operating over a period of time, shapes the general perspectives of the bureaucratic intellectual; he comes increasingly to think in technical and instrumental terms of ways of implementing policies *within a given situation.*

For the unattached intellectual, such shifts in perspective of his bureaucratic colleague often seem a "sell-out." This familiar type of conflict results from the differing positions of the two types of intellectuals within the social structure with, inevitably, some differences in perspective. The unattached intellectual can continue to be adamant in abiding

---

9. What we have attempted to do here is to clarify, through a concrete illustration, an essential implication of Weber's conception of the role of *Wertbeziehung* in intellectual inquiry. Weber points out that observations are focused on certain aspects of the concrete situation in terms of values which govern and define what is considered as "significant." It remains then to explore various fixed points in the social structure, the values which are current at these points and thus to determine the effective relation between social structure and intellectual activity. See Max Weber, *Gesammelte Aufsätze zur Wissenschaftslehre* (Tübingen, 1922), 177-184.

by his formulations, since these are not translated into action, and he often fails to see aspects of the action problem which are constantly borne in on the bureaucratic intellectual. The bureaucratic intellectual, on the other hand, has limited alternatives. (1) He can accommodate his own social values and special knowledge to the values of the policy-makers. (2) He can seek to alter the prevailing policies of the executives in the bureaucratic apparatus. (3) He can respond in terms of a schizoid dissociation between his own values and those of the bureaucracy, by regarding his function as purely technical and without value-implications. The first response involves an incorporation of the bureaucracy's values and sometimes a change in the intellectual's prior outlook. The second, when the isolated intellectual seeks to pit his own grounded views against those of the total apparatus, ordinarily involves ineffectual conflict which is often the prelude to the intellectual's flight from the bureaucracy. The third response which, we suppose, is the most frequent, leads to the "technician role." Since this role is supported by the occupational mores of the intellectual—"As a man of science, I do not indulge in value judgments"—it reduces the conflict otherwise experienced in implementing policies largely at variance with one's own judgments. In short, segmentation of roles permits the intellectual to preserve his sense of personal integrity, although he participates in programs which run counter to his own values.

All this suggests that the unattached and bureaucratic intellectual perform quite different functions with respect to social policy. The unattached intellectual can serve as a gadfly, a critic of established policies by publicly indicating some of their implications and consequences. To a limited degree, then, he may affect the climate of decision. With the growth of mass communication, this function has taken on even greater importance than it had in the past. The bureaucratic intellectual, on the other hand, save in the relatively rare cases where he actually defines policy, is largely limited to developing more effective modes of implementing decisions and of introducing alternative possibilities for action which do not violate the values of the bureaucracy. This suggests that unattached intellectuals may be serving common purposes, even during the war crisis, as effectively as, though differently from, the intellectuals who are devoting "their energies to the war effort" by serving in a public bureaucracy.

POLICY-MAKERS AND INTELLECTUALS

But even though the bureaucratic intellectual often accommodates himself to the outlook of policy-makers, he may still project *alternative lines of action which run counter to values and objectives of businessmen in government policy positions.* This clash of values often occurs in the very proposals of policies. It probably underlies an outburst such as the following by a policy-maker who has returned to his job as an advertising executive:

The professorial mind, in my estimation, is one of the most dangerous factors in our government today. Instead of the broad view that is theoretically promised, their thinking under the unaccustomed glow of authority takes wing and soars through the clouds unimpeded by facts and unhindered by actuality.

I've had my fill of these slide-rule boys. I've found there's no give to their inelastic, academic minds . . . there is no opinion equal to their own unless it is one of complete agreement or of greater daring in their world of dreams.

They don't want the advice of people who are experienced. Their book-bound, dream-ribbed, class-room minds definitely have no doors or windows leading in.[10]

Such conflicts, however, are less a product of the bureaucratic context than of a more extended clash between the values and interests of intellectuals and businessmen. The attitudes of organized business toward the intellectual as expressed by a journal such as *Nation's Business* are revealing in this connection.[11] They indicate the ways in which the intellectual comes into conflict with established economic values and interests.

Intellectuals' appraisals of the consequences of current economic practices and arrangements, which they do not regard as sacrosanct, invite forthright attacks by businessmen who identify themselves with these practices as technically efficient and morally right. This is one source of the charge levelled at the intellectual that he lacks practicality. He does not come to terms with "the facts of the case," these "facts" being current practices. "Theoretical economists" who envisage alternative arrangements are pilloried as "sickly sentimentalists" in contrast to the "practical men" who carry on the nation's business. And since these alternatives have usually not been put into effect, all such prospective arrangements can be promptly tagged as "utopian." Thus, the attack on "the lofty intellects who write the guide books to economic Utopias."

The identification of the businessman with his usual routines and cultural axioms does not make him ready to accept changes in these routines and axioms. The following unhappy jingle is a not atypical plea of the man of affairs who wants to get on with his job:

> Work for the office-holders,
> > Professor and theorist and clerk,
> Work to support the scolders
> > who are damning you while you work.

---

10. Lou R. Maxon, in a statement issued in connection with his resignation from the Office of Price Administration, *New York Times*, July 15, 1943, 15.

11. This brief summary is based upon a sample of all references to intellectuals, professors, etc. contained in *Nation's Business* for six selected years in the period between 1928 and 1943.

Closely allied to his challenge of business-class mores is the intellectual's use of historical and critical analysis. The world of business affairs is ordinarily experienced by those most directly involved in it as a datum, a given, not analyzable into distinct elements which can, perhaps, be differently recombined.[12] The intellectual's analysis is consequently perceived as "unrealistic" and "theoretical" (in the invidious sense). It is not surprising, then, that businessmen have made an epithet of "theory," and reject "professorial abstraction developed in the mists of intellectual rookeries."

In addition to these direct sources of conflict, there are lines of cleavage as a result of the different positions of intellectuals and organized business in the social structure. However concerned the intellectual may be with bettering his own economic status, institutional controls require him to view this as a by-product rather than as the immediate purpose of his activity. The role of the businessman, on the other hand, is firmly and traditionally defined as that of maximizing his economic returns (by legitimate means) with all other aspects of his role subsidiary to that institutionally defined objective. There are, then, two opposed designs for living, two contrasting sets of cultural imperatives. At least some of the mutual suspicion and recriminations derive from this institutionalized opposition of outlook. The businessman may question and impugn the integrity of the intellectual's mores. Or, he may seek to assimilate these mores to his own. Thus, intellectuals are also held to be primarily self-interested: their quest for knowledge is viewed as *merely* an effort to improve their position, as in the following definition of "a professor book":

an impractical book written by a professor largely, the reader feels, because the professor must get his name affixed to a publication.

Or, the businessman may seek to devaluate the social personality of the intellectual. Among those who have had little formal education, this may readily lead to anti-intellectualism with graduate degrees becoming a symbol of disrepute. The businessman with higher formal education has, at one time, been subordinated to professors. In this capacity, he has had occasion to learn of the values and standards of the professorial existence which, in the ideal pattern, are in some respects at variance with those of the business world. Having been emancipated from college, the businessman may act defensively if only because he has a vestige of guilt in not conforming to the disinterested values to which he was exposed as a student. He may seize the opportunity to assert his full emancipation by devaluating his one-time superordinate, thus effecting a reversal of roles. This is not unlike a type of conflict which arises in the family as the child moves from the age of dependency and subordination to adulthood and independent achievement. Thus, we are told

12. This is adapted from Mannheim's formulation, *Ideology and Utopia*, 246.

that professors are characteristically "men who have spent years in addressing immature intellects [and therefore] are impatient of opposition." And the reversal of roles is acclaimed, in a forthright fashion, when professors are reminded of their indebtedness to those who make it possible for them to survive, as in the comment on "so-called intellectuals . . . who come mostly from college communities where they have been privileged to use expensive apparatus and facilities and seldom counted the cost to the taxpayers or honored the system which produced the benevolent donors of the buildings and equipment, and oftentimes the bread-and-butter salaries."

FRUSTRATIONS OF THE INTELLECTUAL IN BUREAUCRACY

With such patterns of conflict as a background, it is not at all surprising that the intellectual commonly experiences a series of frustrations, once he becomes an integral part of a bureaucracy which is in some measure controlled by those who can neither live with him nor without him.[13] The honeymoon of intellectuals and policy-makers is often nasty, brutish, and short. This has an understandable sociological basis. The intellectual, before he enters upon his bureaucratic post, is wont to consider his intellectual problems in abstraction from the demands of specific other persons. He may feel that a problem is solved on its own merits. Once he finds himself in a bureaucracy, he discovers that the intellectual task itself is closely connected with social relations within the bureaucracy. His selection of problems for study must be guided by what he knows or thinks he knows of his clients or prospective clients; his formulation of the problem, his analyses and reports must be geared to the same relationship to a client. In short, where he had previously experienced a sense of intellectual autonomy—whether real or spurious is for the moment unimportant—he now becomes aware of *visible controls* over the nature and direction of his inquiries. This sense of constraint, particularly when he is by no means clear about the exact wants of the client or if clear, when he disagrees with the nature of these wants, is registered in frustration. The resultant conflicts between the criteria of choosing and analyzing problems as an unattached intellectual and as a bureaucratic intellectual often leads to the flight from bureaucracy and the escape to assumed autonomy.

The high turnover of expert personnel in public bureaucracies is not

---

13. It would be interesting to circulate the following observation by Joseph Stalin among American policymakers. ". . . no ruling class has yet managed to get along without its own intellectuals. The problem is not to discourage these comrades." And again: " 'Specialist-baiting' has always been considered and continues to be a harmful and shameful manifestation." [Judging from the cases of Vavilov and Varga, among many others, Stalin's policy changed again.]

merely a matter of client dissatisfaction or of criticism by outside groups, such as Congress. It is often the product of the cumulative frustrations experienced by the intellectual who has been previously conditioned to a sense of personal autonomy and cannot abide the visible constraints imposed by a formal organization. Thus, a psychiatrist recently observed a marked rise in the euphoria and optimism of his friends. He was at a loss to explain this, and at first assumed that it was a result of United Nations victories. Only later did he realize that he had encountered a series of friends who had just left Washington bureaucracy for good. They were exhibiting euphoria born of release from frustration.

So, too, Stouffer reports his wartime observation:

> In the Washington Mêlée one cannot keep the Alpine detachment which is the glory of university research in times of peace. There are many frustrations. . . . All the agencies doing work in sociology or social psychology, such as the Office of War Information, Office of Strategic Services, Military Intelligence and others, have much the same experience.[14]

It is instructive to examine some of the more familiar types of frustrations which often culminate in disillusionment, for these throw light on the possibilities and limitations of the bureaucratic intellectual in affecting policy. These frustrations can be classified into two main groups: (1) those deriving from conflict of values between the intellectual and the policy-maker, and (2) from the bureaucratic type of organization itself.

1. *Conflicts of values between intellectual and policy-makers:*

a. Occasionally the bureaucratic intellectual finds himself the target for conflict arising from different universes of discourse of the policy-maker and himself. Research which appears trivial from an immediately practical standpoint may be highly significant for its theoretic implications and may later illumine a series of practical problems. The intellectual is in time compelled to accept new criteria of significance.

b. Research findings may be exploited for purposes which run counter to the values of the intellectual; his recommendations for policy based on the weight of the evidence may be ignored and a counter-policy introduced.

c. The intellectual will often not be willing to commit himself on the basis of what seems to him flimsy evidence, whereas the policy-maker must do so because of the urgency for action.

d. Specialists may experience frustrations from being required to work in fields which are outside their sphere of competence, since policy-makers are at times not clear on significant differences between specialists.

2. *Frustrations arising from bureaucratic organization:*

a. Since bureaucracies are organized for action, questions are often asked of intellectuals for which they have no immediate answer. Or, this may invite the "deadline neurosis"; problems may be raised which it is impossible to solve within the allotted time.

---

14. Samuel A. Stouffer, "Social science and the soldier," in *American Society in Wartime*, ed. by W. F. Ogburn (1943), 116.

The problem of the deadline has perhaps been best described by Robert Louis Stevenson in an entirely different context:

"This is no cabinet science, in which things are tested to a scruple; we theorize with a pistol to our head; we are confronted with a new set of conditions on which we have not only to pass judgment, but to take action, before the hour is at an end."

b. Lines of communication between policy-makers and intellectuals may be clogged, leading typically to frustrations.

1) Since policy-makers often do not keep intellectuals informed of impending problems of policy, it is difficult for the latter to determine what are relevant data.

2) Or, there may be the problem of having research findings reach the appropriate policy-maker, who is confronted with a mass of material emanating from different sources.

3) Or, the findings on their way to the policy-maker may be emasculated and distorted by intervening personnel.

4) Or, finally, there is the problem of so formulating the findings that the most significant results will be intelligible to and engage the interest of the policy-maker. The "processing of the material" may require simplification to the point where some of the more complex though significant findings are discarded.

c. Despite all precautions, the intellectual's findings may not be used by those for whom it is intended. This eliminates the very rationale of the intellectual's work and dissipates his interest in his work, leading to the "boondoggling neurosis." (Correlatively, even occasional use of research findings, no matter how limited the context in which these have been put to use, serves to reinvigorate the morale of the intellectual.)

1) The policy-maker will at times reject funded research in the social sciences on the assumption that his first-hand experience has given him a more secure understanding of the situation than the intellectual can possibly attain. This is the more likely to occur if the findings suggest changes in familiar routines and practices, since it is seldom that the intellectual can demonstrate the greater effectiveness of proposed as compared with current arrangements.

This excursion into one phase of the intellectual's role in our society is intended primarily to formulate certain hypotheses. The collection of life-histories, diaries, and journal-books of intellectuals in public bureaucracies, direct participant-observation and historical data can provide a firm and fruitful basis for research in this field.[15]

---

15. Since this was written, an initial step in this direction has been taken by Julian L. Woodward, "Making government opinion research bear upon operations," *American Sociological Review*, 1944, 9, 670-677. See also R. K. Merton, "The role of applied social science in the formation of policy," *Philosophy of Science*, July 1949, 16, 161-181.

VIII CONTRIBUTIONS TO THE THEORY OF REFERENCE GROUP BEHAVIOR*

THIS CHAPTER PROCEEDS on the assumption that there is two-way traffic between social theory and empirical research. Systematic empirical materials help advance social theory by imposing the task and by affording the opportunity for interpretation along lines often unpremeditated, and social theory, in turn, defines the scope and enlarges the predictive value of empirical findings by indicating the conditions under which they hold. The systematic data of *The American Soldier*,[1] in all their numerous variety, provide a useful occasion for examining the interplay of social theory and applied social research.

More particularly, we attempt to identify and to order the fairly numerous researches in *The American Soldier* which, by implication or by explicit statement, bear upon the theory of *reference group behavior*. (The empirical realities which this term denotes will presently be considered in some detail. It should be said here, however, that although the *term* "reference group" is not employed in these volumes, any more than it has yet found full acceptance in the vocabulary of sociology as distinct from social psychology, reference group *concepts* play an important part in the interpretative apparatus utilized by the Research Branch of the Information and Education Division of the War Department.)

At two points, we deal briefly with related subjects which are not, however, part and parcel of reference group theory. We review the statistical indices of group attributes and social structure as variously adopted in these researches, and attempt to indicate, though very briefly and programmatically, the specific value of *systematically* incorporating such indices in further research. And, in equally brief fashion, we point

---

* In collaboration with Alice S. Rossi.

1. The authors of the first of these volumes, "Adjustment during Army Life," are S. A. Stouffer, E. A. Suchman, L. C. DeVinney, S. A. Star, and R. M. Williams, Jr.; of the second, entitled "Combat and Its Aftermath," S. A. Stouffer, A. A. Lumsdaine, M. H. Lumsdaine, R. M. Williams, Jr., M. B. Smith, I. L. Janis, S. A. Star, and L. S. Cottrell, Jr. Both were published in 1949 by the Princeton University Press.

out how data analyzed by the Research Branch from a psychological standpoint can be supplemented and usefully re-worked from the standpoint of functional sociology.

A common procedure for extracting and attempting to develop the theoretical implications of *The American Soldier* is adopted throughout the analysis. This entails the intensive re-examination of *cases* of research reported in these volumes, with an eye to subsuming the findings under higher-level abstractions or generalizations. In the volumes themselves, the authors austerely (and, in our judgment, wisely) limit their analysis to the interpretation of the behavior of soldiers and to the organizational contexts in which that behavior occurred. But manifestly, the analytical concepts hold not merely for the behavior of soldiers. By provisionally generalizing these concepts, we may be in a position to explore the wider implications of the materials for social theory.

Our discussion thus grows out of an internal analysis of every research study in these volumes in which some reference group concept was used by the authors as an interpretative variable. The object of collating these cases is to determine the points at which they invite extensions of the theory of reference group behavior which can be followed up through further strategically focused research. Occasionally, the effort is made to suggest how these theoretical extensions might be incorporated into designs for empirical research which will thus build upon the findings of the Research Branch. In this way, there may be provision for continuity in the interplay between cumulative theory and new research.

The inductive re-examination of cases admits also the linking of these reference group conceptions with other conceptions prevalent in social psychology and sociology which have not ordinarily been connected with the theory of reference group behavior. In the degree that such connections are established, *The American Soldier* will have served a further function of empirical research: the provisional consolidation of presently scattered fragments of theory.

Along these lines, an effort will be made to indicate the coherence between reference group theory and conceptions of functional sociology. It appears that these deal with different facets of the same subject: the one centers on the processes through which men relate themselves to groups and refer their behavior to the values of these groups; the other centers on the consequences of the processes primarily for social structures, but also for the individuals and groups involved in these structures. It will be found that reference group theory and functional sociology address different questions to the same phenomena but that these questions have reciprocal relevance.

Throughout, then, this essay aims to learn from *The American Soldier* what it has to yield for the current state of reference group theory and related theoretical problems. Committed as we are to the notion that the development of social theory requires a large measure of continuity, rather than a collection of self-contained and allegedly definitive results, this means that the present re-working of some of the materials in *The American Soldier* is itself a highly provisional phase in an ongoing development rather than a stable stopping point. Nor is it assumed, of course, that each and all of the extensions of reference group theory here proposed will in fact turn out to be sound; like any other form of human activity, theorizing has its quota of risk. Indeed, it is when every hypothesis provisionally advanced at a particular stage in the development of a discipline turns out to be apparently confirmed that the theorist has cause for alarm, since a record of unvarying success may indicate a defective and overly-compliant apparatus for confirmation rather than an unexceptionably sound theory.

THE CONCEPT OF RELATIVE DEPRIVATION

Of the various concepts employed by the authors of *The American Soldier* to interpret their multiform materials, there is one which takes a major place. This is the concept of relative deprivation. Its central significance is in some measure evidenced by its being one of the two concepts expressly called to the attention of the reader in the chapter introducing the two volumes. As the authors themselves put it, after a brief allusion to the conception of varying profiles, "Other conceptual tools, notably a theory of *relative deprivation,* also are introduced to help in more generally ordering otherwise disparate empirical findings." (I, 52)

Although the concept of relative deprivation is periodically utilized for the interpretation of variations in attitudes among different categories of men, varying, for example, with respect to age, education and marital status, it nowhere finds formal definition in the pages of these volumes. Nevertheless, as we shall presently discover, the outlines of this conception gradually emerge from the various instances in which it is put to use. It is in the very first instance of such use, for example, that the authors refer to the nature of the theoretical utility of the conception and to its possible kinship to other, established concepts of sociological theory:

The idea [of relative deprivation] is simple, almost obvious, but its utility comes in reconciling data, especially in later chapters, where its applicability is not at first too apparent. The idea would seem to have a kinship to and, in part, include such well-known sociological concepts as "social frame of reference," "patterns of expectation," or "definitions of the situation." (I, 125)

This absence of a formal definition of relative deprivation is no great handicap. In any case, the authors escape the well-established tradition of works in sociological theory to be replete with numerous definitions which remain unemployed. In place of an explicit definition of the concept we can assemble an array of all those occasions, scattered through the volumes and dealing with seemingly unrelated types of situations, in which the concept has been put to use by the authors, and in this way we can learn something of the actual operational character of the concept.

The following list represents, albeit in much abbreviated form, every research in which some version of the concept of relative deprivation (or a kindred concept, such as relative status) is explicitly drawn upon in *The American Soldier:*

1. *With reference to the drafted married man: "Comparing himself with his unmarried associates in the Army,* he could feel that induction demanded greater sacrifice from him than from them; and *comparing himself with his married civilian friends,* he could feel that he had been called on for sacrifices which they were escaping altogether." (I, 125)

2. "The average high school graduate or college man was a clear-cut candidate for induction; marginal cases on occupational grounds probably occurred much more often in groups with less educational attainment. On the average, the non high school man who was inducted *could point to more acquaintances* conceivably no more entitled to deferment than himself, who nonetheless had been deferred on occupational grounds . . . when they *compared themselves with their civilian friends* they may have been more likely to feel that they were required to make sacrifices which *others like them* were excused from making." (I, 127)

3. "The concept of *relative deprivation* is particularly helpful in evaluating the role of education in satisfaction with status or job, as well as in some aspects of approval or criticism of the Army. . . . With higher levels of aspiration than the less educated, *the better educated man had more to lose in his own eyes and in the eyes of his friends* by failure to achieve some sort of status in the Army. Hence, frustration was greater for him than for others if a goal he sought was not attained. . . ." (I, 153)

4. ". . . the concept of differential deprivation and reward . . . may help us understand some of the psychological processes relevant to this problem. In general, it is of course true that the overseas soldier, *relative to soldiers still at home,* suffered a greater break with home ties and with many of the amenities of life in the United States to which he was accustomed. But it was also true that, *relative to the combat soldier,* the overseas soldier [in rear areas of an active theater] not in combat and not likely to get into combat suffered far less deprivation than the actual fighting man." (I, 172)

5. "The concept of differential deprivation would lead us to look further for a reason why the actually more deprived group of soldiers seemed little more critical than the less deprived group . . . the less *the differential between officers and men* in the enjoyment of scarce privileges—the extreme case being that of actual combat—the less likely was the enlisted man to be critical of the officers and the easier it was for him to accept the inevitability of deprivation." (I, 181)

6. ". . . as would be expected . . . those soldiers who had advanced slowly *relative to other soldiers of equal longevity* in the Army were the most critical of the Army's promotion opportunities. *But relative rate of advancement can*

be based on different standards by different classes of the Army population.
For example, a grade school man who became a corporal after a year of service
would have had a more rapid rate of promotion *compared with most of his
friends at the same educational level* than would a college man who rose to
the same grade in a year. Hence we would expect, at a given rank and a given
longevity, that the better educated would be more likely than others to complain of the slowness of promotion. . . . A similar phenomenon appeared to
operate between different branches of the service." (I, 250)

7. "From the studies of enlisted men reported previously in this chapter,
it would be expected that attitudes of officers about promotion, like those of
enlisted men, would reflect some relationship with level of expectation and
with level of achievement *relative to that of one's acquaintances.* Thus we
would expect a captain who had been in grade a long time *compared with
other captains* to be less happy about the promotion situation than a lieutenant in grade a relatively short time." (I, 279)

8. ". . . it seems likely that both Northern and Southern Negroes may have
been considerably influenced in their overall adjustment by other psychological
compensations in being stationed in the South, which can be understood if we
look at their situation as one of *relative status.*
"*Relative to most Negro civilians whom he saw in Southern towns,* the
Negro soldier had a position of comparative wealth and dignity." (I, 563)

9. "Putting it simply, the psychological values of Army life to the Negro
soldier in the South *relative to the Southern Negro civilian* greatly exceeded
the psychological values of Army life to the Negro soldier in the North *relative to the Northern Negro civilian.*" (I, 564)

These nine excerpts touch upon the core interpretative statements in
which the notion of relative deprivation or affiliated concepts were expressly utilized to interpret otherwise anomalous or inconsistent findings.[2] To these explicit uses of the concept we shall later add several
research cases not subjected by the authors to interpretation in terms of
reference group concepts which nevertheless seem explicated by such
concepts.

In all these cases, it should be noted, the concept of relative deprivation serves the same theoretical purpose: it is used as an interpretative
intervening variable. The researches were designed to study the sentiments
and attitudes of American soldiers—their attitudes toward induction, for
example, or their appraisals of chances for promotion. These attitudes
are typically taken as the *dependent variables.* The analysis of data finds
that these attitudes differ among soldiers of varying status—for example,
older or married men exhibited more resentment toward induction than
younger or unmarried men; those enjoying the status of high school and
college graduates were less likely to be optimistic about their prospects

---

2. It thus appears, as we shall have occasion to note in some detail, that the concept of relative deprivation grows out of what we have called "the serendipity
pattern" of the impact of empirical research upon theory, namely, "the fairly common experience of observing an *unanticipated, anomalous and strategic datum* which
becomes the occasion for developing a new theory or for extending an existing
theory." See Chapter III

for promotion in the Army. These status attributes are in general taken provisionally as the *independent variables*. Once the relationships between independent and dependent variables are established, the problem is one of accounting for them: of inferring how it comes to be that the better educated are typically less optimistic about their chances for promotion or how it comes to be that the married man exhibits greater resentment over his induction into military service. At this point of interpretation, the concept of relative deprivation is introduced, so that the pattern of analysis becomes somewhat as follows: the married man (independent variable) more often questions the legitimacy of his induction (dependent variable), because he appraises the situation within the frame of reference (interpretative variable) yielded by comparing himself with other married men still in civilian life, who escaped the draft entirely, or with unmarried men in the Army, whose induction did not call for comparable sacrifice. We may thus tag the major function of the concept of relative deprivation as that of a provisional after-the-fact interpretative concept which is intended to help explain the variation in attitudes expressed by soldiers of differing social status. And since after-the-fact interpretations have a distinctive place in the ongoing development of theory, we shall later want to consider this characteristic of the concept of relative deprivation at some length.[3]

The collation of these key excerpts serves as something more than a thin summary of the original materials. Since the studies employing the concept of relative deprivation deal with diverse subject-matters, they are scattered through the pages of *The American Soldier* and thus are not likely to be examined in terms of their mutual theoretical linkages. The juxtaposition of excerpts admits of a virtually *simultaneous inspection* of the several interpretations and, in turn, permits us to detect the central categories which were evidently taken by the Research Branch as the *bases of comparison* presumably implicit in the observed attitudes and evaluations of soldiers. And once the categories of analysis employed by the Research Branch are detected, their logical connections can be

---

3. At this point it need be noted only in passing that it is premature to assume that *ex post facto* interpretations are *in principle* not susceptible to empirical nullification. To argue this, as Nathan Glazer does in his overly-quick rejection of the concept of relative deprivation, is to be opaque to the interplay between theory and research in the *historical development* of a discipline. As we shall see, there is no foundation for saying, as Glazer does, that the notion of relative deprivation cannot conceivably be nullified: "Thus, [with the concept of relative deprivation] a little imagination will permit us to cover any conceivable outcome. . . ." And later, he claims, that the conception "cannot be refuted by facts, and it will be found to hold true whatever the outcome of a given set of data." It will presently become clear that propositions incorporating the concept of relative deprivation are readily subject to empirical nullification, if they are in fact untrue. To appreciate one reason for our stress on empirically-oriented sociological theory as an ongoing *development*, see the consequences of neglecting this fact as exhibited in Nathan Glazer, " 'The American Soldier' as science," *Commentary*, 1949, 8, 487-96.

worked out, thus leading to formulations which seem to have significance for the further development of reference group theory.

If we proceed inductively, we find that the frames of reference for the soldiers under observation by the Research Branch were provisionally assumed to be of three kinds. First of all are those cases in which the attitudes or judgments of the men were held to be influenced by comparison with the situation of others with whom they were in *actual association,* in sustained social relations, such as the "married civilian friends" of the soldier in excerpt 1, or the "acquaintances" of the non-high-school man in excerpt 2.

A second implied basis of comparison is with those men who are in some pertinent respect *of the same status* or in the *same social category,* as in the case of the captain who compares his lot "with other captains" in excerpt 7 without any implication that they are necessarily in direct social interaction.

And third, comparison is assumed with those who are in some pertinent respect of *different status* or in a *different social category,* as in the case of the non-combat soldier compared with combat men in excerpt 4, or the enlisted men compared with officers in excerpt 5 (again without social interaction between them being necessarily implied).

For the most part, as we learn from this inspection of cases, the groups or individuals presumably taken as bases for comparison by soldiers do not fall simply into one *or* another of these three types, but involve various combinations of them. Most commonly, presumed comparison is with *associates* of the same status, as the grade-school man compared with friends of the same educational level in excerpt 6, or with various unassociated "others" who are of a *status similar in some salient respect and dissimilar in other respects,* such as the Negro soldier who compares himself with the Negro civilian in excerpts 8 and 9.

If these attributes of the individuals or groups serving as presumed frames of reference are arranged in a matrix, then the conceptual structure of the notion of relative deprivation (and affiliated concepts) becomes more readily visible. The schematic arrangement enables us to locate, not only the frames of comparative reference most often utilized in the interpretation of data by the Research Branch, but additional possible frames of reference which found little place in their interpretation. It thus affords an occasion for systematically exploring the theoretical nature of relative deprivation as an interpretative tool and for indicating the points at which it possibly deepens and broadens the apposite theory of reference group behavior.

In substance, the groups or individuals taken as points of reference in the nine excerpts are explicitly characterized by these few attributes. The presence of sustained social relations between the individual and those taken as a basis for comparison indicates that they are to this degree, in a common *membership group* or *in-group,* and their absence, that they are in a *non-membership* or *out-group.* When it comes to comparative status, the implied classification is slightly more complex: the individuals comprising the base of comparison may be of the same status as the subject or different, and if different, the status may be higher, lower, or unranked. The array of reference points implied in the interpretations of the Research Branch thus appears as follows:

ATTRIBUTES OF INDIVIDUALS, SOCIAL CATEGORIES AND GROUPS TAKEN AS A FRAME OF COMPARATIVE REFERENCE BY INDIVIDUALS*

IN SUSTAINED SOCIAL RELATIONS WITH INDIVIDUAL	SAME STATUS	DIFFERENT SOCIAL STATUS		
		Higher	Lower	Unranked
Yes—(membership- or in-group)	# 1 married friends # 2 non high school acquaintances # 6 friends at same educational level	# 5 officers	# 8, 9 Negro civilians in South	# 3 friends # 7 acquaintances
	ORIENTATIONS OF INDIVIDUAL TO			
No—(non-membership or out-group)	# 4 soldiers in U.S. or in active combat # 6 soldiers of equal longevity # 7 other captains	# 5 officers	# 8, 9 Negro civilians in South	

* The numbers refer to the appropriate excerpts which are here being provisionally classified.

Examination of this matrix of variables implied by the notion of relative deprivation at once directs attention to several empirical and theoretical problems. These problems, as will presently become evident, not only bear specifically upon the concept of relative deprivation but more generally upon a theory of reference group behavior.

It will be noted from the preliminary survey of cases contained in the matrix that, at times, the authors of *The American Soldier* assume that individuals take as a base for self-reference the situation of people with whom they are in direct social interaction: primarily, the in-group of friends and associates. At others, the assumed frame of reference is yielded by social categories of people—combat soldiers, other captains, etc.–with whom the individual is not in sustained social relations. In order to highlight the connection of the concept of relative deprivation with reference group theory, these "others" with whom the individual does not interact are here designated as non-membership groups or out-groups.[4] Since both membership groups and non-membership groups, in-groups and out-groups, have in fact been taken as assumed social frames of reference in these interpretations, this at once leads to a general question of central importance to a developing theory of reference group behavior: *under which conditions are associates within one's own groups taken as a frame of reference for self-evaluation and attitude-formation, and under which conditions do out-groups or non-membership groups provide the significant frame of reference?*

Reference groups are, in principle, almost innumerable: any of the groups of which one is a member, and these are comparatively few, as well as groups of which one is not a member, and these are, of course, legion, can become points of reference for shaping one's attitudes, evaluations and behavior. And this gives rise to another set of problems requiring theoretical formulation and further empirical inquiry. For, as the matrix arrangement of cases drawn from *The American Soldier* plainly suggests, the individual may be oriented toward any one *or more* of the various kinds of groups and statuses—membership groups and non-membership groups, statuses like his own or if different, either higher, lower, or not socially ranked with respect to his own. This, then, locates a further problem: if *multiple* groups or statuses, with their possibly divergent or even contradictory norms and standards, are taken as a frame of reference by the individual, how are these discrepancies resolved?[5]

---

4. We recognize that this sentence is replete with implicit problems which it would be premature to consider at this point. It involves, for example, the problem of criteria of "membership" in a group. Insofar as frequency of social interaction is one such criterion, we must recognize that the boundaries between groups are anything but sharply drawn. Rather, "members" of given groups are variously connected with other groups of which they are not *conventionally* regarded as members, though the sociologist might have ample basis for including them in these latter groups, by virtue of their frequent social interaction with its conventional membership. So, too, we are here momentarily by-passing the question of distinctions between social *groups* and social *categories,* the latter referring to established statuses between the occupants of which there may be little or no interaction. It will also be noticed by some that the formulation contained in *The American Soldier* extends the formulations by such theorists of social psychology as George H. Mead who confined himself to *membership groups* as significant frames of reference in his concept of the "generalized other" and in his account of the formation of self-attitudes. All this bears only passing mention at this point since it will be considered at a more appropriate place.

5. Though this problem is reminiscent of the traditional but only slightly clarified problem of conflict between multiple group *affiliations* or multiple *roles,* it is by no means identical with it. For, as we have seen, frames of reference are yielded not only by one's *own* membership groups or one's own statuses, but by non-membership groups and other statuses, as well.

These initial questions may help establish the range of our inquiry. That men act in a social frame of reference yielded by the groups of which they are a part is a notion undoubtedly ancient and probably sound. Were this alone the concern of reference group theory, it would merely be a new term for an old focus in sociology, which has always been centered on the group determination of behavior. There is, however, the further fact that men frequently orient themselves to groups *other than their own* in shaping their behavior and evaluations, and it is the problems centered about this fact of orientation to non-membership groups that constitute the distinctive concern of reference group theory. Ultimately, of course, the theory must be generalized to the point where it can account for *both* membership- and non-membership-group orientations, but immediately its major task is to search out the processes through which individuals relate themselves to groups to which they do *not* belong.

In general, then, reference group theory aims to systematize the determinants and consequences of those processes of evaluation and self-appraisal in which the individual takes the values or standards of other individuals and groups as a comparative frame of reference.[6]

From our brief preliminary examination, it appears that the researches in *The American Soldier* utilizing the concept of relative deprivation can act as a catalyst quickening theoretical clarification and the formulation of problems for further empirical study. But the precise nature of these formulations can be better seen through a detailed examination of several of these cases after we have more definitely connected the concept of relative deprivation with the theory of reference group behavior.

RELATIVE *DEPRIVATION* OR *RELATIVE* DEPRIVATION

In developing their concept of relative deprivation, the authors of *The American Soldier* have, on the whole, centered their attention on the deprivation component rather than the relative component of the concept. They have, so to say, focused on relative *deprivation* rather than on *relative* deprivation. The reason for this seems both apparent and understandable, in view of the conspicuously deprivational character of the Army situations with which they dealt. By and large, American men viewed service in the armed forces as at best a grim and reluctantly accepted necessity:

The vast majority of men did not come into the Army voluntarily . . . the acceptance of the soldier role probably tended to be passive in character, at least with respect to initial attitudes . . . the passive attitude toward military

---

6. This summary and elliptical statement will be amplified in later sections of the chapter.

service implied a relative absence of identification with broad social goals which would serve to deflect attention away from the day-to-day frustrations in the new environment. Recruits were therefore likely to be sharply aware of the deprivational features of Army life. (I, 208-9)

It was, then, the patterns of response to a basically deprivational situation which most often called for study and it was primarily in the service of interpreting these patterns of response that the concept of relative deprivation was developed. As the term, relative deprivation, itself suggests, the concept was primarily utilized to help account for feelings of dissatisfaction, particularly in cases where the objective situation would at first glance not seem likely to provoke such feelings. This is not to say that the concept was wholly confined to interpreting the feelings of dissatisfaction, deprivation, or injustice among soldiers, since the presumed practice of comparing one's own situation with that of others often resulted in a state of relative satisfaction. In the main, however, satisfactions stemming from such comparison with others are seen in the role of offsetting excessive dissatisfaction in cases of multiple comparison: for example, the dissatisfaction of the noncombat man overseas, presumably reinforced by comparison with those serving in the United States, is tempered by satisfaction with his status as compared with the combat man. (I, 173)

As the authors themselves evidently recognize, "deprivation" is the incidental and particularized component of the concept of relative deprivation, whereas the more significant nucleus of the concept is its stress upon social and psychological experience as "relative." This may be seen from the text at the point where the authors introduce the notion of relative deprivation and suggest its kinship to such other sociological concepts as "social frame of reference, patterns of expectation, or definitions of the situation." (I, 125) It is the *relative* component, the standards of comparison in self-evaluation, that these concepts have in common.

By freeing the concept of relative deprivation from confinement to the particular data which it was initially designed to interpret, it may become generalized and related to a larger body of theory. Relative deprivation can provisionally be regarded as a special concept in reference group theory. And since *The American Soldier* provides systematic empirical data and not merely discursive views on the concept of relative deprivation, the way is possibly opened for progressively clarifying crucial variables so that further cumulative research bearing on the theory can be mapped out.

All this, however, is still programmatic. Whether *The American Soldier* does indeed have these functions for reference group theory can only be determined through inspection, at closer range than we have yet attempted, of the researches in these volumes bearing upon the theory.

The analysis of these several cases is intended to document and to elaborate the emergence of those problems of reference group theory briefly foreshadowed in the foregoing pages and to indicate further related problems which have not yet received notice. Toward this end, the essential facts and basic interpretation as these are set out by the Research Branch will be summarized for each case, and followed by a statement of its apparent implications for the advancement of reference group theory.

By way of preview, it may be said that these cases generate the formulation of a wide range of specific problems which will be taken up in detail and which are here roughly indicated by the following list of headings:

> *Membership-groups operating as reference groups;*
> *Conflicting reference groups and mutually sustaining reference groups;*
> *Uniformities of behavior derived from reference group theory;*
> *Statistical indices of social structure;*
> *Reference group theory and social mobility;*
> *Functions of positive orientations to non-membership groups;*
> *Social processes sustaining or curbing these orientations;*
> *Psychological and social functions of institutions regulating passage from*
> *one membership group to another;*
> *and*
> *A review of concepts kindred to reference group theory.*

MEMBERSHIP GROUP AS REFERENCE GROUP

Case #1. This research deals with soldiers' evaluations of promotion opportunities as these were elicited by the question, "Do you think a soldier with ability has a good chance for promotion?" A generalized finding, necessarily and too much abbreviated in this summary, holds that for each level of longevity, rank and education, "the *less* the promotion opportunity afforded by a branch or combination of branches, the *more favorable* the opinion tends to be toward promotion opportunity." (I, 256) Within the limits of the data in hand,[7] this paradoxical response of greater satisfaction with opportunities for mobility in the very branches characterized by less mobility finds clear demonstration. Thus, although the Air Corps had a conspicuously high rate of promotion, Air Corps men were definitely far more critical of chances for promotion than, say, men in the Military Police, where the objective chances for promotion "were about the worst in any branch of the Army." So, too, at any given rank and longevity, the better educated soldiers, despite their notably

---

7. It is important that we introduce this caveat, for it is scarcely probable that this relationship between actual mobility rates and individual satisfaction with mobility chances holds throughout the entire range of variation. If promotion rates were reduced to practically zero in some of these groups, would one then find an even more "favorable opinion" of promotion chances? Presumably, the relationship is curvilinear, and this requires the sociologist to work out toward the conditions under which the observed linear relation fails to obtain.

higher rates of promotion in general, were the more critical of opportunities for promotion.

This paradox is provisionally explained by the Research Branch as a result of evaluations occurring within the frame of reference provided by group rates of promotion. A generally high rate of mobility induces excessive hopes and expectations among members of the group so that each is more likely to experience a sense of frustration in his present position and disaffection with the chances for promotion. As it is put by the authors, "Without reference to the theory that such opinions represent a relationship between their expectations and their achievements *relative to others in the same boat with them,* such a finding would be paradoxical indeed." (I, 251, italics supplied)

Theoretical implications. First of all, it should be noted that it was an anomalous finding which apparently elicited the hypothesis that evaluations of promotion chances are a function of expectations and achievements "relative to others in the same boat with them." And, in turn, the raw uninterpreted finding appears anomalous only because it is inconsistent with the commonsense assumption that, in general, evaluations will correspond to the objective facts of the case. According to common sense, marked differences in objective rates of promotion would presumably be reflected in corresponding differences in assessments of chances for promotion. Had such correspondences been empirically found, there would seemingly have been little occasion for advancing this hypothesis of a group frame of reference. As it turns out, the data suggest that men define the situation differently. But it is not enough to mention these "definitions of the situation"; it is necessary to *account for* them. And the function of the concept of relative deprivation (as with other concepts of reference groups) is precisely that of helping to account for observed definitions of a situation.

In this case, it required *systematic* empirical data, such as those assembled in *The American Soldier,* to *detect* the anomalous pattern, not detectable through impressionistic observation. And this illustrates a basic role of systematic empirical research in reaching unanticipated, anomalous and strategic findings that exert pressure for initiating or extending theory.[8] The data and the hypothesis advanced to account for them open up further theoretical and research problems, which can here receive bare mention rather than the full exposition they deserve.

The hypothesis makes certain important assumptions about *the* group taken as a point of reference by the soldiers and thus affecting their level of satisfaction with promotion opportunities. This assumption is stated, as we have seen, in the form that evaluations are "relative to others in

---

8. This "creative function" of empirical research for theory warrants greater attention than is accorded it in Chapter III of this book.

the same boat." And the data are consistent with the view that four groups or social categories have presumably been taken as a context or frame of reference: men with similar longevity, similar educational status, similar rank, and in the same branch of the Service.

Now, this hypothesis, suitably generalized, raises all manner of further questions germane to reference group theory and requiring renewed inquiry and analysis. Which conditions predispose toward this pattern of selecting people of the same status or group as significant points of reference? The idiomatic phrase, "in the same boat," raises the same sociological problems as the idiomatic phrase, "keeping up with the Joneses." Who are the specific Joneses, in various social structures, with whom people try to keep up? their close associates? people in immediately higher social or income strata with whom they have contact? When are the Joneses people whom one never meets, but whom one hears about (through public media of communication, for example)? How does it happen that some select the Joneses to keep up with, others the Cabots, or the Cassidys, and finally that some don't try to keep up at all?

In other words, the hypothesis advanced in *The American Soldier* regarding individuals of similar status being taken as frames of reference for self-evaluations at once opens up an interrelated array of problems, amenable to research and constituting important further links in the development of reference group theory. When are one's membership-groups *not* taken as reference groups in arriving at evaluations? After all, many men were apparently aware of the differences between the table of organization of the Air Corps and their own branch. When would these mobility rates among men *not* in the same boat affect their own level of satisfaction? And these sociological problems, though they might have originated elsewhere, were in fact generated by the anomalous empirical findings developed and provisionally interpreted in this study.

That new systematic experience, such as that represented by the data and hypothesis of *The American Soldier,* does indeed generate the formulation of further theoretical questions is suggested by glancing briefly at the somewhat contrasting work of a notable theorist in social psychology, George H. Mead, who did not steep himself in *systematic* empirical materials. Mead was, of course, a forerunner and an important forerunner in the history of reference group theory, particularly with respect to his central conception, variously expressed in his basic writings, but adequately enough captured in the statement that "The individual experiences himself as such, not directly, but only indirectly, from the particular standpoints of other individual members *of the same group,* or from the generalized standpoint of the social group as a whole *to which he belongs.*"[9]

In this formulation and in numerous others like it,[10] Mead in effect advances the hypothesis that it is the groups of which the individual *is a member* that yield the significant frame of reference for self-evaluations. And this he *illustrates* abundantly with anecdotal instances drawn from his varied personal experience and insightful reflection. But, possibly because he was not exposed to *systematic* empirical evidence, which might prove seemingly inconsistent with this formulation *at specific points,* he was not driven to ask whether, indeed, the group taken as a point of reference by the individual is invariably the group of which he is a member. The terms "another," "the other" and "others" turn up on literally hundreds of occasions in Mead's exposition of the thesis that the development of the social self entails response to the attitudes of "another" or of "others." But the varying status of "these others" presumably taken as frames of self-reference is glossed over, except for the repeated statement that they are members of "the" group. Thus, Mead, and those of his followers who also eschew empirical research, had little occasion to move ahead to the question of conditions under which non-membership-groups may also constitute a significant frame of reference.

Not only does the research from *The American Soldier* point directly to that question, but it leads further to the problems raised by the facts of *multiple* group affiliations and *multiple* reference groups. It reminds us that theory and research must move on to consider the *dynamics of selection* of reference groups among the individual's several membership groups: when do individuals orient themselves to others in their occupational group, in their congeniality groups, or in their religious group? How can we characterize the *structure of the social situation* which leads to one rather than another of these several group affiliations being taken as the significant context?

Following out the hypothesis advanced in the text, we note as well the problem raised by the simultaneous operation of multiple reference groups. Further steps call for study of the *dynamic processes* involved in the theoretically supposed counter-tendencies induced by multiple reference groups. For example, what are the dynamics of evaluation, and not merely the final evaluation, of the mobility system among college graduates relatively new to the Military Police: on the hypothesis advanced in *The American Soldier,* they would be moved, through reference to the status of other college graduates, toward dissatisfaction, but as comparatively new replacements and as M.P.'s they would be moved

---

9. George H. Mead, *Mind, Self and Society* (The University of Chicago Press, 1934), 138 (italics supplied).

10. For example, see *ibid.,* 151-156, 193-194.

toward relative satisfaction. How are these counter-tendencies ultimately resolved in the evaluation which comes to the notice of the observer?

Turning finally to the dependent variable in this study, we note that it consists in soldiers' evaluations of the *institutional system* of promotion in the Army, and not to *self-evaluations* of personal achievement within that system.[11] The men were in effect asked to appraise the system of promotion in terms of its effectiveness and legitimacy, as can be seen from the carefully worded question which elicited their judgments: "Do you think a soldier with ability has a good chance for promotion?"

This introduces a problem, deserving attention which it has not yet received: do the two types of evaluations, self-appraisals and appraisals of institutional arrangements, involve similar mechanisms of reference group behavior? At this point, it is clear that research is needed to discover the structure of those social situations which typically elicit self-evaluations or internalized judgments—for example, where comparison with the achievements of specified others leads to invidious self-depreciation, to a sense of personal inadequacy—and the structure of those situations which typically lead to evaluations of institutions or externalized judgments—for example, where comparison with others leads to a sense of institutional inadequacies, to the judgment that the social system militates against any close correspondence between individual merit and social reward.

Here, as with many of *The American Soldier* researches, the implications of procedure, analysis, and interpretation are of course not confined to further studies of behavior of soldiers. They bear upon some of the more strategic areas of study in the larger social system. For example, the sociological factors which lead men to consider their own, relatively low, social position as legitimate, as well as those which lead them to construe their position as a result of defective and possibly unjustified social arrangements clearly comprise a problem area of paramount theoretical and political importance. When are relatively slim life-chances taken by men as a normal and expectable state of affairs which they attribute to their own personal inadequacies and when are they regarded as the results of an arbitrary social system of mobility, in which rewards are not proportioned to ability?[12] The concepts of relative deprivation

---

11. True, as the text implies, the institutional evaluations probably reflect soldiers' assessments of their own position as compared with their legitimate expectations, but this is not at issue here. The reference group hypothesis attempts to account for variations in the nature of these expectations in terms of the social contexts provided by the distribution of statuses in significant in-groups.

12. Such questions have of course been raised on numerous previous occasions. But they have ordinarily been regarded as distinct and self-contained problems of interest in their own right and not as special problems subsumable under a theory of reference group behavior. For example, it has been suggested that conspicuously "successful" individuals who have risen rapidly in a social hierarchy and who are

and of relative reward help transfer these much-discussed but little-analyzed patterns of behavior from the realm of impressionistic speculation to that of systematic research.

MULTIPLE REFERENCE GROUPS

Several researches in *The American Soldier* afford occasion for looking into theoretical problems arising from the conception that multiple reference groups provide contexts for evaluations by individuals. Two of these cases have been selected for attention here because they apparently exhibit different patterns of multiple comparison: in the first of these, multiple reference groups provide contexts which operate at cross-purposes; in the second, they provide contexts which are mutually sustaining.

Conflicting reference groups. Case #2. During the latter part of 1943 and the early part of 1944, the Research Branch conducted a series of surveys from which they developed a picture of differences in attitudes (reflecting personal adjustment) of noncombat men overseas and of men stationed in the United States. Though consistent, the differences in attitudes were not large. Among noncoms still in the United States, for example, 41 per cent reported themselves as "usually in good spirits" in comparison with 32 per cent of those overseas; 76 per cent of the one held that the "Army is run pretty well or very well" compared with 63 per cent of the other. (I, 167, Chart IV) But since other surveys found that the major concern of the men overseas was to get back home (I, 187), the authors observe that considerably greater differences in attitudes expressing personal adjustment might well have been expected.

Three factors are tentatively adduced to account for the absence of greater differences, factors operating to curb the expectable[13] degree of dissatisfaction expressed by the noncombat soldier overseas. Of these,

---

much in the public eye, function as models or reference-figures testifying to a mobility-system in which, apparently, careers are still open to talents. For some, these success-models are living testimony to the legitimacy of the institutional system and in this comparative context, the individual deflects criticism of the system onto himself. See Merton, Fiske and Curtis, *Mass Persuasion*, 152ff. But these observations remain impressionistic and anecdotal, since they do not provide *systematic* designs for inquiry into this behavior along the lines suggested by the researches of *The American Soldier*.

13. Here we see again that the concept of relative deprivation (just as the notion of "definition of the situation" generally) is introduced to account for an apparently anomalous finding. In this case, the finding seemingly deviates, not from common sense expectation merely, but from other facts uncovered in the course of research. It would thus seem to illustrate the type of serendipity pattern in research in which "the observation is anomalous, surprising, either because it seems inconsistent with prevailing theory or with other established facts. In either case, the seeming inconsistency provokes curiosity; it stimulates the investigator to 'make sense of the datum.'"

we attend only to the interpretative concept of "differential deprivation and reward"[14] which, it will be remembered from an earlier excerpt,

may help us understand some of the psychological processes relevant to this problem. In general, it is of course true that the overseas soldier, *relative to soldiers still at home,* suffered a greater break with home ties and with many of the amenities of life in the United States to which he was accustomed. But it was also true that, *relative to the combat soldier,* the overseas soldier not in combat and not likely to enter into combat suffered far less deprivation than the actual fighting man. (I, 172)

Theoretical implications. In effect, the authors suggest that two contexts of comparison, operating at cross-purposes, affected the evaluations of overseas noncombat troops. What, then, can be learned from this case about the grounds on which certain contexts rather than others become pertinent for such evaluations?

It should be noted at the outset that the status of those constituting the contexts of evaluation is, in some significant respect, *similar* to the status of the men making the evaluation. Thus, the soldiers still at home are similar in that they too are not in combat, and the combat soldiers are similar in that they too are overseas. Beyond this, other similarities and dissimilarities, pertinent to the situation, affect the resulting evaluations in contrasting ways. Thus, the overseas noncombat soldier is, by the standards of Army life, worse off than the soldier at home in that he is comparatively deprived of amenities and cut off from social ties, and better off than the combat soldier in that he is not exposed to the same measure of deprivation and risk. It is as though he had said, "Bad off as we are, the others are worse off," a comparison not seldom adopted by those who would accommodate themselves to their position. His definition of his situation is then presumably the resultant of these counteracting patterns of comparison.

This suggests the general hypothesis that some similarity in status attributes between the individual and the reference group must be perceived or imagined, in order for the comparison to occur at all. Once this minimal similarity obtains,[15] other similarities and differences perti-

---

14. The other two are, first, physical selection since men overseas had to meet more rigorous standards and second, "a sense of the significance of one's army job." In this latter connection, the authors remark: "While the difference between theaters . . . cannot prove or disprove hypotheses, the fact that, on the average, United States-overseas differences on attitudes toward Army jobs were negligible or reversed—as compared with United States-overseas differences in personal esprit or attitudes toward the Army—is a fact not to be overlooked." (I, 173)

15. This minimum of status similarity apparently presupposed by reference group behavior clearly requires systematic study. *Some* similarity in status can of course always be found, depending only on the breadth of the status category. One can compare oneself with others, if only in the most general social capacity of "human being." And more germane to the case in question, the overseas combat man could (and did) compare himself with the noncombat man back home by virtue of their similar status as soldiers, and with civilians by virtue of their similar status as young

nent to the situation, will provide the context for shaping evaluations. Consequently, this focuses the attention of the theorist immediately upon the factors which produce a sense of pertinent similarity between statuses, since these will help determine which groups are called into play as comparative contexts. The underlying similarities of status among members of in-groups, singled out by Mead as *the* social context, thus appear as only one special, though obviously important, basis for the selection of reference groups. Out-groups may also involve *some* similarity of status.

By implication, the hypothesis of the Research Branch at this point provides a clue to the factors affecting the selection of reference groups. The hypothesis does not hold that the two categories of men—the combat men overseas and the noncombat men at home—constituted the *only* ones with which *any particular individual* among the overseas combat men compared himself. He may indeed have compared his lot with that of numerous and diverse others—a civilian friend in a cushy job back home, a cousin enjoying life as a war correspondent, an undrafted movie star whom he had read about in a magazine. But such comparisons by an individual, precisely because they involve personal frames of reference, might well be idiosyncratic. They would not provide contexts *common* to (many or most of) the individuals in the status of overseas noncombat men. To the degree that they are idiosyncratic, they would vary at random among the various categories of soldiers. Consequently, they would not aggregate into statistically significant differences of attitudes between *groups* or *social categories* of soldiers.

In other words, the statistics of *The American Soldier* on differential definitions of their situation among combat men,[16] overseas noncombat men and men still in the United States are taken to manifest the impact of *socially structured* reference groups more or less common to men in each category. It is not mere indolence or lack of insight which keeps the sociologist from seeking to track down all the comparative contexts which hold for any given individual; it is, rather, that many of these contexts are idiosyncratic, not shared by a large fraction of other individuals within the same group or social category. The comparative statistics in *The American Soldier* are plainly not intended to manifest and cannot manifest those numerous private contexts peculiar to individuals and hence varying at random to the social category. One does not look to these sociological data for idiosyncratic contexts of appraisal.

---

adult American males. The theoretical and research problem at this point is to determine how the structure of the social situation encourages certain status-similarities to become the basis for such comparisons, and leads other status-similarities to be ignored as "irrelevant."

16. *The American Soldier* does not supply data on the attitudes of combat men at this point in the text, although apposite data are found at other places in the volumes. (*e.g.*, I, 111)

The reference groups here hypothesized, then, are not mere artifacts of the authors' arbitrary scheme of classification. Instead, they appear to be frames of reference held in common by a proportion of individuals within a social category sufficiently large to give rise to definitions of the situation characteristic of that category. And these frames of reference are common because they are patterned by the social structure. In the present case, for example, the degree of closeness to combat provides a socially organized and socially emphasized basis of comparison among the three categories of soldiers—overseas combat, overseas noncombat, and troops back home. It is, accordingly, categories such as these which provide the *common* comparative contexts for definition of the situation among these men. This is not to deny that other contexts may be of great consequence to particular individuals within each of these social categories. But these become relevant for the sociologist only if they are shared sufficiently to lead to group differences in evaluations.

In these pages, *The American Soldier* affords a clue, and possibly an important clue, for solving the sociological problem of finding the common residual which constitutes the reference groups distinctive for those in a social status category.

There is another problem implicit here about which little can be learned from this case: what are the patterns of response among members of a group or status category when they are subject to multiple reference groups operating at cross-purposes? In the present case, the net evaluation of their lot among overseas noncombat men apparently represented a compromise, intermediate between the evaluations of non-combat men at home and of men in actual combat. But it is not implied by the authors of *The American Soldier* that this is the only pattern of response under such circumstances. It is possible, for example, that when several membership groups exert diverse and conflicting pressures for self-appraisal, the individual tends to adopt other, non-membership groups as a frame of reference. In any event, there arises the large and imperfectly defined problem, previously alluded to, of searching out the processes of coming to terms with such conflicting pressures.[17] That the social scientists of the Research Branch were cognizant of this line of inquiry, emerging from their wartime studies, is suggested by the fact

---

17. Thus, a study of political behavior found that individuals, under cross-pressure, were more likely to delay their final vote decision. And as the senior author goes on to say: "But such delay is not the only possible reaction. Other alternatives range all the way from individual neurotic reactions, such as an inability to make any decision at all, to intellectual solutions which might lead to new social movements. Many of the baffling questions about the relationship between individual attitudes and social environment may be answered when these problems of cross-pressures and reactions to them are thoroughly and properly studied." Lazarsfeld, Berelson, and Gaudet, *The People's Choice* (New York: Columbia University Press, 1948, second edition), xxii.

that the director, Stouffer, is now developing researches on the varying patterns of response to the simultaneous but conflicting demands of primary groups and of formal organizational authorities.[18]

Mutually sustaining reference groups. Case #3. In its bare outlines, this study (I, 122-130) is concerned with the feelings of legitimacy ascribed by men to their induction into service. Patterns of response to the question, "At the time you came into the Army,[19] did you think you should have been deferred?" showed that married men, over 20 years of age, who had not been graduated from high school were most likely to maintain that they should have been deferred. In this status category, 41 per cent, as compared, for example, with only 10 per cent of unmarried high school graduates under 20 years of age, claimed that they should not have been inducted at all. More generally, it is found that the statuses of age, marital condition and educational level are consistently related with willingness for military service.

Since the hypotheses advanced to account for these findings are essentially of the same type for each of the three status categories, we need concern ourselves here with only one of these for illustrative purposes. As we have seen in an excerpt from this case, the authors provisionally explain the greater reluctance for service of married men in terms of the standards of comparison yielded by reference to two other status categories. The key interpretative passage bears repetition at this point:

Comparing himself with his unmarried associates in the Army, he could feel that induction demanded greater sacrifice from him than from them; and *comparing himself with his married civilian friends* he could feel that he had been called on for sacrifices which they were escaping altogether. Hence the married man, on the average, was more likely than others to come into the Army with reluctance and, possibly, a sense of injustice. (I, 125, italics supplied)

Theoretical implications. However brief and tentative the interpreta-

---

18. Samuel Stouffer, "An analysis of conflicting social norms," *American Sociological Review,* 1949, 14, 707-717.

19. Since it is not germane to our chief purpose, we have made no effort throughout this paper to report the numerous technical steps taken by the Research Branch to determine the adequacy of their data. But readers of *The American Soldier* will be well aware of the diverse and often imaginative procedures adopted to cross-check each set of data. In the present case, for example, it is shown that the responses to this question were not merely a reflection of the soldiers' sentiments *subsequent* to induction. For "when asked of new recruits, whose report on their feelings about induction could not be colored by months or years of subsequent Army experience, the [same kind of] question discriminated significantly between recruits who *later* became psychoneurotics and other men." (I, 123n) This note is intended to emphasize, once and for all, that our summary of a research case does not at all reproduce those subtle and cumulative details which often lend weight to the data in hand. For these details, rather than the more general questions to which they give rise, a firsthand study of *The American Soldier* is necessary.

tion, it helps us to locate and to formulate several further problems involved in developing a theory of reference group behavior.

First of all, it reinforces the supposition, hinted in the preceding case, that it is the institutional definitions of the social structure which may focus the attention of members of a group or occupants of a social status upon certain *common* reference groups. Nor does this refer only to the fact that soldiers will take the official institutional norms (the rules governing induction and exemption) as a *direct* basis for judging the legitimacy of their own induction into the service. These same rules, since they are defined in terms of such statuses as marital condition and age, also focus attention on certain groups or statuses with which individuals subject to service will compare themselves. This is, in effect, implied by the authors who, referring to the greater sacrifices entailed by induction of the married man, go on to say: "This was officially recognized by draft boards. . . . The very fact that draft boards were more liberal with married than with single men provided numerous examples to the drafted married man of *others in his shoes* who got relatively better breaks than he did." (I, 125, italics supplied) The institutional norms evoke comparisons with others similar in *particular* aspects of status—"others in his shoes"—thus encouraging *common* reference groups for these married soldiers. In addition to these common reference groups, as previously stated, there may well have been all manner of idiosyncratic reference groups, which, since they vary at random, would not have resulted in the statistically discernible reluctance for service which was comparatively marked among married men.

A second problem is highlighted by the hypothesis which uniformly assumes that the married soldier compares himself with like-statused individuals with whom he is or has been in *actual social relations: associates* in the Army or civilian *friends*. This, then, raises a question concerning reference group behavior when the frame of comparative reference is provided by *impersonal status categories* in general (other married men, noncoms, *etc.*) and by those representatives of these status categories with whom he is in *sustained social relations*. Which, for example, most affects the evaluations of the individual when these operate at cross-purposes (a problem clearly visible in the matrix of variables set out earlier in this paper)?

This question leads at once to the comparative significance of general status categories and intimate subgroups of which one is a member. Suppose, for example, that all or almost all of a married soldier's married associates have also been drafted, even though, *in general*, this status category has a smaller proportion of inductions than the category of the unmarried male. Which basis of comparison will, on the average, prove more effective? Will he compare himself with the other drafted benedicts in his clique or subgroup and consequently be the more ready to accept induction for himself, or will he compare himself with the larger status category of married men, who are in general more often deferred, and consequently feel aggrieved over his own induction? The question has, of course, more general bearing. For example, are workers' expectations regarding their personal prospects of future employment shaped more by the present employment of themselves and their associates on the job or by high rates of unemployment prevailing in the occupation at large?

This case from *The American Soldier* thus points to the need for cumulative research on *the relative effectiveness of frames of reference yielded by associates and by more general status categories.* It suggests the salient items of observation which must be incorporated in such projected studies, so that this problem, at least in its major outlines, can lend itself to research, here and now, not in some remote future. Such projected studies could readily include items of data on the norms or situation of close associates as well as data on knowledge about the norms or situation prevailing in the given status at large. Subsequent analysis would then be in terms of systematic comparison of individuals in the *same status* but with immediate *associates* who have distinctly opposed norms or who are in contrasting situations. Replicated studies including such materials would substantially advance our present understanding of the workings of reference group behavior.[20]

Third, the theory assumes that individuals comparing their own lot with that of others have some *knowledge* of the situation in which these others find themselves. More concretely, it assumes that the individual *knows about* the comparative rates of induction among married and single men, or the degree of unemployment in their occupation at large.[21] Or, if the individual is taken to be positively oriented toward the norms of a non-membership group, the theory of course assumes that he has some knowledge of these norms. Thus, the theory of reference group behavior must include in its fuller psychological elaboration some treatment of the dynamics of perception (of individuals, groups and norms)

---

20. Thus, a current unpublished research in the sociology and social psychology of housing by R. K. Merton, P. J. S. West, and M. Jahoda, *Patterns of Social Life*, includes a study of the comparative effectiveness of "primary environment of opinion" (constituted by the opinions of one's close associates) and of "secondary environment of opinion" (constituted by the opinions of those with whom one is not in close association). When these operate at cross-purposes, it appears that the primary environment does take some measure of precedence.

21. It may of course turn out that, under certain conditions, individuals extrapolate their knowledge of the situation of associates in a given social category to that social category at large. Or, it may develop that the situation of one's associates is accorded greater weight by the individual than the contrasting situation which he knows to obtain in the social category at large. These are questions amenable to empirical research and salient for reference group theory.

and in its sociological elaboration, some treatment of channels of communication through which this knowledge is gained. Which processes make for accurate or distorted images of the situation of other individuals and groups (taken as a frame of reference)? Which forms of social organization maximize the probabilities of correct perception of other individuals and groups, and which make for distorted perception? Since *some* perceptual and cognitive elements are definitely *implied* even in a description of reference group behavior, it will be necessary for these elements to be explicitly incorporated into the theory.

A fourth problem emerging from this case concerns the empirical status of reference group concepts. In this study, as well as in others we consider here, the interpretative concept of relative deprivation was introduced *after* the field research was completed.[22] This being the case, there was no provision for the collection of *independent systematic*[23] *evidence* on the operation of such social frameworks of individual judgments. That a significant proportion of married soldiers did indeed compare their lot with that of married civilian friends and unmarried associates in the Army in arriving at their judgment remains, so far as the data in hand go, an assumption. These comparisons are inferred, rather than factually demonstrated, intervening variables. But they need not remain assumptions. They not only happen to square with the facts in hand, but are of a kind which can be directly tested in future inquiries employing the concept of reference group.[24] These studies can be de-

---

22. Although the concept is after-the-fact of *data collection*, it was introduced early enough in the *analysis* to permit its use in suggesting types of tabulations which would otherwise not have been undertaken. From the interpretative standpoint, therefore, relative deprivation was not confined to use as an *ex post facto* conception.

23. The emphasis on *systematic* data is essential, for *The American Soldier* has abundant indications that *in many cases* assumed reference groups were indeed taken as a context of comparison. For example, their text includes remarks by overseas soldiers which clearly indicate that the soldiers back home are sometimes taken as a point of reference in assessing their own situation: "I think I've had my share being overseas over two years. That's plenty for any man. . . . Let them USO boys get some of this chow once in a while, then they will know what it is to sleep in the mud with mosquitoes buzzing around them like a P-38." "We should have a chance to breathe a little fresh air for a while. But I guess you better keep them USO boys back there or there won't be any USO." "It is hard as hell to be here and read in every paper that comes from home where Pvt. Joe Dokes is home again on furlough after tough duty as a guard in Radio City." "We receive letters from soldiers who have not yet left the States and who are on their second furlough." (I, 188) These remarks also contain passing allusions to the source of information regarding the situation of the men back home: "read in every paper," "we receive letters," *etc.* But such telling anecdotal materials are properly enough not regarded as a basis for *systematic* analysis by the authors of *The American Soldier*.

24. A recent example of the possibility of now anticipating the need for data on reference group behavior is provided by the 1948 voting study in Elmira, (since published as B. Berelson, P. F. Lazarsfeld and W. N. McPhee, *Voting*, University of Chicago Press, 1954). Under a grant from the Rockefeller Foundation for the study of panel techniques in social research, a conference at Swarthmore on reference group concepts was arranged, with an eye to having materials bearing on these concepts

signed to incorporate systematic data on the groups which individuals actually do take as frames of reference for their behavior and can thus determine whether variations in attitude and behavior correspond to variations in reference group contexts.

This possibility of converting the intervening variable of reference groups from assumption into fact brings us to a fifth problem. Before plunging into research on the conditions under which individuals compare themselves with *specified* other individuals or groups, it is necessary to consider the psychological status of these comparisons. For when individuals *explicitly* and consciously adopt such frames of reference, sociological researches involving interviews with large numbers of people face no great procedural difficulties. Appropriate questions can elicit the needed information on the groups, status categories or individuals which are taken as a frame of reference. But there is, of course, no reason to assume that comparisons of self with others are uniformly conscious. Numerous experimental studies in social psychology have shown that individuals *unwittingly* respond to different frames of reference introduced by the experimenter. To the extent that unwitting reference groups are involved in the ordinary routines of daily life, research techniques must be extended to detect their operation.

Appropriate research procedures must also be designed to discover which reference groups are spontaneously and explicitly brought into play, as distinguished from the study of responses to reference group contexts provided by the experimenter or suggested by the interviewer. Both interview and experimental studies have heretofore been largely centered on responses to reference group contexts supplied for the subjects. These studies can be further advanced by providing ordered arrays of comparative contexts, somewhat as follows:

> "Compared with others on your work-team [or other membership-group], do you feel you are getting a fair income for what you do?"
> "Compared with the men in the front office, do you . . . etc. . . .?"
> "Compared with the president of the firm, do you . . . etc. . . .?"

Or similarly, information about the salaries of various individuals and groups could be given an experimental group and withheld from a matched group of workers to determine whether the subsequent self-

---

introduced into the Elmira voting study. *The American Soldier* provides numerous further conceptions which can be similarly incorporated in further research. It is this process of an ongoing interplay between theory and empirical research which is overlooked by verdicts such as Glazer's that the concept of relative deprivation "cannot be refuted by facts." (See footnote 3 of this chapter.) A theoretical concept emerging or developed in the course of one inquiry, if it has any empirical relevance at all, can then be utilized (and if defective, modified or nullified) in subsequent researches. If it is to be creative at all, research cannot be *confined* to the testing of predetermined hypotheses. New concepts and hypotheses emerge in the process of inquiry, and these become the basis for further inquiry. This, we take it, is precisely how continuity in science occurs.

appraisals and satisfactions of the experimental group are modified by possible reference groups supplied by the investigator.

But such tentative types of inquiry, in which the particular reference groups are provided, do not, of course, enter into the uncharted region of the *spontaneous selection of reference groups* in varying situations. Why will A, in one situation, compare himself with B, and in another, with C? Or, more concretely and illustratively: when do workers compare their lot with that of fellow-workers in close association, and when with others of markedly different status? which aspects of the social structure and which psychological processes limit the range of individuals and groups regarded as pertinent frames of reference? It is this type of problem—the processes shaping the selection of reference groups —that stands in most conspicuous need of research.[25]

UNIFORMITIES OF BEHAVIOR DERIVED FROM REFERENCE GROUP THEORY

To this point, we have examined researches in which the concept of relative deprivation was explicitly utilized by Stouffer and his associates to interpret empirical findings. In doing so, we have attempted, first, to indicate how this concept can be incorporated in a more general, though still primitive, theory of reference group behavior and second, how these studies give rise to further empirical and theoretical problems that can become the object of new and cumulative research.

We want now to consider whether the theory of reference groups does indeed have wider applicability than the seemingly special concept of relative deprivation. Fortunately, the numerous researches of *The American Soldier* enable us to check this, at least to some degree. For some of these researches involve findings which are apparently not germane to the concept of relative deprivation—since they deal with self-images, but not with levels of satisfaction with one's lot—yet which can, we believe, be explicated by applying reference group conceptions to them. In the course of seeing whether this theory permits us to detect sociological uniformities underlying apparently disparate patterns of behavior, we shall also have occasion to add to the list of specific problems needing solution if reference group theory is to be advanced.

Case #4 (II, 242-72). Combat groups were in general subject to high personnel turnover. It is true that some outfits were trained and entered into combat with few changes in personnel, but even in these

---

25. A notable beginning is found in the pioneering study by Herbert H. Hyman, *The Psychology of Status*, Archives of Psychology, No. 269, 1942. Hyman sought to have his subjects report the groups or individuals which they had taken for comparison with their own status. This kind of direct questioning can of course elicit only the conscious and remembered frames of comparison. But the advancement of reference group theory has suffered by the general failure to follow up Hyman's suggestive lead on spontaneously emerging frames of group reference.

instances, casualties required frequent replacements. The Research Branch seized upon the sociologically significant fact that inexperienced soldiers thus found themselves in two distinctly different social structures: some being for a time in homogeneous outfits comprised wholly of similarly green troops, and others, in divisions with combat veterans. And here the study took a decisive sociological turn. Unlike the ordinary polling studies in social psychology, which compare *aggregates of individuals of different status* (age, sex, class, *etc.*), they did not merely compare the attitudes of inexperienced and of veteran troops. This would have been only a comparison of aggregates of men in two distinct statuses, an important type of comparison but of severely limited value for sociology. Rather, they defined this as an occasion for studying the impact of *group contexts* upon the attitudes of types of individuals, a problem which is of course old, older than sociology itself, but which has less often been the object of systematic empirical research than of impressionistic discussion.

The Research Branch therefore centered upon the group contexts in which these troops found themselves: green troops in outfits comprised wholly by their own kind; equally inexperienced replacements in divisions otherwise composed of combat veterans; and the veterans themselves in these divisions.[26] Questions were put to these three groups of soldiers in several of what the Research Branch calls "attitude areas" (willingness for combat, confidence in their ability to take charge of a group in combat, appraisal of their physical condition, and so on). These surveys found apparently diverse *patterns of differences* in response among the three groups. In the first "attitude area," for example, veterans expressed greater reluctance to get into combat than the troops in green outfits, with the replacements being intermediate to the two. Whereas 45 per cent of the green troops were "ready to get into an actual battle zone," this dropped to 28 per cent among the replacements and to only 15 per cent among the veterans. It is, of course, the contrast between the green troops and the replacements which is most significant, since these were alike in their *individual attribute* of lack of combat experience, but different with respect to the *kind of group* in which they found themselves. This same pattern, with the replacement *intermediate* to those of the veteran and green troops, occurred in responses to questions about attitudes toward noncoms.

But, the Research Branch reports, this is only one pattern of response. Quite another pattern was found with regard to the men's confidence in their ability "to take charge of a group of men" in combat. As some

---

26. There is, of course, a fourth group context which might have entered strategically into the systematic comparison, namely, the divisions comprised wholly of combat veterans, except that the replacement practices of the Army did not make it possible for the Research Branch to include such all-veteran divisions in this study.

might expect on commonsense grounds, the veterans more often expressed confidence in their capacity to fulfill this role than did the green troops in green outfits. But it is of crucial significance that, unlike the first instance of willingness for combat, where the replacements were intermediate in their responses, in this case, they were consistently the least confident of the three groups.[27]

Again, on yet another type of "attitude"—toward his own physical condition—the replacement was virtually indistinguishable from the other green troops, but far more likely than the veteran to consider himself "in good physical condition."

These three sets of data, then, seem to show three different patterns of response, in the first of which the replacement responds more like the veteran than the green troops; in the second, most remote from the veteran and also unlike other green troops; and in the third, quite like his counterpart in green outfits. And since these are diverse patterns, the Research Branch has advanced diverse interpretations. With regard to the replacements' approximation to the veterans' reluctance to go into combat, it is suggested that "to some extent the replacements took over the attitudes of the combat veterans around them, whose views on combat would have for them high prestige." (II, 250) With regard to capacity for leading a group in combat, where the replacements differ most from the veterans, it is suggested that "for the veterans, experience was their strong point, and also the point at which replacements in contact with them felt the greatest inferiority, standing as they did in the shadow of the veterans." (II, 251) And when the replacement is quite like his counterpart in green outfits, as with appraisals of physical condition, this is tentatively explained by saying that these judgments probably reflect an actual (objective) difference in physical condition between veterans and others.

Theoretical implications. It will be at once granted that this poses an intriguing challenge and problem for sociological theory. For the response-behavior of the replacements seems to exhibit almost random variation, a situation distasteful to the theorist whose task it is to perceive underlying uniformities amid such apparent disorder. It is reminiscent of the situation confronting Durkheim when he found an immense variety of suicide rates, differing among the sexes, rural-urban

---

27. Were there opportunity here for a full re-analysis of these data, it would be necessary to take account of problems of "question reliability," since three distinct index-questions in this "attitude area" of "self-confidence" led to somewhat different patterns of response. However, that is not essential for the purposes in hand, particularly since we are here concerned primarily with the replacements, who were *consistently* less confident than the veterans and green troops on all three items. (For figures, see II, 252.) See also the analysis of questions in this study by P. L. Kendall and P. F. Lazarsfeld, "Problems of Survey Analysis," in R. K. Merton and P. F. Lazarsfeld, *Continuities in Social Research* (Glencoe, Illinois: The Free Press, 1950), 133-196.

areas, military and civilian populations, religious groups, and so on. Rather than advance new and separate interpretations of each set of differentials, he attempted to derive these numerous variations from a limited set of propositions. So here, these various patterns of response of replacements set sociological theory the task of discerning the significant variables and conditions which bring about this seeming diversity of response-behavior.

As is well known, the first step in the search for sociological order amid apparent disorder is to re-examine, in theoretical terms, the *concepts* in terms of which the data are reported. More often than not, it will be found that these concepts may profit by clarification and reformulation. That appears to be the case here. These several sets of data are all reported as *attitudes* falling into distinct "attitude-areas." The theorist might at once consider the possibility that basic conceptual differences in these data might be obscured by use of a single crudely defined concept.[28] The single blanket concept of "attitude" may also fail to direct the analyst's attention to the appropriate body of theory for interpreting the data. And finally, by tacitly including significantly different elements in the data under this one undifferentiated concept, the empirical findings may exhibit anomalies, contradictions, and lack of uniformities which are only apparent, not real.

What does a conceptual reformulation of these data show? The first variable, "willingness for combat," may indeed be usefully described as an "attitude" in the approximate sense of "a mental and neural *state of readiness,* organized through experience, exerting a directive or dynamic influence upon the individual's response to all objects and situations with which it is related."[29] But the second variable, "self-confidence in leadership capacities," as here indexed, appears not so much a preparatory set for behavior, as a *self-image and a self-appraisal.* Two consequences flow from this provisional reformulation of a single "attitude" concept into the two concepts of attitude and of self-appraisal. First, it is no longer assumed that the data bearing on these two variables need manifest the same comparative distributions: that now becomes a moot question and not a tacit presumption. And second, the reformulation in terms of self-appraisal leads us at once to the reference group theory of self-appraisals.

---

28. In the introduction, Stouffer calls special attention to the looseness of the concept "attitude" as adopted in these studies: ". . . in the main work of the Research Branch and in most of the text of the present volumes there is no operational definition of attitudes—whence, concepts like 'attitudes,' 'tendencies,' and 'opinions' are used more or less loosely and even sometimes interchangeably. . . ." (I, 42) We are here engaged in exploring some of the empirical and theoretical consequences of the *respecification* of a concept. For a clear statement of this procedure, see W. J. Goode and P. K. Hatt, *Methods in Social Research* (New York: McGraw Hill, 1952), 48-53.

29. The particular definition cited is that by G. W. Allport, but various current conceptions of "attitude" have essentially this same core-denotation.

Reformulation of the concept in which the dependent variables are stated thus provides a tentative link with theory of the past: we are not forced to improvise wholly new hypotheses, standing alone and unconnected with a general body of theory, but can, perhaps, derive these findings from an established set of hypotheses centered about the structure, functions and dynamic mechanisms of self-appraisals in diverse group contexts. This is, moreover, the theory which incorporates the concept of relative deprivation, used elsewhere in these volumes, but not here.

With this new conceptual basis, we are prepared to re-examine the data of *The American Soldier* to see whether they do indeed exhibit the anomaly of three distinct patterns of response under the same conditions. If a general theory is to move out from these data and beyond the interpretations advanced in the text, then it should be able to incorporate these seemingly different patterns of response as expressions of an underlying regularity.

Stemming then from the theoretic background provided by James, Cooley and Mead, and by Hyman, Sherif and Newcomb, the hypothesis holds that, insofar as subordinate or prospective group members are motivated to affiliate themselves with a group, they will tend to assimilate the sentiments and conform with the values of the authoritative and prestigeful stratum in that group. The function of conformity is acceptance by the group, just as progressive acceptance by the group reinforces the tendency toward conformity. And the values of these "significant others" constitute the mirrors in which individuals see their self-image and reach self-appraisals. Applied to the specific case in hand, the significant others in the membership-group are similarly inexperienced men for the green soldier in a green outfit, whereas for the replacement, the significant others are experienced veterans, with their distinctive sets of values and sentiments.

In applying the general hypothesis, it must be anticipated that the replacements, as "outsiders" motivated to affiliate themselves with the prestigeful and authoritative stratum (the veterans), would more nearly conform to *all* of the veterans' values and sentiments here under inspection. We should be clear on this point. If its interpretative utility is to be properly assessed, the hypothesis must stand on its own feet, and not be modified or abandoned because the text of *The American Soldier* reports that the responses of replacements in these distinct "attitude areas" were in fact different. The present hypothesis gives us a set of instructions to the effect that we must re-examine these reportedly different patterns in order to determine whether they are actually different, or merely speciously so.

In a provisional way, and to the extent that the reported data allow us to say, it appears that the differences are only apparent. Underlying these manifest differences in the percentage distribution of replies to the given questions by veterans, replacements, and green troops, are regularities of response corresponding to those anticipated in the hypothesis.

Thus, first, with respect to willingness for combat, the sentiments of veterans held, in effect, that "combat is hell," and consequently, veterans most frequently expressed reluctance to enter into combat. The green troops, in contrast, who had more lately quitted civilian ranks, were more likely to have at the outset the values of the wartime civilian population, with all its "conventional stereotypes" of combat as affording occasions for dramatic heroism. This is in fact borne out by the text at another place and in another connection, where it is reported that "probably the strongest group code [among combat men] . . . was the taboo against any talk of a flagwaving variety. . . . The core of the attitude *among combat men* seemed to be that any talk that did not subordinate idealistic values and patriotism to the harsher realities of the combat situation was hypocritical, and a person who expressed such ideas a hypocrite."[30]

In this first instance, then, our hypothesis drawn from reference group theory would lead us to anticipate that the replacements, seeking affiliation with the authoritative and prestigeful stratum of veterans, will move from the civilian-like values toward the more tough-minded values of the veterans. And this, as we know, is indeed the case. For replacements, the assumed function of assimilating the values of the veterans is to find more ready acceptance by the higher-status group, in a setting where the subordinate group of replacements does not have independent claims to legitimate prestige.

But if the hypothesis is consistent with the first set of data on willingness for combat, can it also hold for the second set of data dealing with the so-called attitude of self-confidence regarding capacity for leadership, particularly since it was found that, in this instance, the replies of replacements were *remote* from those of the veterans, even more so than the replies of the green troops? Indeed, the text refers to this as a "different" or "divergent" pattern of response. To be sure, the manifest distribution of replies differs from the first. But, viewed in terms

---

30. II, 150 (italics supplied). Essentially the same point of a contrast in values regarding combat between the civilian population and combat men is made at numerous places in the two volumes; *e.g.*, at II, 111-112, 151; I, 484. Notice should also be taken of Chart VIII in Chapter 3 of volume II, showing that veterans were far more likely than inexperienced troops to say that "this war is not worth fighting." And finally, it should be said that this contrast between the definitions of the combat situation by civilians and by combat men is drawn by Brewster Smith, who also conducted the analysis of replacement behavior now under review.

of reference group theory, it is, we believe, only another expression of the same underlying dynamic regularities of behavior in this group context.

This can be tested by applying the hypothesis. In the case of self-confidence, as we have seen, we deal with a self-appraisal rather than with an attitude in the sense of a preparatory set for action. The values and sentiments of the veteran stratum hold, in effect, that "actual combat experience is needed to prepare a private to take charge of a group of men in combat."[31] Now, if, as the hypothesis anticipates, replacements seek to assimilate *this* value and judge themselves accordingly, if they see themselves in the mirror provided by the values of the prestigeful veterans, they can only appraise themselves as, by and large, unprepared for spontaneous leadership in battle. On the hypothesis, the replacements would, in short, behave just as they do, being most likely to say that they are *not* ready to take charge of men in combat (involving a lower self-estimate than that found among the green troops, *not* vis-à-vis the veterans). Thus, although their *distribution* of replies differs markedly from that of the veterans, leading the Research Branch to describe this as another pattern of response, the replacements are engaging in the same pattern of behavior in the two instances—when this is construed in terms of reference group theory. They are assimilating the values of the veterans, and thus presumably affiliating themselves with this authoritative and prestigeful stratum. In the first instance of "willingness for combat," this calls only for direct reaffirmation of the veterans' sentiments, leading the replacements' distribution of responses to resemble that of the veterans. In the second instance of self-confidence in leadership capacity, they also assimilate the veteran standards but since this is not merely an attitude but a self-appraisal, they apply these standards to themselves, find themselves comparatively wanting, and thus give distributions of responses to the self-appraisal questions differing from those of the veterans. Thus, a uniformity of social process apparently underlies the different patterns of manifest replies.

The same hypothesis can be tested anew on other items from these data on "attitudes" of veterans, replacements, and green troops; for example, those dealing with "attitudes toward physical condition." In this case, the green troops and replacements respond alike, with 57 per cent and 56 per cent respectively saying that they are in good physical condition, whereas only 35 per cent of the veterans make that claim. This is reported as a third pattern of response, again on the manifest

---

31. The statistical data of replies to the question, "Do you think you have been giving enough training and experience so that you could do a good job of taking charge of a group of men on your own in combat," constitute one basis for the view that veterans hold this value. Discussions of the values of combat men, especially in II, Chapter 3, bear this out.

empirical level of response-frequencies, leading the Research Branch to another interpretation of this apparently new pattern: the similarity of answers by replacements and green troops, it is suggested, "undoubtedly parallels similarity in the men's actual physical condition."[32]

Here, it is said, the responses represent, not an assimilation of veterans' attitudes, but more nearly a faithful reporting of objective differences in the physical condition of fatigued veterans—"beat-up Joes"— and of the fresh replacements and green troops.

But this only poses another problem for theory: under which conditions do men respond by reporting the objective situation rather than a socially reflected image?[33] Does this third, apparently different, pattern of response require a new hypothesis? It seems that, again, no additional *ad hoc* variables need be introduced, although in the absence of the required data, this must of course remain for future research to examine. It appears that the veterans do not hold poor physical condition as a distinctive and positive social *value* (except, as the text indicates, as a possible rationalization for escaping further combat) in the same sense that they hold the belief that "combat is hell" or that "combat experience equips a private to take charge of men in combat." Replacements seeking to affiliate themselves with the prestigeful and socially validated veterans will therefore not be served by asserting that they are in poor physical shape, that they, too, are in effect "beat-up Joes." If anything, this claim would only be the occasion for rejection of replacements by veterans, since it would represent, not a bid for affiliation with the group, but for equality of *status*. Moreover, the replacements' recognition of their comparatively good physical condition does not affirm a counter-value, which might also threaten their acceptance by the veterans. Within the same group context, then, there is no functional or motivational basis for replacements to reproduce the self-judgments of the veterans, and apparently objective differences in the physical con-

---

32. II, 263. This refers to their "absolute" ratings in response to the question, "Do you think that you are in good physical condition?" Alternative questions which refer to "combat" conditions possibly introduce the factor of replacements' assimilated reluctance for combat; they tend to be intermediate to veterans and green troops in their responses to these.

33. Here, as elsewhere, a slightly more generalized formulation of the problem directs our attention to the saliency of data now presented in various, and unconnected, pages of *The American Soldier*. At several points in these volumes, recourse is had to the assumption that soldiers' replies represent "objective reporting" rather than group-conditioned judgments. But, without a general formulation, the need for collating these and for clarifying the theoretical issue is not likely to be perceived. See, for example, the interpretation of responses of "nonreturnees in predominantly returnee outfits," where it is said: "In part this agreement between returnees and nonreturnees suggests that there was *some basis in fact* as well as in attitude for the returnees' preference for and greater comfort in their own outfits. But these data may not be taken as sure corroboration of this point, since they may be, at least in part, simply evidence that the attitudes of returnees affected the opinions of the non-returnees around them as well." (II, 515, 517)

dition of fatigued veterans and of fresh replacements and green troops find expression.

In so far as differences in these three patterns of manifest response can be theoretically derived from a functional theory of reference group behavior, this case illustrates one major service of theory for applied social research: the reconstruction through conceptual clarification of apparent irregularities in data leads to the provisional discovery of underlying functional and dynamic regularities. But, as we have suggested, the avenues between social theory and applied research carry two-way traffic: not only can theory reformulate some of the materials in *The American Soldier,* but on the basis of the same materials we can specify the types of further sociological indices and observations needed to achieve continuity and cumulation in the theory of value-assimilation, the group context of self-appraisals, and the objective assessment of situations. A brief list of such indices must stand in lieu of a detailed analysis of their potential for the advancement of this theory.[34]

1. *Index of actual social relations:* There is plainly need for systematic data on the social relations actually obtaining between the prestigeful and authoritative stratum, and the newcomers to a group. Is there an empirically discoverable tendency for those in most frequent or most enduring affiliative contact to exhibit value-assimilation?

2. *Index of motivations of incoming group members:* The theory presupposes a concern among newcomers to affiliate themselves with the higher status group. For research purposes, it would of course be necessary to divide newcomers in terms of the presence, absence, or degree of such motivations. A derivative analytical procedure, moving in another direction, would consist in taking such affiliative motivations not as given, but as problematical, in turn requiring explanation.

3. *Index of social cohesion and of associated values:* Do the newcomers represent a scattered *aggregate* of individuals, or an organized subgroup? If the latter, do they have their own group values with distinctive claims to moral legitimacy? And in such instances, does continuous contact lead to more nearly reciprocal, rather than one-sided, assimilation?[35]

---

34. The reader might be tempted to say that most of the following have been recognized as probably significant variables from the earliest days of modern sociology. But here, as at many points in this paper, it must be said that there is a great difference—in fact, all the difference—between impressionistic and sporadic references to such variables, and *systematic* incorporation of these variables into research. Only through the latter procedure will theory and research both advance. Impressionism is no adequate substitute, if only *because it is so flexible and vague in character as not to admit of decisive nullification of a provisional hypothesis.* As Nietzsche, not ordinarily one to understand the ethos of science, put it in an insightful moment, "It is certainly not the least charm of a theory that it is refutable." It is the object of systematic incorporation of variables into research to allow for nullification as well as confirmation, a rather difficult assignment for an author, wedded to a theory, and not exposed to data sufficiently incriminating to have him divorce himself from that theory.

35. It will be noted that the materials in *The American Soldier* did not allow in general for study of the effects of replacements upon veterans, a problem manifestly involved in an extended setting of the problem. However, the Research Branch

Inclusion of indices such as these, and systematic use of the panel-interview method, as well as direct observation, would encompass systematic study of the *processes* of value-assimilation as part of reference group behavior, and not only, as in the applied researches of *The American Soldier*, the study of certain net results of such processes. There could then be, for example, inquiry into the possibly circular and cumulative process[36] through which value-assimilation furthers social contact between the groups which in turn reinforces value-assimilation, greater social acceptability and increased social contact.

An entirely different sequence of empirical and theoretical inquiry is suggested by the re-analysis of these data on group contexts of value-assimilation. Under which conditions do we find such changed evaluations of entire groups or social strata (whether this be called "perspectivistic thinking," or "false-consciousness")? Does it occur primarily when members of this group identify their fate with that of another group, so that they no longer faithfully express their own distinctive interests and values in the present? In other words, within which context of social structure does such "distortion" of group values occur, and in which is there a response more nearly appropriate to the situation?

Following out this one set of data—found on a few pages among the many hundreds of *The American Soldier*—seems to have involved the following procedures and to have had the following results:

First, a clarification of concepts has allowed an apparent disorder or variation in some reported findings to be interpreted as diverse expressions of underlying sociological uniformities, thus serving the theoretical objective of *parsimony*, found whenever several empirical generalizations are derived from a more general formulation.

Second, reconceptualization operated to this end by suggesting the relevance of a previously developed body of theoretic propositions, thus reducing the *ad hoc* nature of current interpretations and making for *continuity* of present findings and theories of the past. In a measure, this is the same theory implied by the concept of relative deprivation which, though utilized elsewhere in *The American Soldier*, was not applied to this particular set of empirical materials.

Third, generalizing the concepts (beyond the immediate descriptive categories of veterans, replacements, and green troops), points to the possibility that these generic formulations are pertinent, not only for the

---

was clearly sensitive to the problem. At one point, for example, they were able to determine, roughly, if veterans' pride in their company was affected by a comparatively high proportion of replacements. (See II, 255-257)

36. For an example of the type of process analysis required to treat problems of this kind, see P. F. Lazarsfeld and R. K. Merton, "Friendship as social process: a substantive and methodological analysis," in M. Berger, T. Abel and C. H. Page (eds.) *Freedom and Control in Modern Society*, (New York: D. Van Nostrand, 1954), 18-66.

specifically military situation, but for a wider range of situations corresponding to the requirements of the theoretic formulations, thus extending the *scope* of data to which these can perhaps be applied.

And finally, the very existence of such systematic data permitting provisional reconceptualization may importantly advance the development of theory, by highlighting the need for a series of sociological indices to be incorporated into research on these problems, thus providing for further *cumulation* of sociological knowledge by linking past theory, present data, and future research.

Although undertaken as an applied social research, *The American Soldier* has, then, the potential by-products of furthering the parsimony, continuity, scope and cumulation of sociological theory. And, as is not infrequently the case with applied research, the by-products may prove more significant for the discipline of sociology than the direct application of findings.

STATISTICAL INDICES OF
SOCIAL STRUCTURE

Before continuing with our review of problems in reference group theory, it will be useful to consider explicitly the implications of these researches for the study of social contexts. From the foregoing examination of the researches on assessment of promotion opportunities and on replacements' self-evaluations, it can be seen that *The American Soldier* is a fertile source for the development of relatively precise, statistical indices of social structure. In these and other studies, the survey data are analyzed in terms of the distribution of responses by social units (companies, divisions, branches of service). And in their analyses relating frequency distributions or rates characterizing social units to the responses of individuals and subgroups within these diverse units, they have moved well beyond the point ordinarily reached in studies of social ecology.

Like the use of statistical indicators in ecology for depicting different kinds of social units on an areal basis, *The American Soldier* provides indices of attributes of social structure, but *unlike* the ecological studies, *The American Soldier* goes on to make a *systematic analysis of the attitudes or evaluations of like-statused individuals within diverse social structures.*

This *combination* of indices suggests numerous statistical indices of group attributes or social structure which can be built into future sociological research. Moreover, the use of frequency distributions or proportions or rates as indices of social structures has the special merit of reminding us that these structures often vary in terms of degree, and not necessarily in terms of all-or-none qualities. For instance, social systems do not provide simply for mobility *or* for fixity of its members; they exhibit varying rates of mobility.[37] They are not simply heterogeneous *or* homogeneous, but have varying degrees of heterogeneity.[38] They are not integrated *or* unintegrated, cohesive *or* dispersive, but have varying degrees of integration and cohesion.[39]

Because statistical indices of such attributes of social systems have seldom been utilized in conjunction with indices of individual behavior, comparative sociology has been largely limited to loose and indecisive findings. Relatively strict comparison has been lacking as most of us most of the time have been confined to talking about "different" social structures rather than studying structures shown to differ in specifiable degree. When statistical indices of group attributes have been adopted— for example, variations in racial proportions among groups—these have typically not been *combined* with systematic comparisons of the behavior of like-statused people within these distinctive groups. And, correlatively, when relatively precise measures of individual attitudes have been obtained, these have seldom been combined with similarly definite measures of social structure. Thus, social psychology has in the past decade or so moved toward the systematic use of indices of individual attitudes and sentiments primarily among aggregates of mutually unrelated individuals.

The studies of the Research Branch suggest the feasibility and the importance of developing indices *both* of social structure and of the behavior of individuals situated within the structure. Their occasional comparisons of the status-structure of different branches of the Army thus involve indices of stratification similar to those provided by frequency distributions of a population among the several social classes. Once such indices are established, it becomes possible to have systematic, not anecdotal, comparisons of the behavior of people of similar class status living within differently proportioned class structures. This will result in advancing beyond the more familiar characterizations of "the

---

37. See, for example, the use of indices of comparative rates of social mobility in the Air Forces, Service Forces, Ground Forces, *etc.* as a social context for individual evaluations of promotion-chances. I, 251 ff.

38. See, for example, the indices of social heterogeneity of companies provided by proportions of replacements in outfits as a social context for individual expressions of pride in company. II, 255 ff. A similar procedure has been adopted in a study of individual racial attitudes within the contexts of subareas in a biracial housing development which are characterized by differing proportions of Negroes and whites. Merton, West and Jahoda, *op. cit.*

39. Consider how contemporary sociology can improve upon Durkheim's early study of suicide which *assumed* varying degrees of social cohesion and integration among Catholics and Protestants, military and civilian groups, etc. As noted in Chapter II, "the degree of integration is an empirical variable, changing for the same society from time to time and differing among various societies." Statistical indicators of integration and cohesion would permit systematic study, with a rigor not possible in Durkheim's day, of the bearing of such variations of social context upon the behavior of individuals variously located within the group.

middle-class man" or "the working-class man" to determine their characteristic behavior within differently constituted class systems. In the same fashion, other types of social differentiation can be indexed by the frequency distributions of various statuses (education, race, age, *etc.*) and combined with the systematic study of individuals similarly situated within these varying structures.[40]

In this respect, *The American Soldier* may represent a prelude to the immediate future in which indices of mobility rates, cultural change, group cohesion and social differentiation will be regularly and systematically incorporated into comparative studies of social structure. And once this is done, it will become possible to compare the patterns of reference group behavior of like-statused individuals within these various social systems.

REFERENCE GROUP THEORY AND SOCIAL MOBILITY

Other researches reported in *The American Soldier* which do not make explicit use of the concept of relative deprivation or kindred concepts can also be recast in terms of reference group theory. One of the more rigorous and seminal of these is the panel study of relationships between the conformity of enlisted men to official values of the Army and their subsequent promotion.

This study also illustrates the widely-known but seldom elucidated point that the same social research can be variously analyzed in at least three separate, though related, respects: its documented empirical findings, its methodology or logic of procedure, and its theoretical implications.

Since the methodology and the empirical findings of this study have been amply discussed—the one in the paper by Kendall and Lazarsfeld, the other in *The American Soldier* itself—we need not concern ourselves with them here. Instead, we limit our discussion to some of its theoretical implications.

These implications divide into three related kinds. First, the implications for reference group theory as the empirical findings are reexamined within the context of that theory. Second are the implications which enable us to connect reference group theory with hypotheses of functional sociology. And third, the implications which, once suitably generalized, enable us to see that this study bears, not only on the conformity-and-mobility patterns of American soldiers in World War II, but possibly also on more general and seemingly disparate patterns of

---

40. Berelson, Lazarsfeld and McPhee, *Voting* makes extensive use of such procedures, providing further evidence, perhaps, of continuity in social research.

For a more detailed account of sociological indices, see Section 2 of the paper by Kendall and Lazarsfeld, in *Continuities in Social Research*.

behavior, such as group defection, renegadism, social climbing, and the like.

Tracing out these implications comprises a large order which can scarcely be entirely filled, not because of limitations of space but because of limitations of our own sociological knowledge. But even an approximation to achieving our purpose should help us recognize the theoretical linkages between presently separated types of social behavior.

We begin by following our now customary practice of briefly sketching out the chief findings of the study as these are set forth in *The American Soldier.*

Case #5 (I, 258-275). This research was concerned, not with *rates* of promotion which were determined by changes in the table of organization, but with the *incidence* of promotion: which men were the more likely to be advanced? Since the decision of the commanding officer regarding promotions was by no means based upon objective tests of capacity or performance by enlisted men, there was much occasion for interpersonal relations and sentiments to play their part in affecting this decision. Accordingly, the Research Branch advanced the hypothesis that, "One factor which hardly would have failed to enter to some extent into the judgment of an officer in selecting a man for promotion was his conformity to the officially approved military mores." (I, 259) It is noted further, and we shall have occasion to return to this point in some detail, that "in making subjective judgments, the commanding officer necessarily laid himself wide open to charges of favoritism and particularly of succumbing to the wiles of those enlisted men most skilled at 'bucking.'" (I, 264)

A panel study of three groups of enlisted men was designed to find out whether the men who expressed attitudes in accord with the established military mores subsequently received promotions in proportions significantly higher than the others. This was consistently found to be the case. For example, "of the privates who in September 1943 said they did not think the Army's control was too strict, 19 per cent had become Pfc's by January 1944, while only 12 per cent of the other privates had become Pfc's." (I, 261-2) So, too, when men in the three samples are arranged according to their scores on a "quasi-scale of attitudes of conformity," it was uniformly found in all three groups "that the men whose attitudes were most conformist were the ones most likely to be promoted subsequently." (I, 263)[41]

---

41. As the authors themselves say and as Kendall and Lazarsfeld indicate in some detail, these data do not conclusively demonstrate that conformist attitudes, rather than other correlates of these attitudes, made for significantly higher likelihood of promotion. In principle, only a completely controlled experiment, obviously not feasible in the present instance, would demonstrate this beyond all reasonable doubt. But controlled experiment aside, this panel study, holding constant the factors of age and education which had been found to be related both to attitudes and promotion

Theoretical Implications. In discussing this panel study, we want to bring into the open some of the connections between reference group theory and functional sociology which have remained implicit to this point,—an objective to which this study lends itself particularly well, since the findings of the study can be readily reformulated in terms of both kinds of theory, and are then seen to bear upon a range of behavior wider than that considered in the study itself.

The value of such reformulation for social theory is perhaps best seen in connection with the independent variable of "conformity." It is clear, when one thinks about it, that the type of attitude described as conformist in this study is at the polar extreme from what is ordinarily called "social conformity." For in the vocabulary of sociology, social conformity usually denotes conformity to the norms and expectations current in the individual's *own* membership-group. But in this study, conformity refers, not to the norms of the immediate primary group constituted by enlisted men but to the quite different norms contained in the official military mores. Indeed, as data in *The American Soldier* make clear, the norms of the in-groups of associated enlisted men and the official norms of the Army and of the stratum of officers were often at odds.[42] In the language of reference group theory, therefore, attitudes of conformity to the official mores can be described as a positive orientation to the norms of a non-membership group that is taken as a frame of reference. Such conformity to norms of an out-group is thus equivalent to what is ordinarily called nonconformity, that is, nonconformity to the norms of the in-group.[43]

This preliminary reformulation leads directly to two interrelated questions which we have until now implied rather than considered explicitly:

---

goes a long way toward demonstrating a relationship between the incidence of conformist attitudes and subsequent advancement. In this respect, the study moves well beyond the point reached by the use of less rigorous data, indicating a static correlation between rank and conformist attitudes, inasmuch as it can show that those with conformist attitudes were more likely to be *subsequently* promoted. See I, 272-3.

42. Although the absolute percentages of men endorsing a given sentiment cannot of course be taken at face value since these percentages are affected by the sheer phrasing of the sentiment, it is nevertheless suggestive that data presented earlier in the volume (*e.g.*, I, 147 ff.) find only a small minority of the samples of enlisted men in this study adhering to the officially approved attitudes. By and large, a significantly larger proportion of officers abide by these attitudes.

43. There is nothing fixed about the boundaries separating in-groups from out-groups, membership-groups from non-membership-groups. These change with the changing situation. Vis-à-vis civilians or an alien group, men in the Army may regard themselves and be regarded as members of an in-group; yet, in another context, enlisted men may regard themselves and be regarded as an in-group in distinction to the out-group of officers. Since these concepts are relative to the situation, rather than absolute, there is no paradox in referring to the officers as an out-group for enlisted men in one context, and as members of the more inclusive in-group, in another context. On the general point, see Chapters IX and XI.

what are the consequences, functional and dysfunctional, of positive orientation to the values of a group other than one's own? And further, which social processes initiate, sustain or curb such orientations?

Functions of positive orientation to non-membership groups: anticipatory socialization. In considering, however briefly, the possible consequences of this pattern of conformity to non-membership group norms, it is advisable to distinguish between the consequences for the individuals exhibiting this behavior, the sub-group in which they find themselves, and the social system comprising both of these.

For the individual who adopts the values of a group to which he aspires but does not belong, this orientation may serve the twin functions of aiding his rise into that group and of easing his adjustment after he has become part of it. That this first function was indeed served is the gist of the finding in *The American Soldier* that those privates who accepted the official values of the Army hierarchy were more likely than others to be promoted. The hypothesis regarding the second function still remains to be tested. But it would not, in principle, be difficult to discover empirically whether those men who, through a kind of *anticipatory socialization,* take on the values of the non-membership group to which they aspire, find readier acceptance by that group and make an easier adjustment to it. This would require the development of indices of group acceptance and adjustment, and a comparison, in terms of these indices, of those newcomers to a group who had previously oriented themselves to the group's values and those who had not. More concretely, in the present instance, it would have entailed a comparative study among the privates promoted to higher rank, of the subsequent group adjustment of those who had undergone the hypothesized preparation for status shifts and those who had previously held fast to the values of their in-group of enlisted men. Indices of later adjustment could be related to indices of prior value-orientation. This would constitute a systematic empirical test of a functional hypothesis.

It appears, further, that anticipatory socialization is functional for the individual only within a relatively open social structure providing for mobility. For only in such a structure would such attitudinal and behavior preparation for status shifts be followed by actual changes of status in a substantial proportion of cases. By the same token, the same pattern of anticipatory socialization would be dysfunctional for the individual in a relatively closed social structure, where he would not find acceptance by the group to which he aspires and would probably lose acceptance, because of his outgroup orientation, by the group to which he belongs. This latter type of case will be recognized as that of the marginal man, poised on the edge of several groups but fully accepted by none of them.

Thus, the often-studied case of the marginal man[44] and the case of the enlisted man who takes the official military mores as a positive frame of reference can be identified, in a functional theory of reference group behavior, as special cases of anticipatory socialization. The marginal man pattern represents the special case in a relatively closed social system, in which the members of one group take as a positive frame of reference the norms of a group from which they are excluded in principle. Within such a social structure, anticipatory socialization becomes dysfunctional for the individual who becomes the victim of aspirations he cannot achieve and hopes he cannot satisfy. But, as the panel study seems to indicate, precisely the same kind of reference group behavior within a relatively open social system is functional for the individual at least to the degree of helping him to achieve the status to which he aspires. The same reference group behavior in different social structures has different consequences.

To this point, then, we find that positive orientation toward the norms of a non-membership group is precipitated by a passage between membership-groups, either in fact or in fantasy, and that the functional or dysfunctional consequences evidently depend upon the relatively open or closed character of the social structure in which this ocurs. And what would, at first glance, seem entirely unrelated and disparate forms of behavior—the behavior of such marginal men as the Cape Coloured or the Eurasian, and of enlisted men adopting the values of military strata other than their own—are seen, after appropriate conceptualization, as special cases of reference group behavior.

Although anticipatory socialization may be functional for the *individual* in an open social system, it is apparently dysfunctional for the solidarity of the *group* or *stratum* to which he belongs. For allegiance to the contrasting mores of another group means defection from the mores of the in-group. And accordingly, as we shall presently see, the in-group responds by putting all manner of social restraints upon such positive orientations to certain out-group norms.

From the standpoint of the larger social system, the Army as a whole, positive orientation toward the official mores would appear to be functional in supporting the legitimacy of the structure and in keeping the structure of authority intact. (This is presumably what is meant when the text of *The American Soldier* refers to these conformist attitudes as "favorable from the Army's point of view.") But manifestly, much research needs to be done before one can say that this is indeed the case. It is possible, for example, that the secondary effects of such orientations

---

44. Qualitative descriptions of the behavior of marginal men, as summarized, for example, by E. V. Stonequist, *The Marginal Man* (New York, Scribner's, 1937), can be analytically recast as that special and restricted case of reference group behavior in which the individual seeks to abandon one membership group for another to which he is socially forbidden access.

may be so deleterious to the solidarity of the primary groups of enlisted men that their morale sags. A concrete research question might help clarify the problem: are outfits with relatively large minorities of men positively oriented to the official Army values more likely to exhibit signs of anomie and personal disorganization (*e.g.* non-battle casualties)? In such situations, does the personal "success" of conformists (promotion) only serve to depress the morale of the others by rewarding those who depart from the in-group mores?

In this panel study, as well as in several of the others we have reviewed here—for example, the study of soldiers' evaluations of the justification for their induction into the Army—reference group behavior is evidently related to the legitimacy ascribed to institutional arrangements. Thus, the older married soldier is less likely to think it "fair" that he was inducted; most enlisted men think it "unfair" that promotions are presumably based on "who you know, not what you know"; and so on. In part, this apparent emphasis on legitimacy is of course an artifact of the research: many of the questions put to soldiers had to do with their conception of the legitimate or illegitimate character of their situation or of prevailing institutional arrangements. But the researchers' own focus of interest was in turn the result of their having observed that soldiers were, to a significant degree, actually concerned with such issues of institutional legitimacy, as the spontaneous comments of enlisted men often indicate.[45]

This bears notice because imputations of legitimacy to social arrangements seem functionally related to reference group behavior. They apparently affect *the range of the inter-group or inter-individual comparisons* that will typically be made. If the structure of a rigid system of stratification, for example, is generally defined as legitimate, if the rights, perquisites and obligations of each stratum are generally held to be morally right, then the individuals within each stratum will be the less likely to take the situation of the other strata as a context for appraisal of their own lot. They will, presumably, tend to confine their comparisons to other members of their own or neighboring social stratum. If, however, the system of stratification is under wide dispute, then members of some strata are more likely to contrast their own situation with that of others, and shape their self-appraisals accordingly. This variation in the structure of systems and in the degree of legitimacy imputed to the rules of the game may help account for the often-noticed

45. For example, in response to the question, "If you could talk with the President of the United States, what are the three most important questions you would want to ask him about war and your part in it?", a substantial proportion of both Negro and white troops evidently raised questions regarding the legitimacy of current practices and arrangements in the Army. The Negro troops of course centered on unjust practices of race discrimination, but 31 per cent of the white troops also introduced "questions and criticisms of Army life." (I, 504 *et passim.*)

fact that the degree of dissatisfaction with their lot is often less among the people in severely depressed social strata in a relatively rigid social system, than among those strata who are apparently "better off" in a more mobile social system. At any rate, the *range of groups* taken as effective bases of comparison in different social systems may well turn out to be closely connected with the degree to which legitimacy is ascribed to the prevailing social structure.

Though much remains to be said, this is perhaps enough to suggest that the pattern of anticipatory socialization may have diverse consequences for the individuals manifesting it, the groups to which they belong, and the more inclusive social structure. And through such re-examination of this panel study on the personal rewards of conformity, it becomes possible to specify some additional types of problems involved in a more comprehensive functional analysis of such reference group behavior. For example:

1. Since only a fraction of the in-group orient themselves positively toward the values of a non-membership group, it is necessary to discover the social position and personality types of those most likely to do so. For instance, are isolates in the group particularly ready to take up these alien values?

2. Much attention has been paid to the processes making for positive orientation to the norms of one's own group. But what are the processes making for such orientations to other groups or strata? Do relatively high rates of mobility serve to reinforce these latter orientations? (It will be remembered that *The American Soldier* provides data tangential to this point in the discussion of rates of promotion and assessment of promotion chances.) Suitably adapted, such data on actual rates of mobility, aspirations, and anticipatory socialization to the norms of a higher social stratum would extend a functional theory of conformist and deviant behavior.

3. What connections, if any, subsist between varying rates of mobility and acceptance of the legitimacy of the system of stratification by individuals diversely located in that system? Since it appears that systems with very low rates of mobility may achieve wide acceptance, what other interpretative variables need be included to account for the relationship between rates of mobility and imputations of legitimacy?

4. In civilian or military life, are the mobile individuals who are most ready to reaffirm the values of a power-holding or prestige-holding group the sooner accepted by that group? Does this operate effectively primarily as a latent function, in which the mobile individuals adopt these values because they experience them as superior, rather than deliberately adopting them only to gain acceptance? If such orientations are definitely motivated by the wish to belong, do they then become self-defeating, with the mobile individuals being characterized as strainers, strivers (or, in the Army, as brown-nosers bucking for promotion)?

Social processes sustaining and curbing positive orientations to non-membership groups. In the course of considering the functions of anticipatory socialization, we have made passing allusion to social processes which sustain or curb this pattern of behavior. Since it is precisely the data concerning such processes which are not easily caught up in the type of survey materials on attitudes primarily utilized in *The American Soldier,* and since these processes are central to any theory of reference group behavior, they merit further consideration.

As we have seen, what is anticipatory socialization from the standpoint of the individual is construed as defection and nonconformity by the group of which he is a member. To the degree that the individual identifies himself with another group, he alienates himself from his own group. Yet although the field of sociology has for generations been concerned with the determinants and consequences of group cohesion, it has given little *systematic* attention to the complementary subject of group alienation. When considered at all, it has been confined to such special cases as second-generation immigrants, conflict of loyalties between gang and family, *etc.* In large measure, the subject has been left to the literary observer, who could detect the drama inherent in the situation of the renegade, the traitor, the deserter. The value-laden connotations of these terms used to describe identification with groups other than one's own definitely suggest that these patterns of behavior have been typically regarded from the standpoint of the membership group. (Yet one group's renegade may be another group's convert.) Since the assumption that its members will be loyal is found in every group, else it would have no group character, no dependability of action, transfer of loyalty to another group (particularly a group operating in the same sphere of politics or economy), is regarded primarily in affective terms of sentiment rather than in detached terms of analysis. The renegade or traitor or climber—whatever the folk-phrase may be—more often becomes an object of vilification than an object of sociological study.

The framework of reference group theory, detached from the language of sentiment, enables the sociologist to identify and to locate renegadism, treason, the assimilation of immigrants, class mobility, social climbing, *etc.* as so many special forms of identification with what is at the time a non-membership group. In doing so, it affords the possibility of studying these, not as *wholly* particular and unconnected forms of behavior, but as different expressions of similar processes under significantly different conditions. The transfer of allegiance of upper class individuals from their own to a lower class—whether this be in the pre-revolutionary period of 18th century France or of 20th century Russia—belongs to the same family of sociological problems as the more familiar identification of lower class individuals with a higher class, a subject which has lately begun to absorb the attention of sociologists in a society where upward social mobility is an established value. Our cultural emphases notwithstanding, the phenomenon of topdogs adopting the values of the underdog is as much a reference group phenomenon lending itself to further inquiry as that of the underdogs seeking to become topdogs.

In such defections from the in-group, it may turn out, as has often been suggested, that it is the isolate, nominally in a group but only slightly incorporated in its network of social relations, who is most likely to become positively oriented toward non-membership groups. But, even if generally true, this is a static correlation and, therefore, only partly illuminating. What needs to be uncovered is the process through which this correlation comes to hold. Judging from some of the qualitative data in *The American Soldier* and from other studies of group defection, there is continued and cumulative interplay between a deterioration of *social relations* within the membership group and positive *attitudes* toward the norms of a non-membership group.

What the individual experiences as estrangement from a group of which he is a member tends to be experienced by his associates as repudiation of the group, and this ordinarily evokes a hostile response. As social relations between the individual and the rest of the group deteriorate, the norms of the group become less binding for him. For since he is progressively seceding from the group and being penalized by it, he is the less likely to experience rewards for adherence to the group's norms. Once initiated, this process seems to move toward a cumulative detachment from the group, in terms of attitudes and values as well as in terms of social relations. And to the degree that he orients himself toward out-group values, perhaps affirming them verbally and expressing them in action, he only widens the gap and reinforces the hostility between himself and his in-group associates. Through the interplay of dissociation and progressive alienation from the group values, he may become doubly motivated to orient himself toward the values of another group and to affiliate himself with it. There then remains the distinct question of the objective possibility of affiliating himself with his reference group. If the possibility is negligible or absent, then the alienated individual becomes socially rootless. But if the social system realistically allows for such change in group affiliations, then the individual estranged from the one group has all the more motivation to belong to the other.

This hypothetical account of dissociation and alienation, which of course only touches upon the processes which call for research in the field of reference group behavior, seems roughly in accord with qualitative data in *The American Soldier* on what was variously called brown-nosing, bucking for promotion, and sucking up. Excerpts from the diary of an enlisted man illustrate the interplay between dissociation and alienation: the outward-oriented man is too sedulous in abiding by the official mores—"But you're *supposed* to [work over there]. The lieutenant said you were supposed to."—this evokes group hostility expressed in epithets and ridicule—"Everybody is making sucking, kissing noises at K and S now"—followed by increasing dissociation within the group— "Ostracism was visible, but mild . . . few were friendly toward them . . . occasions arose where people avoided their company"—and more frequent association with men representing the non-membership reference group—"W, S and K sucked all afternoon; hung around lieutenants and asked bright questions." In this briefly summarized account, one sees the mechanisms of the in-group operating to curb positive orientation to the official mores[46] as well as the process through which this orientation develops among those who take these mores as their major frame of reference, considering their ties with the in-group as of only secondary importance.

Judging from implications of this panel research on conformity-and-mobility, then, there is room for study of the consequences of reference group behavior patterns as well as for study of their determinants. Moreover, the consequences pertinent for sociology are not merely those for the individuals engaging in this behavior, but for the groups of which they are a part. There develops also the possibility that the extent to which legitimacy is accorded the structure of these groups and the status of their members may affect the range of groups or strata which they ordinarily take as a frame of reference in assessing their own situation. And finally, this panel research calls attention to the need for close study of those processes in group life which sustain or curb positive orientations to non-membership groups, thus perhaps leading to a linking of reference group theory and current theories of social organization.

PSYCHOLOGICAL AND SOCIAL FUNCTIONS

In our review of the foregoing case, an effort was made to distinguish between the consequences of positive orientation toward a non-membership group for the individual, the membership-group and the larger social system. If, as we assume, an established pattern of behavior typically has such diverse consequences, it can be usefully examined from both a psychological and sociological standpoint. On occasion, *The American Soldier* analyzes behavior only in terms of a psychological framework. In some of these instances, the same situation may be profitably re-examined in terms of its implications for a framework of functional sociology.[47] This is not to say that the sociological orientation is necessarily "superior" to the psychological, or that it is necessarily at

---

46. "An official War Department pamphlet given to new recruits attempted to give "bucking" a blessing: " 'Bucking' implies all the things a soldier can honestly do to gain attention and promotion. The Army encourages individuals to put extra effort into drill, extra 'spit and polish' into personal appearance. At times this may make things uncomfortable for others who prefer to take things easier, but it stimulates a spirit of competition and improvement which makes ours a better Army." I, 264.

47. It is interesting to see how one's professional background apparently shapes one's description of *The American Soldier*. In his review of the book, Gordon W. Allport, the psychologist, refers to what he calls its "sociologistic bias." And here, a pair of sociologists are saying, in effect, that it has a marked "psychological orientation." The authors might well take comfort in the twin "charges."

odds with it. But it *is* different. And by regarding these materials from a perspective differing from that in the text itself, we may, perhaps, bring out further implications of these applied researches for social theory.

Case #6 (II, 272-84). Among the cases exhibiting a marked psychological orientation is the brief account of the experiences of men in replacement depots, those army stations through which they filtered from their training outfits to some depleted combat outfit in need of personnel. The author paints a vivid psychological portrait of the replacement depot: of the "apparently irreducible sources of psychological disturbance" characteristic of the depot, with its replacements handled in bulk and impersonally by permanent depot cadre, having only a casual status, and lacking the "support of social ties and the security of having an established niche in some organization." Probably, "the most salient psychological characteristic of depot life . . . was that the situation led to a state of anxious uncertainty without opportunity for resolving the tension." (II, 274) One consequence of the depot experience was to make the replacement "welcome many aspects of a permanent assignment." While this did not mean they welcomed combat itself, "even in this regard . . . the termination of anxious uncertainty was probably in some respects a psychological gain. The new combat man could say to himself, for better or for worse, 'This is it.'" (II, 176)

The Research Branch, then, was centrally concerned with the question: what were the effects of these experiences upon *the replacement?* But the same data involve another type of problem, this time from the standpoint of functional sociology: the problem, not of the effect of the depot upon the replacement, but upon his subsequent incorporation in a combat group.

Functional analysis of this situation would begin by conceptualizing the social role of the replacement depot, which falls into the category of an organization providing for *the movement of individuals from one group to another.* As typically follows upon a somewhat more generalized description of a situation, other situations nominally different on a common-sense level, are seen as belonging to the same general category. Materials presently scattered in the numerous pages of *The American Soldier* become cases in point of this pattern of transition from one group to another: for example, the replacement depot is, *in this respect,* essentially no different from the reassignment station as an intermediary between a combat outfit and a new domestic post. Furthermore, sociologists have long been interested in the standardized social patterns providing for passage from one group to another in various institutional areas, for example, the transition of the high school graduate to a first year at college.

The personal and social difficulties involved in such transfers are assumed to arise primarily from the dual process of breaking down old group affiliations (or of putting them into secondary place) and of building new group ties. That, in a sense, is comparable to the process of the recruit's initial absorption into his first army outfit, with all the attendant growing pains of group-formation. But in this special setting, the individual is immeasurably eased in his adjustment since it is not a problem peculiar to him. Every other member of the newly-forming group is experiencing a similar problem, whether he is a first-year college student or a raw army recruit.

Once he is a part of this group, however, transfer to another already established group is quite a different matter, as any child who is transferred from one school to another in mid-semester can report. In this case, his initial exposure to the new group is most apt to involve an intensification of old ties—his old friends, his former teachers, his old school are imbued with disproportionately great affect. This is much the same phenomenon as that of soldiers separated from their old combat outfits and settling into new domestic army stations. One study in *The American Soldier* reports that such returnees place tremendous importance on being permitted to "continue to wear the insignia of their old units" (II, 507-8),—just as the abruptly transferred school child may intensify his old group ties. Both reflect resistance to a sudden weaning from a former group affiliation. The school child, being a lone individual, presents no challenge to the unity of the new group,* and in time, he is usually taken into the ranks. But should a sizable number of new youngsters confront the group with their emphasis on old school ties, we might well find a need emerging for an "educational depot," to forestall the dysfunctional consequences of these challenges to the unity of the group. This is precisely the problem of the army situation. Being built on fragile enough grounds, the unity of an army outfit might be seriously impaired by the introduction of a sizable number of replacements, if their former group

---

* On this, see how C. S. Lewis, in the first part of his autobiography, mockingly describes the functional requirement for 'fagging' (hazing) in the English public schools or, at least, in the one school which he had the fortune to attend. "The interesting thing is that the public-school system had thus produced the very thing which it was advertised to prevent or cure. For you must understand (if you have not been dipped in that tradition yourself) that the whole thing was devised to 'knock the nonsense' out of the smaller boys and 'put them in their place.' 'If the junior boys weren't fagged,' as my brother once said, 'they would become insufferable.' . . . Obviously a certain grave danger was ever present to the minds of those who built up the Wyvernian hierarchy. It seemed to them self-evident that, if you left things to themselves, boys of nineteen who played rugger for the county and boxed for the school would everywhere be knocked down and sat on by boys of thirteen. And that, you know, would be a very shocking spectacle. The most elaborate mechanism, therefore, had to be devised for protecting the strong against the weak, the close corporation of Old Hands against the parcel of newcomers who were strangers to one another and to everyone in the place, the poor, trembling lions against the furious and ravening sheep." C. S. Lewis, *Surprised by Joy: The Shape of My Early Life* (New York: Harcourt, Brace and Company, 1955), 104-106.

attachment had not broken down prior to their admittance to the new outfit.

Thus from the perspective of the replacements' eventual ease of absorption into a combat group, new to them, as well as from the point of view of their potential effect upon the group they enter, there may well be a functional requirement for their *not* being transferred immediately from the training outfit to the outfit with which they will shortly serve in combat. One alternative is that which was in fact the practice utilized during the war years: filtering the newly trained soldier through replacement depots. This suggests the latent function possibly performed by the replacement depot: it may serve to loosen the soldier's previous army group ties, thus making him more amenable to ready absorption into his combat outfit. In much the same way that the sandhog adjusts to normal atmospheric pressure at the end of a day's work under water by going through de-compression chambers, so the soldier is *"de-grouped"* by passing through replacement depots. This would seem all the more important in view of the speed with which replacements were actually sent into combat upon joining a combat outfit. In one study, it was found that *half* the replacement infantrymen went into combat less than three days after joining their outfit.

In other words, the excessive psychological anxiety noted by the Research Branch as characteristic of depot life may also be regarded as a behavioral index of a state of temporary "grouplessness." But whichever is emphasized—the underlying sociological phenomenon of grouplessness or the external and visible psychological anxiety—the functional sociologist would seek to trace out its organizational consequences, *i.e.*, its impact on the absorption of the replacement into his most important army group, the unit with which he serves in combat.[48]

This anxiety accompanying the degrouping process may well be dysfunctional for the individual soldier at the time he is experiencing it, and for some soldiers, it may have had serious effects upon overall personal adjustment. Yet this same process of de-grouping may have

---

48. We have previously mentioned the similarity between the function of the replacement depot and that of the reassignment station through which the returnee soldier is transferred from his combat outfit to his domestic army post. An examination of the study of the returnee in *The American Soldier* (II—Chapter on problems of Rotation and Reconversion) suggests that the degrouping process of the returnee is of much longer duration, for the returnee has been removed from his most cohesive army group. Thus in a survey of returnees and non-overseas men in which the soldiers were asked about their sense of belonging to their new outfit, the returnees were much more apt to say they did not feel they belonged to their outfits than the non-returnees, *even though in a large proportion of the cases the returnees had been with the outfit longer than the non-returnees.* In the Air Force, for example, 34 per cent of the returnees and 15 per cent of the non-returnees said they did not feel they "belonged" to their outfits. The difference between returnee and non-returnee in other branches of the Army decreases slightly from the difference of 17 per cent in the more cohesive air corps to 11 per cent in the quartermaster corps. (II, 507) The rapidity and ease of the de-grouping process and subsequent re-absorption into a new group would appear to depend on the intensity of the former group ties.

functional consequences for other organizational units, particularly the combat outfit in which the de-grouped replacement is the more readily absorbed.[49] Empirical test of this hypothesis could be provided by an extension of the procedure adopted in the study of returnees (see the foregoing footnote). For each level of men's attachment to their previous outfit, it could be determined, first, whether the longer the period that men have spent in a replacement depot, the more effectively they have divested themselves of their previous group solidarity, and second, whether those men who had been thus "de-grouped" were the more effectively incorporated into their new combat outfit. To the extent that this was found to be the case, it would have bearing on the more general problem of factors and processes affecting the passage from old to new membership groups. And, in some measure, this would supplement the perceptive analysis of the replacement depot provided by *The American Soldier*.

CONCEPTS KINDRED TO REFERENCE GROUP THEORY

From allusions scattered throughout the foregoing discussion, it is evident that certain facts of reference group behavior were noted long before the term, reference group, was coined by Hyman in his important

---

49. To note this possible function of anxiety is not thereby to *advocate* anxiety. For even as a concomitant of the de-grouping process, not all such anxiety situations are functional for the social organization. In the case of the officer candidate schools, for example, which "can be conceived of as an ordeal," one consequence of a high anxiety situation was to strip the officer candidate of any vestige of his former enlisted man's values, which apparently militated against his subsequent ability to see the enlisted man's point of view. After an analysis of the "ordeal" of an officer candidate school in case-study terms, it is said: ". . . there is enough plausibility in this account of the transmission of culture to suggest that we have in this process an explanation of why so many officers, themselves formerly enlisted men, seemed to fail as officers to carry over their enlisted experience and try to see the enlisted man's point of view in handling their men." (I, 391) From the hierarchy-conscious perspective of the Army, this may or may not be considered objectionable. But the evidence seems clear that enlisted men—products of a culture system which expounds the worth of democratic equality—functioned best when they believed the gap between themselves and their leaders was not inflexible, when they felt their officers had relatively few special privileges they did not have, and so on. (I, 369) But, in other cases, the functional consequences of the de-grouping process for the Army's objectives may far outweigh the temporary dysfunctional consequences to the individual exposed to the replacement depot. From the standpoint of a narrowly defined conception of social engineering, this might lead to recommendations for the extension of "de-grouping" through explicit provision for such transitional organizations or statuses in various institutional orders. But this would presuppose an exclusive concern with organizational objectives—e.g., increased efficiency of a fighting machine—which one need not be ready to advocate. In this instance, for example, one's values may lead one to conclude that organizational efficiency, through de-grouping with its attendant anxieties, exacts too high a price. This is scarcely the first time that such moral problems of social engineering have occurred. It might be found, as so many 19th century writers asserted, that hunger, acute anxiety and insecurity are powerful incentives for work. Were this confirmed, it scarcely follows that the sociologist would *advocate* hunger as a prod to work.

study of 1942.[50] Thus, half a century ago, DuBois noted that "A white Philadelphian with $1,500 a year can call himself poor and live simply. A Negro with $1,500 a year ranks with the richest of his race and must usually spend more in proportion than his white neighbor in rent, dress and entertainment."[51] But though the specific fact that self-appraisals are *relative* to "the" group framework was often remarked, it was not conceptualized in terms general enough to lead to systematic research on the implications of the fact. Such a term as "reference group" is useful, not because the term itself helps explain behavior, but because it does not easily allow us to overlook this component in self-appraisals. The very generality of the term leads to the perception of similarities beneath apparent dissimilarities of behavior.

But apart from these isolated observations, there have been several lines of development in sociology and social psychology which now give promise of merging in a functional theory of reference group behavior. Each of these has, after its own fashion, made major contributions, but in retrospect, the impressive fact is that, in large measure, their mutual implications have not yet been consolidated. As is generally known, these are the conceptions of in- and out-groups set forth by Sumner, the ideas regarding the social self developed by James, Cooley and Mead, the

---

50. H. Hyman, *The Psychology of Status*.

51. W. E. B. DuBois, *The Philadelphia Negro*, 1899, as quoted by E. F. Frazier, *The Negro in the United States* (New York: Macmillan, 1949, 299n). Frazier develops the observation further to indicate the cross-pressures to which the Negro professional man is subject. "The Negro professional man or clerical worker often feels under great compulsion to keep up the requirements of upper-class behavior in the Negro group and at the same time act in the role of a middle-class professional or white collar worker in the community at large." And he goes on to say, in effect, that changing networks of social relations—increasing integration "into the larger community"—shift the balance of pertinent reference groups, when he remarks that "As the Negro becomes increasingly integrated into the larger community, the professional man or woman or clerical worker is escaping from the obligations of the upper-class role in the Negro community and *can orient his behavior with reference to* his middle-class status." *Ibid.*, 300, italics supplied.

Interestingly enough, technical problems in developing samples for public opinion polls *forced* attention to the same fact that economic status is relative to the income distribution of the environing community. Thus: "The owner of a small shoe store in Dubuque, Iowa, who is married, has no children, and enjoys an income of $5,000 a year, finds himself thrown with the prosperous people of the town. . . . He finds himself, economically, close to 'the top of the heap' in Dubuque. His association with other prosperous people inclines him to regard his fate as being rather intimately bound up with that of the properous people elsewhere. . . . Give the same $5,000 a year income to an assistant sales manager who lives in New York City and has two daughters of school age, and you will find that he does not regard himself as belonging to the same economic level as the Dubuque shoe dealer, nor does he think or vote like that man on many important subjects." Elmo Roper, "Classifying respondents by economic status," *Public Opinion Quarterly*, 1940, 4, 270; see also, S. S. Wilks, "Representative sampling and poll reliability," *ibid.*, 263: "A $3000-a-year salary in a small Arkansas town means one thing and a $3000-a-year salary in New York City means something entirely different. The problem of economic status in sampling is handled at present on what amounts to a relative basis in each sampling locality. . . ."

more recent systematic researches on reference group behavior represented by the work of Hyman, Sherif and Newcomb, and the very numerous special studies on concrete problems of human behavior such as those dealing with acculturation, assimilation, the marginal man, social mobility, multiple roles, conflicting loyalties, cross-pressures, and the like.

The general and, in this truncated form, uninstructive fact that men are variously oriented to groups besides their own was captured in the terminology invented by Sumner to distinguish between "ourselves, the we-group, or in-group, and everybody else, or the other-groups, out-groups."[52] Sumner proceeded to describe the relations between these types of groups. Essentially, these somewhat premature observations held that conditions of amity and order obtain in the in-group whereas the relation to out-groups is that of hostility, plunder and exploitation. That this is the case (under unspecified conditions) Sumner was able to show through numerous *illustrations* drawn from history and ethnology. But in adopting a descriptive, rather than an analytical, outlook on the facts of the case, he inevitably blurred and obscured the otherwise conspicuous fact that, under certain conditions, the out-group becomes a basis of *positive*, not merely hostile, reference[53] and that the science of sociology is thereby committed to determine the conditions under which one or the other orientation to out-groups obtained. In short, the initial distinction put Sumner well on the way toward opening up a series of problems regarding reference group behavior. But this avenue to the development of a theory of reference group behavior, in principle open to those who would explore it since the appearance of *Folkways* in 1906, was not followed up by systematic research.

With only the slight exaggeration inevitable in having a single sentence summarize a large number of facts, it may be said that the anticipations of reference group theory by James, Cooley, and Mead also remained almost wholly undeveloped for a generation or more. Particularly among sociologists their conceptions were treated, not as a beginning but as a virtual conclusion, repeatedly quoted and illustrated with new examples of multiple selves, the looking-glass self, responses

---

52. W. G. Sumner, *Folkways*, 12.

53. This case of discontinuity in reference group theory is all the more significant since Sumner of course recognized, in other contexts, that what he called "imitation" or "emulation" of out-group patterns of behavior did occur. But these observations were not systematically linked with his prior distinctions between in- and out-groups in such a way that they resulted in a series of analytical problems regarding the diverse patterns of reference group behavior under varied conditions. So, too, he commented on the parvenu (107) who is, of course, passing from one in-group to another, but again without developing the theoretical and analytical questions highlighted by such shifts in group membership. He has, in short, numerous observations pertinent to problems of reference groups, but these remain scattered and unconnected rather than analytically drawn together and seen as cognate.

to the significant gestures of "others," and so on. And because the words of the forefathers became final words, little was built upon their insightful suggestions. They were honored, not in the manner in which men of science do honor to their predecessors, by extending and elaborating their formulations on the basis of cumulatively developed problems and systematic researches bearing on these problems, but in the manner in which littérateurs honor their predecessors, by repeatedly quoting "definitive" passages from the masters' works.

Certain social psychologists, among whom Hyman, Sherif, and Newcomb[54] are representative, have somewhat advanced this theory by designing empirical researches which would feed back into theoretical formulations of reference group behavior. And since their data were systematic rather than anecdotal, they soon found themselves confronted with many of the same theoretical problems which emerge from the researches of *The American Soldier*. Newcomb's study, in particular, centered not only on the reference group contexts of attitudes, perceptions, and judgments, but also considered the social organization which affected the selection of reference groups.

The researches of *The American Soldier* belong to this last line of development, consisting of numerous empirical studies of ostensibly different types of behavior, which nevertheless involve similar social and psychological processes. Since social scientists are equipped with some, though not nearly enough, methods for the study of reference group behavior in the ordinary course of everyday life, they need not look only to the contrived situations of the social-psychology laboratory, which leaves outside its walls the established social relations which comprise the organization of groups in society. An Army private bucking for promotion may only in a narrow and theoretically superficial sense be regarded as engaging in behavior different from that of an immigrant assimilating the values of a native group, or of a lower-middle-class individual conforming to his conception of upper-middle-class patterns of behavior, or of a boy in a slum area orienting himself to the values of a settlement house worker rather than the values of the street corner gang, or of a Bennington student abandoning the conservative beliefs of her parents to adopt the more liberal ideas of her college associates, or of a lower-class Catholic departing from the pattern of his in-group by casting a Republican vote, or of an eighteenth century French aristocrat aligning himself with a revolutionary group of the time. However these may differ in detail, they are not necessarily unconnected forms of

---

54. Hyman, *op. cit.;* M. Sherif's *Psychology of Social Norms* (New York: Harper, 1936) moved toward a conception of reference groups more fully developed in his later book, *An Outline of Social Psychology*. T. M. Newcomb's monograph, *Personality and Social Change* (New York: Dryden Press, 1943) represented a major step forward in this development, and his *Social Psychology* (New York: Dryden Press, 1950) includes more recent researches.

behavior "belonging," respectively, to the jurisdictions of the sociology of military life, race and ethnic relations, social mobility, delinquency (or "social disorganization"), educational sociology, political sociology and the sociology of revolution.

Such conventional divisions in terms of superficially distinct spheres of human behavior serve to obscure the similarity of social and psychological processes with which more abstract conceptions, such as those of reference group theory, are concerned. As can be seen from the matrix of variables in the first part of this paper, the combination of elements may differ, thus giving rise to overtly distinctive forms of behavior, but these may nevertheless be only different expressions of similar processes under different conditions. They may all represent cases of individuals becoming identified with reference groups to which they aspire or in which they have just achieved membership. And to the extent that this is so, the observed behaviors can, in principle, be derived from a few relatively general conceptions holding for them all, rather than having their similarity obscured by varying terminologies, such as promotion, assimilation (and acculturation), class striving (and over-conformity), socialization, social deviation, renegadism, or again, relative deprivation, role conflict, cross-pressures and false consciousness.

The early development of reference group conceptions is studded with instances in which particular historical occurrences in the society led sociologists to focus on spheres of social behavior in which patterns of reference group behavior happened to be conspicuous. Thus, studies of assimilation, clearly a process in which there is reference to the culture of non-membership groups, were precipitated by waves of immigration to this country and the subsequent throes of absorption of people of diverse cultural background. So, too, growing sociological interest in mobility between social classes and in "false consciousness" whereby men identify themselves with classes "to which they do not belong," seems in part a response to open public discussion of classes, and to a possibly heightened sense of class conflict. In such instances, the sociologists' choice of subject-matter was more nearly dictated by concrete practical problems than by the requirements of systematic theory. As a result, there was a marked tendency for the interpretative conceptions to remain *particularized* to the special sphere of behavior under consideration. Distinctive concepts appropriate for each sphere were developed as separate and almost isolated tools of analysis, and their theoretical overlappings and connections were often lost to view. Specialization of inquiry in terms of the concrete practical problems generated by social change sometimes developed at the expense of a more general body of theory. Special cases usurped attention and special concepts were introduced, but the task of their theoretical consolidation was only barely begun.

Though our brief examination of cases has provided only intimations to this effect, they are perhaps enough to lend weight to the possibility that these are not unrelated forms of social behavior but concrete manifestations of underlying patterns of reference group behavior.[55] It seems probable that if special inquiries trace out the theoretical connections between these forms of behavior, they will develop one of those theories of the middle range which consolidate otherwise segregated hypotheses and empirical uniformities. The wider, more inclusive conception would mean, for example, that research on the adjustment-patterns of immigrants would contribute its share to the same theory that helps direct research on, say, factors in social mobility. And these steps toward consolidation would result in a more rapid cumulation of reference group theory, since research on diverse departments of human behavior would become mutually stimulating and sustaining. At least, that seems to be the import of this preliminary review of reference group conceptions in *The American Soldier.*

---

55. A historian of science has commented on comparable problems of theoretical consolidation in the natural and physical sciences: ". . . of all forms of mental activity the most difficult to induce . . . is the art of handling the same bundle of data as before, but placing them in a new system of relations with one another and giving them a different framework, all of which virtually means putting on a different kind of thinking-cap for the moment." H. Butterfield, *The Origins of Modern Science* (London: Bell, 1949), 1.

IX CONTINUITIES IN THE THEORY OF REFERENCE GROUPS AND SOCIAL STRUCTURE

THE CONCEPT of reference group formally originated in the field of social psychology. This field focuses primarily on the responses of individuals to their interpersonal and more extended social environment. As a result, when experimental research and theoretical inquiry into problems of reference groups once got under way, they centered largely upon study of the determinants of selection of reference groups by individuals and the consequences of this for the personality. But as the preceding chapter has periodically indicated, the concept of reference group also has a distinctive place in the theory of sociology, with its focus on the structure and functions of the social environments in which individuals are located.

The socio-psychological and the sociological theory of reference groups are not, of course, sharply separable; in part, they overlap and in part, they complement one another. But they are nevertheless distinct levels of theoretical analysis which it is useful to distinguish periodically for the purpose of uncovering distinctive theoretical problems. To be sure, it may be that ultimately, social psychology and sociology are indivisibly one just as it may be that ultimately all science is one. But for the time being, it proves more useful to take note of the differences between these types and levels of theory, in order that they may be more systematically related. At all events, it is from this perspective that I undertook to examine continuities in the theory of reference groups since the foregoing chapter was first written. During this period of some six years, much has been learned and, in the process, many gaps in knowledge have been detected. It is in this sense that the pages which follow are organized in terms of theoretical problems, both of reference groups and of associated matters of social structure generally.

PROBLEMATICS OF REFERENCE GROUP THEORY

Basic Concepts

As a field of inquiry is intensively cultivated, its basic concepts become progressively clarified. Concepts which proved adequate in a first approximation must be further specified as the results of inquiry cumulate. As more specific concepts are developed, they are often distinguished terminologically in order to fix the distinction in mind.[1] This effort to clarify basic concepts represents one line of recent continuity in the development of reference group theory.

PROBLEM 1.

CLARIFYING THE CONCEPT OF REFERENCE GROUP

That men act in a social frame of reference yielded by the groups of which they are a part is a notion undoubtedly ancient and probably sound. Were this alone the concern of reference group theory, it would merely be a new term for an old focus in sociology, which has always centered on the group determination of behavior. There is, however, the further fact that men frequently orient themselves to groups *other than their own* in shaping their behavior and evaluations, and it is the problems centered about this fact of orientation to non-membership groups that constitute the distinctive concern of reference group theory. Ultimately, of course, the theory must be generalized to the point where it can account for *both* membership and non-membership group orientations, but immediately its major task is to search out the processes through which individuals relate themselves to groups to which they do *not* belong. (Page 234)

As theoretical innovations, great or small, are introduced into the field of inquiry, they are apt to be re-assimilated by some into the antecedent theory of the field, with the result that the *distinctive* advance is blurred or altogether obscured. That it is necessary to emphasize the respects in which reference group theory extends the long-established conception of group determination of behavior is evident from a recent effort at reassimilation of this kind. It has been urged, for example, that "in spite of the enthusiasm of some proponents there is *actually nothing new* in reference group theory."[2] And again, "The proposition that men think, feel, and see things from a standpoint peculiar to the group in which they participate is an old one, repeatedly emphasized by students of anthropology and of the sociology of knowledge. . . . The concept of reference group actually introduces a minor refinement in the long familiar theory. . . ."[3]

It is clear how one can arrive at the conclusion that reference group theory is *nothing but* a reiteration of the notion that thought, sentiment and perception are shaped by the group(s) in which people take part, so that the theory presents "nothing actually new." It is only necessary to adopt the common expedient of ignoring the *distinctive* ideas in this

---

1. The progressive clarification of concepts as an integral phase of sociological theorizing has been examined in Chapter II.

2. Tamotsu Shibutani, "Reference groups as perspectives," *American Journal of Sociology*, 1955, 60, 563 [italics supplied].

3. *Ibid.,* 565.

developing theory, and so to identify it with long familiar conceptions. To make the new seem old by the device of ignoring the new to focus on the old is not at all a new practice. Yet there seems to be some lack of conviction in this judgment, as the author concludes his review of the matter by recognizing a distinctive characteristic of the concept of reference groups which "summarizes differential associations and loyalties and thus facilitates the study of selective perception [although, as we shall see, scarcely selective perception alone]. It becomes, therefore," he adds, "an indispensable tool for comprehending the diversity and dynamic character of the kind of society in which we live [although not, presumably, this 'kind of society' alone]."[4] Whether it can be properly described as an "indispensable tool" waits to be seen.

PROBLEM 1.1.

FUNCTIONAL TYPES OF REFERENCE GROUPS

Throughout the preceding chapter, there are numerous but unsystematic allusions to several functional kinds of reference groups. They are said to provide "a frame of reference for self-evaluation and attitude-formation"; there is said to be a need for "systematic study of the processes of value-assimilation as part of reference group behavior"; there is a short comment "on the reference group contexts of attitudes, perceptions, and judgments." But, as subsequent inquiry has shown, these uncoordinated allusions to implicitly different kinds of reference group behavior are no substitute for a considered and methodical ordering of these kinds.

Several recent papers have been directed to the problem of identifying the major types of reference groups in terms of their characteristic functions for the behavior of those oriented toward them. The papers[5] are in substantial agreement in explicitly distinguishing two[6] major types of reference groups along the lines vaguely adumbrated in the preceding chapter: the first is the "normative type" which sets and maintains standards for the individual and the second is the "comparison type" which provides a frame of comparison relative to which the individual evaluates himself and others. The first is a source of values assimilated by designated individuals (who may or may not be members of the

---

4. *Ibid.,* 569.

5. Harold H. Kelley, "Two functions of reference groups," in G. E. Swanson, T. M. Newcomb and E. L. Hartley (editors), *Readings in Social Psychology,* (New York: Henry Holt & Co., 1952), 410-414; Shibutani, *op. cit.;* Ralph H. Turner, "Role-taking, role standpoint, and reference-group behavior," *American Journal of Sociology,* 1956, 61, 316-328.

6. Shibutani has indicated a third ostensible type: groups to which men aspire. But as Turner has properly indicated, this is not another type for "The desire to be accepted is depicted [by sociologists] as the mechanism which leads to the adoption of the values and perspectives of the reference group." Turner, *op. cit.,* 327.

group), as in the case we have reviewed of replacements in the Army assimilating the values of veterans. The second is instead a context for evaluating the relative position of oneself and others, as in the cases cited by DuBois, Roper and Wilks of the social meaning of economic status as relative to the economic structure of the environing community. The two types are only analytically distinct, since the same reference group can of course serve both functions.

To be distinguished from both types of reference groups are the groups, identified by Turner, "whose members constitute merely conditions" for the action of individuals.[7] These "interaction groups," as Turner calls them, are simply parts of the social environment of the individual just as physical objects are part of his geographic environment; he must take them into account in working toward his purposes but they are not of normative or comparative significance to him.

These distinctions open up various problems: do each of the two types of reference group behavior involve distinctive social and psychological mechanisms? Which structural conditions of a society make for much or for little *comparative* reference behavior—roughly, for the invidious and non-invidious comparisons of the kind examined by Veblen? Do membership and non-membership groups differ in the extent to which they characteristically serve the comparative and the normative functions? Questions of this order follow almost directly from the distinction between these functional types of reference groups.

PROBLEM 1.2.

THE CONCEPT OF GROUP AND GROUP MEMBERSHIP

The distinction between membership and non-membership group quite evidently involves "the problem of criteria of 'membership' in a group," as we have seen. (Page 233) But as a recent critique has forcefully noted,[8] these criteria cannot be allowed to remain implicit. Yet they largely have remained implicit, in sociological writings at large as in the preceding essay. One office of reference group theory is to clarify the conceptual criteria of membership in a group.

As has been repeatedly indicated in the preceding pages, and as will be periodically indicated in the pages that follow, the now-established term "reference *group*" is something of a misnomer. For the term is applied not only to groups, but to individuals and to social categories as well. The distinction between reference groups and reference individuals will be examined in a later section; here, the effort is made to differ-

---

7. Turner, *op. cit.*, 328. I make no effort to reproduce here the details of Turner's instructive division of the various kinds of group-orientation that have until now been caught up in the general concept of reference group.

8. Norman Kaplan, *Reference Group Theory and Voting Behavior*, Columbia University doctoral dissertation, 1955, 35-47 (unpublished).

entiate conceptually the quite disparate sociological data now commonly described as reference *groups.*

A point of departure is supplied by the short and incomplete statements on the concepts of groups and group membership in the preceding chapter.

In so far as frequency of interaction is one such criterion [of membership in a group], we must recognize that the boundaries between groups are anything but sharply drawn. Rather, "members" of given groups are variously connected with other groups of which they are not *conventionally* regarded as members, though the sociologist might have ample basis for including them in these latter groups, by virtue of their frequent social interaction with its conventional membership. So, too, we are here momentarily [a "moment" which has evidently stretched into six calendar years] by-passing the question of distinctions between social *groups* and social *categories,* the latter referring to established statuses between the occupants of which there may be little or no interaction. (Page 233, n. 4)

There is nothing fixed about the boundaries separating in-groups from out-groups, membership groups from non-membership groups. These change with the changing situation. Vis-a-vis civilians or an alien group, men in the Army may regard themselves and be regarded as members of an in-group; yet, in another context, enlisted men may regard themselves and be regarded as an in-group in distinction to the out-group of officers. Since these concepts are relative to the situation, rather than absolute, there is no paradox in referring to the officers as an out-group for enlisted men in one context, and as members of the more inclusive in-group, in another context. (Page 264, n. 43)

To which a critic aptly retorts, "There may well be no paradox, but we may certainly insist on explicit criteria for the designation of a particular group as a membership group in the one instance and as a nonmembership group in the other."[9] Since the critic, Norman Kaplan, does not, however, go on to supply these criteria, it may be useful to re-examine and to systematize the various kinds of social formations loosely designated as "groups," "social categories," and the like. Some of the pertinent criteria are unsystematically mentioned in the foregoing passages, but they have yet to be brought out for methodical examination.

First of all, it is generally understood that the *sociological* concept of a group refers to a number of people who interact with one another in accord with established patterns.[10] This is sometimes phrased as a number of people having established and characteristic social relations. The two statements are, however, equivalent, since "social relations" are themselves patterned forms of social interaction, enduring sufficiently to become identifiable parts of a social structure. This one *objective* criterion of the group has been indicated in the foregoing allusion to "fre-

---

9. *Ibid.,* 32.

10. For an example, see George C. Homans, *The Human Group* (New York: Harcourt, Brace and Company, 1950), 1, 82-86.

quency of interaction." It is of course permissible to adopt this single criterion as sufficient, but if the purpose is to develop a concept which will be sociologically useful, other criteria are called for.[11]

A second criterion of a group, which remained only implicit in the cited passages, is that the interacting persons *define themselves* as "members," *i.e.*, that they have patterned expectations of forms of interaction which are morally binding on them and on other "members," but not on those regarded as "outside" the group. This criterion has been casually indicated in the cited passages in occasional allusions to the fact that people "regard themselves" as members of groups.

The correlative and third criterion is that the persons in interaction be *defined by others* as "belonging to the group," these others including fellow-members and non-members. In the case of formal groups, these definitions tend to be explicit; in the case of informal groups, they are often tacit, being symbolized by behavior rather than expressed in so many words.

To the extent that these three criteria—enduring and morally established forms of social interaction, self-definition as a member and the same definition by others—are fully met, those involved in the sustained interaction are clearly identifiable as comprising groups. Both the objective criterion of interaction and the subjective criteria of social definitions combine to effect relatively clear boundaries of membership and non-membership. When the subjective definitions are blurred, the form of the observed social interaction loses its distinctive character and there develops the familiar type of case in which the sociological observer detects "group formations" which are not necessarily experienced as such by those involved in them.

As has been implied and now needs to be said, group boundaries are not necessarily fixed but are dynamically changing in response to specifiable *situational contexts*. A changed situation may bring about significant changes in the rate of social interaction so that one-time members objectively leave the group, even though they do not explicitly "resign" or "drop out." Particularly in those informal groups lacking explicit definitions of group membership by self and others, such changes in the rate of social interaction may blur the boundaries of the group. This may be considered one of the functional properties of informal groups: their stability in part depending upon this relative ambiguity of membership. By the same token, this creates *practical*, not *theoretical*, difficulties for the sociologist who is concerned with identifying the membership of informal groups. This points to the need for reexamining and rejecting some of the connotations of the terms "member" and "non-member"; the terms are not fully faithful to the facts, for there appear

---

11. For an extensive set of such criteria, see P. A. Sorokin, *Society, Culture, and Personality* (New York: Harper & Brothers, 1947), 70 ff.

to be *degrees* of membership which are in part indicated by the rates of social interaction with others in the group. This is implied in such terms, occasionally used by sociologists, as "nominal" group member or "peripheral" group member. A nominal group member is one who is *defined* by others as engaged in the group system of social interaction but who, in actual fact, has ceased to interact with the others in the group. A peripheral group member is one who has so reduced his rate of social interaction with the others in the group as to have relatively little of his behavior controlled by them. Changes in the objective situation—for example, a change in the spatial distribution of current group members—may make for a relatively high ratio of nominal to actual members.

In the same way, situational changes may affect the self- and other-definitions of group membership. For since rates of social interaction are not evenly distributed among the members of a group, any continuing event which increases the interaction among some and reduces the interaction among others will tend to make for *sub-group* formations. As the term implies, sub-groups are structurally constituted by those who develop distinctive social relations among themselves which are not shared with other members of the larger group. All groups are potentially vulnerable to such sub-group formations. The forces making for these differentiated groups may be non-culturally objective: for example, those group members continually in closest propinquity are apt to form distinctive sub-groups. Special interests, peculiar to certain statuses or strata in the larger group, may also make for sub-group formations; for example, to the extent that the *interests* of enlisted men and of officers in an army are not identical and differ in patterned respects. Sentiments and values, peculiar to constituent statuses or strata, can also work in the same direction to produce sub-groups. When these three varied types of differentiating forces converge, there develops one of those kinds of *social re-definitions* to which we have referred in saying that, on some occasions, members of an in-group may become differentiated into constituent in-groups and out-groups. An "issue" which crystallizes the distinctive interests, or sentiments, or both, of potential sub-groups can mobilize both the behavior and the attitudes which result in new group formations.

As long as the conceptual language commonly in use to describe group structure connotes a static condition of group membership, it will appear paradoxical that the *same individuals* must on occasion be described as being in the same group and on other occasions, as being in different (and perhaps mutually hostile) groups. But if it is recognized that group membership and group structure are dynamic, that these are only the conceptualized resultants of forces at work within a group, it becomes clear that the boundaries of groups are in constant process of objective change, as registered by rates of social interaction, and of social re-definition, as registered by self- and other-definitions of membership.[12]

PROBLEM 1.3.

THE CONCEPT OF NON-MEMBERSHIP

Just as *membership* in a group is far from being a self-evident concept and requires explicit sociological criteria if it is to be conceptually identifiable, so with *non-membership*. To be sure, "non-members" are those who do not meet the interactional and definitional criteria of membership, and it might therefore seem that the definition of members would suffice to define residual persons as non-members. But residual definitions are notoriously apt to obscure significant features of that which is being defined only negatively.[13] That is the case with the residual concept of non-membership.

For the category of "non-membership," if defined only in negative terms to comprise those who do not meet the criteria of membership, serves to obscure basic distinctions in kinds of non-membership; distinctions which have particular relevance for reference group theory. That this is so can be seen by drawing certain implications from the important and long-neglected concept of "completeness" of a group as introduced by Simmel.[14] The concept of completeness refers to a group property measured by the proportion of *potential members*—those who satisfy the requirements for membership as established by the group—who are *actual members*. Trade unions, professional associations, alumni groups are only the most conspicuous kinds of examples of organizations with varying degrees of completeness.

The group property of completeness, as Simmel properly emphasizes, must be clearly distinguished from the group property of size. In effect, this means that groups of the same absolute size (as measured by the number of members) may have quite different degrees of completeness (as measured by the proportion of potential members who are actually members). And correlatively, this means that groups of the same absolute size may have markedly different degrees of *social power*, according to whether they encompass all potential members or varying proportions

---

12. This general concept of the shifting boundaries of group membership is considered again in Chapter XI, 425. Apropos of such social re-definitions being situationally determined is the ironic observation by Albert Einstein in an address at the Sorbonne: "If my theory of relativity is proven successful, Germany will claim me as a German and France will declare that I am a citizen of the world. Should my theory prove untrue, France will say I am a German and Germany will declare that I am a Jew."

13. For a cogent statement of the idea of residual categories, see Talcott Parsons, *The Structure of Social Action*, 16-20, 192.

14. *The Sociology of Georg Simmel*, translated and edited by Kurt H. Wolff (Glencoe, Illinois: The Free Press, 1950), 95.

of them. Recognition of the relation between completeness and power is, of course, one of the major reasons why associations of men in particular statuses will seek to enlarge their membership to include as large as possible a proportion of the potential membership. The more nearly complete the group, the greater the power and influence it can exercise.

This short formulation of the concept of completeness is only a seeming disgression from the re-examination of the concepts of members and non-members of a group. For, as Simmel apparently sensed, the concept of completeness implies that there are distinct and structurally different *kinds of non-members* of a group. Non-members do not constitute a single, homogeneous social category. They differ in their patterned relations to the group of which they are not members. This is evidently implicit in the observation by Simmel that "the person who ideally, as it were, belongs in the group but remains outside it, by his mere indifference, his non-affiliation, positively harms the group. This non-membership may take the form of competition, as in the case of workers' coalitions; or it may show the outsider the limits of the power which the group wields; or it may damage the group because it cannot even be constituted unless *all* potential candidates join as members, as is the case in certain industrial cartels."[15]

1. *Eligibility and ineligibility for membership:* This suggests a first attribute in terms of which the residual category of non-members can be further specified: non-members who are ineligible for membership can be usefully distinguished from those who are eligible but continue to remain unaffiliated with the group. The distinction between eligible and ineligible non-members can serve to clarify the conditions under which non-members are likely to become positively oriented toward the norms of a group. Other attributes of non-membership being equal— and we shall be considering these other attributes directly—non-members eligible for membership will presumably be more likely to adopt the norms of the group as a positive frame of reference.

The attributes of eligibility and ineligibility provide only one basis for further specifying the residual concept of non-membership. At least three other sets of attributes can be systematically identified and connected with distinctive patterns of reference group behavior.

2. *Attitudes toward becoming members:* Non-members also differ in their patterned attitudes toward becoming members: (a) some may aspire to membership in the group; (b) others may be indifferent toward such affiliation; and (c) still others may be motivated to remain unaffiliated with the group. Reference group theory has of course incorporated the first of these motivated attitudes toward membership as constituting one mechanism making for positive orientation of non-members toward the norms of a group. The preceding chapter is one

---

15. *Ibid.*, 95.

among many analyses dealing with the special case of the "individual who adopts the values of a group to which he aspires but does not belong."[16]

By combining the two attributes of the group-defined eligibility status of non-members and the self-defined attitudes of non-members toward membership, it becomes possible to establish a systematic array of identifiable types of psycho-social relations of non-members to designated groups. In this way, it becomes evident that non-members aspiring to acceptance by a group constitute only one among several distinct types of non-members.

Group-defined Status of Non-members

NON-MEMBERS' ATTITUDES TOWARD MEMBERSHIP	ELIGIBLE FOR MEMBERSHIP	INELIGIBLE
Aspire to belong	Candidate for membership	Marginal man
Indifferent to affiliation	Potential member	Detached non-member
Motivated not to belong	Autonomous non-member	Antagonistic non-member (out-group)

In the preceding chapter, as in reference group theory at large, only some of these discernible types of non-members have been specifically identified. From all indications, this identification of types has been partial and highly selective because it arose from direct descriptions of observed patterns of behavior rather than being analytically derived from combinations of defined attributes of non-members in relation to designated groups. As we have noted, the first of these types—the individuals who aspire to groups of which they are not yet members—has been singled out for special attention in reference group theory. But as has also been implied in these earlier analyses, and as the foregoing paradigm indicates anew, aspirants to group membership divide into two significantly different kinds, depending on the group-defined criteria of eligibility for membership status. They differ in their structurally defined position and consequently, in the functional and dysfunctional consequences of their engaging in anticipatory socialization by adopting the values of the group to which they aspire but do not belong.[17]

The eligible aspirant for membership—who has been identified as the "candidate" for membership—is both motivated to select the non-membership group as his reference group and apt to be rewarded by

16. Page 265 of this volume and the short discussion of this point on page 234. Indeed, Muzafer Sherif and Carolyn W. Sherif, *Groups in Harmony and Tension* (New York: Harper & Brothers, 1953), 161, make this an integral part of their definition of reference groups: "those to which the individual relates himself as a part or to which he aspires to relate himself psychologically."

17. Similar types have been worked out on the same basis by Leonard Broom, "Toward a cumulative social science," *Research Studies of the State College of Washington*, 1951, 29, 67-75.

the group for doing so. The ineligible aspirant, however, engaging in this anticipatory socialization becomes a marginal man, apt to be rejected by his membership group for repudiating its values and unable to find acceptance by the group which he seeks to enter.

The second major class of non-members—those who are wholly indifferent to the prospect of group-membership—consists of those who do not orient themselves at all to the group in question. They are entirely outside its orbit. It constitutes no part of *their* reference groups. Nevertheless, this type too can instructively be subdivided into those who are eligible for membership and may therefore become points of reference for the group which may seek to draw them into its orbit, and the ineligible and indifferent non-members who constitute what Turner has described as merely conditions for action by the group.[18] As we shall soon see, these two types of non-members have distinct status depending on whether or not the group seeks to enlarge its approach to completeness.

The third class of non-members are, on the contrary, oriented toward the group in question but are variously motivated not to seek membership in it. The non-members who actively avoid the membership for which they are eligible are, in the words of Simmel, those to whom "the axiom applies, 'Who is not for me is against me.'"[19] And as Simmel has also implied, the eligible individuals who expressly reject membership pose more of a threat to the group in certain respects than the antagonists, who could not in any case become members. Rejection by eligibles symbolizes the relative weakness of the group by emphasizing its incompleteness of membership just as it symbolizes the relative dubiety of its norms and values which are not accepted by those to whom they should in principle apply. For both these motivated non-affiliates, the group is (or may readily become) a *negative* reference group, as we shall see in the section dealing with this type of group.

Joint consideration of the attributes of eligibility or ineligibility and of attitudes toward membership in a designated group thus differentiates distinct types of non-membership, rather than implicitly treating non-members as all of a piece. Each of these types of non-members is in turn apt to develop distinctive patterns of reference group behavior vis-à-vis the indicated group to which they do not belong. It locates, by anticipation, the non-members who are positively oriented toward the group, those who are negatively oriented toward it, and the large and important category of non-members who are not oriented toward it at

18. This is an adaptation of the conception advanced by Turner and reported in the early part of this chapter. Turner calls our attention to *groups* which comprise merely conditions for persons not in them; we here consider the correlative pattern of *non-members* comprising conditions for groups which do not define them as prospective members.

19. Simmel, *op. cit.*, 95.

all, *i.e.*, for whom the group in question is not a reference group.

At least two additional sets of attributes of non-members and non-membership groups need to be taken into account in order to locate, structurally and psychologically, distinctive orientations to non-membership groups. These are the group-defined concern or absence of concern with incorporating eligible non-members into the group, and the distinction between non-members who have been and those who have never been members of the group.

3. *Open and closed groups:* Just as individuals differ in aspirations to affiliate themselves with particular groups, so do groups differ in their concern to enlarge or to restrict their membership. This is to say that groups, and social structures generally, may be relatively open or closed, as has long since been noted in sociological theory.[20]

Here again, a point of departure is provided by Simmel. Groups do not uniformly seek to enlarge their membership; some, on the contrary, are so organized as to restrict membership, even to the extent of excluding those who are formally eligible for membership. This is particularly the case for élites, either self-constituted or socially recognized. Nor is this policy of exclusion *entirely* a matter of preserving the prestige and the power of the group, although these considerations may concretely enter into the policy. As Simmel says in effect, it may also be a structural requirement for an élite to remain relatively small, if its distinctive social relations are to be maintained.[21] Ready extension of membership may also depreciate the symbolic worth of group affiliation by extending it to numerous others. For these various structural and self-interested reasons, certain groups remain relatively closed.

For the same formal reasons, other types of groups seek to be relatively open in an effort to enlarge their membership. Political parties in

---

20. For a fairly recent formulation, see Sorokin, *op. cit.*, 175. The "relatively open or closed character of the social structure" is related to reference group behavior and its consequences in the preceding chapter, but is not systematically related to other attributes of non-members and non-membership groups. It should be expressly noted also that not only systems of social classes can be usefully regarded as variously open or closed, but all groups and social categories can be so regarded.

21. Simmel's observations read as follows: "Thus the tendency of extreme numerical limitation . . . is not only due to the egoistic disinclination to share a ruling position but also to the instinct [*sic;* read: tacit understanding] that the vital conditions of an aristocracy can be maintained only if the number of its members is small, relatively and absolutely. . . . [Under certain conditions,] there is nothing left but to draw at a certain point a hard line against expansion, and to stem the quantitatively closed group against whatever outside elements may want to enter it, *no matter how much they may be entitled to do so.* The aristocratic nature often becomes conscious of itself only in this situation, in this increased solidarity in the face of a tendency to expand." Simmel, *op. cit.*, 90-91 [italics supplied]. Need it be said that in thus *recognizing* the structural requirement of relative closure for an élite, Simmel is not *advocating* the policy of exclusion?

democratic political systems,[22] industrial unions and certain religious bodies, for example, are structurally and functionally so constituted that they seek to enlarge their membership to the fullest. Proselytizing organizations are not, of course, confined to the political or the religious realm; they can be found in a variety of institutional spheres. Such open organizations aim at becoming both membership groups and reference groups for all those who formally meet their criteria of eligibility. On occasion, the criteria may be successively made less exacting in order to enlarge the numbers of non-members who can acquire membership, this giving rise to the familiar structural pattern of conflict between "high standards of admissibility" and "large numbers of members."[23]

Depending on the open or closed character of the group, then, non-members are variously apt to orient themselves to it as a reference group. This was the basis for suggesting in the previous chapter that non-membership groups are more likely to be adopted as reference groups in those social systems having high rates of social mobility than in those which are relatively closed. The structural context of mobility-rates determines whether such anticipatory orientation on the part of non-members will be functional or dysfunctional for them. In an open system, the positive orientation to non-membership groups will more often be rewarded by subsequent inclusion in the group; in a closed system, it will more often lead to frustrated aims and marginal status. Through this more or less recognized system of patterned rewards and punishments, open systems encourage a high rate and closed systems a low rate of positive reference to non-membership groups.[24]

4. *Time perspectives on non-membership: former members and continued non-members:* Like other sociological concepts of status, non-membership has been usually construed statically, in terms of the *current* status of the individual. And as with these other concepts, it requires a distinct effort of mind to escape from this static context and to incorporate into the conceptual scheme "what everybody knows," namely, that not only his current status but also his past history of statuses affect the present and future behavior of the individual. Thus, it is only re-

---

22. Political parties manifestly do not have this character in all political systems. Sociologically considered, Lenin's Bolshevik doctrine advocated the closed élite principle of confining membership in the party to disciplined and indoctrinated professional revolutionaries in contrast to the Menshevik doctrine of Martov and Trotsky which advocated the open mass principle of membership. Organizations in various institutional spheres have attempted to combine the "open" and "closed" principles by all manner of structural devices for stratifying the membership.

23. This is the counterpart in the field of social organization to the equally familiar conflict in the field of popular culture and mass communications. The objective of maximizing the audience—the "mass principle of popularity"—conflicts with the objective of maintaining "high standards" of cultural content—the "élite principle of taste." Interestingly enough, it is not uncommon for the same people who reject the élite principle of organization to advocate the élite principle of popular culture.

24. In this connection, see the section on "reference group theory and social mobility" in the preceding chapter.

cently that sociological studies of class-typed behavior have systematically, rather than sporadically, distinguished among individuals currently
in the same social class in terms of their past history of class status,
finding, as one might expect, significant differences of reference group
behavior between those who are downwardly mobile, upwardly mobile
or stationary in their class position.[25] In much the same way, a study of
friendship as social process has distinguished among those who, at a
particular time of observation, appear in the same category (for example,
as like-minded friends) but who nevertheless differ in terms of their
mutual relationships and values at an earlier time of observation. It then
becomes possible to connect such past differences to their probable relationship at another, and still later, time of observation.[26]

The category of non-member can similarly be conceptualized dynamically, in terms of the past history of membership, by distinguishing
between those who were formerly members of the group and those who
have never been in the group. As we have seen, non-members have been
considered dynamically in terms of their orientations toward the future,
as in the case of those aspiring to membership in the group. But they
have not been so considered in terms of structural dynamics, dealing
with their past relations with the group. Yet it would seem plausible
that former members would differ in their reference group behavior
from the other non-members who have never been in the group.

It can be provisionally assumed that membership in a group which
has involved deep-seated attachments and sentiments cannot be easily
abandoned without psychological residue. This is to say that former
members of a group previously significant to them are likely to remain
ambivalent, rather than wholly indifferent, toward it. Of course, numerous structural conditions can mitigate or eliminate this ambivalence; for
example, complete spatial and social separation from the group may
reduce the occasions on which it is salient to the former member. Put
in terms of our classification of "non-members' attitudes toward membership," this means that former members are apt to be motivated not
to belong rather than being merely indifferent to affiliation. The group
remains pertinent precisely because they are alienated or estranged
from it; it is therefore likely to become a negative reference group.

By focusing on the special kind of non-member who was formerly a

25. Bruno Bettelheim and Morris Janowitz, *The Dynamics of Prejudice* (New
York: Harper & Brothers, 1950); Joseph Greenblum and Leonard I. Pearlin,
"Vertical mobility and prejudice: a socio-psychological analysis," in Reinhard Bendix
and Seymour Martin Lipset (editors), *Class, Status and Power*, (Glencoe, Illinois:
The Free Press, 1953), 480-491.

26. Paul F. Lazarsfeld and Robert K. Merton, "Friendship as social process: a
substantive and methodological analysis," in Morroe Berger, Theodore Abel and
Charles H. Page (editors), *Freedom and Control in Modern Society,* (New York:
D. Van Nostrand Company, 1954), 18-66. For an extension of this analysis, see the
forthcoming paper by John W. Riley, Jr. and Matilda White Riley, "The study of
psychological mechanisms in sociological research."

member of a group significant to him, it becomes possible to link up the concept of negative reference group—soon to be considered in detail—with the analysis of deviant behavior and social control developed by Parsons. As he points out,

> . . . alienation is conceived *always* to be part of an ambivalent motivational structure, while conformity need not be. Where there is no longer *any* attachment to the object and/or internalization of the normative pattern, the attitude is not alienation but *indifference*. Both social object and pattern have become only neutral objects of the situation which are no longer a focus of ego's cathectic need-system. The conflict in such a case would have been solved by full resolution, through substitution of a new object, through inhibition or extinction of the need-disposition, and/or through internalization of a new normative pattern.[27]

But this full affective attachment to a former membership group need not, and perhaps typically does not, occur. It is then the case that former members of a group often convert it into a negative reference group toward which they are *dependently hostile*, rather than simply indifferent. For precisely because the loss or rejection of membership does not promptly eradicate the former attachment to the group, ambivalence rather than indifference is apt to result. This gives rise to what Parsons calls "compulsive alienation," in this case, an abiding and rigid rejection of the norms of the repudiated group.[28]

The ambivalent ex-member thus has a double orientation: toward finding some substitute group affiliation and toward coping with his earlier attachment to his former membership group. This may account for the often noted tendency of such individuals to become even more strongly attached to the newfound membership group than is the case for those born into the group, and correlatively, to become more hostile toward their former group than is the case among their newfound associates. Michels is one among many to have the impression that the "renegade" is both more devoted to his new group affiliates and more hostile to the group he has left than are the people traditionally affiliated with his new group. The revolutionary of bourgeois origins, he suggests, is more violent in his opposition to the bourgeoisie than are his fellow-revolutionaries of proletarian origins. Should this impression be found empirically true, then the process of membership and reference group behavior we are tracing here may help account for the doubly reinforced

---

27. Parsons, *The Social System*, 254. *Cf.* the discussion of processes of alienation and estrangement in the preceding chapter of this volume, 269-271.

28. The type of ambivalence in which the alienative component dominates is pictured by Parsons as follows: ". . . the fact that the attachment to alter as a person [or as a group] and to the normative pattern is still a fundamental need means that ego must defend himself against the tendency to express this need-disposition. He must therefore not only express his negative reaction, but be doubly sure that the conformative element does not gain the upper hand and risk his having to inhibit the negative again. Therefore his refusal to conform with alter's expectations becomes compulsive." *Ibid.*, 255.

affect: a kind of reaction-formation in which identification with the new is supported by repudiation of the old, both being expressed with disproportionate affect.

Correlatively, the behavior of the repudiated membership group toward the former member tends to be more hostile and bitter than that directed toward people who have always been members of an out-group, or toward people who have never been in the group though eligible for membership. Here, too, there is double affect. In one part, this stems from the threat to the group's values which are being repudiated by individuals who have previously accepted them, for this implies that the former members have in effect put them to test and found these values wanting. This is symbolically more damaging than the opposition to these values by members of an out-group who have never lived in accord with them. This latter case can be interpreted by the group as a matter of pure ignorance, a definition difficult to sustain when applied to a former member of the group. In another part, the ex-member's acceptance of the values of his new group can be taken to symbolize the fragility of the loyalties within the repudiated group. If it can happen once, it can happen again. The estranged ex-member is thus a living symbol both of the inferiority imputed to the group's values and of the tenuous character of group loyalties.

It may not be too much to suggest that the vernacular registers this tendency of the group to respond with marked affect toward those who abandon membership in it. Witness the extensive array of affectively toned terms designating ex-members: renegade, apostate, turncoat, heretic, traitor, secessionist, deserter and the like; it is difficult to find neutrally-toned vernacular denoting the same fact. The shades of meaning distinguishing these terms of abuse ordinarily turn on the subsequent orientation of the ex-member toward the group he has left. The renegade not only repudiates the norms of the group and membership in it, but joins the opposition. The apostate substitutes another and, from the standpoint of the group, a less exalted set of beliefs for those he has previously professed. The turncoat compounds these social felonies by being motivated to shift his allegiance not through inner conviction but through hope of gain. But whatever the nuances of opprobrium in these epithets, they agree in implying that the orientation to the former group is not lightly abandoned, so that the group may become an object of indifference. Just as the new convert is more royalist than the king, so the ex-royalist is more republican than the *citoyen*, born and bred.[29]

---

29. Ample case material attesting this pattern can be found, in the present historical scene, in the behavior of the many ex-Communists turned American patriot and of the few ex-patriots turned Communist. This would require study supplementing that by Gabriel A. Almond *et al.*, *The Appeals of Communism* (Princeton: Princeton University Press, 1954); on these types, see Lewis Coser, *The Functions of Social Conflict* (Glencoe: The Free Press, 1956), 67-72.

Systematic empirical inquiry into the reference group behavior of these two kinds of non-members has yet to be undertaken. But there would seem to be ample theoretical support for the assumption that the orientations toward non-membership groups will differ substantially between ex-members and those who never were members of the groups under review. Unless the concept of non-membership is specified in these terms, however, the problem itself can scarcely be formulated.

This preliminary sketch of attributes of non-members may be enough to establish the point that it is not theoretically adequate to retain the concept of non-membership as a residual and implicitly homogeneous category. Non-members differ in terms of their eligibility for membership in the group, their attitudes toward becoming members, the open or closed structure of the group for those people who are formally eligible and their previous status in relation to the current non-membership group. As these attributes jointly differ, so do the social role and the psychological situation of the non-member, and with this, presumably, his orientation toward the non-membership reference group.

PROBLEM 1.4.

THE CONCEPTS OF IN-GROUP AND OUT-GROUP

From the foregoing review it is evident that membership groups are not co-terminous with in-groups, nor non-membership groups with out-groups, although the contrary may seem to be implied by William Graham Sumner in the famous passage which first introduced the concepts of in-group and out-group. At the outset, Sumner is speaking primarily of "primitive society" but, before he is through, he has much the same to say about more complex societies:

. . . a differentiation arises between ourselves, the we-group, or in-group, and everybody else, or the others-groups, out-groups. The insiders in a we-group are in a relation of peace, order, law, government and industry, to each other. Their relation to all outsiders, or others-groups, is one of war and plunder, except as agreements have modified it. . . .

The relation of comradeship and peace in the we-group and that of hostility and war towards others-groups are correlative to each other. . . . Loyalty to *the group*, sacrifice for it, hatred and contempt for outsiders, brotherhood within, warlikeness without—all grow together, products of the same situation.[30]

---

30. W. G. Sumner, *Folkways*, 12-13 [italics supplied]. Sumner goes on to refer to "ethnocentrism" as "the technical name for this view of things in which one's own group is the center of everything, and all others are *scaled and rated with reference to it*"; an early but not systematically developed allusion to the self-appraisal function of reference groups, even in point of terminology. He defines "patriotism" as "loyalty to the civic group to which one belongs by birth or other group bond" and "chauvinism" as a name for "boastful and truculent self-assertion." These are all considered to be distinctive expressions of the same general pattern: "comradeship" in the in-group and "hostility" toward the out-group rising and waning together.

Following this lead, we sociologists have been wont to repeat, rather than to test in its many implications, the thesis advanced by Sumner. Rather than regarding the in-group as that special kind of membership group which is characterized by inner-cohesion-and-outer-hostility, we have tended to develop the practice, encouraged by Sumner's own ambiguous formulations, of assuming that all membership groups exhibit the characteristics of the in-group. Nor are sociologists alone in this practice. On every side, it is taken for granted that solidarity within the group promotes hostility toward those outside the group, and conversely, in a cumulative spiral of inner-cohesion-and-outer-hostility. At first glance, and in its largest reaches, there is much to support this view. Intense nationalism, as the historical record shows and as contemporary life makes abundantly clear, is typically accompanied by hostility toward other nationalist societies. Attacks or threats of attack by each only strengthens the cohesion of the other and sets the stage for even greater hostility toward the outsider. The identifiable cases conforming to this pattern of group interaction are too numerous and too notorious to allow one to deny the existence of the pattern. What can be questioned, however, and indeed is being questioned here, is whether this is the *only* pattern that connects up the inner cohesion of groups and their external relations, whether, in effect, all membership groups operate in the fashion described by Sumner.

This turns out to be not a matter of logic, but a matter of fact. For, as has been indicated, there is a tendency to assume that from the standpoint of their members, all groups are "in-groups," and consequently, it is inferred that membership groups generally exhibit Sumner's syndrome of behaviors. Yet inquiry shows that this is not the case.[31]

Lacking any but the most primitive conceptions of psychology, Sumner too soon and without warrant concluded that deep allegiance to one group generates antipathy (or, at the least, indifference) toward other groups. Coming out of the evolutionary tradition of social thought, with its emphasis on society as well as nature being red in tooth and claw, Sumner described an important but special case as though it were the general case. He assumed, and his assumption has been echoed as established truth on numerous occasions since his day, that intense loyalty to a group necessarily generates hostility toward those outside the group.

Reference group theory which *systematically* takes account of *positive* orientations toward non-membership groups can serve as a corrective of this prematurely restricted conclusion. In-groups and out-groups are often sub-groups within a larger social organization, and are always

---

31. Merton, West and Jahoda, *Patterns of Social Life,* Chapter 8 (ms.) shows that the pattern of inner-cohesion-and-outer-hostility is only one of several patterns exhibited by membership groups in their relations with other groups. Common observation bears this out, but the conceptual fixity and the connotations of the in-group concept have tended to obscure this readily observable fact.

potentially so, since a new social integration can encompass previously separated groups. This is to say, that just as we have noted structural and situational conditions which make for sub-group formations, so we can observe, under determinate conditions, tendencies toward inter-group integrations. It is not social reality but our own socially conditioned preoccupations which lead some of us to focus on processes of social differentiation at the cost of neglecting processes of social consolidation. Reference group theory treats both types of social processes.

PROBLEM 1.5.

CONCEPTS OF GROUPS, COLLECTIVITIES, AND SOCIAL CATEGORIES

The term *group* has often been stretched to the breaking-point, and not only in reference group theory, by being used to designate large numbers of people among the greatest part of whom there is no social interaction, although they do share a body of social norms. This loose usage is found in such expressions as "nationality group" to designate the total population of a nation (as distinct from its more appropriate usage for associations whose members are of the same nationality). Failing to meet the criterion of social interaction, these social structures should be conceptually and terminologically distinguished from groups. After the usage of Leopold von Wiese and Howard Becker, Florian Znanecki, and Talcott Parsons, they can be designated as *collectivities*:[32] people who have a sense of solidarity by virtue of sharing common values and who have acquired an attendant sense of moral obligation to fulfill role-expectations. All groups are, of course, collectivities, but those collectivities which lack the criterion of interaction among members are not groups. Nor should the distinction be considered purely taxonomic: the operation of social control in groups and in other collectivities differs as a result of differences in the systems of interaction. Moreover, collectivities are potentials for group-formation: the common fund of values can facilitate sustained social interaction among parts of the collectivity.

Distinct from both groups and collectivities are the *social categories*. As we have identified them in the preceding chapter, social categories are aggregates of social statuses, the occupants of which are not in social interaction. These have *like* social characteristics—of sex, age, marital condition, income, and so on—but are not necessarily oriented toward a distinctive and *common* body of norms.[33] Having like statuses, and consequently *similar* interests and values, social categories can be mobilized

---

32. Leopold von Wiese and Howard Becker, *Systematic Sociology*, Chapter XLII: Florian Znaniecki, *Social Actions* (New York: Farrar & Rinehart, 1936), 364-65; Parsons, *The Social System*, 41, 77-78.

33. For the distinction between "like" and "common," see R. M. MacIver and C. H. Page, *Society* (New York: Rinehart and Company, 1949), 32-33.

into collectivities or into groups. When operating as groups, members of the same social category can be thought of as *peer groups* or companies of equals (although the usage has developed of confining the term peer group to groups whose members are of equal age).

Upon examination, then, the concept of reference "group" can be seen to include, in undifferentiated fashion, social formations of quite different kinds: membership and non-membership groups, collectivities, and social categories. It remains to be seen whether reference group behavior differs as one or another of these broad types of social formations is taken as a frame of reference. In any event, as we shall see, it raises the problem of how the structure of the society makes for the selection of others with whom individuals are in actual association as the reference group and how, in the absence of such direct association, it makes for the selection of reference groups among collectivities or social categories.

PROBLEM 1.6.

POSITIVE AND NEGATIVE REFERENCE GROUPS

In examining the several types of non-members, we took passing note that some of these characteristically develop ambivalence toward groups of which they were once members. But it is not only non-membership groups which operate as negative reference groups; this may be the case for membership groups as well. As early as 1943, in his classic study of value-assimilation by college students,[34] Newcomb had indicated that the norms of a reference group may be rejected and he subsequently went on to distinguish, more analytically, positive and negative reference groups.[35] The positive type involves motivated assimilation of the norms of the group or the standards of the group as a basis for self-appraisal; the negative type involves motivated rejection, *i.e.*, not merely non-acceptance of norms but the formation of counter-norms.

Studies of reference groups have exhibited a distinct tendency to focus on those groups whose norms and values are *adopted* by designated individuals. Accordingly, the concept of the negative reference group has yet to be made a focus of sustained inquiry. Yet it would appear that it holds promise of consolidating a wide array of social behavior which, on the surface, seems to be discrete and wholly unconnected. As Newcomb indicates, it conceptualizes such patterns of behavior as "adolescent rebellion" against parents. On the psychological plane, it provides a link with the conceptions of negativism and negativistic personalities. On the sociological plane, it is a general concept

---

34. Theodore M. Newcomb, *Personality and Social Change* (New York: Dryden Press, 1943).

35. Theodore M. Newcomb, *Social Psychology* (New York: Dryden Press, 1950), 227; also Newcomb's analysis in Muzafer Sherif, *An Outline of Social Psychology* (New York: Harper & Brothers, 1948), 139-155.

designed to earmark that pattern of hostile relations between groups or collectivities in which the actions, attitudes and values of one are *dependent* upon the action, attitudes and values of the other to which it stands in opposition. For an example: Charles Singer, the historian of science, has suggested that even the outstanding schools of medicine in ancient Greece rejected the concept of infection in disease precisely because it was held by the "barbarians."[36] In much the same way, it has often been noted that many Americans will reject out of hand conceptions which have merit in their own right, simply because they originated in Soviet Russia or are currently popular there. It would appear that many Russians do much the same for conceptions tagged as American. Numerous experimental studies of "negative prestige" in which a value-laden statement or an empirically demonstrable truth are rejected when attributed to repudiated public figures have also demonstrated the operation of similar processes.

Just as there has evolved a psychological theory of negativistic personalities, so there can develop a sociological theory of the negative reference group which consolidates presently scattered evidences of this phenomenon in widely disparate spheres of behavior. Inquiry could profitably take off from the theoretically significant fact that certain attitudes, values and knowledge which are personally and socially functional may be repudiated simply because they are identified with a negative reference group. Such inquiry would advance our understanding of the basic problem of conditions under which individuals and groups continue to engage in behavior which is dysfunctional to them. It would have the distinct though collateral merit of helping to enlarge the focus of sociological research and theory, now so much concerned with conditions making for functional behavior to those making for the *maintenance* of dysfunctional patterns of behavior in society.

The foregoing examination of the concepts of groups, membership and non-membership, in- and out-groups, collectivities and social categories, and positive and negative reference groups is intended to help clarify some of the more general concepts of reference group theory and to help generate problems for further inquiry. Concepts bearing on more specific components of the theory have also been lately re-examined, as will become evident in the following review of substantive and methodological problems.

The Selection of Reference Groups: Determinants

The scope and objectives of reference group theory were described in the preceding chapter in terms of systematizing "the determinants and consequences of those processes of evaluation and self-appraisal in which

---

36. Cited in H. T. Pledge, *Science Since 1500* (London: H. M. Stationery Office, 1939), 163.

the individual takes the values or standards of other individuals and groups as a comparative frame of reference." As we have seen, this statement should be extended to include normative, as well as comparative, frames of reference. In other respects, however, the statement can be allowed to remain intact as a synoptic formulation of what is involved in this field of inquiry. In particular, the distinction between determinants and consequences needs to be preserved, for although these are dynamically interdependent, each has its characteristic set of theoretic problems. Similarly, there is need to distinguish between reference *individuals* and reference *groups* in order to work out eventually the precise nature of the mechanisms which relate the two.

PROBLEM 2.

SELECTION OF REFERENCE GROUPS AND OF REFERENCE INDIVIDUALS

Ever since the term "reference group" was introduced by Hyman, social scientists have adopted the terminological convention of having the term include behavior oriented both to groups *and* to particular individuals. This elliptical designation was evidently adopted wholly for the purpose of brevity; the term "reference group and reference individual" would simply have been too clumsy and heavy-handed an expression to survive for long. But whatever the reasons for the abbreviated expression, the very terminology itself has tended to fix the definition of problems by social scientists (after the fashion more generally indicated in Chapter II, 92). Research and theory have tended to focus on reference *groups* to the relative neglect of reference *individuals*.

From the outset, it should be suggested that the selection of reference individuals is presumably no more idiosyncratic than the selection of reference groups. Almost irrespective of provenience, sociological theory holds that identification with groups and with individuals occupying designated statuses does not occur at random but tends to be patterned by the environing structure of established social relationships and by prevailing cultural definitions. One among many examples of this pattern is provided by Malinowski's account of the ways in which the identifications and hostilities of the Oedipus complex are shaped by the organization of roles in the family structure. Much still remains to be discovered, however, about the social as well as psychological mechanisms through which the social and cultural structure systematically patterns the selection of reference individuals *within* a reference group.

The *reference individual* has often been described as a *role-model*. Yet, as the terms themselves imply, the assumption that these are conceptually synonymous obscures a basic difference in the matters to which they respectively refer. The person who identifies himself with a reference individual will seek to approximate the behavior and values of that individual in his several roles. The concept of role model can be though* of as more restricted in scope, denoting a more limited identification with an individual in only one or a selected few of his roles. To be sure, a role model may become a reference individual as his multiple roles are adopted for emulation rather than emulation remaining confined to the one role on the basis of which the initial psychological relationship was established. Just as roles can be segregated from one another in the course of social interaction, so they can be in the form of reference orientations. Emulation of a peer, a parent or a public figure may be restricted to limited segments of their behavior and values and this can be usefully described as adoption of a role model. Or, emulation may be extended to a wider array of behaviors and values of these persons who can then be described as reference individuals.

The conceptual distinction generates the problem of the processes making for selection of persons as role models or as reference individuals. To say that partial identification occurs in the first instance, and full identification in the second, is only to put the problem in somewhat different language, rather than to solve it. The circumstances making for full or partial identification still remain to be discovered. The patterns of social interaction, for example, may set limits upon the sheer possibility of selecting certain persons as reference individuals. If the interaction is segmental and confined to certain role relationships, this alone would allow the emergence only of a role model rather than a more comprehensive reference individual (except in fantasy). The partial identification in terms of the one role, however, may motivate a search for more extensive knowledge of the behavior and values of the role model in other spheres. This type of process seems to be involved in the familiar and widespread interest in the private lives of public figures who are serving as role models for many. Partial identification with culture heroes of the past and present may extend to full identification, thus generating an active concern with their behavior and values, far removed from the role in which they came to prominence. Biographers, editors of "fan" magazines and "gossip columnists" thrive on this assumed tendency for role models to become reference individuals.

Valuable clues to the determinants of selection of reference individuals might be afforded by studying *sequences* of reference individuals selected by the same individuals. Presumably, there will be distinct shifts in reference individuals and role models as people move through sequences of statuses during their life cycle. This would again imply that much of such selection is not idiosyncratic but is patterned by structurally determined and statistically frequent career sequences, actual, anticipated or desired. Such developmental studies as well as structural comparisons at one point in time should serve to enlarge our highly imperfect understanding of the determinants of selecting reference individuals and role models.

A correlative problem centers on the selection of reference individuals in the *milieu,* the immediate social environment constituted by the social relationships in which the individual is directly engaged,[36a] and in the larger society, including public figures with whom there is no direct social interaction. The structure of social *milieux* obviously varies: for example, some have a fairly stable structure with enduring social relationships among substantially the same people; others may have both a relatively unstable structure and many and rapid changes of personnel. And as Otto Fenichel has observed, such rapid turnover, often with consequent effects upon patterns of social relations, may "make lasting identifications impossible."[37] It may also dispose those people who lack local reference individuals to turn to more distant figures with whom they identify themselves.

Manifestly, these few observations only skirt the large array of problems developing in this part of reference group theory. They say nothing, for instance, about the question whether identification with a reference group is necessarily mediated by identification with individual members of that group. But what has been said may be enough to indicate that the distinctions between role models, reference individuals, and reference groups help generate a distinctive set of problems for investigation.

PROBLEM 3.

SELECTION AMONG POTENTIAL REFERENCE GROUPS: MEMBERSHIP GROUPS VERSUS NON-MEMBERSHIP GROUPS

Reference groups are, in principle, almost innumerable: any of the groups of which one is a member, and these are comparatively few, as well as groups of which one is not a member, and these are, of course, legion, can become points of reference for shaping one's attitudes, evaluations and behavior. (Page 233)

Under which conditions are associates within one's own groups taken as a frame of reference for self-evaluation and attitude-formation, and under which conditions do . . . non-membership groups provide the significant frame of reference? (Page 233)

These earlier formulations were evidently intended to set the stage for the problem of theoretically construing the social, cultural, and psychological determinants of selection from the large potential of reference groups. They center on the general problem of identifying the

---

36a. I have tried to suggest, in a discussion of this matter, that recent sociological and socio-psychological inquiry has "developed an over-emphasis on the *milieu,* as contrasted with the larger social structure, in dealing with the social environment of human behavior." See "Session 2" in Witmer and Kotinsky (editors), *New Perspectives for Research in Juvenile Delinquency,* 25 ff. Some penetrating observations on some of the problems which this practice generates will be found in Theodore Caplow, "The definition and measurement of ambiences," *Social Forces,* 1955, 34, 28-33.

37. In his treatise, misleadingly because over-restrictively, entitled *The Psychoanalytic Theory of Neurosis* (New York: W. W. Norton & Co., 1945), 505.

forces and contexts making for selection *either* of membership groups *or* of non-membership groups as frames of significant reference, a problem which remains central to reference group theory.

In contrast to other parts of the developing theory, this part has been accorded relatively little attention during the past few years. Much research has been directed toward identifying the conditions making for choice of some rather than other membership groups, as we shall presently see, but little to the conditions making for choice of non-membership groups. The work which has been done, however, tends to confirm previous conjectures or hypotheses and to formulate additional problems.

One such conjecture (which, in any case, carries the matter forward only a short distance) held that individuals "motivated to affiliate themselves with a group" will tend to adopt the values of that non-membership group. (Page 254) This limited hypothesis has lately been extended by Eisenstadt who finds, among a sample of immigrants to Israel, that the selection of reference groups is largely governed by the capacity of certain groups to "confer some prestige in terms of the institutional structure of the society."[38] To the extent that status-conferral represents a major basis for the selection of non-membership groups, the social structure, which assigns varying degrees of prestige and authority to groups and which determines the degree of accessibility to them, will tend to pattern this selection for those variously located in the society.

It has been further conjectured that "isolates" in a group may be particularly ready to adopt the values of non-membership groups as normative frames of reference (Page 268). This hypothesis has also been further developed by Blau, who suggests that in particular those socially non-mobile persons "who are relatively isolated" include "the social striver, the individual who adopts the style of life of a more prestigeful class to which he does not belong, and the disenchanted member of the élite, the individual who adopts the political orientation of a less powerful class than his own."[39]

Finally, in this short list of hypotheses, it has been suggested that social systems with relatively high rates of social mobility will tend to make for widespread orientation to non-membership groups as reference groups. (Page 268) For it is in such societies that aspirations to rise into other groups and strata will be frequent and anticipatory socialization will be functional. At least one study is consistent with this supposition. Stern and Keller have examined the reference groups spontaneously selected by a small sample of the French population and find that these afford little evidence "of orientation to non-membership

---

38. S. M. Eisenstadt, "Reference group behavior and social integration: an explorative study," *American Sociological Review*, 1954, 19, 175-185, at 177.

39. Peter M. Blau, "Social mobility and interpersonal relations," *American Sociological Review*, 1956, 21, 290-295, at 291.

groups." They go on to observe, with respect to the structural context of this pattern of selection, that "one of the characteristics of French society is the relative immobility of social groups. Similar investigations undertaken in other social systems may yield different results. Our findings should be tested in a society where there is less traditionalism than is the case in France, and where upward social mobility is more prevalent. If we were to take a society such as the United States in which basic needs are more widely satisfied, presumably the pattern of reference group behavior would be quite different."[40]

Although we are still some considerable distance from having a theoretically evolved and empirically substantiated set of hypotheses about the determinants of selecting non-membership groups as reference groups, enough has been learned to indicate the contours of further inquiry. Concrete patterns of reference group behavior vary, presumably, according to the types of personality and social status of those exhibiting this behavior and the structural context within which it occurs. Research on personality differentials in such behavior has been prefigured in current studies but is still negligible. Somewhat more attention is being given to status-differentials in relation to reference group behavior, particularly with regard to isolated and integrated members of groups and with regard to socially mobile or stationary persons.

Particularly instructive are the beginnings of comparative studies in different societies which are designed to discover the ways in which differing structural contexts affect the *rates and distribution* of identifiable patterns of reference group behavior. Studies such as those by Eisenstadt, and by Stern and Keller, which have been cited, and by Mitchell,[40a] can be suitably extended to take account of further theoretical problems of the kind under review and can be reproduced in other strategically selected societies to provide a genuinely comparative analysis of reference group behavior. Specifically, in dealing with the problem of the conditions under which non-membership groups are selected as reference groups, only such comparative study will enable sociologists to escape the culture-bound limits of generalizations which may not be recognized as being in fact applicable only to certain types of social systems. This consideration, which is of course germane to a much broader range of sociological problems, has particular force for reference group theory which, until lately, has been developed almost exclusively in the United States. This circumstance of intellectual his-

---

40. Eric Stern and Suzanne Keller, "Spontaneous group references in France," *Public Opinion Quarterly*, 1953, 17, 208-217, at 216-217.

40a. See the working paper for the 29th Study Session of the International Institute of Differing Civilizations, London, September 1955, 13-16, prepared by J. Clyde Mitchell, "The African middle classes in British Central Africa," which examines the emergence of Europeans as a normative reference group for indigenous Africans.

tory could easily introduce a cumulative bias into findings unless the tendency were counteracted by comparative studies of reference group behavior within quite disparate structural contexts.

PROBLEM 4.

THE SELECTION OF REFERENCE GROUPS AMONG MEMBERSHIP GROUPS

. . . theory and research must move on to consider the *dynamics of selection* of reference groups among the individual's several membership groups: when do individuals orient themselves to others in their occupational group, or in their congeniality groups, or in their religious groups? How can we characterize the *structure of the social situation* which leads to one rather than another of these several group affiliations being taken as the significant context? (Page 239)

It has been repeatedly suggested in foregoing pages that the *distinctive* focus of reference group theory is afforded by the fact that men often orient themselves to groups *other than their own* in shaping their behavior and evaluations. It is distinctive in the sense that sociological theory has tended until recently to center systematically on the influences of groups upon their members and to consider only incidentally the influences of non-membership groups. This is far from saying that non-membership groups constitute the *exclusive* focus for reference group theory. Nevertheless, the suggested shift in emphasis can easily be taken to mean that only non-membership groups are of any consequence for reference group behavior;[41] a misapprehension which cannot be scotched too soon.

In actual fact, of course, the great bulk of work in this field continues to focus on the determinants and consequences of taking the norms and values of membership groups as frames of normative and comparative reference. In part, this remains the focus of inquiry because of the generally acknowledged fact that it is the groups of which one is a member that most often and most prominently affect one's behavior. In smaller part, this focus results from the still pervasive and substantial difficulty of devising suitable research tools which will adequately identify the influence of groups upon those who are not members of them. But whatever the reasons, it is the selection among membership groups which continues to engage the attention of those studying reference group behavior and it is the theoretical structure of this problem which calls for detailed examination.

The foregoing questions about the dynamics of selection among membership groups, pertinent as they may be, have not been put in that explicit form which brings out the character of the theoretic problem. This is to say that the questions *imply*, but do not *systematize*, the com-

---

41. Norman Kaplan, *Reference Group Theory and Voting Behavior,* 30 ff., calls emphatic attention to the judgment that exclusive focus on non-membership groups would be plainly unwarranted.

ponent problems which must be settled before methodical substantive answers can be found. Each of these component problems needs to be formulated and examined in its own right, before their inter-connections can be grasped.

Problem 4.1.

The classification of types of membership groups

Questions about which of several membership groups are selected as reference groups (such as those set out in the statement of Problem 4) evidently assume that there are distinct kinds of membership groups but they do not explicitly confront the still-unsolved problem of developing a methodical classification of these types. Taxonomy is far from being the whole of sociological theory. It is, however, an indispensable part. When we examine the current condition of sociological theory in the matter of conceptualizing and classifying types of groups, we must regretfully conclude that a sociological Linnaeus or Cuvier has yet to put in an appearance. Failing such a decisive turn of events, it may nevertheless be useful to call attention, yet again, to the theoretical significance and current status of the problem of systematically classifying types of groups.

The statement introducing Problem 4 can be taken as a reasonably typical example of theoretical inadequacy and can thus help reformulate the problem of classification. By referring *illustratively* to occupational, congeniality, and religious groups, the statement exhibits the practice prevailing among sociologists of adopting substantive lists of groups as these are described in the vernacular. This can be and has been extended into a long allusive list: trade unions and lodges; fraternities, sororities and sodalities generally; gangs, cliques, and friendship-groups; ethnic, occupational, recreational, political, religious, kinship, and educational groups, and so on through a lengthening list limited only by the multiplicity of groups and terms current in society. Yet it would appear that lists such as these bear no striking resemblance to a theoretically grounded classification.

Cross-cutting these descriptive lists of groups are numerous and various classifications—often in the form of dichotomies—based upon one or more criteria. As time is measured in the still-short history of modern sociology, some of these classifications have come to be venerable, much respected, and little improved for two generations or more.[42] But from

---

42. In his inventory of sociological concepts in 1932, Earle E. Eubank could muster thirty-nine distinct classifications of groups, some based upon structure, others upon function, still others upon the nature of the prevailing social relations. And in view of what I have described as the recent "rediscovery of the primary group," consider what Eubank had to say about the publication of B. Warren Brown's book, *Social Groups,* in 1926: "This little volume is a tangible evidence of the fact that the group has been discovered, or more accurately, *re*-discovered during

present indications, these classifications of groups and those which have come after are all destined to be precursors of more exacting and theoretically viable classifications which have yet to be developed. There is some merit in specifying ignorance as a prelude to concerted attack upon problems still unsolved yet clearly important. For some purposes, it has proved useful to work with such current classifications as primary groups and secondary groups, in-groups and out-groups, conflict groups and accommodation groups, "small groups" (classified in terms of number of members into dyads, triads, and so on) and, presumably, "large groups," associations and communities. But manifestly, these do not constitute more than the beginnings of theoretically derived classifications adequate to meet the need for analyzing the operation of group structures.

The problem of developing suitable classifications of groups is of course long-standing, having engaged the attention of a long line of sociological observers from Aristotle to the present day. However these many efforts differ otherwise, the best of them are agreed on the fundamental logical requirement that an effective classification will be not merely grossly descriptive of observed "types" but will derive from combinations of values of designated group properties.[43] The decisive problem is, of course, that of identifying the theoretically strategic group properties which serve systematically to discriminate the operation of each resultant type of group from the others.[44] A comprehensive effort

---

recent years. In its new rôle and with its new implications it becomes not only the central concept under the category of societal forms, but the central concept of Sociology as a whole. It reveals that in a new sense, one far more significant than formerly, Sociology has become 'the science of the group.' But what is this group, this re-discovered 'something,' which is being suggested as our sociological cornerstone?" Eubank, *The Concepts of Sociology* (New York: D. C. Heath and Company, 1932), 132-168, and for the quoted observation, 134. With the experience, if not necessarily the wisdom, gained through hindsight, it can only be hoped that the more recent rediscovery will prove more productive and sequential than the one which was enthusiastically hailed by Eubank a generation ago.

43. Sorokin has seen and stated this requirement with distinct clarity in his *Society, Culture, and Personality*, 159-163 as has Parsons in his seminal note on the concepts of *Gemeinschaft* and *Gesellschaft*, 686-694 of *The Structure of Social Action*. I describe the note as "seminal" because, from all appearances, this analysis of the concrete relationships designated by Tönnies and Weber is the source of Parsons' later classification of "pattern-variables." These are but two of many discussions of the point under review, as indicated in the following note.

44. Among the numerous formulations of the problem and consequent efforts to bring it to heel, see George A. Lundberg, "Some problems of group classification and measurement," *American Sociological Review*, 1940, 5, 351-360; an apposite discussion by Howard Becker, "Constructive typology in the social sciences," *American Sociological Review*, 1940, 5, 40-55; the many papers by R. M. Stogdill, among them in particular, "The organization of working relationships: twenty sociometric indices," *Sociometry*, 1951, 14, 336-373 and "Leadership, membership and organization," *Psychological Bulletin*, 1950, 47, 1-14; and from the same laboratory of "leadership studies" at Ohio State University, John K. Hemphill, *Situational Factors in Leadership* (Columbus: The Ohio State University, 1949), esp. Chapter 3 on "group description"; for a further series of papers and a methodical statement of the problem, P. F. Lazarsfeld and M. Rosenberg, editors, *The Language of Social Re-*

to do precisely this has been reported by P. A. Sorokin[45] with a resulting classification which awaits further systematic use in current research.

In contrast with the substantial agreement among sociologists that strategic classifications of groups must meet the *logical* requirement of being derived from combinations of group-properties, there is widespread disagreement about the *substantive* question of which group-properties provide the basis for most instructive classifications. Since the substantive problem is so much in flux, it may be useful to review in brief a provisional list of such group-properties which have been found, upon inspection and analysis of sociological writings[46] dealing with groups and organizations, to constitute theoretically significant properties of group structure. To say that the following annotated list is but an incomplete draft—or, to appropriate a more fitting description, "the draft of a draft"—is true enough, but in the still unfixed course of theoretical development, it may have some use, nevertheless.

PROBLEM 4.2.

PROVISIONAL LIST OF GROUP-PROPERTIES

1. *Clarity or vagueness of social definitions of membership in the group:* Groups differ widely in the degree of distinctness with which

---

search, Section IV; E. Wight Bakke, *Organization and the Individual* (New Haven: Yale University Press, 1952); for a systematic development of scales to measure group-dimensions, the important and cumulative inquiries by Matilda White Riley, John W. Riley, Jr., Jackson Toby and associates, *Sociological Studies in Scale Analysis* (New Brunswick: Rutgers University Press, 1954); and Edgar F. Borgatta and Leonard S. Cottrell, Jr., "On the classification of groups," *Sociometry and the Science of Man*, 1955, 18, 409-422, who begin with a statement of the precise problem under discussion: "Even if the assumption is made that certain collectivities are groups and others are not, and that there is a difference in kind, when the effort is made to specify the differences, we find ourselves considering variables on which all collectivities could be ordered, and in terms of which they could be variously classified for different purposes. Thus, the question shifts from whether an aggregate is a group or not to one concerning the degree to which such an aggregate is characterized by a specified complex of variables assumed to be components of 'groupness.' Such a formulation points to the necessity for identifying the relevant critical component variables in terms of which any collection of persons may be assessed and, at any given point, be classified."

45. Sorokin, *op. cit.*, Chapter 9, "Classification of Organized Groups." This well-known classification is not summarized here; it can be readily examined with an eye to the extent to which the group properties entering into that classification overlap or are identical with some of those provisionally set out in the following pages.

46. I make no effort to cite the sociological materials which furnished the points of departure for this list of group properties; it should be said, however, that Georg Simmel's writings were, beyond comparison, the most fruitful for the purpose. I wish also to acknowledge the helpful criticisms and suggestions by the students in my graduate seminar on Selected Problems in the Theory of Organization: Chaim Adler, Bernard Blishen, Richard Cloward, Peter M. G. Harris, Russell Heddendorf, James A. Jones, Walter B. Klink, William N. McPhee, William Nicholls, Simone Pare, Gene Peterson, Charlton R. Price, James Price, George S. Rosenberg, Robert Somers, Nechama Tec and Kenneth Weingarten. I am particularly indebted to Terence K. Hopkins who served as my assistant throughout the year's work.

membership can be defined, ranging from some informal groups with indistinct boundaries which can only be identified through systematic inquiry to those with clear-cut and formalized processes of "admission" to membership. This property is presumably related to other group-properties, such as modes of social control. If membership in a group is not clearly defined, the problem of exerting effective control over those who may regard themselves as only nominal or peripheral members would presumably be accentuated; the orientation toward the role-requirements of members would be uncertain and indefinite. It should be noted that this is being stated as a property of the *group*, not in terms of idiosyncratic variations of definition by particular individuals. The group may have clearly defined and easily recognized criteria of membership or these may be vague and difficult to identify, by members of the group or by non-members in the environing society.

2. *Degree of engagement of members in the group:* This property refers to the scope and intensity of the involvement of members in the group. At one extreme, are groups which involve and regulate the sentiments and behavior of members in almost all of their selves and roles; these can be described, in non-invidious terms, as "totalitarian groups." At the other extreme, groups involve and regulate only a limited segment of members' selves and roles; these are described as "segmental groups."

This is conceived not in terms of the attitudes and identification with the group which individual members *happen* to have, but rather in terms of a group-property: the extent to which the degree of engagement in the group is *normatively* prescribed and actually realized. This general conception has, of course, been often utilized in sociology: in a complex society, the individual is normally involved in a large variety of distinct roles, each of which may engage only a small part of his total personality; in less differentiated societies, group affiliation tends to engage a considerably larger share of each member's personality. It seems likely that the greater the culturally defined degree of engagement in a group, the greater the probability that it will serve as a reference group with respect to varied evaluations and behavior.

3. *Actual duration of membership in the group:*

4. *Expected duration of membership in the group:* Although these two properties can vary independently, they are related and can be considered jointly. They refer, respectively, to the actual duration of membership in the group and to the patterned expectation of impending duration. In some groups and organizations, membership has a fixed term of duration, both in fact and in expectation; schools provide one of many such instances. In others, one or both of these affiliations are of indefinitely extended duration. At least one study of the matter[47] has found that the *expectation* of relative permanence or transiency works

---

47. Merton, West and Jahoda, *Patterns of Social Life, passim.*

independently of the actual duration of residence to affect the behavior of those in a community. Groups and organizations manifestly differ in the composition of their membership in these two respects.

5. *Actual duration of the group:*

6. *Expected duration of the group:* Just as individual membership differs in these respects, so do groups and organizations, considered as going concerns. The actual "age" of a group is a property which presumably affects other properties of the group: its flexibility, relative standing, system of normative controls, etc.[48] The actual duration of a group should, however, be distinguished from patterned expectations of the probable duration of the group: whether it is an association established "temporarily" to meet a need which, once met, involves self-liquidation[49] or whether it is established with the expectation of unlimited duration for the indefinitely prolonged future. Variations in the expected duration would presumably affect the self-selection of members, the kind and degree of involvement of members, the internal structure of the organization, its power, and other properties still to be considered.

7. *Absolute size of a group, or of component parts of a group.* This property refers to the number of people comprising the group. Yet this seemingly simple matter of counting the number of members evidently involves prior assumptions and decisions by the sociologist, as can be seen from the foregoing analyses of the concept of group membership. What are to be taken as criteria of membership: objectively measured rates of social interaction patterned in accord with the role-expectations of others; self-definitions of individuals as belonging to the group; definition by (a specified large proportion) of others ascribing membership to individuals? On occasion, the absolute size of a group is taken to mean, not the number of *people* in it, but the number of *positions* in its organization. In this latter sense, the often-asserted connection between growth in size and growth in complexity of social structure of course becomes a tautology.

But however measured, the property of *absolute size* of a group, or of component parts of a group, must be explicitly distinguished from the property of *relative size*.

---

48. The most thorough-going and long-continued study of this property of the actual life-span of groups and organizations has been conducted by P. A. Sorokin. See his *Social and Cultural Dynamics*, IV, 85 ff., and Chapter 34 of his *Society, Culture, and Personality*, which includes an extended bibliography.

49. For a sociological case-study of adaptation of such a self-defined association in the case of the National Foundation for Infantile Paralysis after the discovery of the Salk vaccine, see David Sills, *The Volunteer Way: A Study in the Sociology of Voluntary Associations*, Columbia University, Department of Sociology, doctoral dissertation, 1956 (to be published). See the correlative observation by Chester I. Barnard: "An organization must disintegrate if it cannot accomplish its purpose. A very large number of successful organizations come into being and then disappear for this reason. Hence most continuous organizations require repeated adoption of new purposes." *The Functions of the Executive*, 91.

8. *Relative size of a group, or of component parts of a group:*[50] This property has often been lost to view even when it is implicitly involved in the sociological analysis of a group or social organization. It refers to the number of people in a group (or in a designated stratum of the group) *relative* to the number of people in other groups in the same institutional sphere (or, for special purposes, relative to groups in other institutional spheres). This is to say, that groups or organizations of the same relative size will function differently depending upon their absolute size, and correlatively, groups of the same absolute size will function differently depending upon their size relative to other groups in the social environment. (This seems to hold for groups, associations and communities.) For example, communities which have the same *relative* racial composition—say, with ten per cent Negro and the rest white—will have sociologically different situations, depending on whether the absolute size of the community is a hundred or a hundred thousand. Correlatively, a community of a thousand will have a significantly different social structure, depending on whether it is environed by other communities of like absolute size or by communities of much larger or smaller size.

All this is to say that groups and organizations of a particular absolute size will have differing status and functions in a society in which there are other similar groups and organizations of substantially larger or smaller absolute size than when it exists in a society with comparable groups and organizations of the same size. For example, the same-sized university in the United States and in England will have quite different relative size. This general conception is of course expressed in such folk-notions as a 'big fish in a small pond becoming a distinctly small fish in a big pond.' But as is usually the case with such idiomatic phrases which

---

50. The concepts of absolute and relative size have been distilled from the following passage in Simmel's *Sociology,* and have been given a somewhat different denotation. "The structural differences among groups, that are produced by mere numerical differences, become even more evident in the roles played by certain prominent and effective members. It is obvious that a given number of such members has a different significance in a large group than in a small one. As the group changes quantitatively, the effectiveness of these members also changes. But it must be noted that this effectiveness is modified *even if the number of outstanding members rises or falls in exact proportion to that of the whole group.* The role of one millionaire who lives in a city of ten thousand middle-class people, and the general physiognomy which that city receives from his presence, are totally different from the significance which fifty millionaires, or, rather, each of them, have for a city of 500,000 population—in spite of the fact that the numerical relation between the millionaire and his fellow citizens, which alone (it would seem) should determine that significance, has remained unchanged. . . . The peculiar feature is that the *absolute* numbers of the total group and of its prominent elements so remarkably determine the relations within the group—in spite of the fact that their numerical ratio remains the same." *The Sociology of Georg Simmel,* 97-98 [first italics supplied].

It may be noted that the sociological force of this distinction between absolute numbers and relative proportions is emphasized in the analysis of social structure and anomie and in the study of influentials. See the note on page 175 of Chapter V and note 16 on page 411 of Chapter X.

register some aspect of the human condition and of social reality, the implications of these phrases have not been *methodically* caught up in further analysis. Furthermore, the folk idiom characteristically neglects the consideration that the same pond may be relatively small or large, depending on its location. At all events, it appears that the concepts of absolute and relative size have direct bearing on reference group theory.

9. *Open or closed character of a group:* This property has been discussed at some length earlier in this chapter; as may be recalled, it refers to criteria for membership in the group, which may tend to make the group relatively open and accessible or relatively closed and restrictive. It denotes the degree of exclusivity of membership. In each institutional sphere, some groups aim to maintain a relatively limited membership; others, to achieve maximum expansion of membership. This property is presumably related to other properties of the group: its relative standing, degree of "completeness," of autonomy, of tolerated deviation, and so forth. In view of the earlier discussion, this probably requires no further review at this point.

10. *"Completeness": ratio of actual to potential members:* As we have also seen at some length, the property of completeness, isolated by Simmel but largely ignored by sociologists since his day, refers to the ratio of actual members of a group or organization to its potential members, *i.e.*, to those who satisfy the operative criteria for membership. It need only be reiterated that this property is variously related to other properties of the group. The relative standing of a group in the community, for example, may be affected (though not necessarily in linear fashion) by the extent to which it approaches completeness, as distinct from its relative or absolute size. For example, the American Nurses' Association, with its 178,000 members in 1956, considerably outnumbers the American Medical Association, which claims about 140,000 members. However, the organization of physicians has the highest proportion among all professional associations of those eligible for membership actually being in the association, with about 65 per cent of all licensed physicians; the organization of nurses, despite its larger absolute size, has a distinctly smaller percentage—about 41 per cent of employed professional nurses—in "organized nursing." (Both of these, however, represent substantially higher approximations to completeness than most other professional associations.) All apart from other group-properties which make for differences in social standing and power of an association, it is clear that the A.M.A., with its higher proportion of eligibles actually in the organizational fold, is in a position to claim higher standing and to exercise greater power than the A.N.A., with its larger membership. Nevertheless, the connections between absolute size, degree of completeness, social standing, and power still remain to be worked out. In saying that the property of completeness does not necessarily have a linear relation to such matters as prestige and power we want to take note of the type of

organization which, in order to develop and maintain élite status, selects only a fixed number of members from among those who satisfy the criteria of eligibility for membership.

11. *Degree of social differentiation:* This property refers to the number of statuses and roles operationally distinguished within the organization of the group. At least since the time of Spencer, it has been noted that there is a distinct tendency for growth in the size of a group to go hand in hand with increasing differentiation.[51] Nevertheless, it is also empirically the case that organizations of the same absolute size differ considerably in the extent to which they involve differentiated statuses. Organizations may assign many members to each of relatively few statuses, or multiply structurally distinct statuses, with fewer members assigned to each.

This property does not, of course, refer only to the hierarchic differentiation of statuses (which is only that special form described as social stratification). Yet social differentiation is often identified with social stratification, partly, perhaps, as a result of the tendency for differentiated statuses to be variously evaluated (and thereby ranked) by members of the society. But as the concept of the division of labor reminds us, there can be much or little differentiation of status on the *same* plane of stratification: jobs differentiated in terms of function, for example, may be similarly ranked.

12. *Shape and height of stratification:* This refers to the number of socially distinguished and ranked strata, to the relative size of each stratum, and to the relative social distance between strata. Since these properties of groups and societies have been accorded a great deal of attention, they require no further discussion at this point.[51a]

13. *Types and degrees of social cohesion:* Since at least the work of Durkheim, the degree of social cohesion has been recognized as a group-property which affects a wide variety of behavior and role-performance by members of a group. Three types of social cohesion can be usefully distinguished in terms of the basis of cohesion.[52] All three types may be variously found in any particular group or society, but this does not gainsay the differences among them; groups and societies differ in the

---

51. This empirical generalization was of course central to Herbert Spencer's theory of social structure. See Part II, "The Inductions of Sociology," of *The Principles of Sociology* (New York and London: D. Appleton and Company, 1925), I, 447-600. For a recent empirical study of this relationship, see F. W. Terrien and D. L. Mills, "The effect of changing size upon the internal structure of organizations," *American Sociological Review*, 1955, 20, 11-14.

51a. For a comprehensive comparative study of this subject, see Bernard Barber, *Social Stratification* (New York: Harcourt Brace, 1957).

52. Other and more elaborate typologies have been developed. For a series of pertinent papers, see W. S. Landecker, "Types of integration and their measurement," *American Journal of Sociology*, 1951, 56, 332-340; "Integration and group structure: an area for research," *Social Forces*, 1951-52, 30, 394-400; "Institutions and social integration," *Papers of the Michigan Academy of Science, Arts and Letters*, 1954, 39, 477-493.

extent to which the degree of social cohesion found in them depends upon one or another of these bases.

a) Culturally induced social cohesion: resulting from common norms and values internalized by members of the group;

b) Organizationally induced social cohesion: resulting from realization of personal and group goals through the interdependent activities of others in the group;

c) Social cohesion induced by the structural context: resulting, for example, from contrasts of in-groups and out-groups, conflicts with other groups, and the like.[53]

It remains to be seen how the bases on which groups cohere are consistently related to other properties of the group.

14. *The potential of fission or unity of a group:* This complex property can be usefully thought of as a resultant of #11 (the degree of social differentiation) and #13 (the degree of social cohesion). It refers to a distinctive variable of group life: some groups exhibit a propensity for successive and often unplanned subdivision to the point where emerging sub-groups develop into autonomous groups; others tend to re-incorporate emerging sub-groups into the larger organization so that they serve to reinforce the structure and functions of that organization.[54]

---

53. Not only social scientists, but also statesmen and "men of public affairs" have often noted this source of social cohesion. For two among indefinitely many such observations, consider the passage quoted from Winston Churchill in Chapter I of this book (page 45), and the following passage from Thomas Jefferson's autobiography: "During the war of Independence, while the pressure of an external enemy hooped us together, and their enterprises kept us necessarily on the alert, the spirit of the people, excited by danger, was a supplement to the Confederation, and urged them to zealous exertions, whether claimed by that instrument or not; but, when peace and safety were restored, and every man became engaged in useful and profitable occupation, less attention was paid to the calls of Congress." *The Writings of Thomas Jefferson* (Washington, D.C.: The Thomas Jefferson Memorial Association, 1903), I, 116.

A careful analysis of this uniformity of inter-group relations is supplied by Lewis A. Coser, *The Functions of Social Conflict,* Chapter V, entitled "Conflict with Out-Groups and Group Structure."

54. For an instructive processual analysis of the formation of sub-groups in relation to the larger encompassing group, see George A. Theodorson, "Elements in the progressive development of small groups," *Social Forces,* 1953, 31, 311-320. Note also the following observation in Harriet Martineau, *The Positive Philosohy of Auguste Comte* (London, 1896), 228, which Theodorson appropriately adopts as the epigraph for his paper: "The true general spirit of social dynamics consists in conceiving of each of these social states as the necessary result of the preceding, and the indispensable mover of the following, according to the axiom of Leibnitz, 'The present is big with the future.' In this view, the object of science is the discovery of the laws which govern this continuity, and the aggregate of which determines the course of human development."

Current theories of stochastic process in groups constitute a more exacting probabilistic version of this central conception. For an analysis of social relations as process carried out in this vein, see Lazarsfeld and Merton, "Friendship as social process: a substantive and methodological analysis," in M. Berger, T. Abel and C. H. Page (editors), *Freedom and Control in Modern Society,* 18-66, esp. Part Two.

Political parties, for example, seem to differ greatly in this regard: some divide into numerous "splinter parties," others maintain a monolithic unity. Again: some groups exhibit a distinct propensity for "colonizing," for forming dependent groups in their own image, some of these later becoming independent of the parent group.

15. *Extent of social interaction within the group:* This property refers to the expected and the actual extent of social interaction between occupants of designated statuses in the group. In some groups, substantial social interaction is limited to those in "adjacent" statuses in the hierarchy (peers, and immediate inferiors and superiors), as this is registered in the conception of "going through channels." Other groups and organizations provide more patterned occasions for interaction between those of considerably different rank, as, for example, in the concept of a hierarchized group nevertheless consisting of a "company of equals." It should be noted, however, that in actual fact, the first kind of group often has more social interaction between distinct unequals than is structurally indicated (*e.g.* informal means of communicating without going through channels), just as the second kind often has less interaction between unequals than the normative prescriptions would indicate.

16. *Character of the social relations obtaining in the group:* This property has traditionally been adopted as the major one distinguishing various types of groups, as can be seen from such established classifications as primary and secondary groups, in-group and out-group, *Gemeinschaft* and *Gesellschaft*, formal and informal group, etc. It is in connection with this property, also, that Parsons has developed his well-known system of pattern variables in terms of which the relations in the role structure of a social system can be analytically characterized: affectivity vs. affective neutrality, self-orientation vs. collectivity-orientation, universalism vs. particularism, achievement vs. ascription, and specificity vs. diffuseness.[55] Combinations of values of these five variables serve to characterize distinctively concrete social relationships prevailing in a group.

17. *Degree of expected conformity to norms of group: toleration of deviant behavior and institutionalized departures from the strict definitions of group-norms.* This property refers to the extent of patterned leeway in the behavior of group members which is ordinarily accepted by others in the group. Some groups and organizations tend to require strict adherence to norms, with minimum provision for departures from them at the discretion of members; this is what is often meant by "bureaucracy," used as a term of abuse. Others permit a wide range of departure from norms, as, for example, in groups which pride themselves on making large allowance for individuality and creativity. The stereo-

---

55. Parsons, *The Social System,* 58-88.

typed image of the Prussian bureaucracy would approximate the first type; some organizations devoted to learning and research in Western societies would approximate the second type. In concrete fact, of course, the first type allows more discretion than is popularly assumed and the second type, less. Nevertheless, this does not mean that groups and organizations do not differ in this property.

Evasions of the norms may become functional for the group, and often, as a prelude to structural change in the group, there develops a more or less persistent phase in which these evasions become institutionally patterned. It is this pattern which I have described as the "institutionalized evasion of institutional rules."[56] This is a complicated phase of change in social structure which requires far more detailed examination than is suitable here. It may be said, however, that the pattern of institutionalized evasions develops when practical exigencies confronting the group or collectivity (or significantly large parts of them) require adaptive behavior which is at odds with long-standing norms, sentiments, and practices, or correlatively, when newly-imposed requirements for behavior are at odds with these deep-rooted norms, sentiments, and practices.[57] In the first case, the norms and sentiments are for a time ostensibly retained intact, while tacitly recognized departures from them become progressively accepted in their own right. In the second case, the newly-imposed institutional demands are in fact evaded while the slowly-changing norms and sentiments continue to govern actual behavior. It may be conjectured that an appreciable amount of tolerated deviation from norms is functionally required for the stability of complex social structures.

18. *The system of normative controls:* This property refers to pat-

---

56. For a variety of examples of institutionalized evasions in different institutional spheres, see Wilbert E. Moore, *Industrial Relations and the Social Order* (New York: The Macmillan Company, 1951, rev. ed.), 114; Logan Wilson, *The Academic Man* (New York: Oxford University Press, 1941), 218-219; Robin Williams, *American Society*, 360-365; George Eaton Simpson and J. Milton Yinger, *Racial and Cultural Minorities*, 658-660; J. H. Fichter, "The marginal Catholic," *Social Forces*, 1953, 32, 167-173, at 169.

57. In view of the developments following upon the decision of the Supreme Court on May 17, 1954 declaring that racial segregation in public education is unconstitutional, it may be germane to quote the following applications of the conception of institutionalized evasions, as stated in 1948: "In an unfavorable cultural climate—and this does not necessarily exclude the benign regions of the Far South—the immediate resort will probably have to be that of working through legal and administrative federal controls over extreme discrimination, with full recognition that, in all probability, these regulations will be systematically evaded for some time to come. In such cultural regions, we may expect nullification of the law as the common practice, perhaps as common as was the case in the nation at large with respect to the Eighteenth Amendment, often with the connivance of local officers of the law. The large gap between the new law and local mores will not *at once* produce significant change of prevailing practices; token punishments of violation will probably be more common than effective control. At best, one may assume that significant change will be fitful, and excruciatingly slow. But secular changes in the economy may in due course lend support to the new legal framework of control

terned processes of normative control which regulate the behavior of members of the group. Groups and organizations differ in the extent to which they exercise control through expressly formulated rules (law); through less definitely formulated but definitely patterned expectations of behavior which are reinforced by sentiment and supporting moral doctrine (mores); and through routinized, often habitual but less strongly affective, expectations (folkways). At the one extreme, the delimited and officially promulgated norms are enforced by agents assigned this role; at the other, the norms are enforced by the 'spontaneous' yet socially patterned responses of other members of the group, even though they have not been allocated specific roles for this purpose. It remains still to be seen how the system of normative control is regularly related to the numerous other properties of groups and organizations.

19. *Degree of visibility or observability within the group:* This property refers to the extent to which the norms and the role-performances within a group are readily open to observation by others (status-inferiors, peers, and status-superiors). It is a more extended idea than that which American sociologists have long described as 'social visibility,' meaning by this the degree to which the status-identity (especially of class, caste, race and ethnicity) of individuals is readily visible. The property of visibility or observability, in this more extended sense, requires much more study than has yet been accorded it; partly, because there are indications that it enters *tacitly* into many analyses of group-structure and behavior; partly, because its numerous implications for social process and structure are only now becoming evident, long after it was obliquely and brilliantly introduced by Simmel; and partly, because it has direct bearing on one of the principal problems of reference group theory (as we shall see at length in a later section of this chapter).

In typically essayistic form, Simmel alludes to this property in his account of the sociological character of aristocracies: "There is also an absolute limit [upon numbers] beyond which the aristocratic form of the group can no longer be maintained. The point at which it breaks down it determined in part by external, in part by psychological circumstances. If it is to be effective as a whole, the aristocratic group must be 'visible or observable'[58] by every single member of it. Every element [of the group] must still be personally acquainted with every other."

Simmel intuitively sensed the central importance of the group-property of ready visibility, but not having access to the backlog of theory

over discrimination. As the economic shoe pinches because the illiberals do not fully mobilize the resources of industrial manpower nor extend their local markets through equitable wage-payments, they may slowly abandon some discriminatory practices as they come to find that these do not always pay—even the discriminator." R. K. Merton, "Discrimination and the American creed," in R. M. MacIver, editor, *Discrimination and National Welfare* (New York: Harper & Brothers, 1949), 99-126, at 120 and 101.

58. The original term here is *übersehbar*. In Englishing this passage, Kurt Wolff translates this word as 'surveyable,' which is, of course, an appropriate approxima-

which has developed only since he wrote, he could not systematize this insight, consider the group structure, as well as the group size, which affected variability in this property, and work out its relations to systems of control which operate to maintain the stability of groups. With the recent emergence of "information theory," it becomes evident that Simmel had noted a property of groups which profoundly affects their be-havior and development as going concerns. For it can now be said, without stooping to indulgence in merely analogical and poorly under-stood figures of speech, that social groups so differ in organization that some promote efficient "feed-back" of "information" to those who pri-marily regulate the behavior of members, while others provide little by way of efficient feed-back. The structural conditions which make for ready observability or visibility of role-performance will of course pro-vide appropriate feed-back when the role-performance departs from the patterned expectations of the group. For under such conditions, the re-sponses of other members of the group, tending to bring the deviant back into line with the norms, will begin to operate soon after the deviant behavior has occurred. Collaterally, when there are structural impediments to such direct and immediate observability, deviant be-havior can cumulate, depart even more widely from the prevailing norms before coming to the notice of others in the group, and then often elicit an "over-reaction" which serves only to alienate the deviants, rather than to "correct" their deviations. These structural hindrances to the flow of information (which would appear to be the present-day counterpart to Simmel's concept of observability) will in this manner interfere with the relatively steady state of the group and produce fitful and irregular oscillations of social control.

Much research has lately dealt with matters bordering on this prop-erty of groups. This appears particularly in the form of studies of the ways in which communication nets, established through experimentally

---

tion. The sense of the original seems somewhat better approximated, however, by the words "visible" or "observable," with the connotation of being visible at a glance, of being readily observable. At any rate, this is the reason for departing at this point from the excellent translation by Wolff. See Simmel, *Soziologie*, 50, and *The Sociology of Georg Simmel*, 90.

As is generally recognized, at least from the days when Santayana, as a student at Berlin, was writing William James that "I have discovered a *Privatdocent*, Dr. Simmel, whose lectures interest me very much," Simmel often wrote as though he truly believed that "there are some enterprises in which a careful disorderliness is the true method." He did not work systematically with such a variable as "visibility" but instead alluded sporadically to it. His excursus on the "sociology of the senses," for example, bears implicitly upon the concept of visibility, but Simmel leaves it to his already heavily indebted readers to ferret out the connections. *Soziologie*, 646-665. In his book on *The Functions of Social Conflict*, which attempts to sys-tematize some of Simmel's numerous insights, Lewis A. Coser aptly quotes the observation of José Ortega y Gasset on Simmel's style of work: "That acute mind— a sort of philosophical squirrel—never considered his subject a problem in itself, but instead took it as a platform upon which to execute his marvelous analytical exer-cises.'" Nowhere is this judgment better sustained than in Simmel's intermittent use of the concept of visibility or observability.

simplified group structures, affect the rate, extent, and character of information-flow, with attendant consequences not only for task-performance but also for social control. It is perhaps enough, in this short discussion, to cite only a few of these studies and especially the ones by Alex Bavelas and his associates, which seem to me to be among the most far-reaching of recent inquiries into the matter.[59]

Other studies, designed largely in terms of social psychology rather than of social structure, have begun to explore patterned differentials in information about the sentiments of group members which obtain among leaders and among rank-and-file members.[60] These are plainly a prelude to a phase of social research in which the two types of studies—structural and socio-psychological—are consolidated. In this way, the observability of role-performance and of sentiments will be related to the structure of the group and the flow of information, to the operation of social control.

Sociological field studies which bear upon one or another aspect of observability in the sense being developed here include Blau's examination of the use of statistical measures which register the amount and character of role-performance in a bureaucracy with attendant consequences for social control[61] and an analysis of friendship regarded as social process which takes as a major variable the circumstances making for ready expression of sentiments among pairs of friends, or for continued suppression of these sentiments.[62]

Since the social science inquiries into communication in relation to social organization have grown immense and are still in process of theoretical consolidation, they require little more than bare allusion here. But the essential point under review is that once observability is conceived as a property of groups, it directs attention to the ways in which the structure of the group affects the input of information and the output (of response) which thereupon works to exert social control.

In much the same way, as has been intimated and as we shall presently see, the property of observability is necessarily implied if not ex-

---

59. Alex Bavelas, "Communication patterns in task-oriented groups," in Daniel Lerner and Harold D. Lasswell (editors), *The Policy Sciences* (Stanford: Stanford University Press, 1951), 193-202, and the further inquiries stemming from the Bavelas group; George A. Heise and George A. Miller, "Problem solving by small groups using various communication nets," *Journal of Abnormal and Social Psychology*, 1951, 46, 327-336; Henry Quastler (editor), *Information Theory in Psychology: Problems and Methods* (Glencoe: The Free Press, 1955); Harold Guetzkow and Herbert A. Simon, "The impact of certain communication nets upon organization and performance in task-oriented groups," *Management Science*, 1955, 1, 233-250.

60. Kalma Chowdhry and T. M. Newcomb, "The relative abilities of leaders and non-leaders to estimate opinions of their own groups," *Journal of Abnormal and Social Psychology*, 1952, 47, 51-57. This study and related ones will be considered in terms of their implications at greater length in a later part of this chapter which undertakes to consider observability in some detail.

61. Blau, *The Dynamics of Bureaucracy*, esp. Chapter III, "Statistical Records of Performance."

62. Lazarsfeld and Merton, *op. cit.*, esp. Part II.

pressly taken into account in reference group theory, for variability in the knowledge about the norms of the group manifestly affects the respect in which it can be taken as a frame of normative reference. But this can more appropriately be considered later, when this listing of group-properties has been completed.

20. *Ecological structure of the group:* This refers primarily to the one ecological variable of the spatial distribution of the members of a group since other variables, commonly included in the theory of ecology, are considered elsewhere. It is evident that groups differ in this respect: the members may be spatially adjacent and highly concentrated or widely separated and thinly dispersed. Recent studies of this property uniformly show that the extent of spatial and functional propinquity affects the formation of social relations, the types of social control, and the degree of involvement of members with the group.[63] It is presumably related also to the observability of role-performance.

21. *Autonomy or dependence of the group:* Groups differ in the extent to which they are self-contained or dependent, for fulfilling their functions and achieving their purposes, upon other groups and institutions in the larger society. Groups may continue to operate even though they do not themselves meet one or more of their functional requirements, so long as these requirements are met for them by other groups in the society. The appearance of full autonomy, sociologically considered, is often deceiving. For example, the *kibbutzim* in Israel could not, apparently, retain their essentially socialist character were it not that other parts of the Israeli economy and society were meeting some of their essential requirements and were it not for the resources provided by those outside Israel.[64] This conception of varying degrees of social self-sufficiency of a group or community has been most carefully developed and studied empirically by rural sociologists; it would seem to be pertinent in other than the rural sectors of society.

---

63. As a set of examples of the connection between spatial distance and the formation of social relations in a local community, see R. K. Merton, "The social psychology of housing," in Wayne Dennis (editor), *Current Trends in Social Psychology* (Pittsburgh: University of Pittsburgh Press, 1948), 163-217, esp. at 203-209; Leon Festinger, Stanley Schachter and Kurt Back, *Social Pressures in Informal Groups: A Study of Human Factors in Housing* (New York: Harper & Brothers, 1950), esp. Chapter 3; Theodore Caplow and Robert Forman, "Neighborhood interaction in a homogeneous community," *American Sociological Review*, 1950, 15, 357-366; H. J. Gans, "The sociology of new towns," *Sociology and Social Research*, 1956, 40, 231-239. The sociological studies of the relations of spatial distribution of people to their social behavior and social relationships are by now considerable; a codification of findings from these scores of studies would presumably justify the effort.

64. Eva Rosenfeld, *Institutional Change in the Israeli Collectives*, doctoral dissertation in sociology, Columbia University, 1952; Melford E. Spiro, *Kibbutz: Venture in Utopia* (Cambridge: Harvard University Press, 1956); Barber, *Social Stratification*. Simmel had observed that "Socialistic or nearly socialistic societies have been possible only in very small groups and have always failed in larger ones." *Sociology of Georg Simmel*, 87-88. It turns out, upon further examination, that this empirical generalization is conditional upon other group-properties which Simmel unsystematically introduces in dealing with specific historical instances.

22. _Degree of stability of the group:_ This property refers to the capacity of a group to withstand opposition from without, to maintain its structure, and to change in orderly sequence. It does not refer to rate of turnover in personnel which is another, though probably related, property. Furthermore, it differs from social cohesion (#13) which is connected with stability but is not coterminous with it. In referring to this as a "capacity" rather than an empirically observed degree of stability, I intend to make explicit the consideration that the observed stability of a group is contingent on the degree of environmental stress and not only on its own internal structure, as is indicated in the discussion that follows.

23. _Degree of stability of the structural context of the group:_ This refers to the capacity of the social environment of a particular group to maintain its character. It probably has complex relations with the property of stability of the group. For example: a stable social environment may make for greater empirical stability of groups operating within it, as they cumulatively build up accommodative and adaptive relations with the environment. However, a highly stable environment may create conditions of stress for groups which are in process of marked change. This is the sort of situation, conceived in terms of social structure rather than of culture, which is presumably caught up in Ogburn's notion of cultural lag.

24. _Modes of maintaining stability of the group, and of the structural context:_ As Simmel frequently observed in effect, groups and their structural contexts differ in the processes through which they maintain stability, either through comparative _rigidity_ or through comparative _flexibility_. That is to say, they may retain their character as groups both structurally and functionally when confronted with stress, or they may retain their functional character by appropriate changes of structure in response to stress. This long-standing idea requires considerable clarification but even in these crude terms, it appears that groups differ significantly in the characteristic ways in which they adapt to internal and external stress.

25. _Relative social standing of groups:_ Just as individuals are socially ranked in terms of prestige and access to opportunity for culturally valued returns, so with groups. Sociologists take it for granted that occupational statuses are evaluatively ranked and that occupants of these statuses tend to be correspondingly ranked. But we are somewhat more capricious in our research practice when it comes to incorporating systematic data on the relative rank of groups and organizations.[65] Yet everyday observation indicates some of the many respects in which the

---

65. One of the distinctive contributions of the Warner studies is precisely the substantial beginning of analysis of the relative rank of groups and organizations; see, for example, W. Lloyd Warner and P. S. Lunt, _The Social Life of a Modern Community_ (New Haven: Yale University Press, 1941).

concern with the standing of a group is significant: the process of competition, as Park and Burgess observed a generation ago and as the evolutionists consistently emphasized, involves not only the relative position of individuals but also of groups, organizations, and societies.

26. *Relative power of groups:* This refers to the varying capacity of a group to enforce its collective decisions upon (a) its members and (b) its social environment. It is assumed here that the relative power of a group is a resultant of other group-properties, but analysis of this complex problem is still in its beginnings.[66]

To halt the listing of group-properties at this point is of course arbitrary, for there are probably as many more, if indeed not others beyond those, which have been either sporadically or systematically studied by sociologists. But this list does not pretend to be exhaustive; it is, at best, propaedeutic. It is only a short step toward the theoretically enjoined objective of developing a conceptual scheme for the characterization of social groups. Some such scheme is obviously required if the multitudinous facts about groups and group structure are to be brought together in the form of consolidated knowledge.

Quite the contrary view may be held of this provisional list: not that it is manifestly far from being complete, but that it is already far too long. For how can we cope with the implied task of simultaneously characterizing each group under examination in terms of all twenty-six properties? To do so would patently mean that few groups will be found to be structurally similar in all these numerous respects. Consequently, uniformities of behavior linked with group structure will be difficult, if not impossible, to detect.

All this of course represents no new problem, and surely not one confined to sociological classifications. It is a problem which must be solved anew in evolving a useful classification in any discipline. But the general methods of arriving at a solution are reasonably well known from much cumulative experience. First of all, the proposed list of properties may give rise to several classifications, each having its distinctive use. It is not presupposed that a single classification must be developed on the basis of a large number of distinct properties. Second, it will doubtless turn out that some properties can be deduced from others and need not therefore be considered independently. We have suggested several such possibilities in the foregoing list. Finally, it is probably the case that some of these (and other) apparent group-properties will turn out to be "insignificant," that they do not lead to the discovery of discernible order in the facts. But the utility of a pre-

66. The work upon which Robert S. Lynd is currently engaged promises to cast light on this problem. See also Floyd Hunter, *Community Power Structure* (Chapel Hill: University of North Carolina Press, 1953); Roland J. Pellegrin and Charles H. Coates, "Absentee-owned corporations and community power structure," *American Journal of Sociology*, 1956, 61, 413-419.

liminary list of this sort is that it provides a point of departure for "experimenting" with alternative classifications, rather than adopting *ad hoc* classifications evolved for a momentary purpose.

There is, however, one large obstacle which must be surmounted before further classifications of groups can prove useful. This is the difficulty of developing *standardized measures* of each of the properties under review. There is a phase in the development of a discipline in which *ad hoc* measures and indices are evolved anew in each study, so that although the *words* referring to the property remain much the same, the aspect of the phenomenon they actually designate varies substantially. As long as "social cohesion," for example, is variously "measured" by such rough indicators as acceptance of group norms, reciprocal "liking" of group members as registered by sociometric choices, a sense of "group-belongingness," and so on, it is at least possible that the same term is being used to denote distinct, though related, aspects of the group. Standardization of nomenclature and of measures is a problem which has confronted most sciences, at one time or another in the course of their development, and it may not be too much to suppose that sociology is reaching the stage where efforts will be made to solve this problem, rather than to continue living with it through a series of uneasy and fitful adjustments.

Yet, in emphasizing what we do not yet know and what we have not yet accomplished, we should not neglect the considerable amount that is known and has been accomplished. There has developed, in the last generation or two, a store of knowledge about many, perhaps most, of the properties put together in the preceding list. Perhaps even more in point, there is a growing tendency among sociologists to think in terms of the elements and properties of group structure, rather than to rest content with purely descriptive accounts of various groups. If there is not sufficient occasion for unalloyed optimism, there is even less for sour pessimism.

And now, we may bring to a close what might appear to be a long excursus on group-properties but which is, in sober logic, actually presupposed by such innocent-sounding questions as those introducing Problem 4 of current reference group theory:

. . . when do individuals orient themselves to others in their occupational group, or in their congeniality groups, or in their religious groups? How can we characterize the *structure of the social situation* which leads to one rather than another of these several group affiliations being taken as the significant context?

For, as should now be plain, these questions assume that the useful way of classifying groups is in terms of the institutional activities in which they are engaged: such as work, play and phatic communion, and religiosity. Yet the assumption is at best debatable. True, in sociological science as in the process of growing up, it is generally wiser, if indeed not inevitable, to learn to walk before learning to run. For still some time in the future, as for so long in the past, it may prove both wise and expedient to trace out the choice of reference groups among membership groups, concretely described—of the family rather than of one's age peers, of occupational groups rather than of religious groups. The information gained from inquiries carried forward on this plane of concreteness will doubtless have its uses. But it should be recognized in advance that, from the standpoint of a systematic theory of reference group behavior, this can only constitute interim research—perhaps an indispensable prelude, but still only a prelude, to the discovery of uniformities in the selection of *types* of groups as reference groups under designated conditions.

With this proviso, it will be useful to continue with the formulation of problems involved in the dynamics of selection of reference groups from membership groups, together with the review of studies bearing upon these problems. As matters now stand, what is the status of theory and fact about the conditions and processes making for the choice of some, rather than other, membership groups as normative and comparative frames of reference?

PROBLEM 4.3.

VARIATION IN REFERENCE GROUPS FOR
DIFFERING VALUES AND NORMS

Although this has only slowly worked its way into reference group theory, it has long been assumed that different groups become relevant to differing spheres of behavior by individuals. This is only to say that, tacitly if not always explicitly, reference groups operate as such in conjunction with distinct kinds of evaluation and behavior. As we have seen, when considering the group-property (#2) of degree of engagement in the group, some groups presumably take on pertinence for a wide variety of behaviors, and others for only a few.

Intimations to this effect are numerous in social science. From its beginnings, for example, sociometry has assumed that certain individuals tend to be selected as preferred associates in the realm of work, and others, in the realm of play.[67] In the same way, it cannot be tacitly assumed that the same groups uniformly serve as reference groups for the same individuals in every phase of their behavior. Put in these direct terms, this statement has all the earmarks of a commonplace, ponderously announced. Yet the practice of alluding to reference groups, with-

---

67. This basic and once-mentioned, obvious, but otherwise easily-overlooked consideration entered into the technique of sociometric analysis as this was first introduced by J. L. Moreno, in his influential work, *Who Shall Survive?* (Washington, D.C.: Nervous and Mental Disease Monograph, Series No. 58, 1934).

out relating these at once to the particular form of behavior or evaluation involved, manages to escape the constraining implications of this commonplace. Furthermore, neither layman nor sociologist appear to know much, as yet, about the uniformities of selecting some rather than other groups as frames of reference in connection with specified kinds of behavior and evaluation. What little is known suggests that the obvious common-sense supposition which holds that the functionally or substantively pertinent group invariably becomes the reference group is far from true; it is not the case, for example, that one's religious affiliation alone determines which group will be adopted as a frame of normative reference on religious matters or that one's trade union will necessarily govern one's economic outlook. The complexity of reference group behavior does not appear to be cut to this engagingly simple pattern.

Numerous other observers have emphasized the general point that the same individuals or groups are not uniformly taken as guides to behavior and evaluation in different social spheres. For a time, this was put in the language designed to describe the workings of leadership. As one example, consider the observation by Saul Alinsky that a "man looks up to a particular person as a leader, one whose judgment he has confidence in, in political matters, but when he is confronted with the problem of finances he will turn to one of his associates in his fraternal society. And so on down the line. He may have in his orbit of activities five or six individuals to whom he will turn on different matters. It is obvious then that one rarely stumbles across what might be defined as a complete leader—a person who has a following of 40 or 50 people in every sphere of activity. . . ."[68] Since this is described as merely an impression gained from his field observation, Alinsky expresses his confidence that more systematic "investigation will disclose" this to be the case. One such inquiry, reported in the next chapter of this book devoted to a study of what I believe is more properly described as "the influential" rather than the leader, finds that

> . . . influentials differ widely with respect to the *number of spheres* of activity in which they exert interpersonal influence. Some influentials, and these may be termed *monomorphic*, are repeatedly cited as exerting influence, but only in one rather narrowly defined area—*e.g.*, the area of politics, *or* of canons of good taste, *or* of fashion. The monomorphic influentials are the "experts" in a limited field, and their influence does not diffuse into other spheres of decision. Others, and this includes a good number of the top influentials, are *polymorphic*, exerting interpersonal influence in a variety of (sometimes seemingly unrelated) spheres. (Pages 413-414)

But, as this discussion goes on to suggest, sociologists are now prepared to move beyond the empirical generalization that relatively few

---

68. Saul D. Alinsky, *Reveille for Radicals* (Chicago: University of Chicago Press, 1946), 90.

influentials exert diversified influence in various spheres of activity, and relatively many confine their influence to only one sphere. Manifestly, the next steps of inquiry must identify the conditions under which one or another of these patterns of influence is apt to emerge.

The most comprehensive study of this general problem of unitary or diverse influence is found in the book by Katz and Lazarsfeld.[69] Here, again, the empirically prevailing pattern of influence is reported to be that restricted to a single area of norms and activity: "The fact that a woman is a leader in one area has no bearing on the likelihood that she will be a leader in another."

This problem is one of several affording an occasion for consolidating[70] into a theory of the middle range the findings and hypotheses concerning influentials and opinion leaders, and those concerning reference group behavior. For it becomes evident that the first set of inquiries deals, in effect, with phenomena of reference groups and reference individuals, examined from the perspective of *those who provide these frames of normative and comparative evaluation.* In these studies, attention is focused on the types of individuals and groups which come to operate as single or multiple sources of orientation for others, with only secondary attention to detailed analysis of the condition of those for whom these individuals and groups are influential. The second set of inquiries, in contrast, centers on those who adopt one or another group or individual as sources of guidance and orientation, and is only secondarily concerned with the detailed analysis of the individuals and groups which exercise this influence. But since "reference group behavior" involves social relationships which are, of course, two-sided, it becomes clear that the next steps in investigation of this field of behavior will require simultaneous analysis both of the individuals adopting various reference groups and of the groups which provide these frames of reference. It may be hazarded that, until now, the relative independence of these two lines of inquiry has actually been advantageous for the advancement of the theory of social influence, for the many points of convergence which are now detectible add to our confidence in the validity of both lines of inquiry, on the ground that independent identical error is less probable than independent identical truth. But however this may turn out, the often separate studies of social influence, focused on individuals and groups exerting influence, and of reference group behavior,

---

69. Elihu Katz and Paul F. Lazarsfeld, *Personal Influence,* Part Two and, in particular, chapter XV, summarizing the findings of the study.

70. This is one of numerous instances in which it is possible to detect the consolidation of distinct theories, as this process of theorizing is briefly described in the Introduction of this book and toward the close of Chapter II. This possible consolidation has been noticed by S. N. Eisenstadt, "Studies in reference group behaviour," *Human Relations,* 1954, 7, 191-216, at 204-206. He properly cites as germane the study by Morris Janowitz, *The Community Press in an Urban Setting* (Glencoe: The Free Press. 1952).

focused on those being influenced, clearly need to be theoretically consolidated into sociological conceptions capable of dealing with both
simultaneously.

Against this somewhat enlarged background, the import of several
recent studies of the selection of some rather than other membership
groups as reference groups takes on added sociological significance.
These studies are avowedly bare beginnings, but perhaps all the more
symptomatic of impending developments for that very reason. The study
by Ralph Turner, for one example, begins with the premise (germane to
the second in our list of group-properties) that "reference group literature has not always stressed the extent to which groups are *segmentally*
rather than totally relevant to an individual's values."[71] Turner thereupon proceeds to mend this defect by inquiring into the distinctive
membership groups selected as frames of reference for differing kinds
of values: values centered on occupational success, designated types of
ethical and moral values, and values having to do with what Turner
describes as "richness of life." I do not undertake to summarize his
findings here; they are, as Turner says, suggestive rather than compelling. The essential point is that distinct patterns of selection emerge,
which relate types of values to types of reference groups. For example,
group affiliations which are matters of achievement, rather than of social
ascription, tend to be more often relevant for the acceptance of values
by the particular kind of "future-oriented men" constituting Turner's
sample. Again, the values and standards of even these groups to which
individuals aspire for membership are not uniformly accepted. If this
latter finding first appears to qualify as a truism, further consideration
suggests that it may be one of those truisms which had better be carefully explored rather than disregarded as self-evident. For it directs attention to the conditions making for *resistance* to the norms and values
of a potential reference group, rather than restrictively dealing only with
those which make for adoption of these norms and values, a general
orientation which Solomon Asch[72] has manfully tried to restore to its
proper important place in the face of a prevailing tendency in the social
and psychological sciences to consider primarily the coercive or constraining influence of the group. This is only to suggest that the study of
"individual autonomy" and of social constraint are opposite sides of the

---

71. Ralph H. Turner, "Reference groups of future-oriented men," *Social Forces*,
1955, 34, 130-136, at 131.

72. Among his significant studies of this matter, see the following: S. E. Asch,
H. Block and M. Hertzman, "Studies in the principles of judgments and attitudes:
I. Two basic principles of judgment," *Journal of Psychology*, 1938, 5, 219-251; S. E.
Asch, "Studies in the principles of judgments and attitudes: II. Determination of
judgments by group and ego standards," *Journal of Social Psychology*, 1940, 12,
433-465. For a comprehensive statement of the theoretical considerations involved
in these and later studies, see S. E. Asch, *Social Psychology* (New York: Prentice-
Hall, Inc., 1952).

same theoretical coin, rather than, as is sometimes still inadvertently supposed, the study of "the individual" vs. "the group."

It appears that the consideration of "different reference groups for different norms and values" is rising to the level of studied sociological attention. The same issue of the journal in which Turner reports his study, for example, includes a collateral, but independent, paper by Rosen, which has the same central purpose. Again, the formulation is one which states the obvious, but takes the truism seriously and tries to develop it further: "Significant others are not necessarily referents for all areas of the individual's behavior."[73] And again, in place of a summary of findings, I select only that one which seems to have import for continuing inquiry. Rosen reports the seemingly anomalous finding that those individuals in his sample who are in fact most "traditionalist" in their religious attitudes and behavior are *not*, as one might suppose on the basis of ready-to-hand common sense, the ones who are most apt to feel that they are living up to traditional norms. The application of reference group theory clarifies the seeming paradox. For those who are most "traditional" or "orthodox" in their religious behavior tend to be those whose parents have particularly demanding standards of religious orthodoxy, and it is in the context of these more exacting standards, that these individuals more often appraise themselves as falling short in their behavior. This finding can be readily consolidated with established conceptions of self-appraisal being dependent upon various and group-derived standards of judgment. It has the merit of reminding us of what is generally known but only fitfully recognized: the individual's sense of being "at one with himself" is often only the result of being "at one" with the standards of a group in which he is affectively engaged. The sense of personal autonomy does not *necessarily* mean the rejection of normative constraints by all groups.

A third, and suggestive, paper by Eisenstadt[74] is most comprehensively directed toward the problem of the selection of differing reference groups as this is affected by the character of the values and norms involved in the situation. However limited the precision of his data, Eisenstadt's analysis of the problem represents a distinct step forward. He begins by discriminating types of social norms, fully recognizing that the classification leaves ample room for improvement. The five types of norms which he distinguishes—to leave them unmentioned here may perhaps have the not inconsiderable merit of directing the reader to the original paper—are later grouped into two major types: (1) the norms which explicitly relate "ultimate values" of the group to the appropriate role-behavior in particular networks of social interaction; and (2) the

---

73. Bernard C. Rosen, "The reference group approach to the parental factor in attitude and behavior formation," *Social Forces*, 1955, 34, 137-144.

74. S. N. Eisenstadt, "Studies in reference group behaviour: I. Reference norms and the social structure," *Human Relations*, 1954, 7, 191-216.

norms which serve to rank the relative importance of various roles or spheres of behavior, thus serving to mitigate potential conflicts between inconsistent role-definitions.

Just as we have seen in the course of listing group-properties that this is a prelude to the classification of groups, so this classification of norms is preliminary to the definition of theoretical problems. Among these problems, the basic one concerns the conditions under which one or the other of these general types of reference norms is evoked and maintained as a mechanism of social control. The first type, Eisenstadt provisionally concludes, which serves to reaffirm the enduring values underlying a particular situation of social interaction, tends to be evoked under the condition in which, for one or another reason, the social routines of the group are significantly disturbed. With mild and fitting paraphrase, this conclusion can be stated as follows: a reference orientation toward this pervasive type of norm, relating ultimate values to specific situations of social interaction, serves as a mechanism of social control, under conditions of impending or actual disorganization, *within* sub-systems of a society rather than under conditions of potential conflict *between* different subsystems. (Eisenstadt, 202) The second type of norm tends to be called into play when diverse and conflicting definitions of the social situation by different groups present the individual with a choice between conflicting roles.[75]

It must be admitted that these conceptions seem important to me because of their theoretical congeniality, which Eisenstadt observes, with some of the conceptions set forth in the preceding chapter of this book. But apart from such extraneous considerations, they have the distinct merit of focusing attention, in the development of a *sociological* theory of reference group behavior, upon the *institutional and structural conditions* which make for one or another selection of reference groups, and which, furthermore, serve one or another social function for the group.[76] And though studies of the kind briefly reported here are

---

75. It is in connection with this problem that the theory of reference group behavior links up with the neighboring theory of social roles and role-conflict. The social structure, cultural values, and situational pressures interact to produce a choice among alternative and sometimes conflicting roles, according to patterns which are only now beginning to be understood and then, only in their bare outlines. See, for example, the paper by Samuel Stouffer, "An analysis of conflicting social norms," *American Sociological Review*, 1949, 14, 707-717, and the subsequent papers by Stouffer and by Jackson Toby, growing out of this one. See also the analysis of role-selection in a situation of acute social pressures by Lewis M. Killian, "The significance of multiple-group membership in disaster," *American Journal of Sociology*, 1952, 67, 309-314.

76. The allusion here is to statements of problems of the following sort which have been set out in the preceding chapter: "The theoretical and research problem at this point is to determine [*i.e.*, find out] how the *structure of the social situation* encourages certain status-similarities to become the basis for such comparisons, and leads other status-similarities to be ignored as 'irrelevant.'" (Page 243, n. 15) Again: the problem is to identify "frames of reference held in common by a propor-

avowed by their authors to be only preliminary, they do represent a beginning toward the solution of the problem of how some, rather than other, membership groups come to be selected as frames of reference for various kinds of evaluation, comparison, and attitude-formation.

PROBLEM 4.4.

SELECTION OF REFERENCE GROUPS AMONG STATUS-CATEGORIES OR SUB-GROUPS INVOLVING SUSTAINED INTERACTION

. . . [what is] the comparative significance of general status categories and intimate sub-groups of which one is a member. . . . For example, are workers' expectations regarding their personal prospects of future employment shaped more by the present employment of themselves and their associates on the job or by high rates of unemployment prevailing in the occupation at large?

This case from *The American Soldier* thus points to the need for cumulative research on *the relative effectiveness of frames of reference yielded by associates and by more general status categories.* It suggests the salient items of observation which must be incorporated in such projected studies, so that this problem . . . can lend itself to research, here and now, not in some remote future. Such projected studies could readily include items of data on knowledge about the norms or situation prevailing in the given status at large. Subsequent analysis would then be in terms of systematic comparison of individuals in the *same status* but with immediate *associates* who have distinctly opposed norms or who are in contrasting situations. (Page 247)

What was projected in this passage as a hope for research focused on the problem has since become, notably in the research constituting the "Elmira study" of voting behavior, something of an actuality. Thus, in one part of the Elmira study centered on the details of reference group behavior,[77] it is noted that the data described in this passage are precisely those "provided in the voting study and, whenever possible, it is this type of analysis" which is used. This monograph includes a substantial fund of relevant findings, which again I do not try to summarize in detail. An example may serve to indicate the general tenor of these findings. It is found that the immediate associates (co-workers) in a formal organization (a trade union) evidently shape the individual's perception of the political complexion of the total organization. Men

---

tion of individuals within a social category sufficiently large to give rise to definitions of the situation characteristic of that category. And these frames of reference are common because they are patterned by the social structure." (Page 244) Further: ". . . it is the institutional definitions of the social structure which may focus the attention of members of a group or occupants of a social status upon certain *common* reference groups. . . . In addition to these common reference groups, . . . there may well . . . [be] . . . all manner of idiosyncratic reference groups which . . . vary at random. . . ." (Page 246). It is this sociological orientation toward reference groups which Eisenstadt is engaged in specifying and developing. It may not be too much to say that, in the field of reference group theory, continuity, rather than abrupt discontinuity, is becoming the prevailing pattern of development.

77. Norman Kaplan, *Reference Group Theory and Voting Behavior*, previously cited, 79 and, for the example, 156 ff.

with Republican co-workers are far more likely to perceive their union as voting predominantly Republican than individuals with Democratic co-workers. Nevertheless, it appears from the data in hand that the union *as a whole* served as a political reference group for some members of the union while for others, immediate associates in the union served the reference function. This finding leads to the further problem of identifying the circumstances which make for one or the other pattern of reference group selection.

The basic book reporting the Elmira study[78] directs itself to this general problem, as can be seen from the following excerpts, which are so compact that to paraphrase would be only to periphrase:

> . . . what of the inevitable discords between the small cluster of personal associates with whom the individual voter lives and the larger community in which he lives? It is customary to say that what matters for the voter is the social environment *close* to him; and so it does. When the primary group of friends or co-workers is united in political opinion, then the respondent's vote is firm. When Democratic primary groups are "solid," the party vote is not significantly lower than for "solid" Republican groups (i.e., each side loses only about 12 or 15 per cent in deviations). The strong community majority for the Republicans has little effect because it has little access to persons within homogeneous Democratic groups.
>
> But when the primary environment is internally *divided* the effect of the distant community can be seen. Then the Republicans get a higher proportion of the vote. If friends and co-workers are divided two-to-one Republican, the vote goes about three-fourths Republican; but, if they are two-to-one Democratic, the vote goes only about half Democratic. It is as though the average vote in *mixed* primary groups was moved some distance to the Republican side. *The impact of the larger community is thus most evident among voters with discordant or disagreeing primary groups. When the voter's close associates do not provide him with a single, clear political direction—when instead they offer an alternative—then wider associations in the surrounding community reinforce one position over the other.*
>
> The same effect can be seen within each socioeconomic status and religious category. With supporting friends of the "right" party (the traditional party of the stratum), each of the subgroups is 90 per cent "solid" in vote. But, in almost every intermediate case, the Republican-disposed category with a mixed group of friends retains a stronger vote for its party than its Democratic counterpart. Protestants with one Democratic friend (of three) "lose" only 15 per cent of their vote to the Democrats, but Catholics with one Republican

78. Bernard R. Berelson, Paul F. Lazarsfeld and William N. McPhee, *Voting: A Study of Opinion Formation in a Presidential Campaign*, (Chicago: The University of Chicago Press, 1954), 98-101, and *passim*. I have taken the liberty of italicizing those sentences which seem to have most general theoretical significance just as I have deliberately included the homely, but informative, parallel between the race track and a newly-identified social process in the local community. The lowly social status of the analogy should surely not render it taboo among sociologists, at least not in the historical light of, say, the origins of the theory of probability in the gambling house, as the problems of the dice-thrower successively enlisted the interest of d'Imola, Pacioli, Cardan, Tartaglia, Pascal, Fermat and Jacques Bernoulli. If we may compare great things with smaller ones, the force of the analogy holds.

friend "lose" 36 per cent of theirs (see Chart XLV [advice which is here strongly recommended to those who take intellectual delight in a creative sociological analysis of empirical materials]).

In general, then, the Republicans get more than their random share of the adjustment to a conflicting environment, because of the pervasive Republican atmosphere of Elmira that thus tends to perpetuate itself. The surrounding majority gets the benefit of the operation of cross-pressures. One might call this the "breakage" effect, borrowing a term from horse-racing circles. In the parimutuel system people bet against and influence one another. But, when the result is settled in round sums, the odd pennies left over—the breakage—go to the track or to the state in the background. In our case the breakage in small-group adjustment goes to the Republican community. At any one moment the breakage may be trivial, as it is at the track; but over a period of time it is considerable. For example, the heavier Republican vote of older people in Elmira may be the result of just such attrition from the give-and-take of primary groups. With advancing age, a steady toll is taken of former Democrats in the Republican community.

Findings such as these confirm some of the assumptions of fact contained in the long-established conception of pluralism which holds that associations can (and in the political doctrine of pluralism, should) *mediate* between individuals and the larger society and polity.[79] Analytically, this is a sound conception of the social structure, but only as a first approximation. To start with, the conception need not be confined, as it traditionally was in the writings of the pluralists, to the struggle for power among privately organized associations and the state. It is not only the formal and conscious exercise of power which is thus affected by the social structure, but the entire span of social influence, including that which is informal and unwitting.

Secondly, and Nisbet's profound analysis makes this abundantly evident, it is not "individuals," tacitly conceived as "sand heap of disconnected particles of humanity," who are protected in their liberties by the associations which stand between them and the sovereign state, but "persons," diversely engaged in primary groups, such as the family, companionships, and local groups. That figment of the truly isolated individual, which was so powerfully conceived in the time-honored Chapter XIII of Hobbes's *Leviathan,* and which was since caught up in the assumptions of the liberal pluralists, is a fiction which present-day sociology has shown, beyond all reasonable doubt, to be both untrue and superfluous.

Thirdly, as it now appears, even the primary groups in which persons are in some measure involved, do not have uniform effects upon the orientations of their members. On occasion, the values of the groups

---

79. For instructive sociological analyses of pluralism, not only as a political theory but also as a conception of social structure, see Robert A. Nisbet, *The Quest for Community* (New York: Oxford University Press, 1953) and Clark Kerr, "Industrial relations and the liberal pluralist," *Proceedings of the Seventh Annual Meeting of the Industrial Relations Research Association.*

providing the social *milieu* of individuals are not all (or mostly) of a piece, and in such cases, the potential effects of these groups become neutralized. Moreover, when conflicting value-orientations obtain in the primary groups, and the modal orientations of the larger social environment are pronounced, the mediating role of the primary group becomes lessened or even negligible, and the influence of the larger society becomes more binding. This, at least, is the direction which tentative inferences from this set of findings in the Elmira study might appropriately take.

Another type of implication in these findings bears upon the theoretical place of "small group research" in the development of reference group theory, and the more general sociological theory of groups. It is plain that the Elmira findings could not have been readily made if the behavior under examination had been that of a few individuals brought together for a short time to constitute a "small group" in one or another sociological laboratory. For the essential requirement of the problem is that the behavior of these individuals be examined within the twin contexts of long-standing intimate relationships ("friendship" or "coworkers") and of the normative and behavioral structure of the environing community. It is precisely this kind of *sociological* problem, which implicates actively functioning social structures with enduring affective significance for individuals within them, that characteristically falls through the sieve of experimentally contrived "small groups" of individuals brought together on an *ad hoc* basis for limited purposes, with limited involvement in the "group" and all this for a limited time. This is not of course to question the worth of experimental small group research; it is only to urge that this design of inquiry is appropriate for a limited range of sociological problems and inappropriate for a probably greater range of others. It is only to say that for problems, such as the one under review, in which the inter-connections between affectively significant and enduring networks of personal relations and the larger social structure are precisely the connections being explored, the otherwise instructive designs of experimental small group inquiry are not calculated to be adequate. One may venture to express the hope and to profess the confidence that, before long, sociologists and social psychologists will have identified the theoretical problems which are most effectively amenable to investigation in experimental small group research and to distinguish these from the problems which are more effectively studied within the ordinary routines of everyday social life.[79a]

79a. For an example of detailed sociological data on conflicting reference groups, see the dossier of evidence compiled in *The Worker-Priests: A Collective Documentation*, translated from the French by John Petrie (London: Routledge and Kegan Paul, 1956). The *patterned* opposition of roles emerging among the French priest-workers can be instructively interpreted in terms of the conceptions just reviewed; they would be difficult, if not impossible, to reproduce, in theoretically comparable form, within the confines of a laboratory.

Reference Group Behavior: Structural Elements

The preceding section of this examination of continuities in the theory of reference groups and social structure has concerned itself with what is presently known of the *determinants* of the selection of groups—membership and non-membership groups, alternative types of membership groups, and groups involving sustained personal relations as distinct from those abstract aggregates comprised by categories of social status and as distinct from the larger community and society in which individuals also find their place. A variety of specific theoretical and empirical problems have been examined in their bearings on determinants of selection. Since we shall not undertake at this time to do more than mention some of the consequences and functions of reference group behavior, we should examine at least a few of the structural elements which are centrally involved in reference group behavior, conceived as a social process. As has been intimated in the foregoing list of group-properties believed to be germane to the further development of reference group theory, the element of "observability" or "visibility" plays a commanding part in this process. It therefore requires explicit consideration.

PROBLEM 5.

OBSERVABILITY OR VISIBILITY: PATTERNED AVENUES OF INFORMATION ABOUT NORMS, VALUES, AND ROLE-PERFORMANCE

Reference group theory of course "assumes that individuals comparing their own lot with that of others have some *knowledge* of the situation in which these others find themselves. . . . Or, if the individual is taken to be . . . oriented toward the norms of a non-membership group, the theory of course assumes that he has some knowledge of these norms. Thus, the theory of reference group behavior must include in its fuller psychological elaboration some treatment of the dynamics of perception (of individuals, groups and norms) and in its sociological elaboration, some treatment of channels of communication through which this knowledge is gained. Which processes make for accurate or distorted images of the situation of other individuals and groups (taken as a frame of reference)? Which forms of social organization maximize the probabilities of correct perception of other individuals and groups, and which make for distorted perception? Since *some* perceptual and cognitive elements are definitely *implied* even in a description of reference group behavior, it will be necessary for these elements to be explicitly incorporated into the theory." (Pages 247-248)

This statement of the conception that there are patterned variations in the extent of knowledge about the norms and values of a reference group remains tolerably adequate at this writing. But through the inadvertence of returning repeatedly to the matter of accurate or distorted perception, the statement may possibly mis-direct attention exclusively to the large and important problems of the psychology of perception and away from the large and important problems of the ways in which the variability of group structure affect readiness of access to information about the norms and values prevailing in groups.

That the concept of reference group behavior presupposes some knowledge or image of the norms and values obtaining in the group is practically self-evident and has of course been recognized for some time. In the account of his Bennington study, for example, Newcomb noted that not all students were aware of the distinct trend away from conservatism as students move through successive years of college. He went on to observe that "Obviously, those not aware of the dominant community trend could not be using the community as a reference group for an attitude."[80] Newcomb thereupon included, in his design of inquiry, a measure of the awareness of this trend among students. "Obvious" as this component of the theory evidently is, it is nevertheless the case that many studies of reference group behavior have not explicitly provided for the systematic collection of evidence indicating varying degrees of awareness of the norms prevailing in groups ostensibly serving as reference groups.[81]

However, the matter of knowledgeability or awareness of the norms and values prevailing in a group is more than an empirical datum incorporated into analyses of the determinants of reference group selection. It is not only a datum, but is also sociologically problematical. Knowledge of these norms, that is to say, does not merely *happen* to vary empirically among individuals; the availability and extent of such knowledge is also presumably patterned by the group structure. And this generates some theoretically significant problems for further analysis. In which ways does group structure affect the distribution of knowledge about the values and norms actually held by members of the group?

That such differences in knowledge of group norms actually exist is not only a matter of conventional assumption, but has been systematically shown by studies such as the one by Chowdhry and Newcomb (to which I have referred in the short discussion of "visibility" or "observability" as a group-property). In Newcomb's later summary of findings,

80. Newcomb, in Sherif, *An Outline of Social Psychology*, 143.

81. For a detailed and methodical examination of this point, see Chapter III of Norman Kaplan, *op. cit.* Kaplan appropriately observes that two distinct kinds of "awareness" are variously involved in reference group behavior: awareness that a group or individual is being used as a frame of value reference and awareness (knowledge) only of the norms held by designated others (who may be unwittingly serving as frames of reference). The reason for emphasizing these "obvious" presuppositions of the theory is artlessly simple: they have often proved so obvious as to be wholly overlooked in the design of research on reference groups.

he noted that in every one of the groups (of from 20 to 40 members, including a student religious group, a community political group, a medical sorority, and a workers' education group), "the leaders were more accurate judges of the attitudes of the total membership than were nonleaders *on relevant but not on non-relevant items.*" A relevant item was defined as one closely related to the purposes of the group; an irrelevant item as one only remotely related. Religious attitudes were thus considered relevant to the religious group but not for the political group. Newcomb goes on to observe that

> If the leaders' judgments had turned out to be superior on the non-relevant items, too, . . . [this] would have meant that leaders are good all-round judges of other people's attitudes, regardless of the particular norms of the group. This would suggest that the leader of one group could rather readily be interchanged with the leader of a quite different group. The actual findings, of course, do not support this conclusion. They suggest, rather, that the leader's *position is a special one* in terms of the group's specific norms. Incidentally, since these leaders had not been members of their respective groups any longer than had the average non-leader, it cannot be concluded that either their positions of leadership or their familiarity with group norms resulted from "seniority."[82]

Findings of this kind on the variability of knowledge about the norms obtaining in a group have lately been multiplied in *social psychology.*[83] These provide important beginnings for developing collateral *sociological* studies of the processes through which the structure of groups leads to such differentials in the visibility of norms obtaining in those groups. Such studies, complementing the socio-psychological

---

82. This summary of the study is provided by Newcomb, *Social Psychology,* 658-659. I have italicized the phrase implying a concept of group structure which will now be examined and I have taken the occasion to correct an obvious typographical error in the final sentence, by substituting the compound word "non-leader" for the word "non-member" which inadvertently found its way into print.

As Chowdhry and Newcomb themselves make clear, a single study, even so imaginative a study as this one, is not enough to establish the interpretation put upon the observed facts. Another study, designed to follow up the interpretation of the Chowdhry-Newcomb study, suggests that the more accurate assessment of group attitudes by leaders need not result only from their strategic position in the communication structure. "Leaders may know best the opinions of their groups because they, more than any other member, were influential in formulating these opinions." Limited experimental evidence is reported in support of this explanation of the facts. I should add, only, that this need not be taken as an *alternative* social process which brings about greater knowledge of group-values, attitudes, and opinions among "'leaders,'" but as a *complementary* social process which reinforces the one indicated by Chowdhry and Newcomb. My reason for this suggestion will become evident in the pages that follow. See George A. Talland, "The assessment of group opinions by leaders, and their influence on its formation," *Journal of Abnormal and Social Psychology,* 1954, 49, 431-434. (I am indebted to my colleague, Richard Christie, for having called my attention to the paper by Talland.)

83. These are summarized at various places in the *Handbook of Social Psychology,* edited by Gardner Lindzey (Cambridge, Mass.: Addison-Wesley Publishing Company, Inc., 1954), for example, in Chapters 17, 21, 22, and 28.

studies, need to be focused on the *positions or statuses* occupied by individuals in the group structure and not, as the italicized observation by Newcomb makes clear, upon individual differences in perceptual sensitivity. To work out the details of the required sociological studies at this point would take us far afield, but some limited indications may serve the immediate purpose.

Empirical sociological studies of patterned differentials in knowledge about the distribution of values and norms in the group could profitably begin with the theoretical point that authority in groups does not ordinarily operate as it outwardly appears: through the issuance of orders. As Barnard, among others,[84] has observed, authority is the attribute of a communication by virtue of which it is accepted by a "member" of the group as governing his action. In this conception, "the decision as to whether an order has authority or not lies with the persons to whom it is addressed, and does not reside in 'persons of authority' or those who issue these orders." In short, authority is sociologically regarded as a patterned social relationship, rather than as the attribute of an individual ("a leader").

As in other cases, so in this one: the conceptualization of a problem makes an appreciable difference in the way further analysis proceeds. If authority is conceived as a trait of an individual rather than as a social relationship, inquiry turns to the particular psychological characteristics which make for one rather than another type of individual having his orders generally accepted. Important as it patently is, this is not a problem which falls within the theoretical competence of sociology. But construed as a social relationship, authority becomes amenable to sociological investigation.

Barnard provides a lead for analyzing the place of visibility or observability in the exercise of authority. He maintains, provisionally but definitely, that those in positions of authority exercise it effectively and have their "orders" accepted only as these orders, in turn, conform to the norms of the group or organization. If this seems paradoxical, it seems so only because of unexamined preconceptions to the contrary. For "authority," in the lexicon of the much-advertised man-in-the-street, seems to reside in the individuals issuing commands, and not in the consequent activities of those to whom the commands are issued. Yet, on renewed examination, all this appears less paradoxical, for plainly "authority" is only an idle hope if it does not result in the acceptance of

84. C. I. Barnard, *The Functions of the Executive,* Chapter XII and specifically at 163. For further examination of the difference between "leadership," as construed in social psychology, and "authority," as construed in sociology, see J. F. Wolpert, "Toward a sociology of authority," in A. W. Gouldner, *Studies in Leadership* (New York: Harper & Bros., 1950), 679-701; Robert Bierstedt, "The problem of authority," in Berger, Abel and Page (editors), *Freedom and Control in Modern Society,* 67-81, esp. at 71-72; Elliott Jaques, *The Changing Culture of a Factory* (New York: Dryden, 1952), Chapters 9 and 10.

orders. And the basic point of this conception is that these orders will *ordinarily* not be accepted if they depart considerably from the norms operating within the group.[85]

All this is not to say, of course, that those in authority are *nothing but* passive followers of the prevailing norms. It only means that "authority" does not confer *carte blanche* upon those who possess it, that it does not carry with it unconditional power to do as one would like. To be continuously effective, authority must be exercised within the constraining limits provided by the norms of the group. Nevertheless, it is also true that authority provides occasion for modifying the norms and for introducing new patterns of behavior regarded as consistent with these new norms as well as with previously existing norms. In short, authority involves less in the way of unconditional power than is popularly supposed and more in the way of conditional power than that available to individual rank-and-file members of the group.

In the present context, I am primarily concerned with the first of these attributes of authority: its constraint by group norms. For this plainly requires that those in authority have substantial knowledge of these norms; a greater knowledge, presumably, than that held by other individual members of the group. Otherwise, orders issued by authority will often and unwittingly violate these norms and cumulatively reduce the effective authority of those who issue them. Orders will not be followed, or followed only under duress, with the result that the once legitimate authority becomes progressively converted into the exercise of "naked power." This outcome does, of course, sometimes occur, and precisely for the reasons we have just reviewed. But when authority remains more or less intact, it does so because "orders" are contained well within the limits set by the group norms which those in authority take into account. We must therefore consider the mechanisms of social structure which operate to provide those in authority with the needed information.

Until now, we have centered on the functional requirement for the effective exercise of authority of having adequate information about the *norms and values* of the group and, implicitly, about the attitudes of its members. It should now be further noted that comparable information is also functionally required about the actual behavior of members of the group, about their *role-performance*. The two types of information are closely connected, but they are distinctly different. Visibility of both norms and of role-performance is required if the structure of authority is to operate effectively.

85. Barnard based his conception on numerous observations of behavior and reflection upon this in large formal organizations. Since he wrote, detailed investigations have confirmed this conception; for example, the ingenious experiment reported by F. Merei, "Group leadership and institutionalization," *Human Relations*, 1949, 2, 23-39.

PROBLEM 5.1.

MECHANISMS OF OBSERVABILITY OF NORMS
AND OF ROLE-PERFORMANCE

All this is to say that studies are needed not only to establish the initial facts of the case—whether authorities in effectively operating groups, both formal and informal, generally do have greater knowledge than others of the norms and behavior obtaining in the group—but also to identify the structural arrangements and group processes which provide for such visibility. Although there is no backlog of systematic studies of this matter, it is possible even now to piece together some facts and guesses bearing upon social mechanisms serving this function of providing observability.

The identification of these mechanism begins with a central fact about the exercise of social control by members of a group in general and by those in positions of authority in particular. This is a fact which is often neglected in studies of social control largely because it is taken for granted. Yet, as everybody knows, it is precisely some of the matters which are taken for granted which have a way of rising up to plague those engaged in the search for knowledge. This is the fact to which we have alluded before and now find it necessary to repeat: whether they realize it or not, people who are effectively engaged in exercising social control must in some sense be informed about the norms (or morally regulated and expected behavior) obtaining in the group, just as they must be informed about the actual behavior of members of the group. Lacking the first kind of information, those in authority will sometimes call for behavior which is not consistent with the norms of the group and will find, often to their indignant surprise, that their expectations ("orders") are not being fulfilled, or are being fulfilled only "under protest" (that is to say, that present conformity to orders is at the price of diminishing spontaneous conformity to orders in the future). In either case, this constitutes an abridgment of authority. Otherwise said, and this only appears to return us to our theoretical point of departure, effective and stable authority involves the functional requirement of fairly full information about the actual (not the assumed) norms of the group and the actual (not the assumed) role-performance of its members.

Which mechanisms—which arrangements of the parts and processes of group structure—serve to meet these functional requirements of effective authority? To ask the question is not, of course, to assume that all groups everywhere always have these mechanisms. It is only to say that to the extent that groups do *not* have mechanisms adequate to meet these requirements, authority and social control will diminish. And as we all know, this has been the fate of many groups which fell apart, for a group cannot persist without a substantial measure of social control.

1. *Differentials in communication:* One such mechanism, and not necessarily a mechanism expressly planned for the purpose, is provided by the distinctive networks of communication in which the "authorities" in a group are typically engaged. This has been compactly described by Homans in two connected statements: "The higher a man's social rank, the larger will be the number of persons that originate interaction for him, either directly or through intermediaries." And "The higher a man's social rank, the larger the number of persons for whom he originates interaction, either directly or through intermediaries."[86] The structure is generally so arranged that those in authority are at a nexus of two-way communication, with the result that they are better informed about norms and behavior than are those holding other positions in the group. Again, it should be said that this is an organizational tendency, rather than a description of concrete fact. Effective organization requires that those in authority be located at junctures in the network of communication where they are regularly apprised of the norms actually obtaining in the group.

As a result of the same structure, occupants of authoritative positions tend to be better informed than others of the character of role-performance in the group. A great multiplicity of organizational devices have been evolved at one time or another in the effort to meet this functional requirement of visibility. In small and informal groups, this often comes to be met without the use of structural devices deliberately introduced for the purpose: the patterns of social interaction serve to keep the "leaders" in touch with the group-related activities of members of the group. In large and formal organization, specific mechanisms must be invented, mechanisms which can be broadly regarded as "accounting procedures." Whether these involve double-entry bookkeeping in private or public business, "grading" students in educational institutions, or conducting "morale surveys" in military or industrial establishments, they have substantially the same function of informing those in authority about the quality and quantity of performance of organizational roles, in order that the activities of the group can be the more effectively controlled and coordinated.

However, the use of mechanisms to meet the functional requirement

---

86. George C. Homans, *The Human Group* (New York: Harcourt, Brace and Company, 1950), 182, and for further apposite analysis, the whole of Chapter 16. I have found Homans's book the single most informative source on this matter of the structure and functions of "communication" in the exercise of social control within groups and organizations. Homans expresses his indebtedness to the basic work of Barnard, and this is amply justified. It should be noted, however, that Homans has considerably developed and systematized the ideas making up Barnard's theory of authority. The next step is to study the mechanisms through which groups and organizations come to meet the functional requirement of having those occupying positions of authority adequately informed about *both* norms and role-performance.

of visibility is itself limited by the norms of the group. If the authorities try to keep informed about details of role-performance to an extent that exceeds the normative expectations of members of the group, this will meet with resistance or expressed opposition. Few groups, it appears, so fully absorb the loyalties of members that they will readily accept unrestricted observability of their role-performance. This attitude is sometimes described as a "need for privacy." But however apt this phrase may be as a *description* of opposition to unremitting observation of what one is doing, it can scarcely be regarded as an explanation, in spite of the seemingly explanatory character of the idea of "need."

Resistance to full visibility of one's behavior appears, rather, to result from structural properties of group life. *Some* measure of leeway in conforming to role-expectations is presupposed in all groups. To have to meet the strict requirements of a role at all times, without some degree of deviation, is to experience insufficient allowances for individual differences in capacity and training and for situational exigencies which make strict conformity extremely difficult. This is one of the sources of what has been elsewhere noted in this book as socially patterned, or even institutionalized, evasions of institutional rules. But if the structure of the group makes for full surveillance of activities, even tolerated departures from the strict letter of prescribed role-requirements will come to be psychologically taxing. Members of the group must then decide anew how far they can depart from the norms, without invoking punitive sanctions, just as the authorities must decide anew whether the basic formal structure of the group is being undermined by the observed deviations of behavior. It is in this sense that authorities can have "excessive knowledge" of what is actually going on, so that this becomes dysfunctional for the system of social control.

Resistance to full visibility of activities is of course accentuated by an (assumed or actual) cleavage of interests between authoritative strata and governed strata. The strong hostility toward "close supervision" in business and industry evidently expresses this doubly reinforced objection to the surveillance of role-performance. For much the same reasons, the people who insist on close compliance to the official rules become regarded as organizational martinets, engaged in advancing their own interests by not permitting customarily tolerated departures from the rules. But the presumed malevolence or self-interest of the observer only accentuates the antipathy toward having one's every activity subject to observation. To be sure, the telescreens of 1984 excite horror because the Thought Police have institutionally-malevolent reasons for wanting to watch what any of the subjects of Oceania are doing at any given moment. Yet all malevolence aside, the autonomy of the person is experienced as threatened by having no private—that is to say, wholly separate and secret—life, immune to observation by others. Robert

Owen's good-will toward his employees in New Lanark was conceded even by those of his contemporaries who doubted his sanity; yet, when he installed what he called his "silent monitor" to observe at a glance the conduct of each of his workers, it can be supposed that they did not entirely welcome the thought that their benevolent big brother was in a position to know precisely how well or ill they were doing.

To notice that there is resistance to full visibility of one's conduct, empirically familiar as it is (presumably, to people in all societies), serves an important theoretic purpose as well. It suggests that it may be useful to think in terms of there being, for various social structures, some *functionally optimum degree of visibility*. It indicates, further, that this optimum does not coincide with complete visibility. Nor is this simply to say that people *happen* to want some "privacy," for true as this may be, it is not analytically helpful. Nor, after the fashion of the cultural relativists, is it enough merely to say that this "need for privacy" *happens* to vary among cultures, or among various social strata with their distinctive subcultures within an overarching society. True as it is that this variation occurs, it is not the case, our theory suggests, that this results simply from the accidents of history. Rather, we are led to the idea that differing social structures *require*, for their effective operation, differing degrees of visibility. Correlatively, it is being suggested that differing social structures require arrangements for insulation from full and uninhibited visibility if they are to function adequately: arrangements which, in the vernacular, are described as needs for privacy, or as the importance of secrecy.

It is possible to suggest, if not yet to demonstrate, the functional character of curbs upon full observability of conduct. Particularly in complex social life, in which most people have at one time or another departed from the strict normative requirements of the society, the unflagging and literal application of these normative standards, upon pain of punishment for all departures from them, would result almost in "a war, as is of every man, against every man." For full, continuous, and ready compliance with strict group standards would be possible only in a social vacuum that never existed. It is not possible in any societies known to man. The social function of permissiveness, the function of some measure of small delinquencies remaining unobserved or if observed, unacknowledged, is that of enabling the social structure to operate without undue strain. There is a band of behavior which, though it deviates from the strict letter of the law (or of the moral code), is socially allowed, without undue comment and without the application of sanctions. This is the band of institutionalized evasion which apparently varies in breadth from group to group, under varying conditions of exigency. In times of acute stress upon the group or society, in which it is threatened with disruption, there is, evidently, a narrowing of this band of permitted or allowable deviations; martial law exhibits this shift in the demand for strict conformity. At other times, when the same group or society is not subject to grave dangers, the band of permissiveness widens, and unless visibility is enforced and public attention is drawn to deviations from the literal normative standards, these departures are allowed to continue.

As is so often the case, the man of letters succeeds better than the social scientist in *depicting,* in unmistakable and vivid colors, the social situation which the scientist has abstractly analyzed. George Orwell and Aldous Huxley, among our contemporaries, have succeeded in portraying the horror of full observability of conduct. But they have had to extrapolate tendencies variously developing in present-day societies into a hypothetical future in order to paint this fiendish portrait of a society with unrestricted visibility. Long before societies emerged which could stimulate this short flight of the imagination, the Victorian novelist and essayist, William Makepeace Thackeray, was able to portray a horrendous society in which all deviations from social norms were promptly detected, and thereupon punished. Consider only the following passage from his essay, "On Being Found Out":

Just picture to yourself everybody who does wrong being found out, and punished accordingly. Fancy all the boys in all the schools being whipped; and then the assistants, and then the headmaster. . . . Fancy the provost-marshal being tied up, having previously superintended the correction of the whole army. . . . After the clergyman has cried his peccavi, suppose we hoist up a bishop, and give him a couple of dozen! (I see my Lord Bishop of Double-Gloucester sitting in a very uneasy posture on his right reverend bench.) After we have cast off the bishop, what are we to say to the Minister who appointed him? . . . The butchery is too horrible. The hand drops powerless, appalled at the quantity of birch it must cut and brandish. I am glad we are not all found out, I say again; and protest, my dear brethren, against our having our deserts. . . . Would you have your wife and children know you exactly for what you are, and esteem you precisely at your worth? If so, my friend, you will live in a dreary house, and you will have but a chilly fireside. . . . You don't fancy you *are,* as you seem to them. No such thing, my man. Put away that monstrous conceit, and be thankful that *they* have not found you out.

If prompted by practices in public schools of his time, Thackeray's imagination was limited in scope, it nevertheless was able to seize upon the essential point: full visibility of conduct and unrestrained enforcement of the letter of normative standards would convert a society into a jungle. It is this central idea which is contained in the concept that some limits upon full visibility of behavior are functionally required for the effective operation of a society. It is, of course, this same requirement which has set limits upon the ready accessibility of personal data to the psychologist and sociologist who, with fine disinterested purpose, wishes to enlarge the observability of human conduct. This is why, it may be said, the social scientist is so often an object of ambivalence. This is why his inquiries are so often regarded as mere "snooping" into "private affairs." Were it not for other, countervailing mechanisms in society—such as the institutionalization of "privileged communications," or "data to be treated in utter confidence"—neither the social scientist dependent upon free access to data on human behavior, nor the other professionals, such as the doctor, lawyer, and clergyman, who must also have this information, would be able to carry out their social roles. But since these social roles are institutionally defined to include unflagging restrictions on making observed departures from the code known to others, the band of observability of deviant behavior can be safely enlarged, without interfering with the functional necessity for "privacy," "secrecy," or "ignorance."[87]

It is one thing to say that visibility of role-performance can be judged as excessive by the standards of the group; it is quite another to say that the norms nevertheless allow greater access to such information to those in authority than to the run of others in the group. Differentials in visibility are not merely givens or "happenstances"; they are resultants of functional requirements being met by the structure of the group and by the norms which support that structure.

2. *Differentials in motivation:* Not only does the structure of groups provide greater access to information about operating norms and role-performance to those in positions of authority, but the institutional definitions of the roles of men in these positions provides them with greater motivation to seek out this information. This kind of inquisitiveness is not merely a matter of individual personality disposition, although, to be sure, personal proclivities may reinforce the socially defined requirements of the role. In formal groups or informal, the acknowledged leaders have distinctive responsibility, both for what goes on within the group and for what will relate the group to its social environment. They are motivated to keep in touch with what is happening, if only because they will be held accountable for it.

Correlatively, members of the group are motivated to gain assent of their superiors to contemplated new forms of action. To act without such support is to jeopardize their position. That is why subordinates gen-

---

87. Orwell's *1984* and Huxley's *Brave New World* of course require no citation to be further identified. The account of the "silent monitor" in New Lanark is proudly included in *The Life of Robert Owen,* Written by Himself [at the age of 86], (London: Effingham Wilson, 1857), I, 80-81. Thackeray's essay will be found in his collected works.

Just as Simmel sensed the sociological significance of observability, so he sensed the significance of its counterpart, "secrecy." See *The Sociology of Georg Simmel,* 307-376. His "instinct for the [sociological] jugular" seldom failed him, although he frequently became bored with going on from there. In further point is the paper by Wilbert E. Moore and Melvin M. Tumin, "Some social functions of ignorance," *American Sociological Review,* 1949, 14, 787-795.

erally "clear" with superiors before taking any but routinized action. This procedure is of course built into the structure of highly organized bureaucracies. But what is more telling, and as Whyte, Homans, and others have noted, this practice occurs in the most informal groups as well. Clearance may involve only a seemingly casual exchange of remarks, but this can be readily identified as the functional equivalent of "going through channels" in formal and more complex organizations.

In this way, the institutionalized motivations of superiors and inferiors in groups can become complementary and mutually supporting. To some extent, the responsible superior is motivated to keep informed of changing behavior and expectations; to some extent, the dependent subordinate is motivated to inform the superior before taking innovative action. Structure and motivation both serve to keep those in authority better informed than rank-and-file members of the group.

3. *Obstacles to visibility:* But this is of course only part of the story. Countervailing motivations and social processes operate to reduce visibility by authorities from the high level which would automatically obtain, if only the preceding mechanisms were at work. Some of these countervailing tendencies are well-known and need only be mentioned here.[87a]

Those occupying the uppermost ranks in complex groups or organizations cannot keep in direct touch with all those in all the other strata. It is not only that this is physically impossible; even if it were possible, it would be organizationally dysfunctional. For if they are to preserve the structure of authority, they too must generally work "through channels." Otherwise, as Simmel and others have in effect noted, they will undermine the authority of those intermediate to the topmost authorities and the lower echelons of the organization. As a result, the topmost strata may come to hear only what their immediate subordinates want them to hear. Observability is filtered through structural layers of personnel and the finally distilled information may be variously at odds with the actual situation of operating norms and role-performance in the organization.[88]

Furthermore, authority tends to isolate those who possess it to a

---

87a. They are partly considered, for example, by Homans, *op. cit.*, 438-439, and elsewhere in the same book.

88. "Folk-knowledge" often includes recognition of this structural tendency in complex societies. The defenders of Hitler seized upon this fact of complex organization to explain that "he did not really know" about the extermination camps of Nazi Germany. But this, it seems from the historical record, is to do injustice to Hitler's organizational acumen: his channels of communication operated more efficiently than this would allow. History holds him accountable for mass slaughter not only because institutional leaders are generally held accountable for the behavior of their underlings, but also because Hitler builded "better" than he knew: he had considerable observability of what was actually going on. Except toward the end of his thousand-year empire, he was kept well informed: this phase of the organized efficiency of Nazism provided ample basis for accountability.

high degree. Since they normally interact with near-equals in the hierarchy, the more complex the organization the greater the possibility that
they will be shut off, for a time, from changes in attitudes and norms in
the lower (and not only the lowermost) strata of the organization. This
circumstance of social structure often makes for an informational lag.
Considerable numbers of people in the organization may become alienated from established norms long before this comes to the attention of
the authorities whose job it is to uphold these norms. As a result of this
structural insulation, they may not know about changes in the operating
norms until these changes have become far advanced. Given this structural source of defective communication, such changes in the controlling
norms may come to the attention of "the authorities" only when they
discover that orders which they assumed to be well within the limits
of the norms prevailing in the organization do not meet with the expected conformity. Under such circumstances and to this extent, authority dwindles. Belated concessions to the now-patently changed norms of
the organization serve only to make apparent to all how much the
previously existing authority has declined. In some cases, when this
process has run its course before it is recognized by those ostensibly in
command, authority is abdicated.

The functional importance of a tolerable degree of visibility of norms
and role-performance by those in positions of authority tends to be, but
in specific cases need not be, organizationally recognized. When the
structure of the group or organization fails to meet the hypothetically
minimum requirement of "sufficient" visibility, a new structure of authority is instituted, or the social organization falls apart. This theoretical
claim, which requires more systematic empirical study than has yet been
accorded it, links up the theory of reference group behavior with the
theory of social organization. These two strands of sociological theory
can be interwoven with a third composed of ideas about the functional
requirements of personality for occupying positions of sustained authority and for maintaining visibility of organizational norms and role-
performance.

4. *Social selection of personality types suited to maintain visibility:*
As a requirement for the effective exercise of authority, visibility presupposes the operation of mechanisms for selecting organizational leaders
having the functionally appropriate type of personality. This statement
can be easily banalized. It can be taken to say that people in positions
of authority would do well to have a "capacity for leadership," in which
event it becomes that sorrowful thing: an advanced case of platitude
complicated by redundancy. If, however, the statement is understood to
say that *specific* attributes of personality are required to maintain effective observability of group norms and of role-performance, it then opens
up questions which deserve, and may ultimately receive, empirically

sound answers. The vast and, at times, it would seem, almost limitless literature on the personality traits of "leaders" and of those cast in other functional roles doubtless includes much information which bears upon the question now under review. No effort is made here to examine and to collate these materials. Instead, I refer only to some instructive conjectures by Shils[89] which seem to me to bear directly upon the problem of the requirements of personality which must be met to maintain ready visibility of norms and role-performance.

Shils comes upon this problem when he asks why it is that nativist-Fascist movements in the United States have proved to be either short-lived or, after a brief span of power if not of glory, relatively ineffectual. After all, there appear to be patches of cultural soil where nativism should thrive. As Shils puts the matter, "The Middle West and Southern California are well strewn with small scale nativist-fundamentalist agitators of the type which might be called Fascist. Yet they have never had any success in the United States despite their numbers and despite the existence in the Middle and Far Western population of a vein of xenophobia, populist, anti-urban and anti-plutocratic sentiment, distrust of intellectuals—in fact very much of what [some] would regard as the ingredients of Fascism. Since an *Ethos* or general value system are not the same as differentiated behavior in a system of roles, these people have never been able to constitute a significant movement."

Part of the explanation for this seeming paradox seems to turn upon the inadequacies of personality of the nativist leaders, seen from the standpoint of that functional requirement of effective authority in social systems which I have been describing as observability or visibility. The nativist leaders generally seem to lack the following requisite characteristics of personality identified by Shils:

—sufficient sensitivity to the expectations of others;
—orientation toward the approval of colleagues and constituency (which need not involve, of course, slavish subjection to such approval);
—a capacity for persisting in a course of organizational action;
—a substantial minimum capacity for trusting others, so that one is alerted to their several and shared values;
—a capacity for controlling and inhibiting immediate responses to situations to allow for considered judgment of organizational consequences of action;
—a capacity for distinguishing systematically between occasions calling for behavior expressive of one's own sentiments, instrumental behavior and behavior enacting shared values;
—a capacity for acting to maintain the authority of their own lieutenants by not insisting on relating themselves directly to their constituency.[90]

---

89. E. A. Shils, "Authoritarianism: 'right' and 'left,'" in Richard Christie and Marie Jahoda, *Studies in the Scope and Method of 'The Authoritarian Personality,'* 24-49, esp. at 44-48.

90. These items are partial paraphrase of Shils's compact statement of the case; *ibid.,* 44 ff.

These are some of the personality variables which serve to make it readily possible for those dressed in authority to remain responsive without being dependently subordinated to their actual and potential following. But whether these requirements of personality are met by organizational leaders is itself a result of the social processes of selection of leaders, and Shils goes on to describe the defects in the machinery of selection by nativist movements; defects which need only be applauded here rather than described in detail.

The essential theoretical point is that certain personality constellations are functionally required by the role of organizational leader just as certain selective processes in the social structure are functionally required for appropriate personalities to be placed in positions of authority where they can effectively observe norms and role-performance.

5. *The argument on visibility thus far:* The immediately preceding pages have singled out for attention a sociological variable of some importance to reference group theory in particular and to organizational theory in general. This variable of visibility has been examined only in some of its principal outlines. Even so, it was necessary to move somewhat afield from reference group theory, as narrowly conceived, to take up the matter of visibility in the broader sphere of social organization.

In the course of this review, it was provisionally suggested that from the standpoint of sociological theory, visibility is the counterpart in social structure of what, from the standpoint of psychological theory, is social perception. The sociological study of visibility is addressed to the problems of how *social structures make for* ready or difficult awareness of the norms prevailing in the group and of the extent to which members of the group live up to these norms. In the same way that a comprehensive theory of social organization provides a place for the structural patterns of visibility, a comprehensive theory of perception provides a place for the psychological processes making for those differential sensitivities to social situations which have been described as "social perception."[91]

"Visibility," then, is a name for the extent to which the structure of a social organization provides occasion to those variously located in that structure to perceive the norms obtaining in the organization and the character of role-performance by those manning the organization. It refers to an attribute of social structure, not to the perceptions which individuals *happen* to have. Patterned differentials in visibility were explored by comparing those in positions of authority with those in sub-

---

91. For an informed review and assessment of this latter field of inquiry, see Jerome S. Bruner and Renato Tagiuri, "The perception of people," in Lindzey, *Handbook of Social Psychology,* II, 634-654, and further review articles cited in the bibliography of that paper.

ordinate positions. This led to a short review of some social mechanisms facilitating or curbing visibility.

Mechanisms refer to structures and processes considered in terms of their functional significance for designated requirements of the social organization; in this case, the requirement of visibility as an element entering into social control. Two of these mechanisms were said to be, first, the location of "authorities" in strategic positions within the network of communication and, second, the structurally induced motivations for authorities, who are held accountable for the successes and failures of the organization, to keep informed about norms and activities. Correlatively, we examined structural and processual barriers to visibility by those in authority and noted that further structural devices are required to surmount these barriers. Finally, notice was taken of the kinds of personality requirements which must be met if those in positions of authority are to make systematic use of the structurally arranged opportunities for visibility.

All this may seem to be a prolonged excursus from the subject of structural elements and processes entering into reference group behavior. In part, it is a digression into the wider theory of social organization. But in greater part, it bears directly upon one of the principal presuppositions of reference group theory, the presupposition that there must be patterned ways in which people become acquainted with the norms and activities in the groups which they select as evaluative and comparative frames of reference. Social scientists have barely begun to examine the mechanisms which make for greater or less knowledge about the norms and activities of groups, on the part of insiders and of outsiders. Until this is further clarified by new theoretical formulations and associated empirical inquiry, reference group theory will remain, to this degree, decidedly limited and, in this respect, incomplete.

Next steps toward the advancement of this part of reference group theory can at least be prefigured. For, once visibility is recognized as an integral component of reference group processes, numerous questions, hypotheses, and guesses quickly come to mind. Is the observability of *non*-membership groups characteristically greater with respect to their *norms and values* than with respect to the patterns of behavior actually obtaining in them? Is there, in somewhat other words, a tendency for outsiders to develop unrealistic images of non-membership groups which, if they are positive reference groups, lead toward unqualified idealization (as the official norms are taken at face value) or, if they are negative reference groups, lead toward unqualified condemnation (as the official norms are experienced as wholly alien to the outsider's deep-seated values)? Correlatively, do people ordinarily discount the expressed values of their membership groups, knowing, even if they do not formulate this knowledge, that actual behavior only approximates these values as they are embodied in social roles? More generally: are there, in fact, patterned differences in the visibility of norms and of activities, depending on whether the group in question is one of which the individual is a member, one to which he aspires, or one which he rejects out of hand?

Questions of this order are not without implications. For example, consider the notoriously familiar case of the new convert to a group. It is often been said, and this is probably part of the truth, that the convert becomes overly-zealous in his conformity to the norms of the group because he considers himself to be on trial and wishes to ensure his acceptance. But true as it may be to describe the convert's ardent conformity in these terms of socially induced motivation, is it a large part of the whole truth? The concept of differentials in observability suggests that it is not. For apart from this matter of motivation, the convert may also be peculiarly conformist for want of having had first-hand knowledge of the nuances of allowable and patterned departures from the norms of the group which he has lately joined. As a result, and unlike long-established members of the group who have acquired this knowledge unwittingly in the course of their socialization, the convert tries to live up to the strict letter of these norms. He becomes a rigid conformist. But the theoretically significant point is that he exhibits this extreme conformity, not necessarily because his is a "rigid personality," but because, in the absence of close familiarity with the norms of his newfound group, he has no alternative but to make the official norms his compelling guide to behavior. Very often, as everybody knows, the new convert—whether of a religious, political, or "social" persuasion—becomes a prig, narrowly engrossed in the satisfaction of acting in conformity with the rules.[92]

From the standpoint of visibility of norms, the sociological counterpart to priggishness is the concept that rank imposes obligations: *noblesse oblige*. Those of established high rank in a group or society—those of nobility in other than an historically provincial sense—know the rules of the game, that is, know the norms, and know their way around. They

---

92. To describe this manner of man as a prig is not to indulge in calling names. The prig is a well-defined social type. Since I cannot improve upon the description of this social type beyond that provided by an anonymous volume of essays quoted in Fowler's *Modern English Usage*, I borrow the description: " 'A prig is a believer in red tape; that is, he exalts the method above the work done. A prig, like the Pharisee, says: "God, I thank thee that I am not as other men are"—except that he often substitutes *Self* for *God*. A prig is one who works out his paltry accounts to the last farthing, while his millionaire neighbour lets accounts take care of themselves. A prig expects others to square themselves to his very inadequate measuring-rod, & condemns them with confidence if they do not. A p. is wise beyond his years in all the things that do not matter. A p. cracks nuts with a steam hammer: that is, calls in the first principles of morality to decide whether he may, or must, do something of as little importance as drinking a glass of beer. On the whole, one may, perhaps, say that all his different characteristics come from the combination, in varying proportions, of three things—the desire to do his duty, the belief that he knows better than other people, & blindness to the difference in value between different things.' "

also tend to have the power to enforce their will. In this measure, they have a socially validated sense of personal security. Precisely because of all this, they are expected not to exercise their power to the limit. ("He to whom much is permitted should take least advantage of it.") Unlike the neophyte, insecure in status, the man of established rank can freely depart from the strict norms, particularly when it is not to his advantage to do so. For to insist on the strict letter of the norm would generally be only to insist on his differential advantages of position, just as to depart from the norm is generally to provide greater leeway to the many subordinate to him in station, rank, and esteem. The social structure being what it is, a prig of low rank may be tolerated, if not liked, but a prig of high rank, standing to gain disproportionately by his insistence upon the letter of the norm, will be twice condemned and hated; once, because he does not temper the norm to the exigencies of the situation, and in this he is like others who fail to recognize that norms are only guide-lines, and twice, because he profits by making a virtue of strict conformity. Only when he plainly loses by unqualified conformity to the norms he would enforce upon himself and others, is the man of established rank reluctantly and ambivalently admired. He is then defined as a man of principle, rather than as a self-serving prig.

In all this, the variable of visibility is an indispensable, though sometimes obscured, component. To remove this variable from the shadows of inattention which obscure it, it may be helpful to examine, however briefly, a kind of sociological inquiry which centers upon the ways in which the opinion of "publics" and "constituencies" come to the attention of those in high places. For the attitudes, opinions, sentiments, and expectations of organized groups and of unorganized masses presumably constitute a social frame of reference for action by authoritative persons only as these are known, or are thought to be known, by these persons. In short, it is public opinion as observed and not public opinion as it might in fact be, which variously affects, if it does not determine, the decisions of authorities.

PROBLEM 5.2.

OBSERVABILITY OF PUBLIC OPINION BY DECISION-MAKERS

It has often been remarked that "public opinion" must be an informed opinion if it is to be well-founded, that is, if it is to be oriented to the realities of the situation. This is not under discussion here. Rather, we are concerned with the correlative question of how the social structure provides for those in authoritative positions to become informed about the state of public opinion. For public opinion is significant in affecting the actual course of affairs and in providing a frame of reference for the decisions of authoritative persons largely to the extent that it is observable.

Organized "pressure groups," of course, provide the most conspicuous basis for observability of the ostensible state of opinion. Indeed, the pressure group may be conceived as an organizational device for bringing certain interests, sentiments, and points of view to the attention of influentials, power-holders, and authorities, and for making clear the consequences of nonconformity to these. The operation of pressure groups has been extensively studied,[93] and though much doubtless remains to be learned about the conditions under which they are variously effective, this is not of immediate interest here. Rather, we consider the cloudier question of how various kinds of social machinery make for observability of *unorganized* interests, sentiments, and orientations. It is partly the expressive behavior, partly the instrumental behavior, of large and often unorganized collectivities and the patterned procedures for making this visible to the holders of power which are still poorly understood and require further study.[94]

---

93. A thorough-going review and analysis of these studies is provided by V. O. Key, *Politics, Parties, and Pressure Groups* (New York: Thomas Y. Crowell, 1952, 3d ed.).

94. There is, of course, an ancient tradition of thought dedicated to the problem of how to make the voices of the people heard, particularly in the realm of politics. There is also something of a short tradition of empirical inquiry into this matter, the part with which I am most directly familiar being that developed by the Columbia University Bureau of Applied Social Research. Initially, these studies centered on the communications from audiences directed to those who are dependent on having an audience; *e.g.*, Jeanette Sayre, "Progress in radio fan-mail analysis," *Public Opinion Quarterly*, 1939, 3, 272-278. This was later extended to include systematic analyses of the mail reaching political representatives; *e.g.*, Herta Herzog and Rowena Wyant, "Voting via the senate mailbag," *Public Opinion Quarterly*, 1941, 5, 358-382; 590-624. In 1948, a completed but still-unpublished monograph was devoted to the analysis of a sample of the 20,000 letters, postcards, and telegrams addressed to Dwight D. Eisenhower, largely directed toward urging him to become, in spite of his announced reluctance, a candidate for the presidency of the United States—Robert K. Merton, Leila A. Sussmann, Marie Jahoda and Joan Doris, *Mass Pressure: The 1948 Presidential Draft of Eisenhower*. Leila A. Sussmann is now engaged in a detailed study of the mail addressed to Franklin D. Roosevelt; a part of this study having been published under the title, "FDR and the White House mail," *Public Opinion Quarterly*, 1956, 20, 5-16. See also the papers that follow in the same number of this quarterly under the general title, "Communication to the policy-maker: petition and pressure."

The invention of public opinion polls provided a new and, though imperfect, an increasingly utilized avenue for observability of mass opinion and mass behavior. It would take us far afield to consider this in detail. For pertinent studies of the use of the polls and of other evidence of mass opinion by legislators and public officials, see: Martin Kriesberg, "What Congressmen and administrators think of the polls," *Public Opinion Quarterly*, 1945, 9, 333-337, which reports that a small sample of some fifty senators and representatives held that their access to political sentiments and opinions of the public was primarily through personal mail and, in successively smaller degree, through direct personal contact with their constituency, newspapers, and finally, the polls. See also, Lewis E. Gleeck, "96 Congressmen make up their minds," *Public Opinion Quarterly*, 1940, 4, 3-23; George F. Lewis, Jr. "The Congressmen look at the polls," *Public Opinion Quarterly*, 1940, 4, 229-231. For short-run reactions to the use of polls as a means of gauging public sentiment which followed upon the alleged polling debacle of 1948, see R. K. Merton and Paul K.

Organized social life itself generates motivations for developing social arrangements which will provide a functionally adequate degree of observability. To an appreciable extent, the authoritative strata are motivated to discover the values, norms, interests, and behavior of the other strata in order that their decisions can take these circumstances into account just as, to a certain extent, the rank-and-file are motivated to make their values, norms, interests, and behavior known to the authoritative makers of social policy in order that these will be taken into account. (It is only under special conditions that these strata are motivated to block such observability.) But the motivations are not enough to produce the event. The social organization must provide the machinery which will enable this information to come to the attention of the appropriate authoritative strata.

The social procedures and devices serving this function have historically been most varied. They have ranged from use of the Napoleonic police spy and "public opinion expert," such as Barère, to the contemporary public opinion poll. But though these have varied in organizational character and in specific purpose, they have uniformly had the function of providing authorities with some image of the prevailing "state of opinion." For even when authorities seek to circumvent or to reshape the interests and values of their constituency, to say nothing of the cases in which they aim to act in accord with the expectations of their constituency, it is helpful, if not imperative, to know what these expectations are. Whatever the form of organization—dictatorial or democratic—some substantial degree of observability is a functional requirement. The machinery of observability differs in different social structures, but, in some measure, its functions seem to be universal to group life.

This is not to say, of course, that the function is uniformly and adequately met. Complex social structures have historically struggled along with patently inadequate arrangements for apprising authorities of the feelings and values of their constituency. Often, authorities have had to resort to educated guesses based upon shreds of evidence. Jefferson, for example, observes in his *Autobiography* that the legislators of Virginia had considered a bill which would provide for "a future and general emancipation," but "it was found that the public mind would not yet

---

Hatt, "Election polling forecasts and public images of social science," *Public Opinion Quarterly*, 1949, 13, 185-222.

Stephen K. Bailey and Howard Samuel, *Congress at Work* (New York: Henry Holt and Co., 1952); Stephen K. Bailey, *Congress Makes A Law* (New York: Columbia University Press, 1950); and Morton Grodzins, *Americans Betrayed: Politics and the Japanese Evacuation* (Chicago: University of Chicago Press, 1949) are three impressive analyses of the role of public sentiment in affecting public decisions which provide valuable data on observability of mass opinion.

bear the proposition . . ." Again, Lincoln made a valiant but, in the end, defeated effort to read all the letters addressed to him in the White House that he might know what the people were thinking. Since then, the masses of mail sent to American presidents has increased steadily and shot up to spectacular new heights during the incumbency of Franklin D. Roosevelt.[95]

In the absence of social machinery for detecting the import of a large volume of messages, observability may lessen rather than increase. (Communications theorists have clearly identified the processes through which an excess of messages produces confusion.) The story told by Sandburg of Lincoln's effort to cope with the growing volume of documents directed to him can serve as a sociological parable of an excess of messages:[96]

> The first few months of Lincoln's administration: . . . he read each paper carefully through, remarking, "I never sign a document I have not first read."
> Later: "Won't you read these papers to me?"
> Still later: he requests merely "a synopsis of the contents."
> And, in the fourth year of his incumbency: his most frequent response was "Show me where you want my name."

Apart from formal provision for it, large and complex organizations come to develop the functional equivalent of a continuing plebiscite, partial and not binding in force, which serves, with varying degrees of error, to acquaint the authorities with the wishes of "the membership." Furthermore, as Sussmann points out,[97] mass communications to the authorities perform other functions than that of serving as an (imperfect) index of public sentiment. When judiciously employed, they serve also to strengthen the hand of some authorities in conflict with others. Roosevelt's administration, for example, made masterly use of this organizational weapon. When C.W.A. was ended, more than 50,000 letters and 7,000 telegrams were sent to the White House protesting the decision, and these, in Sherwood's words, "could not possibly be ignored."[98] In the same way, authorities, who in all organizations and not only in political ones, have responsibility for external relations can draw upon the expressed sentiments of their constituency to support their policies

---

95. Sussmann, op. cit., 6-9, summarizes the evidence on volume of mail. As one dramatic example, 450,000 communications reached the White House during Roosevelt's first week in office.

96. Carl Sandburg, Abraham Lincoln: The War Years (New York: Harcourt, Brace & Company, 1939), III, 414.

97. For an instructive summary of the multiple functions of such mass mail, see Sussmann, op. cit. For a critical and programmatic statement of the need for studying public opinion as it is brought "to bear on those who have to act in response" to it, see Herbert Blumer, "Public opinion and public opinion polling," American Sociological Review, 1948, 13, 542-549, and the discussion of this paper by Theodore M. Newcomb and by Julian Woodward, 549-554.

98. Robert E. Sherwood, Roosevelt and Hopkins: An Intimate History (New York: Harper & Brothers, 198), 56.

governing these relations.[99] Finally, this kind of observability provides for *direct* communication with topmost authority without undermining the authority of intermediates.[100]

This quick sketch of patterns of communication which emerge to meet, at least in part, the functional requirement of observability or visibility of course leaves much unsaid. It may, however, underscore the major point, no less important because it is obvious, that reference group theory must systematically incorporate the variable of observability of norms, values, and role-performance obtaining in the groups taken as a frame of reference. Until now, studies of reference group behavior have largely neglected this variable. At best, these studies have included evidence on the perceptions of the norms and values in potential reference groups; they have also, but less often, included the sociological counterpart of the structural arrangements which make for greater or less validity of these perceptions among those variously located in the structure of communication. The two lines of inquiry have been largely developed independently, and it may be one of the uses of reference group theory to bring them together and to consolidate them.

PROBLEM 6.

NONCONFORMITY AS A TYPE OF REFERENCE GROUP BEHAVIOR

At various places in the preceding chapter and in earlier parts of this one, it has been suggested that conformist and nonconformist behavior can be adequately *described*, to say nothing of being adequately *analyzed*, only if this behavior is related to the membership groups and non-membership groups taken as frames of normative and evaluative reference.

For example: ". . . in the vocabulary of sociology, social conformity

---

99. For one among an indefinitely large number of examples, see Sherwood's account of Hopkins's conferences with Stalin after the death of Roosevelt. Hopkins emphasized the important role of "the general state of American opinion" in affecting current foreign policies and went on to assure Stalin "with all the earnestness at his command that this body of American public opinion who had been the constant support of the Roosevelt policies were seriously disturbed about their relations with Russia. In fact, in the last six weeks deterioration of public opinion [how this was assessed is not told] had been so serious as to affect adversely the relations between our two countries. Mr. Hopkins said that it was not simple or easy to put a finger on the precise reasons for this deterioration but he must emphasize that without the support of public opinion and particularly of the supporters of President Roosevelt it would be very difficult for President Truman to carry forward President Roosevelt's policy." *Ibid.*, 888-889.

100. Sussmann, *op. cit.*, 12. "Perhaps the chief reason Roosevelt put such high value on his mail was that he considered it one of his best lines of communication with the 'common people.' He was only too well aware of the biases of the élite-controlled mass media. . . . He was persuaded of the limitations of official information channels. Frances Perkins quotes him as having once told her, '. . . official channels of communication and information are often pretty rigid. . . . People making such studies rarely get near the common people.'"

usually denotes conformity to the norms and expectations current in the individual's *own* membership group. . . . [And, as we have seen] conformity to norms of an out-group is thus equivalent to what is ordinarily called nonconformity, that is, nonconformity to the norms of the in-group." (264) This gives rise, it was pointed out, to "two interrelated questions . . . : what are the consequences, functional and dysfunctional, of positive orientation to the values of a group other than one's own? And further, which social processes initiate, sustain, or curb such orientations?" (265)

Since this was put into print, I have re-examined that seedbed of ideas about what is now called reference group behavior—Chapter 8 of Cooley's *Human Nature and the Social Order*—and have found that, as long ago as 1902, Cooley had conceived of nonconformity in much the same terms. In one of its two principal aspects—the other being what he described as "rebellious impulse or 'contrary suggestion,'" that is, a personality trait of negativism or alienation—nonconformity

may be regarded as a remoter conformity. The rebellion is only partial and apparent; and the one who seems to be out of step with the procession is really keeping time to another music. As Thoreau said, he hears a different drummer. If a boy refuses the occupation his parents and friends think best for him, and persists in working at something strange and fantastic, like art or science, it is sure to be the case that his most vivid life *is not with those about him at all*, but with the masters he has known through books, or perhaps seen and heard for a few moments.

Environment, in the sense of social influence actually at work, is far from the definite and obvious thing it is often assumed to be. Our real environment consists[100a] of those images which are most present to our thoughts, and in the case of a vigorous, growing mind, these are likely to be quite *different from what is most present to the senses. The group to which we give allegiance, and to whose standards we try to conform, is determined by our own selective affinity, choosing among all the personal influences accessible to us; and so far as we select with any independence of our palpable companions, we have the appearance of non-conformity.*

All non-conformity that is affirmative or constructive must *act by this selection of remoter relations;* opposition, by itself, being sterile, and meaning nothing beyond personal peculiarity. There is, therefore, *no definite line between conformity and non-conformity; there is simply a more or less characteristic and unusual way of selecting and combining accessible influences.*[101]

100a. This is plainly an over-statement of the case, sufficiently extreme as to be almost self-correcting. Trying to emphasize the idea, much needed at the time he was writing, that the social environment does not consist *only* of the people with whom one is in direct interaction, Cooley pushes himself to the other, and no more tenable, extreme of asserting that this environment consists of *nothing but images* of other men and standards. A naive objectivism cannot be rectified by an equally naive subjectivism. It is evident from the rest of his writings, however, that Cooley did not in practice subscribe to the literal tenets of the extreme idealism which he expresses in this passage.

101. Charles H. Cooley, *Human Nature and the Social Order* (New York: Charles Scribner's Sons, 1902; reprinted by The Free Press, 1956), 301-302, and the whole of Chapter 8, entitled "Emulation." I have italicized those parts of this passage

Whatever the history of this concept of nonconformity, it now appears that the concept provides a basis for consolidating the theory of "deviant behavior" (partly[102] as this has been set out in Chapters IV and V dealing with anomie) and the theory of reference group behavior. For once nonconformity is conceived as typically being conformity with the values, standards, and expectations of reference individuals and groups, it becomes conceptually distinguished from other forms of deviant behavior. Truly "private" nonconformity, wholly unconnected with past, present, or realistically prospective reference groups, is what psychologists have identified as "autism," capricious thought and action far removed from external reality.[103] It is not private nonconformity but rather public nonconformity which is of interest here.

When nonconformity represents conformity to the values, standards, and practices of an earlier condition of society which are still enduring but not uniformly accepted, it is often described as "conservatism." Pejoratively, and sometimes exactly, it is described as "reactionary,"

which bear most directly upon reference group theory. What Cooley there asserts as fact has since become a series of *problems* being accorded empirical study.

To say that reference group theory is in part a rediscovery of what had long lain fallow in these notable pages by Cooley would be a true reading of the antecedent history of the idea of reference groups. But it would be a mistake to say that reference group theory is *nothing but* such a rediscovery. The circumstance of seminal ideas and hints remaining unproductive until the course of intellectual development has given them new significance is a familiar episode in the history of human thought. Indeed, rediscoveries commonly occur precisely in this form: a cumulation of scientific knowledge results in making clearly relevant ideas and observations long existing in the public print. These have been largely ignored, however, because their relevance was not evident and, in the earlier condition of the discipline, could not easily have been evident to the perhaps wiser but less informed observers of that earlier day. In this reasonably strict sense, these ideas are "before their time." Later, when they can be joined with other ideas and instrumentalities of inquiry which have been developed in the interim, they take on a new significance. This should make it plain that in taking notice of Cooley's long-neglected observations—these pages have not, to my knowledge, been a starting-point for sustained and cumulative inquiry since they first appeared—I do not intend to detract from the accomplishments of present-day social scientists who have been independently developing the theory of reference groups. I do not intend to play the game of the "adumbrationists" by robbing latter-day Peters of their merits in order to pay all due respect to the Pauls of an earlier day. This is intended only to indicate a discontinuity in the development of this theory involving, as we can now see in retrospect, a gap of forty years or more.

102. I do not cite other writings which have lately developed the theory of deviant behavior because these have been examined in some little detail in preceding chapters. It should be said, however, that the chapter devoted to "deviant behavior and the mechanisms of social control" in Parsons's *The Social System* provides one substantial basis for the kind of theoretical consolidation which is being proposed. Indeed, at one point in that chapter (292n.), Parsons makes an anticipatory allusion to "one of several points at which the theory of 'reference groups' becomes of great importance to the analysis of social systems." But such consolidation is not the work of a day, and will require the concerted efforts of many before its seeming prospects can be realized.

103. The place of autistic thinking in the theory of social psychology has been examined by Theodore Newcomb, *Social Psychology*, 101-103; 287-294; 303-310.

particularly when it constitutes an effort to re-introduce values and practices which have been superseded or have simply fallen into neglect. When nonconformity represents conformity to values, standards, and practices which have not yet been institutionalized but are regarded as making up the normative system of future reference groups, it is often described as "radicalism." Pejoratively, and sometimes exactly, it is described as "utopianism," particularly when it is believed to represent a perfect state of society impossible of attainment.[104] But since social and political tags such as these have more than a purely descriptive function, they are seldom used as objective designations but come to be pinned on varied types of nonconformity.

In these terms, reference group theory calls for a sustained distinction among the various kinds of behavior presently described by sociologists as "deviant behavior." What is here being identified as "nonconformity," in its established historical sense, must plainly be distinguished from such other kinds of deviant behavior as (most forms of) crime and delinquency. These kinds of "deviant behavior" differ structurally, culturally, and functionally.[104a] It cannot be assumed, therefore, that they are all *adequately* caught up in a single concept of "deviant behavior"; this is a matter for inquiry, not for assumption.

At first appearance, the behavior of the nonconformist and of the criminal may seem to be structurally the same. In both cases, they are not living up to the morally-rooted expectations of the others with whom they are engaged in a system of interlocking statuses and roles. In both cases, also, others in the social system will act in such ways as to try to bring the behavior of the "deviants" back into accord with established expectations. Whatever differences may exist between the two are often obscured since the nonconformist is not infrequently declared to be a criminal. Nevertheless, underlying these surface similarities are profound differences.

In the first place, the nonconformist does not, like the criminal, try to hide his departures from the prevailing norms of the group. Instead, he announces his dissent. This links up with a second difference: the nonconformist challenges the legitimacy of the norms and expectations he rejects or at least challenges their applicability to certain situations; the criminal generally acknowledges their legitimacy. Generally, he does

---

104. Compare the account of ideological and utopian mentalities by Karl Mannheim, *Ideology and Utopia* (New York: Harcourt, Brace and Company, 1936), esp. 173-237.

104a. The differences have been indicated in the fifth type of adaptation to anomie identified in the paradigm set out in Chapter IV, which indicates that both reigning cultural goals and institutional means are repudiated, and *supplanted by* new values which are shared and accorded legitimacy. (Pages 140, 155-57). For a further discussion of this latter type of "deviant behavior," see Katherine Organski, *Change in Tribal South Africa* (unpublished doctoral dissertation, Columbia University, Department of Sociology, 1956).

not argue that theft is right and murder, virtuous. He simply finds it expedient or expressive of his state of mind to violate the norms and to evade them. Thirdly, and correlatively, the nonconformist aims to change the norms of the group, to supplant what he takes to be morally illegitimate norms with norms having an alternative moral basis. The criminal, in contrast, tries only to escape the force of the norms now existing. The nonconformist typically appeals to a "higher morality"; except as an expedient for self-defense, the criminal appeals to extenuating circumstances. Finally, and crucially, the nonconformist is, however reluctantly and subconsciously, assumed to depart from prevailing norms for wholly or largely disinterested purposes; the criminal is assumed to deviate from the norms in order to serve his own interests. The preceding characteristics of the two tend to bear out these distinct assumptions. Knowing the punitive consequences which his public behavior will call into play, the nonconformist nevertheless acts in accord with his sentiments and values; knowing the consequences of his action, the criminal makes every effort to evade them by concealing his deviations from public view.

In the cultural realm, as well, the nonconformist and the criminal differ basically (even, it should be repeated, when the society, as a nearly last resort of social control, tags the nonconformist as "nothing more" than a criminal. For, public definitions and appearances notwithstanding, it is widely felt that the nonconformist, of political, religious, or ethical persuasion, is in fact considerably more than a mere criminal.) In terms of sociological theory, the differences between the cultural plane and the plane of social structure (to which we have referred in the preceding paragraphs) are fundamental, even though they may be obscured by the fact that the *same* historical complexes of behavior have implications for *both*. Without going into detail in this matter, for that would take us even farther afield, we can at least point to the different levels of analysis which these represent.

On the plane of social structure, nonconformist and other deviant behavior activates mechanisms of social control on the part of those involved in interlocking networks of social status and social role with the "deviant." His failure to live up to the expectations of those with whom he is in *direct* relationship constitutes a punitive experience for them, and they in turn respond by penalizing him for his departures from the established role-expectations. In an important sense, then, the role-partners of the deviant tend to behave in terms of their *own interests;* the deviant makes life miserable or difficult for them, and they try to bring him back into line, with the result that they can go about their normal business of life.

On the cultural plane, this same behavior on the part of the "orthodox" members of the social system occurs, even when they are *not directly* engaged in a system of social relations with the deviant. Their hostile reaction to the deviant is, in this fairly strict sense, *disinterested*. They have nothing or little to lose by his departure from established norms and role-expectations; their own situation is not, in fact, appreciably damaged by his "misbehavior." Nevertheless, they too respond with hostility, since they have internalized the moral norms now being violated and experience the behavior which in effect repudiates these norms, or threatens their continued social validity, as a denial of the worth of what they, and their groups, hold dear. The form which such reprisals take is best described as "moral indignation," a disinterested attack on those who depart from the norms of the group, even when such departures do not interfere with the performance of one's own roles, since one is not directly socially related to the deviant.[105]

Were it not for this reservoir of moral indignation, the mechanisms of social control would be severely limited in their operation. They would be confined only to the action of people who are *directly* disadvantaged by nonconformist and deviant behavior. In actual fact, however, moral indignation and disinterested opposition to nonconformity and deviant behavior serve to lend greater strength to the mechanisms of social control, for not only the relatively small number of people directly injured by deviance—for example, the parents of the kidnapped child—but also the larger collectivity, adhering to the culturally established norms, are activated to bring the deviant (and, by anticipation, other prospective deviants) back into line.

On the cultural plane, the nonconformist, with his appeal to a higher

---

105. The functional rationale of moral indignation was classically stated, albeit in the archaic vocabulary of Natural Law, by Hobbes in Chapter XV of the *Leviathan*. As a reminder: "Again, the Injustice of Manners, is the disposition, or aptitude to do Injurie; and is Injustice before it proceed to Act; and without supposing any individuall person injured. But the Injustice of an Action, (that is to say Injury), supposeth an individuall person Injured; namely him, to whom the Covenant was made: And therefore many times the injury is received by one man, when the dammage redoundeth to another. As when the Master commandeth his servant to give mony to a stranger; if it be not done, the Injury is done to the Master, whom he had before Covenanted to obey; but the dammage redoundeth to the stranger, to whom he had no Obligation; and therefore could not Injure him. And so also in Commonwealths, private men may remit to one another their debts; but not robberies or other violences, whereby they are endammaged; because the detaining of Debt, is an injury to themselves; but Robbery and Violence, are Injuries to the Person of the Common-wealth." This is the case for disinterested objection to violation of norms. Although it is, by the author's own testimony, only a bare beginning of investigation into this matter, in more recent times, the *locus classicus* of the theory of moral indignation is Svend Ranulf, *Moral Indignation and Middle Class Psychology* (Copenhagen: Levin & Munksgaard, 1938). As Ranulf makes abundantly plain, his own work derives, in direct sociological descent, from the fundamental theory about the workings of moral indignation advanced, in the most influential if not the first instance, by Emile Durkheim. The earlier monograph on this subject by Ranulf should also be consulted: *The Jealousy of the Gods and Criminal Law at Athens: A Contribution to the Sociology of Moral Indignation* (Copenhagen: Levin & Munksgaard; London: Williams & Norgate Ltd, 1933). 2 vols.

morality, can, in historically propitious circumstances and unlike the mere delinquent, draw upon the latent store of moral indignation. In some measure, his nonconformity appeals either to the moral values of an earlier day which have been lost to view or to moral values of a time which will come to pass. It thus has the prospect, if not always the reality, of obtaining the assent of other, initially less courageous and venturesome members of society. His nonconformity is not a private dereliction, but a thrust toward a new morality (or a restoration of an old and almost forgotten morality). He appeals, in short, to a past or future reference group. He re-activates a forgotten set of values, stand- ards, and practices, or activates a set which is not blemished by existing concessions and expedient compromises with current realities. In all this, the nonconformist is far removed from the orthodox criminal who has nothing old to restore and nothing new to suggest, but seeks only to satisfy his private interests or to express his private sentiments. Although the law of the land may not always make the distinction, in terms of cultural dynamics, the nonconformist and the run-of-the-household criminal are poles apart.

What has been briefly said about the cultural and social-structural planes of criminal behavior and nonconformity does not, of course, tell the whole story. But it may suffice for immediate purposes. Both kinds of departures from norms of the group can be and have been described as "deviant behavior"—and in a first loose approximation, this is not mistaken—but, on the planes of social structure and of culture, they are, in a more exacting approximation, nevertheless distinct. It may now be suggested that they characteristically differ also on the plane of per- sonality. To be sure, the personalities of those who head up historically significant movements of nonconformity *may* on occasion bear more than a passing resemblance to the personalities of those engaged in self- interested petty and major crime. But to emphasize these occasional and superficial similarities at the expense of characteristic and deep-seated differences would be to declare the intellectual bankruptcy of academic psychology. Whatever psychology may seem to pronounce to the con- trary, those courageous highwaymen of seventeenth-century England, John Nevinson and his much-advertised successor, Dick Turpin, were not of a piece with that courageous nonconformist, Oliver Cromwell. And if one's political or religious sympathies serve to make this self- evident and not needing statement, one should re-examine those his- torical judgments which would make of Trotsky or of Nehru little more than criminals with sizable followings.

It is possible that the unconscious motivations of some nonconform- ists resemble those of mere criminals. In both instances, behavior may be compulsive, designed to expiate a personal sense of sin. Violation of existing norms may serve to legitimize the guilty act by sharing it with others. Nevertheless, since the social norms which are being violated are functionally quite distinct, in the cases of the nonconformist and of the criminal, the psychological meaning of the violation is also different. Just as the conceptual scheme of sociology may, in a first approximation, be so gross as to couple, without distinction, nonconformity with established but morally suspect norms and deviation from unquestioned norms, so the conceptual scheme of psychology, with its ideas of guilt, defense mechanisms, reaction formation, and the like, may blur basic differences by consigning socially disparate behaviors to the same motivational bin. This, admittedly, is to state the issue, rather than to resolve it. But it may have the theoretical merit of reminding us that, in the search for generalizations about human behavior, we are not infrequently apt to submerge or to neglect behaviorally significant differences. To do this is to indulge in the intellectually questionable practice of reductionism. It is to indulge oneself in the fallacy of assuming, as William James unforgettably described it, that "a Beethoven string-quartet is truly . . . a scraping of horses' tails on cats' bowels, and may be exhaustively described in such terms. . . ."[106]

The historically significant nonconformist is, in terms of social structure, culture, and personality, a distinct type of social deviant. Following the ancient adage that "the nature of anything is best known from the examination of extreme cases," we should take note of the extreme nonconformist who enters upon his public course of nonconformity with full knowledge that he runs the risk, so high a risk as to be almost a certainty, of severe punishment for his behavior by the group. This kind of man is, in the fairly strict sense, a martyr—that is, one who sacrifices self for principle. Adhering to the norms and values of some reference group other than the group to whose expectations he will not conform, he is

---

106. William James, *The Will to Believe* (New York: Longmans, Green, and Co., 1937), 76. Or, as James has put the theoretical issue in more general terms, it is to engage in "vicious abstractionism: a way of using concepts which may be thus described: We conceive a concrete situation by singling out some salient or important feature in it, and classing it under that; then, instead of adding to its previous characters all the positive consequences which the new way of conceiving it may bring, we proceed to use our concept privatively; reducing the originally rich phenomenon to the naked suggestions of that name abstractly taken, treating it as a case of 'nothing but' that concept, and acting as if all the other characters from out of which the concept is abstracted were expunged. Abstraction, functioning in this way, becomes a means of arrest far more than a means of advance in thought. It mutilates things; it creates difficulties and finds impossibilities; and more than half the trouble that metaphysicians and logicians give themselves over the paradoxes and dialectic puzzles of the universe may, I am convinced, be traced to this relatively simple source. *The viciously privative employment of abstract characters and class names* is, I am persuaded, one of the great original sins of the rationalistic mind." As sociologists and psychologists have ample occasion to know, this source of trouble is not confined to the metaphysicians and logicians. William James, *The Meaning of Truth: A Sequel to "Pragmatism,"* (New York: Longmans, Green, and Co., 1932), 249-250.

prepared to accept, if not to welcome,[107] the almost certain and painful consequences of dissent.

The *psychological* sources of the martyr's behavior are one thing; its *sociological* character is something else. The motives of the martyr may be any among a wide variety: an expression of primary narcissism, a need for punishment, a wish for active mastery of a seemingly intransigent outer reality in behalf of loved ones.[108] All this is as it may be. Within the social context, however, this type of nonconformity uniformly involves public repudiation of certain established values and practices and adherence to alternative values and practices at the price of almost inevitable punishment being inflicted on oneself by others. Functionally, such nonconformity can serve to institute social and cultural change. In this connection, it should be noted that the reactions of others to this kind of nonconformist are apt to be more complex than an outer appearance of unalloyed hostility might suggest.

The avowed nonconformist tends to be regarded with mingled feelings of hate, admiration, and love, even by those who still cling to the values and practices being put in question. Acting openly rather than

---

107. Should he give signs of actually welcoming the punitive consequences, however, he is apt to be contemptuously described as trying "to make a martyr of himself." Common long before the advent of Freud, this phrasing reflects popular recognition of the possibility that ostensibly disinterested subjection of self to punishment by others may turn out, upon further analysis, to be either self-serving or responsive to a "pathological" psychological need. Only in special institutional circumstances, does masochism enjoy the respect of others. In such socially patterned and often ritually enjoined circumstances, the masochistic character can be admirably suited to the effective performance of the social role. But generally, to make a public virtue of a private necessity is to be judged guilty of a double misdemeanor: for this claims reward for seemingly disinterested but actually self-centered action, and it disrupts the mutual trust required in a stable society by casting doubt on the moral validity of actually disinterested conduct by others.

108. The vocabulary of motivation, it is widely agreed, leaves much to be desired. These remarks should not be construed into the idea that "motives" *are* separate impulses, each of which "produces" its distinctive form of behavior. Even without the benefit of a systematic psychological theory, Cooley had some general thoughts on this matter which are, if anything, more apt today than when he set them out, two generations ago. For example: "The egoism-altruism way of speaking falsifies the facts at the most vital point possible by assuming that our impulses relating to persons are separable into two classes, the I impulses and the You impulses, in much the same way that physical persons are separable; whereas a primary fact throughout the range of sentiment is a fusion of persons, so that the impulse belongs not to one or the other, but precisely to the common ground that both occupy, to their intercourse or mingling." Again: ". . . 'altruistic' is used to imply something more than kindly or benevolent, some radical psychological or moral distinction between this sentiment or class of sentiments and others called egoistic, and this distinction appears not to exist. All social sentiments are altruistic in the sense that they involve reference to another person; few are so in the sense that they exclude the self. The idea of a division on this line appears to flow from a vague presumption that personal ideas must have a separateness answering to that of material bodies." Cooley, *Human Nature and the Social Order*, 128, 129-130. It might be said that when Comte coined the term "altruism" and defined it as he did, he helped create the kind of fallacy which Cooley tried to counteract.

secretively, and evidently aware that he invites severe sanctions by the group, the nonconformist tends to elicit some measure of respect, although this may be buried in thick layers of overt hostility and hatred among those who have a sense that their sentiments, their interests, and their status are threatened by the words and actions of the nonconformist. The positive component of the ambivalence is the tribute paid to disinterested conduct. The nonconformist is felt to have courage, that is to say, a demonstrated capacity to run large risks, especially for disinterested purposes.[109] In some degree, courage (though perhaps of a lesser degree) is felt to be exhibited when men run large risks even for private self-interested or alien purposes, as in the familiar case of the "daring criminal" or the "courageous enemy" who are, in this degree, admired even as they are condemned. For since courage is potentially a social virtue—that is, functional for the persistence and development of groups in accord with ultimate values—it elicits respect, even in those complex instances where it is apparently being used, not for the group, but against it.

Even this short review of the matter may serve to clarify functional differences between the two kinds of deviant behavior. Under certain conditions, public nonconformity can have the manifest and latent functions of changing standards of conduct and values which have become dysfunctional for the group. Other, private forms of deviant behavior have the manifest function of serving the interests of the deviant and, under conditions which have been partly identified by Durkheim, George Mead and Radcliffe-Brown, the latent function of re-activating sentiments of the group which have grown so weak as no longer to be effective regulators of behavior. To lump together these functionally (and not only morally) different forms of conduct in the one concept of "deviant behavior" is to obscure their sociological import. After all, it seems safe to suppose that, unlike John Brown's, Al Capone's soul will not go marching on. Or again: Eugene V. Debs and Albert B. Fall, Harding's

---

109. Instances of this can of course be multiplied almost without number. Consider only the case of John Brown, that traitor, murderer and courageous fanatic willing to die in the cause of freedom as he saw that cause. In the estimate of Carl Sandburg, "Brown had been so calmly and religiously glad to be hanged publicly, before all men and nations, that he could not be dismissed lightly from the thoughts of men." And so, the governor of the state which, after a fair trial had him hanged, had this to say: "Brown is a bundle of the best nerves I ever saw, cut and thrust, bleeding and in bonds. He is a man of clear head, of courage, fortitude. He is a fanatic, vain and garrulous, but firm and truthful and intelligent.'" So far as "deviant behavior" is that which the norms and standards of society would have it so, plainly the social definition of Brown's terrifying crimes differs from those many others who were *only* horse thieves. In his account of this great act of nonconformity, Carl Sandburg is both historian and spokesman for American culture: *Abraham Lincoln: The Prairie Years* (New York: Harcourt, Brace & Company, 1926), II, 188-195.

Secretary of the Interior of Teapot Dome notoriety who proved unable to hold a firm grip on the public purse, were both clapped into jail under the laws of American society because they had engaged in "deviant behavior." Yet Harding, the exponent of normalcy, found it possible to release the nonconformist Debs from prison by a belated act of executive clemency, whereas Coolidge, pledged to extend the region of normalcy, did not find it possible to release the deviant Fall.

Unless the distinction between types of nonconformist and deviant behavior is maintained, conceptually and terminologically, sociology will by inadvertence continue on the path it has sometimes begun to tread and become that science of society which implicitly sees virtue only in social conformity. If sociology does not systematically develop the distinctions between the social structure and functions of these diverse forms of deviant behavior, it will in effect—though not, I believe, deliberately—place a premium on the value to the group of conformity to its prevailing standards and to imply that nonconformity is necessarily dysfunctional to the group.[110] Yet, as has been emphasized at several places in this book, it is not infrequently the case that the nonconforming minority in a society represents the interests and ultimate values of the group more effectively than the conforming majority.[111] This, it

---

110. The American cultural value of the right to dissent is too deeply established for it to have no controlling effect upon behavior, even under conditions of stress. In terms of the sociology of knowledge, which sees intellectual work as variously responsive to underlying social conditions, there is special significance in a major empirical study of forces making for acceptance, rejection, and support of political and other nonconformists—Samuel A. Stouffer, *Communism, Conformity, and Civil Liberties* (New York: Doubleday & Company, 1955). This study proceeds from the assumption that these types of nonconformity differ significantly from other types of deviant behavior. Moreover, it is addressed to the problem of uncovering the bases of acceptance and rejection of nonconformists, a problem which has only been touched upon in the foregoing pages.

Also much in point is a recent sociological experiment focused on the correlative problem of conditions under which social conformity is dysfunctional to selected purposes of the group. See Harold H. Kelley and Martin M. Shapiro, "An experiment on conformity to group norms where conformity is detrimental to group achievement," *American Sociological Review*, 1954, 19, 667-677.

111. See that remarkable account of public nonconformity in the history of the United States Senate written by Senator John F. Kennedy—*Profiles in Courage: Decisive Moments in the Lives of Celebrated Americans* (New York: Harper & Brothers, 1955). This is a record of eight senators who refused to conform to prevailing expectations in spite of the extreme pressures exerted upon them—pressures involving a fatal risk to their political careers, defamation of their character, and repudiation by their constituents. Oriented to reference groups other than those then in power, these men could feel that their reputation and their principles would be later vindicated and their nonconformity appreciated. This compact and detailed record of "hard and unpopular decisions" is, among other things, instructive for a further development of a theory of nonconformity as part of a wider theory of reference group behavior. It provides valuable clinical information on the use of social pressures in advance of the anticipated act of nonconformity, the multiple reference groups involved in a basic public decision, the structural fact of maximum ob-

should be repeated, is not a moral but a functional judgment, not a statement in ethical theory but a statement in sociological theory. It is a statement, finally, which once made, will probably be accepted by the same social observers who, by using an insufficiently differentiated concept of "deviant behavior," deny in their sociological analysis what they affirm in their ethical precepts.

Problem 7.

The structural context of reference group behavior: role-sets, status-sets, and status-sequences

Having examined the workings of *observability* and diverse types of nonconformity and deviance in the process of reference group behavior, we have now to examine the social structure of roles and statuses which provides the context for reference group behavior. This is no small task and, as in preceding sections of this chapter, we shall do little more than sketch out a way of thinking about this matter and consider the problems which this generates for further inquiry. This requires us to consider and to develop somewhat the theory of social roles and social status.

For some time now, at least since the influential writings of Ralph Linton on the subject, it has been recognized that two concepts—social status and social role—are fundamental to the description, and to the analysis, of a social structure.[112]

By status Linton meant a position in a social system occupied by designated individuals; by role, the behavioral enacting of the patterned expectations attributed to that position. Status and role, in these terms, are concepts serving to connect the culturally defined expectations with the patterned behavior and relationships which comprise social structure. Linton went on to observe that each person in society inevitably occupies multiple statuses and that, for each of these statuses, there is *an* associated role.[113] This proved to be a useful first approximation, as later

---

servability which confronts such public figures as Senators, the complications resulting from unclear and imperfect definitions of role-obligations, the structural fact that the observability of constituency-opinion is slight and thus provides room for autonomous decision, the patterning of motivation for overt conformity whatever the covert opinion of the public man, the sense in which posterity can in fact be taken as a significant reference group, and the multiple values which can put personal security, popular esteem, and the preservation of public relations in a place second to the value of autonomous belief. It is, in short, a book of singular importance to social scientists interested in the theory of reference group behavior.

112. To say that Linton was not "the first" to introduce these twin concepts into social science would be as true as it is irrelevant. For the fact is that it was only after his famous Chapter VIII in *The Study of Man* (New York: Appleton-Century, 1936) that these concepts, and their implications, became systematically incorporated into a developing theory of social structure.

113. Cf. *ibid.*, and particularly, Linton's later work which, it might be suggested, has apparently not been accorded the notice it deserves: *The Cultural Background of Personality* (New York: Appleton-Century, 1945), esp. 76 ff.

social research amply testifies. In this first approximation, however, Linton assumed that each status has *its distinctive role*.[114]

Without engaging in heavier deliberation than the subject deserves, we must note that a particular social status involves, not a single associated role, but an array of associated roles. This is a basic characteristic of social structure. This fact of structure can be registered by a distinctive term, *role-set*, by which I mean that *complement of role relationships which persons have by virtue of occupying a particular social status.* As one example: the single status of medical student entails not only the role of a student in relation to his teachers, but also an array of other roles relating the occupant of that status to other students, nurses, physicians, social workers, medical technicians, etc.[115] Again: the status of public school teacher has its distinctive role-set, relating the teacher to his pupils, to colleagues, the school principal and superintendent, the Board of Education, and, on frequent occasion, to local patriotic organizations, to professional organizations of teachers, Parent-Teachers Associations, and the like.

It should be plain that the role-set differs from the structural pattern which has long been identified by sociologists as that of "multiple roles." For in the established usage, multiple roles refer to the complex of roles associated, not with a *single* social status, but with the *various* statuses (often, in differing institutional spheres) in which individuals find themselves—the roles, for example, connected with the distinct statuses of teacher, wife, mother, Catholic, Republican, and so on. We designate

114. As one among many instances of this conception, see Linton's observation that "a particular status within a social system can be occupied, and *its associated rôle* known and exercised, by a number of individuals simultaneously." *The Cultural Background of Personality*, 77. On occasion, Linton did make passing mention of "roles connected with the . . . status," but did not work out the structural implications of multiple roles being associated with a single status. *The Study of Man*, 127, provides one such statement.

Theodore Newcomb has clearly seen that each position in a system of roles involves multiple role-relations. *Social Psychology*, 285-286.

115. For a preliminary analysis of the role-set of the medical student which is of direct import for reference group theory, see Mary Jean Huntington, "The development of a professional self-image," in R. K. Merton, P. L. Kendall and G. G. Reader (editors), *The Student-Physician: Introductory Studies in the Sociology of Medical Education* (Cambridge: Harvard University Press, 1957), this being part of the studies conducted by the Columbia University Bureau of Applied Social Research under a grant from the Commonwealth Fund. Also, Merton, in Witmer and Kotinsky, *op. cit.*, 47-50. Hans L. Zetterberg, *An Action Theory* (*ms.*) takes up these concepts and associated problems in Chapter V.

As in other fields, the cumulation of theory in sociology presses for the development of concepts in determinate directions. This is at least illustrated by the development of concepts similar to those of role-set, status-set and status-sequences, though with differing terminology, in a paper by Frederick L. Bates, "Position, role, and status: a reformulation of concepts," *Social Forces*, 1956, 34, 313-321. Theoretically compatible ideas have also been developed by Neal Gross, in his forthcoming study of school executives.

this complement of social statuses of an individual as his *status-set,* each of the statuses in turn having its distinctive role-set.

The concepts of role-set and of status-set are structural and refer to parts of the social structure *at a particular time.* Considered as changing in the course of time, the succession of statuses occurring with sufficient frequency as to be socially patterned will be designated as a *status-sequence,* as in the case, for example, of the statuses successively occupied by a medical student, intern, resident, and independent medical practitioner. In much the same sense, of course, we can observe *sequences of role-sets and status-sets.*

The patterned arrangements of role-sets, status-sets and status-sequences can be held to comprise the social structure. The concepts remind us, in the unlikely event that we need to be reminded of this insistent and obstinate fact, that even the seemingly simple social structure is extremely complex. For operating social structures must somehow manage to organize these sets and sequences of statuses and roles so that an appreciable degree of social order obtains, sufficient to enable most of the people most of the time to go about their business of social life without having to improvise adjustments anew in each newly confronted situation.

The concepts serve further to help us identify some of the substantive problems of social structure which require analysis. Which social processes tend to make for disturbance or disruption of the role-set, creating conditions of structural instability? Through which social mechanisms do the roles in the role-set become articulated so that conflict among them becomes less than it would otherwise be?

PROBLEM 7.1.

STRUCTURAL SOURCES OF INSTABILITY IN THE ROLE-SET

It would seem that the basic source of disturbance in the role-set is the structural circumstance that any one occupying a particular status has role-partners who are differently located in the social structure. As a result, these others have, in some measure, values and moral expectations differing from those held by the occupant of the status in question. The fact, for example, that the members of a school board are often in social and economic strata quite different from that of the public school teacher will mean that, in certain respects, their values and expectations differ from those of the teacher. The individual teacher may thus be readily subject to conflicting role-expectations among his professional colleagues and among the influential members of the school board and, at times, derivatively, of the superintendent of schools. What is an educational frill for the one may be judged as an essential of education by the other. These disparate and inconsistent evaluations complicate the task of coming to terms with them all. What holds conspicuously for the status of the teacher holds, in varying degree, for the occupants of other statuses who are structurally related, in their role-set, to others who themselves occupy diverse statuses.

As things now stand, this appears to be the major structural basis for potential disturbance of a stable role-set. The question does not arise, of course, in those special circumstances in which all those in the role-set have the same values and same role-expectations. But this is a special and, perhaps historically rare, situation. More often, it would seem, and particularly in highly differentiated societies, the role-partners are drawn from diverse social statuses with, to some degree, correspondingly different social values. To the extent that this obtains, the characteristic situation should be one of disorder, rather than of relative order. And yet, although historical societies vary in the extent to which this is true, it seems generally the case that a substantial degree of order rather than of acute disorder prevails. This, then, gives rise to the problem of identifying the social mechanisms through which some reasonable degree of articulation among the roles in role-sets is secured or, correlatively, the social mechanisms which break down so that structurally established role-sets do not remain relatively stabilized.

PROBLEM 7.2.

SOCIAL MECHANISMS FOR THE ARTICULATION OF ROLES IN THE ROLE-SET

Before beginning to examine some of these mechanisms, we should reiterate that it is not being assumed that, as a matter of historical fact, all role-sets do operate with substantial efficiency. We are concerned, not with a broad historical generalization that social order prevails but with the analytical problem of identifying the social mechanisms which operate to produce a greater degree of social order than would obtain, if these mechanisms were not called into play. Otherwise put, it is sociology, not history, which is of immediate interest here.

1. *The mechanism of differing intensity of role-involvement among those in the role-set:* Role-partners are variously concerned with the behavior of those in a particular social status. This means that the role-expectations of those in the role-set are not maintained with the same degree of intensity. For some, this role-relationship may be of only peripheral concern; for others, it may be central. As an hypothetical example: the parents of children in a public school may be more directly engaged in appraising and controlling the behavior of teachers than, say, the members of a local patriotic organization who have no children in the school. The values of the parents and of the patriotic organization may be at odds in numerous respects and may call for quite different behavior on the part of the teacher. But if the expectations of the one group in the role-set of the teacher are central to their concerns and interests, and the expectations of the other group, only peripheral, this

eases the problem of the teacher seeking to come to terms with these disparate expectations.

We have noted before, in the listing of structural properties of groups, that there is patterned variation in the scope and intensity of involvement of group members in their statuses and roles. Such variation serves to cushion the disturbance to a role-set involving conflicting expectations of the behavior of those occupying a particular status. The teacher, for whom this status holds primary significance, is in this degree better able to withstand the demands for conformity with the differing expectations of those in his role-set for whom this relationship has only peripheral significance. This is not to say, of course, that teachers are not vulnerable to these expectations which are at odds with their professional commitments. It is only to say that they are less vulnerable than they would otherwise be (or sometimes are) when the powerful members of their role-set are only little concerned with this particular relationship. Were all those involved in the role-set of the teacher *equally* concerned with this relationship, the plight of the teacher would be considerably more sorrowful than it presently is. What holds for the particular case of the teacher presumably holds for the occupants of any other status: the impact upon them of diverse expectations of appropriate behavior among those in their role-set can be structurally mitigated by differentials of involvement in the relationship among those constituting their role-set.

All this is to say that the workings of each role-set under observation need to be examined in terms of the mechanisms making for differing degrees of involvement in the role-relationship among the diverse people making up the role-set.

2. *The mechanism of differences in the power of those involved in a role-set:* A second mechanism which affects the stability of a role-set is potentially provided by the distribution of power. By power, in this connection, is meant nothing more than the observed and predictable capacity for imposing one's own will in a social action, even against the resistance of others taking part in that action.[116]

The members of a role-set are not apt to be equally powerful in shaping the behavior of occupants of a particular status. However, it does not follow that the individual, group, or stratum in the role-set which is *separately* most powerful uniformly succeeds in imposing its expectations upon the status-occupants—say, the teacher. This would be so only in the circumstance when the one member of the role-set has an effective monopoly of power, either to the exclusion of all others or outweighing the combined power of the others. Failing this special situa-

---

116. This will be recognized as Max Weber's conception of power, and one not far removed from other contemporary versions of the concept. *From Max Weber: Essays in Sociology,* 180 ff.

tion, the individuals subject to conflicting expectations among the members of their role-set can effect, deliberately or unwittingly, *coalitions of power* among them which enable these individuals to go their own way. The conflict is then not so much between the status-occupants and the diverse members of their role-set as between the members of the role-set itself. The counterpoise to any one powerful member of the role-set is at times provided by a coalition of lesser powers in combination. The familiar pattern of "balance of power" is not confined to power struggles among nations; in less easily visible form, it can be found in the workings of role-sets generally, as the child who succeeds in having his father's decision offset his mother's contrasting decision has ample occasion to know. When conflicting powers in the role-set neutralize one another, the status-occupant has relative freedom to proceed as he intended in the first place.

Thus, even in those potentially unstable structures in which the members of a role-set hold distinct and contrasting expectations of what the status-occupant should do, the latter is not wholly at the mercy of the most powerful among them. Moreover, a high degree of involvement in his status reinforces his relative power. For to the extent that powerful members of his role-set are not primarily concerned with this particular relationship in the same degree as the status-occupant, they will not be motivated to exercise their potential power to the full. Within wide margins of his role-activity, the status-occupant will then be free to act, uncontrolled because unnoticed.

This does not mean, of course, that the status-occupant subject to conflicting expectations[117] among members of his role-set is in fact im-

---

117. In a sprightly and informed lecture, William G. Carr, the executive secretary of the National Education Association, has summarized some of the conflicting pressures exerted upon school curricula by voluntary organizations, such as the American Legion, the Association for the United Nations, the National Safety Council, the Better Business Bureau, the American Federation of Labor, and the Daughters of the American Revolution. His summary may serve through concrete example to indicate the extent of competing expectations among those in the complex role-set of school superintendents and local school boards in as differentiated a society as our own. Sometimes, Mr. Carr reports, these voluntary organizations "speak their collective opinions temperately, sometimes scurrilously, but always insistently. They organize contests, drives, collections, exhibits, special days, special weeks, and anniversaries that run all year long.

"They demand that the public schools give more attention to Little League baseball, first aid, mental hygiene, speech correction, Spanish in the first grade, military preparedness, international understanding, modern music, world history, American history, and local history, geography and homemaking, Canada and South America, the Arabs and the Israeli, the Turks and the Greeks, Christopher Columbus and Leif Ericsson, Robert E. Lee and Woodrow Wilson, nutrition, care of the teeth, free enterprise, labor relations, cancer prevention, human relationships, atomic energy, the use of firearms, the Constitution, tobacco, temperance, kindness to animals, Esperanto, the 3 R's, the 3 C's and the 4 F's, use of the typewriter and legible penmanship, moral values, physical fitness, ethical concepts, civil defense, religious literacy, thrift, law observance, consumer education, narcotics, mathematics, dramatics, physics, ceramics, and (that latest of all educational discoveries) phonics.

mune to control by them. It is only to say that the power-structure of role-sets is often such that the status-occupant more nearly has autonomy than would be the case if this structure of competing powers did not obtain.

3. *The mechanism of insulating role-activities from observability by members of the role-set:* The occupant of a status does not engage in continuous interaction with all those in his role-set. This is not an incidental fact, but is integral to the operation of role-sets. The interaction with each member (individual or groups) of the role-set is variously limited and intermittent; it is not equally sustained throughout the range of relationships entailed by the social status. This fundamental fact of role-structure allows for role-behavior which is at odds with the expectations of some in the role-set to proceed without undue stress. For, as we have seen at some length, effective social control presupposes an appreciable degree of *observability* of role-behavior. To the extent that the role-structure insulates the status-occupant from direct observation by some of his role-set, he is not uniformly subject to competing pressures. It should be emphasized that we are dealing here with a fact of social structure, not with individual adjustments whereby this or that person *happens* to conceal parts of his role-behavior from certain members of his role-set.

The structural fact is that social statuses differ in the extent to which some of the associated role-behavior is insulated from ready observability by all members of the role-set. Variations in this structurally imposed attribute of social statuses accordingly complicate the problem of coping with the disparate expectations of those in the role-set. Thus, occupants of all occupational statuses sometimes face difficult decisions which involve their sense of personal integrity, *i.e.* of living up to the norms and standards basically governing the performance of their occupational role. But these statuses differ in the extent of ready observability of occupational behavior. As Senator Kennedy notes, in that book to which we have made admiring reference, few, if any, occupations face such difficult decisions "in the glare of the spotlight as do those in public office. Few, if any, face the same dread finality of decision that confronts a Senator facing an important call of the roll."[118]

In contrast, other social statuses have a functionally significant in-

---

"Each of these groups is anxious to avoid overloading the curriculum. All any of them ask is that the nonessentials be dropped in order to get their material in. Most of them insist that they do not want a special course—they just want their ideas to permeate the entire daily program. Every one of them proclaims a firm belief in local control of education and an apprehensive hatred of national control.

"Nevertheless, if their national organization program in education is not adopted forthwith, many of them use the pressure of the press, the radiance of the radio, and all the props of propaganda to bypass their elected local school board." An address at the inauguration of Hollis Leland Caswell, Teachers College, Columbia University, November 21-22, 1955, 10.

118. Kennedy, *op. cit.*, 8.

sulation from easy observability by some of those in the role-set. The status of the university teacher provides one example. The norm which holds that what is said in the class-rooms of universities is privileged, in the sense of being restricted to the professor and his students, has this function of maintaining a degree of autonomy for the teacher. For if this were uniformly made available to all those comprising the role-set of the teacher, he might be driven to teach not what he knows or what the evidence leads him to believe, but what will placate the numerous and diverse expectations of all those concerned with "the education of youth." This would soon serve to lower the level of instruction to the lowest common denominator. It would be to transform teaching and place it on the plane of the television show, concerned to do whatever is needed to improve its popularity rating. It is, of course, this exemption from observability from all and sundry who may wish to impose their will upon the instructor which is an integral part of academic freedom, conceived as a functional complex of values and norms.

More broadly, the concept of privileged information and confidential communication in the professions—law and medicine, teaching and the ministry—has the same function of insulating clients from ready observability of their behavior and beliefs by others in their role-set. If the physician or priest were free to tell all they have learned about the private lives of their clients, they could not adequately discharge their functions. More, as we have seen in our review of observability, if the facts of all role-behavior and all attitudes were freely available to anyone, social structures could not operate. What is sometimes called "the need for privacy"—that is, insulation of actions and thoughts from surveillance by others—is the individual counterpart to the functional requirement of social structure that some measure of exemption from full observability be provided for. Otherwise, the pressure to live up to the details of all (and often conflicting) social norms would become literally unbearable; in a complex society, schizophrenic behavior would become the rule rather than the formidable exception it already is. "Privacy" is not merely a personal predilection; it is an important functional requirement for the effective operation of social structure. Social systems must provide for some appropriate measure, as they say in France, of *quant-à-soi*—a portion of the self which is kept apart, immune from social surveillance.

The mechanism of insulation from observability can, of course, miscarry. Were the politician or statesman fully removed from the public spotlight, social control of his behavior would be correspondingly reduced. Anonymous power anonymously exercised does not make for a stable structure of social relations meeting the values of the society, as the history of secret police amply testifies. The teacher who is fully insulated from observation by peers and superiors may fail to live up to the minimum requirements of his status. The physician in his private practice who is largely exempt from the judgment of competent colleagues may allow his role-performance to sink below tolerable standards. The secret policeman may violate the values of the society, and not be detected.

All this means that some measure of observability of role-performance by members of the role-set is required, if the indispensable social requirement of accountability is to be met. This statement obviously does not contradict earlier statements to the effect that some measure of insulation from observability is also required for the effective operation of social structures. Instead, the two statements, taken in conjunction, hold again that there is some optimum of observability, difficult as yet to identify in measurable terms and doubtless varying for different social statuses, which will simultaneously make for accountability of role-performance and for autonomy of role-performance, rather than for a frightened acquiescence with the distribution of power that happens, at a given moment, to obtain in the role-set. Varying patterns of observability can operate to enable the occupants of social statuses to cope with the conflicting expectations among members of their role-sets.

4. *The mechanism making for observability by members of the role-set of their conflicting demands upon the occupants of a social status:* This mechanism is implied by the two foregoing accounts of the power structure and patterns of insulation from observability; it therefore needs only passing comment here. As long as members of the role-set are happily ignorant that their demands upon the occupants of a status are incompatible, each member may press his own case upon the status-occupants. The pattern is then many against one. But when it is made plain that the demands of some members of the role-set are in full contradiction with the demands of other members, it becomes the task of the role-set, rather than the task of the status-occupant, to resolve these contradictions, either by a struggle for exclusive power or by some degree of compromise. As the conflict becomes abundantly manifest, the pressure upon the status-occupant becomes temporarily relieved.

In such cases, the occupant of the status subjected to conflicting demands and expectations can become cast in the role of the *tertius gaudens,* the third (or more often, the nth) party who draws advantage from the conflict of the others.[119] The status-occupant, originally at the focus of

---

119. The classical analysis of the *tertius gaudens* pattern is still that by Georg Simmel, *Sociology,* 154-169, 232-239. There is at least the promise that this will be advanced by current inquiry; *e.g.,* Theodore M. Mills, "The coalition pattern in three person groups," *American Sociological Review,* 1954, 19, 657-667; Fred L. Strodtbeck, "The family as a three-person group," *ibid.,* 1954, 19, 23-29; T. M. Mills, "Power relations in three-person groups," *ibid.,* 1953, 18, 351-357. Such studies of three-*person* groups are akin to the problem under review but they are not, of course, identical with the matter of patterned relations between three social *strata.* Inquiry into this latter problem is now under way in a seminar on Selected Problems in the Theory of Organization at Columbia University.

the conflict, virtually becomes a more or less influential bystander whose function it is to high-light the conflicting demands by members of his role-set and to make it a problem for them, rather than for him, to resolve *their* contradictory demands. Often enough, this serves to change the structure of the situation.

This social mechanism can be thought of as working to eliminate one form of what Floyd H. Allport described as "pluralistic ignorance," that is, the pattern in which individual members of a group *assume* that they are virtually alone in holding the social attitudes and expectations they do, all unknowing that others privately share them.[120] This is a frequently observed condition of a group which is so organized that mutual observability among its members is slight. This basic notion of pluralistic ignorance can, however, be usefully enlarged to take account of a formally similar but substantively different condition. This is the condition now under review, in which the members of a role-set do not know that their expectations of the behavior appropriate for the occupants of a particular status are *different* from those held by other members of the role-set. There are two patterns of pluralistic ignorance—the unfounded assumption that one's own attitudes and expectations are unshared and the unfounded assumption that they are uniformly shared.

Confronted with contradictory demands by members of his role-set, each of whom assumes that the legitimacy of his demands is beyond dispute, the occupant of a status can act to make these contradictions manifest. To some extent, depending upon the structure of power, this re-directs the conflict so that it is one between members of the role-set, rather than, as was at first the case, between them and the occupant of the status. It is the members of the role-set who are now in a position in which *they* are being required to articulate their role-expectations. At the very least, this serves to make evident that it is not willful misfeasance on the part of the status-occupant which keeps him from conforming to all of the contradictory expectations imposed upon him. In some instances, the replacing of pluralistic ignorance by common knowledge serves to make for a re-definition of what can properly be expected of the status-occupant. In other cases, the process serves simply to allow him to go his own way, while the members of his role-set are engaged in their conflict. In both instances, this making manifest of contradictory expectations serves to articulate the role-set beyond that which would occur, if this mechanism were not at work.

5. *The mechanism of social support by others in similar social statuses with similar difficulties of coping with an unintegrated role-set:* This

---

120. Floyd H. Allport, *Social Psychology* (Boston: Houghton Mifflin Co., 1924). The notion of pluralistic ignorance was considerably developed by R. L. Schanck, "A study of a community and its groups and institutions conceived of as behaviors of individuals," *Psychological Monographs*, 1932, 43, No. 2.

mechanism presupposes the not unusual structural situation that others occupying the same social status have much the same problems of dealing with their role-sets. Whatever he may believe to the contrary, the occupant of a social status is usually not alone. The very fact that it is a *social status* means that there are others more or less like-circumstanced. The actual and potential experience of confronting conflicting role-expectations among those in one's role-set is to this extent common to occupants of the status. The individual subject to these conflicts need not, therefore, meet them as a wholly private problem which must be handled in a wholly private fashion. Such conflicts of role-expectations become patterned and shared by occupants of the same social status.

These facts of social structure afford a basis for understanding the formation of organizations and normative systems among those occupying the same social status. Occupational and professional associations, for example, constitute a structural response to the problems of coping with the power structure and (potentially or actually) conflicting demands by those in the role-set of the status. They constitute social formations designed to counter the power of the role-set; of being, not merely amenable to these demands, but of helping to shape them. The organization of status-occupants—so familiar a part of the social landscape of differentiated societies—serves to develop a normative system which anticipates and thereby mitigates the conflicting demands made of those in this status. They provide social support to the individual status-occupant. They minimize the need for his improvising private adjustments to conflict situations.

It is this same function, it might be said, which also constitutes part of the sociological significance of the emergence of professional codes which are designed to state in advance what the socially supported behavior of the status-occupant should be. Not, of course, that such codes operate with automatic efficiency, serving to eliminate in advance those demands judged illegitimate in terms of the code and serving to indicate unequivocally which action the status-occupant should take when confronted with conflicting demands. Codification, of ethical as of cognitive matters, implies abstraction. The codes still need to be interpreted before being applied to concrete instances.[121] Nevertheless, social support is provided by consensus among status-peers as this con-

---

121. There is no obvious end to the interpretation of codes governing status-behavior in occupations, religion, politics, and all the other institutional areas of society. But for a recent detailed and compact collection of such interpretations, see the 900-page volume, *Opinions of the Committees on Professional Ethics* of the Association of the Bar of the City of New York and the New York County Lawyers' Association, published under the auspices of the William Nelson Cromwell Foundation by Columbia University Press, 1956. The decisive point is, not that there is full unanimity on the appropriate status-behavior in designated situations, but that the individual lawyer is not required to settle these matters exclusively on the basis of his own reading of the situation. Professionally, he is not alone.

sensus is recorded in the code or is expressed in the judgments of status-peers oriented toward the code. The function of such codes becomes all the more significant in those cases in which status-occupants are vulnerable to pressures from their role-set precisely because they are relatively isolated from one another. Thus, thousands of librarians sparsely distributed among the towns and villages of the nation and not infrequently subject to censorial pressures received strong support from the code on censorship developed by the American Library Association in conjunction with the American Book Publishers Council.[122] This kind of social support for conformity to the requirements of the status when confronted with pressures by the role-set to depart from these requirements serves to counteract the instability of role-performance which would otherwise develop.

6. *Abridging the role-set: disruption of role-relationships:* This is, of course, the limiting case in modes of coping with incompatible demands upon status-occupants by members of the role-set. Certain relationships are broken off, leaving a consensus of role-expectations among those that remain. But this mode of adaptation is possible only under special and limited conditions. It can be effectively utilized only in those circumstances where it is still possible for the status-occupant to perform his other roles, without the support of those with whom he has discontinued relations. Otherwise put, this requires that the remaining relationships in the role-set are not substantially damaged by this device. It presupposes that social structure provides the option to discontinue some relations in the role-set as, for example, in a network of personal friendships. By and large, however, this option is far from unlimited, since the role-set is not so much a matter of personal choice as a matter of the social structure in which the status is embedded. Under these conditions, the option is apt to be that of the status-occupant removing himself from the status rather than that of removing the role-set, or an appreciable part of it, from the status. Typically, the individual goes, and the social structure remains.

PROBLEM 7.3.

RESIDUAL CONFLICT IN THE ROLE-SET

There can be little doubt but that these are only some of the mechanisms working to articulate the expectations of those in the role-set. Inquiry will uncover others, just as it will probably modify the preceding account of those we have provisionally identified. But I believe that the logical structure of this analysis may remain largely intact. This can be briefly recapitulated.

---

122. For the code, see *The Freedom to Read* (Chicago: American Library Association, 1953); for an analysis of the general issue, see Richard P. McKeon, R. K. Merton and Walter Gellhorn, *Freedom to Read* (1957).

First, it is assumed that each social status has its organized complement of role-relationships which can be thought of as comprising a role-set.

Second, the relationships are not only between the occupant of the particular status and each member of the role-set but, always potentially and often actually, between members of the role-set itself.

Third, to some extent, those in the role-set and especially those occupying disparate social statuses, may have differing expectations (moral and actuarial) of the behavior of the status-occupant.

Fourth, this gives rise to the problem of their diverse expectations being sufficiently articulated for the status- and role-structure to operate with a modicum of effectiveness.

Fifth, inadequate articulation of these role-expectations tends to call one or more social mechanisms into play, which operate to reduce the amount of patterned role-conflict below that which would be involved if these mechanisms were not operating.

Sixth, finally and importantly, even when these mechanisms are at work, they may not, in particular instances, prove sufficient to reduce the conflict of expectations among those comprising the role-set below the level required for the role-system to operate with substantial efficiency. This residual conflict within the role-set may be enough to interfere materially with the effective performance of roles by the occupant of the status in question. Indeed, it will probably turn out that this condition is the most frequent—role-systems operating at considerably less than full efficiency. Without trying to draw out tempting analogies with other types of systems, I suggest that this is not unlike the case of engines—whether Newcomen's atmospheric engine or Parsons's turbine—which cannot fully utilize heat energy.

We do not yet know some of the requirements for maximum articulation of the relations between the occupant of a status and members of his role-set, on the one hand, and for maximum articulation of the values and expectations among those comprising the role-set, on the other. But as we have seen, even those requirements which can now be identified are not readily satisfied, without fault, in social systems. To the extent that they are not, social systems are forced to limp along with that measure of ineffectiveness and inefficiency which is often tolerated because the realistic prospect of decided improvement seems so remote as sometimes not to be visible at all.

PROBLEM 7.4.

THE SOCIAL DYNAMICS OF ADAPTATION IN STATUS-SETS AND STATUS-SEQUENCES

The status-set, it will be remembered, refers to the complex of distinct positions assigned to individuals both within and among social systems. Just as there are problems of articulating the role-set, so there

REFERENCE GROUPS AND SOCIAL STRUCTURE

are problems of articulating the status-set. In some measure, these problems are similar, though not identical, in structure. For this reason and also, it must be admitted, because this paper has already run to unconscionable length, I make no effort here even to sketch out the entire array of problems which can now be identified. It may be useful, however, to refer to a few of these, if only to indicate the general character which further analysis might take.

Status-sets plainly provide one basic form of interdependence between the institutions and subsystems of a society. This stems from the familiar fact that the same persons are engaged in distinct social systems. It should be noted, furthermore, that, just as groups and societies differ in the number and complexity of social statuses comprising part of their structure, so individual people differ in the number and complexity of statuses comprising their status-sets. Not everyone in a "complex social structure" has the same complexity of status-sets. As a parochial example of one extreme, consider the actually enumerable though seemingly endless statuses occupied at the same time by Nicholas Murray Butler, and as an hypothetical example of the other extreme, the relatively few statuses occupied by a rentier-scholar who has actually succeeded in withdrawing himself from most social systems—busy at his work though formally "unemployed," unmarried and unmated, unconcerned with political, religious, civic, educational, military and other organizations. The problems of articulating the role-requirements of the complex status-set in the one instance and of the simple status-set in the second are presumably of quite differing order.

Complex status-sets not only make for some form of liaison between subsystems in a society; they confront the occupants of these statuses with distinctly different degrees of difficulty in organizing their role-activities. Furthermore, primary socialization in certain statuses, with their characteristic value-orientations, may so affect the formation of personality as to make it sometimes more, sometimes less, difficult to act out the requirements of other statuses.

Counteracting such difficulties which are potentially involved in complex status-sets are several types of social process. For one thing, people are not perceived by others as occupying only one status, even though this may be the controlling status in a particular social relationship. Employers often recognize that employees also have families and, on patterned occasions, temper their expectations of employee-behavior to the exigencies of this fact. The employee who is known to have experienced a death in his immediate family is, as a matter of course, held, for the time being, to less demanding occupational requirements. This social perception of competing obligations entailed in status-sets serves to cushion and to modify the demands and expectations by members of the role-sets associated with some of these statuses.

This kind of continuing adaptation is in turn related to the values of the society. To the extent that there is a *prior* consensus on the relative "importance" of conflicting status-obligations, this reduces the internal conflict of decision by those occupying these statuses and eases the accommodation on the part of those involved in their role-sets.

There are, of course, forces militating against such ready adaptations. Those involved in the role-set of the individual in one of his statuses have their own patterned activities disturbed when he does not live up to his role-obligations. To some extent, they become motivated to hold him to performance of his role. If self-interested motivation were in fact all-compelling, this would make for even more stress in status-systems than actually occurs. Members of each role-set would in effect be pulling and hauling against those in other role-sets, with the occupant of the several statuses continuously in the middle. But self-interested motivation is not all, and this provides patterned leeway in accommodating to conflicting demands.

In psychological terms, empathy—the sympathetic understanding of the lot of the other—serves to reduce the pressures exerted upon people caught up in conflicts of status-obligations. To call it "psychological," however, is not to suggest that empathy is nothing but an individual trait of personality which people happen to have in varying degree; the extent to which empathy obtains among the members of a society is in part a function of the underlying social structure. For those who are in the role-sets of the individual subjected to conflicting status-obligations are in turn occupants of multiple statuses, formerly or presently, actually or potentially, subject to similar stresses. This structural circumstance at least facilitates the development of empathy. ("There, but for the grace of God, go I.")

Social structures are not without powers of learned adaptations, successively transmitted through changed cultural mandates. This helps mitigate the frequency and intensity of conflict in the status-set. For the greater the frequency with which patterned conflict between the obligations of multiple statuses occurs, the more likely that new norms will evolve to govern these situations by assigning priorities of obligation. This means that each individual caught up in these stressful situations need not improvise new adjustments. It means, further, that members of his role-sets will in effect make it easier for him to settle the difficulty, by accepting his "decision" if it is in accord with these functionally evolved standards of priority.

Social mechanisms for reducing such conflict can also be considered in terms of status-sequences—that is, the succession of statuses through which an appreciable proportion of people move. Consider sequences of what Linton called *achieved* (or, more generally, what may be called *acquired*) *statuses:* statuses into which individuals move by virtue of their own achievements rather than having been placed in them by virtue of fortunate or unfortunate birth, (which would be *ascribed* statuses). The principal idea here holds that the components of status-sets are not combined at random. A process of self-selection—both social and psychological—operates to reduce the prospects of random assortments of statuses. Values internalized by people in prior dominant statuses are such as to make it less likely (than would be the case in the absence of these values) that they will be motivated to enter statuses with values incompatible with their own. (Once again, as throughout our account of mechanisms, it is not being implied that this process invariably operates with full and automatic efficiency; but it does operate.)

As a result of this process of self-selection of successive statuses, the status-set at any one time is more nearly integrated than it would otherwise be. In terms of the value-orientations already developed, people reject certain statuses which they could achieve, because they find them repugnant, and select other prospective statuses, because they find them congenial. An extreme case will illuminate the general theoretical point: those reared as Christian Scientists and committed to this faith do not ordinarily become physicians. To say that this is self-evident is of course precisely the point. These two successive statuses—Christian Science and medicine—do not occur with any frequency as a result of the process of self-selection. But what holds for this conspicuous and extreme case may be supposed to hold, with much less visibility and regularity, for other successions of statuses. It is this same theoretical idea, after all, which was employed by Max Weber in his analysis of the Protestant Ethic in relation to business enterprise. He was saying, in effect, that owing to the process of self-selection, along the lines we have sketched, a statistically frequent status-set included both affiliation with ascetic Protestant sects and capitalistic business. In due course, moreover, these two statuses developed increasingly compatible definitions of social roles. In short, they operated to reduce the actual conflict between statuses in a statistically frequent status-set below the level which would have obtained, were it not for the operation of these mechanisms of self-selection and of progressive re-definition of status-obligations.

By the same mechanism, it becomes possible for statuses which are "neutral" to one another to turn up with considerable frequency in the same status-sets. By "neutral" is meant only that the values and obligations of the respective statuses are such that they are *not likely* to enter into conflict. (Concretely, of course, almost any pair of statuses may, under certain conditions, have conflicting requirements; some pairs, however, are more clearly subject to such conflict than others. Other pairs may be mutually reinforcing, as we have seen, and still others may simply be neutral.) For example, it is concretely possible that a locomotive engineer will be more subject to conflicting status-demands if he is of Italian rather than of Irish extraction, but the social system being what it is, this combination of statuses would seem to have high neutrality. The pattern of mutually indifferent statuses provides for some measure of variability in status-sets without entailing conflict among statuses. It helps account for the demonstrable fact that, although the statuses in a status-set are not randomly assorted, they are also not fully and tightly integrated.

The concepts of status-set and status-sequence help generate other problems for the functional analysis of social structures.[123] But the foregoing sketch may be enough to suggest the nature of these problems. That these are, in turn, connected with problems of reference group behavior is also evident, and these connections will not be examined here.

CONSEQUENCES OF REFERENCE GROUP BEHAVIOR

In concluding this report on continuities in the theory of reference group behavior and social structure, I simply mention, rather than analyze, selected problems of the *consequences* of differing types of reference group behavior. To consider these in the detail which is now possible would be to make this a full-length book rather than an interim report.

PROBLEM 8.

THE FUNCTIONS AND DYSFUNCTIONS OF REFERENCE GROUP BEHAVIOR

As was suggested in the preceding chapter and in earlier portions of this one, there is "coherence between reference group theory and conceptions of functional sociology. It appears that these deal with different facets of the same subject: the one centers on the processes through which men relate themselves to groups and refer their behavior to the values of these groups; the other centers on the consequences of these processes, primarily for social structures but also for the individuals and groups involved in these structures." (226)[124]

We have already met intimations of some of the provisionally identified social functions of reference group behavior in preceding sections. We now consider one of these, the function of anticipatory socialization: the acquisition of values and orientations found in statuses and groups in which one is not yet engaged but which one is likely to enter.

---

123. To report on some of the further attendant problems would take us too far afield. But it should be noted that *role-gradations* (the gradual rather sudden changes of roles in status-sequences) operate to mitigate difficulties of the type described by Ruth Benedict, in her "Continuities and discontinuities in cultural conditioning," *Psychiatry*, 1938, 1, 161-167.

124. This same orientation is adopted by Eisenstadt, with interesting results. See his "Studies in reference group behaviour," *Human Relations*, 1954, 7, 191-216, esp. 192, where he observes: "Instead of asking at the beginning what are the ways in which reference groups influence an individual's behaviour, we could ask why such an orientation is necessary at all from the point of view both of a given social system and of the individual's personality. What are the functions which such orientation fulfils in the social life-space of an individual and in his participation in the society of which he is a member?"

It serves to prepare the individual for future statuses in his status-sequence. An explicit, deliberate, and often formal part of this process is of course what is meant by education and training. But much of such preparation is *implicit, unwitting,* and *informal,* and it is particularly to this that the notion of anticipatory socialization directs our attention.

Such informal preparation for the roles to be performed in connection with future statuses tends to have a distinctive character. It does not ordinarily involve specialized personnel designated to train for these roles, or it results from the preparation unwittingly and collaterally provided by such personnel. Even in schools, anticipatory socialization proceeds beyond the boundaries of what is formally provided for. By the same token, anticipatory socialization is not didactic. The individual responds to the cues in behavioral situations, more or less unwittingly draws implications from these for future role-behavior, and thus becomes oriented toward a status he does not yet occupy. Typically, he does not expressly codify the values and role-requirements he is learning.

Conducing to this function of anticipatory socialization is the structural circumstance of what can be called "role-gradations." The individual moves more or less continuously through a sequence of statuses and associated roles, each phase of which does not greatly differ from the one which has gone before. Although his "official" (socially acknowledged) transfer into a new status may seem to be sudden, more often than not this is only because the informal antecedent preparation has gone unnoticed. There is less discontinuity in status-sequences than might appear on the social surface, with its celebrative *rites de passage* and legally enacted changes of status.

In status- and role-sequences, the individual is more or less continuously subject to appraisal, by others, of the adequacy of his current role-performance. Tendencies to regress to the behavior of an earlier role are curbed, by re-assertion of the newly-won status. ("You're a big boy now. . . .") Correlatively, tendencies to advance "prematurely" to prospective roles are curbed ("Some day, of course, but you're not far enough along now. . . .") In effect, by orientation to the norms of prospective statuses, the individual engages in trial behavior and tends to move at a pace which is controlled by the responses of those in his current role-set.

Little enough is known of the time-orientations toward statuses and roles which cultures hold should obtain at each phase of the life cycle, and even less of those which actually do obtain.[125] In their minute-by-

---

125. One paper dealing with four cultures bears upon this to some extent: Marian W. Smith, "Different cultural concepts of past, present and future: a study of ego extension," *Psychiatry,* 1952, 15, 395-400. Another paper begins to examine the possibility that there may be "various temporal goal orientations in the various levels of social class" by a preliminary study of something over a hundred children from lower and middle strata in the United States; Lawrence L. LeShan, "Time orientation and social class," *Journal of Abnormal and Social Psychology,* 1952, 47, 589-592.

minute record of the behavior of one boy throughout the course of one day, Barker and Wright[126] find that somewhat short of half the boy's behavior was definitely oriented toward his current roles, a very small part (some four per cent of the "behavior-units") toward future roles, and even less toward past roles. Parallel data for representative numbers of people drawn from differing societies and social strata are not available, so that the matter remains entirely conjectural. It has been said, for example, that in youth, the long future looks vague and almost limitless; the past seems negligible; and so the present and immediate future hold primary significance. The middle years, the same supposition holds, tend to involve somewhat more of a balance among the three, whereas old age is oriented primarily toward the past. But these are guesses at best, and not very instructive guesses, at that. The patterns of orientation toward past, present, and future statuses at different stages of the life cycle almost surely vary according to variations of culture and position in the social structure. But systematic knowledge about this is yet to come. It can be supposed, however, that as these time-orientations vary, the selection of reference groups varies and so, also, their function of providing anticipatory socialization.

What is true of this one function of reference groups seems to hold for other functions which have been identified in the studies of reference group behavior previously cited in this paper. But these functions (and dysfunctions) of reference groups have only begun to be explored and, as things now stand, they might best be considered in a later interim report.[127]

126. R. G. Barker and H. F. Wright, *One Boy's Day* (New York: Harper & Brothers, 1951).

127. Basic contributions to the theory of reference groups are to be found in the revised edition of Muzafer Sherif and Carolyn W. Sherif, *An Outline of Social Psychology* (New York: Harper & Brothers, 1956). To my regret, this came to my attention only after this book was in page proof.

X PATTERNS OF INFLUENCE: LOCAL AND COSMOPOLITAN INFLUENTIALS

T HIS IS AN exploratory study focused upon the place of mass communications in patterns of interpersonal influence. Based primarily upon interviews with eighty-six men and women drawn from diverse social and economic strata in "Rovere," a town of 11,000 on the Eastern seaboard, it is essentially a case study rather than a statistical analysis[1] of influence patterns. The initial substantive aim of this pilot study was fourfold: (1) to identify types of people regarded as variously influential by their fellows; (2) to relate patterns of communications behavior to their roles as influential persons; (3) to gain clues to the chief avenues through which they came to acquire influence; and (4) to set out hypotheses for more systematic study of the workings of interpersonal influence in the local community.

The body of this report is devoted to an analysis of basically different types of influential persons: types which we shall call the "local" and the "cosmopolitan." But before turning to these substantive materials, there may be some interest in glancing briefly at two procedural and methodo‑ logical detours encountered on the way. The first detour was taken when an applied research in sociology, originally devoted to a delimited practical problem, gave rise to theoretic constructs which unexpectedly emerged in the process of investigation. Although the pilot study was in the beginning undertaken to learn the functions served by a national newsmagazine for various types of readers—a problem in the sociology of mass communications—it was soon reoriented as a result of initial impressions and findings. For it appeared that the magazine was utilized in markedly different ways by people who exercised varying degrees of interpersonal influence in their community. In rapidly retracing our steps over the second detour, we shall meet the obstacle which required us to devise alternative schemes for analyzing the same qualitative data.

---

1. Although figures summarizing our case-study materials are cited from time to time, these are merely heuristic, not demonstrative, in character. They serve only to indicate the sources of interpretative hypotheses which await detailed, systematic inquiry.

The plain fact is that our initial analysis was quite unproductive. With the emergence of the concepts of local and cosmopolitan *influentials*, however, the "same" qualitative data led to productive results which have since lent themselves to elaboration. After this brief procedural review of these two phases of our qualitative analysis, we shall be better prepared to assess the substantive account of local and cosmopolitan influentials.

CONVERSION OF AN APPLIED INTO A THEORETIC RESEARCH

The practical problem which gave rise to this inquiry was clear enough.[2] The research department of a national newsmagazine sought to learn how one could locate the areas of personal influence in a community. Further, what were the characteristics, including magazine readership, of these influential persons? Was this magazine reaching the "key" persons in networks of personal relations? And however this might be, what patterns of use of this magazine were made by influential people in comparison with rank-and-file readers?

As the practical problem was formulated, it at once led to a focus on evolving *methods of identifying persons* with varying degrees of inter-personal influence. Obviously, one could not determine whether readers of this newsmagazine were or were not disproportionately comprised of those who may be called "influentials," unless procedures for locating and identifying influentials were at hand. Furthermore, the very fact that a research was initiated to deal with this problem indicated that some plausible indices of influence were considered inadequate by the client. Such seeming indices of influence as occupation, income, prop-erty-ownership, and organizational affiliations of readers were available in the files of the newsmagazine or were readily obtainable through a canvass of readers. A research directed toward evolving more effective indices of influence was thus premised on the hypothesis that although people of high "social status" *may* exert relatively great interpersonal influence, social status is not an adequate index. Some individuals of high status apparently wield little interpersonal influence, and some of low-status have considerable interpersonal influence. New qualitative in-

---

2. It is tempting to pursue the digression which this suggests. The clients were presumably concerned with learning more about patterns of interpersonal influence largely, if not wholly, because the "influentiality theme" might aid them in selling advertisements. (Frank Stewart lists 43 national magazines which use as "copy themes some variation of the idea that their readers are persons possessing influence.") This practical objective fused with the existence of a research department to suggest the need for research in this field. And, as we shall see, once the research was initiated, its objectives became diversified, spreading into subproblems only remotely related to the original objectives. The functions of applied research for pertinent theory need to be systematically explored; some beginnings are set forth in Chapter III of this volume.

vestigation was needed to evolve more direct indices of interpersonal influence.

But, as is not infrequently the case, it was assumed that the problem had been adequately stated at the outset. Do the readers of this magazine disproportionately comprise people of influence and, in any case, do influentials put the magazine to different uses than do rank-and-file readers? Actually, this was a *premature specification* of the problem, as we realized only after the pilot study had been under way for some time. For, as we discovered, it is not so much a matter of identifying *influentials* (and the use they make of newsmagazines) but of detecting *types of influentials* (and the associated differences in their orientation toward newsmagazines as agencies of information concerning the larger society rather than their own local community).

The major shift in this study, as we shall see, occurred with the recognition that the *practical problem had been overspecified* in its initial formulation. This overspecification for a time diverted our attention from salient alternatives of investigation. Only when the initial problem had been reformulated, only when the search for means of identifying influentials was converted into a search for types of influentials likely to differ in their communications behavior, did the research prove productive both in its applied and in its theoretic dimensions. Only then did data, not previously assimilable by our interpretative scheme, "fall into place." Only then were we able to account for diverse and previously unconnected observational data through a limited number of concepts and propositions.

As we shall see in the central part of this report, it required a restatement of the problem before we were in a position to advance toward both the applied and the theoretic objectives of the inquiry.

Two Phases of Qualitative Analysis of Influentials

Following upon the reformulation of the problem, we were concerned with devising procedures, however crude, for enabling informants to single out people (apart from their immediate family) who exerted significant "influence" upon them in the course of social interaction.[3] We were not concerned with influence exercised indirectly through major political, market, and other administrative decisions which affect large numbers of people.[4] In prolonged interviews, informants were led to

---

3. Nothing will be said in this paper of the procedures developed in preliminary fashion for the identification of people exerting various degrees of interpersonal influence. For a report of these procedures as adapted in a subsequent research, see Frank A. Stewart, "A sociometric study of influence in Southtown," *Sociometry*, 1947, 10, 11-31. The requisite methodology has been notably developed in a research on influence in a Midwestern community conducted by the Bureau of Applied Social Research of Columbia University, Elihu Katz and P. F. Lazarsfeld, *Personal Influence* (Glencoe, Illinois: The Free Press, 1955).

4. For a brief discussion of the concept of interpersonal influence as provisionally employed in this exploratory study, see Addendum at close of this Chapter.

mention people to whom they turned for help or advice regarding various types of personal decisions (decisions ranging from choice of a job or educational plans for self and children to selections of books, plays or furniture). Informants were invited, further, to indicate those persons who, so far as they knew, were generally sought out for advice in these several spheres. Such tentative identifications of individuals exercising interpersonal influence were of course linked with reasons advanced by informants for singling out these individuals rather than others.

In the course of these interviews, our eighty-six informants came to mention a total of 379 people who, in one respect or another, were said to have exerted influence upon them in a concrete situation involving decisions. Some people turned up repeatedly in this canvass. (There were 1043 "mentions" referring to 379 persons, some of whom were referred to on thirty or more occasions.) Of the 379, fifty-seven, or 15 per cent, were mentioned four or more times and this was provisionally taken as our working criterion of "influentiality." As we shall presently see, this wholly tentative and arbitrary criterion enabled us to identify cases in which we could examine the operation of interpersonal influence. Thirty of these influential people were subsequently interviewed with regard to their own evaluation and image of their influence, evaluations of the influence exercised by others upon them, situations in which they exerted influence, their communications behavior, and the like. All this comprised the data for analysis.

This is not the place to report in detail the first, rather unproductive, phase of our analysis of the communications behavior of influentials. But by briefly considering how and why this gave rise to an alternative kind of analysis, something may be gained toward a *codification* of methods of qualitative analysis.[5] Just enough will be said to indicate how the data exerted pressure upon the research worker for successively so modifying his concepts that, with the recasting of the data in terms of the new concepts, there emerged a set of suggestive uniformities in place of the previously untidy aggregation of facts.

In what we now know to be the relatively sterile first phase of our analysis, we not only distinguished the influentials from the rank-and-

---

5. This part of our report, then, is a bid to the sociological fraternity for the practice of incorporating in publications a detailed account of the ways in which qualitative analyses *actually* developed. Only when a considerable body of such reports are available will it be possible to *codify* methods of qualitative analysis with something of the clarity with which quantitative methods have been articulated. The present report suffers from the deletion of concrete materials illustrating the successive shifts in the categories of analysis; the few details reported here are drawn from a more extensive monograph on file in the Bureau of Applied Social Research. However, this may be sufficient to emphasize the need for increasingly detailed accounts of qualitative analyses in sociology which report not only the *final product* but also the sequential steps taken to obtain this product. In the view of the Bureau, this codification is devoutly to be desired both for the *collection* and the *analysis* of qualitative sociological data.

file, but went on to distinguish influentials according to their dynamic position in the local *influence-structure*. Thus, distinctions were drawn between the currently influential (occupying a supposedly stable position), the potentially influential (the rising star—still upward mobile), the waning influential (passed the zenith—now downward mobile), and the dormant influential (possessing the *objective* attributes of the influential but not exploiting these for the exercise of influence). The non-influentials were in turn divided into the rank-and-file (with a limited range of social contacts in which they are typically the recipients rather than the dispensers of advice) and the isolates (largely shut off from social contacts).

This classification proved to be logically impeccable, empirically applicable, and virtually sterile. To be sure, our data could readily be arranged in these categories. But this resulted in few clear-cut uniformities of communications behavior or of other patterns of behavior. In short, the distinctions were valid but relatively fruitless for our purposes. But since, as L. J. Henderson once remarked, "almost any classification is better than none," this did lead to some scattered clues concerning the functions of newsmagazines and other communications for those occupying various positions in the influence-structure. Thus, we found that some influentials characteristically use the newsmagazine not so much for self-clarification as for the clarification of others who look to them for guidance and orientation. It also seemed clear that the functions of the newsmagazine differ greatly for the rank-and-file and the influential reader. For the one, it largely serves a private, personal function; for the other, a public function. For the rank-and-file reader, the information found in the newsmagazine is a *commodity for personal consumption,* extending his *own* conception of the world of public events whereas for the influential, it is a *commodity for exchange,* to be traded for further increments of prestige, by enabling him to act as an interpreter of national and international affairs. It aids him in being an opinion-leader.

But at best, this first classification resulted in a welter of discrete impressions not closely related one to the others. It did not enable us to account for the diverse behaviors of influentials. Somewhat more than half of the influentials read newsmagazines, for example, but our classification gave no systematic clue as to why the others did not. The sterility of this phase of our analysis *motivated the search* for new working concepts, but it was a series of observations incidentally turned up in the course of this analysis which directed attention to the *actual concepts* with which we came to operate.

Above all else, one strategic *fact* shaped the second phase of the analysis. The interviews with influentials had been centered on their relations with*in* the town. Yet, in response to the same set of queries, some influentials spoke wholly in terms of the local situation in Rovere, whereas others managed to incorporate frequent references to matters far beyond the reaches of Rovere. A question concerning the impact of the war upon the Rovere economy would elicit in the one instance a response dealing exclusively with problems within the town and in the other, to remarks about the national economy or international trade. It was this characteristic patterning of response within a peculiarly local or a more extended frame of reference—a patterning which could, perhaps, have been anticipated but which was not—that led to the conception of two major types of influentials: the "local" and the "cosmopolitan."

Whereas the first classification had dealt with phases in the cycle of personal influence, the second was in terms of influentials' *orientation*[6] toward local and larger social structures. The one centered on position within the influence-structure; the other on the grounds for influence and the ways in which this influence was exercised.

With the emergence of the concepts of local and cosmopolitan influentials, a number of new uniformities at once came to light. The "same" materials took on quite new implications as they were re-examined and re-analyzed in terms of these concepts. Facts which found no pertinent place in the first analysis became not only relevant but critical in the second. Thus the varying types of career-patterns of influentials—whether these developed largely within Rovere or were furthered in Rovere after having been initiated elsewhere—came to be an integral part of the second analysis whereas they had been "interesting" but unincorporated data in the first. Such seemingly diverse matters as geographic mobility, participation in networks of personal relations and in voluntary organizations, the translation of influence-potentials into influence-operations, patterns of communications behavior—all these were found to be expressions of these major orientations toward the local community: orientations ranging from virtually exclusive concern with the local area to central concern with the great world outside.

In this prelude to the main body of the report, then, we have noted two matters of procedural and methodological interest. We have seen first, that an applied social research, originally focused upon a severely limited objective, gave rise to a more extended inquiry bearing upon a sociological theory of patterns of interpersonal influence. And, second, we have briefly reviewed the circumstances pressing for a modification of qualitative concepts, with the consequent rearrangement of discrete facts into coherent patterns and uniformities. With this brief introduction, we are prepared for the substantive account of two basically different types of influentials and their respective patterns of communications behavior.

---

6. A word of explanation is needed for this concept of "orientation." The social orientation differs from the social role. Role refers to the manner in which the rights and duties inherent in a social position are put into practice; orientation, as here conceived, refers to the theme underlying the complex of social roles performed by an individual. It is the (tacit or explicit) theme which finds expression in each of the complex of social roles in which the individual is implicated.

TYPES OF INFLUENTIALS: THE LOCAL AND THE COSMOPOLITAN

The terms "local" and "cosmopolitan"[7] do not refer, of course, to the regions in which interpersonal influence is exercised. Both types of influentials are effective almost exclusively within the local community. Rovere has few residents who command a following outside that community.[*]

The chief criterion for distinguishing the two is found in their *orientation* toward Rovere. The localite largely confines his interests to this community. Rovere is essentially his world. Devoting little thought or energy to the Great Society, he is preoccupied with local problems, to the virtual exclusion of the national and international scene. He is, strictly speaking, parochial.

Contrariwise with the cosmopolitan type. He has some interest in Rovere and must of course maintain a minimum of relations within the community since he, too, exerts influence there. But he is also oriented significantly to the world outside Rovere, and regards himself as an integral part of that world. He resides in Rovere but lives in the Great Society. If the local type is parochial, the cosmopolitan is ecumenical.

Of the thirty influentials interviewed at length, fourteen were independently assessed by three analysts[8] as "cosmopolitan" on the basis

---

7. Upon identification of the two types of influentials, these terms were adopted from Carle C. Zimmerman, who uses them as translations of Toennies' well-known distinction between *Gemeinschaft* (localistic) and *Gesellschaft* (cosmopolitan). The sociologically informed reader will recognize essentially the same distinction, though with different terminologies, in the writings of Simmel, Cooley, Weber, Durkheim, among many others. Although these terms have commonly been used to refer to types of social organization and of social relationships, they are here applied to empirical materials on types of influential persons. *Cf.* Ferdinand Toennies, *Fundamental Concepts of Sociology* (New York, 1940), a translation by C. P. Loomis of his classic book, *Gemeinschaft und Gesellschaft,* and more importantly, a later article bearing the same title. See also Carle C. Zimmerman, *The Changing Community,* (New York and London: Harper & Brothers, 1938), especially 80 ff. For a compact summary of similar concepts in the sociological literature, see Leopold von Wiese and Howard Becker, *Systematic Sociology* (New York: John Wiley & Sons, 1932), especially 223-226n.

* The concept of influentials has been taken up in a study of the influence-structure of a suburb which houses men of national reputation and influence. As the authors say, "It is hardly surprising then that the personal characteristics of these 'influentials' differ from those of the lower-ranking cosmopolitan influential in Rovere." Kenneth P. Adler and Davis Bobrow, "Interest and influence in foreign affairs," *Public Opinion Quarterly,* 1956, 20, 89-101. See also Floyd Hunter, *Power Structure: A Study of Decision-Makers* (Chapel Hill: University of North Carolina Press, 1953).

8. This complete coincidence of assessments is scarcely to be expected in a larger sample. But the cosmopolitan and local syndromes were so clearly defined for this handful of cases, that there was little doubt concerning the "diagnoses." A full-fledged investigation would evolve more formal criteria, along the lines implied in the following discussion, and would, accordingly, evolve an intermediate type which approaches neither the local nor the cosmopolitan pole.

of case-materials exhibiting their orientation toward the Rovere community, and sixteen, as "local."

These orientations found characteristic expression in a variety of contexts. For example, influentials were launched upon a statement of their outlook by the quasi-projective question: "Do you worry much about the news?" (This was the autumn of 1943, when "the news" was, for most, equivalent to news about the war.) The responses, typically quite lengthy, readily lent themselves to classification in terms of the chief foci of interest of the influentials. One set of comments was focused on problems of a national and international order. They expressed concern with the difficulties which would attend the emergence of a stable postwar world; they talked at length about the problems of building an international organization to secure the peace; and the like. The second set of comments referred to the war news almost wholly in terms of what it implied for interviewees personally or for their associates in Rovere. They seized upon a question about "the news" as an occasion for reviewing the immediate flow of problems which the war had introduced into the town.

Classifying influentials into these two categories, we find that twelve of the fourteen[9] cosmopolitans typically replied within the framework of international and national problems, whereas only four of the sixteen locals spoke in this vein. Each type of influential singled out distinctively different elements from the flow of events. A vaguely formulated question enabled each to project his basic orientations into his replies.

All other differences between the local and cosmopolitan influentials seem to stem from their difference in basic orientation.[10] The group-profiles indicate the tendency of local influentials to be devoted to localism: they are more likely to have lived in Rovere for a long period, are profoundly interested in meeting many townspeople, do not wish to move from the town, are more likely to be interested in local politics, *etc.* Such items, which suggest great disparity between the two types of influentials, are our main concern in the following sections. There we will find that the difference in basic orientation is bound up with a variety of other differences: (1) in the structures of social relations in which each type is implicated; (2) in the roads they have traveled to

---

9. It should be repeated that the figures cited at this point, as throughout the study, should not be taken as representative of a parent population. They are cited only to illustrate the heuristic purpose they served in suggesting clues to the operation of diverse patterns of interpersonal influence. As is so often the fact with quantitative summaries of case-studies, these figures do not confirm interpretations, but merely suggest interpretations. The tentative interpretations in turn provide a point of departure for designing quantitative studies based upon adequate samples, as in Katz and Lazarsfeld, *op. cit.*

10. Nothing is said here of the objective *determinants* of these differences in orientation. To ascertain these determinants is an additional and distinctly important task, not essayed in the present study.

their present positions in the influence-structure; (3) in the utilization of their present status for the exercise of interpersonal influence; and (4) in their communications behavior.

STRUCTURES OF SOCIAL RELATIONS

Roots in the Community

Local and cosmopolitan influentials differ rather markedly in their attachment to Rovere. The local influentials are great local patriots and the thought of leaving Rovere seems seldom to come to mind. As one of them gropingly expressed it:

Rovere is the greatest town in the world. It has something that is nowhere else in the world, though I can't quite say what it is.

When asked directly if they had "ever thought of leaving Rovere," thirteen of the sixteen local influentials replied emphatically that they would never consider it, and the other three expressed a strong preference to remain, although they believed they would leave under certain conditions. None felt that they would be equally satisfied with life in any other community. Not so with the cosmopolitans. Only three of these claim to be wedded to Rovere for life. Four express their present willingness to live elsewhere, and the remaining seven would be willing to leave under certain conditions. Cosmopolitans' responses such as these do not turn up at all among the locals:

I've been on the verge of leaving for other jobs several times.

I am only waiting for my son to take over my practice, before I go out to California.

These basic differences in attitude toward Rovere are linked with the different runs of experience of local and cosmopolitan influentials. The cosmopolitans have been more mobile. The locals were typically born in Rovere or in its immediate vicinity. Whereas 14 of the 16 locals have lived in Rovere for over twenty-five years, this is true for fewer than half of the cosmopolitans. The cosmopolitans are typically recent arrivals who have lived in a succession of communities in different parts of the country.

Nor does this appear to be a result of differences in the age-composition of the local and cosmopolitan groups. True, the cosmopolitans are more likely to be younger than the local influentials. But for those over forty-five, the cosmopolitans seem to be comparative newcomers and the locals Rovere-born-and-bred.

From the case-materials, we can infer the bases of the marked attachment to Rovere characteristic of the local influentials. In the process of making their mark, these influentials have become thoroughly *adapted to the community* and dubious of the possibility of doing as well elsewhere. From the vantage point of his seventy years, a local judge reports his sense of full incorporation in the community:

> I wouldn't think of leaving Rovere. The people here are very good, very responsive. They like me and I'm grateful to God for the feeling that the people in Rovere trust me and look up to me as their guide and leader.

Thus, the strong sense of identification with Rovere among local influentials is linked with their typically local origins and career patterns in this community. Economically and sentimentally, they are deeply rooted in Rovere.

So far as attachment to Rovere is concerned, the cosmopolitans differ from the locals in virtually every respect. Not only are they relative newcomers; they do not feel themselves rooted in the town. Having characteristically lived elsewhere, they feel that Rovere, "a pleasant enough town," is only one of many. They are also aware, through actual experience, that they can advance their careers in other communities. They do not, consequently, look upon Rovere as comprising the outermost limits of a secure and satisfactory existence. Their wider range of experience has modified their orientation toward their present community.

Sociability: Networks of Personal Relations

In the course of the interview, influentials were given an occasion to voice their attitudes toward "knowing many people" in the community. Attitudes differed sharply between the two types. Thirteen of the sixteen local influentials in contrast to four of the fourteen cosmopolitans expressed marked interest in establishing frequent contacts with many people.

This difference becomes more instructive when examined in qualitative terms. The local influential is typically concerned with knowing *as many* people as possible. He is a quantitativist in the sphere of social contacts. Numbers count. In the words of an influential police officer (who thus echoes the sentiments of another "local," the Mayor):

> I have lots of friends in Rovere, if I do say so myself. I like to know everybody. If I stand on a corner, I can speak to 500 people in two hours. Knowing people helps when a promotion comes up, for instance. Everybody mentions you for the job. Influential people who know you talk to other people. Jack Flye [the Mayor] said to me one day, "Bill," he said, "you have more friends in town than I do. I wish I had all the friends you have that you don't even know of." It made me feel good. . . .

This typical attitude fits into what we know of the local type of influential. What is more, it suggests that the career-function of personal contacts and personal relations is recognized by local influentials themselves. Nor is this concern with personal contact merely a consequence of the occupations of local influentials. Businessmen, professionals, and local government officials among them all join in the same paeans on the desirability of many and varied contacts. A bank president recapitulates the same story in terms of his experience and outlook:

> I have always been glad to meet people. . . . It really started when I became a teller. The teller is the most important position in a bank as far as meeting people goes. As teller, you must meet everyone. You learn to know everybody by his first name. You don't have the same opportunity again to meet people. Right now we have a teller who is very capable but two or three people have come to me complaining about him. He is unfriendly with them. I told him, you've got to have a kind word for everyone. It's a personal and a business matter.

This keynote brings out the decisive interest of local influentials in all manner of personal contacts which enable them to establish themselves when they need political, business, or other support. Influentials in this group act on the explicit assumption that they can be locally prominent and influential by lining up enough people who know them and are hence willing to help them as well as be helped by them.

The cosmopolitan influentials, on the other hand, have notably little interest in meeting *as many* people as possible.[11] They are more selective in their choice of friends and acquaintances. They typically stress the importance of confining themselves to friends with whom "they can really talk," with whom they can "exchange ideas." If the local influentials are quantitativists, the cosmopolitans are qualitativists in this regard. It is not *how many* people they know but the *kind of people* they know that counts.[12]

The contrast with the prevailing attitudes of local influentials is brought out in these remarks by cosmopolitan influentials:

> I don't care to know people unless there is something to the person.

> I am not interested in quantity. I like to know about other people; it broadens your own education. I enjoy meeting people with knowledge and standing. Masses of humanity I don't go into. I like to meet people of equal mentality, learning and experience.

Just as with the local influentials, so here the basic attitude cuts across occupational and educational lines. Professional men among the

---

11. This was interestingly confirmed in the following fashion. Our informants were confronted with a random list of names of Rovere residents and were asked to identify each. Local influentials recognized more names than any other group of informants, and cosmopolitans, in turn, knew more persons than the non-influential informants.

12. In this pilot study, we have confined ourselves to the expression of attitudes toward personal contacts and relations. A detailed inquiry would examine the quantum and quality of *actual* personal relations characteristic of the local and cosmopolitan influentials.

cosmopolitans, for example, do not emphasize the importance of a wide and extensive acquaintanceship, if one is to build up a practice. In contrast to a "local" attorney who speaks of the "advantage to me to know as many people as possible," a "cosmopolitan" attorney waxes poetic and exclusive all in one, saying:

> I have never gone out and sought people. I have no pleasure in just going around and calling. As Polonius advised Laertes,
>   "Those friends thou hast, and their adoption tried,
>   Grapple them to thy soul with hoops of steel,
>   But do not dull the palm with entertainment
>   Of each new-hatch'd unfledged comrade. . . ."

In a later section of this study, we shall see that these diverse orientations of locals and cosmopolitans toward personal relations can be interpreted as a function of their distinctive modes of achieving influence. At the moment, it is sufficient to note that locals seek to enter into manifold networks of personal relations, whereas the cosmopolitans, *on the same status level*, explicitly limit the range of these relations.

Participation In Voluntary Organizations

In considering the sociability of locals and cosmopolitans, we examined their attitudes toward informal, personal relationships. But what of their roles in the more formal agencies for social contact: the voluntary organizations?

As might be anticipated, both types of influentials are affiliated with more organizations than rank-and-file members of the population. Cosmopolitan influentials belong to an average of eight organizations per individual, and the local influentials, to an average of six. This suggests the possibility that cosmopolitans make greater use of organizational channels to influence than of personal contacts, whereas locals, on the whole, operate contrariwise.

But as with sociability, so with organizations: the more instructive facts are qualitative rather than quantitative. It is not so much that the cosmopolitans belong to *more* organizations than the locals. Should a rigorous inquiry bear out this impression, it would still not locate the strategic organizational differences between the two. It is, rather, that they belong to different types of organizations. And once again, these differences reinforce what we have learned about the two kinds of influentials.

The local influentials evidently crowd into those organizations which are largely designed for "making contacts," for establishing personal ties. Thus, they are found largely in the secret societies (Masons), fraternal organizations (Elks), and local service clubs—the Rotary, Lions, and the Kiwanis, the most powerful organization of this type in Rovere. Their participation appears to be less a matter of furthering the nominal

objectives of these organizations than of using them as *contact centers.*
In the forthright words of one local influential, a businessman:

I get to know people through the service clubs; Kiwanis, Rotary, Lions. I
now belong only to the Kiwanis. Kiwanis is different from any other service
club. You have to be asked to join. They pick you out first, check you first.
Quite a few influential people are there and I get to meet them at lunch every
week.

The cosmopolitans, on the other hand, tend to belong to those organizations in which they can exercise their special skills and knowledge.
They are found in professional societies and in hobby groups. At the
time of the inquiry, in 1943, they were more often involved in Civilian
Defense organizations where again they were presumably more concerned with furthering the objectives of the organization than with
establishing personal ties.

Much the same contrast appears in the array of public offices held
by the two types of influentials. Seven of each type hold some public
office, although the locals have an average somewhat under one office.
The primary difference is in the *type* of office held. The locals tend to
hold political posts—street commissioner, mayor, township board, etc.—
ordinarily obtained through political and personal relationships. The
cosmopolitans, on the other hand, more often appear in public positions
which involve not merely political operations but the utilization of special
skills and knowledge (*e.g.*, Board of Health, Housing Committee, Board
of Education).

From all this we can set out the hypothesis that participation in
voluntary associations* has somewhat different functions for cosmopolitan and local influentials. Cosmopolitans are concerned with associations
primarily because of the activities of these organizations. They are means
for extending or exhibiting their skills and knowledge. Locals are primarily interested in associations not for their activities, but because these
provide a means for extending personal relationships. The basic orientations of locals and cosmopolitan influentials are thus diversely expressed
in organizational behavior as in other respects.

AVENUES TO INTERPERSONAL INFLUENCE

The foregoing differences in attachment to Rovere, sociability, and
organizational behavior help direct us to the different avenues to influence traveled by the locals and the cosmopolitans. And in mapping these
avenues we shall fill in the background needed to interpret the differences in communications behavior characteristic of the two types of
influentials.

---

* For types and functions of participation in such organizations, see Bernard
Barber, "Participation and mass apathy in associations," in Alvin W. Gouldner, (ed.)
Studies in Leadership (New York: Harper & Brothers, 1950), 477-504.

The locals have largely grown up in and with the town. For the most part, they have gone to school there, leaving only temporarily for their college and professional studies. They held their first jobs in Rovere and earned their first dollars from Rovere people. When they came to work out their career-pattern, Rovere was obviously the place in which to do so. It was the only town with which they were thoroughly familiar, in which they knew the ins and outs of politics, business, and social life. It was the only community which they knew and, equally important, which knew them. Here they had developed numerous personal relationships.

And this leads to the decisive attribute of the local influentials' path to success: far more than with the cosmopolitans, *their influence rests on an elaborate network of personal relationships.* In a formula which at once simplifies and highlights the essential fact, we can say: *the influence of local influentials rests not so much on what they know but on whom they know.*

Thus, the concern of the local influential with personal relations is in part the product and in part the instrument of his particular type of influence. The "local boy who makes good," it seems, is likely to make it through good personal relations. Since he is involved in personal relations long before he has entered seriously upon his career, it is the path of less resistance for him to continue to rely upon these relations as far as possible in his later career.

With the cosmopolitan influential, all this changes. Typically a newcomer to the community, he does not and cannot utilize personal ties as his chief claim to attention. He usually comes into the town fully equipped with the prestige and skills associated with his business or profession and his "worldly" experience. He begins his climb in the prestige-structure at a relatively high level. It is the prestige of his previous achievements and previously acquired skills which make him eligible for a place in the local influence-structure. Personal relations are much more the product than the instrumentality of his influence.

These differences in the location of career-patterns have some interesting consequences for the problems confronting the two types of influentials. First of all, there is some evidence, though far from conclusive, that the rise of the locals to influentiality is slow compared with that of the cosmopolitans. Dr. A, a minister, cosmopolitan, and reader of newsmagazines, remarked upon the ease with which he had made his mark locally:

> The advantage of being a minister is that *you don't have to* prove yourself. You are immediately accepted and received in all homes, including the best ones. [Italics inserted]

However sanguine this observation may be, it reflects the essential point that the newcomer who has "arrived" in the outside world, sooner takes his place among those with some measure of influence in the local community. In contrast, the local influentials *do* "have to prove" themselves. Thus, the local bank president who required some forty years to rise from his job as messenger boy, speaks feelingly of the slow, long road on which "I worked my way up."

The age-composition of the local and cosmopolitan influentials is also a straw in the wind with regard to the rate of rise to influence. All but two of the sixteen locals are over forty-five years of age, whereas fewer than two-thirds of the cosmopolitans are in this older age group.

Not only may the rate of ascent to influence be slower for the local than for the cosmopolitan, but the ascent involves some special difficulties deriving from the local's personal relations. It appears that these relations may hinder as well as help the local boy to "make good." He must overcome the obstacle of being intimately known to the community when he was "just a kid." He must somehow enable others to recognize his consistent change in status. Most importantly, people to whom he was once subordinate must be brought to the point of now recognizing him as, in some sense, superordinate. Recognition of this problem is not new. Kipling follows Matthew 13 in observing that "prophets have honour all over the Earth, except in the village where they were born." The problem of ascent in the influence-structure for the home-town individual may be precisely located in sociological terms: change of status within a group, particularly if it is fairly rapid, calls for the revamping of attitudes toward the mobile individual and the remaking of relations with him. The pre-existent structure of personal relations for a time thus restrains the ascent of the local influential. Only when he has broken through these established conceptions of him, will others accept the reversal of roles entailed in the rise of the local man to influence. A Rovere attorney, numbered among the local influentials, describes the pattern concisely:

> When I first opened up, people knew me so well in town that they treated me as if I still were a kid. It was hard to overcome. But after I took interest in various public and civic affairs, and became chairman of the Democratic organization and ran for the State legislature—knowing full well I wouldn't be elected—they started to take me seriously.

The cosmopolitan does not face the necessity for breaking down local preconceptions of himself before it is possible to have his status as an influential "taken seriously." As we have seen, his credentials are found in the prestige and authority of his attainments elsewhere. He thus manifests less interest in a wide range of personal contacts for two reasons. First, his influence stems from prestige rather than from reciprocities with others in the community. Secondly, the problem of disengaging himself from obsolete images of him as "a boy" does not exist for him, and consequently does not focus his attention upon personal relations as it does for the local influential.

The separate roads to influence traveled by the locals and cosmopolitans thus help account for their diverging orientations toward the local community, with all that these orientations entail.

SOCIAL STATUS IN ACTION:
INTERPERSONAL INFLUENCE

At this point, it may occur to the reader that the distinction between the local and cosmopolitan influentials is merely a reflection of differences in education or occupation. This does not appear to be the case.

It is true that the cosmopolitans among our interviewees have received more formal education than the locals. All but one of the cosmopolitans as compared with half of the locals are at least graduates of high school. It is also true that half of the locals are in "big business," as gauged by Rovere standards, whereas only two of the fourteen cosmopolitans fall in this group; and furthermore, that half of the cosmopolitan influentials are professional people as compared with fewer than a third of the locals.

But these differences in occupational or educational status do not appear to determine the diverse types of influentials. When we compare the behavior and orientations of professionals among the locals and cosmopolitans, their characteristic differences persist, even though they have the same types of occupation and have received the same type of education. Educational and occupational differences may *contribute* to the differences between the two types of influentials but they are not the *source* of these differences. Even as a professional, the local influential is more of a businessman and politician in his behavior and outlook than is the cosmopolitan. He utilizes personal relationships as an avenue to influence conspicuously more than does his cosmopolitan counterpart. In short, *it is the pattern of utilizing social status and not the formal contours of the status itself which is decisive.*[13]

While occupational status may be a major support for the cosmopolitan's rise to influence, it is merely an adjunct for the local. Whereas all five of the local professionals actively pursue local politics, the cosmopolitan professionals practically ignore organized political activity in Rovere. (Their offices tend to be honorary appointments.) Far from occupation serving to explain the differences between them, it appears that the same occupation has a different role in interpersonal influence according to whether it is pursued by a local or a cosmopolitan. This

---

13. The importance of actively seeking influence is evident from an analysis of "the upward mobile type," set forth in the monograph upon which this report is based. See also Granville Hicks, *Small Town* (New York: The Macmillan Co., 1946), 154, who describes a man who is evidently a local influential in these terms: "He is a typical politician, a born manipulator, a man who worships influence, *works hard to acquire it,* and does his best to convince other people that he has it." (Italics supplied)

bears out our earlier impression that "objective attributes" (education, occupation, etc.) do not suffice as indices of people exercising interpersonal influence.

The influential businessman, who among our small number of interviewees is found almost exclusively among the locals, typically utilizes his personal relations to enhance his influence. It is altogether likely that a larger sample would include businessmen who are cosmopolitan influentials and whose behavior differs significantly in this respect. Thus, Mr. H., regarded as exerting great influence in Rovere, illustrates the cosmopolitan big-business type. He arrived in Rovere as a top executive in a local manufacturing plant. He has established few personal ties. But he is sought out for advice precisely because he has "been around" and has the aura of a man familiar with the outside world of affairs. His influence rests upon an imputed expertness rather than upon sympathetic understanding of others.

This adds another dimension to the distinction between the two types of influential. It appears that the cosmopolitan influential has a following because *he knows;* the local influential, because *he understands.* The one is sought out for his specialized skills and experience; the other, for his intimate appreciation of intangible but affectively significant details. The two patterns are reflected in prevalent conceptions of the difference between "the extremely competent but impersonal medical specialist" and the "old family doctor." Or again, it is not unlike the difference between the "impersonal social welfare worker" and the "friendly precinct captain," which we have considered in Chapter I. It is not merely that the local political captain provides food-baskets and jobs, legal and extra-legal advice, that he sets to rights minor scrapes with the law, helps the bright poor boy to a political scholarship in a local college, looks after the bereaved—that he helps in a whole series of crises when a fellow needs a friend, and, above all, a friend who "knows the score" and can do something about it. It is not merely that he provides aid which gives him interpersonal influence. It is *the manner in which the aid is provided.* After all, specialized agencies do exist for dispensing this assistance. Welfare agencies, settlement houses, legal aid clinics, hospital clinics, public relief departments—these and many other organizations are available. But in contrast to the professional techniques of the welfare worker which often represent in the mind of the recipient the cold, bureaucratic dispensation of limited aid following upon detailed investigation are the unprofessional techniques of the precinct captain who asks no questions, exacts no compliance with legal rules of eligibility and does not "snoop" into private affairs. The precinct captain is a prototype of the "local" influential.

Interpersonal influence stemming from specialized expertness typically involves some social distance between the advice-giver and the

advice-seeker, whereas influence stemming from sympathetic understanding typically entails close personal relations. The first is the pattern
of the cosmopolitan influential; the second, of the local influential. Thus,
the operation of these patterns of influence gives a clue to the distinctive
orientations of the two types of influentials.[13a]

13a. All this still leaves open the problem of working out the patterns of social
interaction and of influence-relations *between* local and cosmopolitan influentials.
This problem has been explored in a current study of high schools in relation to the
value-structure of the environing community, a study by Paul F. Lazarsfeld in
collaboration with Richard Christie, Frank A. Pinner, Arnold Rogow, Louis Schneider
and Arthur Brodbeck.

In the course of this study, Frank A. Pinner found that school boards and school
superintendents evidently varied in their orientation: some were distinctly "local,"
others "cosmopolitan" in orientation. Nor is this, it appears, simply a matter of historical "accident." Pinner suggests that communities of different types tend to elect
people of differing orientation to the high school board. This, in turn, creates special
circumstances affecting the interaction of the school board and the school superintendent, depending on the primary orientation of both. The orientations of school
boards are also, it seems, linked up with the degree of control exercised over educational policies. The influentials in one community "being profoundly interested in
local affairs, were bound to subject all community functions to constant scrutiny and
to accept or reject policies as they seemed to be in agreement with or contradictory
to commonly accepted standards [in the local community]. By the same token, the
[other] district was a 'loosely' organized area in more than the sheer geographical
sense. Interest in local affairs was not equally shared by those who, in view of their
social and economic position, were capable of exerting some influence. As a result,
the policies controlling the operation of the high school need not represent the consensus of the influential groups in the community; rather, a large number of potentially influential people could, by default, leave the running of high school affairs
to some group of citizens who happened to take an interest in high school affairs.

"Degrees of 'looseness' and 'tightness' of a community structure are perhaps best
measured in terms of the administration's opportunity for maneuvering."

The study of the *interaction* between groups having differing composition in
terms of local and cosmopolitan influentials represents a definite advance upon the
ideas set forth in this paper. The concept of "tight" and "loose" community structures, as connected with the prevailingly local or cosmopolitan orientations of those
in strategically placed positions represents another advance. It is of more than passing interest that this conception of "loose" and "tight" social structures has been
independently *developed* by those engaged in the afore-mentioned study and, at a
far remove, by Bryce F. Ryan and Murray A. Straus, "The integration of Sinhalese
Society," *Research Studies of the State College of Washington*, 1954, 22, 179-227,
esp. 198 ff and 219 ff. It is important to emphasize that these conceptions are being
developed in the course of systematic emirical inquiry; else one becomes the professional adumbrationist who makes it his business to show that there is literally
nothing new under the sun, by the simple expedient of excising all that is new and
reducing it only to the old. It is only in this limited sense that one will find the
"same" central idea of "rigid" and "flexible" social structures in the writings of that
man of innumerable seminal ideas, Georg Simmel. See his essay, translated a half-
century ago by Albion W. Small and published in the *American Journal of Sociology*
during its early and impoverished years when American sociologists of intellectual
taste were compelled to draw upon the intellectual capital of European sociologists:
"The persistence of social groups," *American Journal of Sociology*, 1898, 3, 662-
698; 829-836; 1898, 4, 35-50. The most compact formulation of the ideas in question is this one: "The group may be preserved (1) by conserving with the utmost
tenacity its firmness and rigidity of form, so that the group may meet approaching
dangers with substantial resistance, and may preserve the relation of its elements
through all change of external conditions; (2) by the highest possible variability

There is reason to believe that further inquiry will find differing proportions of local and cosmopolitan influentials in different types of community structures. At least this implication can be provisionally drawn from the ongoing studies of technological and social change in a Pennsylvania city during the past fifty years being conducted by Dorothy S. Thomas, Thomas C. Cochran and their colleagues.* Their detailed historical and sociological analysis yields the finding that the city comprised two distinct types of population: "fairly permanent residents, many of whom had been born there, and a migrating group that continually came and went." On the basis of crude statistics of turnover of population in other American cities, the investigators conclude further that this condition is fairly widespread. It may well be that the first, more nearly permanent group includes the local type of influential and the second, relatively transient group, the cosmopolitan. Diverse types of communities presumably have differing proportions of the two kinds of population and of the two kinds of influentials.

Other recent studies have found more directly that the proportions and social situations of the two types of influentials vary as the social structure of the community varies. Eisenstadt reports, for example, that a traditional Yemenite community almost entirely lacks the cosmopolitan type, whereas both cosmopolitans and locals play their distinctive roles in several other communities under observation.** On the basis of Stouffer's study of civil liberties, David Riesman suggests ways in which the roles of local and cosmopolitan influentials may differ in different social structures. Cosmopolitans who take on positions of formal leadership in the community, he suggests, may be obliged to become middlemen of tolerance, as they are caught between the upper millstone of the tolerant élite and the nether one of the intolerant majority, and thus become shaped into being less tolerant than their former associates and

---

of its form, so that adaptation of form may be quickly accomplished in response to change of external conditions, so that the form of the group may adjust itself to any demand of circumstance." (831)

Evidently, the more it changes, the less it is the same thing. The re-emerging concepts of loose and tight social structures resemble the Simmelian observations; they are nevertheless significantly different in their implications.

* As reported by Thomas C. Cochran, "History and the social sciences," in *Relazioni del X Congresso Internazionale di Scienze Storiche* (Rome, 4-11 September 1955), I, 481-504, at 487-88 on the basis of Sidney Goldstein, *Patterns of Internal Migration in Norristown, Pennsylvania, 1900-1950,* 2 volumes (Ph.D. thesis, multigraphed), University of Pennsylvania, 1953.

** S. N. Eisenstadt, "Communication systems and social structure: an exploratory comparative study," *Public Opinion Quarterly,* 1955, 19, 154-167. A study of a small Southern town reports that the two types of influentials cannot be distinguished there; the present suggestion holds that, with the accumulation of research, it is no longer enough to report the presence or absence of the types of influentials. Rather, it is sociologically pertinent to search out the attributes of the social structure which make for varying proportions of these identifiable types of influentials. See A. Alexander Fanelli, "A typology of community leadership based on influence and interaction within the leader subsystem," *Social Forces,* 1956, 34, 332-338.

more so than their constituency. As a result of differing structural context, also, cosmopolitans among the community leaders, themselves more "tolerant" of civil liberties than others, may be in more vulnerable situations in the South than in the East and West. For Stouffer has found that among all but the college-educated, Southerners are far less tolerant of civil liberties than Northerners of like education; "This means," Riesman points out, "that the college graduate in the South is, in these respects, quite sharply cut off from the rest of the community, including even those with some college attendance, for although education is everywhere associated with tolerance, the gradations are much less steep in the North. Moreover, much the same is true in the South for metropolitan communities against smaller cities, though in this dimension there are substantial differences in the East as well."†

From this evidence which is only now being accumulated, it would seem that the emergence of the two types of influentials depends upon characteristic forms of environing social structure with their distinctive functional requirements.

Against this background of analysis it is now possible to consider more fully the utilization of mass communications by the local and the orientations of the two types of influentials.

THE COMMUNICATIONS BEHAVIOR OF INFLUENTIALS

It appears that communications behavior is part and parcel of the routines of life and basic orientations characteristic of the two types of influentials. Their selections of magazines, newspapers, and radio programs at once reflect and reinforce the basic orientations. Although the *motives* for their selection of materials from the vast flow of mass communications may vary widely, the psychological and social *functions* fulfilled by the selection are fairly limited. Since the local and cosmopolitan make distinctly different demands of their social environment, they utilize mass communications for distinctly different results.

Patterns and Functions of Magazine Reading

Cosmopolitan influentials apparently read more magazines—subscribing to four or five—than the locals, with their subscriptions to two or three. This is to be anticipated from what we know of their respective routines of life and orientations. The cosmopolitans, with their extra-local interests, devote themselves more fully to the kind of vicarious experience set forth in journals, whereas the locals are more immediately

---

† Samuel A. Stouffer, *Communism, Conformity, and Civil Liberties* (New York: Doubleday & Company 1955) provides the findings under review by David Riesman in his article, "Orbits of tolerance, interviewers, and elites," *Public Opinion Quarterly,* 1956, 20, 49-73.

concerned with direct interpersonal relations. The one tends to read about the great world outside, the other, to act in the little world inside. Their reading practices reflect their ways of life.

It is the variations in the *types* of magazines read by the locals and cosmopolitans, however, which more directly indicate the functions of these reading patterns. The influential reader of the newsmagazine, for example, is prevalently of the cosmopolitan rather than the local type. This is entirely expectable, in the light of the functions fulfilled by a magazine such as *Time*.

The newsmagazine provides news and views on a broad front. Promising to give its version of the news behind the news, it deals with current developments in national and international politics, industry and business, education, science, the arts. These constitute the very spheres in which the influence of the cosmopolitans is to be found; for, as we have seen, they are considered the expert arbiters of "good taste," or "culture," and of trends in the Great Society. By the same token, the national newsmagazine had little to say to the local influentials. It does not, after all, devote much space to Rovere and its environs. The reading of *Time* will contribute neither to the locals' understanding of Rovere life nor to their influence in the town. It is an entirely dispensable luxury.

For the cosmopolitan, however, the newsmagazine serves several functions. It provides a transmission-belt for the diffusion of "culture" from the outside world to the "cultural leaders" of Rovere. (This is particularly true for the women among the cosmopolitans.) Among the little coteries and clubs of like-minded cosmopolitans, it provides the stuff of conversation. It enables the cultural élite of Rovere's middle class to remain well in advance of those who seek them out for advice in matters of taste or for opinions concerning the trend of international developments. *Time* not only builds a bridge across the gulf between the cosmopolitan influential and the influenced; it helps maintain the gulf separating the knower from the uninformed. It thus supplies diverse gratifications for the cosmopolitans of Rovere. It enables them to retain a kind of contact with the world outside and reduces their sense of cultural isolation. It gives some a sense of "self-improvement," as they "keep up with things." It enables them to buttress their own position in the community, by enabling them to flourish their credentials of knowledge-ability when the occasion demands.

But since these are not the grounds of influence for the local influentials, since their social roles do not entail judgments about "culture" and the world at large, journals such as *Time* are superfluous.

Gratifications derived from mass communications, therefore, are not merely psychological in nature; they are also a product of the distinctive *social roles* of those who make use of these communications. It is not that the newsmagazine is *one man's meat* and *another man's poison.* It is, rather, that the newsmagazine is meat for one *social type* and poison for another *social type.* The analysis of the functions of mass communications requires prior analysis of the social roles which determine the uses to which these communications can and will be put. Had the social contexts of interpersonal influence not been explored, we could not have anticipated the selection of *Time* by one type of influential and its rejection by another.

Much the same can be said of the further magazine-reading of Rovere influentials. It so happens that for our handful of cases, the reading of *Time* most clearly differentiates the locals and the cosmopolitans. But the same patterns of selection operate with other magazines. *Atlantic Monthly, Harper's, National Geographic*—the so-called "class" magazines which devote much of their content to foreign and national affairs and to the arts are read by twice as many cosmopolitans as locals. For virtually all other magazines, there seems to be no difference between the two. *Reader's Digest* and *Life* appear with equal frequency. A large-scale study could readily check the impression that *upon the same educational level,* local and cosmopolitan influentials have different patterns of magazine reading and that these can be explained in terms of the magazines satisfying distinctly different functions for the two groups.

Patterns and Functions of Newspaper Reading

Reading national newsmagazines is an act above and beyond the call of dutiful newspaper reading. It implies an interest in being "in on things," in "developing responsible opinions," in having a "distinctive point of view." Interestingly enough, it appears that the patterns of newspaper reading also reflect the different orientations of the local and the cosmopolitan influential.

Locals read more newspapers, but this is wholly accounted for by their greater proclivity for Rovere and other local newspapers (in a nearby city). The picture is quite different for metropolitan newspapers. Every one of the cosmopolitans reads the *New York Times* or the *New York Herald Tribune,* or both, while the locals less often turn to these papers with their wide and analytical coverage of world news. The contrast extends to details. Almost half of the locals read New York tabloids, with their capsule treatments of world affairs and their emphasis on "human interest" news—murder, divorce, and daring crimes appear to be major foci of contemporary human interest—but only one cosmopolitan includes a tabloid in his newspaper diet. However these statistical distributions might turn out in a detailed study, the consistency of these exploratory facts suggests that the basic orientations of influentials are also expressed in their patterns of newspaper reading.

Patterns and Functions of Listening to Radio News Commentators

There is some evidence that the predilection of cosmopolitans for an impersonal, analytical understanding of world events is reflected in their routines of listening to radio news commentators. On the basis of an earlier study by the Bureau of Applied Social Research, commentators were classified according to the degree to which they "analyzed" rather than "reported" news, particularly world news. The cosmopolitans prefer the more analytical commentators (Swing, Hughes) while the locals are more interested in those who forego analysis and are virtually newscasters (Thomas, Goddard, etc.).

Even in the realm of "extra-local news," the locals manage to import a localistic criterion. They distinctly prefer those commentators who typically convert news and public issues into *personalized* anecdotes. Gabriel Heatter with his infusions of sentiment into political and economic affairs is a favorite of the locals but not of the cosmopolitans. So, too, with Walter Winchell, who reports the Broadway version of intimate gossip across the backfence and personalizes national and international issues. The local influentials seek out the personal ingredients in the impersonal array of world news.

Communications behavior thus appears to reflect the basic orientations of local and cosmopolitan influentials. Further inquiry should provide a sound statistical check and make more rigorous tests of these impressions. Do locals and influentials who read "the *same*" magazines, for example, actually select the same contents in these magazines? Or do the locals characteristically focus upon the "personalized and localistic" components in the editorial material, whereas the cosmopolitans seek out the more impersonal and "informative" components? To what uses do these different types of readers put the materials which they have read? In other words, how do the contents of mass communications enter into the flow of interpersonal influence?[14] Studies in the sociology of mass communications must supplement analyses in terms of personal attributes of readers and listeners with analyses of their social roles and their implication in networks of interpersonal relations.

PATTERNS OF RECIPROCAL EVALUATIONS

To this point, we have been examining the influentials: their diverse modes of exerting interpersonal influence, their avenues to positions of influence, their communications behavior. But, after all, we consider these persons as influential only because they are so reported by our

---

14. This is precisely the focus in the study of influence patterns by Katz and Lazarsfeld, *op. cit.*

informants.[15] What can we learn about patterns of interpersonal influence by looking at patterns of reciprocal evaluations? What can we learn by looking at the relations between the mentionee and the mentioner, between those who emerge as variously influential and those whose judgments have defined them as influential?

THE INFLUENTIAL AND THE INFLUENCED

Although one often speaks of "men of influence," it is clear that this phrase is an elliptical way of saying: "men who exert influence upon a certain number of other people in certain situations." As noted in the postscript to this chapter, interpersonal influence implies an asymmetrical *relation* between people. Influence is not an abstract attribute of a person, it is a process implicating two or more people. Accordingly, in an analysis of these patterns, we must look not *only* at the man who is influential, but also at the people who are influenced by him. Otherwise put, we have much to learn by exploring the question: who is influential for whom?

This general question at once divides into a series of more specific questions. Who are influential for people variously located in the influence-structure? Are people more often subject to influence by those above them in the influence-structure or by people in their own stratum of influence?

When the Rovere informants are divided into "top influentials" (those mentioned by 15 per cent or more of our informants), the "middle influentials" (mentioned by 5 to 14 per cent), and the "rank-and-file" (mentioned by fewer than 5 per cent), and when we relate these to their identifications of people who exert influence upon them, several clear impressions emerge. There is an impressive agreement on every level of the influence-structure concerning the people who belong at the top of the structure. Very largely, it is the *same* people who are reported as influential, irrespective of the position in the influence-structure of those who do the judging. From two-thirds to three-quarters of mentions by the three strata are concentrated on the top 15 per cent of influentials.

However, differences among the several strata in the influence structure do occur. Informants in each influence-stratum report a larger proportion of people in their own stratum as influential for them than do

---

15. It should be repeated that interpersonal influence is here regarded as not simply a matter of evaluation, but as a matter of fact. Whether the *judgments* of informants and *objective observation* would lead to the same results must remain an open question. This exploratory study has utilized informants' reports in order to locate certain types of problems with respect to interpersonal influence; a full-fledged inquiry would utilize observation as well as interviews to ascertain the actual degree of interpersonal influence and the spheres in which this is exercised.

informants in the other strata. More concretely: the top influentials are more likely to mention others among the top influentials than are middle influentials or rank-and-file informants; the middle influentials are more likely to mention other middle influentials than are either the top influentials or the rank-and-file; and the rank-and-file more often mention people in this stratum than do the other informants. One thus gains the impression that although a relatively few people—the top influentials— exert influence upon people on all levels of the influence-structure, there occurs a secondary tendency for people to be otherwise most influenced by their peers in that structure. If this proves to be generally true, it is a most important fact concerning the operation of interpersonal influence.

The striking concentration of interpersonal influence may divert our attention from the entire distribution of influence. This could easily lead to mistaken inferences. Despite this concentration, it appears likely that *more personal decisions in a community may be the result of advice by the many people ranking low in the influence-structure than by the few ranked at the top.* For although the top influentials *individually* have a large measure of interpersonal influence, they are likely to be so few in number that they *collectively* have a minor share of the total amount of interpersonal influence in the community. And correlatively, although *each person* among the middle-influentials and the rank-and- file has relatively little influence, they may *collectively* account for the greater share of interpersonal influence, since these strata include the great bulk of people in the community.[16] To take the Southtown data as indicative, the top 4 per cent of the influentials were cited in about 40 per cent of all instances of influence, but the fact remains that the residual 60 per cent referred to people ranking lower in the local influ- ence-structure. Much the same was found in the present pilot study. Our Rovere inquiry is sufficient to formulate, though not, of course, to con- firm the central point: a few individuals at the top may have a large *individual* quantum of influence, but the *total* amount of influence of this comparatively small group may be less than that exercised by the large numbers of people found toward the lower ranges of the influ- ence-structure.

Our pilot study has thus far yielded two major impressions concern- ing the structure of influence which await further inquiry: (1) people

---

16. The empirical force of this consideration is like that found in studies of the social distribution of genius or talent (or, for that matter, of the distribution of purchasing power). It has been repeatedly found that the upper social and educa- tional strata have a relatively higher proportion of "geniuses" or "talents." But since the numbers in these strata are small, the great bulk of geniuses or talents actually come from lower social strata. From the standpoint of the society, of course, it is the *absolute number* and not the *proportion* coming from any given social stratum which matters.

in each influence stratum are more likely to be influenced by their peers in this structure than are people in the other strata and (2) despite the great concentration of interpersonal influence among a relatively few individuals, the bulk of such influence is widely dispersed among the large number of people in the lower reaches of that structure.

A third impression deserving further inquiry is suggestive of the pattern through which interpersonal influence percolates down through the influence-structure. From the Rovere data, it appears that this structure involves a "chain of influence," with the links in the chain constituted by persons in adjacent strata of influence. People in each influence-stratum are more likely to regard as influential people who are in the stratum *immediately above* their own than are informants in other strata, either above or further below. Thus rank-and-file informants looking upward toward their adjacent stratum (the middle influentials) more often mention these people as influential than do the top influentials, and middle influentials, in turn, more often mention the top influentials than do the rank-and-file. This suggests that some opinions and advice originated (or derived from mass communications) by the top influentials may be passed on progressively down the line. Other opinions, originating at lower levels in the structure, may be successively transmitted through adjacent successively lower strata. Our limited materials provide only a straw in the wind. In a full-scale inquiry dealing with several strata of influentials, this impression of a pattern of the percolation of interpersonal influence could be put to a decisive test.

We have thus far considered these patterns solely in terms of the position of the influenced and the influencer in the local influence-structure. Manifestly, it would be rewarding to examine the same patterns from the standpoint of the location of people in other social systems. The generic problem can be stated briefly enough: to what extent and in which situations does interpersonal influence operate largely *within* one's own social group or stratum or category (age, sex, class- power-stratum, prestige-stratum, etc.) and when does it operate largely *between* groups, strata, or social categories? Since the outlines of this problem were set forth in the introductory sections and since the problem is, *mutatis mutandis,* much the same as the foregoing, only a few symptomatic questions need be raised here.

Do men and women generally turn to others of their own age, their own sex, their own social class or religious group for advice and guidance? How, for example, does age enter into the pattern? How general is the tendency, detectible in both the Rovere and the Southtown materials, for people to be influenced by those somewhat older than themselves? How does this differ among various types of communities and among the various subcultures in our society? When does a youngster turn to a more seasoned veteran for advice and when does he talk it out with another youngster.[17] So, too, much remains to be learned about the canalizing of influence along sex lines. The Rovere and Southtown studies both found a distinct tendency for men to report the influence of other men, whereas women reported male and female influentials in almost equal numbers. Further inquiry would undoubtedly detect spheres of influence virtually monopolized by men, others by women, and still others shared in more or less equal measure.[18]

Similarly, although the major flow of interpersonal influence appears to be from the upper social strata downward, there is a discernible stream in the opposite direction. What needs to be learned is the type of situation in which people are primarily influenced by others on the same status level, and by those on a higher or lower level. It is needful to search out particularly the deviate cases where people ranking high in some status-hierarchy (power, class, prestige) are influenced by others of lower standing. Thus, in a handful of cases, upper-status people in Rovere report having been influenced by people generally regarded as lacking in substantial influence. Indeed, our case materials suggest the possibility that people at the top, presumably with a large share of self-assurance and security of status, are more likely than middle-status individuals, possibly less secure in their position, to turn for occasional advice to people toward the bottom of the hierarchy. Although these cases are in general probably few in number, they may yield great insight into the workings of interpersonal influence. As in the case with the concentration of influence, there is the danger here that the research worker may confine himself to the major patterns, thus losing sight of the instructive subsidiary patternings of influence.

Questions of this order, growing out of our initial inquiry, can be readily multiplied. But these may perhaps suffice as prototypes. Clearly, all of these questions must be raised anew for each distinct sphere of influence, since it is altogether likely that the patterns will differ according to the sphere of activity and attitude in which influence is exercised. Though this has been presupposed throughout our account, the special problem of spheres of influence requires distinct, though brief, examination.

SPHERES OF INFLUENCE:
MONOMORPHIC AND POLYMORPHIC

In Rovere, influentials differ widely with respect to the *number of*

---

17. Here, as for all other questions raised in this section, it is understood that observed patterns will differ for different *spheres of influence*. This need not therefore be repeated anew for each battery of questions. The general problem of spheres of influence will be briefly discussed in the following section.

18. Substantial beginnings of answers to questions such as these are provided by Katz and Lazarsfeld, *op. cit.*

spheres of activity in which they exert interpersonal influence. Some influentials, and these may be termed *monomorphic*, are repeatedly cited as exerting influence, but only in one rather narrowly defined area—e.g. the area of politics, *or* of canons of good taste, *or* of fashion. The monomorphic influentials are the "experts" in a limited field, and their influence does not diffuse into other spheres of decision. Others, and this includes a good number of the top influentials, are *polymorphic*, exerting interpersonal influence in a variety of (sometimes seemingly unrelated) spheres. Although the types were readily identifiable in the Rovere study, much remains to be learned about them. Above all, the dynamics of these types needs to be established. Under which conditions does the influential remain monomorphic? Is this a stable type—or, is it rather a *stage* in the development of influence, such that the monomorphic in due course tends to become polymorphic through the operation of the transfer of prestige from one sphere to others (the "halo effect")? Perhaps monomorphic influence occurs only in certain spheres involving high specialization of skill and little public recognition. Under such conditions, a monomorphic influential—the biophysicist, for example—may be asked for advice only on matters touching upon his special sphere of competence—"what should we do about a National Science Foundation?"— and his influence may be such that monomorphic influence soon gives way to the polymorphic exercise of interpersonal influence in diverse respects: "authority" may be generalized and transferred.

We may go on to inquire into the comparative number of spheres in which the local and the cosmopolitan influentials are effective. One gains the impression from the Rovere materials that locals and cosmopolitans not only exert influence in different spheres, but also that the locals are the more likely to be polymorphic and the cosmopolitans, monomorphic. Apparently, the influence of the locals, based largely on their personal "connections," ramifies into many and diverse spheres; influence of the cosmopolitans, more often stemming from certain types of seeming expertness, tends to be more narrowly circumscribed.

So, too, it will be instructive to learn whether the *same* individuals exert monomorphic influence upon some persons and polymorphic influences upon others. It may turn out, for example, that influentials advising people of their own social stratum characteristically do so in a variety of fields whereas they are influential for a more limited range of decisions for followers of a lower social stratum. However this may be, it should not be assumed that *individuals* "are" monomorphic or polymorphic, but rather that they *operate* as the one type or the other, according to the structure of the situation.*

---

* S. N. Eisenstadt reports that this distinction is "clearly discernible" among various groups of European immigrants in Israel. See his "Communication processes

All this highlights the need to clarify such terms as "men of influence" or "opinion-leaders." An individual may be regarded as influential when he has a large following in one sphere of activity just as another may be so regarded because he has several small followings in diverse spheres. Further inquiry into interpersonal influence must seek to identify the monomorphic and polymorphic influentials, locate these within the local social structure and establish the dynamics of change from one type to the other.

A final suggestion is needed for future studies into the interpersonal influence-structure of a community. This preliminary inquiry strongly suggests (and this is borne out by the Southtown study) that formal criteria such as education, income, participation in voluntary organizations, number of references in the local newspaper and the like,[19] do not provide adequate indicators of those individuals who exert a significant measure of interpersonal influence. Systematic interviewing supplemented by direct observation are required. Otherwise put, location within various social hierarchies of wealth, power, and class does not predetermine location within a local structure of interpersonal influence.

ADDENDUM: THE PROVISIONAL CONCEPT OF INTERPERSONAL INFLUENCE

Confined to the subject of "interpersonal influence," this study does not deal with social influence in general. Interpersonal influence refers to the direct interaction of persons in so far as this affects the *future* behavior or attitude of participants (such that this differs from what it would have been in the absence of interaction).[20]

The strategic significance of the concept of "influence" in social science has lately become increasingly evident. Among the numerous recent developments of this conception, I single out only the analysis by

---

among immigrants in Israel," *Public Opinion Quarterly*, 1952, 16, 42-58. Robert E. Agger has traced the types of influence exercised by polymorphic influentials in matter of school policy, local government, and community welfare in a small town. "Power attributions in the local community: theoretical and research considerations," *Social Forces*, 1956, 34, 322-331.

19. Influence through mass media is patently not the same as interpersonal influence. It is suggestive, for example, that neither in Rovere nor in Frank Stewart's Southtown was the editor of the local newspaper included among those exerting appreciable interpersonal influence.

20. This is adapted from the formulation by Herbert Goldhamer and Edward A. Shils. "Types of power and status," *American Journal of Sociology*, 1939, 45, 171-182. The reasons for modifying their formulation will become progressively clear. My emphasis upon *future* behavior or attitude can be readily understood. If "influence" referred to any and all alterations of behavior it would be virtually identical with "social interaction," since all interaction has an effect, however slight, upon behavior in the immediate situation. One does not act precisely the same in the presence of others as in isolation.

James G. March[20a] which, avowedly tentative as it is, represents a distinct forward step. Influence is successively defined in terms compatible with the foregoing conception as that "which induces a change in the state of the organism different from that [which is] predictable." It is a particular instance of causality, plainly not co-extensive with it. As March indicates, however, we can identify cases of manifest behavior which *can* be predicted on the basis of information about the state of the person and which, nevertheless, may have been interpersonally influenced. (March prefers to speak of the state of "the individual organism." For the sociologist, the organism is in some respects more inclusive a concept than the person, including as it does biological and other non-social attributes, and in other respects, less inclusive, excluding as it typically does the social position and relations of the person.) He makes the important observation, in the light of this conception, that "Although it is frequently possible to establish the fact that interpersonal influence has occurred, it is peculiarly difficult to establish the fact that no such influence has taken place. Partly for this reason, a distinction needs to be made between the influence relationship between two events (*e.g.,* "A votes yes," "B votes yes") and the relationship between two individuals (*e.g.* A, B)." (435)

These conceptions afford March a basis for appraising the worth and limitations of current methods of measuring influence. Although this need not be re-examined here, it is important to take note of March's general conclusion that, until now, these measurements have been *ad hoc* rather than theoretically derived and standardized. As he concludes, "It is extraordinary—but true—that despite the fact that there are currently in use a significant number of distinctly different methods of measuring 'influence,' it is not at all clear under what conditions they provide comparable answers. It is, of course, possible, though rarely useful, to define a concept by a measurement technique [which is not derived from a set of systematic ideas about the substantive concept]; but in the absence of some knowledge of the inter-correlations involved, one cannot define the same concept by several different measurement procedures. Yet this is the current state of influence measurement. Similarly, one can find few serious attempts in the literature to relate formal definitions of influence either to measurement methods or to the main body of social science theory." (450-451)

20a. James G. March, "An introduction to the theory and measurement of influence," *The American Political Science Review*, 1955, 49, 431-451. March draws substantially upon the work of his colleague, Herbert A. Simon, *e.g.* "Notes on the observation and measurement of political power," *Journal of Politics*, 1953, 15, 500-516. See also L. Festinger, H. B. Gerard, B. Hymovitch, H. H. Kelley and B. Raven, "The influence process in the presence of extreme deviates," *Human Relations*, 1952, 5, 327-346.

The observation is true and what is equally in point, useful. It serves to *specify our ignorance* in this matter of developing measures connected with the concept of influence and, as the history of thought, both great and small, attests, *specified* ignorance is often a first step toward supplanting that ignorance with knowledge.

Problems of interpersonal influence have been less often singled out for systematic attention by sociologists than they have been touched upon in discussions of social stratification. The reasons for this are clear enough. Interpersonal influence implies an *asymmetrical social relation:* there is the influencer and the influenced, with respect to any given behavior or attitude. Of course, reciprocal influence often occurs. But even in such instances, the degree of influence in both directions is seldom equal and is seldom exerted upon the same behavior. It is this asymmetrical character of interpersonal influence which accounts for its being bound up with discussions of social stratification generally. For however much the various analyses of stratification differ, they of course agree that stratification implies asymmetrical social positions (i.e., ranks). (If positions were completely symmetrical, if all were in fact *equal* in rank, the concept of stratification would be superfluous.)[20b]

As a result of being caught up in general discussions of stratification rather than being the immediate focus of inquiry, the concept of interpersonal influence has become confusingly merged with related concepts. To clarify our provisional concept of interpersonal influence, therefore, it is necessary to locate it within the framework of stratification analyses.

Numerous recent discussions of stratification have given rise to a vast array of related concepts and terms. Among these, we find

terms for generic social position: status, rank, situs, socio-economic status, locus, stratum, station, standing;

20b. Compare the observation by March on one similarity between causal relations and more narrowly conceived influence relations. "Both relations are asymmetrical. That is, the statement that A *causes* B excludes the possibility that B *causes* A. Similarly, the statement that A *influences* B excludes the possibility that B *influences* A. Here again, much of the confusion in the theoretical discussion of influence stems from the failure to distinguish the influence relationship between events (i.e., subsets of activities by individuals) and the influence relationship between individuals (i.e., the complete sets of activities by individuals). The fact that it appears to be possible to speak of asymmetries holding between events but not so frequently possible to speak of influence asymmetries between individuals (e.g., the sharing of influence may often be exhibited in the form of influence specialization according to 'area') suggests that the appropriate model for the description of an influence relationship between two individuals is one in which the influence-related activities of the individuals are partitioned into mutually-exclusive sets in such a way that within each set asymmetry holds between the individual agents of the activities." *Ibid.*, 436, and the previously cited "notes" by Simon.

Correlatively, these asymmetries provide a basis for distinguishing *influentials* who wield influence in many spheres of conduct and opinion and those who do so in one sphere or few.

terms for specific social position: upper-, middle-, lower-class, parvenu, *arrivés, declassés,* aristocracy, etc.;

terms for stratification structures: open-class system, *Ständesystem,* caste, prestige-hierarchy, economic-, political-, social-hierarchy, etc.;

terms for attributes of position (sources, symbols, criteria, determinants): wealth, power, prestige, achievement, ascription, style of life, status honor, authority, *etc.;*

terms referring to the operation of the position: the exercising of power, control, influence, exclusion, domination, subordination, discrimination, coercion, manipulation, *etc.*

This selected array of terms suggests that terminologies may have been multiplied beyond strict necessity and that there is a large number of problems attending the interrelations of these concepts. It suggests, further, that populations may be socially stratified in different hierarchies. In ways not too clearly understood, these several hierarchies of stratification are inter-related. But we cannot *assume* that they are identical. The sociological problem here is manifestly to explore the interrelations between the several hierarchies, and not to blur the problem by *assuming* that they can be merged into a composite system of ranking.[21]

In the present study, therefore, we assume that *position in a local structure of interpersonal influence may be related to position in other hierarchies but is not identical with it.* This assumption has both empirical and conceptual basis. Empirical support is provided by a study

---

21. The *locus classicus* for this formulation is Max Weber's analysis of class, status, and power, now available in an English translation by Hans H. Gerth and C. Wright Mills, *From Max Weber: Essays in Sociology* (New York: Oxford University Press, 1946), 180 ff. and in a translation by A. R. Henderson and Talcott Parsons, *The Theory of Social and Economic Organization* (London: Wm. Hodge, 1947), 390-395. More recent discussions have in some measure built upon the foundation laid down by Weber. Among the numerous accounts, see Talcott Parsons, "A revised analytical approach to the theory of social stratification," in Reinhard Bendix and S. M. Lipset (eds.), *Class, Status and Power: A Reader in Social Stratification* (Glencoe, Illinois: The Free Press, 1953), 92-128; Kingsley Davis, "A conceptual analysis of stratification," *American Sociological Review,* 1942, 7, 309-321; Emile Benoit-Smullyan, "Status, status types and status interrelations," *American Sociological Review,* 1944, 9, 151-161, and Bernard Barber, *Social Stratification* (New York: Harcourt, Brace, 1957).

For empirical efforts to clarify these problems, see W. L. Warner and P. S. Lunt, *The Social Life of a Modern Community* (New Haven: Yale University Press, 1941); Harold F. Kaufman, *Prestige Classes in a New York Rural Community* (Cornell University Agricultural Experiment Station, Memoir 260, March 1944) and the same author's *Defining Prestige in a Rural Community,* Sociometry Monographs, No. 10 (Beacon, N. Y.: Beacon House, 1946); A. B. Hollingshead, "Selected characteristics of classes in a middle western community," *American Sociological Review,* 1947, 12, 385-395; C. Wright Mills, "The middle classes in middle-sized cities," *American Sociological Review,* 1946, 11, 520-529.

The largest accumulation of recent data bearing upon this problem is to be found in the Warner-Lunt volume, but the analysis suffers from the absence of the type of conceptual distinctions supplied by Weber.

of political behavior[22] which found that "the opinion-leaders are not identical with the socially prominent people in the community or the richest people or the civic leaders." By briefly exploring types of relations between several systems of stratification, we find further grounds for this assumption.

Although they may be variously correlated, interpersonal influence, social class, prestige and power do *not* coincide. Ranked in terms of the size and source of income and accumulated wealth, some members of "the upper middle class" may be found to exert less direct influence upon the decisions of a few associates than some members of "the lower class" exert upon *their* many associates. People ranking high in a certain kind of prestige-hierarchy—based, say, on genealogical criteria—may have little interpersonal influence upon all those who are not concerned with their particular spheres of activity and opinion (e.g., the arts, fashion, "good taste"). Even the closely related concepts of power and interpersonal influence are not identical. Men with power to affect the economic life-chances of a large group may exert little interpersonal influence in other spheres: the power to withhold jobs from people may not result in directly influencing their political or associational or religious behavior.

So, too, with the other interrelations. People high in a prestige-hierarchy may not have the power to enforce decisions on others in many types of specified situations. (The power to exclude certain people from membership in an "exclusive" club should be distinguished from the power to exclude them from gaining a livelihood in their current occupation.) People high in a power-hierarchy may have little prestige (the political boss and the successful racketeer being only the more stereotyped instances).

In short, positions in the class, power, and prestige hierarchies contribute to the potential for interpersonal influence, but do not determine the extent to which influence actually occurs.

Just as the *bases* of interpersonal influence vary, so do its *forms*. Influence may thus take such forms as:

coercion (force, violence);
domination (commands, without threat of force);
manipulation (when the influencer's objectives are not made explicit);[23]
clarification (in which the setting forth of alternative lines of action affects subsequent behavior);
prototypes for imitation (in which the person exerting influence is not aware that interaction has resulted in modification of the others' subsequent behavior or attitude);

---

22. Lazarsfeld, Berelson and Gaudet, *The People's Choice*, 50 and chapter XVI.

23. Cf. Goldhamer and Shils, *op. cit.*, 171-172. Since these authors confine themselves to a discussion of power, they deal only with force, domination, and manipulation. See also K. Davis, *op. cit.*, 319, who adds "exchange" to the forms of influence.

advice (consisting of opinions and recommendations, but not commands); and *exchange* (in which each person openly modifies the situation so as to lead the other to given forms of behavior).

In the present inquiry, we have been primarily concerned with influence in the form of clarification, advice, and as a prototype for imitation. We are *not* here concerned with the indirect exercise of power through market, political, and other administrative behavior, with its effects upon large numbers of people. It is the people who emerge as having an appreciable measure of *interpersonal* influence, manifested directly in 'heir relations with others, who are the objects of inquiry.

XI   THE SELF-FULFILLING PROPHECY

IN A SERIES OF WORKS seldom consulted outside the academic fraternity, W. I. Thomas, the dean of American sociologists, set forth a theorem basic to the social sciences: "If men define situations as real, they are real in their consequences." Were the Thomas theorem and its implications more widely known more men would understand more of the workings of our society. Though it lacks the sweep and precision of a Newtonian theorem, it possesses the same gift of relevance, being instructively applicable to many, if indeed not most, social processes.

THE THOMAS THEOREM

"If men define situations as real, they are real in their consequences," wrote Professor Thomas. The suspicion that he was driving at a crucial point becomes all the more insistent when we note that essentially the same theorem had been repeatedly set forth by disciplined and observant minds long before Thomas.

When we find such otherwise discrepant minds as the redoubtable Bishop Bossuet in his passionate seventeenth-century defense of Catholic orthodoxy, the ironic Mandeville in his eighteenth-century allegory honeycombed with observations on the paradoxes of human society, the irascible genius Marx in his revision of Hegel's theory of historical change, the seminal Freud in works which have perhaps gone further than any others of his day toward modifying man's outlook on man, and the erudite, dogmatic, and occasionally sound Yale professor, William Graham Sumner, who lives on as the Karl Marx of the middle classes— when we find this mixed company (and I select from a longer if less distinguished list) agreeing on the truth and the pertinence of what is substantially the Thomas theorem, we may conclude that perhaps it is worth our attention as well.

To what, then, are Thomas and Bossuet, Mandeville, Marx, Freud and Sumner directing our attention?

The first part of the theorem provides an unceasing reminder that men respond not only to the objective features of a situation, but also, and at times primarily, to the meaning this situation has for them. And once they have assigned some meaning to the situation, their consequent behavior and some of the consequences of that behavior are determined by the ascribed meaning. But this is still rather abstract, and abstractions have a way of becoming unintelligible if they are not occasionally tied to concrete data. What is a case in point?

A SOCIOLOGICAL PARABLE

It is the year 1932. The Last National Bank is a flourishing institution. A large part of its resources is liquid without being watered. Cartwright Millingville has ample reason to be proud of the banking institution over which he presides. Until Black Wednesday. As he enters his bank, he notices that business is unusually brisk. A little odd, that, since the men at the A.M.O.K. steel plant and the K.O.M.A. mattress factory are not usually paid until Saturday. Yet here are two dozen men, obviously from the factories, queued up in front of the tellers' cages. As he turns into his private office, the president muses rather compassionately: "Hope they haven't been laid off in midweek. They should be in the shop at this hour."

But speculations of this sort have never made for a thriving bank, and Millingville turns to the pile of documents upon his desk. His precise signature is affixed to fewer than a score of papers when he is disturbed by the absence of something familiar and the intrusion of something alien. The low discreet hum of bank business has given way to a strange and annoying stridency of many voices. A situation has been defined as real. And that is the beginning of what ends as Black Wednesday—the last Wednesday, it might be noted, of the Last National Bank.

Cartwright Millingville had never heard of the Thomas theorem. But he had no difficulty in recognizing its workings. He knew that, despite the comparative liquidity of the bank's assets, a rumor of insolvency, once believed by enough depositors, would result in the insolvency of the bank. And by the close of Black Wednesday—and Blacker Thursday —when the long lines of anxious depositors, each frantically seeking to salvage his own, grew to longer lines of even more anxious depositors, it turned out that he was right.

The stable financial structure of the bank had depended upon one set of definitions of the situation: belief in the validity of the interlocking system of economic promises men live by. Once depositors had defined the situation otherwise, once they questioned the possibility of having these promises fulfilled, the consequences of this unreal definition were real enough.

A familiar type-case this, and one doesn't need the Thomas theorem to understand how it happened—not, at least, if one is old enough to have voted for Franklin Roosevelt in 1932. But with the aid of the theorem the tragic history of Millingville's bank can perhaps be converted into a sociological parable which may help us understand not only what happened to hundreds of banks in the '30's but also what happens to the relations between Negro and white, between Protestant and Catholic and Jew in these days.

The parable tells us that public definitions of a situation (prophecies or predictions) become an integral part of the situation and thus affect subsequent developments. This is peculiar to human affairs. It is not found in the world of nature, untouched by human hands. Predictions of the return of Halley's comet do not influence its orbit. But the rumored insolvency of Millingville's bank did affect the actual outcome. The prophecy of collapse led to its own fulfillment.

So common is the pattern of the self-fulfilling prophecy that each of us has his favored specimen. Consider the case of the examination neurosis. Convinced that he is destined to fail, the anxious student devotes more time to worry than to study and then turns in a poor examination. The initially fallacious anxiety is transformed into an entirely justified fear. Or it is believed that war between two nations is inevitable. Actuated by this conviction, representatives of the two nations become progressively alienated, apprehensively countering each "offensive" move of the other with a "defensive" move of their own. Stockpiles of armaments, raw materials, and armed men grow larger and eventually the anticipation of war helps create the actuality.

The self-fulfilling prophecy is, in the beginning, a *false* definition of the situation evoking a new behavior which makes the originally false conception come *true*. The specious validity of the self-fulfilling prophecy perpetuates a reign of error. For the prophet will cite the actual course of events as proof that he was right from the very beginning. (Yet we know that Millingville's bank was solvent, that it would have survived for many years had not the misleading rumor *created* the very conditions of its own fulfillment.) Such are the perversities of social logic.

It is the self-fulfilling prophecy which goes far toward explaining the dynamics of ethnic and racial conflict in the America of today. That this is the case, at least for relations between Negroes and whites, may be gathered from the fifteen hundred pages which make up Gunnar Myrdal's *An American Dilemma*. That the self-fulfilling prophecy may have even more general bearing upon the relations between ethnic groups than Myrdal has indicated is the thesis of the considerably briefer discussion that follows.[1]

---

1. Counterpart of the self-fulfilling prophecy is the "suicidal prophecy" which so alters human behavior from what would have been its course had the prophecy not been made, that it *fails* to be borne out. The prophecy destroys itself. This important type is not considered here. For examples of both types of social prophecy, see R. M.

SOCIAL BELIEFS AND SOCIAL REALITY

As a result of their failure to comprehend the operation of the self-fulfilling prophecy, many Americans of good will (sometimes reluctantly) retain enduring ethnic and racial prejudices. They experience these beliefs, not as prejudices, not as prejudgments, but as irresistible products of their own observation. "The facts of the case" permit them no other conclusion.

Thus our fair-minded white citizen strongly supports a policy of excluding Negroes from his labor union. His views are, of course, based not upon prejudice, but upon the cold hard facts. And the facts seem clear enough. Negroes, "lately from the nonindustrial South, are undisciplined in traditions of trade unionism and the art of collective bargaining." The Negro is a strikebreaker. The Negro, with his "low standard of living," rushes in to take jobs at less than prevailing wages. The Negro is, in short, "a traitor to the working class," and should manifestly be excluded from union organizations. So run the facts of the case as seen by our tolerant but hard-headed union member, innocent of any understanding of the self-fulfilling prophecy as a basic process of society.

Our unionist fails to see, of course, that he and his kind have produced the very "facts" which he observes. For by defining the situation as one in which Negroes are held to be incorrigibly at odds with principles of unionism and by excluding Negroes from unions, he invited a series of consequences which indeed made it difficult if not impossible for many Negroes to avoid the role of scab. Out of work after World War I, and kept out of unions, thousands of Negroes could not resist strikebound employers who held a door invitingly open upon a world of jobs from which they were otherwise excluded.

History creates its own test of the theory of self-fulfilling prophecies. That Negroes were strikebreakers because they were excluded from unions (and from a wide range of jobs) rather than excluded because they were strikebreakers can be seen from the virtual disappearance of Negroes as scabs in industries where they have gained admission to unions in the last decades.

The application of the Thomas theorem also suggests how the tragic, often vicious, circle of self-fulfilling prophecies can be broken. The initial definition of the situation which has set the circle in motion must be abandoned. Only when the original assumption is questioned and a new definition of the situation introduced, does the consequent flow of events give the lie to the assumption. Only then does the belief no longer father the reality.

But to question these deep-rooted definitions of the situation is no

---

MacIver, *The More Perfect Union* (New York: Macmillan, 1948); for a general statement, see Merton, "The unanticipated consequences of purposive social action," *op. cit.*

simple act of the will. The will, or for that matter, good will, cannot be turned on and off like a faucet. Social intelligence and good will are themselves *products* of distinct social forces. They are not brought into being by mass propaganda and mass education, in the usual sense of these terms so dear to the sociological panaceans. In the social realm, no more than in the psychological realm, do false ideas quietly vanish when confronted with the truth. One does not expect a paranoiac to abandon his hard-won distortions and delusions upon being informed that they are altogether groundless. If psychic ills could be cured merely by the dissemination of truth, the psychiatrists of this country would be suffering from technological unemployment rather than from overwork. Nor will a continuing "educational campaign" itself destroy racial prejudice and discrimination.

This is not a particularly popular position. The appeal to education as a cure-all for the most varied social problems is rooted deep in the mores of America. Yet it is nonetheless illusory for all that. For how would this program of racial education proceed? Who is to do the educating? The teachers in our communities? But, in some measure like many other Americans, the teachers share the same prejudices they are being urged to combat. And when they don't, aren't they being asked to serve as conscientious martyrs in the cause of educational utopianism? How long the tenure of an elementary school teacher in Alabama or Mississippi or Georgia who attempted meticulously to disabuse his young pupils of the racial beliefs they acquired at home? Education may serve as an operational adjunct but not as the chief basis for any but excruciatingly slow change in the prevailing patterns of race relations.

To understand further why educational campaigns cannot be counted on to eliminate prevailing ethnic hostilities, we must examine the operation of in-groups and out-groups in our society. Ethnic out-groups, to adopt Sumner's useful bit of sociological jargon, consist of all those who are believed to differ significantly from "ourselves" in terms of nationality, race, or religion. Counterpart of the ethnic out-group is of course the ethnic in-group, constituted by those who "belong." There is nothing fixed or eternal about the lines separating the in-group from out-groups. As situations change, the lines of separation change. For a large number of white Americans, Joe Louis is a member of an out-group—when the situation is defined in racial terms. On another occasion, when Louis defeated the nazified Schmeling, many of these same white Americans acclaimed him as a member of the (national) in-group. National loyalty took precedence over racial separatism. These abrupt shifts in group boundaries sometimes prove embarrassing. Thus, when Negro-Americans ran away with the honors in the Olympic games held in Berlin, the Nazis, pointing to the second-class citizenship assigned Negroes in various regions of this country, denied that the United States had really won the games, since the Negro athletes were by our own admission "not full-fledged" Americans. And what could Bilbo or Rankin say to that?

Under the benevolent guidance of the dominant in-group, ethnic out-groups are continuously subjected to a lively process of prejudice which, I think, goes far toward vitiating mass education and mass propaganda for ethnic tolerance. This is the process whereby "in-group virtues become out-group vices," to paraphrase a remark by the sociologist Donald Young. Or, more colloquially and perhaps more instructively, it may be called the "damned-if-you-do and damned-if-you-don't" process in ethnic and racial relations.

IN-GROUP VIRTUES AND OUT-GROUP VICES

To discover that ethnic out-groups are damned if they do embrace the values of white Protestant society and damned if they don't, we have first to turn to one of the in-group culture heroes, examine the qualities with which he is endowed by biographers and popular belief, and thus distill the qualities of mind and action and character which are generally regarded as altogether admirable.

Periodic public opinion polls are not needed to justify the selection of Abe Lincoln as the culture hero who most fully embodies the cardinal American virtues. As the Lynds point out in *Middletown*, the people of that typical small city allow George Washington alone to join Lincoln as the greatest of Americans. He is claimed as their very own by almost as many well-to-do Republicans as by less well-to-do Democrats.[2]

Even the inevitable schoolboy knows that Lincoln was thrifty, hard-

---

2. On Lincoln as culture hero, see the perceptive essay, "Getting Right with Lincoln," by David Donald, *Lincoln Reconsidered* (New York: Alfred A. Knopf, 1956), 3-18.

Though Lincoln nominally remains, of course, the symbolic leader of the Republicans, this may be just another paradox of political history of the same kind which Lincoln noted in his day with regard to Jefferson and the Democrats.

"Remembering, too, that the Jefferson party was formed upon its supposed superior devotion to the personal rights of men, holding the rights of property to be secondary only, and greatly inferior, and assuming that the so-called Democrats of to-day are the Jefferson, and their opponents the anti-Jefferson, party, it will be equally interesting to note how completely the two have changed hands as to the principle upon which they were originally supposed to be divided. The Democrats of to-day hold the liberty of one man to be absolutely nothing, when in conflict with another man's right of property; Republicans, on the contrary, are for both the man and the dollar, but in case of conflict the man before the dollar.

"I remember being once much amused at seeing two partially intoxicated men engaged in a fight with their great-coats on, which fight, after a long and rather harmless contest, ended in each having fought himself out of his own coat and into that of the other. If the two leading parties of this day are really identical with the two in the days of Jefferson and Adams, they have performed the same feat as the two drunken men."

Abraham Lincoln, in a letter to H. L. Pierce and others, April 6, 1859, in *Complete Works of Abraham Lincoln*, edited by John G. Nicolay and John Hay, (New York, 1894), V, 125-126.

working, eager for knowledge, ambitious, devoted to the rights of the average man, and eminently successful in climbing the ladder of opportunity from the lowermost rung of laborer to the respectable heights of merchant and lawyer. (We need follow his dizzying ascent no further.)

If one did not know that these attributes and achievements are numbered high among the values of middle-class America, one would soon discover it by glancing through the Lynds' account of "The Middletown Spirit." For there we find the image of the Great Emancipator fully reflected in the values in which Middletown believes. And since these are their values, it is not surprising to find the Middletowns of America condemning and disparaging those individuals and groups who fail, presumably, to exhibit these virtues. If it appears to the white in-group that Negroes are *not* educated in the same measure as themselves, that they have an "unduly" high proportion of unskilled workers and an "unduly" low proportion of successful business and professional men, that they are thriftless, and so on through the catalogue of middle-class virtue and sin, it is not difficult to understand the charge that the Negro is "inferior" to the white.

Sensitized to the workings of the self-fulfilling prophecy, we should be prepared to find that the anti-Negro charges which are not patently false are only speciously true. The allegations are true in the Pickwickian sense that we have found self-fulfilling prophecies in general to be true. Thus, if the dominant in-group believes that Negroes are inferior, and sees to it that funds for education are not "wasted on these incompetents" and then proclaims as final evidence of this inferiority that Negroes have proportionately "only" one-fifth as many college graduates as whites, one can scarcely be amazed by this transparent bit of social legerdemain. Having seen the rabbit carefully though not too adroitly placed in the hat, we can only look askance at the triumphant air with which it is finally produced. (In fact, it is a little embarrassing to note that a larger proportion of Negro than of white high school graduates have gone on to college; apparently, the Negroes who are hardy enough to scale the high walls of discrimination represent an even more highly selected group than the run-of-the-high-school white population.)

So, too, when the gentleman from Mississippi (a state which spends five times as much on the average white pupil as on the average Negro pupil) proclaims the essential inferiority of the Negro by pointing to the per capita ratio of physicians among Negroes as less than one-fourth that of whites, we are impressed more by his scrambled logic than by his profound prejudices. So plain is the mechanism of the self-fulfilling prophecy in these instances that only those forever devoted to the victory of sentiment over fact can take these specious evidences seriously. Yet the spurious evidence often creates a genuine belief. Self-hypnosis through one's own propaganda is a not infrequent phase of the self-fulfilling prophecy.

So much for out-groups being damned if they don't (apparently) manifest in-group virtues. It is a tasteless bit of ethnocentrism, seasoned with self-interest. But what of the second phase of this process? Can one seriously mean that out-groups are also damned if they *do* possess these virtues? One can.

Through a faultlessly bisymmetrical prejudice, ethnic and racial out-groups get it coming and going. The systematic condemnation of the out-grouper continues largely *irrespective of what he does.* More: through a freakish exercise of capricious judicial logic, the victim is punished for the crime. Superficial appearances notwithstanding, prejudice and discrimination aimed at the out-group are not a result of what the out-group does, but are rooted deep in the structure of our society and the social psychology of its members.

To understand how this happens, we must examine the moral alchemy through which the in-group readily transmutes virtue into vice and vice into virtue, as the occasion may demand. Our studies will proceed by the case-method.

We begin with the engagingly simple formula of moral alchemy: the same behavior must be differently evaluated according to the person who exhibits it. For example, the proficient alchemist will at once know that the word "firm" is properly declined as follows:

> I am firm,
> Thou art obstinate,
> He is pigheaded.

There are some, unversed in the skills of this science, who will tell you that one and the same term should be applied to all three instances of identical behavior. Such unalchemical nonsense should simply be ignored.

With this experiment in mind, we are prepared to observe how the very same behavior undergoes a complete change of evaluation in its transition from the in-group Abe Lincoln to the out-group Abe Cohen or Abe Kurokawa. We proceed systematically. Did Lincoln work far into the night? This testifies that he was industrious, resolute, perseverant, and eager to realize his capacities to the full. Do the out-group Jews or Japanese keep these same hours? This only bears witness to their sweatshop mentality, their ruthless undercutting of American standards, their unfair competitive practices. Is the in-group hero frugal, thrifty, and sparing? Then the out-group villain is stingy, miserly and pennypinching. All honor is due the in-group Abe for his having been smart, shrewd, and intelligent and, by the same token, all contempt is owing the out-group Abes for their being sharp, cunning, crafty, and too clever by far. Did the indomitable Lincoln refuse to remain content with a life of work with the hands? Did he prefer to make use of his brain?

Then, all praise for his plucky climb up the shaky ladder of opportunity. But, of course, the eschewing of manual work for brain work among the merchants and lawyers of the out-group deserves nothing but censure for a parasitic way of life. Was Abe Lincoln eager to learn the accumulated wisdom of the ages by unending study? The trouble with the Jew is that he's a greasy grind, with his head always in a book, while decent people are going to a show or a ball game. Was the resolute Lincoln unwilling to limit his standards to those of his provincial community? That is what we should expect of a man of vision. And if the out-groupers criticize the vulnerable areas in our society, then send 'em back where they came from. Did Lincoln, rising high above his origins, never forget the rights of the common man and applaud the right of workers to strike? This testifies only that, like all real Americans, this greatest of Americans was deathlessly devoted to the cause of freedom. But, as you examine the statistics on strikes, remember that these un-American practices are the result of out-groupers pursuing their evil agitation among otherwise contented workers.

Once stated, the classical formula of moral alchemy is clear enough. Through the adroit use of these rich vocabularies of encomium and opprobrium, the in-group readily transmutes its own virtues into others' vices. But why do so many in-groupers qualify as moral alchemists? Why are so many in the dominant in-group so fully devoted to this continuing experiment in moral transmutation?

An explanation may be found by putting ourselves at some distance from this country and following the anthropologist Malinowski to the Trobriand Islands. For there we find an instructively similar pattern. Among the Trobrianders, to a degree which Americans, despite Hollywood and the confession magazines, have apparently not yet approximated, success with women confers honor and prestige on a man. Sexual prowess is a positive value, a moral virtue. But if a rank-and-file Trobriander has "too much" sexual success, if he achieves "too many" triumphs of the heart, an achievement which should of course be limited to the elite, the chiefs or men of power, then this glorious record becomes a scandal and an abomination. The chiefs are quick *to resent any personal achievement not warranted by social position.* The moral virtues remain virtues only so long as they are jealously confined to the proper in-group. The right activity by the wrong people becomes a thing of contempt, not of honor. For clearly, only in this way, by holding these virtues exclusively to themselves, can the men of power retain their distinction, their prestige, and their power. No wiser procedure could be devised to hold intact a system of social stratification and social power.

The Trobrianders could teach us more. For it seems clear that the chiefs have not calculatingly devised this program of entrenchment. Their behavior is spontaneous, unthinking, and immediate. Their resentment of "too much" ambition or "too much" success in the ordinary Trobriander is not contrived, it is genuine. It just happens that this prompt emotional response to the "misplaced" manifestation of in-group virtues also serves the useful expedient of reinforcing the chiefs' special claims to the good things of Trobriand life. Nothing could be more remote from the truth and more distorted a reading of the facts than to assume that this conversion of in-group virtues into out-group vices is part of a calculated deliberate plot of Trobriand chiefs to keep Trobriand commoners in their place. It is merely that the chiefs have been indoctrinated with an appreciation of the proper order of things, and see it as their heavy burden to enforce the mediocrity of others.

Nor, in quick revulsion from the culpabilities of the moral alchemists, need we succumb to the equivalent error of simply upending the moral status of the in-group and the out-groups. It is not that Jews and Negroes are one and all angelic while Gentiles and whites are one and all fiendish. It is not that individual virtue will now be found exclusively on the wrong side of the ethnic-racial tracks and individual viciousness on the right side. It is conceivable even that there are as many corrupt and vicious men and women among Negroes and Jews as among Gentile whites. It is only that the ugly fence which encloses the in-group happens to exclude the people who make up the out-groups from being treated with the decency ordinarily accorded human beings.

SOCIAL FUNCTIONS AND DYSFUNCTIONS

We have only to look at the consequences of this peculiar moral alchemy to see that there is no paradox at all in damning out-groupers when they do and when they don't exhibit in-group virtues. Condemnation on these two scores performs one and the same social function. Seeming opposites coalesce. When Negroes are tagged as incorrigibly inferior because they (apparently) don't manifest these virtues, this confirms the natural rightness of their being assigned an inferior status in society. And when Jews or Japanese are tagged as having too many of the in-group values, it becomes plain that they must be securely controlled by the high walls of discrimination. In both cases, the special status assigned the several out-groups can be seen to be eminently reasonable.

Yet this distinctly reasonable arrangement persists in having most unreasonable consequences, both logical and social. Consider only a few of these.

In some contexts, the limitations enforced upon the out-group—say, rationing the number of Jews permitted to enter colleges and professional schools—logically imply a fear of the alleged superiority of the out-group. Were it otherwise, no discrimination need be practiced. The unyielding, impersonal forces of academic competition would soon trim down the number of Jewish (or Japanese or Negro) students to an "appropriate" size.

This implied belief in the superiority of the out-group seems premature. There is simply not enough scientific evidence to demonstrate Jewish or Japanese or Negro superiority. The effort of the in-group discriminator to supplant the myth of Aryan superiority with the myth of non-Aryan superiority is condemned to failure by science. Moreover, such myths are ill-advised. Eventually, life in a world of myth must collide with fact in the world of reality. As a matter of simple self-interest and social therapy, therefore, it might be wise for the in-group to abandon the myth and cling to the reality.

The pattern of being damned-if-you-do and damned-if-you-don't has further consequences—among the out-groups themselves. The response to alleged deficiencies is as clear as it is predictable. If one is repeatedly told that one is inferior, that one lacks any positive accomplishments, it is all too human to seize upon every bit of evidence to the contrary. The in-group definitions force upon the allegedly inferior out-group a defensive tendency to magnify and exalt "race accomplishments." As the distinguished Negro sociologist, Franklin Frazier, has noted, the Negro newspapers are "intensely race conscious and exhibit considerable pride in the achievements of the Negro, most of which are meagre performances as measured by broader standards." Self-glorification, found in some measure among all groups, becomes a frequent counter-response to persistent belittlement from without.

It is the damnation of out-groups for excessive achievement, however, which gives rise to truly bizarre behavior. For, after a time and often as a matter of self-defense, these out-groups become persuaded that their virtues really are vices. And this provides the final episode in a tragi-comedy of inverted values.

Let us try to follow the plot through its intricate maze of self-contradictions. Respectful admiration for the arduous climb from office boy to president is rooted deep in American culture. This long and strenuous ascent carries with it a two-fold testimonial: it testifies that careers are abundantly open to genuine talent in American society and it testifies to the worth of the man who has distinguished himself by his heroic rise. It would be invidious to choose among the many stalwart figures who have fought their way up, against all odds, until they have reached the pinnacle, there to sit at the head of the long conference table in the longer conference room of The Board. Taken at random, the saga of Frederick H. Ecker, chairman of the board of one of the largest privately managed corporations in the world, the Metropolitan Life Insurance Company, will suffice as the prototype. From a menial and poorly paid job, he rose to a position of eminence. Appropriately enough, an unceasing flow of honors has come to this man of large power and large achievement. It so happens, though it is a matter personal to this eminent man of finance, that Mr. Ecker is a Presbyterian. Yet at last report, no elder of the Presbyterian church has risen publicly to announce that Mr. Ecker's successful career should not be taken too seriously, that, after all, relatively few Presbyterians have risen from rags to riches and that Presbyterians do not actually "control" the world of finance—or life insurance, or investment housing. Rather, one would suppose, Presbyterian elders join with other Americans imbued with middle-class standards of success to felicitate the eminently successful Mr. Ecker and to acclaim other sons of the faith who have risen to almost equal heights. Secure in their in-group status, they point the finger of pride rather than the finger of dismay at individual success.

Prompted by the practice of moral alchemy, noteworthy achievements by out-groupers elicit other responses. Patently, if achievement is a vice, the achievements must be disclaimed—or at least, discounted. Under these conditions, what is an occasion for Presbyterian pride must become an occasion for Jewish dismay. If the Jew is condemned for his educational or professional or scientific or economic success, then, understandably enough, many Jews will come to feel that these accomplishments must be minimized in simple self-defense. Thus is the circle of paradox closed by out-groupers busily engaged in assuring the powerful in-group that they have not, in fact, been guilty of inordinate contributions to science, the professions, the arts, the government, and the economy.

In a society which ordinarily looks upon wealth as a warrant of ability, an out-group is compelled by the inverted attitudes of the dominant in-group to deny that many men of wealth are among its members. "Among the 200 largest non-banking corporations . . . only ten have a Jew as president or chairman of the board." Is this an observation of an anti-Semite, intent on proving the incapacity and inferiority of Jews who have done so little "to build the corporations which have built America?" No; it is a retort of the Anti-Defamation League of B'nai B'rith to anti-Semitic propaganda.

In a society where, as a recent survey by the National Opinion Research Center has shown, the profession of medicine ranks higher in social prestige than any other of ninety occupations (save that of United States Supreme Court Justice), we find some Jewish spokesmen manoeuvred by the attacking in-group into the fantastic position of announcing their "deep concern" over the number of Jews in medical practice, which is "disproportionate to the number of Jews in other occupations." In a nation suffering from a notorious undersupply of physicians, the Jewish doctor becomes a deplorable occasion for deep concern, rather than receiving applause for his hard-won acquisition of knowledge and skills and for his social utility. Only when the New York

Yankees publicly announce deep concern over their numerous World Series titles, so disproportionate to the number of triumphs achieved by other major league teams, will this self-abnegation seem part of the normal order of things.

In a culture which consistently judges the professionals higher in social value than even the most skilled hewers of wood and drawers of water, the out-group finds itself in the anomalous position of pointing with defensive relief to the large number of Jewish painters and paper hangers, plasterers and electricians, plumbers and sheet-metal workers.

But the ultimate reversal of values is yet to be noted. Each succeeding census finds more and more Americans in the city and its suburbs. Americans have travelled the road to urbanization until fewer than one-fifth of the nation's population live on farms. Plainly, it is high time for the Methodist and the Catholic, the Baptist and the Episcopalian to recognize the iniquity of this trek of their coreligionists to the city. For, as is well known, one of the central accusations levelled against the Jew is his heinous tendency to live in cities. Jewish leaders, therefore, find themselves in the incredible position of defensively urging their people to move into the very farm areas being hastily vacated by city-bound hordes of Christians. Perhaps this is not altogether necessary. As the Jewish crime of urbanism becomes ever more popular among the in-group, it may be reshaped into transcendent virtue. But, admittedly, one can't be certain. For in this daft confusion of inverted values, it soon becomes impossible to determine when virtue is sin and sin, moral perfection.

Amid this confusion, one fact remains unambiguous. The Jews, like other peoples, have made distinguished contributions to world culture. Consider only an abbreviated catalogue. In the field of creative literature (and with acknowledgment of large variations in the calibre of achievement), Jewish authors include Heine, Karl Kraus, Börne, Hofmannsthal, Schnitzler, Kafka. In the realm of musical composition, there are Meyerbeer, Felix Mendelssohn, Offenbach, Mahler, and Schönberg. Among the musical virtuosi, consider only Rosenthal, Schnabel, Godowsky, Pachmann, Kreisler, Hubermann, Milstein, Elman, Heifetz, Joachim, and Menuhin. And among scientists of a stature sufficient to merit the Nobel prize, examine the familiar list which includes Beranyi, Mayerhof, Ehrlich, Michelson, Lippmann, Haber, Willstätter, and Einstein. Or in the esoteric and imaginative universe of mathematical invention, take note only of Kronecker, the creator of the modern theory of numbers; Hermann Minkowski,* who supplied the mathematical foundations of

---

* Obviously, the forename must be explicitly mentioned here, else Hermann Minkowski, the mathematician, may be confused with Eugen Minkowski, who contributed so notably to our knowledge of schizophrenia, or with Mieczyslaw Minkowski, high in the ranks of brain anatomists, or even with Oskar Minkowski, discoverer of pancreatic diabetes.

the special theory of relativity; or Jacobi, with his basic work in the theory of elliptical functions. And so through each special province of cultural achievement, we are supplied with a list of pre-eminent men and women who happened to be Jews.

And who is thus busily engaged in singing the praises of the Jews? Who has so assiduously compiled the list of many hundreds of distinguished Jews who contributed so notably to science, literature and the arts—a list from which these few cases were excerpted? A philo-Semite, eager to demonstrate that his people have contributed their due share to world culture? No, by now we should know better than that. The complete list will be found in the thirty-sixth edition of the anti-Semitic handbook by the racist Fritsch. In accord with the alchemical formula for transmuting in-group virtues into out-group vices, he presents this as a roll call of sinister spirits who have usurped the accomplishments properly owing the Aryan in-group.

Once we comprehend the predominant role of the in-group in defining the situation, the further paradox of the seemingly opposed behavior of the Negro out-group and the Jewish out-group falls away. The behavior of both minority groups is in response to the majority-group allegations.

If the Negroes are accused of inferiority, and their alleged failure to contribute to world culture is cited in support of this accusation, the human urge for self-respect and a concern for security often leads them *defensively* to magnify each and every achievement by members of the race. If Jews are accused of excessive achievements and excessive ambitions, and lists of pre-eminent Jews are compiled in support of this accusation, then the urge for security leads them *defensively* to minimize the actual achievements of members of the group. Apparently opposed types of behavior have the same psychological and social functions. Self-assertion and self-effacement become the devices for seeking to cope with condemnation for alleged group deficiency and condemnation for alleged group excesses, respectively. And with a fine sense of moral superiority, the secure in-group looks on these curious performances by the out-groups with mingled derision and contempt.

ENACTED INSTITUTIONAL CHANGE

Will this desolate tragi-comedy run on and on, marked only by minor changes in the cast? Not necessarily.

Were moral scruples and a sense of decency the only bases for bringing the play to an end, one would indeed expect it to continue an indefinitely long run. In and of themselves, moral sentiments are not much more effective in curing social ills than in curing physical ills. Moral sentiments no doubt help to motivate efforts for change, but they are no substitute for hard-headed instrumentalities for achieving the objective, as the thickly populated graveyard of soft-headed utopias bears witness.

There are ample indications that a deliberate and planned halt can be put to the workings of the self-fulfilling prophecy and the vicious circle in society. The sequel to our sociological parable of the Last National Bank provides one clue to the way in which this can be achieved. During the fabulous '20's, when Coolidge undoubtedly caused a Republican era of lush prosperity, an average of 635 banks a year quietly suspended operations. And during the four years immediately before and after The Crash, when Hoover undoubtedly did not cause a Republican era of sluggish depression, this zoomed to the more spectacular average of 2,276 bank suspensions annually. But, interestingly enough, in the twelve years following the establishment of the Federal Deposit Insurance Corporation and the enactment of other banking legislation while Roosevelt presided over Democratic depression and revival, recession and boom, bank suspensions dropped to a niggardly average of 28 a year. Perhaps money panics have not been institutionally exorcized by legislation. Nevertheless, millions of depositors no longer have occasion to give way to panic-motivated runs on banks simply because deliberate institutional change has removed the grounds for panic. Occasions for racial hostility are no more inborn psychological constants than are occasions for panic. Despite the teachings of amateur psychologists, blind panic and racial aggression are not rooted in human nature. These patterns of human behavior are largely a product of the modifiable structure of society.

For a further clue, return to our instance of widespread hostility of white unionists toward the Negro strikebreakers brought into industry by employers after the close of the very first World War. Once the initial definition of Negroes as not deserving of union membership had largely broken down, the Negro, with a wider range of work opportunities, no longer found it necessary to enter industry through the doors held open by strike-bound employers. Again, appropriate institutional change broke through the tragic circle of the self-fulfilling prophecy. Deliberate social change gave the lie to the firm conviction that "it just ain't in the nature of the nigra" to join co-operatively with his white fellows in trade unions.

A final instance is drawn from a study of a bi-racial housing project. Located in Pittsburgh, this community of Hilltown is made up of fifty per cent Negro families and fifty per cent white. It is not a twentieth-century utopia. There is some interpersonal friction here as elsewhere. But in a community made up of equal numbers of the two races, fewer than a fifth of the whites and less than a third of the Negroes report that this friction occurs between members of *different* races. By their own testimony, it is very largely confined to disagreements *within* each racial group. Yet only one in every twenty-five whites initially *expected* relations between the races in this community to run smoothly, whereas five times as many expected serious trouble, the remainder anticipating a tolerable, if not altogether pleasant, situation. So much for expectations. Upon reviewing their actual experience, three of every four of the most apprehensive whites subsequently found that the "races get along fairly well," after all. This is not the place to report the findings of this study in detail, but substantially these demonstrate anew that under *appropriate institutional and administrative conditions,* the experience of interracial amity can supplant the fear of interracial conflict.

These changes, and others of the same kind, do not occur automatically. *The self-fulfilling prophecy, whereby fears are translated into reality, operates only in the absence of deliberate institutional controls.* And it is only with the rejection of social fatalism implied in the notion of unchangeable human nature that the tragic circle of fear, social disaster, and reinforced fear can be broken.

Ethnic prejudices do die—but slowly. They can be helped over the threshold of oblivion, not by insisting that it is unreasonable and unworthy of them to survive, but by cutting off the sustenance now provided them by certain institutions of our society.

If we find ourselves doubting man's capacity to control man and his society, if we persist in our tendency to find in the patterns of the past the chart of the future, it is perhaps time to take up anew the wisdom of Tocqueville's century-old remark: "I am tempted to believe that what we call necessary institutions are often no more than institutions to which we have grown accustomed, and that in matters of social constitution the field of possibilities is much more extensive than men living in their various societies are ready to imagine."

Nor can widespread, even typical, failures in planning human relations between ethnic groups be cited as evidence for pessimism. In the world laboratory of the sociologist, as in the more secluded laboratories of the physicist and chemist, it is the successful experiment which is decisive and not the thousand-and-one failures which preceded it. More is learned from the single success than from the multiple failures. A single success proves it can be done. Thereafter, it is necessary only to learn what made it work. This, at least, is what I take to be the sociological sense of those revealing words of Thomas Love Peacock: "Whatever is, is possible."

Part III

THE SOCIOLOGY OF KNOWLEDGE AND MASS COMMUNICATIONS

INTRODUCTION

P ART III CONSISTS OF three chapters, two critically reviewing some general and special problems in the sociology of knowledge, and the third, written in collaboration with Paul F. Lazarsfeld, summarizing a limited range of studies in the sociology of opinion and mass communications. The juxtaposition of the two fields is anything but casual. For though they have developed largely independently of one another, it is the office of this introduction to suggest that the effective cultivation of each would be aided by consolidating some of the theoretic conceptions, research methods, and empirical findings of both. And to see the substantial similarities between the two, the reader has only to compare the general summary of the sociology of knowledge provided in Chapter XII of this book with the general summary of mass communications research provided by Lazarsfeld in the symposium, *Current Trends in Social Psychology*, edited by Wayne Dennis.

Indeed, the two can be regarded as species of that genus of research which is concerned with the interplay between social structure and communications. The one emerged and has been most assiduously cultivated in Europe and the other, until now, has been far more common in America. If the label be not taken literally, therefore, the sociology of knowledge may be called the "European species," and the sociology of mass communications, the "American species." (That these labels cannot be strictly applied is evident: after all, Charles Beard was long an exponent of the native-American version of the sociology of knowledge, just as Paul Lazarsfeld, for example, conducted some of his earliest researches on mass communications in Vienna.) Although both sociological specialisms are devoted to the interplay between ideas and social structure, each has its distinctive foci of attention.

In these fields we have instructive examples of the two contrasting emphases in sociological theory described earlier in these pages (particularly in Chapter II and in the Introduction to Part I). The sociology of knowledge belongs for the most part to the camp of global theorists, in which the breadth and significance of the problem justifies one's dedication to it, sometimes quite apart from the present possibility of materially advancing beyond ingenious speculations and impressionistic conclusions. By and large, the sociologists of knowledge have been among those raising high the banner which reads: "We don't know that what we say is true, but it is at least significant."

The sociologists and psychologists engaged in the study of public opinion and mass communications are most often found in the opposed camp of the empiricists, with a somewhat different motto emblazoned on their banner: "We don't know that what we say is particularly significant, but it is at least true." Here the emphasis has been heavy on the assembling of data relating to the general subject, data which have substantial standing as evidence, though they are not beyond all dispute. But, until recently, there has been little concern with the bearing of these data on theoretic problems, and the amassing of practical information has been mistaken for the collection of scientifically pertinent observations.

It will not only serve to introduce the chapters in Part III, but may possibly be of interest in its own right to compare these European and American variants of the sociological study of communications. To do so is to gain the strong impression that those distinctive emphases are bound up with the environing social structures in which they developed, although the present discussion will do little more than suggest a few of these possible connections between the social structure and the social theory, in a manner only preliminary to an actual investigation of the matter. The comparison has the further objective of advocating the consolidation of these related fields of sociological inquiry, aiming toward that happy combination of the two which possesses the scientific virtues of both and the superfluous vices of neither.

COMPARISON OF *WISSENSSOZIOLOGIE* AND MASS COMMUNICATIONS RESEARCH

The distinctive orientations of these coordinate, complementary and partly overlapping fields of inquiry are compounded of and expressed in a variety of related aspects: their characteristic subject-matter and definition of problems, their conceptions of data, their utilization of research techniques, and the social organization of their research activities.

Subject-Matter and Definition of Problems

The European variant is devoted to digging up the social roots of knowledge, to searching out the ways in which knowledge and thought are affected by the environing social structure. The chief focus here is the shaping of intellectual perspectives by society. In this discipline, as I suggest in the chapters following, knowledge and thought are so loosely construed that they come to include almost all ideas and beliefs. At the core of the discipline, nevertheless, is a sociological interest in the social contexts of that knowledge which is more or less certified by systematic evidence. That is to say, the sociology of knowledge is most directly concerned with the intellectual products of experts, whether in science or philosophy, in economic or political thought.

Although it too includes some interest in the current state of knowledge (or level of information, as it is characteristically and significantly called), the American variant has its focus in the sociological study of popular belief. It is especially focused on *opinion*, rather than *knowledge*. These are not, of course, black and white distinctions. Not being arbitrary, the line between them has not the sharpness of, say, an international boundary. Opinion shades into knowledge, which is only that part of opinion socially certified by particular criteria of evidence. And just as opinion may grow into knowledge, so ostensible knowledge may degenerate into opinion merely. But, except at the margins, the distinction holds, and it is expressed in the distinctive foci of the European and American variants of the sociology of communications.

If the American version is primarily concerned with public opinion, with mass beliefs, with what has come to be called "popular culture," the European version centers on more esoteric doctrines, on those complex systems of knowledge which become reshaped and often distorted in their subsequent passage into popular culture.

These differences in focus carry with them further differences: the European variant being concerned with knowledge, comes to deal with the intellectual élite; the American variant, concerned with widely held opinion, deals with the masses. The one centers on the esoteric doctrines of the few, the other on the exoteric beliefs of the many. This divergence of interest has immediate bearing on every phase of research techniques, as we shall see; it is clear, for example, that a research interview designed to yield information from a scientist or man of literature will differ materially from a research interview intended for a cross-section of the population at large.

The orientations of the two variants show further distinctive correlations of subtle details. The European division refers, on the cognitive plane, to *knowledge;* the American to *information*. Knowledge implies a *body* of facts or ideas, whereas information carries no such implication of *systematically connected* facts or ideas. The American variant accordingly *studies the isolated fragments of information* available to masses of people; the European variant typically *thinks about a total structure of knowledge* available to a few. The American emphasis has been on *aggregates* of discrete tidbits of information, the European on *systems* of doctrine. For the European, it is essential to analyze the system of tenets in all their complex interrelation, with an eye to conceptual unity, levels of abstraction and concreteness, and categorization (*e.g.*, morphological or analytic). For the American, it is essential to detect, through the techniques of factor analysis for example, the clusters of ideas (or attitudes) which empirically occur. The one stresses relations which subsist logically; the other stresses relations which occur empirically. The European is interested in political labels only as they direct him to systems of political ideas which he will then construe in all their subtlety and complexity, seeking to show their (assumed) relation to one or another social stratum. The American is interested in discrete political beliefs, and in these, only as they enable the investigator to classify ("code") people under some general political label or category, which can then be shown, not assumed, to have greater currency in one or another social stratum. If the European analyzes the ideology of political movements, the American investigates the opinions of voters and nonvoters.

These distinctive foci could be further expounded and illustrated, but perhaps enough has been said to indicate that out of a broadly common subject matter, the European sociology of knowledge and the American sociology of mass communications select distinctive problems for distinctive interpretation. And gradually, the loose impression emerges which can be baldly and too simply summarized thus: the American knows what he is talking about, and that is not much; the European knows not what he is talking about, and that is a great deal.

Perspectives on Data and Facts

The European and American variants have notably different conceptions of what constitutes raw empirical data, of what is needed to convert these raw data into certified facts, and of the place of these facts, diversely arrived at, in the development of sociological science.

On the whole, the European is hospitable and even cordial in his receptivity to candidates for the status of an empirical datum. An impression derived from a few documents, particularly if these documents refer to a time or place sufficiently remote, will pass muster as fact about widespread currents of thought or about generally held doctrines. If the intellectual status of an author is high enough and the scope of his attainments broad enough, his impressions, sometimes his casual impressions of prevailing beliefs, will be typically taken as reports of sociological fact. Or, a generalization stated positively enough and generally enough will be taken as an empirical datum.

To seek a few illustrations is to find an embarrassment of riches. A Mannheim, for example, will summarize the state of mind of the "lower classes in the post-medieval period," saying that "only bit by bit did they arrive at an awareness of their social and political significance." Or, he may regard it as not only significant but true that "all progressive groups regard the idea as coming before the deed," this ostensibly being a matter of thorough observation rather than of definition. Or, he may submit an hypothesis as instructive as the following, an hypothesis compounded of several assumptions of fact: ". . . the more actively an ascendant party collaborates in a parliamentary coalition, and the more it gives up its original utopian impulses and with it its broad perspective, the more its power to transform society is likely to be absorbed by its interest in concrete and isolated details. Quite parallel to the change that may be observed in the political realm runs a change in the scientific outlook which conforms to political demands, i.e., what was once merely a formal scheme and an abstract, total view, tends to dissolve into the investigation of specific and discrete problems." Suggestive and nearly apodictic, and if true, shedding so much light on so much that the intellectual has experienced and perhaps casually noted in the course of living in political society, such a statement tempts one to regard it as fact rather than as hypothesis. What is more, as is often the case with sociological formulations of the European variety, the statement seems to catch up so many details of experience that the reader seldom goes on to consider the vast labors of empirical research required before this can be regarded as more than an interesting hypothesis. It quickly gains an unearned status as generalized fact.

It will be noted that observations such as these drawn from the sociology of knowledge typically pertain to the historical past, presumably summing up the typical or modal behavior of large numbers of people (entire social strata or groups). In any strict empirical sense, the data justifying such large summary statements have of course not been systematically gathered, for the good and sufficient reason that they are nowhere to be found. The opinions of thousands of ordinary men in the distant past can only be surmised or imaginatively reconstructed; they are in fact lost in history, unless one adopts the convenient fiction that the *impressions* of mass or collective opinion as set down by a few observers of that day can be regarded as attested social *facts* today.

In contrast to all this, the American variant places its primary emphasis on establishing empirically the facts of the case under scrutiny. Before seeking to determine *why* it is that certain schools of thought are more addicted to the "investigation of specific and discrete problems," it would first attempt to learn whether this is indeed the case. Of course, this emphasis, like that of the European variant, has the defects of its qualities. Very often, the strong concern with empirical test leads prematurely to a curbing of imaginative hypotheses: the nose is held so close to the empirical grindstone that one cannot look up to see beyond the limits of the immediate task.

The European variant, with its large purposes, almost disdains to establish the very facts it purports to explain. By passing over the diffi-cult and often laborious task of determining the facts of the case, by going directly on to explanations of the assumed facts, the sociologist of knowledge may succeed only in putting the cart well before the horse. As everyone knows, if this procedure makes for movement at all, it generally makes for retrogressive movement—perhaps in the realm of knowledge as in the realm of transportation. What is worse, occasionally the horse disappears entirely, and the theoretical cart is left motionless until it is harnessed to new facts. The saving grace here is that more than once in the history of science, an explanatory idea has turned out to be productive even when the facts it was first designed to explain later turn out not to be facts at all. But one can scarcely count on these fruitful errors.

The American variant, with its small vision, focuses so much on the establishment of fact that it considers only occasionally the theoretic pertinence of the facts, once established. Here the problem is not so much that the cart and horse have reversed places; it is rather that too often there is no theoretic cart at all. The horse may indeed move ahead, but since he pulls no cart, his swift journey is profitless, unless some European comes along belatedly to hitch his wagon on behind. Yet, as we know, *ex post facto* theories are properly suspect.

These diverse orientations toward facts and data relate also to the selection of subject-matter and the definition of problems for investiga-tion. The American variant, with its emphasis on empirical confirmation, devotes little attention to the historical past, since the adequacy of data on public opinion and group beliefs in the past becomes suspect when judged by the criteria applied to comparable data regarding group be-liefs today. This may partly account for the American tendency to deal primarily with problems of the short-run: the responses to propaganda materials, the experimental comparison of propaganda effectiveness of diverse media, and the like. The virtual neglect of historical materials is not for want of interest in or recognition of the importance of long-run effects but only because these, it is believed, require data which cannot be obtained.

With their more hospitable attitude toward impressionistic mass data, the European group can indulge their interest in such long-run problems as the movement of political ideologies in relation to shifts in *systems* of class stratification (not merely the shift of individuals from one class to another within a system). The historical data of the Euro-peans typically rest on assumptions empirically explored for the present by the Americans. Thus, a Max Weber (or some of his numerous tribe of epigoni) may write of the Puritan beliefs obtaining widely in the seventeenth century, basing his factual conclusions on the literate few, who set down their beliefs and impressions of others' beliefs in books which we can now read. But, of course, this leaves untouched, and untouchable, the independent question of the extent to which these beliefs as set down in books express the beliefs of the larger and, so far as history goes, wholly inarticulate population (to say nothing of different strata within that population). This relation between what is found in publications and the actual beliefs (or attitudes) of the underlying population which is taken for granted by the European variant becomes a problem amenable to research by the American variant. When newspapers or magazines or books are found to express a shift in belief-system or general outlook, and this is provisionally taken as a reflection of changing beliefs or outlook in an associated population (class, group or region), representatives of the American variant, even the less radically empiricist among them, go on to indicate that it would be important "to discover by some independent means the attitude of the general populace. Our verification here could be gained only by interviews with cross-sections of the public in the two periods to see if the shift in values indicated by this changing concentration in the magazine [or other mass medium] is the reflection of an actual value shift in the underlying population." (Lazarsfeld, op. cit., 224.) But since no techniques have yet been developed for interviewing cross-sections of populations in the remote past, thus testing the impressions gained from the scattered historical documents which remain, the American sociologist of mass communications tends to confine himself to the historical present. Possibly by assembling the raw materials of public opinion, beliefs and knowledge today, he may help lay the foundations for the sociologist of knowledge who would empirically study long-run trends in opinion, beliefs and knowledge tomorrow.

If the European prefers to deal with long-run developments through the study of historical data, where some of the data regarding group and mass beliefs may be disputed and the conclusions thereby impugned, the American prefers to deal meticulously with the short-run instance, using data which have been more fully fashioned to meet the needs of the scientific problem and confining himself to the immediate responses of individuals to an immediate situation cut out of the long stretches of history. But in dealing empirically with the more restricted problem, he may, of course, be excising from the research the very problems which are of central concern. The European holds high the banner of preserving intact the problem in which he is basically interested, even though it can be only a matter of speculation; the American raises aloft the standard affirming adequacy of empirical data at any price, even at the price of surrendering the problem which first led to the inquiry. The empirical rigor of the American persuasion involves a self-denying ordinance in which significant long-term movements of ideas in relation to changes in social structure are pretty much abandoned as a feasible subject for study; the speculative proclivity of the European persuasion involves plenary self-indulgence in which impressions of mass developments are taken for facts, and in which few violate the established convention of avoiding embarrassing questions about the evidence ultimately supporting these alleged facts of mass behavior or belief.

Thus it is that the European variant comes to talk about important matters in an empirically questionable fashion whereas the American talks about possibly more trivial matters in an empirically rigorous fashion. The European imagines and the American looks; the American investigates the short-run, the European speculates on the long run.

Again, it is to be considered at just which points the rigor of the first and the breadth of the second are inevitably antagonistic, and for the rest, to work out the means of bringing them together.

Research Techniques and Procedures

The two variants exhibit characteristic differences in their concern with research techniques for the collection of data and for their subsequent analysis.

For the European sociologist of knowledge, the very term *research technique* has an alien and unfriendly ring. It is considered almost intellectually debasing to set forth the prosaic details of *how* an analysis in the sociology of knowledge was conducted. Tracing his intellectual lineage from history, discursive philosophy and the arts, the European feels that this would be to expose the scaffolding of his analysis and, even worse, to lavish that loving care on the scaffolding which should be preserved only for the finished structure. In this tradition, the role of the research technician wins neither praise nor understanding. There are, to be sure, established and often elaborate techniques for testing the authenticity of historical documents, for determining their probable date, and the like. But techniques for the *analysis* of the data rather than for authentication of the document receive only slight attention.

It is quite another matter with the American student of mass communications. In the course of the last decades in which research in this field has been systematically pursued, a vast and varied array of techniques has marched into view. Interview techniques in all their numerous variety (group and individual, nondirective and structured, exploratory and focused, the single cross section interview and the repeated panel interview), questionnaires, opinionnaires and attitude tests, attitude scales of the Thurstone, the Guttman and the Lazarsfeld type, controlled experiment and controlled observation, content-analysis (whether symbol-counts, or item, thematic, structural and campaign analysis), the Lazarsfeld-Stanton program analyzer—these few are only a sampling of the diverse procedures evolved for research in mass communications.[1] The very abundance of the American techniques only diminishes by contrast the meagre list of the European techniques. And the contrast can scarcely fail to disclose other facets of difference in the two orientations to the sociological study of communications.

The attitude toward the problem of *reliability* of observations among the European and American variants can be applied as a touchstone by which to gauge their more general orientation toward techniques. Reliability, by which is meant roughly, the consistency between independent observations of the same material, is almost entirely absent as a *problem* for the European student. By and large, each student of the sociology of knowledge exercises his own capacities in his own way to establish the content and meanings of his documents. It would be regarded as an affront to the integrity or dignity of the investigator to suggest that the document he has analyzed must be independently analyzed by others in order to establish the degree of reliability, of agreement among the several observers of the same materials. The insult would be only compounded if one went on to say that large discrepancies between such independent analyses must cast doubt on the adequacy of one or the other. The very notion of reliability of categorization (*i.e.*, the extent to which independent categorizations of the same empirical materials coincide) has seldom found expression in the design of researches by the sociologist of knowledge.

This systematic neglect of the problem of reliability may possibly be inherited by the sociologist of knowledge from the historians among his intellectual antecedents. For in the writings of historians the diversity of interpretation is typically taken not so much as a problem to be solved, but as fate. If recognized at all, it is recognized with an air of resignation, tinged with a bit of pride in the artistic and therefore individualized diversity of observation and interpretation. Thus, in the introduction to the first magisterial volume of his projected four volumes on Thomas Jefferson, Dumas Malone makes the following disclaimer, not unrepresentative of the attitudes of other historians toward their own work: "Others will interpret the *same* man and the *same* events differently; this is practically inevitable, since he was a central figure

---

1. See, for example, the techniques set forth in the following publications of the Columbia University Bureau of Applied Social Research: P. F. Lazarsfeld and F. Stanton, (editors), *Radio Research, 1941*, (New York: Duell, Sloan and Pearce, 1941); *Radio Research, 1942-1943*, (New York: Duell, Sloan and Pearce, 1944); *Communications Research, 1948-1949*, (New York: Harper and Brothers, 1949); also the recent volume reporting the studies of the Research Branch of the Army's Information and Education Division, Carl I. Hovland, A. A. Lumsdaine, F. D. Sheffield, *Experiments on Mass Communications*, (Princeton University Press, 1949); and the volume on the War Communications Research Project by H. D. Lasswell, Nathan Leites and Associates, *Language of Politics*, (New York: George W. Stewart, 1949).

in historic controversies which are still echoing." (Emphasis supplied.)

This doctrine of different interpretations of the *same* events has become so thoroughly established among historians that it is almost certain to turn up, in one form or another, in the preface to most historical writings. If history is placed in the tradition of the humanities, of literature and art, this conception becomes at once understandable. In the context of the arts, this disclaimer of any final interpretation is at once an expression, however conventionalized, of professional modesty and a description of repeated experience: historians do commonly revise interpretations of men, events, and social movements. Nor do scientists, for that matter, expect a 'final' interpretation, although their attitude toward variety of interpretation is notably different.

To understand this implied attitude toward reliability, as expressed among historians and sociologists of knowledge, does not require us to quarrel with the doctrine of an inevitable diversity of interpretation. But the understanding will be improved if this doctrine is contrasted with the point of view which typically occurs in the writings of scientists, very definitely in the writings of physical scientists and, in some measure, in the writings of social scientists. Where the historian awaits with equanimity and almost with happy resignation *different* interpretations of the *same* data, his scientific colleagues regard this as a sign of an unstable resting point, casting doubt on the reliability of observation as well as on the adequacy of interpretation. How odd would be the preface to a work of chemistry in which it were asserted after the fashion of the historian, that "others will interpret the *same* data on combustion differently; this is practically inevitable. . . ." Differences in theoretic interpretation may indeed occur in science and often do; this is not the point in issue. But the differences are conceived as evidence of inadequacies in the conceptual scheme or possibly in the original observations, and research is instituted to eliminate these differences.

It is, in fact, because effort is centered on successfully eliminating these differences of interpretation in science, because consensus is sought in place of diversity, that we can, with justification, speak of the *cumulative* nature of science. Among other things, cumulation requires reliability of initial observation. And by the same token, because the arts center on difference—as expressions of the artist's distinctive and personal, if not private, perceptions—they are not, in the same sense, cumulative. Works of art accumulate in the limited sense of having more and more products of art available to men in society; they can be placed side by side. Whereas works of science are as a matter of course placed one upon the others to comprise a structure of interlocking and mutually sustaining theories which permit the understanding of numerous observations. Toward this end, reliability of observation is of course a necessity.

This brief digression on a possible source of the European's unconcern with reliability as a technical problem may highlight the bases of his more general unconcern with research techniques. There is a very substantial orientation toward the humanities which persists in the sociology of knowledge and with this, an aversion to standardizing observational data and the interpretation of the data.

In contrast, the technical concern of the American variant forces systematic attention to such problems as those of reliability. Once systematic attention is given these problems, their nature is more precisely understood. The finding, for example, of an American student of mass communications that in content-analysis, "the more complex the category, the lower the reliability" is of a kind which simply does not occur in the European sociology of knowledge. This example also indicates the price paid for technical precision, in this early stage of the discipline. For since it has been uniformly found that reliability declines as complexity of categorization increases, there has been a marked pressure for working with very simple, one-dimensional categories, in order to achieve high reliability. At the extreme, content-analyses will deal with such abstract categories as "favorable, neutral, and unfavorable," "positive, neutral, and negative." And this often surrenders the very problem which gave rise to the research, without necessarily putting theoretically relevant facts in its place. To the European, this is a Pyrrhic victory. It means that reliability has been won by surrendering theoretic relevance.

But all this would seem to take a figure of speech too seriously, to assume that the European and the American divisions are indeed distinct intellectual species, incapable of interbreeding and deprived of a common progeny. Of course, this is not the case. To take a purely local instance, the last chapter of this book reports an early use of techniques of content-analysis in the sociology of knowledge, an analysis designed to determine systematically, rather than impressionistically, the foci of research attention among seventeenth century English scientists, and to establish, crudely but objectively, the extent of connections between economic needs and the direction of scientific research in that period.

There are indications that it was anything but mere sociological pollyannism to suggest, earlier in this introduction, that the virtues of each variant be combined to the exclusion of the vices of both. Here and there, this has been accomplished. Such cross-fertilization produces a vigorous hybrid, with the theoretically interesting categories of the one, and the empirical research techniques of the other. A content analysis of popular biographies in mass circulation magazines by Leo Lowenthal affords a promising specimen of what can be anticipated as this union becomes more frequent.[2] In tracing the shifts of subject-matter

---

2. Leo Lowenthal, "Biographies in popular magazines," P. F. Lazarsfeld and F. Stanton, (editors), *Radio Research, 1942-1943*, (New York: Duell, Sloan and Pearce, 1944).

in these popular biographies, from "idols of production" to "idols of consumption," Lowenthal employs categories drawn from an important European tradition of social theory. And to determine whether the shift is fact or fancy, he substitutes the systematic content-analysis of the American variant for the impressionism of the European. The hybrid is distinctly superior to either of the two pure strains.

Another area of research in which the concern with techniques among the European variant is nil and among the American uppermost is that of the *audiences* for cultural products. The European does not wholly blink the fact that doctrines require audiences if they are to be effective, but he does not pursue this systematically or seriously. He resorts to occasional, thin and dubious data. If a book has had a resounding popular success, or if the number of editions can be ascertained, or if, in a few instances, the number of copies distributed can be determined, this is assumed, under the conventions of the European tradition, to tell something significant about the audience. Or perhaps reviews, extracts from occasional diaries or journals of a few scattered readers, or impressionistic guesses by contemporaries are treated as impressive and significant evidence regarding the size, nature and composition of audiences, and their responses.

It is of course much otherwise with the American variant. What is a large research gap in the European sociology of knowledge becomes a major focus of interest in the American study of mass communications. Elaborate and exacting techniques have been developed for measuring not only the *size* of audiences in the several mass media, but also their composition, preferences and, to some degree, their responses.

One reason for this difference in focus upon audience research is the major difference in the central problems in the two fields. Above all, the sociologist of knowledge seeks the social determinants of the intellectual's perspectives, how he came to hold his ideas. He is ordinarily interested in the audience, therefore, only as it has an impact on the intellectual, and, therefore, it is enough for him to consider the audience only as it is taken into account by the intellectual. The student of mass communications, on the other hand, has almost from the beginning been concerned primarily with the *impact* of the mass media *upon* audiences. The European variant focuses on the structural determinants of thought; the American, on the social and psychological consequences of the diffusion of opinion. The one centers on the source, the other on the result. The European asks, how does it come to be that these particular ideas appear at all; the American asks, once introduced, how do these ideas affect behavior?

Given these differences in intellectual focus, it is easy to see why the European variant has neglected audience research and why the American variant has been devoted to it. It may also be asked whether these intellectual foci are in turn products of the structural context in which they appear. There are indications that this is the case. As Lazarsfeld and others have pointed out, mass communications research developed very largely in response to market requirements. The severe competition for advertising among the several mass media and among agencies within each medium has provoked an economic demand for objective measures of size, composition and responses of audiences (of newspapers, magazines, radio and television). And in their quest for the largest possible share of the advertising dollar, each mass medium and each agency becomes alerted to possible deficiencies in the audience yardsticks employed by competitors, thus introducing a considerable pressure for evolving rigorous and objective measures not easily vul-nerable to criticism. In addition to such market pressures, recent military interest in propaganda has also made for a focus on audience measure-ment since, with propaganda as with advertisements, the sponsors want to know if these have reached their intended audiences and whether they have attained their intended effects. In the academic community where the sociology of knowledge has largely developed, there has not been the same intense and unyielding economic pressure for technically objective measures of audiences nor, often enough, the appropriate re-sources of research staff to test these measures, once they were pro-visionally developed. This variation in the social contexts of the two fields has led them to develop markedly different foci of research atten-tion.

Not only have these market and military demands made for great interest among students of mass communications in audience measure-ment, they have also helped shape the categories in terms of which the audience is described or measured. After all, the purpose of a research helps determine its categories and concepts. The categories of audience measurement have accordingly been primarily those of income strati-fication (a kind of datum obviously important to those ultimately con-cerned with selling and marketing their commodities), sex, age and education (obviously important for those seeking to learn the advertising outlets most appropriate for reaching special groups). But since such categories as sex, age, education and income happen also to correspond to some of the chief statuses in the social structure, the procedures evolved for audience measurement by the students of mass communica-tion are of direct interest to the sociologist as well.

Here again we note that a socially induced emphasis on particular intellectual problems may deflect research interest from other problems with as great or greater sociological interest, but with perceptibly little value for *immediate* market or military purposes. The immediate task of applied research sometimes obscures the long-distance tasks of basic research. Dynamic categories, with little direct bearing on commercial interests, such as "false consciousness" (operationally defined, for example, by marked discrepancy between an objectively low economic status and an ideological identification with upper economic strata) or various types of economically mobile individuals have as yet played little part in the description of audiences.

Whereas the European variant (*Wissenssoziologie*) has done little research on the audiences for various intellectual and cultural products, the American variant (mass communications research) has done a great deal, and the categories of this research have, until the recent past, been shaped not so much by the needs of sociological or psychological theory as by the practical needs of those groups and agencies which have created the demand for audience research. Under direct market pressures and military needs, definite research techniques are developed and these techniques initially bear the marks of their origin; they are strongly conditioned by the practical uses to which they are first to be put.

The question of whether or not this technical research in mass communications later becomes independent of its social origins is itself a problem of interest for the sociology of science. Under which conditions does the research fostered by market and military interests take on a functional autonomy in which techniques and findings enter into the public domain of social science? It is possible that we have here, so much under our eyes as not to be noticed at all, a parallel in the social sciences to what happened in the physical sciences during the seventeenth century. At that time, it will be remembered, it was not the old universities but the new scientific societies which provided the impetus to experimental advances in science, and this impetus was itself not unrelated to the practical demands laid upon the developing physical sciences. So now, in the field of mass communications research, industry and government have largely supplied the venture-capital in support of social research needed for their own ends at a time and in a field where universities were reluctant, or unable, to provide such support. In the process, techniques were developed, personnel trained and findings reached. Now, it would seem, the process continues and as these demonstrations of the actual and potential value of the research come to the attention of the universities, they provide resources for research, basic and applied, in this field as in other fields of social science. It would be interesting to pursue this further: have the researches oriented toward the needs of government and industry been too closely harnessed to the immediate pressing problem, providing too little occasion for dealing with more nearly fundamental questions of social science? Do we find that social science is neither sufficiently advanced, nor industry and government sufficiently mature to lead to the large-scale support of basic research in social science as in physical science? These are questions growing directly out of the social history of research in mass communications, and they are questions of immediate concern for the sociologist of knowledge.

The Social Organization of Research

As with subject-matter, definition of problems, conceptions of empirical data, and attitude toward techniques, so with the organization of research personnel: the European and American variants take up distinctive and different positions. The Europeans have typically worked as lone scholars, exploring publications accessible in libraries, perhaps with the aid of one or two assistants under their direct and continuous supervision. Increasingly, the Americans have worked as research teams or as large research organizations comprising a number of teams.

These differences in the social organization of research feed into and sustain the other differences we have noted. They reinforce the different attitudes toward research techniques, for example, and the attitudes toward such technical problems as the one we have briefly reviewed, the problem of reliability.

Undoubtedly, the lone European scholars in the sociology of knowledge are abstractly aware of the need for reliable categorization of their empirical data, in so far as their studies involve systematic empirical data at all. Undoubtedly, too, they typically seek and perhaps achieve consistency in the classification of their materials, abiding by the criteria of classification in the apparently rare instances when these are expressly stated. But the lone scholar is not constrained *by the very structure of his work situation* to deal systematically with reliability as a technical problem. It is a remote and unlikely possibility that some other scholar, off at some other place in the academic community, would independently hit upon precisely the same collection of empirical materials, utilizing the same categories, the same criteria for these categories and conducting the same intellectual operations. Nor, given the tradition to the contrary, is it likely that deliberate replication of the same study would occur. There is, consequently, very little in the organization of the European's work situation constraining him to deal *systematically* with the tough problem of reliability of observation or reliability of analysis.

On the other hand, the very different social organization of American research in mass communications virtually forces attention to such technical problems as reliability. Empirical studies in mass communications ordinarily require the systematic coverage of large amounts of data. The magnitude of the data is such that it is usually far beyond the capacity of the lone scholar to assemble, and the routine operations so prodigally expensive of time that they are ordinarily beyond his means to pay. If these inquiries are to be made at all, they require the collaboration of numbers of research workers organized into teams. Recent examples are provided by Lasswell's War Communications Research Project at the

Library of Congress, by Hovland's mass communications section of the Research Branch of the Army's Information and Education Division, and by the division on communications research of the Columbia University Bureau of Applied Social Research.

With such research organization, the problem of reliability becomes so compelling that it cannot be neglected or scantily regarded. The need for reliability of observation and analysis which, of course, exists in the field of research at large, becomes the more visible and the more insistent in the miniature confines of the research team. Different researchers at work on the same empirical materials and performing the same operations must presumably reach the same results (within tolerable limits of variation). Thus, the very structure of the immediate work group with its several and diverse collaborators reinforces the perennial concern of science, including social science, with objectivity: the interpersonal and intergroup reliability of data. After all, if the content of mass communications is classified or coded by several coders, this inevitably raises the question of whether the same results are indeed reached by the different coders (observers). Not only does the question thus become manifest and demanding, it can without too great difficulty be answered, by arranging to compare several independent codings of the same material. In this sense, then, "it is no accident" that such research groups as Lasswell's War Communications Research Project devoted great attention to reliability of content analysis, whereas Mannheim's study of German conservatism, based also on documentary content but conducted by a lone scholar after the European fashion, does not systematically treat the question of reliability as a problem at all.

In these ways, perhaps, divergent tendencies have been reinforced by the differing social structures of the two types of research—the lone scholar, with his loneliness mitigated by a few assistants, in the European tradition of the sociology of knowledge, and the research team, its diversity made coherent by an overarching objective, in the American tradition of mass communications research.

Further Queries and Problems

It would probably be instructive to pursue further comparisons between those variant forms of communications research. How, for example, do the social origins of the personnel conducting the researches in the two fields compare? Do they differ in accord with the different social functions of the two types of research? Are the sociologists of knowledge more often, as Mannheim in effect suggests, men *marginal* to different social systems, thus able to perceive if not to reconcile the diverse intellectual perspectives of different groups, whereas the researchers on mass communications are more often men mobile *within* an economic or social system, searching out the data needed by those who operate organizations, seek markets and control large numbers of people? Does the emergence of the sociology of knowledge in Europe relate to the basic cleavages between radically opposed social systems such that there seemed to many no established system within which they might significantly apply their skills and such that they were led to search for a meaningful social system in the first instance?

But questions of this large order move well beyond the limits of this introduction. This review of the European variant of communications research—namely, the sociology of knowledge—and the American variant —namely, the sociology of opinion and mass communications—may provide a setting for the three chapters that follow.

Chapter XII is intended as a systematic review and appraisal of some basic contributions to the sociology of knowledge. It will be at once noticed that these contributions are primarily European and that they have, for the most part, little to say about procedures of analysis and only slightly more to report by way of systematic empirical findings. But the genesis of many important questions of sociological research will be found in their systems of thought.

The next chapter treats in some detail the contributions of Karl Mannheim to the sociology of knowledge, and permits a more thorough exploration of a few problems barely mentioned in the more general discussion of Chapter XII.

The last chapter in Part III—dealing with radio and film propaganda —reviews recent studies almost entirely from the standpoint of the research technician. Thus it centers on research techniques for the study of propaganda rather than on the correlative questions of the functional role of propaganda in societies of diverse kinds. It remains to be seen if the research techniques reviewed in that chapter are pertinent only for the limited array of problems presently set by market and military exigencies, or if they are pertinent also for problems inevitably arising in any large social structure. Does a socialist society, for example, any less than a capitalist society face problems of social incentive and motivation, of informing and persuading large numbers of men of the purposes and ends which should be pursued, and of having them adopt the expeditious ways of moving toward those ends? One may ask, further, if the need for technical social knowledge *must* be forgotten by those who find revolting the uses to which this knowledge is on occasion put. By the same token, one may ask if the exclusive concern with minute technical particulars may not represent a premature and not overly productive restriction of the sociological problem to the point where the research has no perceivable implications for sociology or for society. These are questions far more easily raised than answered, though the discussion in Chapter XIV may at the least provide raw materials for those concerned with working toward these answers.

XII

THE SOCIOLOGY OF KNOWLEDGE

T HE LAST GENERATION has witnessed the emergence of a special field of sociological inquiry: the sociology of knowledge (*Wissenssoziologie*). The term "knowledge" must be interpreted very broadly indeed, since studies in this area have dealt with virtually the entire gamut of cultural products (ideas, ideologies, juristic and ethical beliefs, philosophy, science, technology). But whatever the conception of knowledge, the orientation of this discipline remains largely the same: it is primarily concerned with the relations between knowledge and other existential factors in the society or culture. General and even vague as this formulation of the central purpose may be, a more specific statement will not serve to include the diverse approaches which have been developed.

Manifestly, then, the sociology of knowledge is concerned with problems which have had a long history. So much is this the case, that the discipline has found its first historian, Ernst Gruenwald.[1] But our primary concern is not with the many antecedents of current theories. There are indeed few present-day observations which have not found previous expression in suggestive aperçus. King Henry IV was being reminded that "Thy wish was father, Harry, to that thought" only a few years before Bacon was writing that "The human understanding is no dry light but receives an infusion from the will and affections; whence proceed sciences which may be called 'sciences as one would.'" And Nietzsche had set down a host of aphorisms on the ways in which needs determined the perspectives through which we interpret the world so that even sense perceptions are permeated with value-preferences. The antecedents of *Wissenssoziologie* only go to support Whitehead's ob-

---

1. Nothing will be said of this history in this paper. Ernst Gruenwald provides a sketch of the early developments, at least from the so-called era of Enlightenment in *Das Problem der Soziologie des Wissens*, (Wien-Leipzig: Wilhelm Braumueller, 1934). For a survey, see H. Otto Dahlke, "The sociology of knowledge," H. E. Barnes, Howard and F. B. Becker, eds., *Contemporary Social Theory*, (New York: Appleton-Century, 1940), 64-89.

servation that "to come very near to a true theory, and to grasp its precise application, are two very different things, as the history of science teaches us. Everything of importance has been said before by somebody who did not discover it."

THE SOCIAL CONTEXT

Quite apart from its historical and intellectual origins, there is the further question of the basis of contemporary interest in the sociology of knowledge. As is well known, the sociology of knowledge, as a distinct discipline, has been especially cultivated in Germany and France. Only within the last decades, have American sociologists come to devote increasing attention to problems in this area. The growth of publications and, as a decisive test of its academic respectability, the increasing number of doctoral dissertations in the field partly testify to this rise of interest.

An immediate and obviously inadequate explanation of this development would point to the recent transfer of European sociological thought by sociologists who have lately come to this country. To be sure, these scholars were among the culture-bearers of *Wissenssoziologie*. But this merely provided availability of these conceptions and no more accounts for their actual acceptance than would mere availability in any other instance of culture diffusion. American thought proved receptive to the sociology of knowledge largely because it dealt with problems, concepts, and theories which are increasingly pertinent to our contemporary social situation, because our society has come to have certain characteristics of those European societies in which the discipline was initially developed.

The sociology of knowledge takes on pertinence under a definite complex of social and cultural conditions.[2] With increasing social conflict, differences in the values, attitudes and modes of thought of groups develop to the point where the orientation which these groups previously had in common is overshadowed by incompatible differences. Not only do there develop distinct universes of discourse, but the existence of any one universe challenges the validity and legitimacy of the others. The co-existence of these conflicting perspectives and interpretations within the same society leads to an active and reciprocal *distrust* between groups. Within a context of distrust, one no longer inquires into the content of beliefs and assertions to determine whether they are valid or not, one no longer confronts the assertions with relevant evidence, but introduces an entirely new question: how does it happen that these views are maintained? Thought becomes functionalized; it is interpreted in terms of its psychological or economic or social or racial sources and functions.

---

2. See Karl Mannheim, *Ideology and Utopia*, 5-12; Sorokin, *Social and Cultural Dynamics*, II, 412-413.

In general, this type of functionalizing occurs when statements are doubted, when they appear so palpably implausible or absurd or biased that one need no longer examine the evidence for or against the statement but only the grounds for its being asserted at all.[3] Such alien statements are "explained by" or "imputed to" special interests, unwitting motives, distorted perspectives, social position, etc. In folk thought, this involves reciprocal attacks on the integrity of opponents; in more systematic thought, it leads to reciprocal ideological analyses. On both levels, it feeds upon and nourishes collective insecurities.

Within this social context, an array of interpretations of man and culture which share certain common presuppositions finds widespread currency. Not only ideological analysis and *Wissenssoziologie*, but also psycho-analysis, Marxism, semanticism, propaganda analysis, Paretanism and, to some extent, functional analysis have, despite their other differences, a similar outlook on the role of ideas. On the one hand, there is the realm of verbalization and ideas (ideologies, rationalizations, emotive expressions, distortions, folklore, derivations), all of which are viewed as expressive or derivative or deceptive (of self and others), all of which are functionally related to some substratum. On the other hand are the previously conceived substrata (relations of production, social position, basic impulses, psychological conflict, interests and sentiments, interpersonal relations, and residues). And throughout runs the basic theme of the unwitting determination of ideas by the substrata; the emphasis on the distinction between the real and the illusory, between reality and appearance in the sphere of human thought, belief, and conduct. And whatever the intention of the analysts, their analyses tend to have an acrid quality: they tend to indict, secularize, ironicize, satirize, alienate, devalue the intrinsic content of the avowed belief or point of view. Consider only the overtones of terms chosen in these contexts to refer to beliefs, ideas and thought: vital lies, myths, illusions, derivations, folklore, rationalizations, ideologies, verbal façade, pseudo-reasons, etc.

What these schemes of analysis have in common is the practice of discounting the *face value* of statements, beliefs, and idea-systems by re-examining them within a new context which supplies the "real meaning." Statements ordinarily viewed in terms of their manifest content are debunked, whatever the intention of the analyst, by relating this content to attributes of the speaker or of the society in which he lives. The

---

3. Freud had observed this tendency to seek out the "origins" rather than to test the validity of statements which seem palpably absurd to us. Thus, suppose someone maintains that the center of the earth is made of jam. "The result of our intellectual objection will be a *diversion of our interests; instead of their being directed on to the investigation itself,* as to whether the interior of the earth is really made of jam or not, *we shall wonder what kind of man it must be who can get such an idea into his head. . . .*" Sigmund Freud, *New Introductory Lectures,* (New York: W. W. Norton, 1933), 49. On the social level, a radical difference of outlook of various social groups leads not only to *ad hominem* attacks, but also to "functionalized explanations."

professional iconoclast, the trained debunker, the ideological analyst and their respective systems of thought thrive in a society where large groups of people have already become alienated from common values; where separate universes of discourse are linked with reciprocal distrust. Ideological analysis systematizes the lack of faith in reigning symbols which has become widespread; hence its pertinence and popularity. The ideological analyst does not so much create a following as he speaks for a following to whom his analyses "make sense," *i.e.,* conform to their previously unanalyzed experience.[4]

In a society where reciprocal distrust finds such folk-expression as "what's in it for him?"; where "buncombe" and "bunk" have been idiom for nearly a century and "debunk" for a generation; where advertising and propaganda have generated active resistance to the acceptance of statements at face-value; where pseudo-*Gemeinschaft* behavior as a device for improving one's economic and political position is documented in a best-seller on how to win friends who may be influenced; where social relationships are increasingly instrumentalized so that the individual comes to view others as seeking primarily to control, manipulate and exploit him; where growing cynicism involves a progressive detachment from significant group relationships and a considerable degree of self-estrangement; where uncertainty about one's own motives is voiced in the indecisive phrase, "I may be rationalizing, but . . ."; where defenses against traumatic disillusionment may consist in remaining permanently disillusioned by reducing expectations about the integrity of others through discounting their motives and abilities in advance;—in such a society, systematic ideological analysis and a derived sociology of knowledge take on a socially grounded pertinence and cogency. And American academicians, presented with schemes of analysis which appear to order the chaos of cultural conflict, contending values and points of view, have promptly seized upon and assimilated these analytical schemes.

The "Copernican revolution" in this area of inquiry consisted in the hypothesis that not only error or illusion or unauthenticated belief but also the discovery of truth was socially (historically) conditioned. As long as attention was focused on the social determinants of ideology, illusion, myth, and moral norms, the sociology of knowledge could not emerge. It was abundantly clear that in accounting for error or uncertified opinion, some extra-theoretic factors were involved, that some

---

4. The concept of *pertinence* was assumed by the Marxist harbingers of *Wissenssoziologie.* "The theoretical conclusions of the Communists are in no way based on ideas or principles that have been invented, or discovered, by this or that would-be universal reformer. *They merely express, in general terms, the actual relations* springing from an existing class struggle, from a historical movement going on under our very eyes. . . ." Karl Marx and Friedrich Engels, *The Communist Manifesto,* in *Karl Marx, Selected Works,* I, 219.

special explanation was needed, since the reality of the object could not account for error. In the case of confirmed or certified knowledge, however, it was long assumed that it could be adequately accounted for in terms of a direct object-interpreter relation. The sociology of knowledge came into being with the signal hypothesis that even truths were to be held socially accountable, were to be related to the historical society in which they emerged.

To outline even the main currents of the sociology of knowledge in brief compass is to present none adequately and to do violence to all. The diversity of formulations—of a Marx or Scheler or Durkheim; the varying problems—from the social determination of categorical systems to that of class-bound political ideologies; the enormous differences in scope—from the all-encompassing categorizing of intellectual history to the social location of the thought of Negro scholars in the last decades; the various limits assigned to the discipline—from a comprehensive sociological epistemology to the empirical relations of particular social structures and ideas; the proliferation of concepts—ideas, belief-systems, positive knowledge, thought, systems of truth, superstructure, etc.; the diverse methods of validation—from plausible but undocumented imputations to meticulous historical and statistical analyses—in the light of all this, an effort to deal with both analytical apparatus and empirical studies in a few pages must sacrifice detail to scope.

To introduce a basis of comparability among the welter of studies which have appeared in this field, we must adopt some scheme of analysis. The following paradigm is intended as a step in this direction. It is, undoubtedly, a partial and, it is to be hoped, a temporary classification which will disappear as it gives way to an improved and more exacting analytical model. But it does provide a basis for taking an inventory of extant findings in the field; for indicating contradictory, contrary and consistent results; setting forth the conceptual apparatus now in use; determining the nature of problems which have occupied workers in this field; assessing the character of the evidence which they have brought to bear upon these problems; ferreting out the characteristic lacunae and weaknesses in current types of interpretation. Full-fledged theory in the sociology of knowledge lends itself to classification in terms of the following paradigm.

PARADIGM FOR THE SOCIOLOGY OF KNOWLEDGE

1. Where *is the existential basis of mental productions located?*

a. *social bases:* social position, class, generation, occupational role, mode of production, group structures (university, bureaucracy, academies, sects, political parties), "historical situation," interests, society, ethnic affiliation, social mobility, power structure, social processes (competition, conflict, etc.).

b. *cultural bases:* values, ethos, climate of opinion, *Volksgeist, Zeitgeist,* type of culture, culture mentality, *Weltanschauungen,* etc.

2. What *mental productions are being sociologically analyzed?*

a. *spheres of:* moral beliefs, ideologies, ideas, the categories of thought, philosophy, religious beliefs, social norms, positive science, technology, etc.

b. *which aspects are analyzed:* their selection (foci of attention), level of abstraction, presuppositions (what is taken as data and what as problematical), conceptual content, models of verification, objectives of intellectual activity, etc.

3. How *are mental productions related to the existential basis?*

a. *causal or functional relations:* determination, cause, correspondence, necessary condition, conditioning, functional interdependence, interaction, dependence, etc.

b. *symbolic or organismic or meaningful relations:* consistency, harmony, coherence, unity, congruence, compatibility (and antonyms); expression, realization, symbolic expression, *Strukturzusammenhang,* structural identities, inner connection, stylistic analogies, logicomeaningful integration, identity of meaning, etc.

c. *ambiguous terms to designate relations:* correspondence, reflection, bound up with, in close connection with, etc.

4. Why? *manifest and latent functions imputed to these existentially conditioned mental productions.*

a. to maintain power, promote stability, orientation, exploitation, obscure actual social relationships, provide motivation, canalize behavior, divert criticism, deflect hostility, provide reassurance, control nature, coordinate social relationships, etc.

5. When *do the imputed relations of the existential base and knowledge obtain?*

a. historicist theories (confined to particular societies or cultures).

b. general analytical theories.

There are, of course, additional categories for classifying and analyzing studies in the sociology of knowledge, which are not fully explored here. Thus, the perennial problem of the implications of existential influences upon knowledge for the epistemological status of that knowledge has been hotly debated from the very outset. Solutions to this problem, which assume that a sociology of knowledge is necessarily a sociological theory of knowledge, range from the claim that the "genesis of thought has no necessary relation to its validity" to the extreme relativist position that truth is "merely" a function of a social or cultural basis, that it rests solely upon social consensus and, consequently, that any culturally accepted theory of truth has a claim to validity equal to that of any other.

But the foregoing paradigm serves to organize the distinctive approaches and conclusions in this field sufficiently for our purposes.

The chief approaches to be considered here are those of Marx,

Scheler, Mannheim, Durkheim and Sorokin. Current work in this area is largely oriented toward one or another of these theories, either through a modified application of their conceptions or through counter-developments. Other sources of studies in this field indigenous to American thought, such as pragmatism, will be advisedly omitted, since they have not yet been formulated with specific reference to the sociology of knowledge nor have they been embodied in research to any notable extent.

THE EXISTENTIAL BASIS

A central point of agreement in all approaches to the sociology of knowledge is the thesis that thought has an existential basis in so far as it is not immanently determined and in so far as one or another of its aspects can be derived from extra-cognitive factors. But this is merely a formal consensus, which gives way to a wide variety of theories concerning the nature of the existential basis.

In this respect, as in others, Marxism is the storm-center of *Wissenssoziologie*. Without entering into the exegetic problem of closely identifying Marxism—we have only to recall Marx's *"je ne suis pas Marxiste"*—we can trace out its formulations primarily in the writings of Marx and Engels. Whatever other changes may have occurred in the development of their theory during the half-century of their work, they consistently held fast to the thesis that "relations of production" constitute the "real foundation" for the superstructure of ideas. "The mode of production in material life determines the general character of the social, political and intellectual processes of life. It is not the consciousness of men that determines their existence, but on the contrary, their social existence determines their consciousness."[5] In seeking to functionalize ideas, *i.e.*, to relate the ideas of individuals to their sociological bases, Marx locates them within the class structure. He assumes, not so much that other influences are not at all operative, but that class is a primary determinant and, as such, the single most fruitful point of departure for analysis. This he makes explicit in his first preface to *Capital:* ". . . here individuals are dealt with *only in so far* as they are the personifications of economic categories, embodiments of particular class-relations and class-interests."[6] In abstracting from other variables and in regarding men in their economic and class roles, Marx hypothesizes that these roles are primary determinants and thus leaves as an open question *the extent to which they adequately account for thought and be-*

5. Karl Marx, *A Contribution to the Critique of Political Economy,* (Chicago: C. H. Kerr, 1904), 11-12.

6. Karl Marx, *Capitol,* I, 15; *cf.* Marx and Engels, *The German Ideology,* (New York: International Publishers, 1939), 76; *cf.* Max Weber, *Gesammelte Aufsaetze zur Wissenschaftslehre,* 205.

havior in any given case. In point of fact, one line of development of Marxism, from the early *German Ideology* to the latter writings of Engels, consists in a progressive definition (and delimitation) of the extent to which the relations of production do in fact condition knowledge and forms of thought.

However, both Marx and Engels, repeatedly and with increasing insistence, emphasized that the ideologies of a social stratum need not stem only from persons who are *objectively* located in that stratum. As early as the *Communist Manifesto,* Marx and Engels had indicated that as the ruling class approaches dissolution, "a small section . . . joins the revolutionary class. . . . Just as, therefore, at an earlier period, a section of the nobility went over to the bourgeoisie, so now a portion of the bourgeoisie goes over to the proletariat, and in particular, a portion of *the bourgeois ideologists,* who have *raised themselves* to the level of comprehending theoretically the historical movement as a whole."[7]

Ideologies are socially located by analyzing their perspectives and presuppositions and determining how problems are construed: from the standpoint of one or another class. Thought is not mechanistically located by merely establishing the class position of the thinker. It is attributed to that class for which it is "appropriate," to the class whose social situation with its class conflicts, aspirations, fears, restraints and objective possibilities within the given sociohistorical context is being expressed. Marx's most explicit formulation holds:

> One must not form the narrow-minded idea that the petty bourgeoisie wants on principle to enforce an egoistic class interest. It believes, rather, that the *special* conditions of its emancipation are the *general* conditions through which alone modern society can be saved and the class struggle avoided. Just as little must one imagine that the democratic representatives are all shopkeepers or are full of enthusiasm for them. *So far as their education and their individual position are concerned,* they may be as widely separated from them as heaven from earth. *What makes them representatives of the petty bourgeosie is the fact that in their minds {im Kopfe} they do not exceed the limits which the latter do not exceed in their life activities,* that they are consequently driven to the same problems and solutions in theory to which material interest and social position drive the latter in practice. *This is ueberhaupt the relationship of the political and literary representatives of a class to the class which they represent.*[8]

But if we cannot derive ideas from the objective class position of their exponents, this leaves a wide margin of indeterminacy. It then becomes a further problem to discover why some identify themselves with the characteristic outlook of the class stratum in which they objectively find themselves whereas others adopt the presuppositions of a

7. Marx and Engels, *The Communist Manifesto,* in *Karl Marx, Selected Works,* I, 216.

8. Karl Marx. *Der Achtzehnte Brumaire des Louis Bonaparte,* (Hamburg, 1885), 36 (italics inserted).

class stratum other than "their own." An empirical description of the fact is no adequate substitute for its theoretical explanation.

In dealing with existential bases, Max Scheler characteristically places his own hypothesis in opposition to other prevalent theories.[9] He draws a distinction between cultural sociology and what he calls the sociology of real factors (*Realsoziologie*). Cultural data are "ideal," in the realm of ideas and values: "real factors" are oriented toward effecting changes in the reality of nature or society. The former are defined by ideal goals or intentions; the latter derive from an "impulse structure" (*Triebstruktur, e.g.,* sex, hunger, power). It is a basic error, he holds, of all naturalistic theories to maintain that real factors—whether race, geopolitics, political power structure, or the relations of economic production—unequivocally determine the realm of meaningful ideas. He also rejects all ideological, spiritualistic, and personalistic conceptions which err in viewing the history of existential conditions as a unilinear unfolding of the history of mind. He ascribes complete autonomy and a determinate sequence to these real factors, though he inconsistently holds that value-laden ideas serve to guide and direct their development. Ideas as such initially have no social effectiveness. The "purer" the idea, the greater its impotence, so far as dynamic effect on society is concerned. Ideas do not become actualized, embodied in cultural developments, unless they are bound up in some fashion with interests, impulses, emotions or collective tendencies and their incorporation in institutional structures.[10] Only then—and in this limited respect, naturalistic theories (*e.g.,* Marxism) are justified—do they exercise some definite influence. Should ideas not be grounded in the imminent development of real factors, they are doomed to become sterile Utopias.

Naturalistic theories are further in error, Scheler holds, in tacitly assuming the *independent variable* to be one and the same throughout history. There is no constant independent variable but there is, in the course of history, a definite sequence in which the primary factors prevail, a sequence which can be summed up in a "law of three phases." In the initial phase, blood-ties and associated kinship institutions constitute the independent variable; later, political power and finally, economic factors. There is, then, no constancy in the effective primacy of existential factors but rather an ordered variability. Thus, Scheler sought

---

9. This account is based upon Scheler's most elaborate discussion, "Probleme einer Soziologie des Wissens," in his *Die Wissensformen und die Gesellschaft* (Leipzig: Der Neue-Geist Verlag, 1926), 1-229. This essay is an extended and improved version of an essay in his *Versuche zu einer Soziologie des Wissens,* (Muenchen: Duncker und Humblot, 1924), 5-146. For further discussions of Scheler, see P. A. Schillp, "The formal problems of Scheler's sociology of knowledge," *The Philosophical Review,* March, 1927, 36, 101-20; Howard Becker and H. O. Dahlke, "Max Scheler's sociology of knowledge," *Philosophy and Phenomenological Research,* 2: 310-322, March, 1942.

10. Scheler, *Die Wissensformen . . .,* 7, 32.

to relativize the very notion of historical determinants.[11] He claims not only to have confirmed his law of the three phases inductively but to have derived it from a theory of human impulses.

Scheler's conception of *Realfaktoren*—race and kinship, the structure of power, factors of production, qualitative and quantitative aspects of population, geographical and geopolitical factors—hardly constitutes a usefully defined category. It is of small value to subsume such diverse elements under one rubric, and, indeed, his own empirical studies and those of his disciples do not profit from this array of factors. But in suggesting a variation of significant existential factors, though not in the ordered sequence which he failed to establish, he moves in the direction which subsequent research has followed.

Thus, Mannheim derives from Marx primarily by extending his conception of existential bases. Given the *fact* of multiple group affiliation, the problem becomes one of determining *which* of these affiliations are decisive in fixing perspectives, models of thought, definitions of the given, etc. Unlike "a dogmatic Marxism," he does not assume that class position is alone ultimately determinant. He finds, for example, that an organically integrated group conceives of history as a continuous movement toward the realization of its goals, whereas socially uprooted and loosely integrated groups espouse an historical intuition which stresses the fortuitous and imponderable. It is only through exploring the variety of group formations—generations, status groups, sects, occupational groups—and their characteristic modes of thought that there can be found an existential basis corresponding to the great variety of perspectives and knowledge which actually obtain.[12]

Though representing a different tradition, this is substantially the position taken by Durkheim. In an early study with Mauss of primitive forms of classification, he maintained that the genesis of the categories of thought is to be found in the group structure and relations and that the categories vary with changes in the social organization.[13] In seeking to account for the social origins of the categories, Durkheim postulates that individuals are more directly and inclusively oriented toward the groups in which they live than they are toward nature. The primarily

---

11. *Ibid.*, 25-45. It should be noted that Marx has long since rejected out of hand a similar conception of shifts in independent variables which was made the basis for an attack on his *Critique of Political Economy;* see *Capital,* I, 94n.

12. Karl Mannheim, *Ideology and Utopia,* 247-8. In view of the recent extensive discussions of Mannheim's work, it will not be treated at length in this essay. For the writer's appraisal, see Chapter XIII of this book.

13. Emile Durkheim and Marcel Mauss, "De quelques formes primitives de classification," *L'Année Sociologique,* 1901-02, 6, 1-72, ". . . even ideas as abstract as those of time and space are, at each moment of their history, in close relation with the corresponding social organization." As Marcel Granet has indicated, this paper contains some pages on Chinese thought which have been held by specialists to mark a new era in the field of sinological studies.

significant experiences are mediated through social relationships, which leave their impress on the character of thought and knowledge.[14] Thus, in his study of primitive forms of thought, he deals with the periodic recurrence of social activities (ceremonies, feasts, rites), the clan structure and the spatial configurations of group meetings as among the existential bases of thought. And, applying Durkheim's formulations to ancient Chinese thought, Granet attributes their typical conceptions of time and space to such bases as the feudal organization and the rhythmic alternation of concentrated and dispersed group life.[15]

In sharp distinction from the foregoing conceptions of existential bases is Sorokin's idealistic and emanationist theory, which seeks to derive every aspect of knowledge, not from an existential social basis, but from varying "culture mentalities." These mentalities are constructed of "major premises": thus, the ideational mentality conceives of reality as "non-material, ever-lasting Being"; its needs as primarily spiritual and their full satisfaction through "self imposed minimization or elimination of most physical needs."[16] Contrariwise, the sensate mentality limits reality to what can be perceived through the senses, it is primarily concerned with physical needs which it seeks to satisfy to a maximum, not through self-modification, but through change of the external world. The chief intermediate type of mentality is the idealistic, which represents a virtual balance of the foregoing types. It is these mentalities, *i.e.*, the major premises of each culture, from which systems of truth and knowledge are derived. And here we come to the self-contained emanationism of an idealistic position: it appears plainly tautological to say, as Sorokin does, that "in a sensate society and culture the Sensate system of truth based upon the testimony of the organs of senses has to be dominant."[17] For sensate mentality has already been *defined* as one conceiving of "reality as only that which is presented to the sense organs."[18]

Moreover, an emanationist phrasing such as this by-passes some of the basic questions raised by other approaches to the analysis of existential conditions. Thus, Sorokin considers the failure of the sensate "system of truth" (empiricism) to monopolize a sensate culture as evidence that the culture is not "fully integrated." But this surrenders inquiry into the bases of those very differences of thought with which our contemporary world is concerned. This is true of other categories and principles of knowledge for which he seeks to apply a sociological accounting. For example, in our present sensate culture, he finds that "materialism" is less prevalent than "idealism," "temporalism" and "eternalism" are al-

---

14. Emile Durkheim, *The Elementary Forms of the Religious Life*, 443-4; see also Hans Kelsen, *Society and Nature* (University of Chicago Press, 1943), 30.

15. Marcel Granet, *La pensée chinoise*, (Paris: La Renaissance du Livre, 1934), *e.g.* 84-104.

16. Sorokin, *Social and Cultural Dynamics*, I, 72-73.

17. *Ibid.*, II, 5.

18. *Ibid.*, I, 73.

most equally current; so, too, with "realism" and "nominalism," "singularism" and "universalism," etc. Since there are these diversities within a culture, the overall characterization of the culture as sensate provides no basis for indicating which groups subscribe to one mode of thought, and which to another. Sorokin does not systematically explore varying existential bases *within* a society or culture; he looks to the "dominant" tendencies and imputes these to the culture as a whole.[19] Our contemporary society, quite apart from the *differences* of intellectual outlook of divers classes and groups, is viewed as an integral exemplification of sensate culture. On its own premises, Sorokin's approach is primarily suited for an overall characterization of cultures, not for analyzing connections between varied existential conditions and thought within a society.

TYPES OF KNOWLEDGE

Even a cursory survey is enough to show that the term "knowledge" has been so broadly conceived as to refer to every type of idea and every mode of thought ranging from folk belief to positive science. Knowledge has often come to be assimilated to the term "culture" so that not only the exact sciences but ethical convictions, epistemological postulates, material predications, synthetic judgments, political beliefs, the categories of thought, eschatological doxies, moral norms, ontological assumptions, and observations of empirical fact are more or less indiscriminately held to be "existentially conditioned."[20] The question is, of course, whether these diverse kinds of "knowledge" stand in the same relationship to their sociological basis, or whether it is necessary to discriminate between spheres of knowledge precisely because this relationship differs for the various types. For the most part, there has been a systematic ambiguity concerning this problem.

Only in his later writings did Engels come to recognize that the concept of ideological superstructure included a variety of "ideological forms" which differ *significantly, i.e.*, are not equally and similarly conditioned by the material basis. Marx's failure to take up this problem systematically[21] accounts for much of the initial vagueness about *what* is comprised by the superstructure and how these several "ideological"

---

19. One "exception" to this practice is found in his contrast between the prevalent tendency of the "clergy and religious landed aristocracy to become the leading and organizing classes in the Ideational, and the capitalistic bourgeoisie, intelligentsia, professionals, and secular officials in the Sensate culture. . . ." III, 250. And see his account of the diffusion of culture among social classes, IV, 221 ff.

20. *Cf.* Merton, *op. cit.*, 133-135; Kurt H. Wolff, "The sociology of knowledge: emphasis on an empirical attitude," *Philosophy of Science*, 10: 104-123, 1943; Talcott Parsons, "The role of ideas in social action," *Essays in Sociological Theory*, Chapter VI.

21. This is presumably the ground for Scheler's remark: "A specific thesis of the economic conception of history is the subsumption of the laws of development of *all* knowledge under the laws of development of ideologies." *Die Wissensformen . . .*, 21.

spheres are related to the modes of production. It was largely the task of Engels to attempt this clarification. In differentiating the blanket term "ideology," Engels granted a degree of autonomy to law.

As soon as the new division of labor which creates professional lawyers becomes necessary, another new and independent sphere is opened up which, for all its general dependence on production and trade, still has its own capacity for reacting upon these spheres as well. In a modern state, law must not only correspond to the general economic position and be its expression, but must also be an expression which is *consistent in itself,* and which does not, owing to inner contradictions, look glaringly inconsistent. And in order to achieve this, the faithful reflection of economic conditions is more and more infringed upon. All the more so the more rarely it happens that a code of law is the blunt, unmitigated, unadulterated expression of the domination of a class—this in itself would already offend the "conception of justice."[22]

If this is true of law, with its close connection with economic pressures, it is all the more true of other spheres of the "ideological super-structure." Philosophy, religion, science are particularly constrained by the pre-existing stock of knowledge and belief, and are only indirectly and ultimately influenced by economic factors.[23] In these fields, it is not possible to "derive" the content and development of belief and knowledge merely from an analysis of the historical situation:

Political, juridical, philosophical, religious, literary, artistic, etc., development is based on economic development. But all these react upon one another and also upon the economic base. It is not that the economic position is the *cause and alone active,* while everything else only has a passive effect. There is, rather, interaction on the basis of the economic necessity, which *ultimately* always asserts itself.[24]

But to say that the economic basis "ultimately" asserts itself is to say that the ideological spheres exhibit some degree of independent development, as indeed Engels goes on to observe:

The further the particular sphere which we are investigating is removed from the economic sphere and approaches that of pure abstract ideology, the more shall we find it exhibiting accidents [i.e., deviations from the "expected"] in its development, the more will its curve run in zig-zag.[25]

Finally, there is an even more restricted conception of the sociological status of natural science. In one well-known passage, Marx expressly distinguishes natural science from ideological spheres.

---

22. Engels, letter to Conrad Schmidt, 27 October, 1890, in *Marx, Selected Works,* I, 385.

23. *Ibid.,* I, 386.

24. Engels, letter to Heinz Starkenburg, 25 January, 1894, *ibid.,* I, 392.

25. *Ibid.,* I, 393; *cf.* Engels, *Feuerbach,* (Chicago: C. H. Kerr, 1903) 117 ff. "It is well known that certain periods of highest development of art stand in *no direct connection* with the general development of society, nor with the material basis and the skeleton structure of its organization." Marx, Introduction, *A Contribution to the Critique of Political Economy,* 309-10.

With the change of the economic foundation the entire immense super-structure is more or less rapidly transformed. In considering such trans-formations the distinction should always be made between the material transformation of the economic conditions of production *which can be deter-mined with the precision of natural science,* and the legal, political, religious, aesthetic or philosophic—in short, ideological forms in which men become conscious of this conflict and fight it out.[26]

Thus, natural science and political economy, which can match its precision, are granted a status quite distinct from that of ideology. The conceptual content of natural science is not imputed to an economic base: merely its "aims" and "material."

Where would natural science be without industry and commerce? Even this "pure" natural science is provided with an aim, as with its material, *only* through trade and industry, through the sensuous activity of men.[27]

Along the same lines, Engels asserts that the appearance of Marx's materialistic conception of history was itself determined by "necessity," as is indicated by similar views appearing among English and French historians at the time and by Morgan's independent discovery of the same conception.[28]

He goes even further to maintain that socialist theory is itself a proletarian "reflection" of modern class conflict, so that here, at least, the very content of "scientific thought" is held to be socially deter-mined,[29] without vitiating its validity.

There was an incipient tendency in Marxism, then, to consider natural science as standing in a relation to the economic base different from that of other spheres of knowledge and belief. In science, the focus of attention may be socially determined but not, presumably, its con-

---

26. Marx, *A Contribution to the Critique of Political Economy,* 12.

27. Marx and Engels, *The German Ideology,* 36 (italics inserted). See also Engels, *Socialism: Utopian and Scientific,* (Chicago: C. H. Kerr, 1910), 24-25, where the needs of a rising middle class are held to account for the revival of science. The assertion that "only" trade and industry provide the aims is typical of the ex-treme, and untested, statements of relationships which prevail especially in the early Marxist writings. Such terms as "determination" cannot be taken at their face value; they are characteristically used very loosely. The actual *extent* of such relationships between intellectual activity and the material foundations were not investigated by either Marx or Engels.

28. Engels, in *Marx, Selected Works,* I, 393. The occurrence of parallel inde-pendent discoveries and inventions as "proof" of the social determination of knowl-edge was a repeated theme throughout the nineteenth century. As early as 1828, Macaulay in his essay on Dryden had noted concerning Newton's and Leibniz's inven-tion of the calculus: "Mathematical science, indeed, had reached such a point, that if neither of them had existed, the principle must inevitably have occurred to some person within a few years." He cites other cases in point. Victorian manufacturers shared the same view with Marx and Engels. In our own day, this thesis, based on independent duplicate inventions, has been especially emphasized by Dorothy Thomas, Ogburn, and Vierkandt.

29. Engels, *Socialism: Utopian and Scientific,* 97.

ceptual apparatus. In this respect, the social sciences were sometimes held to differ significantly from the natural sciences. Social science tended to be assimilated to the sphere of ideology, a tendency developed by later Marxists into the questionable thesis of a class-bound social science which is inevitably tendentious[30] and into the claim that only "proletarian science" has valid insight into certain aspects of social reality.[31]

Mannheim follows in the Marxist tradition to the extent of exempting the "exact sciences" and "formal knowledge" from existential determination but not "historical, political and social science thinking as well as the thought of everyday life."[32] Social position determines the "perspective," i.e., "the manner in which one views an object, what one perceives in it, and how one construes it in his thinking." The situational determination of thought does not render it invalid; it does, however, particularize the scope of the inquiry and the limits of its validity.[33]

If Marx did not sharply differentiate the superstructure, Scheler goes to the other extreme. He distinguishes a variety of forms of knowledge. To begin with, there are the "relatively natural Weltanschauungen": that which is accepted as given, as neither requiring nor being capable of justification. These are, so to speak, the cultural axioms of groups; what Joseph Glanvill, some three hundred years ago, called a "climate of opinion." A primary task of the sociology of knowledge is to discover the laws of transformation of these Weltanschauungen. And since these outlooks are by no means necessarily valid, it follows that the sociology of knowledge is not concerned merely with tracing the existential bases of truth but also of "social illusion, superstition and socially conditioned errors and forms of deception."[34]

The Weltanschauungen constitute organic growths and develop only in long time-spans. They are scarcely affected by theories. Without adequate evidence, Scheler claims that they can be changed in any fundamental sense only through race-mixture or conceivably through the "mixture" of language and culture. Building upon these very slowly changing Weltanschauungen are the more "artificial" forms of knowledge which may be ordered in seven classes, according to degree of artificial-

---

30. V. I. Lenin, "The three sources and three component parts of Marxism," in Marx, Selected Works, I, 54.

31. Nikolai Bukharin, Historical Materialism, (New York: International Publishers, 1925), xi-xii; B. Hessen in Society at the Cross-Roads, (London: Kniga, 1932) 154; A. I. Timeniev in Marxism and Modern Thought, (New York: Harcourt, Brace, 1935), 310; "Only Marxism, only the ideology of the advanced revolutionary class is scientific."

32. Mannheim, Ideology and Utopia, 150, 243; Mannheim, "Die Bedeutung der Konkurrenz im Gebiete des Geistigen," Verhandlungen des 6. deutschen Soziologentages, (Tuebingen: 1929), 41.

33. Mannheim, Ideology and Utopia, 256, 264.

34. Scheler, Die Wissensformen . . ., 59-61.

ity: 1. myth and legend; 2. knowledge implicit in the natural folk-language; 3. religious knowledge (ranging from the vague emotional intuition to the fixed dogma of a church); 4. the basic types of mystical knowledge; 5. philosophical-metaphysical knowledge; 6. positive knowledge of mathematics, the natural and cultural sciences; 7. technological knowledge.[35] The more artificial these types of knowledge, the more rapidly they change. It is evident, says Scheler, that religions change far more slowly than the various metaphysics, and the latter persist for much longer periods than the results of positive science, which change from hour to hour.

This hypothesis of rates of change bears some points of similarity to Alfred Weber's thesis that civilizational change outruns cultural change and to the Ogburn hypothesis that "material" factors change more rapidly than the "non-material." Scheler's hypothesis shares the limitations of these others as well as several additional shortcomings. He nowhere indicates with any clarity what his principle of classification of types of knowledge—so-called "artificiality"—actually denotes. Why, for example, is "mystical knowledge" conceived as more "artificial" than religious dogmas? He does not at all consider what is entailed by saying that one type of knowledge changes more rapidly than another. Consider his curious equating of new scientific "results" with metaphysical systems; how does one compare the degree of change implied in neo-Kantian philosophy with, say, change in biological theory during the corresponding period? Scheler boldly asserts a seven-fold variation in rates of change and, of course, does not empirically confirm this elaborate claim. In view of the difficulties encountered in testing much simpler hypotheses, it is not at all clear what is gained by setting forth an elaborate hypothesis of this type.

Yet only certain aspects of this knowledge are held to be sociologically determined. On the basis of certain postulates, which need not be considered here, Scheler goes on to assert:

> The sociological character of all knowledge, of all forms of thought, intuition and cognition is unquestionable. Although the *content* and even less the objective validity of all knowledge is not determined by the *controlling perspectives of social interests*, nevertheless this is the case with the *selection* of the objects of knowledge. Moreover, the "forms" of the mental processes by means of which knowledge is acquired are always and necessarily co-determined sociologically, i.e. by the social structure.[36]

Since explanation consists in tracing the relatively new to the familiar and known and since society is "better known" than anything else,[37] it is to be expected that the modes of thought and intuition and the classi-

---

35. *Ibid.*, 62.
36. *Ibid.*, 55.
37. See the same assumption of Durkheim, cited in fn. 14 of this chapter.

fication of knowable things generally, are co-determined (*mitbedingt*) by the division and classification of groups which comprise the society.

Scheler flatly repudiates all forms of sociologism. He seeks to escape a radical relativism by resorting to a metaphysical dualism. He posits a realm of "timeless essences" which in varying degrees enter into the *content of judgments;* a realm utterly distinct from that of historical and social reality which determines the *act* of judgments. As Mandelbaum has aptly summarized this view:

> The realm of essences is to Scheler a realm of possibilities out of which we, bound to time and our interest, first select one set and then another for consideration. Where we as historians turn the spotlight of our attention depends upon our own sociologically determined valuations; what we see there is determined by the set of absolute and timeless values which are implicit in the past with which we are dealing.[38]

This is indeed counter-relativism by fiat. Merely asserting the distinction between essence and existences avoids the incubus of relativism by exorcising it. The concept of eternal essences may be congenial to the metaphysician; it is wholly foreign to empirical inquiry. It is noteworthy that these conceptions play no significant part in Scheler's empirical efforts to establish relations between knowledge and society.

Scheler indicates that different types of knowledge are bound up with particular forms of groups. The content of Plato's theory of ideas required the form and organization of the platonic academy; so, too, the organization of Protestant churches and sects was determined by the content of their beliefs which could exist only in this and in no other type of social organization, as Troeltsch has shown. And, similarly, *Gemeinschaft* types of society have a traditionally defined fund of knowledge which is handed down as conclusive; they are not concerned with discovering or extending knowledge. The very effort to test the traditional knowledge, in so far as it implies doubt, is ruled out as virtually blasphemous. In such a group, the prevailing logic and mode of thought is that of an *"ars demonstrandi"* not of an *"ars inveniendi."* Its methods are prevailingly ontological and dogmatic, not epistemologic and critical; its mode of thought is that of conceptual realism, not nominalistic as in the *Gesellschaft* type of organization; its system of categories, organismic and not mechanistic.[39]

Durkheim extends sociological inquiry into the social genesis of the categories of thought, basing his hypothesis on three types of presump-

---

38. Maurice Mandelbaum, *The Problem of Historical Knowledge,* (New York: Liveright, 1938), 150; Sorokin posits a similar sphere of "timeless ideas," e.g. in his *Sociocultural Causality, Space, Time,* (Durham: Duke University Press, 1943), 215, *passim.*

39. Scheler, *Die Wissensformen . . .,* 22-23; compare a similar characterization of "sacred schools" of thought by Florian Znaniecki, *The Social Role of the Man of Knowledge,* (New York: Columbia University Press, 1940), Chap. 3.

tive evidence. (1) The fact of cultural variation in the categories and the rules of logic "prove that they depend upon factors that are historical and consequently social."[40] (2) Since concepts are imbedded in the very language the individual acquires (and this holds as well for the special terminology of the scientist) and since some of these conceptual terms refer to things which we, as individuals, have never experienced, it is clear that they are a product of the society.[41] And (3), the acceptance or rejection of concepts is not determined *merely* by their objective validity but also by their consistency with other prevailing beliefs.[42]

Yet Durkheim does not subscribe to a type of relativism in which there are merely competing criteria of validity. The social origin of the categories does not render them wholly arbitrary so far as their applicability to nature is concerned. They are, in varying degrees, adequate to their object. But since social structures vary (and with them, the categorical apparatus) there are inescapable "subjective" elements in the particular logical constructions current in a society. These subjective elements "must be progressively rooted out, if we are to approach reality more closely." And this occurs under determinate social conditions. With the extension of intercultural contacts, with the spread of inter-communication between persons drawn from different societies, with the enlargement of the society, the local frame of reference becomes disrupted. "Things can no longer be contained in the social moulds according to which they were primitively classified; they must be organized according to principles which are their own. So logical organization differentiates itself from the social organization and becomes autonomous. Genuinely human thought is not a primitive fact; it is the product of history. . . ."[43] Particularly those conceptions which are subjected to scientifically methodical criticism come to have a greater objective adequacy. Objectivity is itself viewed as a social emergent.

Throughout, Durkheim's dubious epistemology is intertwined with his substantive account of the social roots of concrete designations of temporal, spatial and other units. We need not indulge in the traditional exaltation of the categories as a thing set apart and foreknown, to note that Durkheim was dealing not with them but with conventional divisions of time and space. He observed, in passing, that differences in these respects should not lead us to "neglect the similarities, which are no less essential." If he pioneered in relating variations in systems of concepts to variations in social organization, he did not succeed in establishing the social origin of the categories.

---

40. Durkheim, *Elementary Forms . . .*, 12, 18, 439.

41. *Ibid.*, 433-435.

42. *Ibid.*, 438.

43. *Ibid.*, 444-445; 437.

Like Durkheim, Granet attaches great significance to language as constraining and fixing prevalent concepts and modes of thought. He has shown how the Chinese language is not equipped to note concepts, analyze ideas, or to present doctrines discursively. It has remained intractable to formal precision. The Chinese word does not fix a notion with a definite degree of abstraction and generality, but evokes an indefinite complex of particular images. Thus, there is no word which simply signifies "old man." Rather, a considerable number of words "paint different aspects of old age": *k'i,* those who need a richer diet; *k'ao,* those who have difficulty in breathing, and so on. These concrete evocations entail a multitude of other similarly concrete images of every detail of the mode of life of the aged: those who should be exempt from military service; those for whom funerary material should be held in readiness; those who have a right to carry a staff through the town, etc. These are but a few of the images evoked by *k'i* which, in general, corresponds to the quasi-singular notion of old persons, some 60 to 70 years of age. Words and sentences thus have an entirely concrete, emblematic character.[44]

Just as the language is concrete and evocative, so the most general ideas of ancient Chinese thought were unalterably concrete, none of them comparable to our abstract ideas. Neither time nor space were abstractly conceived. Time proceeds by cycles and is round; space is square. The earth which is square is divided into squares; the walls of towns, fields and camps should form a square. Camps, buildings and towns must be oriented and the selection of the proper orientation is in the hands of a ritual leader. Techniques of the division and management of space—surveying, town development, architecture, political geography—and the geometrical speculations which they presuppose are all linked with a set of social regulations. Particularly as these pertain to periodic assemblies, they reaffirm and reinforce in every detail the symbols which represent space. They account for its square form, its heterogeneous and hierarchic character, a conception of space which could only have arisen in a feudal society.[45]

Though Granet may have established the social grounds of concrete designations of time and space, it is not at all clear that he deals with data comparable to Western conceptions. He considers traditionalized or ritualized or magical conceptions and implicitly compares these with our matter-of-fact, technical or scientific notions. But in a wide range of actual *practices,* the Chinese did not *act* on the assumption that "time is round" and "space, square." When comparable spheres of activity and thought are considered it is questionable that this radical cleavage of

44. Granet, *La Pensée Chinoise,* 37-38, 82 and the whole of Chapter I.
45. *Ibid.,* 87-95.

"categorial systems" occurs, in the sense that there are no common de-
nominators of thought and conception. Granet has demonstrated qualitative differences of concepts in *certain contexts,* but not within such
comparable contexts as, say, that of technical practice. His work testifies
to different foci of intellectual interests in the two spheres and within
the ritualistic sphere, basic differences of outlook, but not unbridgeable
gaps in other spheres. The fallacy which is most prominent in Levy-
Bruhl's concept of the "prelogicality" of the primitive mind thus appears
in the work of Granet as well. As Malinowski and Rivers have shown,
when comparable spheres of thought and activity are considered, no
such irreconcilable differences are found.[46]

Sorokin shares in this same tendency to ascribe entirely disparate
criteria of truth to his different culture types. He has cast into a distinctive idiom the fact of shifts of attention on the part of intellectual
élites in different historical societies. In certain societies, religious conceptions and particular types of metaphysics are at the focus of attention, whereas in other societies, empirical science becomes the center of
interest. But the several "systems of truth" coexist in each of these
societies within certain spheres; the Catholic church has not abandoned
its "ideational" criteria even in this sensate age.

In so far as Sorokin adopts the position of radically different and
disparate criteria of truth, he must locate his own work within this
context. It may be said, though an extensive discussion would be needed
to document it, that he never resolves this problem. His various efforts
to cope with a radically relativistic impasse differ considerably. Thus, at
the very outset, he states that his constructions must be tested in the
same way "as any scientific law. First of all the principle must by nature
be logical; second, it must successfully meet the test of the 'relevant
facts,' that is, it must fit and represent the facts."[47] In Sorokin's own
terminology, he has thereby adopted a scientific position characteristic
of a "sensate system of truth." When he confronts his own epistemologic
position directly, however, he adopts an "integralist" conception of truth
which seeks to assimilate empirical and logical criteria as well as a
"supersensory, super-rational, metalogical act of 'intuition' or 'mystical
experience.' "[48] He thus posits an integration of these diverse systems.
In order to justify the "truth of faith"—the only item which would remove him from the ordinary criteria used in current scientific work—he

---

46. *Cf.* B. Malinowski in *Magic, Science & Religion* (Glencoe: The Free Press,
1948), 9. "Every primitive community is in possession of a considerable store of
knowledge, based on experience and fashioned by reason." See also Emile Benoit-
Smullyan, "Granet's *La Pensée Chinoise,*" *American Sociological Review,* 1936, 1,
487-92.

47. Sorokin, *Social and Cultural Dynamics,* I, 36; *cf.* II, 11-12n.

48. *Ibid.,* IV, Chap. 16; *Sociocultural Causality . . .,* Chap. 5.

indicates that "intuition" plays an important role as a *source* of scientific discovery. But does this meet the issue? The question is not one of the psychological *sources* of valid conclusions, but of the *criteria* and *methods of validation*. Which criteria would Sorokin adopt when "super-sensory" intuitions are not consistent with empirical observation? In such cases, presumably, so far as we can judge from his work rather than from his comments about his work, he accepts the facts and rejects the intuition. All this suggests that Sorokin is discussing under the generic label of "truth" quite distinct and not comparable types of judgments: just as the chemist's analysis of an oil painting is neither consistent nor inconsistent with its aesthetic evaluation, so Sorokin's systems of truth refer to quite different kinds of judgments. And, indeed, he is finally led to say as much, when he remarks that "each of the systems of truth, within its legitimate field of competency, gives us genuine cognition of the respective aspects of reality."[49] But whatever his private opinion of intuition he cannot draw it into his sociology as a *criterion* (rather than a source) of valid conclusions.

RELATIONS OF KNOWLEDGE
TO THE EXISTENTIAL BASIS

Though this problem is obviously the nucleus of every theory in the sociology of knowledge, it has often been treated by implication rather than directly. Yet each type of imputed relation between knowledge and society presupposes an entire theory of sociological method and social causation. The prevailing theories in this field have dealt with one or both of two major types of relation: causal or functional, and the symbolic or organismic or meaningful.[50]

Marx and Engels, of course, dealt solely with some kind of causal relation between the economic basis and ideas, variously terming this relation as "determination, correspondence, reflection, outgrowth, dependence," etc. In addition, there is an "interest" or "need" relation; when strata have (imputed) needs at a particular stage of historical development, there is held to be a definite pressure for appropriate ideas and knowledge to develop. The inadequacies of these divers formulations have risen up to plague those who derive from the Marxist tradition in the present day.[51]

Since Marx held that thought is not a mere "reflection" of objective class position, as we have seen, this raises anew the problem of its

---

49. *Sociocultural Causality* . . ., 230-1n.

50. The distinctions between these have long been considered in European sociological thought. The most elaborate discussion in this country is that of Sorokin, *Social and Cultural Dynamics*, e.g. I, chapters 1-2.

51. *Cf.* the comments of Hans Speier, "The social determination of ideas," *Social Research*, 1938, 5, 182-205; C. Wright Mills, "Language, logic and culture," *American Sociological Review*, 1939, 4, 670-80.

imputation to a determinate basis. The prevailing Marxist hypotheses for coping with this problem involve a theory of history which is the ground for determining whether the ideology is "situationally adequate" for a given stratum in the society: this requires a hypothetical construction of what men *would think and perceive* if they were able to comprehend the historical situation adequately.[52] But such insight into the situation need not *actually* be widely current within particular social strata. This, then, leads to the further problem of "false consciousness," of how ideologies which are neither in conformity with the interests of a class nor situationally adequate come to prevail.

A partial empirical account of false consciousness, implied in the *Manifesto*, rests on the view that the bourgeoisie control the content of culture and thus diffuse doctrines and standards alien to the interests of the proletariat.[53] Or, in more general terms, "the ruling ideas of each age have ever been the ideas of its ruling class." But, this is only a partial account; at most it deals with the false consciousness of the subordinated class. It might, for example, partly explain the fact noted by Marx that even where the peasant proprietor "does belong to the proletariat by his position he does not believe that he does." It would not, however, be pertinent in seeking to account for the false consciousness of the ruling class itself.

Another, though not clearly formulated, theme which bears upon the problem of false consciousness runs throughout Marxist theory. This is the conception of ideology as being an *unwitting, unconscious* expression of "real motives," these being in turn construed in terms of the objective interests of social classes. Thus, there is repeated stress on the unwitting nature of ideologies:

> Ideology is a process accomplished by the so-called thinker consciously indeed but with a false consciousness. The real motives impelling him remain unknown to him, otherwise it would not be an ideological process at all. Hence he imagines false or apparent motives.[54]

The ambiguity of the term "correspondence" to refer to the connection between the material basis and the idea can only be overlooked by the polemical enthusiast. Ideologies are construed as "distortions of the

---

52. *Cf.* the formulation by Mannheim, *Ideology and Utopia*, 175 ff.; Georg Lukács, *Geschichte und Klassenbewusstsein* (Berlin: 1923), 61 ff.; Arthur Child, "The problem of imputation in the sociology of knowledge," *Ethics*, 1941, 51, 200-214.

53. Marx and Engels, *The German Ideology*, p. 39. "In so far as they rule as a class and determine the extent and compass of an epoch, it is self-evident that they do this in their whole range, hence among other things rule also as thinkers, as producers of ideas, and regulate the production and distribution of the ideas of their age. . . ."

54. Engels' letter to Mehring, 14 July 1893, in *Marx, Selected Works*, I, 388-9; *cf.* Marx, *Der Achtzehnte Brumaire*, 33; *Critique of Political Economy*, 12.

social situation";[55] as merely "expressive" of the material conditions;[56] and, whether "distorted" or not, as motivational support for carrying through real changes in the society.[57] It is at this last point, when "illusory" beliefs are conceded to provide motivation for action, that Marxism ascribes a measure of independence to ideologies in the historical process. They are no longer merely epiphenomenal. They enjoy a measure of autonomy. From this develops the notion of interacting factors in which the superstructure, though interdependent with the material basis, is also assumed to have some degree of independence. Engels explicitly recognized that earlier formulations were inadequate in at least two respects: first, that both he and Marx had previously over-emphasized the economic factor and understated the role of reciprocal interaction;[58] and second, that they had "neglected" the formal side—the way in which these ideas develop.[59]

The Marx-Engels views on the connectives of ideas and economic substructure hold, then, that the economic structure constitutes the framework which limits the range of ideas which will prove socially effective; ideas which do not have pertinence for one or another of the conflicting classes may arise, but will be of little consequence. Economic conditions are necessary, but not sufficient, for the emergence and spread of ideas which express either the interests or outlook, or both, of distinct social strata. There is no strict determinism of ideas by economic conditions, but a definite predisposition. Knowing the economic conditions, we can predict the kinds of ideas which can exercise a controlling influence in a direction which can be effective. "Men make their own history, but they do not make it just as they please; they do not make it under circumstances chosen by themselves, but under circumstances directly found, given and transmitted from the past." And in the making of history, ideas and ideologies play a definite role: consider only the view of religion as "the opiate of the masses"; consider further the importance attached by Marx and Engels to making those in the proletariat "aware" of their "own interests." Since there is no fatality in the development of the total social structure, but only a development of economic conditions which make certain lines of change *possible* and probable, idea-systems may play a decisive role in the selection of one alternative which "corresponds" to the real balance of power rather than

---

55. Marx, *Der Achtzehnte Brumaire*, 39, where the democratic Montagnards indulge in self-deception.

56. Engels, *Socialism: Utopian and Scientific*, 26-27. *Cf.* Engels, *Feuerbach*, 122-23. "The failure to exterminate the Protestant heresy *corresponded* to the invincibility of the rising bourgeoisie. . . . Here Calvinism proved itself to be the true religious disguise of the interests of the bourgeoisie of that time. . . ."

57. Marx grants motivational significance to the "illusions" of the burgeoning bourgeoisie, *Der Achtzehnte Brumaire*, 8.

58. Engels, letter to Joseph Bloch, 21 September 1890, in *Marx, Selected Works*, I, 383.

59. Engels, letter to Mehring, 14 July 1893, *ibid.*, I, 390.

another alternative which runs counter to the existing power-situation and is therefore destined to be unstable, precarious and temporary. There is an ultimate compulsive which derives from economic development, but this compulsive does not operate with such detailed finality that no variation of ideas can occur at all.

The Marxist theory of history assumes that, *sooner or later,* idea-systems which are inconsistent with the actually prevailing and incipient power-structure will be rejected in favor of those which more nearly express the actual alignment of power. It is this view that Engels expresses in his metaphor of the "zig-zag course" of abstract ideology: ideologies may temporarily deviate from what is compatible with the current social relations of production, but they are ultimately brought back in line. For this reason, the Marxist analysis of ideology is always bound to be concerned with the "total" historical situation, in order to account both for the temporary deviations and the later accommodation of ideas to the economic compulsives. But for this same reason, Marxist analyses are apt to have an excessive degree of "flexibility," almost to the point where *any* development can be explained away as a temporary aberration or deviation; where "anachronisms" and "lags" become labels for the explaining away of existing beliefs which do not correspond to theoretical expectations; where the concept of "accident" provides a ready means of saving the theory from facts which seem to challenge its validity.[60] Once a theory includes concepts such as "lags," "thrusts," "anachronisms," "accidents," "partial independence" and "ultimate dependence," it becomes so labile and so indistinct, that it can be reconciled with virtually any configuration of data. Here, as in several other theories in the sociology of knowledge, a decisive question must be raised in order to determine whether we have a genuine theory: how can the theory be invalidated? In any given historical situation, which data will contradict and invalidate the theory? Unless this can be answered directly, unless the theory involves statements which can be controverted by definite types of evidence, it remains merely a pseudo-theory which will be compatible with any array of data.

Though Mannheim has gone far toward developing actual research procedures in the substantive sociology of knowledge, he has not appreciably clarified the connectives of thought and society.[61] As he indicates, once a thought-structure has been analyzed, there arises the problem of imputing it to definite groups. This requires not only an empirical investigation of the groups or strata which prevalently think in these terms, but also an interpretation of why these groups, and not others, manifest this type of thought. This latter question implies a social psychology which Mannheim has not systematically developed.

The most serious shortcoming of Durkheim's analysis lies precisely

---

60. *Cf.* Max Weber, *Gesammelte Aufsaetze zur Wissenschaftslehre,* 166-170.
61. This aspect of Mannheim's work is treated in detail in the following chapter.

in his uncritical acceptance of a naive theory of correspondence in which the categories of thought are held to "reflect" certain features of the group organization. Thus "there are societies in Australia and North America where space is conceived in the form of an immense circle, *because* the camp has a circular form . . . the social organization has been the model for the spatial organization and a reproduction of it."[62] In similar fashion, the general notion of time is derived from the specific units of time differentiated in social activities (ceremonies, feats, rites).[63] The category of class and the modes of classification, which involve the notion of a hierarchy, are derived from social grouping and stratification. Those social categories are then "projected into our conception of the new world."[64] In summary, then, categories "express" the different aspects of the social order.[65] Durkheim's sociology of knowledge suffers from his avoidance of a social psychology.

The central relation between ideas and existential factors for Scheler is interaction. Ideas interact with existential factors which serve as selective agencies, releasing or checking the extent to which potential ideas find actual expression. Existential factors do not "create" or "determine" the content of ideas; they merely account for the *difference* between potentiality and actuality; they hinder, retard or quicken the actualization of potential ideas. In a figure reminiscent of Clerk Maxwell's hypothetical daemon, Scheler states: "in a definite fashion and order, existential factors open and close the sluice-gates to the flood of ideas." This formulation, which ascribes to existential factors the function of selection from a self-contained realm of ideas is, according to Scheler, a basic point of agreement between such otherwise divergent theorists as Dilthey, Troeltsch, Max Weber and himself.[66]

Scheler operates as well with the concept of "structural identities" which refers to common presuppositions of knowledge or belief, on the one hand, and of social, economic or political structure on the other.[67] Thus, the rise of mechanistic thought in the sixteenth century, which came to dominate prior organismic thought is inseparable from the new individualism, the incipient dominance of the power-driven machine over the hand-tool, the incipient dissolution of *Gemeinschaft* into *Gesellschaft*, production for a commodity market, rise of the principle of competition in the ethos of western society, etc. The notion of scientific research as an endless process through which a store of knowledge can be accumulated for practical application as the occasion demands and the total divorce of this science from theology and philosophy was not

---

62. Durkheim, *Elementary Forms* . . ., 11-12.
63. *Ibid.*, 10-11.
64. *Ibid.*, 148.
65. *Ibid.*, 440.
66. Scheler, *Die Wissensformen* . . ., 32.
67. *Ibid.*, 56.

possible without the rise of a new principle of infinite acquisition characteristic of modern capitalism.[68]

In discussing such structural identities, Scheler does not ascribe primacy either to the socio-economic sphere or to the sphere of knowledge. Rather, and this Scheler regards as one of the most significant propositions in the field, both are determined by the impulse-structure of the élite which is closely bound up with the prevailing ethos. Thus, modern technology is not merely the application of a pure science based on observation, logic and mathematics. It is far more the product of an orientation toward the control of nature which defined the purposes as well as the conceptual structure of scientific thought. This orientation is largely implicit and is not to be confused with the personal motives of scientists.

With the concept of structural identity, Scheler verges on the concept of cultural integration or *Sinnzusammenhang*. It corresponds to Sorokin's conception of a "meaningful cultural system" involving "the identity of the fundamental principles and values that permeate all its parts," which is distinguished from a "causal system" involving interdependence of parts.[69] Having constructed his types of culture, Sorokin's survey of criteria of truth, ontology, metaphysics, scientific and technologic output, etc., finds a marked tendency toward the meaningful integration of these with the prevailing culture.

Sorokin has boldly confronted the problem of how to determine the *extent* to which such integration occurs, recognizing, despite his vitriolic comments on the statisticians of our sensate age, that to deal with the extent or degree of integration necessarily implies some statistical measure. Accordingly, he developed numerical indexes of the various writings and authors in each period, classified these in their appropriate category, and thus assessed the comparative frequency (and influence) of the various systems of thought. Whatever the technical evaluation of the validity and reliability of these cultural statistics, he has directly acknowledged the problem overlooked by many investigators of integrated culture or *Sinnzusammenhaengen*, namely, the approximate degree or extent of such integration. Moreover, he plainly bases his empirical conclusions very largely upon these statistics.[70] And these conclusions again testify that his approach leads to a statement of the

---

68. *Ibid.*, 25; cf. 482-84.

69. Sorokin, *Social and Cultural Dynamics*, IV, Chap. 1, I, Chap. 1.

70. Despite the basic place of these statistics in his empirical findings, Sorokin adopts a curiously ambivalent attitude toward them, an attitude similar to the attitude toward experiment imputed to Newton: a device to make his prior conclusions "intelligible and to convince the vulgar." Note Sorokin's approval of Park's remark that his statistics are merely a concession to the prevailing sensate mentality and that "if they want 'em, let 'em have 'em." Sorokin, *Sociocultural Causality, Space, Time*, 95n. Sorokin's ambivalence arises from his effort to integrate quite disparate "systems of truth."

problem of connections between existential bases and knowledge, rather than to its solution. Thus, to take a case in point. "Empiricism" is defined as the typical sensate system of truth. The last five centuries, and more particularly the last century represent "sensate culture par excellence!"[71] Yet, even in this flood-tide of sensate culture, Sorokin's statistical indices show only some 53% of influential writings in the field of "empiricism." And in the earlier centuries of this sensate culture,—from the late 16th to the mid-18th—the indices of empiricism are consistently lower than those for rationalism, (which is associated, presumably, with an idealistic rather than a sensate culture).[72] The object of these observations is not to raise the question whether Sorokin's conclusions coincide with his statistical data: it is not to ask why the 16th and 17th centuries are said to have a dominant "sensate system of truth" in view of these data. Rather, it is to indicate that even on Sorokin's own premises, overall characterizations of historical cultures constitute merely a first step, which must be followed by analyses of deviations from the central tendencies of the culture. Once the notion of *extent* of integration is introduced, the existence of types of knowledge which are not integrated with the dominant tendencies cannot be viewed merely as "congeries" or as "contingent." Their *social* bases must be ascertained in a fashion for which an emanationist theory does not provide.

A basic concept which serves to differentiate generalizations about the thought and knowledge of an entire society or culture is that of the "audience" or "public" or what Znaniecki calls "the social circle." Men of knowledge do not orient themselves exclusively toward their data nor toward the total society, but to special segments of that society with their special demands, criteria of validity, of significant knowledge, of pertinent problems, etc. It is through anticipation of these demands and expectations of particular audiences, which can be effectively located in the social structure, that men of knowledge organize their own work, define their data, seize upon problems. Hence, the more differentiated the society, the greater the range of such effective audiences, the greater the variation in the foci of scientific attention, of conceptual formulations and of procedures for certifying claims to knowledge. By linking each of these typologically defined audiences to their distinctive social position, it becomes possible to provide a *wissenssoziologische* account of variations and conflicts of thought within the society, a problem which is necessarily by-passed in an emanationist theory. Thus, the scientists in seventeenth century England and France who were organized in newly established scientific societies addressed themselves to audiences very different from those of the savants who remained exclusively in the traditional universities. The direction of their efforts, toward a "plain,

---

71. Sorokin, *Social and Cultural Dynamics,* II, 51.
72. *Ibid.,* II, 30.

sober, empirical" exploration of specific technical and scientific problems differed considerably from the speculative, unexperimental work of those in the universities. Searching out such variations in effective audiences, exploring their distinctive criteria of significant and valid knowledge,[73] relating these to their position within the society and examining the sociopsychological processes through which these operate to constrain certain modes of thought constitutes a procedure which promises to take research in the sociology of knowledge from the plane of general imputation to that of testable empirical inquiry.[74]

The foregoing account deals with the main substance of prevailing theories in this field. Limitations of space permit only the briefest consideration of one other aspect of these theories singled out in our paradigm: functions imputed to various types of mental productions.[75]

FUNCTIONS OF EXISTENTIALLY CONDITIONED KNOWLEDGE

In addition to providing causal explanations of knowledge, theories ascribe social functions to knowledge, functions which presumably serve to account for its persistence or change. These functional analyses cannot be examined in any detail here, though a detailed study of them would undoubtedly prove rewarding.

The most distinctive feature of the Marxist imputation of function is its ascription, not to the society as a whole, but to distinct strata within the society. This holds not only for ideological thinking but also for natural science. In capitalist society, science and derivative technology are held to become a further instrument of control by the dominant class.[76] Along these same lines, in ferreting out the economic determinants of scientific development, Marxists have often thought it sufficient to show that the scientific results enabled the solution of some

73. The Rickert-Weber concept of "Wertbeziehung" (relevance to value) is but a first step in this direction; there remains the further task of differentiating the various sets of values and relating these to distinctive groups or strata within the society.

74. This is perhaps the most distinctive variation in the sociology of knowledge now developing in American sociological circles, and may almost be viewed as an American acculturation of European approaches. This development characteristically derives from the social psychology of G. H. Mead. Its pertinence in this connection is being indicated by C. W. Mills, Gerard de Gré, and others. See Znaniecki's conception of the "social circle," *op. cit.* See, also, the beginnings of empirical findings along these lines in the more general field of public communications: Paul F. Lazarsfeld and R. K. Merton, "Studies in Radio and Film Propaganda."

75. An appraisal of historicist and ahistorical approaches is necessarily omitted. It may be remarked that this controversy definitely admits of a middle ground.

76. For example, Marx quotes from the 19th century apologist of capitalism, Ure, who, speaking of the invention of the self-acting mule, says: "A creation destined to restore order among the industrious classes. . . . This invention confirms the great doctrine already propounded, that when capital enlists science into her service, the refractory hand of labor will always be taught docility." *Capital,* I, 477.

economic or technological need. But the application of science to a need does not necessarily testify that the need has been significantly involved in leading to the result. Hyperbolic functions were discovered two centuries before they had any practical significance and the study of conic sections had a broken history of two millennia before being applied in science and technology. Can we infer, then, that the "needs" which were ultimately satisfied through such applications served to direct the attention of mathematicians to these fields, that there was, so to speak, a retroactive influence of some two to twenty centuries? Detailed inquiry into the relations between the emergence of needs, recognition of these needs by scientists or by those who direct their selection of problems and the consequences of such recognition is required before the role of needs in determining the thematics of scientific research can be established.[77]

In addition to his claim that the categories are social emergents, Durkheim also indicates their social functions. The functional analysis, however, is intended to account not for the particular categorical system in a society but for the existence of a system common to the society. For purposes of inter-communication and for coordinating men's activities, a common set of categories is indispensable. What the apriorist mistakes for the constraint of an inevitable, native form of understanding is actually "the very authority of society, transferring itself to a certain manner of thought which is the indispensable condition of all common action."[78] There must be a certain minimum of "logical conformity" if joint social activities are to be maintained at all; a common set of categories is a functional necessity. This view is further developed by Sorokin who indicates the several functions served by different systems of social space and time.[79]

FURTHER PROBLEMS AND RECENT STUDIES

From the foregoing discussion, it becomes evident that a wide diversity of problems in this field require further investigation.[80]

Scheler had indicated that the social organization of intellectual activity is significantly related to the character of the knowledge which

77. Compare B. Hessen, *op. cit.*, R. K. Merton, *Science, Technology and Society in 17th Century England,* (Bruges: Osiris History of Science Monographs, 1938), chapters 7-10; J. D. Bernal, *The Social Function of Science* (New York: The Macmillan Co., 1939); J. G. Crowther, *The Social Relations of Science,* (New York: The Macmillan Co., 1941); Bernard Barber, *Science and the Social Order* (Glencoe, Illinois: The Free Press, 1952); Gerard De Gré, *Science as a Social Institution,* (New York: Doubleday & Company, 1955).

78. Durkheim, *Elementary Forms* . . ., 17, 10-11, 443.

79. Sorokin, *Sociocultural Causality, Space, Time, passim.*

80. For further summaries, see Louis Wirth's preface to Mannheim, *Ideology and Utopia,* xxviii-xxxi; J. B. Gittler, "Possibilities of a sociology of science," *Social Forces,* 1940, 18, 350-59.

develops under its auspices. One of the earliest studies of the problem in this country was Veblen's caustic, impressionistic and often perceptive account of the pressures shaping American university life.[81] In more systematic fashion, Wilson has dealt with the methods and criteria of recruitment, the assignment of status and the mechanisms of control of the academic man, thus providing a substantial basis for comparative studies.[82] Setting forth a typology of the roles of men of knowledge, Znaniecki developed a series of hypotheses concerning the relations between these roles and the types of knowledge cultivated; between types of knowledge and the bases of appraisal of the scientist by members of the society; between role-definitions and attitudes toward practical and theoretical knowledge; etc.[83] Much remains to be investigated concerning the bases of class identifications by intellectuals, their alienation from dominant or subordinate strata in the population, their avoidance of or indulgence in researches which have immediate value-implications challenging current institutional arrangements inimical to the attainment of culturally approved goals,[84] the pressures toward technicism and away from dangerous thoughts, the bureaucratization of intellectuals as a process whereby problems of policy are converted into problems of administration, the areas of social life in which expert and positive knowledge are deemed appropriate and those in which the wisdom of the plain man is alone considered necessary—in short, the shifting role of the intellectual and the relation of these changes to the structure, content and influence of his work require growing attention, as changes in the social organization increasingly subject the intellectual to conflicting demands.[85]

Increasingly, it has been assumed that the social structure does not influence science merely by focusing the attention of scientists upon certain problems for research. In addition to the studies to which we have already referred, others have dealt with the ways in which the cultural and social context enters into the conceptual phrasing of scientific prob-

81. Thorstein Veblen, *The Higher Learning in America,* (New York: Huebsch, 1918).

82. Logan Wilson, *The Academic Man; cf.* E. Y. Hartshorne, *The German Universities and National Socialism,* (Harvard University Press, 1937).

83. Florian Znaniecki, *Social Role of the Man of Knowledge.*

84. Gunnar Myrdal in his treatise, *An American Dilemma,* repeatedly indicates the "concealed valuations" of American social scientists studying the American Negro and the effect of these valuations on the formulation of "scientific problems" in this area of research. See especially II, 1027-1064.

85. Mannheim refers to an unpublished monograph on the intellectual; general bibliographies are to be found in his books and in Roberto Michels's article on "Intellectuals," *Encyclopedia of the Social Sciences.* Recent papers include C. W. Mills, "The Social Role of the Intellectual," *Politics,* I, April 1944; R. K. Merton, "Role of the Intellectual in Public Policy," presented at the annual meeting of the American Sociological Society, Dec. 4, 1943 (Chapter VII in the present volume); Arthur Koestler, "The Intelligentsia," *Horizon,* 1944, 9, 162-175.

lems. Darwin's theory of selection was modeled after the prevailing notion of a competitive economic order, a notion which in turn has been assigned an ideological function through its assumption of a natural identity of interests.[86] Russell's half-serious observation on the national characteristics of research in animal learning points to a further type of inquiry into the relations between national culture and conceptual formulations,[87] So, too, Fromm has attempted to show that Freud's "conscious liberalism" tacitly involved a rejection of impulses tabooed by bourgeois society and that Freud himself was in his patricentric character, a typical representative of a society which demands obedience and subjection.[88]

In much the same fashion, it has been indicated that the conception of multiple causation is especially congenial to the academician, who has relative security, is loyal to the status quo from which he derives dignity and sustenance, who leans toward conciliation and sees something valuable in all viewpoints, thus tending toward a taxonomy which enables him to avoid taking sides by stressing the multiplicity of factors and the complexity of problems.[89] Emphases on nature or nurture as prime determinants of human nature have been linked with opposing political orientations. Those who emphasize heredity are political conservatives whereas the environmentalists are prevalently democrats or radicals seek-

---

86. Keynes observed that "The Principle of the Survival of the Fittest could be regarded as one vast generalization of the Ricardian economics." Quoted by Talcott Parsons, *The Structure of Social Action*, 113; *cf.* Alexander Sandow, "Social factors in the origin of Darwinism," *Quarterly Review of Biology*, 13, 316-26.

87. Bertrand Russell, *Philosophy*, (New York: W. W. Norton and Co., 1927), 29-30. Russell remarks that the animals used in psychological research "have all displayed the national characteristics of the observer. Animals studied by Americans rush about frantically, with an incredible display of hustle and pep, and at last achieve the desired result by chance. Animals observed by Germans sit still and think, and at last evolve the solution out of their inner consciousness." Witticism need not be mistaken for irrelevance; the possibility of national differences in the choice and formulation of scientific problems has been repeatedly noted, though not studied systematically. *Cf.* Richard Mueller-Freienfels, *Psychologie der Wissenschaft*, (Leipzig: J. A. Barth, 1936), Chap. 8, which deals with national, as well as class, differences in the choice of problems, 'styles of thought,' etc., without fully acquiescing in the echt-deutsch requirements of a Krieck. This type of interpretation, however, can be carried to a polemical and ungrounded extreme, as in Max Scheler's debunking 'analysis' of English cant. He concludes that, in science, as in all other spheres, the English are incorrigible 'cantians.' Hume's conception of the ego, substance, and continuity as biologically useful self-deceptions was merely purposive cant; so, too, was the characteristic English conception of working hypotheses (Maxwell, Kelvin) as aiding the progress of science but not as truth—a conception which is nothing but a shrewd maneuver to provide momentary control and ordering of the data. All pragmatism implies this opportunistic cant, says Scheler, *Genius des Krieges*, (Leipzig: Verlag der Weissenbuecher, 1915).

88. Erich Fromm, "Die gesellschaftliche Bedingtheit der psychoanalytischen Therapie," *Zeitschrift fuer Sozialforschung*, 1935, 4, 365-397.

89. Lewis S. Feuer, "The economic factor in history," *Science and Society*, 1940, 4, 174-175.

ing social change.[90] But even environmentalists among contemporary American writers on social pathology adopt conceptions of "social adjustment" which implicitly assume the standards of small communiti as norms and characteristically fail to assess the possibility of certain groups achieving their objectives under the prevailing institutional conditions.[91] The imputations of perspectives such as these require more systematic study before they can be accepted, but they indicate recent tendencies to seek out the perspectives of scholars and to relate these to the framework of experience and interests constituted by their respective social positions. The questionable character of imputations which are not based on adequate *comparative* material is illustrated by a recent account of the writings of Negro scholars. The selection of analytical rather than morphological categories, of environmental rather than biological determinants of behavior, of exceptional rather than typical data is ascribed to the caste-induced resentment of Negro writers, without any effort being made to compare the frequency of similar tendencies among white writers.[92]

Vestiges of any tendency to regard the development of science and technology as *wholly* self-contained and advancing irrespective of the social structure are being dissipated by the actual course of historical events. An increasingly visible control and, often, restraint of scientific research and invention has been repeatedly documented, notably in a series of studies by Stern[93] who has also traced the bases of resistance to change in medicine.[94] The basic change in the social organization of Germany has provided a virtual experimental test of the close dependence of the direction and extent of scientific work upon the prevailing power structure and the associated cultural outlook.[95] And the limitations of any unqualified assumption that science or technology represent the basis to which the social structure must adjust become evident in

90. N. Pastore, "The nature-nurture controversy: a sociological approach," *School and Society*, 1943, 57, 373-77.

91. C. Wright Mills, "The professional ideology of social pathologists," *American Journal of Sociology*, 1943, 49, 165-90.

92. William T. Fontaine, " 'Social determination' in the writings of negro scholars," *American Journal of Sociology*, 1944, 49, 302-315.

93. Bernhard J. Stern, "Resistances to the Adoption of Technological Innovations," in National Resources Committee, *Technological Trends and National Policy*, (Washington: U. S. Government Printing Office, 1937), 39-66; "Restraints upon the Utilization of Inventions," *The Annals*, 200: 1-19, 1938, and further references therein; Walton Hamilton, *Patents and Free Enterprise*, (TNEC Monograph No. 31, 1941).

94. Bernhard J. Stern, *Social Factors in Medical Progress*, (New York: Columbia University Press, 1927); *Society and Medical Progress*, (Princeton: Princeton University Press, 1941); cf. Richard H. Shryock, *The Development of Modern Medicine*, (Philadelphia: University of Pennsylvania Press, 1936); Henry E. Sigerist, *Man and Medicine*, (New York: W. W. Norton and Co., 1932).

95. Hartshorne, *German Universities and National Socialism*.

the light of studies showing how science and technology have been put in the service of social or economic demands.[96]

To develop any further the formidable list of problems which require and are receiving empirical investigation would outrun the limits of this chapter. There is only this to be said: the sociology of knowledge is fast outgrowing a prior tendency to confuse provisional hypothesis with unimpeachable dogma; the plenitude of speculative insights which marked its early stages are now being subjected to increasingly rigorous test. Though Toynbee and Sorokin may be correct in speaking of an alternation of periods of fact-finding and generalization in the history of science, it seems that the sociology of knowledge has wedded these two tendencies in what promises to be a fruitful union. Above all, it focuses on problems which are at the very center of contemporary intellectual interest.[97]

96. Only most conspicuously in time of war; see Sorokin's observation that centers of military power tend to be the centers of scientific and technologic development (*Dynamics*, IV, 249-51); *cf.* I. B. Cohen and Bernard Barber, *Science and War* (ms.); R. K. Merton, "Science and military technique," *Scientific Monthly*, 1935, 41, 542-545; Bernal, *op. cit.*; Julian Huxley, *Science and Social Needs*, (New York: Harper and Bros., 1935).

97. For extensive bibliographies, see Bernard Barber, *Science and the Social Order*; Mannheim, *Ideology and Utopia*; Harry E. Barnes, Howard Becker, and Frances B. Becker, eds., *Contemporary Social Theory* (New York: D. Appleton-Century Co., 1940).

XIII

KARL MANNHEIM AND THE SOCIOLOGY OF KNOWLEDGE

*But indeed language has succeeded until recently in
hiding from us almost all the things we talk about.*
—I. A. Richards

T HE DISCIPLINE which its German exponents have called *Wissenssoziologie*—and failing a simpler English term, the turgid Teutonicism
is often retained—has a long history, centered largely on the problem of
objectivity of knowledge.[1] *Systematic* consideration of the social factors
in the acquisition, diffusion and growth of knowledge, however, is a
relatively late development which has its two main roots in French and
German sociological thought.[2] The two lines of development had different antecedents and characteristically different emphases in the choice
of problems. The French, Durkheimian branch derived primarily from
an ethnographical background which stressed the range of variation
among different peoples not only of moral and social structure but of
cognitive orientations as well. The pioneering Durkheim himself, in
well-known passages in his *Les formes élémentaires de la vie religieuse*
(Paris, 1912), presented an audacious analysis of the social origins of
the fundamental categories of thought. Departing in some respects from
Durkheim, Lucien Lévy-Bruhl, in his studies of primitive mentality,
sought to demonstrate irreducible differences between primitive and
civilized mentalities. Other followers of Durkheim have broken through
this primary concern with nonliterate societies and have applied his conceptual scheme to various social aspects of thought and knowledge in
civilized society. These studies testify that the French contributions to

---

1. A sketch of this early development, at least from the so-called Era of Enlightenment, is provided in Ernst Grünwald, *Das Problem der Soziologie des Wissens*,
chapter I. It is not mere antiquarianism to suggest, however, that this history can
be dated from the time of the Greek Enlightenment. Indeed, Pierre-Maxime Schuhl's
exemplary *Essai sur la formation de la pensée grecque* (Paris, 1934) is ample basis
for suggesting an earlier, if equally arbitrary, 'beginning.'

2. One may cavil at this observation by citing suggestive *aperçus* in English
thought from at least the time of Francis Bacon and Hobbes. Likewise, the pragmatic
movement from Peirce and James onward is informed with relevant discussions.
However, these did not constitute systematic analyses of the central *sociological* problems in question. An exhaustive treatment of this field would of course include these
tangential developments.

la sociologie du savoir are largely autochthonous and independent of similar researches in Germany.[3]

THEORETIC ANTECEDENTS

The main German antecedents of *Wissenssoziologie* are found among the immediate precursors of Mannheim. They were by no means of a piece—indeed, they often supported antithetical views but they were largely concerned with the same body of problems. Moreover, in unraveling the intellectual ancestry of Mannheim it cannot be supposed that he followed in all relevant respects the lead of any of these. On the contrary, he joined issue with all of them in one connexion or another and it was precisely these *Auseinandersetzungen* which repeatedly led him to clarify his own position.

Left-wing Hegelianism and Marx in particular have left their impress on Mannheim's work. His position has, in fact, been characterized as "bourgeois Marxism." In Marx and Engels, and in Georg Lukács' stimulating *Geschichte und Klassenbewusstsein*, we find some of Mannheim's basic conceptions: the far-reaching historicism which sees even the categorical apparatus as a function of the social, and particularly the class, structure;[4a] the dynamic conception of knowledge;[4b] the activist interpretation of the dialectic relations between theory and practice;[4c] the

---

3. Not wholly, however, for Durkheim initiated a section in *L'Année sociologique* (1910, 11, 41) on "conditions sociologiques de la connaissance" on the occasion of a review of Wilhelm Jerusalem's article, "Die Soziologie des Erkennens." Again, brief bibliographical indications must be substituted for a detailed discussion of the Durkheim tradition. Maurice Halbwachs, *Les cadres sociaux de la mémoire* (Paris, 1925), develops the thesis that memory, the epistemological relevance of which has been lately stressed by Schlick, Frank and others of the Vienna circle, is a function of the social framework. Marcel Granet, in *La civilisation chinoise* (Paris, 1929) and particularly in his widely-heralded *La pensée chinoise* (Paris, 1934), attributes characteristically Chinese modes of thought to various features of the social structure. Durkheim also influenced various writers on the beginnings of Occidental science: Abel Rey, *La science orientale avant les Grecs* (Paris, 1930), *La jeunesse de la science grecque* (Paris, 1933); Léon Robin, *La pensée grecque et les origines de l'esprit scientifique* (Paris, 1928); P-M. Schuhl, *op. cit.*, and to some extent, Arnold Reymond, *Histoire des sciences exactes et naturelles dans l'antiquité gréco-romaine* (Paris, 1924). His influence is also manifest in various sociological studies of art and literature, preeminently those by Charles Lalo. In this connection, see volumes 16 and 17 of the *Encyclopédie française*, entitled "Arts et littératures dans la société contemporaine" (Paris, 1935-6). The one noteworthy contributor to *Wissenssoziologie* in France who antedated Durkheim and who stemmed from a quasi-Marxist heritage was Georges Sorel. See his *Le procès de Socrate* (Paris, 1889); *Réflexions sur la violence* (Paris, 1908); *Les illusions du progrès* (Paris, 1908).

4a. *E.g.*, Friedrich Engels, "Socialism: Utopian and Scientific," in *Karl Marx: Selected Works*, I, 142 f; *cf. Die deutsche Ideologie, Marx-Engels Gesamtausgabe* (Berlin, 1931), V.

b. Engels, "Ludwig Feuerbach and the Outcome of Classical German Philosophy," *ibid.*, I, 453 f.

c. Marx, "Theses on Feuerbach," *ibid.*, I, 471; *cf. Capital* (Chicago, 1925-6), III, 954.

role of knowledge in shifting human action from the realm of "necessity" to that of "freedom";[4d] the place of contradictions and conflicting social groups in initiating reflexion;[4e] the emphasis on concrete sociology as distinct from the imputation of historically-determined qualities to the abstract individual.[4f]

The neo-Kantians, particularly the so-called Southwest or Baden school—the use of a single rubric for this group of theorists should not obscure their differences attested by numerous disagreements on specific points—likewise contributed to the formation of Mannheim's views. In fact, as we shall see, Mannheim departed less from their central theses than he seems to have realized.[5] From Dilthey, Rickert, Troeltsch and especially Max Weber, he derived much that is fundamental to his thought: the emphases on affective-volitional elements in the direction and formation of thought; a dualism, explicitly repudiated by Mannheim yet persisting in numerous formulations, in the theory of knowledge which draws a distinction between the role of value-elements in the development of the exact sciences and of the *Geisteswissenschaften;* the distinction between *Erkennen* and *Erklären* on the one hand and *Erleben* and *Verstehen* on the other; value-relevance of thought as not involving a fundamental invalidity of empirical judgments.[6] Finally, from the writings of the phenomenologists, Husserl, Jaspers, Heidegger and above all Max Scheler, Mannheim probably derived an emphasis on the accurate observation of facts 'given' in direct experience; a concern with the analysis of *Selbstverständlichkeiten* in social life; relating various types of intellectual cooperation to types of group structure.[7] Mannheim's varied background is reflected in his eclecticism and in a fundamental instability in his conceptual framework.

It must at once be noted that Mannheim's theories have been undergoing constant change so that one cannot with propriety deal with his

---

d. Engels, "Socialism . . .", *op. cit.,* I, 180-1.

e. Marx, "Introduction to the Critique of Political Economy," *ibid.,* I, 356.

f. Marx, "Theses on Feuerbach," *op. cit.,* I, 473.

5. In his essay on "Das Problem einer Soziologie des Wissens," *Archiv für Sozialwissenschaften und Sozialpolitik,* 1925, 599 f., Mannheim explicitly repudiates neo-Kantianism as a point of departure for *Wissenssoziologie.* But see our later discussion in which it is maintained that *in practice,* Mannheim approaches the Rickert-Weber concept of *Wertbeziehung* very closely indeed.

6. See Heinrich Rickert, *Die Grenzen der naturwissenschaftlichen Begriffsbildung,* 4th ed. (Tübingen, 1921), esp. 35-51, 245-271; Wilhelm Dilthey, *Gesammelte Schriften* (Tübingen, 1922), III, 68 f., 169 ff.; Max Weber, *Gesammelte Aufsätze zur Wissenschaftslehre,* 146-214; 403-502.

7. See Edmund Husserl, *Ideas: General Introduction to Pure Phenomenology* (New York, 1931), 187 ff.; Karl Jaspers, *Psychologie der Weltanschauungen* (Berlin, 1925), 20 ff.; 142 ff.; Julius Kraft, *Von Husserl zu Heidegger* (Leipzig, 1932), esp. 87 ff.; Max Scheler, *Versuche zu einer Soziologie des Wissens* (Munich-Leipzig, 1924); *Die Wissensformen und die Gesellschaft* (Leipzig, 1926).

earlier or later studies as equally representing his matured views.[8] Since it is not the object of this paper to trace the development of Mannheim's thought, although such an enterprise might well reward the student of *Wissenssoziologie,* we shall take his more recent works as a key to his present position and refer to the earlier writings only when they throw additional light on this position. This does not, of course, imply the general proposition that later formulations are invariably more accurate and profound than earlier ones, but this appears to be the case in the present instance.

THEORY OF IDEOLOGY

Mannheim derives certain of the basic conceptions of *Wissenssoziologie* from an analysis of the concept *ideology.*[9] Awareness of ideological thought comes when an adversary's assertions are regarded as untrue by virtue of their determination by his life-situation. Since it is not assumed that these distortions are deliberate, the ideology differs from the lie. Indeed, the distinction between the two is essential in as much as it emphasizes the unwitting nature of ideological statements. This, which Mannheim calls the "particular conception of ideology," differs in three fundamental respects from the "total conception." The

---

8. *Cf.* Grünwald, *op. cit.,* 266-7. In order to abbreviate subsequent references and to distinguish between Mannheim's 'early' and 'later' periods, the following alphabetical citations will be used throughout. Inasmuch as the article, "Wissenssoziologie" represents Mannheim's first radical departure from his previous position, this will be taken to mark the emergence of his 'new formulations.'

A. 1923. "Der Historismus," *Archiv für Sozialwissenschaft und Sozialpolitik,* 52, 1-60.

B. 1925. "Das Problem einer Soziologie des Wissens," *ibid.,* 53, 577-652.

C. 1926. "Ideologische und soziologische Interpretation der geistigen Gebilde," *Jahrbuch für Soziologie* (Karlsruhe), 424-40.

D. 1927. "Das konservative Denken," *Archiv für Sozialwissenschaft,* 57, Heft. 1-2, 68-142.

E. 1928. "Das Problem der Generationen," *Kölner Vierteljahrshefte für Soziologie,* 7, 157-185.

F. 1929. "Die Bedeutung der Konkurrenz im Gebiete des Geistigen," *Verhandlungen* des 6. deutschen Soziologentages in Zürich (Tübingen), 35-83.

G. 1929. *Ideologie und Utopie* (Bonn) trans. by Louis Wirth and Edward Shils as parts II-IV (49-236) of *Ideology and Utopia* (New York, 1936); references are to the English edition.

H. 1931. "Wissenssoziologie," *Handwörterbuch der Soziologie,* ed. by Alfred Vierkandt (Stuttgart), 659-680, translated as part V (237-280) of *Ideology and Utopia;* references are to the translation.

I. 1934. "German Sociology," *Politica,* 12-33.

J. 1935. *Mensch und Gesellschaft im Zeitalter des Umbaus* (Leiden).

K. 1936. "Preliminary approach to the problem," written especially for the English edition of *Ideology and Utopia,* pt. I, 1-48.

L. 1940. *Man and Society in an Age of Reconstruction* (New York), a translation by Edward Shils of a revised and considerably enlarged version of J.

9. The correlative concept, "utopia," may be more advantageously discussed at a later point, since it is primarily relevant to Mannheim's views on the criteria of valid propositions.

particular conception views only certain of the opponent's assertions as ideological, that is, it grants to him the *possibility* of non-ideological thought; the total conception designates the opponent's entire system of thought as inevitably ideological. Again, the particular conception necessarily involves analysis on the psychological plane, since it assumes that the adversaries share common criteria of validity whereas the total conception is concerned with the noological level in which the form, content and conceptual framework of a "mode of thought" is conceived as unavoidably bound up with the life-situation. Finally, and as a corollary, the first view involves a "psychology of interests" (in much the same sense that the psychoanalyst operates with "rationalizations") whereas the second seeks only to establish a "correspondence" between the social setting and the system of thought. Thus, the latter conception does not require the imputation of *motives* but rests with the indication of understandable correspondences between modes of thought and the concrete situation.[10] From these differences, it follows that the particular conception is implicitly individualistic, dealing with group ideologies only by "adding" the separate ideologies of its members or by selecting those which are common to the individuals in the group. The total conception, however, seeks to establish the integrated system of thought of a group which is implicit in the judgments of its members. (G, pp. 49-53.) The development from the particular to the total conception of ideology, which Mannheim traces with consummate skill, leads to the problem of false consciousness, "the problem of how such a thing as . . . the totally distorted mind which falsifies everything which comes within its range could ever have arisen." (G, pp. 61-62.)

The particular and total conceptions are for the first time merged in Marxist theory which definitely shifted the emphasis from the psychological to the social plane. One further step was necessary for the emergence of a sociology of knowledge, the shift from a "special" formulation of the concept of ideology to a "general" formulation. In the special formulation, only our adversaries' thought is regarded as wholly a function of their social position; in the general, the thought of all groups, our own included, is so regarded. As Mannheim succinctly puts it, "With the emergence of the general formulation of the total conception of ideology, the simple theory of ideology develops into the sociology of knowledge. What was once the intellectual armament of a party is transformed into a method of research in social and intellectual history generally." (G, p. 69.)

Although the theory of ideology may be conceived as a parent of

---

10. G, 50-51. Compare Scheler, *Versuche* . . ., p. 95. "Vor allem darf hier nicht die Rede sein von Motivationen und subjektiven Absichten der gelehrten und forschenden Individuen: diese können unendlich mannigfaltig sein: technische Aufgaben, Eitelkeit, Ehrgeiz, Gewinnsucht, Wahrheitsliebe, usw."

Wissenssoziologie, it is necessary to disown much of its heritage if it is to be a cognitive rather than a political discipline. The theory of ideology is primarily concerned with discrediting an adversary, *à tout prix,* and is but remotely concerned with reaching valid articulated knowledge of the subject-matter in hand. It is polemical, aiming to dissipate rival points of view. It is implicitly anti-intellectualistic. It would establish truth by fiat, by sheer political domination if necessary. It seeks assent, irrespective of the grounds for acceptance. It is akin to rhetoric rather than to science. The implications of the theory of ideology are such that they must be openly repudiated if they are not to overshadow the essentially cognitive purposes of a sociology of knowledge. In point of fact, Mannheim seeks to eliminate the acutely relativistic and propagandistic elements which persisted in the earlier formulation of *Wissenssoziologie.*

SUBSTANTIVE THEOREMS

Broadly speaking, the sociology of knowledge may be conceived as having two main branches: theory and "an historico-sociological method of research." The theoretical phase is in turn classifiable into (a) "purely empirical investigation through description and structural analysis of the ways in which social relationships, in fact, influence thought"; and (b) "epistemological inquiry concerned with the bearing of this interrelationship upon the problem of validity." (H, p. 277.) The methodological phase is concerned with devising procedures for the construction of ideal types of the *Weltanschauungen* which are implied in the types of thought current in various social strata (social classes, generations, sects, parties, cliques, schools of thought). Through such articulated reconstructions, the concrete modes of thought are to be derived from the social "composition of the groups and strata" which express themselves in this fashion. (H, p. 277. It is apparent, then, that the methodological branch of this discipline is closely linked with the theoretical branch, (a), above). Thus we may revise Mannheim's classification and consider this discipline as involving two main classes of problems: those of a substantive *Wissenssoziologie,* which includes the empirical and procedural aspects, and those pertaining to the epistemological relevance of the sociology of knowledge. Although most commentators on Mannheim's work have centered their attention on his epistemological discussion, it seems more fruitful to devote attention to the substantive sociology of knowledge, as indeed Mannheim himself recognizes. (H, p. 275.)

The scope of the substantive branch is reflected in its problems, concepts, theorems and canons of evidence. Thought is held to be existentially determined when it can be shown that it is not imminent or internally determined and when its genesis, form and content are significantly influenced by extra-theoretical factors. (H, p. 240.) [In Frederick Jackson Turner's words: "Each age writes the history of the past

anew with reference to the conditions uppermost in its own time."] On
the basis of empirical studies, it may be asserted that collective purposes
and social processes lead to an awareness of various problems which
would otherwise be obscured and undetected. It is in this connexion
that Mannheim derives the problems which are the special concern of
Wissenssoziologie itself from intensive horizontal and vertical mobility
in society, for only by thus coming into contact with radically different
modes of thought does the participant-observer come to doubt the general validity of his own received forms of thought. Likewise, it is only
when the usual institutional guarantees of a *Weltanschauung*—e.g., the
Church, the State—are shattered by rapid social change that the multiple
forms of thought come to constitute a problem. Changes in the social
structure such as these lead to the reexamination and questioning of
Selbstverständlichkeiten, of what was formerly taken for granted.
(J, p. 132 f.)

Others of Mannheim's theorems illustrate, in general outline, the
correlations between thought and social structure which he seeks to
establish. He submits the thesis that "even the categories in which experiences are subsumed, collected and ordered vary according to the
social position of the observer." (G, p. 130.) An organically integrated
group conceives of history as a continuous movement toward the realization of its ends; socially uprooted and loosely integrated groups espouse
an ahistorical intuitionism which stresses the fortuitious and imponderable. The well-adjusted conservative mentality is averse to historical
theorizing since the social order, *wie es eigentlich ist,* is viewed as natural and proper, rather than as problematical. Conservatives turn to
defensive philosophical and historical reflections concerning the social
world and their place in it only when the *status quo* is questioned by
opposing groups. Moreover, conservatism tends to view history in terms
of morphological categories which stress the unique character of historical *configurations,* whereas advocates of change adopt an analytical
approach in order to arrive at elements which may be recombined,
through causality or functional integration, into new social structures.
The first view stresses the inherent stability of the social structure as
it is; the second emphasizes changeability and instability by abstracting
the components of this structure and rearranging them anew. In a nation
with expanding economic and territorial horizons, such as the United
States, social scientists concern themselves with detailed investigation
of isolated social problems and assume that the solution of individual
problems will automatically lead to an adequate integration of the entire society. This assumption can flourish only in a society where vast
possibilities and numerous alternatives of action provide a degree of
elasticity which in fact permits some remedy for institutional defects.
Contrariwise, in a nation such as the German, the limited field for action

leads to a realization of the interdependence of social elements and thus to an organic view involving the entire transformation of the social structure rather than piecemeal reformism. (G. pp. 228-9; I, pp. 30-33.)

In similar fashion, Mannheim relates four types of utopian mentality —the Anabaptist chiliastic, the liberal-humanitarian, the conservative and the socialist-communist—to the particular social location and collective purposes of their protagonists. In this connexion, he shows that even the "historical time-sense" of these groups is influenced by their position and aspirations. Anabaptist chiliasm, deriving from the revolutionary ardor and "tense expectations" of oppressed strata, stresses the immediate present, the *hic et nunc*. The bourgeoning middle classes who gave rise to liberal-humanitarianism emphasize the "idea" of *the indeterminate future* which, in due course, will witness the realization of their ethical norms through progressive "enlightenment." The conservatives' time-sense construes *the past* as inexorably leading to and indisputably validating the existing state of society. ("Whatever is, is in its causes just." "One truth is clear, Whatever is, is right.") Finally, the socialist-communist conceptions differentiate historical time in a more complex manner, distinguishing between the *immediate and remote future* while emphasizing that *the concrete present* embraces not only *the past* but also the latent tendencies of *the future*. By formulating these connections between social location, collective aspirations and temporal orientation, Mannheim has advanced a field of study which is being increasingly cultivated.[11]

TYPES OF KNOWLEDGE

It will be noted that the foregoing theorems pertain less to positive knowledge than to political convictions, philosophies of history, ideologies and social beliefs. And this at once opens a basic problem. Which spheres of "thought" are included in Mannheim's theses concerning the existential determination (*Seinsverbundenheit*) of thought? Precisely what is embraced by the term "knowledge" to the analysis of which the discipline of *Wissenssoziologie* is nominally devoted? For the purposes of this discipline, are there significant differences in types of knowledge?

Mannheim does not meet these issues specifically and at length in

---

11. Durkheim's earlier sociological analysis of temporal frames of reference was wholly concerned with preliterate materials and (consequently?) did not treat differences in temporal orientation between groups in the same society. See his *Elementary Forms of the Religious Life*, 1 f. 440 f.; also E. Durkheim and M. Mauss, "De quelques formes primitives de classification," *L'Année sociologique*, 1901-2, 6, 1-71; H. Hubert and M. Mauss, *Mélanges d'histoire des religions* (Paris, 1909), chapter on "La représentation du temps." For more recent discussions, see P. A. Sorokin and R. K. Merton, "Social time," *American Journal of Sociology*, 1937, 42, 615-29; A. I. Hallowell, "Temporal Orientation in Western Civilization and in a Preliterate Society," *American Anthropologist*, 1937, 39, 647-70. Sorokin includes an extensive discussion of this subject in the fourth volume of his *Social and Cultural Dynamics*.

any of his writings. However, his occasional observations and empirical studies imply that he is persistently bedevilled by this fundamental question and, moreover, that he has failed to come to any clearcut, though provisional, conclusion concerning it. His failure in this respect introduces serious discrepancies between some of his theorems and specific empirical inquiries. Knowledge is at times regarded so broadly as to include every type of assertion and every mode of thought from folkloristic maxims to rigorous positive science. Thus, in an earlier formulation, he holds that "historical, political and social science thinking as well as the thought of everyday life" are all existentially determined. (F, p. 41.) Elsewhere, we learn that the social process penetrates into the "perspective" of "most of the domains of knowledge." Likewise, the content of "formal knowledge" [analytic statements? logic? mathematics? formal sociology?] is unaffected by the social or historical situation. (G, p. 150.) Such immunity is enjoyed by the "exact sciences" but not by the "cultural sciences." (H, p. 243.) Elsewhere, ethical convictions, epistemological postulates, material predications, synthetic judgments, political beliefs, the categories of thought, eschatological doxies, moral norms, ontological assumptions and observations of empirical fact are more or less indiscriminately held to be "existentially determined."[12] The identification of different types of inquiry by subsuming them under one rubric serves only to confuse rather than to clarify the mechanisms involved in "existential determination." Different sets of ideas are used to perform different functions, and we are led to logomachy and endless controversy if we insist that they are to be judged as "essentially" similar. Mannheim's work is informed with this fallacy. Had he attended to the familiar distinction between the referential and emotive functions of language, for example, such a miscellany would scarcely have remained undifferentiated. As I. A. Richards has phrased it, "The sense in which we believe a scientific proposition is not the sense in which we believe emotive utterances, whether they are political, 'We will not sheathe the sword,' or critical, 'The progress of poetry is immortal,' or poetic."

Mannheim's failure to distinguish, in practice, the markedly heterogeneous types of knowledge which he asserts to be *seinsverbunden* is particularly striking in view of his familiarity with Alfred Weber's useful distinction between cultural and civilizational knowledge.[13] Fortunately,

---

12. Cf. E, 162; F, 41; K, 22-23; G, 71-72, 150; H, 243, 260, etc. On this point, consult the vigorous criticism by Alexander von Schelting, *Max Weber's Wissenschaftslehre* (Tübingen, 1932), 95, 99,n.2. Note also the relevance of I. A. Richards' observation that "Thought in the strictest sense varies only with evidence; but attitudes and feelings change for all manner of reasons." This is not to deny their interpenetration.

13. As is clear from Mannheim's discussion in A, 37, 48 and his passing comment on Weber's work in another connection, G, 159. For a brief general discussion of this distinction, see R. M. MacIver, *Society* (New York, 1937), 268-81; R. K. Merton, "Civilization and culture," *Sociology and Social Research*, 1936, 21, 103-13

Mannheim's own investigations in substantive *Wissenssoziologie* have been concerned almost wholly with cultural materials (*Weltanschauungen*, eschatologies, political convictions) so that this confusion does not vitiate his empirical studies. However, his more general theorems are rendered questionable by his use of an inadequately differentiated and amorphous category of knowledge. This defect, moreover, interferes with any attempt to ascertain the status of the natural and physical sciences as far as existential determination is concerned. Had Mannheim systematically and explicitly clarified his position in this respect, he would have been less disposed to *assume* that the physical sciences are wholly immune from extra-theoretical influences and, correlatively, less inclined to urge that the social sciences are peculiarly subject to such influences.[14]

CONNECTIVES OF KNOWLEDGE AND SOCIETY

Mannheim's analysis is limited, as well, by his failure to specify the *type* or *mode* of relations between social structure and knowledge. This lacuna leads to vagueness and obscurity at the very heart of his central thesis concerning the "existential *determination* of knowledge" (*Seinsverbundenheit des Wissens*). Mannheim has evidently come to recognize (but not to surmount) this difficulty, for he writes:

Here we do not mean by "determination" a mechanical cause-effect sequence: we leave the meaning of "determination" open, and only empirical investigation will show us how strict is the correlation between life-situation and thought-process, or what scope exists for variations in the correlation.[15] Although it may be agreed that it is unwise to prejudge the types of relations between knowledge and social structure, it is also true that a failure to specify these types virtually precludes the possibility of formulating problems for empirical investigation. For *nolens volens*, the investigator, and Mannheim's own empirical researches are a case in point, includes in his conceptual scheme or tacitly presupposes some conception of these relations. Thus, it is instructive to note briefly the various terms which Mannheim uses to refer to the relations between social position and knowledge. The following list is illustrative [italics inserted].

---

14. For example, the recent empirical investigations by Borkenau, Hessen, Bernal, Sorokin, Merton are at least indicative that the role of extra-scientific factors in determining the direction of natural and of social science development differs rather in degree than in kind. For a theoretical formulation of this view, see Talcott Parsons, *The Structure of Social Action*, 595 f. And, to anticipate our later discussion, there is no basis for assuming that the validity of empirical judgment is *necessarily* any more affected by these extra-scientific influences in the one case than in the other.

15. H, p. 239, n. Wirth and Shils, the translators, add: "The German expression 'Seinverbundenes Wissens' conveys a meaning which leaves the exact nature of the determinism open."

It was *in accord with the needs* of an industrial society . . . to base their collective actions . . . on a rationally justifiable system of ideas. (K, p. 33.)

The generation that followed Romanticism . . . [adopted] a revolutionary view as being *in accord with the needs of the* time. (G, p. 144.)

[This particular conception of ideology] refers to a sphere of errors . . . which . . . follow inevitably and unwittingly from certain *causal determinants.* (G, p. 54.)

. . . a given point of view and a given set of concepts, because they are *bound up with and grow out of* a certain social reality. . . . (G, p. 72.)

When the social situation changes, the system of norms to which it had previously given birth ceases to be *in harmony with it.* The same estrangement goes on with reference to knowledge. . . . (G, p. 76.)

. . . the intellectualistic conception of science, underlying positivism, is itself rooted in a definite *Weltanschauung* and has progressed *in close connection with* definite political interests. (G, p. 148.)

Socially, this intellectualistic outlook had its basis in a middle stratum, in the bourgeoisie and in the intellectual class. This outlook *in accordance with the structural relationship* of the groups representing it, pursued a dynamic middle course. . . . (G, p. 199.)

Ideas, forms of thought, and psychic energies persist and are transformed *in close conjunction with* social forces. It is *never by accident* that they appear at given moments in the social process. (G, p. 223.)

It is no accident that the one group [ascendant *elites*] regards history as a circulation of *elites,* while for the others [*e.g.,* socialists], it is a transformation of the historical-social structure. Each gets to see primarily only that aspect of the social and historical totality towards which it is oriented by its purpose. (G, p. 127.)

The several terms which nominally refer to the types of relations between the sub- and the super-structure are less a matter of stylistic diversity in prose than an indication of Mannheim's fundamental indecision. He uses the generic term "correspondence" (*Entsprechung*) to denote these relations. He has made a variety of unintegrated assumptions in deriving certain forms of thought from certain types of social situations. Some of these merit brief examination.

1. On occasion—despite his explicit denial of any such intention—Mannheim assumes a direct *causation* of forms of thought by social forces. This assumption is usually heralded by the oft-recurring phrase: "It is never an accident that . . ." a given theory will derive from a given kind of group position. (See, *e.g.,* H, pp. 248-9.) In this case, Mannheim adopts the natural-science view of *"Erklärung"* in which the general rule accounts for aspects of the particular instance.

2. A second assumption may be termed the "interest assumption" which holds that ideas and forms of thought are "in accord with," that is, gratifying to, the interests of the subjects. In one form, it is simply a doctrine of the influence of vested interests—economic, political, religious —in which it is to the advantage of the subjects to entertain certain views. Thus, an advantageously situated group will presumably be less receptive than a socially disadvantaged group to talk of extensive social

reform or revolution. The acceptance or rejection may be deliberate or unwitting.[16] This assumption is found in *Vulgärmarxismus* which, repudiated by Mannheim as it was by Marx, is occasionally implicit in the former's writings.

3. A third assumption is that of "focus of attention." According to this, the subject limits his perspective in order to deal with a particular problem, directly practical or theoretical. Here thought is directed by the very formulation of the problem, awareness of which may in turn be attributed to the social position of the subject. Roughly, it may be asserted that this hypothesis is stressed in the substantive sociology of knowledge whereas the "interest hypothesis" is emphasized in the theory of ideology.

4. On quite another level is Mannheim's occasional treatment of certain social structures as simply prerequisite to certain forms of thought. In this, he joins with Scheler in speaking of "certain types of groups in which . . . [these forms of thought] alone can arise and be elaborated." (H, pp. 242-3.) Much of Mannheim's analysis has to do with the establishment of preconditions or even facilitating factors rather than with necessary and sufficient conditions. Instances are numerous. Social mobility *may* lead to reflection, analysis, comprehensiveness of outlook; it may equally well lead to *insouciance,* superficiality, confirmation of one's prejudgments. Or, to take another theorem: the juxtaposition of conflicting views *may* induce reflection, as summarized in the instrumentalists' aphorism, "conflict is the gadfly of thought." But such conflict may also evoke fideism, inconclusive anxieties, skepticism. Or still again, advantageously located classes ("conservatives") *may* be loath to theorize about their situations, but it is hardly permissible to ignore the alienated nobility who turned to the Encyclopedists' social theories or the renegades who are socially bourgeois but spiritually proletarian or their proletarian counterparts who identify themselves with the bourgeois ethos. All this is not to deny the suggested correlations but only to set forth, in company with Mannheim himself, the

---

16. The occasional vogue of such "interest theories" as affording allegedly adequate explanation is itself a *wissenssoziologische* problem which merits further study. Particular varieties are found in some of the inferences drawn from the postulate of an "economic man," the "conspiracy theory" in political science, the excessive extension of "rationalization" and "propaganda" concepts in psychology, the "priestly lie" notion of Voltaire, the "religion-an-opiate-for-the-masses" cliché. Of course, the occasional currency of these views may be due to the fact that "they work," that, up to a certain point, they account for human behavior and are consonant with a wider body of knowledge. It is not irrelevant, however, that in all these doctrines, when action and thought can be ascribed to ulterior (especially if disreputable) motives, the behavior is said to be explained. Curiosity is satisfied: X is a special pleader, a tool of vested interests, a Bolshevik, a Hamiltonian banker. The assumption common to these several versions is the Hobbesian notion of egoism as *the* motive force of conduct. For a penetrating account of the sources and consequences of worries ('theories') about conspiracy, see Edward A. Shils, *The Torment of Secrecy,* (Glencoe, Illinois: The Free Press, 1956).

need for a more circumstantial analysis of the many structural factors which are involved. Mannheim's discussion in terms of prerequisites shades into the view of existential determination as referring simply to empirical correlations between society and knowledge, in which the very uniformity is taken to establish the "correspondence." On this level, analysis is all too often halted once the correlation is indicated.

5. Still another implied relation between social structure and knowledge involves what may be termed an emanationist or quasi-aesthetic assumption. In this view (particularly marked in B and F), Hegelian overtones are not altogether absent. Such terms as "compatibility," "congruity," "harmony," "consistency," and "contrariety" of *Weltanschauungen* usually signalize the emergence of this assumption. The criteria for establishing these relations are left implicit. Thus, we read: "The absence of depth in the plastic arts and the dominance of the purely linear correspond to the manner of experiencing historical time as unilinear progress and evolution."[17] It should be noted, however, that this particular assumption plays no large part in Mannheim's substantive researches. The vestiges which do remain are more significant as a sign of his uncertainty concerning the types of relation between knowledge, culture and society than as an indication of idealistic presuppositions in his theory.[18]

A more extensive discussion of the substantive and methodological aspects of Mannheim's work would include a detailed treatment of the procedures of analysis he has adopted. His attempt to set forth a systematic "code of techniques" suffers from brevity and excessive generality. These failings would only be multiplied by those of any commentator who ventures an epitome of an already epitomized version. (H, pp. 276-8.) However, one obstacle confronting the first of these procedures—an explicit articulation of the presuppositions common to "single expressions and records of thought"—should be noted. At least so far as beliefs are concerned, it is at present often impossible to deter-

---

17. G, 200. Mannheim's frequent comparisons between "styles" in the history of art and in intellectual history usually presupposes the quasi-aesthetic assumption. Compare Scheler, *Versuche . . .*, 92-3, who speaks of the "stilanalogen Beziehungen zwischen Kunst (und den Künsten untereinander), Philosophie, und Wissenschaft der grossen Epochen" and of the "Analogien zwischen der französischen klassischen Tragödie und der französischen mathematischen Physik des 17. und 18. Jahrhunderts, zwischen Shakespeare und Milton und der englischen Physik . . ." and so on. Spengler and Sorokin have developed this theme at some length.

18. This is but a special case of the more general problem of establishing types of social and cultural integration. Mannheim's practice, despite the absence of systematic formulation, marks a distinct advance over that of Marxist epigoni. An explicit formulation of a logic of relations between cultural values is provided by Sorokin, *Social and Cultural Dynamics*, Vol. I, 7-13. In so far as he deals with "cultural integration" and ignores its relation to social organization, Sorokin leans toward an idealistic interpretation. *Cf.* C. Wright Mills, "Language, logic and culture," *American Sociological Review*, 1939, 4, 670-80. For a specific criticism of Mannheim on this point, see Schelting, *op. cit.*, 102-115.

mine whether cultural values are consistent or inconsistent, in advance of the actual social situations in which these values are implicated. Thus, if the question is raised, in abstraction from concrete cases of *behavior*, whether "pacifism" and "abolitionism" are compatible or incompatible, the answer must be indeterminate. One can equally well conclude, on the abstract cultural plane of belief, that these two value-systems are random (mutually irrelevant), consistent or inconsistent. In the case of the Quakers, adherence to both these values involved integrated action for the abolition of slavery without resort to violence whereas Garrison and his disciples, initially advocates of non-resistance, retracted their pacifist views in order to get on with the war to abolish slavery. It should be noted that prior to the occurrence of this situation, there was little basis for assuming any conflict between the values of abolitionism and pacifism. If anything, the cultural analyst might be tempted to consider these values as components of an integrated value-system labelled "humanitarianism." Abstract cultural synthesis which seeks to reconstruct the "underlying unity of outlook" may thus lead to false inferences. Abstractly inconsistent values are often rendered compatible by their distribution among various statuses in the social structure so that they do not result in conflicting demands upon the same persons at the same time. Potential conflict of values may be obviated by their segregation in different universes of discourse and their incorporation in different social roles. Failure to recognize that the organization of values among social roles may render abstractly conflicting values compatible would lead, for example, to the thesis that the Catholic Church maintains incompatible values of celibacy and fertility. In this case, conflict and malintegration is largely avoided, of course, by attaching these values to different statuses within the church organization: celibacy to the status of priest and unrestricted fertility to the married laity. Systems of belief, then, must be examined in terms of their relations with the social organization. This is a cardinal requirement of both *Sinngemässe Zurechnung* and *Faktizitätszurechnung*, as described by Mannheim. (H, pp. 276-7.)

RELATIVISM

There remains now to be considered the most disputed phase of Mannheim's writings, namely, his claims for the epistemological consequences of the sociology of knowledge. These need not be examined in full detail, since many critical expositions are available.[19] Moreover,

---

19. The most elaborate of these is by Schelting, *op. cit.*, pp. 94 f. See also his review of *Ideologie und Utopie* in *American Sociological Review*, 1936, 1, 664-72; Günther Stern, "Ueber die sogenannte 'Seinsverbundenheit' des Bewusstseins," *Archiv für Sozialwissenschaft und Sozialpolitik*, 1930, 44, 492-102; Sjoerd Hofstra, *De sociale Aspecten van Kennis en Wetenschap*, (Amsterdam, 1937), 39-31; Paul Tillich, "Ideologie und Utopie," *Die Gesellschaft*, 1929, 6, 348-55 (privately circulated English translation by James Luther Adams).

Mannheim acknowledges that the substantive results of *Wissenssoziologie* —which comprise the most distinctly rewarding part of the field—do not lead to his epistemological conclusions.

The controversy centers on Mannheim's conception of the general total ideology which, it will be remembered, asserts that "the thought of all parties in all epochs is of an ideological character." This leads at once, it would seem, to radical relativism with its familiar vicious circle in which the very propositions asserting such relativism are *ipso facto* invalid. That Mannheim perceives the logical fallacy and intellectual nihilism implicit in such a position is abundantly clear. Thus, he explicitly disclaims the irresponsible view that "sees in intellectual activity no more than arbitrary personal judgments and propaganda." (G, p. 89, n.) He likewise repudiates "the vague, ill-considered and sterile form of relativism with regard to scientific knowledge which is increasingly prevalent today." (H, p. 237.) How, then, does he escape the relativistic impasse?

In perhaps an unduly simplified form, we may classify Mannheim's efforts to avoid the relativistic fallacy and to establish *points d'appui* for the validity of his own judgments under three major heads: Dynamic Criteria of Validity, Relationism, and Structural Warranties of Validity.

1. *Dynamic Criteria of Validity.* Mannheim introduces several dynamic criteria of the validity of historical judgments. "A theory . . . is wrong if in a given practical situation it uses concepts and categories which, if taken seriously, would prevent man from *adjusting* himself *at that historical stage.*" (G, p. 85; italics inserted.) ". . . knowledge is distorted and ideological when it fails to take account of the new realities applying to a situation, and when it attempts to conceal them by thinking of them in categories which are inappropriate." And in a note, Mannheim adds: "A perception may be *erroneous or inadequate to the situation* by being in advance of it, as well as by being antiquated." (G, p. 86 and n. 1.) It is apparent, however, that the criterion of adjustment or adaptation begs the question unless the type of adjustment is specified.[20] Numerous, even contradictory, theories may enable man to "adjust" in one fashion or another. Social adjustment tends to be a normative rather than an existential concept. Moreover, determination of the "appropriateness" or "inappropriateness" of categories presupposes the very criteria of validity which Mannheim wishes to discard. It is perhaps these obscurities and ambiguities which led him to evolve other criteria of validity by introducing the concept of utopia.

"Only those orientations transcending reality" are utopian "which, when they pass over into conduct, tend to shatter, either partially or

---

20. As had long since been indicated by Max Weber in his discussion of "diesen viel misbrauchten Begriff," the concept of "social adaptation" has a large variety of meanings, most of which are scientifically useless. See his *Wissenschaftslehre,* 477 f.; see further, Schelting, *op. cit.,* 102 f.

wholly, the order of things prevailing at the time." (G, p. 173.) In this sense, utopian, in contrast to ideological, thought is true rather than illusory. The difficulty of this view is at once evident. How, at any given time, is the observer to discriminate between valid utopian thought and distorted ideological thought? Moreover, since, as we have just seen, conceptions may be "inadequate to the situation by being in advance of it," how is one to choose the valid from amongst the invalid "advanced ideas?" Mannheim recognizes these embarrassments, but his solution is of dubious value. It not only involves an *ex post facto* criterion of validity but also precludes the possibility of valid judgments on contemporary ideas, as may be seen from the following passage.

. . . if we look into the past, it seems possible to find a fairly adequate criterion of what [idea] is to be regarded as ideological and what is utopian. This criterion is their realization. Ideas which later turned out to have been only distorted representations of a past or potential social order were ideological, while those which were adequately realized in the succeeding social order were relative utopias. . . . The extent to which ideas are realized constitutes a supplementary and retroactive standard for making distinctions between facts which as long as they are contemporary are buried under the partisan conflict of opinion. (G, p. 184.)

As Schelting has shown, this retroactive criterion presupposes the very criteria of validity which Mannheim wishes to supplant, for how else is the observer to demonstrate that his reading of the historical process is correct? A lengthy and detailed analysis, far beyond the compass of this discussion, would be necessary to demonstrate further difficulties inherent in this position. However, Mannheim moderates this view considerably in another attempt to circumvent radical relativism.

2. *Relationism.* Mannheim sketches three possible positions on the question of the bearing of the genesis of an assertion upon its validity. The first denies "absolute validity" [*sic*] to an assertion when its structural sources are demonstrated.[21] Contrariwise, the second holds that such demonstration has no bearing whatever on the truth-value of the assertion. The third conception, adopted by Mannheim, mediates between these extremes. Identification of the social position of the assertor implies only "the suspicion"—a probability—that the assertion "might represent merely a partial view." Such identification also particularizes the scope of the assertion and fixes the limits of its validity. This attributes to *Wissenssoziologie* a considerably more modest role than was claimed in Mannheim's earlier formulations, as is evident from his own summary.

The analyses characteristic of the sociology of knowledge are, in this sense,

---

21. Throughout, Mannheim imputes a doctrine of "absolute truth" to those who reject a radically relativist position. (*E.g.*, H, 270, 274.) This is gratuitous. One may grant different perspectives, different purposes of inquiry, different conceptual schemes and add only that the various results be translatable or integrated, before they are judged valid.

by no means irrelevant for the determination of the truth of a statement; but these analyses . . . do not by themselves fully reveal the truth because the mere delimitation of the perspectives is by no means a substitute for the immediate and direct discussion between the divergent points of view or for the direct examination of the facts.[22]

In expounding his relationist views, Mannheim clarifies the concept of "perspective" (*Aspektstruktur*), which denotes "the manner in which one views an object, what one perceives in it, and how one construes it in his thinking." Perspectives may be described and imputed to their social sources by considering: "the meaning of the concepts being used; the phenomenon of the counter-concept; the absence of certain concepts; the structure of the categorical apparatus; dominant models of thought; level of abstraction; and the ontology that is presupposed." (H, p. 244.)

By this time, Mannheim has come almost full circle to his point of departure; so much so that his present observations may be readily assimilated to those by Rickert and Max Weber. Situationally determined thought no longer signifies inevitably ideological thought but implies only a certain "probability" that the occupant of a given place in the social structure will think in a certain fashion. (H, p. 264.) The validity of propositions is no longer ascertained through *wissenssoziologische* analysis but through direct investigation of the object. Again, the "particularizing function" of the sociology of knowledge simply assists us in ascertaining the limits within which generalized propositions are valid. What Mannheim calls particularization is, of course, nothing but a new term for a widely recognized methodological precept, namely, that whatever is found true under certain conditions should not be assumed to be true universally or without limits and conditions. Bridgman and Sorokin have termed this the "principle of limits"; Dewey calls its violation *"the* philosophical fallacy"; in its most prosaic and widely known form it is described as the "fallacy of unwarranted extrapolation."

Mannheim's conception of "perspectivism" is substantially the same as the Rickert-Weber conception of *Wertbeziehung* (which holds that values are relevant to formulation of the scientific problem and choice of materials but are not relevant to the validity of the results).[23] Both

---

22. H, 256. Similarly, in his more recent essay, Mannheim writes: "It is, of course, true that in the social sciences, as elsewhere, the ultimate criterion of truth or falsity is to be found in investigation of the object, and the sociology of knowledge is no substitute for this." (K, 4.)

23. See Rickert, *Die Grenzen* . . ., 245-271. ". . . die Geschichte ist *keine wertende* sondern eine *wertbeziehende* Wissenschaft." *Cf.* Weber, *Wissenschaftslehre*, 146-214. "Es gibt keine schlechthin 'objektive' wissenschaftliche Analyse des Kulturlebens oder . . . der 'sozialen Erscheinungen' *unabhängig* von speziellen und 'einseitigen' Gesichtspunkten, nach denen . . . als Forschungsobjekt ausgewählt, analysiert und darstellend gegliedert werden." (170.) But "Die Beziehung der Wirklichkeit auf Wertideen, die ihr Bedeutung verleihen und die Heraushebung und Ordnung der dadurch gefärbten Bestandteile des Wirklichen unter dem Gesichtspunkt ihrer Kulturbedeutung ist ein gänzlich heterogener und disparater Gesichtspunkt gegenüber der Analyse der Wirklichkeit auf Gesetze und ihrer Ordnung in generellen Begriffen." (176.)

views depart from the premises of an inexhaustible multitude of phenomena, the inevitability of selection from these in terms of a conceptual scheme and the relevance of values and social structure to this scheme and the formulation of the problem. Indeed, as early as 1904, Külpe and the psychologists of the Würzburg school had shown experimentally that the nature of problems (*Aufgaben*) largely determined the form and content of perception and observation.[24] The Gestalt psychologists and the Lewin school have more recently extended these findings on the directive influence of *Aufgaben*. Rickert, Weber and especially Mannheim seek to add a sociological dimension to this signal discovery by showing that cultural values and social structure in turn determine the formulation of the *Aufgaben* which direct observation along certain lines. Thus, this particular phase of the sociology of knowledge is clearly integrated with the findings of experimental researches in psychology. It will be noted, however, that these experiments do not indicate that the validity of the observations focused in this manner is thereby to be impugned.

In part, Mannheim's inconsistency in his earlier writings stems from an indefinite distinction between incorrectness (invalidity) and perspective (onesidedness). Perspectival statements are presumably not incorrect, *if* their author recognizes and allows for their partial nature; they are then simply abstract formulations of certain aspects of the concrete situation. They are, however, definitely invalid if they are submitted as significantly complete representations of the phenomena in question (Whitehead's "fallacy of misplaced concreteness"). The line between invalidity and mere perspectivism is, then, scarcely as distinct as Mannheim seems to imply. His present emphasis upon the recognition and proper discounting of perspective as essential to valid thought in social science appears to be little more than a restatement of the notion of *Wertbeziehung* and, as such, returns him to the Rickert-Weber fold from which he presumably departed.[25]

3. *Structural Warranties of Validity.* Thus far, Mannheim has sought

---

24. See O. Külpe, "Versuche über Akstraktion," *Bericht über den Internationalen Kongress für experimentelle Psychologie*, 1904, 56-69; C. C. Pratt, "The present status of introspective technique," *The Journal of Philosophy*, April 24, 1924, 21, 231: "As far as accurate observation and unequivocal report are concerned, an observer is adequate only to those aspects of a given experience which the determining tendency brings clearly into line with the particular *Aufgabe* of the moment; other aspects of that experience fall at various distances outside the sphere of immediate observation and hence cannot be made the objects of scientific description." Cited in Ralph M. Eaton, *Symbolism and Truth* (Cambridge, 1925), 17 f.

25. The discrepancy between this interpretation and that of Schelting, who systematically criticizes Mannheim on the basis of Weber's *Wissenschaftslehre,* is more apparent than real. Schelting treats Mannheim's work as a whole in which the early and later portions are often juxtaposed. Here, we deal with Mannheim's writings as representing a development in the later stages of which the departure from Weber becomes increasingly attenuated.

to provide grounds for validity *within* the limits of given perspectives. He is still faced, however, with the problem of evaluating the relative merits of diverse particular views and further, of validating what he calls the "dynamic syntheses" of these several views. In short, if intellectual anarchy is to be avoided, there must be some common ground for integrating the various particularistic interpretations. In his *Ideologie und Utopie* he submits a solution which, despite modifications, is strongly reminiscent of Hegel and Marx. Hegel's idealistic historicism guaranteed its own truth by positing that the "absolute *Geist*" had come into its own in Hegel's philosophy in as much as history had at long last attained its goal. For Marx, the same kind of postulate finds the proletariat as the present exponents of an imminent historical process which opens to them alone the possibility of undistorted social thought. And Mannheim finds a structural warranty of the validity of social thought in the "classless position" of the "socially unattached intellectuals" (*sozialfreischwebende Intelligenz*). These efforts to rescue oneself from an extreme relativism parallel Munchhausen's feat of extricating himself from a swamp by pulling on his whiskers.

Seinsverbundenheit which for others renders opaque all but a limited perspectival slice of knowledge falls away for the intellectuals. (D, pp. 115-120; F, p. 67 f.) The role of the intelligentsia becomes a kind of reassuring palliative for an implicit relativism. The intellectuals are the observers of the social universe who regard it, if not with detachment, at least with reliable insight, with a synthesizing eye. To them is vouchsafed, as to Marx's proletariat, the outlook which permits a rounded view of the concrete historical situation and, as for Marx, this privilege derives from their peculiar position within the social structure. Thus, Mannheim indicates that the intellectuals are able to comprehend the various conflicting tendencies of the time since they are "recruited from constantly varying social strata and life-situations." (K, p. 10; G, p. 139.) In the *Communist Manifesto*, we read: "the proletariat is recruited from all classes of the population." Mannheim asserts that the intellectuals are structurally free from distorted interpretations in as much as they are "consciously or unconsciously . . . interested in something else than success in the competitive scheme that displaces the present one." (G, p. 232; "es bewusst oder unbewusst stets auch auf etwas anderes ankam, als auf das Hineinarrivieren in die nächste Stufe des sozialen Seins.") Engels, in his essay on Feuerbach, reminds us that "only among the working class does the German aptitude for theory remain unimpaired. . . . Here there is no concern for careers, for profit-making, or for gracious patronage from above." However all this may in fact be, it is clear that in the case of both the intellectuals and the proletariat, mere structural position of the stratum is not in itself enough to validate their conceptions. And indeed, Mannheim seems to have come to this conclusion, for in a later article, he acknowledges the necessity of a "common de-nominator" and a formula for "translating" the results derived from different perspectives. (H, p. 270; "eine Formel der Umrechenbarkeit und Uebersetzbarkeit dieser verschiedenen Perspektiven ineinander . . .") However, in this connection, it is not asserted that only the struc-turally warrantied intellectuals can forge these syntheses. Nor does Mannheim satisfactorily indicate how the "translation of one perspective 'into the terms of another" is, on his view, to be attained. Once given the existential determination of thought, who is there to judge among the babel of competing voices?

It appears then that in drawing epistemological consequences from the sociology of knowledge Mannheim has been led to various un-resolved antinomies. Doubtless further modifications of his position along lately adumbrated lines will bring it to a tenable and integrated system of analysis. As for the veritable revolution in the theory of knowl-edge which he sees as deriving from an appropriate extension of *Wis-senssoziologie*, it can be said that in its bold outlines this epistemology has for some time been familiar to the American mind. It is that of Peirce and James, mediated by Dewey and Mead, in which thought is seen as but one among many types of activity, as inevitably linked with experience, as understandable only in its relations to noncognitive ex-perience, as stimulated by obstacles and temporarily frustrating situa-tions, as involving abstract concepts which must be constantly re-examined in the light of their implications for concrete particulars, as valid only so long as it rests upon an experimental foundation.[26] To this, Mannheim has contributed a valuable analysis of the role of social structure in directing and activating thought.

The critical tone of the foregoing discussion should not be mislead-ing. Mannheim has sketched the broad contours of the sociology of knowledge with remarkable skill and insight. Shorn of their epistemo-logical impedimenta, with their concepts modified by the lessons of further empirical inquiry and with occasional logical inconsistencies eliminated, Mannheim's procedures and substantive findings clarify rela-tions between knowledge and social structure which have hitherto re-mained obscure. Fortunately, Mannheim recognizes that his work is by no means definitive—a term which strikes a harsh discord when applied to any work of science—and we may await considerable enlightenment from further explorations of the territory in which he pioneered.

---

26. In a later book, Mannheim indicates his agreement with many features of pragmatism. J, 170 f. He shares also the precepts of operationalism in several respects which cannot be examined here. See, for example, H, 254, 274-5.

XIV STUDIES IN RADIO AND FILM PROPAGANDA*

HIS IS A REPORT on certain studies of domestic propaganda in radio and motion pictures. Having said this, let us define the term propaganda and let us make the definition hold throughout our discussion. We understand by propaganda any and all sets of symbols which influence opinion, belief or action on issues regarded by the community as controversial. These symbols may be written, printed, spoken, pictorial or musical. If, however, the topic is regarded as beyond debate, it is not subject to propaganda. In our society, the belief that 2 and 2 make 4 cannot, in this sense, be propagandized any more than the moral conviction that mother-son incest is evil. But it is still possible to propagandize the belief that our victory in war is not inevitable; that the poll tax runs counter to certain conceptions of democracy; that it would be unwise, during wartime, to provide citizens with as much fuel oil and gasoline as they wish; that one religious system has greater claim to our allegiance than another. Given a controversial issue, propaganda becomes possible and, it would seem, almost inevitable.

Another general remark. In many quarters, propaganda is often identified with lies, deceit or fraud. In our view, propaganda has no necessary relation to truth or falsity. An authentic account of the sinkings of American merchant ships in time of war may prove to be effective propaganda inducing citizens to accept many deprivations which they would not otherwise accept in good spirit. If we succumb to the view that propaganda and falsity are one, we are well on the way to nihilism. Let us recognize also that an attitude of uncritical distrust may develop as a defense against the acceptance of deprivation or against a barrage of facts and information which invite fear, discomfort or the abandonment of cherished beliefs.

But it is long since time to halt discussions of propaganda in the large; discussions which have all the fascination of speculation uncontrolled by empirical inquiry. To bring certain problems of propaganda

* In collaboration with Paul F. Lazarsfeld.

into clear focus, we must turn to propaganda in the particular, and develop definite procedures for testing our interpretations. It is not that general discussions of propaganda are necessarily invalid; it is only that they tend to outrun our funded knowledge. They are big with the bigness of vacuity.

Possibly this paper errs in the opposite direction. We intend only to report some of the studies conducted in World War II by the Columbia University Bureau of Applied Social Research under the supervision of Dr. Herta Herzog and the authors. One characteristic of these studies is their concern with the ascertainable effects of particular propaganda documents. Another characteristic is their technial orientation; they constitute one basis for advising the writers and producers of this propaganda. The research must be such as to implement immediate decision and action. A dozen years before he fled to Samoa, Robert Louis Stevenson was unwittingly describing the very type of situation which confronts research students operating within the framework of political action:

> This is no cabinet science, in which things are tested to a scruple; we theorize with a pistol to our head; we are confronted with a new set of conditions on which we have not only to pass judgment, but to take action, before the hour is at an end.

The present report, then, deals with research conducted "with a pistol to our head." Our object is to plead that you not pull the trigger.

MODES OF PROPAGANDA ANALYSIS

In one sense, detailed propaganda analysis is not a new development. For at least the past generation, the effects of films, radio programs and newspaper materials have been studied. Until recently, however, these studies have dealt with the over-all effects of the propaganda material as a whole. These researches—for example, those of L. L. Thurstone—have consequently confined their general results to observations of this order:

> An anti-Negro film, "The Birth of a Nation," increased anti-Negro sentiment among tested audiences.
> The film, "Streets of Chance," which portrayed a gambler "as an interesting, likeable character," for some unascertained reason led to an increased condemnation of gambling.
> The film, "All Quiet on the Western Front," led to more marked reactions against war among groups of school children than did the film "Journey's End."

You will notice that such research tells us little about the specific features of the propaganda which provoked these effects. But this is the very question with which the script-writer and the producer are concerned. If they are to benefit from propaganda research, it must be directed toward discovering the typical effects of definite and specific aspects of propaganda as well as its over-all effects. What is the character of effective propaganda under given conditions? In this report, we shall examine samples of recent studies in which definite features of propaganda are linked with definite types of response.

Before turning to methods of analyzing propaganda effects, we should seek to dispel one common illusion. It is clear that, in general, writers of propaganda cannot know how audiences will respond to their material merely by relying on intuition or by observing their own reactions. Several examples, the first of which is educational rather than propagandistic, will illustrate what unexpected responses the writer may elicit.

A skilled writer had drafted the instructions for the use of the second war ration book in as lucid a fashion as he could. Psychological consultants assisted him in the task. Trained interviewers presented the instructions to housewives and observed their reactions. On the basis of these observations, a second draft of instructions was prepared. This also was tested by interviewing, and a modified third draft was finally adopted. A central objective was that of making it clear that ration stamps of different values could be added to reach a given number of points.

It was assumed that since most people have had experience with postage stamps, an analogy might profitably be used in the instructions. Who would have anticipated from the vantage point of his armchair that this simple analogy would elicit comments such as these:

> I didn't realize that you had to mail them.

> There doesn't seem to be any place to stick them.

This trivial example of the unexpected response merely reflects a breakdown in communication. Other illustrations are provided by films which emphasize the cruelty and immorality of the Nazis. Episodes which ostensibly indicate that the Nazis are entirely unconcerned with common human decencies are at times appraised by audiences in purely technical terms: they are taken as illustrations of Nazi efficiency. The emotional and moral implications intended by the producers of these films are overlooked by the audience.

Much the same pattern of the unexpected response is found in radio materials. A talk on X-rays was broadcast under the auspices of a medical society, as part of a campaign seeking to promote "proper" use of health services by members of the community. The speaker, a noted radiologist, attempted to dissuade his listeners from turning to unlicensed practitioners (quacks) for X-ray examinations and treatments. In an effort to make his persuasion effective, he repeatedly stressed "the dangers in the use of and in the making of X-ray examinations." The radiologist's good intentions elicited unexpected anxieties. Some members of the audience—who, in any case, would not have consulted quacks—expressed their newly acquired fears:

It left people not wanting X-rays. It sounded so dangerous. The doctor uses lead and wears gloves. People wouldn't even want to get an X-ray after that. They'd be scared away.

I would feel that maybe it would hurt. From hearing about currents and so on I would think that it would be at least unpleasant.

The pattern of the unanticipated response raises several basic questions. How can we analyze propaganda films, radio and print, in such a way that we can determine what is likely to produce given effects? The procedures for achieving this end have come to be known as *content-analysis*. There are further questions. How can we ascertain responses actually elicited by propaganda? How far can we account for discrepancies between anticipated and actual responses? Can we build a fund of experience and interpretation which will enable us more fully to anticipate responses to various types of propaganda, thus minimizing or precluding undesirable responses by appropriate modification of the propaganda before it is released? Procedures designed to answer these questions we shall call *response-analysis*.

And now we turn to what we consider our main task: to report our experience in the analysis of various types of propaganda during a period of two years. Perhaps by focusing on problems actually encountered in these studies, we can make clear some of the procedures of content- and response-analysis which have been developed.

CONTENT-ANALYSIS

The propaganda document—a pamphlet, film or radio program—is first scrutinized to determine the probable types of responses to its various components, aspects, or to the document-as-a-whole. It may be assumed, perhaps, that anyone who examines the propaganda material will know its content. But this is far from being the case. Content-analysis requires certain procedures, based on clinical experience and funded in psychological or sociological theory, in order to discern the probable responses to the content. Mere impressionism is not enough. The content of a 15-minute radio program or of an hour film can be adequately appraised only through systematic procedures. Just as we need a field glass to perceive an object in the far distance, so we need devices, at times surprisingly simple devices, to perceive a flow of experience which endures over an extended period of time. These devices vary from the one extreme of counting the frequency of certain *key symbols* to the other extreme of determining the *structure* of the propaganda-as-a-whole or of an entire propaganda campaign.

Let us consider a few examples of the simplest type: symbol-analysis.

A radio series of morale programs contained approximately 1000 symbols denoting the United Nations (or its constituents, other than the United States) and the Axis (distributively or collectively). Upon examination of the frequency of these respective sets of symbols in twelve programs, several uniformities emerge which reflect a structure of the programs that runs counter to the manifest intent of the producers. In all but one of the programs, the frequency of United Nations symbols is positively correlated with those pertaining to the Axis: an increase or decrease in the one set of symbols is associated with an increase or decrease in the other. This brought to the fore a significant pattern in these morale programs. Interest in the United Nations is largely confined to their role in the war vis-à-vis the Axis: they are seldom mentioned in any other connection. So far as this morale series is concerned, the United Nations appear to be "foul-weather friends": interest is primarily manifested in them as allies helping to fight the Axis, and not as allies with whom we have sympathetic ties, irrespective of the war. The programs deal with them, not as societies, but only as nations exhibiting military prowess and courage. We salute the heroic dead of the Russians and rejoice that they are enemies of Hitler. We eulogize the British who have so long held the fortress Britain against the Nazis. Or we mourn the fate of the occupied nations and, again, interest in these nations is limited to their experience at the hands of the enemy. Because these are the motifs expressed in allusions to the United Nations, we find the observed association between the frequency of symbols referring to the United Nations and to the Axis. It should be noted that the analysts, and possibly the producers, of this radio series would not have detected this underlying structure had the symbol counts not called it to their attention.

This series of programs also made extensive use of the personification stereotype in referring to the enemy: about 25 per cent of all symbols denoting the enemy refer to Hitler, Mussolini, Goering, *etc.*, whereas only four per cent of references to the United Nations and 11 per cent of those to the United States consist of personifications. This use of simplified personalized stereotypes presents the enemy as consisting essentially of a small band of evil men and implies that once these men are destroyed, all will be well. This kind of personification proves to be all too acceptable to listeners, since it accords with common simplistic ideas; for example, the parallel notion that we must fight crime primarily by punishing criminals and not by preventive measures.

Moreover, we have found that varying distributions of terms used to designate the enemy in documentary films are reflected in the comments of interviewees who have seen these films. Thus, if the single satanic figure, Hitler, or the entire German people, rather than the Nazis, are most frequently identified as the enemy by the film commentator, this is reflected in the pattern of audience responses. We need only remember reactions to the war-guilt clause in the Versailles treaty to realize that the issue has considerable political importance. Current propaganda may be inadvertently ignoring the Fascist or Nazi character of the enemy and thus building up a reservoir of misdirected ill will for the post-war period.

Another example is provided by a pamphlet concerning Negroes. The main themes of the pamphlet were two: It is true that Negroes continue to suffer from discrimination but, none the less, they have made great progress in our democratic society which has enabled many Negroes to achieve individual success and to contribute to the community. In contrast, Hitler has always expressed contempt for colored peoples and, should he win the war, all gains of the Negro would be wiped out. The content of the pamphlet can thus be classified in two categories: material pertaining to "Negro gains and achievements in a democracy," and to "deprivations threatened by a Hitler victory." There were 189 paragraphs and captions: 84 per cent of these dealt with present gains and 16 per cent with potential losses under Nazism. To the producers of the pamphlet, this evidently seemed a reasonable distribution of emphasis on the two themes.

But the pamphlet contained two types of presentation. One was an article by a prominent Negro writer; the other, a series of attention-fixing photographs with short captions. Further thematic analysis found that the photograph-captions and the article presented the two themes in completely different proportions. Some 73 per cent of the items in the article referred to losses under Hitler and 27 per cent to gains in a democracy, whereas 98 per cent of the photographs and captions referred to gains and only two per cent to the Hitler threat.

Now it so happens that a majority of the population, and particularly the Negro population with its lower educational level, generally prefer photographs and captions to a detailed text. They are more likely to look at the former than the latter. The photographs, in this case, almost wholly neglected the theme of Negro losses in the event of a Nazi victory. As a result, the pamphlet largely missed its mark. Certain attitudes of Negroes were tested both before and after they read the pamphlet. Most of the readers experienced pride and a higher ego-level as a result of this testimonial to the achievements and contributions of the race. But the pamphlet failed to canalize special motives for Negroes to push the fight against Nazism in their own interest, since readers had largely overlooked the essential message.

However cursorily, these two examples illustrate ways in which ordinary counts of key-symbols and thematic analysis enable us to discover inadvertent errors of the propagandist. They also serve as a guide to interviews with persons exposed to the propaganda. There are other types of content-analysis which can be briefly summarized:[1]

1. *Symbol-counts:* Consist of identifying and counting specified key-symbols in communications. This merely indicates, in a restricted fashion, the symbols which have been at the focus of attention of audiences. The count of references to the enemy in film commentaries illustrates this type.[2]

2. *One-dimensional classification of symbols:* This is a slight elaboration of the previous type. Symbols are classified according to whether they are employed, broadly speaking, in positive ("favorable") or negative ("unfavorable") contexts. Thus, Britain may be described in + terms (victorious, democratic, courageous) or in − terms (defeated, caste-ridden, perfidious). This type of analysis is a first step in determining the most effective distributions of symbols for reaching a given result. It may serve to check the often ineffectual practice of dealing in black-and-white contrasts. When applied to enemy propaganda, this kind of analysis provides one basis for gauging the relative security or insecurity of the enemy.[3]

3. *Item-analysis:* Classification of segments or sections of the propaganda (*e.g.,* scenes in a film; songs in a radio program; photographs in a pamphlet). This requires selection of significant and insignificant items on the basis of a psychological theory of "attention-value." Will these items tap central or peripheral interests of the audience? How will these items be interpreted by different types of audiences? In several analyses of films, it was possible to predict scenes and sequences which would be at the center of attention of audiences.

4. *Thematic analysis:* Classification of the explicit and implicit (symbolic) themes in propaganda material. This, as distinct from item-analysis, deals with the supposed cumulative significance of a series of items.[4]

5. *Structural analysis:* Concerned with the interrelations of the various themes in propaganda. These relations may be *complementary* (enemy is cruel, we are merciful); *integrated* (enemy is cruel, deceitful, aggressive, irreligious); *interfering* (when themes work at cross-purposes; *e.g.,* theme of Nazi strength produces anxiety.)[5]

6. *Campaign analysis:* Deals with the interrelations of different documents all of which are designed for a general over-all purpose. Whereas structural analysis deals with the relations *within* a single propaganda document, cam-

---

1. A thorough examination of the procedures of content analysis is now available: Bernard Berelson, *Content Analysis in Communications Research* (Glencoe, Illinois: The Free Press, 1951). See also H. D. Lasswell, "A provisional classification of symbol data," *Psychiatry,* 1938, 1, 197-204; Douglas Waples et al., *What Reading Does to People.* Appendix B, (Chicago, 1940); N. C. Leites & I. de Sola Pool. On content analysis. Experimental Division for the Study of Wartime Communications. Document No. 26. September, 1942.

2. See, for example, H. D. Lasswell, "The world attention survey," *Public Opinion Quarterly,* 1941, 3, 452-462.

3. For example, studies by Hans Speier & Ernst Kris, Research Project on Totalitarian Communication, at the New School for Social Research; an unpublished symbol-analysis of the "This Is War" radio series. Bureau of Applied Social Research, Columbia University.

4. For example, a study by Gregory Bateson of a Nazi propaganda film. See, also, Siegfried Kracauer, *Propaganda in the Nazi War Film* (New York: Museum of Modern Art Film Library, 1942).

5. For example, Kracauer, *op. cit.;* also film studies by the Bureau of Applied Social Research.

paign analysis deals with the relations of a series of such documents. Problems of sequence, duration, relative emphasis, timing, as well as the relations mentioned under structural analysis, are involved.[6]

From this summary, we see that a major task of content-analysis is to provide clues to probable responses to the propaganda. But this is not enough. We must see whether these anticipated responses actually occur, whether the content-analysis is essentially valid. This requires interviews with members of audiences; interviews of a special type, which we shall call the "focused interview."[7]

Incidentally, there is interaction between analyses of propaganda content and focused interviews with readers and listeners. A prior content-analysis is indispensable for helping to guide the interview and experience in interviewing sharpens your eye for more adequate content-analysis.

RESPONSE-ANALYSIS

Interviews designed to discover actual responses to propaganda seem, at first sight, a simple task. But in actual experience, it is not so at all. Use of the customary interviewing techniques does not suffice to obtain the needed information. Most people find it difficult to express their reactions to a film or radio program in terms which will be of use to the writer or producer or social scientist.

We have found that respondents fall into two broad classes. If they are highly articulate, they will usually express their advice on how the film "should be presented" or how the radio program "should be revised" to increase its effectiveness. They seek to act as professional critics or consultants, and this is precisely what we do not want. Interview tactics have had to be devised for the purpose of avoiding such consultant attitudes on the part of interviewees and of making it possible for them to report their own immediate responses to the propaganda.

For other subjects who find it difficult to report their responses at all, special interview techniques have been developed to enable them to render their experiences articulate. The entire interview is focused in terms of the propaganda material which is being tested. The interviewer's remarks do not direct attention toward definite aspects of the propaganda. They merely facilitate the respondents' reports of their own centers of attention and of their own reactions to those items which are significant for them. If the figure be permitted, the interviewer provides the respondent with a flashlight which illumines the traces of the film or radio program or printed material in the respondent's mind. It is only after the interviewees have fully reported their reactions to the aspects of the propaganda which they experienced most vividly that the inter-

---

6. For example, studies of political campaigns, public utility propaganda campaigns, bond drives, etc.

7. R. K. Merton, M. Fiske and P. L. Kendall, *The Focused Interview.*

viewer rounds out the discussion by checking these hypotheses derived from content-analysis which have not yet been considered in the interview. The entire interview is recorded verbatim by stenotypists. This permits a later intensive analysis of just which aspects of the propaganda elicited certain types of response.

In general, we may say that a focused interview is valuable according to the extent that it achieves the following objectives:

1. Determines the effective aspects of the propaganda to which the audience has responded.

2. Determines the many-sided nature of these responses in considerable detail.

3. Enables us to test whether the responses which we expected on the basis of content-analysis have actually occurred.

4. Discovers wholly unanticipated responses; that is, responses which were anticipated neither by the writer nor by the content-analyst.

Although all of these objectives of the interview are important, it is the last which is of special practical importance. You will remember our examples of the Negro pamphlet and of the radio talk on X-rays. These were intended to indicate to you that without a content- and response-analysis to aid him, the propagandist sometimes cannot see the forest for the trees. We should suggest, further, that often the propagandist cannot see the thorns for the rose. If a propagandist wishes to convey an idea or create a given impression, he must do it by words, illustrations or other symbols. Once his pamphlet, play, radio program or script is out in the world, it is for the audience to understand him as they will. The story is told of a missionary who pointed to a table and repeatedly said "table" until his audience of non-literates could repeat the word. After some time, he was dismayed to learn that some non-literates referred to a tree as "table," because both were brown. Others called dogs "tables" since both had four legs. In short, each listener had selected some aspect of the complex object, which for the missionary was so well designated as a whole by the word "table." In the same way, it is instructive to see how often the effects of propaganda can be totally unexpected.

The Boomerang Effect

The case we want to consider here is derived from the previously mentioned test of a health program. This had wide implications, should the government seek to maintain the educational and propagandistic functions which it has assumed in an effort to maintain morale during the war. Having had the experience of accepting some measure of government supervision, the American population may prove more receptive to the promotion of public health, nutrition and educational activities in the post-war period.

In this instance, it will be remembered, a representative of a county medical society broadcast a talk on X-rays. He stressed the precautions needed to prevent X-ray burns; he indicated that the local government protects the citizen by a system of licensing X-ray operators and by inspecting equipment; he emphasized the specialized training required to attain competence in this field. The speaker was evidently seeking to prevent his listeners from falling into the hands of quacks who have neither competence nor integrity. Professionally concerned with this problem, he apparently did not realize that his listeners had not accumulated experience comparable to his own. He neglected to integrate the problem into the experience-world of his audience.

It is well known from related fields of investigation that listeners cannot readily assimilate information and attitudes if these are not integrated with their backlog of experience. Had the physician described the procedures used by quacks for obtaining clients, or had he indicated how they might readily be recognized or, even, if he had presented figures on the presumed number of unlicensed operators in this field, his listeners might have assimilated his views and attitudes. Since he did not, he seemed to be pounding at open doors.

> He talked about licensed doctors but he didn't make it too clear. He never said what would happen to you if an unlicensed person did it.

As a result, listeners began to doubt the importance and, at times, the reality of the issue. The physician talked, as it were, into a psychological void which the listeners had somehow to structure for themselves. They had been told of the complexity of X-ray apparatus, and they used this newly acquired information to look at the problem in their own way.

> I don't think the warning is justified at all. Just anyone can't have an X-ray machine. General Electric probably wouldn't sell the equipment to anybody without a license.
> I couldn't conceive that anybody without a license would dare to buy such expensive machinery for about $10,000 only to be caught the next day by somebody who found he didn't have his license.

Possibly intending to meet this problem, the speaker went on to extol the merits of the specialist in general terms. A content-analysis found 63 references in 14 minutes to the conceptions of authority, licensing, and specialization. Since the talk raised issues which it failed to clarify, it led to a *boomerang effect*. The listener became more and more impatient and in the end challenged the X-ray expert himself.

> There are a good many cases where there is a licensed man and he doesn't use the X-ray just right.
> You can get an automobile license but that doesn't prove you can drive. In the same way these people can get a license but that doesn't prove they are competent.

The program stressed the value of proper training for X-ray specialists. But it assumed, erroneously, that listeners had the mental set necessary to identify licensing with appropriate skills. Consequently, the whole emphasis of the speaker led first to impatience, then to disbelief and finally to distrust.

Under certain conditions, then, people respond to propaganda in a fashion opposite to that intended by the author. In the course of our tests, we have found various types of such boomerangs, some of which may be mentioned here. The foregoing "specialist" boomerang illustrates a familiar type: *it results from an erroneous psychological appraisal of the state of mind of the audience.* Propaganda will not produce the expected response unless its content corresponds to the psychological wants of the audience. It is necessary, therefore, to have a continuing flow of intelligence information concerning prevalent attitudes and sentiments in the population, if propaganda is not to invite boomerangs. It is at this point that the familiar types of opinion polls and other mass observation studies are linked with detailed propaganda analysis.

We know, for instance, from public opinion polls that a large proportion of Americans believed, at a time when it was not remotely the case, that we had the largest army, the greatest production of war materials and had contributed most to victory over the Axis. Therefore, films which seek to emphasize the contributions of our allies must be especially designed not to feed this ethnocentrism. If we want to show what the British or the Russians or the Chinese have accomplished, sequences dealing with lend-lease aid or other American contributions must specifically and explicitly indicate the limits of such assistance. Otherwise, we shall find the indicated type of boomerang-effect, where a neglected psychological set of the audience deflects the film to ends other than those for which it was intended.

A second type of boomerang-effect is probably part of the irreducible minimum of boomerang-responses. *It arises from the dilemma confronting the writer who must address his propaganda to a psychologically heterogeneous audience, i.e., the members of which are in different states of mind on the given issue.* Material which is effective for one segment of the audience may produce opposite effects among another segment which is socially and psychologically different.

Let us take a case in point. A radio morale program, broadcast shortly after Pearl Harbor, contained two dominant themes. The first stressed the power and potentiality of the United Nations, being intended to combat defeatism. The second emphasized the strength of the enemy in an effort to combat complacency and over-confidence. The problem is clear enough. Is it not possible that emphasis on our strength will reinforce the complacency of those who are already complacent? And correlatively, that references to enemy strength will support the defeatism of those who are already defeatist?[8] To judge from interview materials, this is evidently what happened.

It is no easy task to avoid opposed reactions by different sections of the audience. It is further complicated by shifts and, it would sometimes seem, by mercurial shifts in the "state of the public mind," such that the prevalent outlook is at one time "complacent" and, at another, "acutely pessimistic." Once again, it appears that if "morale propaganda" is to be functionally appropriate to the situation, there must be a continuing intelligence concerning dominant emotional orientations of the population.

A third type of boomerang is perhaps more significant than the others, for it is one which can be largely eliminated on the basis of adequate propaganda analysis. This we may call the *structural boomerang, which results from different themes in the same piece of propaganda working at cross-purposes.* If the propagandist considers *separately* the several themes in his propaganda and ignores their social and psychological interrelations, he may find that his total propaganda document is ineffective in reaching his ends. Structural analysis of the relations between themes is necessary if this is to be avoided.

A hypothetical case, parallel in essentials to instances which have actually emerged in tests, may serve to illustrate the structural boomerang. Several films, produced before American entrance into the war, included two dominant themes, among others. The first of these emphasized the immense cruelty and sadism of the Nazis as well as their threat to our way of life; a theme vividly exemplified by scenes of mistreatment of civilians simply because of their political or religious convictions. In interviews, sequences such as these are found to evoke profoundly aggressive feelings on the part of many in the audience.

But curiously enough, such aggression directed against the Nazis does not necessarily lead a larger proportion of those who have seen these films than of those who have not to express their willingness for this country to enter the conflict. In fact, there may be at times a slight decrease in the numbers of the "film-group" as compared with the "control-group" who wish to intervene in the war. How does this come about?

On occasion, interview material will show that this apparent absence of effect so far as intervention is concerned derives from the fact that another theme in the film works at cross-purposes. This counteracting theme may stress the skill, experience and enormous size of the Nazi army, exemplifying these by detailed and vivid sequences of Nazi fighting men in action. A theme such as this may serve to elicit fears and anxieties about the prospect of Americans coping with armies as formidable as the Nazi, particularly since we had not yet built up our own forces.

---

8. In fact, there is some experimental evidence, however slight, that persons respond selectively in such manner as to reinforce their current attitudes and sentiments.

Thus, it may develop that the Nazi-strength theme which elicits fears may counteract the Nazi-cruelty theme which elicits aggression. Aggressive feelings may thus not be translated into a realistic desire to have this nation enter the conflict. Adequate structural analysis of such films would have indicated the likelihood that one theme in the film would inhibit the very effects deriving from another theme in the same film. Consequently, although each theme may be effective, as it were—the one in exciting hostility, the other in acquainting Americans with the might of the enemy—the net result with respect to willingness to have us intervene in the war may be nil.

This type of case not only illustrates a type of boomerang-response, but also shows how the focused interview enables us to supplement and enrich the value of the traditional controlled experiment, of the type mentioned at the outset of our discussion. The controlled experiment consists in having two closely matched groups of subjects, one of which has been exposed to the propaganda, the other of which has not. Certain attitudes and sentiments of the two groups are tested twice: once, before the experimental group has been exposed to the propaganda; again, at some time after it has been exposed. If the groups are indeed properly matched, differences in attitude between the two groups which are found in the second test can be ascribed to the propaganda. But let us suppose that, for some attitudes, there is no perceptible difference, as was the case with our subjects' attitude toward American intervention in the war. The controlled experiment will not tell us why there is no change. *Its results show only the net effect of the propaganda on this attitude and not the more intricate dynamics of response which led to this net effect.* But, as we have seen, the failure of the film may be due to the fact that two themes, each of which was effective, produced responses which cancelled each other out. The interview material thus enables us to provide a psychological explanation of responses which may not be registered in the experimental results.

A fourth type of boomerang should be briefly discussed, if only because it is so frequently found in propaganda. *This boomerang results from what we may call,* with due apologies to Whitehead, *the fallacy of misplaced exemplification.* Whenever propaganda deals with matters which are familiar at first-hand to the prospective audience, there is the risk that the particular examples chosen will not be considered representative by some in the audience who consult their own experience. The pamphlet dealing with Negroes and the war which we have previously discussed was largely devoted to the social and economic gains of Negroes under American democracy. This theme was exemplified for the most part by photographs of prominent Negroes, of improved housing conditions and the like. Some 40 per cent of a sample of Negroes discounted the entire pamphlet as "untrue," because of the marked discrepancy between their own experience and observations, on the one hand, and these "examples of progress," on the other.

It should be noted that the truth of the examples does not spare them from producing a boomerang response. The reader consults his own immediate experience and if this does not correspond to the examples contained in the document, he rejects these wholeheartedly. The distrust generated by such apparent discrepancies between "fact" and the "propaganda" tends to be generalized and directed toward the document as a whole.

Moreover, boomerang responses diffuse far beyond the persons who experience them initially. In discussing the document with others, the distrustful reader becomes, as it were, a source of contagious scepticism. He predisposes other potential readers toward the same distrustful attitude. Thus, content-analysis and response-analysis, which eliminate such bases for boomerang responses, serve an important prophylactic function.

Our account has perhaps included enough examples of propaganda analysis to help overcome a perennial difficulty with writers and producers of propaganda. The creative writer often cannot accept the notion that what he has conceived as a unique expression of an inspired moment could possibly be improved or even dealt with by what seems to him a rather mechanical testing procedure. But this is all beside the point. It is not assumed that we are getting at the mind of the artificers, the craftsmen, the artists who contrive this propaganda. It is not believed that our prosy analysis recaptures the deft rhetoric and impressive rhythms which enter into its dramatic effectiveness. It is agreed that we cannot readily teach them their craft. Creative ideas, whether expressed in words, sounds or pictures, cannot be manufactured synthetically.[9] But systematic research is needed to see whether propagandists have achieved their aims. Just as researchers cannot write acceptable scripts, so, we are convinced propagandists often cannot gauge the psychological effects of their products without using techniques such as we have described. It might even be conjectured that it is in the nature of this problem that the propagandist is bound to overlook some of the undesired implications of his work.

This may explain the frequency with which our tests uncover inadequacies which, it would seem, should have been anticipated. But, in

9. We should thus agree whole-heartedly with the views of Aldous Huxley on essentially this same issue. ". . . the man of letters does most of his work not by calculation, not by the application of formulas, but by aesthetic intuition. He has something to say, and sets it down in the words which he finds most satisfying aesthetically After the event comes the critic [read: propaganda analyst], who discovers that he was using a certain kind of literary device, which can be classified in its proper chapter of the cookery-book. The process is largely irreversible. Lacking talent, you cannot, out of the cookery-book, concoct a good work of art." "T. H. Huxley as a man of letters," Huxley Memorial Lecture, 1932, 28; also Remy de Gourmont, *La culture des idées,* 1900, 51.

fact, response-analysis is usually indispensable; it uncovers a host of other inadequacies which we cannot now discuss at any length. This extends to modes of presentation. For example, consider the technique fact, response-analysis is usually indispensable: it uncovers a host of which the radio has adapted from the movies, the quick shift of scenes corresponding to montage in visual presentations. We are confident, on the basis of tests, that this technique in general leads to obscurity for the average radio listener. Continuity is lost. They just don't know what it is all about. They lose interest. In much the same way, historical allusions often fall on deaf ears unless they are carefully explained.

Or consider the question of authenticity in the case of documentary films. Propagandists would probably be surprised to learn how often the audience questions the possibility of having an actual film of Hitler in his mountain retreat, or of the mountainous Goering in a conference room. The propagandist knows that it is a clip from a German film, but the audience does not. Distrust is engendered and spreads. In the same way we have found numerous errors of judgment in the use of radio narrators or of officials' speeches which outrun the endurance of the audience.

We have repeatedly emphasized the need for obtaining detailed evidence of responses to propaganda. As an aid toward this end, we have often used a device called the Program Analyzer. The device, so called because it was first used for radio tests, can also be used for any communication, such as a film, which develops along a time-dimension. The purpose of the Program Analyzer may be briefly explained. Interviews on responses to propaganda must of course be postponed until the film or radio program is over, since we do not wish to interrupt the normal flow of the audience's experience. How, then, can we help the audience to recall their responses to particular aspects of the material? Should the interviewer mention specific scenes or episodes, he would be determining the focus of attention. Moreover, the interviewer's description of the scene would also influence the respondent's account of his experience. The Program Analyzer serves to eliminate these limitations.

While watching a film or listening to a radio program, each subject presses a green button in his right hand whenever he likes what is being presented, and a red button in his left hand when he dislikes it. He does not press either button when he is "indifferent." These responses are recorded on a moving tape which is synchronized with the film or radio program. Thus, members of the audience register their approval or disapproval, *as they respond to the material.* Reasons for and details of these reactions are later determined by the type of focused interview to which we have referred.

Two advantages of this procedure are clear. In the first place, the audience itself selects the sections of the material which are significant enough to be made the object of a detailed interview. Each listener presents, as it were, a general running account of his own reactions by classifying the material into three groups: the items which affect him positively, negatively, or neutrally.

Secondly, the responses recorded on the tape can be cumulated for the audience as a whole to obtain a general "curve of response." This curve lends itself to statistical treatment, enabling us to determine the main sources of favorable and unfavorable response. Above all, it provides, together with prior content-analysis, an extremely useful guide to the focused interview.

TECHNOLOGICAL PROPAGANDA OR THE PROPAGANDA OF FACTS

This discussion has perhaps served its major purpose. It may have given you some conception of procedures used in the psychological analysis of propaganda. Now let us turn to some general conclusions which we have reached in the course of our work.

One of the most conspicuous responses which we observed in our tests is the pervasive distrust of propaganda exhibited by many people. Propaganditis has reached epidemic proportions. Any statement of values is likely to be tagged as "mere propaganda" and at once discounted. Direct expressions of sentiment are suspect. Comments such as the following are typical of the ubiquitous man in the street when he believes that others seek to sway him:

I just think it's too sappy to put over on an adult mind. To me it gave the opposite kind of a reaction than it was supposed to give me. I suppose they wanted to make you feel full of patriotism, but I think it gave me the opposite reaction.

And then at the end—whistling "The Star-Spangled Banner." Everybody believes in the flag, but they don't like it waved in front of their faces.

This distrust of sentiment will not surprise you. There appears to have been relatively little fanfare during the war. As the psychoanalyst, Ernst Kris, has put it, referring to our enemies as well as ourselves, "men went to war in sadness and silence."[10] Or, in the words of a subject in one of our tests:

In this present situation, we haven't seen the boys marching as we did in 1917. We haven't got the feeling of the situation.

What implications does this lack of collective outbursts of enthusiasm have for the propagandist who seeks to rally all support to the war effort?

Our observations suggest that such distrust is levelled primarily against propaganda which obviously seeks to sway or stir people by general appeals to sentiment. Efforts to excite diffuse emotions are dis-

10. It is interesting that, basing his discussion on quite different propaganda materials, Ernst Kris has independently come to much the same conclusions. See his instructive paper "Some problems of war propaganda," *The Psychoanalytic Quarterly* 1943, 12, 381-399.

counted. But this is only a partial scepticism. The same audiences which set up defenses against fervent appeals to patriotic sentiments show a readiness to accept the implications of another type of propaganda, which we may tentatively call *technological propaganda* or *the propaganda of facts*.

Again let us begin with observations made in the course of our own studies. We observed at once a central interest in *detailed circumstantial facts*. Facts are in the saddle. The following comment by a subject in one of our tests reflects this attitude:

A great many people [sic] don't like that rah-rah sort of patriotism that stirs you up. I [sic] like factual things.

This desire for specific, almost technological information, sometimes takes on naive forms, as can be seen from the following remark on a documentary film which stressed the strength of the Nazis:

I was really surprised. I mean I don't believe everything I have read in the papers. But what you actually see with your own eyes and is authentic, you have to believe.

One of the most effective scenes in the aforementioned radio morale program described in great detail how the speed of a convoy is not necessarily determined by the speed of the slowest boat. Wrapped in this layer of technical information was an effective implication that men in the merchant marine willingly sacrifice themselves for the common good. The moral contained in the facts—"surely my sacrifices do not match theirs"—could be accepted by those who would reject a direct appeal of the same type. Films showing battle scenes or bombings prove effective if they focus on the details of the operations rather than stressing the direct propaganda "message" for the audience. *The fact, not the propagandist, speaks.*

We may now ask: why the prevalent interest in "facts"? What are the functions of this interest? *The concrete incident, rich in circumstantial detail, serves as a prototype or model which helps orient people toward a part of the world in which they live. It has orientation-value.* For large sections of the population, the historical events which they experience are wholly bewildering. Nations which are enemies one day are allies the next. The future seems dark with despair or bright with promise. Many have not the time or capacity to understand the trends and the forces behind them, yet they sense how closely these are bound up with their lives. All this accentuates a powerful need for orientation. Concrete facts take on the role of models in terms of which more complicated events can be explained and understood.

Illustrations of this are numerous. Thus, one episode in a radio morale program made a notable impression on the audience: during the last war, Franklin Delano Roosevelt, then Assistant Secretary of the

Navy, accompanied a submarine crew on a trial run, immediately after a series of submarine disasters. This proved far more satisfying and effective than to be told directly of the courage and past experience of our President. It had an *integrating*, explanatory function.

He showed he wasn't a coward; that if the men were willing to go down, he was willing to go; and he's the best man to be president because he's been through the thing himself, and because of the things he's done.

So, too, when films indicate specifically the virtual absence of armored divisions in England after Dunkirk, this type of fact will effectively integrate a variety of discrete points. It will be mentioned repeatedly in interviews. It helps to crystallize, so to speak, the ingenuity and courage of the British in the face of such odds. It proves effective where direct evaluations of the British would evoke scepticism and doubt. *Facts which integrate and "explain" a general course of events comprise one impor- tant component of the propaganda of facts.*

We can make another general observation about the propaganda of facts. We have observed that a certain type of fact which contains the desired propaganda implications appears to be most effective. This is the *"startling fact,"* of the type exploited by "believe it or not" columns and by quiz programs. This is effective for at least three reasons. In the first place, it has great *attention-value*. The startling fact stands out as a "figure" against the "ground." Secondly, such tidbits of information have *diffusion-value*. They readily become part of the currency of conversa- tion and small-talk ("Did you know that . . ."). The propagandistic implications of these are thus often transmitted by word of mouth. Finally, these integrating startling facts have *confidence-value*. They are "cold," as idiom so aptly puts it. They are not likely to elicit the distrust which is so widely latent in the population.

The propaganda of facts has yet another characteristic which marks it off from propaganda which seeks to persuade by clarion calls and direct exhortation. The propaganda of facts does not seek so much to tell people where to go, but rather shows them the path they should choose to get there. It preserves the individual's sense of autonomy. *He* makes the decision. The decision is voluntary, not coerced. It is by in- direction, not by prescription, that the propaganda of facts operates. It has *guidance-value*. The cumulative force of facts carries its own mo- mentum, so to speak. It is virtually a syllogism with an implicit conclu- sion—a conclusion to be drawn by the audience, not by the propagandist. To take a case in point: a pamphlet was recently issued by a war agency, directed to the families of men in the armed service, for the purpose of persuading them not to repeat the contents of letters received from abroad. Little emphasis was placed on the theme that careless words cost lives and ships. Instead, the bulk of the pamphlet was devoted to a detailed description of the methods used by the enemy to construct their total information from bits and patches gathered by agents on different occasions and in different places. Tests showed that the pamphlet succeeded in driving the story home, by permitting the reader to draw the inevitable conclusions from this circumstantial array of facts. The voluntary drawing of conclusions has little likelihood of the aftermath of disillusionment which so often follows upon the propaganda of exhortation. The hammerlike blows of frenzied oratory may produce present acquiescence and later recriminations; autonomous decisions under the cumulative pressure of facts do not exact this price.

Interestingly enough, it appears that our enemies have also discovered the power of technological propaganda. This type of propaganda, as any other tool, may be abused as well as used. The pseudo-facts may supplant the fact. Several observers have commented on the Nazi "stage-managing" of reality. It is reported, for example, that prior to the invasion of Belgium, a German officer made an apparently forced landing in Belgium. On his person were found plans for an invasion quite unlike that actually intended. Or again, there is the case of the first night bombing of Berlin. It is said that the Nazis planted reports of great destruction in Berlin in Swiss and Swedish newspapers, accrediting them to the English. These accounts were rebroadcast over the German domestic radio and the local population was invited to look at the actual damage and see for themselves that the reports were untrue. In this way, probably, many people could not escape the conclusion that the British had lied. The effect of this type of self-indoctrination was probably considerably greater than if the German radio had directly denounced the veracity of the British.

In passing, it might be remarked that the logic of the propaganda of facts is not far removed from the logic of progressive education. It is typical in progressive schools that the teacher does not indicate what the children are to do and believe but rather creates situations which lead them to decide for themselves the conduct and beliefs which the teacher considers appropriate.

Your own experience will demonstrate that the propaganda of facts is not a "new" conception. We are concerned only with formulating this idea in terms which may be of some value in planning morale programs. Widespread distrust and scepticism pushed to the extreme of cynicism are corrosive forces. But, since they are here, they must be considered. If propaganda is restricted wholly to exhortation, it runs the risk of intensifying distrust. The propaganda of facts can be utilized to supplant cynicism with common understandings.

Nor do we suggest that exhortations are wholly a thing of the past. Common values and common attitudes still need to be established among a considerable part of the population if propaganda is to prove effective. But our observations may be useful to those of us who are concerned with a constructive post-war era. We should not wait until post-war problems press in upon us before we recognize that a re-integration of societies must, to some extent, draw upon the instrument of propaganda.

And, finally, we should not exaggerate the role of propaganda. In the long run, no propaganda can prevail if it runs counter to events and forces underlying these events, as the fascists have begun to discover. Propaganda is no substitute for social policy and social action, but it can serve to root both policy and action in the understandings of the people.

Part IV

STUDIES IN THE SOCIOLOGY OF SCIENCE

INTRODUCTION

P ART IV IS COMPRISED of five papers in the sociology of science,[1] a specialized field of research which can be regarded as a subdivision of the sociology of knowledge, dealing as it does with the social environment of that particular kind of knowledge which springs from and returns to controlled experiment or controlled observation.

In broadest outline, the subject-matter of the sociology of science is *the dynamic interdependence* between science, as an ongoing social activity giving rise to cultural and civilizational products, and the environing social structure. The *reciprocal* relations between science and society are the object of inquiry, as those who have seriously applied themselves to studies in the sociology of science have been forced to recognize. But until very recently, the reciprocity of these relations has received uneven attention, the impact of science upon society eliciting much notice, and the impact of society upon science, little.

Possibly because it is so readily apparent, the impact of science upon the social structure, particularly through its technological by-products, has long been the object of concern if not of systematic study. It is plain to see that science is a dynamic force of social change, though not always of changes foreseen and desired. From time to time, during the last century or so, even physical scientists have emerged from their laboratories to acknowledge, with pride and wonder, or to disown, with horror and shame, the social consequences of their work. The explosion over Hiroshima only verified what everyone knew. Science has social consequences.

But if the consequences of science for society have been long perceived, the consequences of diverse social structures for science have not. Very few physical scientists and not many more social scientists have paid attention to the diverse influences of social structure upon the rate of development, the foci of interest and, perhaps, upon the very content of science. It is difficult to say why there is this reluctance to explore the bearing of its social environment upon science. The reluctance may

---

1. For a thorough-going account of this field, see Bernard Barber, *Science and the Social Order* (Glencoe, Ill.: The Free Press, 1952); see also Bernard Barber and R. K. Merton, "Brief bibliography for the sociology of science," *Proceedings of the American Academy of Arts and Sciences*, May 1952, 80, 140-154.

come from the mistaken belief that to admit the sociological fact would be to jeopardize the autonomy of science. Perhaps it is believed that objectivity, so central a value in the ethos of science, is threatened by the fact that science is an organized social activity, that it presupposes support by society, that the measure of this support and the types of research for which it is given differ in different social structures, as does the recruitment of scientific talents. There may be something here of the sentiment that science remains the more pure and unsullied if it is implicitly conceived as developing in a social vacuum. Just as the word "politics" now carries for many the connotation of base corruption, so the phrase "social contexts of science" may connote for some physical scientists the intrusion of concerns alien to science-proper.

Or perhaps the reluctance comes from the equally mistaken belief that to recognize these connections of science and society is to impugn the disinterested motives of the scientist. Their recognition may seem to imply that the scientist seeks, first and foremost, not the advancement of knowledge but the aggrandizement of self. We have noted this familiar type of error at several points throughout this book: the error lies in mistaking the level of motivational analysis for the level of institutional analysis. As indicated in several of the chapters following, scientists may be most variously motivated—by a disinterested desire to learn, by hope of economic gain, by active (or, as Veblen calls it, by idle) curiosity, by aggression or competition, by egotism or altruism. But the same motives in different institutional settings take different social expressions, just as different motivations in a given institutional setting may take approximately the same social expression. In one institutional context, egoism may lead a scientist to advance a branch of science useful for the military arts; in another institutional context, egoism may lead him to work on researches with apparently no miltary use. To consider how and how far social structures canalize the direction of scientific research is not to arraign the scientist for his motives.

But events of history have succeeded where the studies and writings of social scientists have failed. The course of recent history has made it increasingly difficult, even for scientists secluded in their laboratories and rarely moving about in the larger civil and political society, any longer to neglect the fact that science itself is variously dependent on the social structure. To select but a few of these events, there was first the emergence of Nazi Germany with its dramatic impact upon the nature, quality, and direction of the science cultivated in that country. Rather than recognizing this as an extreme and therefore illuminating case of a more general relationship, rather than seeing this as testimony to the fact that science requires particular forms of social structure in order to follow out its own genius, some physical scientists put this down as an exceptional and pathological case, with no implications for the more general situation. During the war, however, the marshalling of the forces of science led more scientists to recognize the interplay between their science and social structure. And most recently, the politicizing of science in Soviet Russia has again led others to the same belated conclusion.

With these developments coming so hard on one another's heels as to seem almost one continuous event, many have come to recognize the connections between science and social structure who previously thought of these connections, if they thought of them at all, as a figment of Marxist sociology. (In his excellent little book, *On Understanding Science,* for example, James B. Conant still refers to "the interconnection between science and society" as a subject "about which so much has been said in recent years by our Marxist friends.") Now, as we have seen in Chapter XII at some length, Marx and Engels did indeed set forth a general conception of these interconnections, and deplored the practice of writing "the history of the sciences as if they had fallen from the skies." But since the time of Marx and Engels, there has been distressingly little empirical study of the relations between science and social structure. The same old historical illustrations, grown venerable with age and threadbare with use, have been periodically trotted out to indicate that technological need sometimes leads scientists to focus upon distinctive problems of research. Through such overconformity to the early conceptions of Marx and Engels, piety has been expressed and the *advancement* of social science has been limited. Or old quotations newly illustrated have been mistaken for research. A pattern of thought and writing has developed which would be appropriate, perhaps, for a religious group where changeless tradition is the thing and ancient revelation must remain intact. But this is scarcely a pattern appropriate to science, including social science, where the founding fathers are honored, not by zealous repetition of their early findings, but by extensions, modifications and, often enough, by rejections of some of their ideas and findings. In the sociology of science, as in other fields, we can profitably return to the wisdom of Whitehead's apothegm: "a science which hesitates to forget its founders is lost."

There is ample institutional evidence of this failure to follow up through empirical research the numerous and now widely recognized problems of the relations between science and the social structure: nowhere among the universities of this country is there an Institute for Research on the Social Relations of Science.

It is to these relations between science and its social environment that the last five chapters of this book are devoted. Written at various times over a period of years, these papers have two main objectives. They seek, first, to trace out the varied modes of interdependence of science and the social structure, treating science itself as a social institution diversely related to the other institutions of the time. And second, they attempt a functional analysis of this interdependence, with special reference to points of integration and malintegration.

Chapter XV sets forth types of linkage between social structure and the development of science, centering particularly on those societies with a highly centralized political core. It traces the points of strain between the institutional norms of science and the institutional norms of political dictatorship. So, too, it indicates the strains, developing in less centralized societies such as our own, between the high evaluation of science and its present utilization for military purposes and for new productive equipment which is sometimes so introduced as to make for unemployment. It develops the suggestion that such social consequences of the present employment of science are laying the groundwork for a revolt against science, however misplaced in the choice of its object this revolt might be. Among the reasons for this hostility toward science is the one expressed in a sentence which a short time ago seemed dubiously figurative and now seems more nearly literal: "Science is held largely responsible for endowing those engines of human destruction which, it is said, may plunge our civilization into everlasting night and confusion."

Chapter XVI consists of a paper complementary to Chapter XV, dealing with the relations between science and a democratic social order. The ethos of the social institution of science is taken to include universalistic criteria of scientific validity and scientific worth, thus involving values easily integrated with the values of a free society in which it is men's capacities and achievements which matter, not their ascribed status or origins. Another component of the ethos of science is 'communism,' in the special sense that the institutional norms of science would make its products part of the public domain, shared by all and owned by none. The strains between this element of the ethos, with its insistence that knowledge must be made available to all equipped to assimilate that knowledge, and the requirement of secrecy, often enjoined by the military and sometimes by economic agencies, are briefly traced. Here again, the recent course of history has made these institutional analyses anything but academic and remote from the affairs of everyday life. Instead, the strains increase and become visible to all. Thus, for example, Karl T. Compton, dedicating in 1949 new research facilities at a Naval Ordnance Laboratory, finds it necessary to remind his hearers: "Unfortunately, secrecy and progress are mutually incompatible. This is always true of science, whether for military purposes or otherwise. Science flourishes and scientists make progress in an atmosphere of free inquiry and free interchange of ideas, with the continued mutual stimulation of active minds working in the same or related fields. Any imposition of secrecy in science is like application of a brake to progress."

Chapter XVII follows out one implication in the preceding chapters to the effect that the economic by-products of science, in the shape of new technologies and productive equipments, react upon the social status of science, and presumably upon its subsequent development. This paper is partly an inquiry into sources of public images of science: of what science seems to do to and for people. There are indications that the social repute of science for the great majority rests upon its manifest and powerful technological by-products. But with the failure to plan the orderly introduction of these advances in technology, many workers find themselves suffering from displacement, obsolescence of skills, discontinuities in employment or prolonged unemployment. This, too, may affect the popular estimate of science. And by adopting the role of technicians, of experts in a subaltern role taking their instructions from executives, engineers and technologists find it possible to abjure all concern with the social consequences of diverse methods of introducing technological change.

Representing two kinds of empirical studies in the sociology of science, the last chapters of this book were the first to be written. Chapter XVIII is devoted to some of the sociological bases for the support of science as a social institution, as this took shape in England of the seventeenth century. It seizes upon and attempts to test an insight implied by Max Weber's hypothesis of the relations between early ascetic Protestantism and capitalism, namely, that this same ascetic Protestantism helped motivate and canalize the activities of men in the direction of experimental science. This is the historical form of the hypothesis. In its more general and analytical form, it holds that science, like all other social institutions, must be supported by the values of the group if it is to develop. There is, consequently, not the least paradox in finding that even so rational an activity as scientific research is grounded on nonrational values. This early excursion into the research problem of the sociological roots of interest in science needs, of course, to be amplified, supplemented, and corrected by other empirical studies for other times and places. Out of such comparative studies there is bound to develop a more substantial understanding of this important sector of the sociology of science.

As the social institution of science becomes securely established, what are the determinants, other than wholly scientific, of the foci of research interest and the selection of problems? It is to this question that the final chapter is addressed, again with England as the place and the seventeenth century as the time. Since this paper first appeared, controversy has grown hot and heavy around the misleading and sterile question of whether the selection of problems for scientific research is or is not affected by practical (economic and technologic) needs of the time. It is the enthusiasts in both camps who succeed in converting a problem of sociological research into political slogans in which the answers are in before the hard work of the inquiry is begun. The significant problem, after all, is not whether such practical influences on the course of scientific development have *ever* occurred, or whether they have *always* proved determining. It is, instead, a matter of multiple questions, each demanding long patient study rather than short impatient answers: to what extent have these influences operated in different times and places? under which sociological conditions do they prove greater and under which, less determining? are they more characteristically found in the early stages of a scientific discipline? what are the diverse consequences, both for the science and for the social structure, of the several patterns through which problems are adopted for research?

As materials bearing upon questions of this order accumulate, another sector of the sociology of science will gain in solid substance. The last chapter of this book is intended to provide a few such materials for a brief period in the early days of science in England.

XV

SCIENCE AND THE
SOCIAL ORDER[1]

About the turn of the century, Max Weber observed that "the belief in the value of scientific truth is not derived from nature but is a product of definite cultures."[2] We may now add: and this belief is readily transmuted into doubt or disbelief. The persistent development of science occurs only in societies of a certain order, subject to a peculiar complex of tacit presuppositions and institutional constraints. What is for us a normal phenomenon which demands no explanation and secures many self-evident cultural values, has been in other times and still is in many places abnormal and infrequent. The continuity of science requires the active participation of interested and capable persons in scientific pursuits. This support of science is assured only by appropriate cultural conditions. It is, then, important to examine those controls which motivate scientific careers, which select and give prestige to certain scientific disciplines and reject or blur others. It will become evident that changes in institutional structure may curtail, modify or possibly prevent the pursuit of science.[3]

SOURCES OF HOSTILITY TOWARD SCIENCE

Hostility toward science may arise under at least two sets of conditions, although the concrete systems of values—humanitarian, economic, political, religious—upon which it is based may vary considerably. The first involves the logical, though not necessarily correct, conclusion that the results or methods of science are inimical to the satisfaction of important values. The second consists largely of non-logical elements. It rests upon the feeling of incompatibility between the sentiments em-

---

1. Read at the American Sociological Society Conference, December 1937. The writer is indebted to Professor Read Bain, Professor Talcott Parsons, Dr. E. Y. Hartshorne and Dr. E. P. Hutchinson for their helpful suggestions.

2. Max Weber, *Gesammelte Aufsätze zur Wissenschaftslehre*, 213; cf. Sorokin, *Social and Cultural Dynamics*, esp. II, Chap. 2.

3. Cf. Merton, *Science, Technology and Society in Seventeenth Century England*, Chap. XI.

bodied in the scientific ethos and those found in other institutions. When ever this feeling is challenged, it is rationalized. Both sets of conditions underlie, in varying degrees, current revolts against science. It might be added that such reasoning and affective responses are also involved in the social approval of science. But in these instances science is thought to facilitate the achievement of approved ends, and basic cultural values are felt to be congruent with those of science rather than emotionally inconsistent with them. The position of science in the modern world may be analyzed, then, as a resultant of two sets of contrary forces, approving and opposing science as a large-scale social activity.

We restrict our examination to a few conspicuous instances of certain revaluation of the social role of science, without implying that the anti-science movement is in any sense thus localized. Much of what is said here can probably be applied to the cases of other times and places.[4]

The situation in Nazi Germany since 1933 illustrates the ways in which logical and non-logical processes converge to modify or curtail scientific activity. In part, the hampering of science is an unintended by-product of changes in political structure and nationalistic credo. In accordance with the dogma of race purity, practically all persons who do not meet the politically imposed criteria of 'Aryan' ancestry and of avowed sympathy with Nazi aims have been eliminated from universities and scientific institutes.[5] Since these outcasts include a considerable number of eminent scientists, one indirect consequence of the racialist purge is the weakening of science in Germany.

Implicit in this racialism is a belief in race defilement through actual or symbolic contact.[6] Scientific research by those of unimpeachable 'Aryan' ancestry who collaborate with non-Aryans or who even accept their scientific theories is either restricted or proscribed. A new racial-political category has been introduced to include these incorrigible Aryans: the category of 'White Jews.' The most prominent member of this new race is the Nobel Prize physicist, Werner Heisenberg, who has persisted in his declaration that Einstein's theory of relativity constitutes an "obvious basis for further research."[7]

---

4. The premature death of E. Y. Hartshorne halted a proposed study of science in the modern world in terms of the analysis introduced in this chapter.

5. See Chapter III of E. Y. Hartshorne, *The German Universities and National Socialism* (Cambridge: Harvard University Press, 1937), on the purge of the universities; cf. *Volk und Werden*, 5, 1937, 320-1, which refers to some of the new requirements for the doctorate.

6. This is one of many phases of the introduction of a caste system in Germany. As R. M. MacIver has observed, "The idea of defilement is common in every caste system." *Society*, 172.

7. Cf. the official organ of the SS, the *Schwarze Korps*, July 15, 1937, 2. In this issue Johannes Stark, the president of the Physikalisch-Technische Reichsanstalt, urges elimination of such collaborations which still continue and protests the appointment of three university professors who have been 'disciples' of non-Aryans. See also Hartshorne, *op. cit.*, 112-3; Alfred Rosenberg, *Wesen, Grundsätze und Ziele der*

In these instances, the sentiments of national and racial purity have clearly prevailed over utilitarian rationality. The application of such criteria has led to a greater proportionate loss to the natural science and medical faculties in German universities than to the theological and juristic faculties, as E. Y. Hartshorne has found.[8] In contrast, utilitarian considerations are foremost when it comes to official policies concerning the directions to be followed by scientific research. Scientific work which promises direct practical benefit to the Nazi party or the Third Reich is to be fostered above all, and research funds are to be re-allocated in accordance with this policy.[9] The rector of Heidelberg University announces that "the question of the scientific significance [*Wissenschaft-lichkeit*] of any knowledge is of quite secondary importance when compared with the question of its utility."[10]

The general tone of anti-intellectualism, with its depreciation of the theorist and its glorification of the man of action,[11] may have long-run rather than immediate bearing upon the place of science in Germany. For should these attitudes become fixed, the most gifted elements of the population may be expected to shun those intellectual disciplines which have thus become disreputable. By the late 30's, effects of this anti-theoretical attitude could be detected in the allocation of academic interests in the German universities.[12]

It would be misleading to suggest that the Nazi government has

Nationalsozialistischen Deutschen Arbeiterpartei, (München: E. Boepple, 1933), 45 ff.; J. Stark, "Philipp Lenard als deutscher Naturforscher," *Nationalsozialistische Monatshefte,* 1936, 71, 106-11, where Heisenberg, Schrödinger, von Laue and Planck are castigated for not having divorced themselves from the 'Jewish physics' of Einstein.

8. The data upon which this statement is based are from an unpublished study by E. Y. Hartshorne.

9. *Cf. Wissenschaft und Vierjahresplan,* Reden anlässlich der Kundgebung des NSD-Dozentenbundes, January 18, 1937; Hartshorne, *op. cit.,* 110 ff.; E. R. Jaensch, *Zur Neugestaltung des deutschen Studententums und der Hochschule,* (Leipzig, J. A. Bart, 1937), esp. 57 ff. In the field of history, for example, Walter Frank, the director of the Reichsinstitut für Geschichte des neuen Deutschlands, "the first German scientific organization which has been created by the spirit of the national-socialistic revolution," testifies that he is the last person to forego sympathy for the study of ancient history, "even that of foreign peoples," but also points out that the funds previously granted the Archaeological Institute must be re-allocated to this new historical body which will "have the honor of writing the history of the National Socialist Revolution." See his *Zukunft und Nation,* (Hamburg, Hanseatische Verlags-anstalt, 1935), esp. 30 ff.

10. Ernst Krieck, *Nationalpolitische Erziehung,* (Leipzig, Armanen Verlag, 1935), (19th Printing), 8.

11. The Nazi theoretician, Alfred Baeumler, writes: "Wenn ein Student heute es ablehnt, sich der politischen Norm zu unterstellen, es z. B ablehnt, an einem Arbeits- oder Wehrsportlager teilzunehmen, weil er damit Zeit für sein Studium versäume, dann zeigt er damit, dass er nichts von dem begriffen hat, was um ihn geschieht. Seine Zeit kann er nur bei einem abstrakten, richtungslosen Studium versäumen." *Männerbund und Wissenschaft,* (Berlin, Junker & Dünnhaupt, 1934), 153.

12. Hartshorne, *op. cit.,* 106 ff.; *cf. Wissenschaft und Vierjahresplan, op. cit.,* 25-6, where it is stated that the present "breathing-spell in scientific productivity" is partly due to the fact that a considerable number of those who might have received

completely repudiated science and intellect. The official attitudes toward science are clearly ambivalent and unstable. (For this reason, any statements concerning science in Nazi Germany are made under correction.) On the one hand, the challenging scepticism of science interferes with the imposition of a new set of values which demand an unquestioning acquiescence. But the new dictatorships must recognize, as did Hobbes who also argued that the State must be all or nothing, that science is power. For military, economic and political reasons, theoretical science —to say nothing of its more respectable sibling, technology—cannot be safely discarded. Experience has shown that the most esoteric researches have found important applications. Unless utility and rationality are dismissed beyond recall, it cannot be forgotten that Clerk Maxwell's speculations on the ether led Hertz to the discovery that culminated in the wireless. And indeed one Nazi spokesman remarks: "As the practice of today rests on the science of yesterday, so is the research of today the practice of tomorrow."[13] Emphasis on utility requires an unbanishable minimum of interest in science which can be enlisted in the service of the State and industry.[14] At the same time, this emphasis leads to a limitation of research in pure science.

SOCIAL PRESSURES ON AUTONOMY OF SCIENCE

An analysis of the role of science in the Nazi state uncovers the following elements and processes. The spread of domination by one segment of the social structure—the State—involves a demand for primary loyalty to it. Scientists, as well as all others, are called upon to relinquish adherence to all institutional norms which, in the opinion of political authorities, conflict with those of the State.[15] The norms of the scientific ethos must be sacrificed, in so far as they demand a repudiation of the politically imposed criteria of scientific validity or of scientific worth. The expansion of political control thus introduces conflicting loyalties. In this respect, the reactions of devout Catholics who resist the efforts of the political authority to redefine the social structure, to encroach upon the preserves which are traditionally those of religion, are of the same order as the resistance of the scientist. From the sociological point of view, the place of science in the totalitarian world is largely the same

---

scientific training have been recruited by the army. Although this is a dubious explanation of that particular situation, a prolonged deflection of interest from theoretical science will probably produce a decline in scientific achievements.

13. Professor Thiessen in *Wissenschaft und Vierjahresplan, op. cit.*, 12.

14. For example, chemistry is highly prized because of its practical importance. As Hitler put it, "we will carry on because we have the fanatic will to help ourselves and because in Germany we have the chemists and inventors who will fulfil our needs." Quoted in *Wissenschaft und Vierjahresplan, op. cit.*, 6; *et passim.*

15. This is clearly put by Reichswissenschaftsminister Bernhard Rust, *Das nationalsozialistische Deutschland und die Wissenschaft*, (Hamburg, Hanseatische Verlagsanstalt, 1936), 1-22, esp. 21.

as that of all other institutions except the newly-dominant State. The basic change consists in placing science in a new social context where it appears to compete at times with loyalty to the state. Thus, coöperation with non-Aryans is redefined as a symbol of political disloyalty. In a liberal order, the limitation of science does not arise in this fashion. For in such structures, a substantial sphere of autonomy—varying in extent, to be sure—is enjoyed by non-political institutions.

The conflict between the totalitarian state and the scientist derives in part, then, from an incompatibility between the ethic of science and the new political code which is imposed upon all, irrespective of occupational creed. The ethos of science[16] involves the functionally necessary demand that theories or generalizations be evaluated in terms of their logical consistency and consonance with facts. The political ethic would introduce the hitherto irrelevant criteria of the race or political creed of the theorist.[17] Modern science has considered the personal equation as a potential source of error and has evolved impersonal criteria for checking such error. It is now called upon to assert that certain scientists, because of their extra-scientific affiliations, are *a priori* incapable of anything but spurious and false theories. In some instances, scientists are required to accept the judgments of scientifically incompetent political leaders concerning *matters of science*. But such politically advisable tactics run counter to the institutionalized norms of science. These, however, are dismissed by the totalitarian state as 'liberalistic' or 'cosmopolitan' or 'bourgeois' prejudices,[18] inasmuch as they cannot be readily integrated with the campaign for an unquestioned political creed.

---

16. The ethos of science refers to an emotionally toned complex of rules, prescriptions, mores, beliefs, values and presuppositions which are held to be binding upon the scientist. Some phases of this complex may be methodologically desirable, but observance of the rules is not dictated solely by methodological considerations. This ethos, as social codes generally, is sustained by the sentiments of those to whom it applies. Transgression is curbed by internalized prohibitions and by disapproving emotional reactions which are mobilized by the supporters of the ethos. Once given an effective ethos of this type, resentment, scorn and other attitudes of antipathy operate almost automatically to stabilize the existing structure. This may be seen in the current resistance of scientists in Germany to marked modifications in the content of this ethos. The ethos may be thought of as the "cultural" as distinct from the "civilizational" component of science. *Cf.* R. K. Merton, "Civilization and culture," *Sociology and Social Research*, 1936, 21, 103-113.

17. *Cf.* Baeumler, *op. cit.*, 145. Also Krieck (*op. cit.*), who states: "Nicht alles, was den Anspruch auf Wissenschaftlichkeit erheben darf, liegt auf der gleichen Rang- und Wertebene; protestantische und katholische, französische und deutsche, germanische und jüdische, humanistische oder rassische Wissenschaft sind zunächst nur Möglichkeiten, noch nicht erfüllte oder gar gleichrangige Werte. Die Entscheidung über den Wert der Wissenschaft fällt aus ihrer 'Gegenwärtigkeit,' aus dem Grad ihrer Fruchtbarkeit, ihrer geschichtsbildenden Kraft. . . ."

18. Thus, says Ernst Krieck: "In the future, one will no more adopt the fiction of an enfeebled neutrality in science than in law, economy, the State or public life generally. The method of science is indeed only a reflection of the method of government." *Nationalpolitische Erziehung*, 6. *Cf.* Baeumler, *op. cit.*, 152; Frank, *Zukunft und Nation*, 10; and contrast with Max Weber's "prejudice" that "Politik gehört nicht in den Hörsaal."

From a broader perspective, the conflict is a phase of institutional dynamics. Science, which has acquired a considerable degree of autonomy and has evolved an institutional complex which engages the allegiance of scientists, now has both its traditional autonomy and its rules of the game—its ethos, in short—challenged by an external authority. The sentiments embodied in the ethos of science—characterized by such terms as intellectual honesty, integrity, organized scepticism, disinterestedness, impersonality—are outraged by the set of new sentiments which the State would impose in the sphere of scientific research. With a shift from the previous structure where limited loci of power are vested in the several fields of human activity to a structure where there is one centralized locus of authority over all phases of behavior, the representatives of each sphere act to resist such changes and to preserve the original structure of pluralistic authority. Although it is customary to think of the scientist as a dispassionate, impersonal individual—and this may not be inaccurate as far as his technical activity is concerned—it must be remembered that the scientist, in company with all other professional workers, has a large emotional investment in his way of life, defined by the institutional norms which govern his activity. The social stability of science can be ensured only if adequate defences are set up against changes imposed from outside the scientific fraternity itself.

This process of preserving institutional integrity and resisting new definitions of social structure which may interfere with the autonomy of science finds expression in yet another direction. It is a basic assumption of modern science that scientific propositions "are invariant with respect to the individual" and group.[19] But in a completely politicized society—where as one Nazi theorist put it, "the universal meaning of the political is recognized"[20]—this assumption is impugned. Scientific findings are held to be merely the expression of race or class or nation.[21] As such doctrines percolate to the laity, they invite a general distrust of science and a depreciation of the prestige of the scientist, whose discoveries appear arbitrary and fickle. This variety of anti-intellectualism which threatens his social position is characteristically enough resisted by the scientist. On the ideological front as well, totalitarianism entails a conflict with the traditional assumptions of modern science.

---

19. H. Levy, *The Universe of Science,* (New York, Century Co., 1933), 189.

20. Baeumler, *Männerbund und Wissenschaft,* 152.

21. It is of considerable interest that totalitarian theorists have adopted the radical relativistic doctrines of *Wissenssoziologie* as a political expedient for discrediting 'liberal' or 'bourgeois' or 'non-Aryan' science. An exit from this cul-de-sac is provided by positing an Archimedean point: the infallibility of *der Führer* and his *Volk*. (*Cf.* General Hermann Goering, *Germany Reborn,* (London, Mathews & Marrot, 1934, 79). Politically effective variations of the 'relationism' of Karl Mannheim (e.g. *Ideology and Utopia*) have been used for propagandistic purposes by such Nazi theorists as Walter Frank, Krieck, Rust, and Rosenberg.

FUNCTIONS OF NORMS OF PURE SCIENCE

One sentiment which is assimilated by the scientist from the very outset of his training pertains to the purity of science. Science must not suffer itself to become the handmaiden of theology or economy or state. The function of this sentiment is likewise to preserve the autonomy of science. For if such extra-scientific criteria of the value of science as presumable consonance with religious doctrines or economic utility or political appropriateness are adopted, science becomes acceptable only in so far as it meets these criteria. In other words, as the pure science sentiment is eliminated, science becomes subject to the direct control of other institutional agencies and its place in society becomes increasingly uncertain. The persistent repudiation by scientists of the application of utilitarian norms to their work has as its chief function the avoidance of this danger, which is particularly marked at the present time. A tacit recognition of this function may be the source of that possibly apocryphal toast at a dinner for scientists in Cambridge: To pure mathematics, and may it never be of any use to anybody!

The exaltation of pure science is thus seen to be a defence against the invasion of norms which limit directions of potential advance and threaten the stability and continuance of scientific research as a valued social activity. Of course, the technological criterion of scientific achievement has also a positive social function for science. The increasing comforts and conveniences deriving from technology and ultimately from science invite the social support of scientific research. They also testify to the integrity of the scientist, since abstract and difficult theories which cannot be understood or evaluated by the laity are presumably proved in a fashion which can be understood by all, *i.e.,* through their technological applications. Readiness to accept the authority of science rests, to a considerable extent, upon its daily demonstration of power. Were it not for such indirect demonstrations, the continued social support of that science which is intellectually incomprehensible to the public would hardly be nourished on faith alone.

At the same time, this stress upon the purity of science has had other consequences which threaten rather than preserve the social esteem of science. It is repeatedly urged that scientists should in their research ignore all considerations other than the advance of knowledge.[22] Atten-

---

22. For example, Pareto writes: "The quest for experimental uniformities is an end in itself." See a typical statement by George A. Lundberg. "It is not the business of a chemist who invents a high explosive to be influenced in his task by considerations as to whether his product will be used to blow up cathedrals or to build tunnels through the mountains. Nor is it the business of the social scientist in arriving at laws of group behavior to permit himself to be influenced by considerations of how his conclusions will coincide with existing notions, or what the effect of his findings on the social order will be." *Trends in American Sociology,* (edited by G. A.

tion is to be focused exclusively on the scientific significance of their work with no concern for the practical uses to which it may be put or for its social repercussions generally. The customary justification of this tenet—which is partly rooted in fact[23] and which, in any event, has definite social functions, as we have just seen—holds that failure to adhere to this injunction will encumber research by increasing the possibility of bias and error. But this *methodological* view overlooks the *social* results of such an attitude. The objective consequences of this attitude have furnished a further basis of revolt against science; an incipient revolt which is found in virtually every society where science has reached a high stage of development. Since the scientist does not or cannot control the direction in which his discoveries are applied, he becomes the subject of reproach and of more violent reactions in so far as these applications are disapproved by the agents of authority or by pressure groups. The antipathy toward the technological products is projected toward science itself. Thus, when newly discovered gases or explosives are applied as military instruments, chemistry as a whole is censured by those whose humanitarian sentiments are outraged. Science is held largely responsible for endowing those engines of human destruction which, it is said, may plunge our civilization into everlasting night and confusion. Or to take another prominent instance, the rapid development of science and related technology has led to an implicitly anti-science movement by vested interests and by those whose sense of economic justice is offended. The eminent Sir Josiah Stamp and a host of less illustrious folk have proposed a moratorium on invention and discovery,[24] in order that man may have a breathing spell in which to adjust his social

Lundberg, R. Bain and N. Anderson), (New York, Harper, 1929), 404-5. Compare the remarks of Read Bain on the "Scientist as Citizen," *Social Forces*, 1933, 11, 412-15.

23. A neurological justification of this view is to be found in E. D. Adrian's essay in *Factors Determining Human Behavior*, (Harvard Tercentenary Publications, Cambridge, 1937), 9. "For discriminative behavior . . . there must be some interest: yet if there is too much the behavior will cease to be discriminative. Under intense emotional stress the behavior tends to conform to one of several stereotyped patterns."

24. Of course, this does not constitute a movement opposed to science as such. Moreover, the destruction of machinery by labor and the suppression of inventions by capital have also occurred in the past. Cf. R. K. Merton, "Fluctuations in the rate of industrial invention," *Quarterly Journal of Economics*, 1935, 49, 464 ff. But this movement mobilizes the opinion that science is to be held strictly accountable for its social effects. Sir Josiah Stamp's suggestion may be found in his address to the British Association for the Advancement of Science, Aberdeen, 6 Sept. 1934. Such moratoria have also been proposed by M. Caillaux (*cf.* John Strachey, *The Coming Struggle for Power*, (New York: 1935, 183), by H. W. Sumners in the U. S. House of Representatives, and by many others. In terms of current humanitarian, social and economic criteria, some of the products of science are more pernicious than beneficial. This evaluation may destroy the rationale of scientific work. As one scientist pathetically put it: if the man of science must be apologetic for his work, I have wasted my life. Cf. *The Frustration of Science* (ed. by F. Soddy), (New York: Norton, 1935), 42 *et passim*.

and economic structure to the constantly changing environment with which he is presented by the "embarrassing fecundity of technology." These proposals have received wide publicity in the press and have been urged with unslackened insistence before scientific bodies and governmental agencies.[25] The opposition comes equally from those representatives of labor who fear the loss of investment in skills which become obsolete before the flood of new technologies and from the ranks of those capitalists who object to the premature obsolescence of their machinery. Although these proposals probably will not be translated into action within the immediate future, they constitute one possible nucleus about which a revolt against science in general may materialize. It is largely immaterial whether these opinions which make science ultimately responsible for undesirable situations are valid or not. W. I. Thomas' sociological theorem—"If men define situations as real, they are real in their consequences"—has been repeatedly verified.

In short, this basis for the re-valuation of science derives from what I have called elsewhere the "imperious immediacy of interest."[26] Concern with the primary goal, the furtherance of knowledge, is coupled with a disregard of those consequences which lie outside the area of immediate interest, but these social results react so as to interfere with the original pursuits. Such behavior may be rational in the sense that it may be expected to lead to the satisfaction of the immediate interest. But it is irrational in the sense that it defeats other values which are not, at the moment, paramount but which are none the less an integral part of the social scale of values. Precisely because scientific research is not conducted in a social vacuum, its effects ramify into other spheres of value and interest. In so far as these effects are deemed socially undesirable, science is charged with responsibility. The goods of science are no longer considered an unqualified blessing. Examined from this perspective, the tenet of pure science and disinterestedness has helped to prepare its own epitaph.

---

25. English scientists have especially reacted against the "prostitution of scientific effort to war purposes." Presidential addresses at annual meetings of the British Association for the Advancement of Science, frequent editorials and letters in *Nature* attest to this movement for "a new awareness of social responsibility among the rising generation of scientific workers." Sir Frederick Gowland Hopkins, Sir John Orr, Professor Soddy, Sir Daniel Hall, Dr. Julian Huxley, J. B. S. Haldane and Professor L. Hogben are among the leaders of the movement. See, for example, the letter signed by twenty-two scientists of Cambridge University urging a program for dissociating science from warfare (*Nature*, 137, 1936, 829). These attempts for concerted action by English scientists contrast sharply with the apathy of scientists in this country toward these questions. (This observation holds for the period prior to the development of atomic weapons.) The basis of this contrast might profitably be investigated. In any event, although this movement may possibly derive from the sentiments, it may serve the function of eliminating one source of hostility toward science in democratic regimes.

26. Merton, "The unanticipated consequences of purposive social action," *op. cit.*

Battle lines are drawn in terms of the question: can a good tree bring forth evil fruit? Those who would cut down or stunt the tree of knowledge because of its accursed fruit are met with the claim that the evil fruit has been grafted on the good tree by the agents of state and economy. It may salve the conscience of the individual man of science to hold that an inadequate social structure has led to the perversion of his discoveries. But this will hardly satisfy an embittered opposition. Just as the *motives* of scientists may range from a passionate desire in the furtherance of knowledge to a profound interest in achieving personal fame and just as the *functions* of scientific research may vary from providing prestige-laden rationalizations of the existing order to enhancing our control of nature, so may other social *effects* of science be considered pernicious to society or result in the modification of the scientific ethos itself. There is a tendency for scientists to assume that the social effects of science *must* be beneficial in the long run. This article of faith performs the function of providing a rationale for scientific research, but it is manifestly not a statement of fact. It involves the confusion of truth and social utility which is characteristically found in the non-logical penumbra of science.

ESOTERIC SCIENCE AS POPULAR MYSTICISM

Another relevant phase of the connections between science and the social order has seldom been recognized. With the increasing complexity of scientific research, a long program of rigorous training is necessary to test or even to understand the new scientific findings. The modern scientist has necessarily subscribed to a cult of unintelligibility. There results an increasing gap between the scientist and the laity. The layman must take on faith the publicized statements about relativity or quanta or other such esoteric subjects. This he has readily done in as much as he has been repeatedly assured that the technologic achievements from which he has presumably benefited ultimately derive from such research. Nonetheless, he retains a certain suspicion of these bizarre theories. Popularized and frequently garbled versions of the new science stress those theories which seem to run counter to common sense. To the public mind, science and esoteric terminology become indissolubly linked. The presumably scientific pronouncements of totalitarian spokesmen on race or economy or history are for the uninstructed laity of the same order as announcements concerning an expanding universe or wave mechanics. In both instances, the laity is in no position to understand these conceptions or to check their scientific validity and in both instances they may not be consistent with common sense. If anything, the myths of totalitarian theorists will seem more plausible and are certainly more comprehensible to the general public than accredited scientific theories, since they are closer to common-sense experience and cultural bias. Partly as a result of scientific advance, therefore, the population at large has become ripe for new mysticisms clothed in apparently scientific jargon. This promotes the success of propaganda generally. The borrowed authority of science becomes a powerful prestige symbol for unscientific doctrines.

PUBLIC HOSTILITY TOWARD ORGANIZED SCEPTICISM

Another feature of the scientific attitude is organized scepticism, which becomes, often enough, iconoclasm.[27] Science may seem to challenge the "comfortable power assumptions" of other institutions,[28] simply by subjecting them to detached scrutiny. Organized scepticism involves a latent questioning of certain bases of established routine, authority, vested procedures and the realm of the 'sacred' generally. It is true that, *logically,* to establish the empirical genesis of beliefs and values is not to deny their validity, but this is often the psychological effect on the naïve mind. Institutionalized symbols and values demand attitudes of loyalty, adherence and respect. Science which asks questions of fact concerning every phase of nature and society comes into psychological, not logical, conflict with other attitudes toward these same data which have been crystallized and frequently ritualized by other institutions. Most institutions demand unqualified faith; but the institution of science makes scepticism a virtue. Every institution involves, in this sense, a sacred area, which is resistant to profane examination in terms of scientific observation and logic. The institution of science itself involves emotional adherence to certain values. But whether it be the sacred sphere of political convictions or religious faith or economic rights, the scientific investigator does not conduct himself in the prescribed uncritical and ritualistic fashion. He does not preserve the cleavage between the sacred and the profane, between that which requires uncritical respect and that which can be objectively analyzed.[29]

It is this which in part lies at the root of revolts against the socalled intrusion of science into other spheres. In the past, this resistance has come for the most part from the church which restrains the scientific examination of sanctified doctrines. Textual criticism of the Bible is still

27. Frank H. Knight, "Economic psychology and the value problem," *Quarterly Journal of Economics,* 1925, 39, 372-409. The unsophisticated scientist, forgetting that scepticism is primarily a methodological canon, permits his scepticism to spill over into the area of value generally. The social functions of symbols are ignored and they are impugned as 'untrue.' Social utility and truth are once again confused.

28. Charles E. Merriam, *Political Power,* (New York, Whittlesey House, 1934), 82-3.

29. For a general discussion of the sacred in these terms, see Durkheim, *The Elementary Forms of the Religious Life,* 37 ff., *et passim.*

suspect. This resistance on the part of organized religion has become less significant as the locus of social power has shifted to economic and political institutions which in their turn evidence an undisguised antagonism toward that generalized scepticism which is felt to challenge the bases of institutional stability. This opposition may exist quite apart from the introduction of certain scientific discoveries which appear to invalidate particular dogmas of church, economy and state. It is rather a diffuse, frequently vague, recognition that scepticism threatens the *status quo*. It must be emphasized again that there is no logical necessity for a conflict between scepticism, within the sphere of science, and the emotional adherences demanded by other institutions. But as a psychological derivative, this conflict invariably appears whenever science extends its research to new fields toward which there are institutionalized attitudes or whenever other institutions extend their area of control. In the totalitarian society, the centralization of institutional control is the major source of opposition to science; in other structures, the extension of scientific research is of greater importance. Dictatorship organizes, centralizes and hence intensifies sources of revolt against science which in a liberal structure remain unorganized, diffuse, and often latent.

In a liberal society, integration derives primarily from the body of cultural norms toward which human activity is oriented. In a dictatorial structure, integration is effected primarily by formal organization and centralization of social control. Readiness to accept this control is instilled by speeding up the process of infusing the body politic with new cultural values, by substituting high-pressure propaganda for the slower process of the diffuse inculcation of social standards. These differences in the mechanisms through which integration is typically effected permit a greater latitude for self-determination and autonomy to various institutions, including science, in the liberal than in the totalitarian structure. Through such rigorous organization, the dictatorial state so intensifies its control over non-political institutions as to lead to a situation which is different in kind as well as degree. For example, reprisals against science can more easily find expression in the Nazi state than in America, where interests are not so organized as to enforce limitations upon science, when these are deemed necessary. Incompatible sentiments must be insulated from one another or integrated with each other if there is to be social stability. But such insulation becomes virtually impossible when there exists centralized control under the aegis of any one sector of social life which imposes, and attempts to enforce, the obligation of adherence to its values and sentiments as a condition of continued existence. In liberal structures the absence of such centralization permits the necessary degree of insulation by guaranteeing to each sphere restricted rights of autonomy and thus enables the gradual integration of temporarily inconsistent elements.

CONCLUSIONS

The main conclusions of this paper may be briefly summarized. There exists a latent and active hostility toward science in many societies, although the extent of this antagonism cannot yet be established. The prestige which science has acquired within the last three centuries is so great that actions curtailing its scope or repudiating it in part are usually coupled with affirmation of the undisturbed integrity of science or "the rebirth of true science." These verbal respects to the pro-science sentiment are frequently at variance with the behavior of those who pay them. In part, the anti-science movement derives from the conflict between the ethos of science and of other social institutions. A corollary of this proposition is that contemporary revolts against science are *formally* similar to previous revolts, although the *concrete* sources are different. Conflict arises when the social effects of applying scientific knowledge are deemed undesirable, when the scientist's scepticism is directed toward the basic values of other institutions, when the expansion of political or religious or economic authority limits the autonomy of the scientist, when anti-intellectualism questions the value and integrity of science and when non-scientific criteria of eligibility for scientific research are introduced.

This paper does not present a program for action in order to withstand threats to the development and autonomy of science. It may be suggested, however, that as long as the locus of social power resides in any one institution other than science and as long as scientists themselves are uncertain of their primary loyalty, their position becomes tenuous and uncertain.

XVI

SCIENCE AND DEMOCRATIC
SOCIAL STRUCTURE

SCIENCE, AS ANY OTHER ACTIVITY involving social collaboration,
is subject to shifting fortunes. Difficult as the very notion may appear to
those reared in a culture which grants science a prominent if not a commanding place in the scheme of things, it is evident that science is not
immune from attack, restraint and repression. Writing a little while ago,
Veblen could observe that the faith of western culture in science was
unbounded, unquestioned, unrivalled. The revolt from science which
then appeared so improbable as to concern only the timid academician
who would ponder all contingencies, however remote, has now been
forced upon the attention of scientist and layman alike. Local contagions
of anti-intellectualism threaten to become epidemic.

SCIENCE AND SOCIETY

Incipient and actual attacks upon the integrity of science have led
*scientists to recognize their dependence on particular types of social
structure.* Manifestos and pronouncements by associations of scientists
are devoted to the relations of science and society. An institution under
attack must re-examine its foundations, restate its objectives, seek out
its rationale. Crisis invites self-appraisal. Now that they have been confronted with challenges to their way of life, scientists have been jarred
into a state of acute self-consciousness: consciousness of self as an integral element of society with corresponding obligations and interests.[1]
A tower of ivory becomes untenable when its walls are under assault.
After a prolonged period of relative security, during which the pursuit
and diffusion of knowledge had risen to a leading place if indeed not to
the first rank in the scale of cultural values, scientists are compelled to
vindicate the ways of science to man. Thus they have come full circle to
the point of the re-emergence of science in the modern world. Three
centuries ago, when the institution of science could claim little inde-

---

1. Since this was written in 1942, it is evident that the explosion at Hiroshima
has jarred many more scientists into an awareness of the social consequences of their
works.

pendent warrant for social support, natural philosophers were likewise led to justify science as a means to the culturally validated ends of economic utility and the glorification of God. The pursuit of science was then no self-evident value. With the unending flow of achievement, however, the instrumental was transformed into the terminal, the means into the end. Thus fortified, the scientist came to regard himself as independent of society and to consider science as a self-validating enterprise which was in society but not of it. A frontal assault on the autonomy of science was required to convert this sanguine isolationism into realistic participation in the revolutionary conflict of cultures. The joining of the issue has led to a clarification and reaffirmation of the ethos of modern science.

Science is a deceptively inclusive word which refers to a variety of distinct though interrelated items. It is commonly used to denote (1) a set of characteristic methods by means of which knowledge is certified; (2) a stock of accumulated knowledge stemming from the application of these methods; (3) a set of cultural values and mores governing the activities termed scientific or (4) any combination of the foregoing. We are here concerned in a preliminary fashion with the cultural structure of science, that is, with one limited aspect of science as an institution. Thus, we shall consider, not the methods of science, but the mores with which they are hedged about. To be sure, methodological canons are often both technical expedients and moral compulsives, but it is solely the latter which is our concern. This is an essay in the sociology of science, not an excursion in methodology. Similarly, we shall not deal with the substantive findings of sciences (hypotheses, uniformities, laws), except as these are pertinent to standardized social sentiments toward science. This is not an adventure in polymathy.

The ethos of science is that affectively toned complex of values and norms which is held to be binding on the man of science.[1a] The norms are expressed in the form of prescriptions, proscriptions, preferences and permissions. They are legitimatized in terms of institutional values. These imperatives, transmitted by precept and example and reenforced by sanctions are in varying degrees internalized by the scientist, thus fashioning his scientific conscience or, if one prefers the latter-day phrase, his superego. Although the ethos of science has not been codified,[2] it can be inferred from the moral consensus of scientists as ex-

---

1a. On the concept of ethos, see Sumner, *Folkways*, 36 ff.; Hans Speier, "The social determination of ideas," *Social Research*, 1938, 5, 196 ff.; Max Scheler, *Schriften aus dem Nachlass* (Berlin, 1933), 1, 225-62. Albert Bayet, in his book on the subject, soon abandons description and analysis for homily; see his *La morale de la science*, (Paris, 1931).

2. As Bayet remarks: "Cette morale [de la science] n'a pas eu ses théoriciens, mais elle a eu ses artisans. Elle n'a pas exprimé son idéal, mais elle l'a servi: il est impliqué dans l'existence même de la science." *Op. cit.*, 43.

pressed in use and wont, in countless writings on the scientific spirit and in moral indignation directed toward contraventions of the ethos.

An examination of the ethos of modern science is but a limited introduction to a larger problem: the comparative study of the institutional structure of science. Although detailed monographs assembling the needed comparative materials are few and scattered, they provide some basis for the provisional assumption that "science is afforded opportunity for development in a democratic order which is integrated with the ethos of science." This is not to say that the pursuit of science is confined to democracies.[3] The most diverse social structures have provided some measure of support to science. We have only to remember that the Accademia del Cimento was sponsored by two Medicis; that Charles II claims historical attention for his grant of a charter to the Royal Society of London and his sponsorship of the Greenwich Observatory; that the Académie des Sciences was founded under the auspices of Louis XIV, on the advice of Colbert; that urged into acquiescence by Leibniz, Frederick I endowed the Berlin Academy, and that the St. Petersburg Academy of Sciences was instituted by Peter the Great (to refute the view that Russians are barbarians). But such historical facts do not imply a random association of science and social structure. There is the further question of the ratio of scientific achievement to scientific potentialities. Science develops in various social structures, to be sure, but which provide an institutional context for the fullest measure of development?

THE ETHOS OF SCIENCE

The institutional goal of science is the extension of certified knowledge. The technical methods employed toward this end provide the relevant definition of knowledge: empirically confirmed and logically consistent predictions. The institutional imperatives (mores) derive from the goal and the methods. The entire structure of technical and moral norms implements the final objective. The technical norm of empirical evidence, adequate, valid and reliable, is a prerequisite for sustained true prediction; the technical norm of logical consistency, a prerequisite for systematic and valid prediction. The mores of science

---

3. Tocqueville went further: "The future will prove whether these passions [for science], at once so rare and so productive, come into being and into growth as easily in the midst of democratic as in aristocratic communities. For myself, I confess that I am slow to believe it." *Democracy in America* (New York, 1898), II, 51. See another reading of the evidence: "It is impossible to establish a simple causal relationship between democracy and science and to state that democratic society alone can furnish the soil suited for the development of science. It cannot be a mere coincidence, however, that science actually has flourished in democratic periods." Henry E. Sigerist, "Science and democracy," *Science and Society*, 1938, 2, 291.

possess a methodologic rationale but they are binding, not only because they are procedurally efficient, but because they are believed right and good. They are moral as well as technical prescriptions.

Four sets of institutional imperatives—universalism, communism, disinterestedness, organized scepticism—comprise the ethos of modern science.

Universalism

Universalism[4] finds immediate expression in the canon that truth claims, whatever their source, are to be subjected to *preestablished impersonal criteria:* consonant with observation and with previously confirmed knowledge. The acceptance or rejection of claims entering the lists of science is not to depend on the personal or social attributes of their protagonist; his race, nationality, religion, class and personal qualities are as such irrelevant. Objectivity precludes particularism. The circumstance that scientifically verified formulations refer to objective sequences and correlations militates against all efforts to impose particularistic criteria of validity. The Haber process cannot be invalidated by a Nuremberg decree nor can an Anglophobe repeal the law of gravitation. The chauvinist may expunge the names of alien scientists from historical textbooks but their formulations remain indispensable to science and technology. However *echt-deutsch* or hundred-per-cent American the final increment, some aliens are accessories before the fact of every new technical advance. The imperative of universalism is rooted deep in the impersonal character of science.

However, the institution of science is but part of a larger social structure with which it is not always integrated. When the larger culture opposes universalism, the ethos of science is subjected to serious strain. Ethnocentrism is not compatible with universalism. Particularly in times of international conflict, when the dominant definition of the situation is such as to emphasize national loyalties, the man of science is subjected to the conflicting imperatives of scientific universalism and of ethnocentric particularism.[4a] The structure of the situation in which he finds

---

4. For a basic analysis of universalism in social relations, see Talcott Parsons, *The Social System.* For an expression of the belief that "science is wholly independent of national boundaries and races and creeds," see the resolution of the Council of the American Association for the Advancement of Science, *Science,* 1938, 87, 10; also, "The advancement of science and society: proposed world association," *Nature,* 1938, 141, 169.

4a. This stands as written in 1942. By 1948, the political leaders of Soviet Russia strengthened their emphasis on Russian nationalism and began to insist on the 'national' character of science. Thus, in an editorial, "Against the Bourgeois ideology of cosmopolitanism," *Voprosy filosofii,* 1948, No. 2, as translated in the *Current Digest of the Soviet Press,* February 1, 1949, Vol. 1, No. 1, p. 9: "Only a cosmopolitan without a homeland, profoundly insensible to the actual fortunes of science, could deny with contemptuous indifference the existence of the many-hued national forms in which science lives and develops. In place of the actual history of science

himself determines the social role which is called into play. The man of science may be converted into a man of war—and act accordingly. Thus, in 1914 the manifesto of 93 German scientists and scholars—among them, Baeyer, Brentano, Ehrlich, Haber, Eduard Meyer, Ostwald, Planck, Schmoller and Wassermann—unloosed a polemic in which German, French and English men arrayed their political selves in the garb of scientists. Dispassionate scientists impugned 'enemy' contributions, charging nationalistic bias, log-rolling, intellectual dishonesty, incompetence and lack of creative capacity.[5] Yet this very deviation from the norm of universalism actually presupposed the legitimacy of the norm. For nationalistic bias is opprobrious only if judged in terms of the standard of universalism; within another institutional context, it is redefined as a virtue, patriotism. Thus by the very process of contemning their violation, the mores are reaffirmed.

Even under counter-pressure, scientists of all nationalities adhered to the universalistic standard in more direct terms. The international, impersonal, virtually anonymous character of science was reaffirmed.[6] (Pasteur: "Le savant a une patrie, la science n'en a pas.") Denial of the norm was conceived as a breach of faith.

Universalism finds further expression in the demand that careers be open to talents. The rationale is provided by the institutional goal. To

---

and the concrete paths of its development, the cosmopolitan substitutes fabricated concepts of a kind of supernational, classless science, deprived, as it were, of all the wealth of national coloration, deprived of the living brilliance and specific character of a people's creative work, and transformed into a sort of disembodied spirit . . . Marxism-Leninism shatters into bits the cosmopolitan fictions concerning supra-class, non-national, 'universal' science, and definitely proves that science, like all culture in modern society, is national in form and class in content." This view confuses two distinct issues: first, the cultural context in any given nation or society may predispose scientists to focus on certain problems, to be sensitive to some and not other problems on the frontiers of science. This has long since been observed. But this is basically different from the second issue: the criteria of validity of claims to scientific knowledge are not matters of national taste and culture. Sooner or later, competing claims to validity are settled by the universalistic facts of nature which are consonant with one and not with another theory. The foregoing passage is of primary interest in illustrating the tendency of ethnocentrism and acute national loyalties to penetrate the very criteria of scientific validity.

5. For an instructive collection of such documents, see Gabriel Pettit and Maurice Leudet, *Les allemands et la science*, (Paris, 1916). Félix Le Dantec, for example, discovers that both Ehrlich and Weismann have perpetrated typically German frauds upon the world of science. ("Le bluff de la science allemande.") Pierre Duhem concludes that the 'geometric spirit' of German science stifled the 'spirit of finesse': *La science allemande* (Paris, 1915). Hermann Kellermann, *Der Krieg der Geister* (Weimar, 1915) is a spirited counterpart. The conflict persisted into the post-war period; see Karl Kherkhof, *Der Krieg gegen die Deutsche Wissenschaft* (Halle, 1933).

6. See the profession of faith by Professor E. Gley (in Pettit and Leudet, *op. cit.*, 181: ". . . il ne peut y avoir une vérité allemande, anglaise, italienne ou japonaise pas plus qu'une française. Et parler de science allemande, anglaise ou française, c'est énoncer une proposition contradictoire à l'idée même de science." See also the affirmations of Grasset and Richet, *ibid.*

restrict scientific careers on grounds other than lack of competence is to prejudice the furtherance of knowledge. Free access to scientific pursuits is a functional imperative. Expediency and morality coincide. Hence the anomaly of a Charles II invoking the mores of science to reprove the Royal Society for their would-be exclusion of John Graunt, the political arithmetician, and his instructions that "if they found any more such tradesmen, they should be sure to admit them without further ado."

Here again the ethos of science may not be consistent with that of the larger society. Scientists may assimilate caste-standards and close their ranks to those of inferior status, irrespective of capacity or achievement. But this provokes an unstable situation. Elaborate ideologies are called forth to obscure the incompatibility of caste-mores and the institutional goal of science. Caste-inferiors must be shown to be inherently incapable of scientific work, or, at the very least, their contributions must be systematically devaluated. "It can be adduced from the history of science that the founders of research in physics, and the great discoverers from Galileo and Newton to the physical pioneers of our own time, were almost exclusively Aryans, predominantly of the Nordic race." The modifying phrase, 'almost exclusively,' is recognized as an insufficient basis for denying outcastes all claims to scientific achievement. Hence the ideology is rounded out by a conception of 'good' and 'bad' science: the realistic, pragmatic science of the Aryan is opposed to the dogmatic, formal science of the non-Aryan.[7] Or, grounds for exclusion are sought in the extra-scientific capacity of men of science as enemies of the state or church.[8] Thus, the exponents of a culture which abjures universalistic standards in general feel constrained to pay lip-service to this value in the realm of science. Universalism is deviously affirmed in theory and suppressed in practice.

However inadequately it may be put into practice, the ethos of democracy includes universalism as a dominant guiding principle. Democratization is tantamount to the progressive elimination of restraints upon the exercise and development of socially valued capacities. Impersonal criteria of accomplishment and not fixation of status characterize the democratic society. In so far as such restraints do persist, they are

---

7. Johannes Stark, *Nature*, 1938, 141, 772; "Philipp Lenard als deutscher Naturforscher," *Nationalsozialistische Monatshefte*, 1936, 7, 106-112. This bears comparison with Duhem's contrast between 'German' and 'French' science.

8. "Wir haben sie ['marxistischen Leugner'] nicht entfernt als Vertreter der Wissenschaft, sondern als Parteigaenger einer politischen Lehre, die den Umsturz aller Ordnungen auf ihre Fahne geschrieben hatte. Und wir mussten hier um so entschlossener zugreifen, als ihnen die herrschende Ideologie einer wertfreien und voraussetzungslosen Wissenschaft ein willkommener Schutz fuer die Fortfuehrung ihrer Plaene zu sein schien. Nicht wir haben uns an der Wuerde der freien Wissenschaft vergangen. . . ." Bernhard Rust, *Das nationalsozialistische Deutschland und die Wissenschaft* (Hamburg, 1936), 13.

viewed as obstacles in the path of full democratization. Thus, in so far as laissez-faire democracy permits the accumulation of differential advantages for certain segments of the population, differentials which are not bound up with demonstrated differences in capacity, the democratic process leads to increasing regulation by political authority. Under changing conditions, new technical forms of organization must be introduced to preserve and extend equality of opportunity. The political apparatus designed to put democratic values into practice may thus vary, but universalistic standards are maintained. To the extent that a society is democratic, it provides scope for the exercise of universalistic criteria in science.

'COMMUNISM'

'Communism,' in the non-technical and extended sense of common ownership of goods, is a second integral element of the scientific ethos. The substantive findings of science are a product of social collaboration and are assigned to the community. They constitute a common heritage in which the equity of the individual producer is severely limited. An eponymous law or theory does not enter into the exclusive possession of the discoverer and his heirs, nor do the mores bestow upon them special rights of use and disposition. Property rights in science are whittled down to a bare minimum by the rationale of the scientific ethic. The scientist's claim to 'his' intellectual 'property' is limited to that of recognition and esteem which, if the institution functions with a modicum of efficiency, is roughly commensurate with the significance of the increments brought to the common fund of knowledge. Eponymy—e.g., the Copernican system, Boyle's law—is thus at once a mnemonic and a commemorative device.

Given such institutional emphasis upon recognition and esteem as the sole property right of the scientist in his discoveries, the concern with scientific priority becomes a 'normal' response. Those controversies over priority which punctuate the history of modern science are generated by the institutional accent on originality.[9] There issues a competitive cooperation. The products of competition are communized,[10]

---

9. Newton spoke from hard-won experience when he remarked that "[natural] philosophy is such an impertinently litigious Lady, that a man had as good be engaged in lawsuits, as have to do with her." Robert Hooke, a socially mobile individual whose rise in status rested solely on his scientific achievements, was notably 'litigious.'

10. Marked by the commercialism of the wider society though it may be, a profession such as medicine accepts scientific knowledge as common property. See R. H. Shryock, "Freedom and interference in medicine," *The Annals*, 1938, 200, 45. ". . . the medical profession . . . has usually frowned upon patents taken out by medical men. . . . The regular profession has . . . maintained this stand against private monopolies ever since the advent of patent law in the seventeenth century." There arises an ambiguous situation in which the socialization of medical practice is rejected in circles where the socialization of knowledge goes unchallenged.

and esteem accrues to the producer. Nations take up claims to priority,[10a] and fresh entries into the commonwealth of science are tagged with the names of nationals: witness the controversy raging over the rival claims of Newton and Leibniz to the differential calculus. But all this does not challenge the status of scientific knowledge as common property.

The institutional conception of science as part of the public domain is linked with the imperative for communication of findings. Secrecy is the antithesis of this norm; full and open communication its enactment.[11] The pressure for diffusion of results is reenforced by the institutional goal of advancing the boundaries of knowledge and by the incentive of recognition which is, of course, contingent upon publication. A scientist who does not communicate his important discoveries to the scientific fraternity—thus, a Henry Cavendish—becomes the target for ambivalent responses. He is esteemed for his talent and, perhaps, for his modesty. But, institutionally considered, his modesty is seriously misplaced, in view of the moral compulsive for sharing the wealth of science. Layman though he is, Aldous Huxley's comment on Cavendish is illuminating in this connection: "Our admiration of his genius is tempered by a certain disapproval; we feel that such a man is selfish and anti-social." The epithets are particularly instructive for they imply the violation of a definite institutional imperative. Even though it serves no ulterior motive, the suppression of scientific discovery is condemned.

The communal character of science is further reflected in the recognition by scientists of their dependence upon a cultural heritage to which

---

10a. Now that the Russians have officially taken up a deep reverence for the Motherland, they come to insist on the importance of determining priorities in scientific discoveries. Thus: "The slightest inattention to questions of priorities in science, the slightest neglect of them, must therefore be condemned, for it plays into the hands of our enemies, who cover their ideological aggression with cosmopolitan talk about the supposed non-existence of questions of priority in science, *i.e.,* the questions regarding which peoples made what contribution to the general store of world culture." And further: "The Russian people has the richest history. In the course of this history it has created the richest culture, and all the other countries of the world have drawn upon it and continue to draw upon it to this day." *Voprosy filosofii, op. cit.,* pp. 10, 12. This is reminiscent of the nationalist claims made in western Europe during the nineteenth century and Nazi claims in the twentieth. (*Cf.* text at footnote 7.) Nationalist particularism does not make for detached appraisals of the course of scientific development.

11. *Cf.* Bernal, who observes: "The growth of modern science coincided with a definite rejection of the ideal of secrecy." Bernal quotes a remarkable passage from Réaumur (*L'Art de convertir le forgé en acier*) in which the moral compulsion for publishing one's researches is explicitly related to other elements in the ethos of science. E.g., ". . . il y eût gens qui trouvèrent étrange que j'eusse publié des secrets, qui ne devoient pas etre revelés . . . est-il bien sur que nos découvertes soient si fort à nous que le Public n'y ait pas droit, qu'elles ne lui appartiennent pas en quelque sorte? . . . resterait il bien des circonstances, où nous soions absolument Maîtres de nos découvertes? . . . Nous nous devons premiérement à notre Patrie, mais nous nous devons aussi au rest du monde; ceux qui travaillent pour perfectionner les Sciences et les Arts, doivent même se regarder commes les citoyens du monde entier." J. D. Bernal, *The Social Function of Science,* 150-51.

they lay no differential claims. Newton's remark—"If I have seen farther it is by standing on the shoulders of giants"—expresses at once a sense of indebtedness to the common heritage and a recognition of the essentially coöperative and cumulative quality of scientific achievement.[12] The humility of scientific genius is not simply culturally appropriate but results from the realization that scientific advance involves the collaboration of past and present generations. It was Carlyle, not Maxwell, who indulged in a mythopoeic conception of history.

The communism of the scientific ethos is incompatible with the definition of technology as 'private property' in a capitalistic economy. Current writings on the 'frustration of science' reflect this conflict. Patents proclaim exclusive rights of use and, often, nonuse. The suppression of invention denies the rationale of scientific production and diffusion, as may be seen from the court's decision in the case of *U. S. v. American Bell Telephone Co.:* "The inventor is one who has discovered something of value. It is his absolute property. He may withhold the knowledge of it from the public. . . ."[13] Responses to this conflict-situation have varied. As a defensive measure, some scientists have come to patent their work to ensure its being made available for public use. Einstein, Millikan, Compton, Langmuir have taken out patents.[14] Scientists have been urged to become promoters of new economic enterprises.[15] Others seek to resolve the conflict by advocating socialism.[16] These proposals—both those which demand economic returns for scientific discoveries and those which demand a change in the social system to let science get on with the job—reflect discrepancies in the conception of intellectual property.

DISINTERESTEDNESS

Science, as is the case with the professions in general, includes disinterestedness as a basic institutional element. Disinterestedness is not to be equated with altruism nor interested action with egoism. Such equivalences confuse institutional and motivational levels of analysis.[17]

---

12. It is of some interest that Newton's aphorism is a standardized phrase which had found repeated expression from at least the twelfth century. It would appear that the dependence of discovery and invention on the existing cultural base had been noted some time before the formulations of modern sociologists. See *Isis*, 1935, 24, 107-9; 1938, 25, 451-2.

13. 167 U. S. 224 (1897), cited by B. J. Stern, "Restraints upon the utilization of inventions," *The Annals*, 1938, 200, 21. For an extended discussion, *cf.* Stern's further studies cited therein; also Walton Hamilton, *Patents and Free Enterprise* (Temporary National Economic Committee Monograph No. 31, 1941).

14. Hamilton, *op. cit.*, 154; J. Robin, *L'oeuvre scientifique, sa protection-juridique,* Paris, 1928.

15. Vannevar Bush, "Trends in engineering research," *Sigma Xi Quarterly*, 1934, 22, 49.

16. Bernal, *op. cit.*, 155 ff.

17. Talcott Parsons, "The professions and social structure," *Social Forces*, 1939, 17, 458-9; *cf.* George Sarton, *The History of Science and the New Humanism* (New York, 1931), 130 ff. The distinction between institutional compulsives and motives is of course a key conception of Marxist sociology.

A passion for knowledge, idle curiosity, altruistic concern with the benefit to humanity and a host of other special motives have been attributed to the scientist. The quest for distinctive motives appears to have been misdirected. *It is rather a distinctive pattern of institutional control of a wide range of motives which characterizes the behavior of scientists.* For once the institution enjoins disinterested activity, it is to the interest of scientists to conform on pain of sanctions and, in so far as the norm has been internalized, on pain of psychological conflict.

The virtual absence of fraud in the annals of science, which appears exceptional when compared with the record of other spheres of activity, has at times been attributed to the personal qualities of scientists. By implication, scientists are recruited from the ranks of those who exhibit an unusual degree of moral integrity. There is, in fact, no satisfactory evidence that such is the case; a more plausible explanation may be found in certain distinctive characteristics of science itself. Involving as it does the verifiability of results, scientific research is under the exacting scrutiny of fellow-experts. Otherwise put—and doubtless the observation can be interpreted as *lese majesty*—the activities of scientists are subject to rigorous policing, to a degree perhaps unparalleled in any other field of activity. The demand for disinterestedness has a firm basis in the public and testable character of science and this circumstance, it may be supposed, has contributed to the integrity of men of science. There is competition in the realm of science, competition which is intensified by the emphasis on priority as a criterion of achievement, and under competitive conditions there may well be generated incentives for eclipsing rivals by illicit means. But such impulses can find scant opportunity for expression in the field of scientific research. Cultism, informal cliques, prolific but trivial publications—these and other techniques may be used for self-aggrandizement.[18] But, in general, spurious claims appear to be negligible and ineffective. The translation of the norm of disinterestedness into practice is effectively supported by the ultimate accountability of scientists to their compeers. The dictates of socialized sentiment and of expediency largely coincide, a situation conducive to institutional stability.

In this connection, the field of science differs somewhat from that of other professions. The scientist does not stand vis-à-vis a lay clientele in the same fashion as do the physician and lawyer, for example. The possibility of exploiting the credulity, ignorance and dependence of the layman is thus considerably reduced. Fraud, chicane and irresponsible claims (quackery) are even less likely than among the 'service' professions. To the extent that the scientist-layman relation does become paramount, there develop incentives for evading the mores of science. The abuse of expert authority and the creation of pseudo-sciences are

---

18. See the account of Logan Wilson, *The Academic Man,* 201 ff.

called into play when the structure of control exercised by qualified compeers is rendered ineffectual.[19]

It is probable that the reputability of science and its lofty ethical status in the estimate of the layman is in no small measure due to technological achievements.[19a] Every new technology bears witness to the integrity of the scientist. Science realizes its claims. However, its authority can be and is appropriated for interested purposes, precisely because the laity is often in no position to distinguish spurious from genuine claims to such authority. The presumably scientific pronouncements of totalitarian spokesmen on race or economy or history are for the uninstructed laity of the same order as newspaper reports of an expanding universe or wave mechanics. In both instances, they cannot be checked by the man-in-the-street and in both instances, they may run counter to common sense. If anything, the myths will seem more plausible and are certainly more comprehensible to the general public than accredited scientific theories, since they are closer to common-sense experience and to cultural bias. Partly as a result of scientific achievements, therefore, the population at large becomes susceptible to new mysticisms expressed in apparently scientific terms. The borrowed authority of science bestows prestige on the unscientific doctrine.

ORGANIZED SCEPTICISM

As we have seen in the preceding chapter, organized scepticism is variously interrelated with the other elements of the scientific ethos. It is both a methodologic and an institutional mandate. The suspension of judgment until 'the facts are at hand' and the detached scrutiny of beliefs in terms of empirical and logical criteria have periodically involved science in conflict with other institutions. Science which asks questions of fact, including potentialities, concerning every aspect of nature and society may come into conflict with other attitudes toward these same data which have been crystallized and often ritualized by other institutions. The scientific investigator does not preserve the cleavage between the sacred and the profane, between that which requires uncritical respect and that which can be objectively analyzed. ("Ein Professor ist ein Mensch der anderer Meinung ist.")

This appears to be the source of revolts against the so-called intrusion of science into other spheres. Such resistance on the part of organized religion has become less significant as compared with that of economic and political groups. The opposition may exist quite apart from the in-

---

19. *Cf.* R. A. Brady, *The Spirit and Structure of German Fascism* (New York, 1937), Chapter II; Martin Gardner, *In the Name of Science* (New York: Putnam's, 1953).

19a. Francis Bacon set forth one of the early and most succinct statements of this popular pragmatism: "What is most useful in practice is most correct in theory." *Novum Organum,* Book II, 4.

troduction of specific scientific discoveries which appear to invalidate particular dogmas of church, economy or state. It is rather a diffuse, frequently vague, apprehension that scepticism threatens the current distribution of power. Conflict becomes accentuated whenever science extends its research to new areas toward which there are institutionalized attitudes or whenever other institutions extend their area of control. In modern totalitarian society, anti-rationalism and the centralization of institutional control both serve to limit the scope provided for scientific activity.

XVII THE MACHINE, THE WORKER AND THE ENGINEER

To suspect the full measure of one's ignorance is a first step toward supplanting this ignorance with knowledge. What is known about the effects of changes in the methods of production upon the problems, behavior, and perspectives of the worker is little indeed; what needs to be known is very great. A short paper dealing with this large subject can at best roughly map out the contours of our ignorance. It is possible only to allude to the order of research findings now at hand, the conditions needed for suitable extension of these findings, and the social organization of further research required to achieve these results.

So widespread and deep-rooted is the belief that technological advance is a self-evident good that men have largely failed to look into the *conditions of society* under which this is indeed the case. If technology is good, it is so because of its human implications, because large numbers of diversely placed men have occasion to regard it as such in the light of their experience. And whether this occurs depends not so much upon the intrinsic character of an advancing technology, which makes for increased capacity to produce an abundance of goods, as upon the structure of society which determines which groups and individuals gain from this increased bounty and which suffer the social dislocations and human costs entailed by the new technology. Many, in our own society, find the pluralistic social effects of the progressive introduction of labor-saving technology to be far from advantageous. Limited as they are, the data on technological unemployment, displacement of labor, obsolescence of skills, discontinuities in employment, and decreases in jobs per unit of product all indicate that workers bear the brunt of failures to plan the orderly introduction of advances in the processes of production.

Research on these matters is not, of course, a panacea for the social dislocations ascribable to the present methods of introducing technological advances; but research can indicate the pertinent facts of the case—that is to say, it can set out the grounds for decisions by those directly affected by the multiform effects of technological change. Social research in this field has been impressively limited, and it will be of some interest to consider why this is the case.

We shall first review the order of findings which have resulted from social research in this general field; then consider some factors affecting the social role of engineers—especially those immediately concerned with the design and construction of the equipments of production—and the social repercussions of their creative work; and finally, suggest some of the more evident problems and potentialities of further research on the social consequences of labor-saving technology.

SOCIAL CONSEQUENCES OF CHANGES IN TECHNOLOGY

Research has detected some of the social repercussions of techno logical change, a few of which will be mentioned here. These range from the most direct effects upon the nature of work life—the social anatomy of the job—to those which bear upon the institutional and structural patterns of the larger society.

Social Anatomy of the Job

It has become plain that new productive processes and equipment inevitably affect *the network of social relations* among workers engaged in production. For men at work in the factory, in the mine, and, for that matter, on the farm, changes in methods of production elicit changes in work routines which modify the immediate social environment of the worker. Modifications of the size and composition of the work team; the range, character, and frequency of contact with associates and supervisers, the status of the worker in the organization, the extent of physical mobility available to him—any and all of these may be collateral effects of the technological change. Although these shifts in the local structure of social relations diversely affect the level of employee satisfaction with the job, they are often unanticipated and unregarded.

The conditions under which such a change is introduced have also been found to determine its impact upon workers. Responding to depressed economic conditions by the introduction of labor-saving technology, management may widen and deepen local pools of unemployment at the very time when workers have few alternatives for employment. Management may thus nourish *the job insecurities and anxieties of workers.* Circumstances such as these understandably lead organized labor to seek a greater part in shaping plans for the introduction of new equipment and processes.

In this connection the tempo of technological change is of critical, though not exclusive, importance. Workers, like executives, seek some measure of control over their day-by-day lives. Changes imposed upon them without their prior knowledge and consent are regarded as a threat to their well-being in much the same fashion as they are by the businessmen subjected to the vicissitudes of the market or to what they consider unpredictable decisions by "those bureaucrats in Washington." Not uncommonly, the worker's stake in the decision has been conscientiously and unrealistically neglected by a management installing labor-saving technology in an effort to maintain or improve the competitive situation of the firm. It has been observed that an environment of uncertainty, fear, and hostility may be skillfully created by quickening the pace of unpresaged changes in technology.

Through the *enforced obsolescence of skills*, labor-saving technology produces acute psychological and social problems for the worker. The difficulty does not lie exclusively in the need for learning new routines of work. The need for discarding acquired skills and, often, the accompanying demotion of status destroys the positive self-image of the worker, stemming from the confident use of those skills. Although this human cost of new methods of production can on occasion be reduced for individual workers through the planned reallocation of jobs, this does not preclude basic changes in the occupational structure of industry at large.

With technological advance, the growing subdivision of work tasks creates numberless new occupations for which, as Roethlisberger has observed, "there exist no occupational names that have any social significance outside of the particular industry, factory or even department in many cases." The splintering of work tasks involves *loss of public identity of the job*. Who but a chosen few, for example, can distinguish a fin sticker in an automobile plant from other radiator-core assemblers? Or, to take a more homely instance, what distinguishes the pride in work of a doughnut sugarer from that of a doughnut pumper, who successfully injects jelly into fried doughnuts with a jelly pump? To the outside world, these esoteric specializations are all of a piece and, consequently, for the outside world there must be other marks of status and significant work activity that count. The alienation of workers from their job and the importance of wages as the chief symbol of social status are both furthered by the absence of social meaning attributable to the task.

Increased specialization of production leads inescapably to a greater need for predictability of work behavior and, therefore, for *increased discipline in the workplace*. The meshing of numerous limited tasks requires that the margin of variation of individual behavior be reduced to a minimum. This trend, first made conspicuous in the beginnings of the factory system by the rebellions of workers against the then unfamiliar discipline of factory life, has become steadily more marked. In practice, this comes to mean an increasing quantum of discipline which, under specified conditions, becomes coercive for the worker.

Institutional and Structural Effects

The political and social as well as the economic by-products of an advancing technology variously affect the structure of society at large. This wider context suggests that workers' attitudes toward the new technology are determined not by it *per se*, but by the collateral uses to which it can be and, at times, has been put as an *instrument of social power*. Technology has been employed not only for the production of goods but also for the management of workmen. It has, in fact, been repeatedly defined as a weapon for subduing the worker by promising to displace him unless he accepts proffered terms of employment.

In the present day, this tactical use of technology in the 'price war' between management and labor need not be phrased as a threat but merely as an observation on the self-contained workings of the market. In an address before the Princeton Bicentennial Conference, for example, it has been stated that "among the compelling pressures that now stimulate management to increased mechanization and technological improvement in the processes of production are fantastic increases in money wages, the abandonment or reduced effectiveness of incentive wages, the intransigence of many labor groups, and an abundant supply of cheap money. Process engineers, tool designers, tool makers are now and will be in demand as never before. Invention and innovation will be at a premium without precedent."

A hundred years ago, these political implications of technology (and of the role assigned to engineers) were somewhat more plainly drawn by enterprisers and their representatives. Andrew Ure, for example, could then describe the self-acting mule as a "creation destined to restore order among the industrious classes. . . . The invention confirms the great doctrine already propounded that when capital enlists science into her service the refractory hand of labor will always be taught docility."

It would be instructive to learn if the avowed or tacit use of technology as a weapon in industrial conflict does in fact break the "intransigence" of workers or instruct them in the virtue of "docility." It is possible, of course, that the planned efficiency of a new machine or process is at times unrealized when its collateral function is that of keeping workmen in their place. Quite conceivably it may be found that the exercise of naked power no more produces a stable structure of social relations in industry than in other spheres of human behavior.

Advances in methods of production, as Elliott Dunlap Smith and Robert S. Lynd, among others, have observed, may enlarge the social cleavage between workmen and operating executives. It may produce a sharper *social stratification of industry*. As the complexities of the new technology make technical education a prerequisite for the operating executive, the prospect of workers rising through the ranks becomes progressively dimmed. To the extent that opportunities for higher education are socially stratified, moreover, managers come increasingly to be drawn from social strata remote from those of workers. Also, since technically trained personnel enter industry at a relatively high level, they have little occasion to share the job experience of workers at an early stage of their careers and tend, accordingly, to have an abstract *knowledge about* rather than a concrete *acquaintance with* the perspective of workers. Finally, with the increasing rationalization of managerial procedures, the relations between operating executives and workmen become increasingly formalized and depersonalized.

These several patterns—progressive closure of opportunities for substantial promotion, the polarization of social origins of workers and of executives, the insulation of managerial personnel from workers' outlooks through changes in their typical career patterns and depersonalization of contact—may in composite contribute to a secular trend toward growing tensions between the men who manage and the men whom they manage.

The impact of technology upon the social organization is not, of course, confined to these subsurface trends in class structure. The interdependence of the industrial structure, tightened by applications of science to industry, infects the decisions of large industrial firms with the public interest. In consequence, government comes increasingly to regulate and to supervise these decisions, at least at the margins where they plainly affect the larger community. This trend toward "big government" forces upon popular attention what analytical observers have long recognized: the spheres of economic and political behavior, far from having only tangential relations, overlap considerably. Labor and management deal not only directly with each other through collective bargaining and administrative decision but also indirectly by exerting pressure upon government. Following in the footsteps of entrepreneur and management, labor enters politics.

The growing requirements of work discipline, deriving from technological integration, go far toward explaining the strategic role of the "big union" in our society. "Big industry" has been finding it more expedient or efficient to deal with unions than with large masses of unorganized workers. For industry has come to learn that discipline is often more effectively achieved with the aid of unions of the workers' own choosing than through exclusive resort to the managerial and supervisory apparatus. Moreover, a condition of technological tenuousness in which the stoppage of any one sector of production threatens to paralyze the entire industry modifies the constellation of power relations. All this confers heightened power and responsibility upon labor.

This cursory review of certain consequences of changes in the techniques of production helps sharpen the moral dilemma involved in the choice of problems for social research in this field. Research focused solely on the impact of new technology upon the *immediate work situation* in a plant leads primarily, if not exclusively, to findings which can be readily adapted for making the technological change more acceptable to the individual worker, though it may, in fact, have adverse consequences for him. The scientific problem may be inadvertently construed as one of discovering methods for accommodating the worker to the change, almost irrespective of the mosaic of consequences which it entails for him and his associates. Capital may also enlist *social* science to teach the worker the value of docility. On the other hand, only through this close study of immediate effects upon work life is one likely to discover methods of introducing changes in methods of production which may appreciably mitigate consequences unfavorable to the worker.

Attention directed solely to the effects upon *the larger social structure* has its limits as well. Research oriented wholly toward secular trends—for example, the pattern of increases in productivity outrunning or keeping pace with increases in total employment—diverts attention from ways and means of minimizing the present impact of technological change upon the worker. This type of research, however, does locate the central sociological problem: discerning the features of our social organization which militate against technological progress resulting in "greater security of livelihood and more satisfactory living standards."

IMPLICATIONS FOR THE ENGINEER

New applications of science to production by the engineer, then, do not merely affect the methods of production. They are inescapably social decisions affecting the routines and satisfactions of men at work on the machine and, in their larger reaches, shaping the very organization of the economy and society.

The central role of engineers as the General Staff of our productive systems only underscores the great importance of their social and political orientations: the social strata with which they identify themselves; the texture of group loyalties woven by their economic position and their occupational careers; the groups to whom they look for direction; the types of social effects of their work which they take into account—in short, only by exploring the entire range of their allegiances, perspectives, and concerns can engineers achieve that self-clarification of their social role which makes for fully responsible participation in society.

But to say that this poses sociological problems for "the" engineer is to make a reference so inclusive and vague as to mean little at all. The large and multifarious family of men called engineers have a far-flung kinship, but they also have much that marks subgroups off, each from the others. There are military, civil, mechanical, chemical, electrical, and metallurgical engineers, and so on down through the hundreds of titles found among the members of national engineering societies. But whatever their specialty, so long as they are concerned with the design, construction, or operation of the equipments and processes of production, they are confronted with social and political implications of their position in our society.

A nascent trend toward full recognition of these implications is curbed by several obstacles, chief among which, it would seem, are (1) the marked specialization and division of scientific labor, (2) the applications of professional codes governing the social outlook of engineers, and (3) the incorporation of engineers into industrial bureaucracies.

Specialization

The intensified division of labor has become a splendid device for escaping social responsibilities. As professions subdivide, each group of specialists finds it increasingly possible to "pass the buck" for the social consequences of their work, on the assumption, it would seem, that in this complex transfer of responsibility there will be no hindmost for the devil to take. When appalled by resulting social dislocations, each specialist, secure in the knowledge that he has performed his task to the best of his ability, can readily disclaim responsibility for them. And, of course, no one group of specialists, the engineer any more than the others, alone initiates these consequences. Rather, within our economic and social structure each technological contribution meshes into a cumulative pattern of effects, some of which none has desired and all have brought about.

The Professional Ethic

Deriving in part from the specialization of functions, engineers, not unlike scientists, come to be indoctrinated with an ethical sense of limited responsibilities. The scientist, busy on his distinctive task of carving out new knowledge from the realm of ignorance, has long disclaimed responsibility for attending to the ways in which this knowledge was applied. (History creates its own symbols. It required an atomic bomb to shake many scientists loose from this tenaciously held doctrine.)

So, in many quarters, it has been held absurd that the engineer should be thought accountable for the social and psychological effects of technology, since it is perfectly clear that these do not come within his special province. After all, it is the engineer's "job"—note how effectively this defines the limits of one's role and, thereby, one's social responsibility—to improve processes of production, and it is "not his concern" to consider their ramified social effects. The occupational code focuses the attention of engineers upon the first links in the chain of consequences of technological innovation and diverts their attention, both as specialists and as citizens, from succeeding links in the chain as, for example, the consequences for wage levels and employment opportunities. "But we have to include consequences impartially"—this is John Dewey putting the issue in more general form. "It is willful folly to fasten upon some single end or consequence which is liked, and permit the view of that to blot from perception all other undesired and undesirable consequences."

Bureaucratic Status

The employment of large numbers of engineers and technologists in industrial bureaucracies further shapes their social perspectives. Knit into a bureaucratic apparatus, many engineers take their place as experts in a subaltern role with fixed spheres of competence and authority and with a severely delimited orientation toward the larger social system. In this status, they are rewarded for viewing themselves as technical auxiliaries. As such, it is not their function to consider the human and social consequences of introducing their efficient equipments and processes or to decide when and how they are to be introduced. These are matters for administrative and managerial concern.

The grounds for assigning these concerns to administrators in business and industrial organizations have seldom been stated as lucidly and instructively as in the following passage by Roethlisberger: ". . . physicists, chemists, mechanical, civil, chemical engineers have a useful way of thinking about and a simple method of dealing with their own class of phenomena. Within this area their judgments are likely to be sound. Outside it their judgments are more questionable. Some of them recognize quite clearly this limitation. They do not want to be concerned with the human factor; they want to design the best tool, the best machine to accomplish certain technical purposes. Whether or not the introduction of this tool or machine will involve the layoff of certain employees, quite rightly, is not their concern as engineers. . . . These men are invaluable to the administrator in any industrial organization."

Max Weber and Thorstein Veblen, among others, have pointed to the danger that this occupational perspective, involving the rationalized abdication of social responsibility in favor of the administrator, may be transferred by engineers beyond the immediate economic enterprise. From this transference of outlook and the resulting trained incapacity for dealing with human affairs there develops a passive and dependent role for engineers and technologists in the realm of political organization, economic institutions, and social policy. The citizen-self threatens to become submerged in the occupational self.

As technical specialists thus attend to "their own" limited tasks, the over-all impact of technology upon the social structure becomes nobody's business through default.

THE NEEDS OF SOCIAL RESEARCH

Engineers may well continue to abjure any direct concern with the social effects of an advancing technology as long as the effects cannot be anticipated and taken into account. To the extent that social scientists have failed to address themselves to this problem, there is no informed basis for the most socially oriented of technologists to act with due social responsibility. Only when those equipped with the skills of social research make available an adequate body of scientific knowledge can those working with the skills of engineering extend their sights from the individual business enterprise to the larger social system.

Just as men for centuries neglected the problems of soil erosion, in part because they were unaware that erosion constituted a significant problem, so they are still neglecting the social erosion ascribable to present methods of introducing rapid technological changes. There is a severely limited market for research in this field. It seems safe to suppose that fewer man-hours of research activity are devoted to the intensive investigation of these problems central to our technological age than, say, to the design of alluring packages for perfumes and other such basic commodities or to the planning of competitive advertisements for the tobacco manufacturers of the nation.

The inauguration of a vast program of social inquiry proportioned to the scale of the problem need not wait upon new research procedures. Methods of social research have been advancing steadily and will undoubtedly become developed further through disciplined experience. The effective development of this program does wait, however, upon decisions concerning the organization of the research teams, sponsorship of the research, and the directions of inquiry.

Organization of the Research Team

Disparate and uncoordinated inquiries by diversely skilled groups have not proved adequate. The problems in this area call for the complementary skills and knowledge of engineers, economists, psychologists, and sociologists. Once this focus of joint inquiry is recognized, systematic efforts to institute a program of collaborative investigation could be begun by representatives of the several professional societies. Common universes of discourse would probably be lacking at the outset, but, as the experience of the TVA suggests, patterns of collaboration between engineers and social scientists can be evolved. The walls insulating the several disciplines raised up by the division of scientific labor can be surmounted if they are recognized for the temporary expedients that they are.

Sponsorship of the Research

Of the limited body of social research in industry, the greater part has been oriented toward the needs of management. The problems selected as the focus of the inquiry—high labor turnover and restricted output, for example—have been largely thus defined by management, sponsorship has been typically by management, the limits and character of experimental changes in the work situation have been passed upon by management, and periodic reports have been made primarily to management. No matter how good or seemingly self-evident the reason, it should be noted that this *is* the typical perspective of social research in industry and that it limits the effective prosecution of the research.

These remarks do not, of course, impugn the validity and usefulness of research oriented toward the needs of management. From the fact that this research continues to be sponsored by management, we can conclude only that it has been found eminently useful and valid, within the limits of the definition of problems. But an intelligence staff for one stratum of the business and industrial population may in due course find itself focusing on problems which are not the chief problems confronting other sectors of that population. It may happen, for example, that devising methods of reducing workers' anxieties through sympathetic and prolonged interviews or through appropriate behavior by supervisors is not among those researches which workers regard as central to their interests. They may be more concerned with having research men uncover the varied consequences, for themselves and for others, of alternative plans governing the introduction of technological changes.

This reminds us that social research itself takes place within a social setting. The social scientist who fails to recognize that his techniques of participant-observation, interviewing, sociogramming, and the like represent an innovation for workers and supervisors greater, perhaps, than technological changes in the plant would indeed be a dubious believer in his own findings. Resistance to this innovation can be anticipated, if only because it is remote from run-of-the-mill experience of most people. Those who have engaged in social research among workers and administrative personnel need not be told of the mingled suspicion, distrust, uneasy amusement, and, often, open hostility with which they were initially met. Unfamiliarity with this type of inquiry, coupled with its apparent inquisitiveness into areas of tension and private affairs, makes for some measure of resistance.

If the research is subsidized by management and if the problems dealt with are relevant primarily to management, the resistance of workers will be all the greater. It is small wonder that in some quarters of organized labor the preliminary efforts at social research in industry are regarded with a measure of suspicion and distrust comparable to that which attended the introduction of scientific management studies in the 1920's. For if workers have occasion to identify the research program as a new-fangled academic device for countering labor organizations or for scientifically substituting symbolic for material rewards, it will create rather than locate problems.

Social research in industry, therefore, must be conducted under the joint auspices of management and labor, irrespective of the source of funds for the research. The cooperation of large numbers of workers will not be achieved unless they know that they will be beneficiaries of an application of scientific method to a field where rule-of-thumb has largely prevailed.

The Directions of Research

The initial task of these research teams would be to search out the specific problems which demand attention. The very fact that they undertake the research would indicate that they are not possessed by the opaque faith that forward strides in technology, howsoever applied, must lead to the common good. They would be expected to think dangerous thoughts. They would not hold cultural and institutional axioms to be beyond inquiry. The focus of their attention would be the institutional arrangements adequate to incorporate the full potentialities for production of an unevenly but continuously advancing technology with an equitable distribution of gains and losses contained in these advances.

During the last decade there has occurred a reaction among social researchers against the earlier tendency to focus on the economic consequences of advances in technology. The center of research attention was shifted to workers' sentiments and social relations on the job. This new emphasis, however, has the defects of its qualities. It is not only the sentiments of workers which are affected by technological change. It is not only their social ties and their status—it is also their incomes, their job chances, and their economic interests. If the new research on human relations in industry is to have maximum pertinence, it must be meshed with the continuing research on the economic implications of labor-saving technology.

Nor can the research be effectively confined to studies of "the worker." To single out the worker as though he represented a self-contained sector of the industrial population is to do violence to the structure of social relations which actually obtains in industry. Presumably, it is not only the worker who is subject to preoccupations, obsessive reveries, defects and distortions of attitude, and irrational dislikes of co-workers or supervisors. It might even turn out that the behavior and decisions of management are appreciably affected by similar psychological patterns and that these, as well as a clear-cut sense of economic interests, go far toward determining decisions on the introduction of labor-saving technology.

In the absence of research jointly sponsored by labor and management and aimed at commonly agreed-upon problems of the role of technology in our society, the alternative is to pursue the present pattern of piecemeal research, directed toward those special problems which it is in the interest of special groups to have examined. It is possible, of course, that this alternative will seem preferable to some. It is altogether possible that the several interested groups will find no basis for agreement on the sponsorship and direction of social research in this field. But then, this too would serve its backhanded purpose. Should research by technologists and social scientists under the joint auspices of management and labor be rejected on these grounds, it would be a significant diagnostic sign of the state which industrial relations have reached.

PURITANISM, PIETISM
AND SCIENCE

Ⅰ N HIS PROLEGOMENA to a cultural sociology Alfred Weber has
discriminated between the processes of society, culture, and civilization.[1]
Since his primary interest lay in differentiating these categories of sociological phenomena, Weber in large measure ignored their specific inter-
relationships, a field of study which is fundamental for the sociologist.
It is precisely this interaction between certain elements of culture and
civilization, with especial reference to seventeenth-century England,
which constitutes the object-matter of the present essay.

THE PURITAN ETHOS

The first section of this paper outlines the Puritan value-complex in
so far as it was related to the notable increase of interest in science
during the latter part of the seventeenth century, while the second
presents the relevant empirical materials concerning the differential
cultivation of natural science by Protestants and other religious affiliates.

It is the thesis of this study that the Puritan ethic, as an ideal-typical
expression of the value-attitudes basic to ascetic Protestantism generally,
so canalized the interests of seventeenth-century Englishmen as to constitute one important *element* in the enhanced cultivation of science.
The deep-rooted religious *interests*[2] of the day demanded in their force-

---

1. Alfred Weber, "Prinzipielles zur Kultursoziologie: Gesellschaftsprozess, Zivili-
sationsprozess und Kulturbewegung," *Archiv für Sozialwissenschaft und Sozialpolitik*,
xlvii 1920, 47, 1-49. See the similar classification by R. M. MacIver, *Society: Its
Structure and Changes,* chap. xii; and the discussion of these studies by Morris Gins-
berg, *Sociology* (London, 1934), 45-52.

2. "Nicht die ethische Theorie theologischer Kompendien, die nur als ein (unter
Umständen allerdings wichtiges) Erkenntnismittel dient, sondern die in den psycholo-
gischen und pragmatischen Zusammenhängen der Religionen gegründeten praktischen
Antriebe zum Handeln sind das, was in Betracht kommt [unter 'Wirtschaftsethik'
einer Religion]." Max Weber, *Gesammelte Aufsätze zur Religionssoziologie* (Tübingen, 1920), 1, 238. As Weber justly indicates, one freely recognizes the fact that
religion is but *one* element in the determination of the religious ethic, but none the
less it is at present an insuperable, and for our purposes, unnecessary task to determine *all* the component elements of this ethic. That problem awaits further analysis
and falls outside the scope of this study.

ful implications the systematic, rational, and empirical study of Nature for the glorification of God in His works and for the control of the corrupt world.

It is possible to determine the extent to which the values of the Puritan ethic stimulated interest in science by surveying the attitudes of the contemporary scientists. Of course, there is a marked possibility that in studying the avowed motives of scientists we are dealing with rationalizations, with derivations, rather than with accurate statements of the actual motives. In such instances, although they may refer to isolated specific cases, the value of our study is by no means vitiated, for these conceivable rationalizations themselves are evidence (Weber's *Erkenntnismitteln*) of the motives which were regarded as socially acceptable, since, as Kenneth Burke puts it, "a terminology of motives is moulded to fit our general orientation as to purposes, instrumentalities, the good life, etc."

Robert Boyle was one of the scientists who attempted explicitly to link the place of science in social life with other cultural values, particularly in his *Usefulness of Experimental Natural Philosophy*. Such attempts were likewise made by John Ray, whose work in natural history was path-breaking and who was characterized by Haller as the greatest botanist in the history of man; Francis Willughby, who was perhaps as eminent in zoology as was Ray in botany; John Wilkins, one of the leading spirits in the "invisible College" which developed into the Royal Society; Oughtred, Wallis, and others. For additional evidence we can turn to the scientific body which, arising about the middle of the century, provoked and stimulated scientific advance more than any other immediate agency: the Royal Society. In this instance we are particularly fortunate in possessing a contemporary account written under the constant supervision of the members of the Society so that it might be representative of their views of the motives and aims of that association. This is Thomas Sprat's widely read *History of the Royal-Society of London,* published in 1667, after it had been examined by Wilkins and other representatives of the Society.[3]

Even a cursory examination of these writings suffices to disclose one outstanding fact: certain elements of the Protestant ethic had pervaded the realm of scientific endeavour and had left their indelible stamp upon the attitudes of scientists toward their work. Discussions of the why and wherefore of science bore a point-to-point correlation with the Puritan

---

3. *Cf.* C. L. Sonnichsen, *The Life and Works of Thomas Sprat* (Harvard University, unpublished doctoral dissertation, 1931), 131 ff., where substantial evidence of the fact that the *History* is representative of the views of the Society is presented. It is of further interest that the statements in Sprat's book concerning the aims of the Society bear a distinct similarity on every score to Boyle's characterizations of the motives and aims of scientists in general. This similarity is evidence of the dominance of the ethos which included these attitudes.

teachings on the same subject. Such a dominant force as was religion in those days was not and perhaps could not be compartmentalized and delimited. Thus, in Boyle's highly commended apologia for science it is maintained that the study of Nature is to the greater glory of God and the Good of Man.[4] This is the motif which recurs in constant measure. The juxtaposition of the spiritual and the material is characteristic. This culture rested securely on a substratum of utilitarian norms which constituted the measuring-rod of the desirability of various activities. The definition of action designed for the greater glory of God was tenuous and vague, but utilitarian standards could easily be applied.

Earlier in the century, this keynote had been sounded in the resonant eloquence of that "veritable apostle of the learned societies," Francis Bacon. Himself the initiator of no scientific discoveries, unable to appreciate the importance of his great contemporaries, Gilbert, Kepler, and Galileo, naïvely believing in the possibility of a scientific method which "places all wits and understandings nearly on a level," a radical empiricist holding mathematics to be of no use in science, he was, nevertheless, highly successful as one of the principal protagonists of a positive social evaluation of science and of the disclaim of a sterile scholasticism. As one would expect from the son of a "learned, eloquent, and religious woman, full of puritanic fervour" who was admittedly influenced by his mother's attitudes, he speaks in the *Advancement of Learning* of the true end of scientific activity as the "glory of the Creator and the relief of man's estate." Since, as is quite clear from many official and private documents, the Baconian teachings constituted the basic principles on which the Royal Society was patterned, it is not strange that the same sentiment is expressed in the charter of the Society.

In his last will and testament, Boyle echoes the same attitude, petitioning the Fellows of the Society in this wise: "Wishing them also a happy success in their laudable attempts, to discover the true Nature of the Works of God; and praying that they and all other Searchers into Physical Truths, may cordially refer their Attainments to the Glory of the Great Author of Nature, and to the Comfort of Mankind."[5] John Wilkins proclaimed the experimental study of Nature to be a most effective means of begetting in men a veneration for God.[6] Francis Willughby was prevailed upon to publish his works—which he had

---

4. Robert Boyle, *Some Considerations touching the Usefulness of Experimental Natural Philosophy* (Oxford, 1664), 22 ff. See, also, the letters of William Oughtred in *Correspondence of Scientific Men of the Seventeenth Century,* edited by S. J. Rigaud (Oxford, 1841), xxxiv, *et passim;* or the letters of John Ray in the *Correspondence of John Ray,* edited by Edwin Lankester (London, 1848), 389, 395, 402, *et passim.*

5. Quoted by Gilbert, Lord Bishop of Sarum, *A Sermon preached at the Funeral of the Hon. Robert Boyle* (London, 1692), 25.

6. *Principles and Duties of Natural Religion* (London, 1710—sixth edition), 236 *et passim.*

deemed unworthy of publication—only when Ray insisted that it was a means of glorifying God.[7] Ray's *Wisdom of God,* which was so well received that five large editions were issued in some twenty years, is a panegyric of those who glorify Him by studying His works.[8]

To a modern, comparatively untouched by religious forces, and noting the almost complete separation, if not opposition, between science and religion today, the recurrence of these pious phrases is apt to signify merely customary usage, and nothing of deep-rooted motivating convictions. To him these excerpts would seem to be a case of *qui nimium probat nihil probat.* But such an interpretation is possible only if one neglects to translate oneself within the framework of seventeenth-century values. Surely such a man as Boyle, who spent considerable sums to have the Bible translated into foreign tongues, was not simply rendering lip service. As G. N. Clark very properly notes in this connection:

> There is . . . always a difficulty in estimating the degree to which what we call religion enters into anything which was said in the seventeenth century in religious language. It is not solved by discounting all theological terms and treating them merely as common form. On the contrary, it is more often necessary to remind ourselves that these words were then seldom used without their accompaniment of meaning, and that their use did generally imply a heightened intensity of feeling.[9]

The second dominant tenet in the Puritan ethos designated social welfare, the good of the many, as a goal ever to be held in mind. Here again the contemporary scientists adopted an objective prescribed by the current values. Science was to be fostered and nurtured as leading to the domination of Nature by technologic invention. The Royal Society, we are told by its worthy historian, "does not intend to stop at some particular benefit, but goes to the root of all noble inventions."[10] But those experiments which do not bring with them immediate gain are not to be condemned, for as the noble Bacon has declared, experiments of Light ultimately conduce to a whole troop of inventions useful to the life and state of man. This power of science to better the material condition of man, he continues, is, apart from its purely mundane value, a good in the light of the Evangelical Doctrine of Salvation by Jesus Christ.

And so on through the principles of Puritanism there was the same point-to-point correlation between them and the attributes, goals, and results of science. Such was the contention of the protagonists of science at that time. Puritanism simply made articulate the basic values of the period. If Puritanism demands systematic, methodic labour, constant diligence in one's calling, what, asks Sprat, more active and industrious

---

7. *Memorials of John Ray,* 14 f.

8. *Wisdom of God* (London, 1691), 126-129, *et passim.*

9. G. N. Clark, *The Seventeenth Century* (Oxford, 1929), 323.

10. Thomas Sprat, *History of the Royal-Society,* 78-79.

and systematic than the Art of Experiment, which "can never be finish'd by the perpetual labours of any one man, nay, scarce by the successive force of the greatest Assembly?".[11] Here is employment enough for the most indefatigable industry, since even those hidden treasures of Nature which are farthest from view may be uncovered by pains and patience.[12]

Does the Puritan eschew idleness because it conduces to sinful thoughts (or interferes with the pursuit of one's vocation)? "What room can there be for low, and little things in a mind so usefully and success-fully employ'd [as in natural philosophy]?".[13] Are plays and play-books pernicious and flesh-pleasing (and subversive of more serious pur-suits)?[14] Then it is the "fittest season for experiments to arise, to teach us a Wisdome, which springs from the depths of Knowledge, to shake off the shadows, and to scatter the mists [of the spiritual distractions brought on by the Theatre]".[15] And finally, is a life of earnest activity within the world to be preferred to monastic asceticism? Then recognize the fact that the study of natural philosophy "fits us not so well for the secrecy of a Closet: It makes us serviceable to the World."[16] In short, science embodies two highly prized values: utilitarianism and em-piricism.

In a sense this explicit coincidence between Puritan tenets and the qualities of science as a calling is casuistry. It is an express attempt to fit the scientist *qua* pious layman into the framework of the prevailing social values. It is a bid for religious and social sanction, since both the constitutional position and the personal authority of the clergy were much more important then than now. But this is not the entire explana-tion. The justificatory efforts of Sprat, Wilkins, Boyle, or Ray do not simply represent opportunistic obsequiousness, but rather an earnest attempt to justify the ways of science to God. The Reformation had transferred the burden of individual salvation from the Church to the individual, and it is this "overwhelming and crushing sense of the re-sponsibility for his own soul" which explains the acute religious interest.

---

11. *Ibid.*, 341-2.

12. *Ray, Wisdom of God,* 125.

13. Sprat, *op. cit.,* 344-5.

14. Richard Baxter, *Christian Directory* (London, 1825—first published in 1664), I, 152; II, 167. *Cf.* Robert Barclay, the Quaker apologist, who specifically suggests "geometrical and mathematical experiments" as innocent divertissements to be sought instead of pernicious plays. *An Apology for the True Christian Divinity* (Phila., 1805 —first written in 1675), 554-5.

15. Sprat, *op. cit.,* 362.

16. *Ibid.*, 365-6. Sprat perspicaciously suggests that monastic asceticism induced by religious scruples was partially responsible for the lack of empiricism of the Schoolmen. "But what sorry kinds of Philosophy must the Schoolmen needs produce, when it was part of their Religion, to separate themselves, as much as they could, from the converse of mankind? When they were so far from being able to discover the secrets of Nature, that they scarce had opportunity to behold enough of its common works." *Ibid.*, 19.

If science were not demonstrably a lawful and desirable calling, it dare not claim the attention of those who felt themselves "ever in the Great Taskmaster's eye." It is to this intensity of feeling that such apologias were due.

The exaltation of the faculty of reason in the Puritan ethos—based partly on the conception of rationality as a curbing device of the passions—inevitably led to a sympathetic attitude toward those activities which demand the constant application of rigorous reasoning. But again, in contrast to medieval rationalism, reason is deemed subservient and auxiliary to empiricism. Sprat is quick to indicate the pre-eminent adequacy of science in this respect.[17] It is on this point probably that Puritanism and the scientific temper are in most salient agreement, for the combination of *rationalism and empiricism* which is so pronounced in the Puritan ethic forms the essence of the spirit of modern science. Puritanism was suffused with the rationalism of neo-Platonism, derived largely through an appropriate modification of Augustine's teachings. But it did not stop there. Associated with the designated necessity of dealing successfully with the practical affairs of life within this world— a derivation from the peculiar twist afforded largely by the Calvinist doctrine of predestination and *certitudo salutis* through successful worldly activity—was an emphasis upon empiricism. These two currents brought to convergence through the logic of an inherently consistent system of values were so associated with the other values of the time as to prepare the way for the acceptance of a similar coalescence in natural science.

Empiricism and rationalism were canonized, beatified, so to speak. It may very well be that the Puritan ethos did not directly influence the method of science and that this was simply a parallel development in the internal history of science, but it is evident that through the psychological compulsion toward certain modes of thought and conduct this value-complex made an empirically-founded science commendable rather than, as in the medieval period, reprehensible or at best acceptable on sufferance. This could not but have directed some talents into scientific fields which otherwise would have engaged in more highly esteemed professions. The fact that science to-day is largely if not completely divorced from religious sanctions is itself of interest as an example of the process of secularization.

The beginnings of such secularization, faintly perceptible in the latter Middle Ages, are manifest in the Puritan ethos. It was in this system

---

17. Sprat, *op. cit.*, 361. Baxter in a fashion representative of the Puritans decried the invasion of "enthusiasm" into religion. Reason must "maintain its authority in the command and government of your thoughts." *CD.*, ii, 199. In like spirit, those who at Wilkins' lodgings laid the foundation of the Royal Society "were invincibly arm'd against all the inchantments of Enthusiasm." Sprat, *op. cit.*, 53.

of values that reason and experience were first markedly considered as independent means of ascertaining even religious truths. Faith which is unquestioning and not "rationally weighed," says Baxter, is not faith, but a dream or fancy or opinion. In effect, this grants to science a power which may ultimately limit that of theology.

Thus, once these processes are clearly understood, it is not surprising or inconsistent that Luther particularly, and Melanchthon less strongly, execrated the cosmology of Copernicus and that Calvin frowned upon the acceptance of many scientific discoveries of his day, while the religious ethic which stemmed from these leaders invited the pursuit of natural science.[18] In so far as the attitudes of the theologians dominate over the, in effect, subversive religious ethic,— as did Calvin's authority in Geneva until the early eighteenth century—science may be greatly impeded. But with the relaxation of this hostile influence and with the development of an ethic, stemming from it and yet differing significantly, science takes on a new life, as was indeed the case in Geneva.

Perhaps the most directly effective element of the Protestant ethic for the sanction of natural science was that which held that the study of nature enables a fuller appreciation of His works and thus leads us to admire the Power, Wisdom, and Goodness of God manifested in His creation. Though this conception was not unknown to medieval thought, the consequences deduced from it were entirely different. Thus Arnaldus of Villanova, in studying the products of the Divine Workshop, adheres strictly to the medieval ideal of determining properties of phenomena from *tables* (in which all combinations are set forth according to the canons of logic). But in the seventeenth century, the contemporary emphasis upon empiricism led to investigating nature primarily through observation.[19] This difference in interpretation of substantially the same doctrine can only be understood in the light of the different values permeating the two cultures.

For a Barrow, Boyle or Wilkins, a Ray or Grew, science found its

---

18. On the basis of this analysis, it is surprising to note the statement *accredited* to Max Weber that the opposition of the Reformers is sufficient reason for not coupling Protestantism with scientific interests. See *Wirtschaftsgeschichte* (München, 1924), 314. This remark is especially unanticipated since it does not at all accord with Weber's discussion of the same point in his other works. *Cf. Religionssoziologie,* I, 141, 564; *Wissenschaft als Beruf* (München, 1921), 19-20. The probable explanation is that the first is not Weber's statement, since the *Wirtschaftsgeschichte* was compiled from classroom notes by two of his students who may have neglected to make the requisite distinctions. It is unlikely that Weber would have made the elementary error of confusing the Reformers' opposition to certain scientific discoveries with the unforeseen consequences of the Protestant ethic, particularly since he expressly warns against the failure to make such discriminations in his *Religionssoziologie.* For perceptive but vague adumbrations of Weber's hypothesis, see Auguste Comte, *Cours de philosophie positive* (Paris, 1864), IV, 127-130.

19. Walter Pagel, "Religious motives in the medical biology of the seventeenth century," *Bulletin of the Institute of the History of Medicine,* 1935, 3, 214-15.

rationale in the end and all of existence: glorification of God. Thus, from Boyle:[20]

> . . . God loving, as He deserves, to be honour'd in all our Faculties, and consequently to be glorified and acknowledg'd by the acts of Reason, as well as by those of Faith, there must be sure a great Disparity betwixt that general, confus'd and lazy Idea we commonly have of His Power and Wisdom, and the Distinct, rational and affecting notions of those Attributes which are form'd by an attentive Inspection of those Creatures in which they are most legible, and which were made chiefly for that very end.

Ray carries this conception to its logical conclusion, for if Nature is the manifestation of His power, then nothing in Nature is too mean for scientific study.[21] The universe and the insect, the macrocosm and microcosm alike, are indications of "divine Reason, running like a Golden Vein, through the whole leaden Mine of Brutal Nature."

Up to this point we have been concerned in the main with the directly felt sanction of science through Puritan values. While this was of great influence, there was another type of relationship which, subtle and difficult of apprehension though it be, was perhaps of paramount significance. It has to do with the preparation of a set of largely implicit assumptions which made for the ready acceptance of the scientific temper characteristic of the seventeenth and subsequent centuries. It is not simply that Protestantism implicitly involved free inquiry, *libre examen,* or decried monastic asceticism. These are important but not exhaustive.

It has become manifest that in each age there is a system of science which rests upon a set of assumptions, usually implicit and seldom questioned by the scientists of the time.[22] The *basic* assumption in modern science "is a widespread, instinctive conviction in the existence of an *Order of Things,* and, in particular, of an Order of Nature."[23] This belief, this faith, for at least since Hume it must be recognized as such, is simply "impervious to the demand for a consistent rationality." In the systems of scientific thought of Galileo, Newton, and of their successors, the testimony of experiment is the ultimate criterion of truth, but the very notion of experiment is ruled out without the prior assumption that Nature constitutes an intelligible order, so that when appropriate ques-

---

20. *Usefulness of Experimental Natural Philosophy,* 53; cf. Ray, *Wisdom of God,* 132; Wilkins, *Natural Religion,* 236 ff.; Isaac Barrow, *Opuscula,* iv, 88 ff.; Nehemiah Grew, *Cosmologia sacra* (London, 1701), who points out that "God is the original End," and that "we are *bound* to study His works."

21. Ray, *Wisdom of God,* 130 ff. Max Weber quotes Swammerdam as saying: "ich bringe Ihnen hier den Nachweis der Vorsehung Gottes in der Anatomie einer Laus." *Wissenchaft als Beruf,* 19.

22. A. E. Heath, in *Isaac Newton: A Memorial Volume,* ed. by W. J. Greenstreet (London, 1927), 133 ff.; E. A. Burtt, *The Metaphysical Foundations of Modern Physical Science* (London, 1925).

23. A. N. Whitehead, *Science and the Modern World* (New York, 1931), 5 ff.

tions are asked, she will answer, so to speak. Hence this assumption is final and absolute.[24] As Professor Whitehead indicated, this "faith in the possibility of science, generated antecedently to the development of modern scientific theory, is an unconscious derivative from medieval theology." But this conviction, prerequisite of modern science though it be, was not sufficient to induce its development. What was needed was a constant interest in searching for this order in nature in an empirico-rational fashion, that is, an *active* interest in this world and its occurrences plus a specific frame of mind. With Protestantism, religion provided this interest: it actually imposed obligations of intense concentration upon secular activity with an emphasis upon experience and reason as bases for action and belief.

Even the Bible as final and complete authority was subject to the interpretation of the individual upon these bases. The similarity in approach and intellectual attitude of this system to that of the contemporary science is of more than passing interest. It could not but mould an attitude of looking at the world of sensuous phenomena which was highly conducive to the willing acceptance, and indeed, preparation for, the same attitude in science. That the similarity is deep-rooted and not superficial may be gathered from the following comment upon Calvin's theology:[25]

Die Gedanken werden objektiviert und zu einem objektiven Lehrsystem aufgebaut und abgerundet. Es bekommt geradezu ein naturwissenschaftliches Gepräge; es ist klar, leicht fassbar und formulierbar, wie alles, was der äusseren Welt angehört, klarer zu gestalten ist als das, was im Tiefsten sich abspielt.

The conviction in immutable law is as pronounced in the theory of predestination as in scientific investigation: "the immutable law is there and must be acknowledged."[26] The similarity between this conception and the scientific assumption is clearly drawn by Hermann Weber:[27]

. . . die Lehre von der Prädestination in ihrem tiefsten Kerne getroffen zu sein, wenn mann sie als Faktum im Sinne eines naturwissenschaftlichen Faktums begreift, nur dass das oberste Prinzip, das auch jedem naturwissenschaftlichen Erscheinungskomplex zugrunde liegt, die im tiefsten erlebte gloria dei ist.

The cultural environment was permeated with this attitude toward natural phenomena which was derived from both science and religion

---

24. *Cf.* E. A. Burtt in *Isaac Newton: A Memorial Volume,* 139. For the classic exposition of this scientific faith, see Newton's "Rules of Reasoning in Philosophy," in his *Principia* (London, 1729 ed.), II, 160 ff.

25. Hermann Weber, *Die Theologie Calvins* (Berlin, 1930), 23.

26. *Ibid.,* 31. The significance of the doctrine of God's foreknowledge for the re-enforcement of the belief in natural law is remarked by H. T. Buckle, *History of Civilization in England* (New York, 1925), 482.

27. *Op. cit.,* 31.

and which enhanced the continued prevalence of conceptions characteristic of the new science.

There remains a supremely important part of this study to be completed. It is not sufficient verification of our hypothesis that the cultural
attitudes induced by the Protestant ethic were favourable to science.
Nor, yet again, that the consciously expressed motivation of many
eminent scientists was provided by this ethic. Nor, still further, that the
cast of thought which is characteristic of modern science, namely, the
combination of empiricism and rationalism and the faith in the validity
of one basic postulate, an apprehensible order in Nature, bears an other
than fortuitious congruency with the values involved in Protestantism.
All this can but provide some evidence of a certain probability of the
connection we are arguing. The most significant test of the hypothesis
is to be found in the confrontation of the results *deduced* from the hypothesis with relevant empirical data. If the Protestant ethic involved an
attitudinal set favourable to science and technology in so many ways,
then we should find amongst Protestants a greater propensity for these
fields of endeavour than one would expect simply on the basis of their
representation in the total population. Moreover, if, as has been frequently suggested,[28] the impression made by this ethic has lasted long
after much of its theological basis has been largely disavowed, then even
in periods subsequent to the seventeenth century, this connection of
Protestantism and science should persist to some degree. The following
section, then, will be devoted to this further test of the hypothesis.

THE PURITAN IMPETUS TO SCIENCE

In the beginnings of the Royal Society there is found a closely
wrought nexus between science and society. The Society itself arose
from an antecedent interest in science and the subsequent activities of
its members provided an appreciable impetus to further scientific advance. The inception of this group is found in the occasional meetings
of devotees of science in 1645 and following. Among the leading spirits
were John Wilkins, John Wallis, and soon afterwards Robert Boyle and
Sir William Petty, upon all of whom religious forces seem to have had a
singularly strong influence.

Wilkins, later an Anglican bishop, was raised at the home of his
maternal grandfather, John Dod, an outstanding Non-conformist theo-
logian, and "his early education had given him a strong bias toward

---

28. As Troeltsch puts it: "The present-day world does not live by logical consistency, any more than any other; spiritual forces can exercise a dominant influence
even where they are avowedly repudiated." *Die Bedeutung des Protestantismus für
die Entstehung der modernen Welt* (München, 1911), 22: *cf.* Georgia Harkness,
John Calvin: The Man and His Ethics (New York, 1931), 7 ff.

Puritanical principles."[29] Wilkins' influence as Warden of Wadham College was profound; under it came Ward, Rooke, Wren, Sprat, and Walter Pope (his half-brother), all of whom were original members of the Royal Society.[30] John Wallis, to whose *Arithmetica Infinitorum* Newton was avowedly indebted for many of his leading mathematical conceptions, was a clergyman with strong leanings toward Puritan principles. The piety of Boyle has already been remarked; the only reason he did not take holy orders, as he said, was because of the "absence of an inner call."[31]

Thedore Haak, the German virtuoso who played so prominent a part in the formation of the Royal Society, was a pronounced Calvinist. Denis Papin, who during his prolonged stay in England contributed notably to science and technology, was a French Calvinist compelled to leave his country to avoid religious persecution. Thomas Sydenham, sometimes called "the English Hippocrates," was an ardent Puritan who fought as one of Cromwell's men. Sir William Petty was a latitudinarian; he had been a follower of Cromwell, and in his writings he evinced clearly the influences of Puritanism. Of Sir Robert Moray, described by Huyghens as the "Soul of the Royal Society," it could be said that "religion was the mainspring of his life, and amidst courts and camps he spent many hours a day in devotion."[32]

It is hardly a fortuitous circumstance that the leading figures of this nuclear group of the Royal Society were divines or eminently religious men, though it is not quite accurate to maintain, as did Dr. Richardson, that the beginnings of the Society occurred in a small group of learned men among whom Puritan *divines* predominated.[33] But it is quite clearly true that the originative spirits of the Society were markedly influenced by Puritan conceptions.

Dean Dorothy Stimson, in a recently published paper, has independently arrived at this same conclusion.[34] She points out that of the

---

29. Memorials of John Ray, 18-19; P. A. W. Henderson, *The Life and Times of John Wilkins* (London, 1910), 36. Moreover, after Wilkins took holy orders, he became chaplain to Lord Viscount Say and Seale, a resolute and effective Puritan.

30. Henderson, *op. cit.*, 72-3.

31. *Dictionary of National Biography*, II, 1028. This reason, effective also for Sir Samuel Morland's turning to mathematics rather than to the ministry, is an example of the direct working of the Protestant ethic which, as exposited by Baxter for example, held that only those who felt an "inner call" should enter the clergy, and that others could better serve society by adopting other accredited secular activities. On Morland, see the "Autobiography of Sir Samuel Morland," in J. O. Halliwell-Phillipps' *Letters Illustrative of the Progress of Science in England* (London, 1841), 116 ff.

32. *Dictionary of National Biography*, xiii, 1299.

33. C. F. Richardson, *English Preachers and Preaching* (New York, 1928), 177.

34. Dorothy Stimson, "Puritanism and the new philosophy in seventeenth-century England," *Bulletin of the Institute of the History of Medicine*, 1935, 3, 321-34.

ten men who constituted the "invisible college," in 1645, only one, Scar-brough, was clearly non-Puritan. About two of the others there is some uncertainty, though Merret had a Puritan training. The others were all definitely Puritan. Moreover, among the original list of members of the Society of 1663, forty-two of the sixty-eight concerning whom informa-tion about their religious orientation is available were clearly Puritan. Considering that the Puritans constituted a relatively small minority in the English population, the fact that they constituted sixty-two per cent of the initial membership of the Society becomes even more striking. Dean Stimson concludes: "that experimental science spread as rapidly as it did in seventeenth-century England seems to me to be in part at least because the moderate Puritans encouraged it."

THE PURITAN INFLUENCE ON
SCIENTIFIC EDUCATION

Nor was this relationship only evidenced among the members of the Royal Society. The emphasis of the Puritans upon utilitarianism and empiricism was likewise manifested in the type of education which they introduced and fostered. The "formal grammar grind" of the schools was criticized by them as much as the formalism of the Church.

Prominent among the Puritans who so consistently sought to intro-duce the new realistic, utilitarian, and empirical education into England was Samuel Hartlib. He formed the connecting link between the various Protestant educators in England and in Europe who were earnestly seek-ing to spread the academic study of science. It was to Hartlib that Milton addressed his tractate on education and Sir William Petty dedicated his "Advice . . . for the Advancement of some particular Parts of Learning," namely, science, technology, and handicraft. Moreover, it was Hartlib who was instrumental in broadcasting the educational ideas of Comenius and in bringing him to England.

The Bohemian Reformist, John Amos Comenius, was one of the most influential educators of this period. Basic to the system of education which he promulgated were the norms of utilitarianism and empiricism: values which could only lead to an emphasis upon the study of science and technology, of *Realia*.[35] In his most influential work, *Didactica Magna*, he summarizes his views:[36]

The task of the pupil will be made easier, if the master, when he teaches him everything, shows him at the same time its practical application in every-day life. This rule must be carefully observed in teaching languages, dialectic, arithmetic, geometry, physics, etc.

---

35. Wilhelm Dilthey, "Pädagogik: Geschichte und Grundlinien des Systems," *Gesammelte Schriften* (Leipzig & Berlin, 1934), 163 ff.

36. J. A. Comenius, *The Great Didactic*, translated by M. W. Keatinge (London, 1896), 292, 337; see also 195, 302, 329, 341.

... the truth and certainty of science depend more on the witness of the senses than on anything else. For things impress themselves directly on the senses, but on the understanding only mediately and through the senses. . . . Science, then, increases in certainty in proportion as it depends on sensuous perception.

Comenius found welcome among Protestant educators in England who subscribed to the same values; individuals such as Hartlib, John Dury, Wilkins, and Haak.[37] At the request of Hartlib, he came to England for the express purpose of making Bacon's Solomon's House a reality. As Comenius himself remarked: "nothing seemed more certain than that the scheme of the great Verulam, of opening in some part of the world a universal college, whose one object should be the advancement of the sciences, would be carried into effect."[38] But this aim was frustrated by the social disorder attendant upon the rebellion in Ireland. However, the Puritan design of advancing science was not entirely without fruit. Cromwell founded the only new English university instituted between the Middle Ages and the nineteenth century, Durham University, "for all the sciences."[39] And in Cambridge, during the height of the Puritan influence there, the study of science was considerably augmented.[40]

In the same vein, the Puritan Hezekiah Woodward, a friend of Hartlib, emphasized realism (things, not words) and the teaching of science.[41] In order to initiate the study of the new science on a much more widespread scale than had hitherto obtained, the Puritans instituted a number of Dissenting Academies. These were schools of university standing opened in various parts of the kingdom. One of the earliest of these was Morton's Academy wherein there was pronounced stress laid upon scientific studies. Charles Morton later went to New England, where he was chosen vice-president of Harvard College, in which "he introduced the systems of science that he used in England."[42] At the influential Northampton Academy, another of the Puritan educational centres, mechanics, hydrostatics, physics, anatomy, and astronomy had an important place in the time-table. These studies were pursued largely with the aid of actual experiments and observations.

But the marked emphasis placed by the Puritans upon science and technology may perhaps best be appreciated by a comparison between the Puritan academies and the universities. The latter, even after they had introduced scientific subjects, continued to give an essentially classical education; the truly cultural studies were those which, if not entirely

37. Robert F. Young, *Comenius in England* (Oxford, 1932), 5-9.
38. *Opera Didactica Omnia* (Amsterdam, 1657), Book II, preface.
39. F. H. Hayward, *The Unknown Cromwell* (London, 1934), 206-30, 315.
40. James B. Mullinger, *Cambridge Characteristics in the Seventeenth Century* (London, 1867), 180-81 *et passim*.
41. Irene Parker, *Dissenting Academies in England* (Cambridge, 1914), 24.
42. *Ibid.*, 62.

useless, were at least definitely nonutilitarian in purpose. The academies, in contrast, held that a truly liberal education was one which was "in touch with life" and which should therefore include as many utilitarian subjects as possible. As Dr. Parker puts it:[43]

. . . the difference between the two educational systems is seen not so much in the introduction into the academies of "modern" subjects and methods as in the fact that among the Nonconformists there was a totally different system at work from that found in the universities. The spirit animating the Dissenters was that which had moved Ramus and Comenius in France and Germany and which in England had actuated Bacon and later Hartlib and his circle.

This comparison of the Puritan academies in England and Protestant educational developments on the Continent is well warranted. The Protestant academies in France devoted much more attention to scientific and utilitarian subjects than did the Catholic institutions.[44] When the Catholics took over many of the Protestant academies, the study of science was considerably diminished.[45] Moreover, as we shall see, even in the predominantly Catholic France, much of the scientific work was being done by Protestants. Protestant exiles from France included a large number of important scientists and inventors.[46]

VALUE-INTEGRATION OF PURITANISM AND SCIENCE

Of course, the mere fact that an individual is *nominally* a Catholic or a Protestant has no bearing upon his attitudes toward science. It is only as he adopts the tenets and implications of the teachings that his religious affiliation becomes significant. For example, it was only when Pascal became thoroughly converted to the teachings of Jansenius that he perceived the "vanity of science." For Jansenius characteristically maintained that above all we must beware of that vain love of science, which though seemingly innocent, is actually a snare "leading men away from the contemplation of eternal truths to rest in the satisfaction of the finite intelligence."[47] Once Pascal was converted to such beliefs, he resolved "to make an end of all those scientific researches to which he had hitherto applied himself."[48] It is the firm acceptance of the values

43. *Ibid.*, 133-4.

44. P. D. Bourchenin, *Etude sur les académies protestantes en France au XVIe et au XVIIe siècle* (Paris, 1882), 445 ff.

45. M. Nicholas, "Les académies protestantes de Montauban et de Nimes," *Bulletin de la société de l'histoire du protestantisme français*, 1858, 4, 35-48.

46. D. C. A. Agnew, *Protestant Exiles from France* (Edinburgh, 1866), 210 ff.

47. Emile Boutroux, *Pascal*, trans. by E. M. Creak (Manchester, 1902), 16.

48. *Ibid.*, 17; *cf.* Jacques Chevalier, *Pascal* (New York, 1930), 143; Pascal's *Pensées*, trans. by O. W. Wright, (Boston, 1884), 224, No. xxvii. "*Vanity of the Sciences.* The science of external things will not console me for ignorance of ethics in times of affliction; but the science of morals will always console me for ignorance of external sciences."

basic to the two creeds which accounts for the difference in the respective scientific contributions of Catholics and Protestants.

The same association of Protestantism and science was marked in the New World. The correspondents and members of the Royal Society who lived in New England were "all trained in Calvinistic thinking."[49] The founders of Harvard sprang from this Calvinistic culture, not from the literary era of the Renaissance or from the scientific movement of the seventeenth century, and their minds were more easily led into the latter than the former channel of thought.[50] This predilection of the Puritans for science is also noted by Professor Morison, who states: "the Puritan clergy, instead of opposing the acceptance of the Copernican theory, were the chief patrons and promoters of the new astronomy, and of other scientific discoveries, in New England."[51] It is significant that the younger John Winthrop, of Massachusetts, later a member of the Royal Society, came to London in 1641 and probably spent some time with Hartlib, Dury, and Comenius in London. Apparently, he suggested to Comenius that he come to New England and found a scientific college there.[52] Some years later, Increase Mather, (President of Harvard College from 1684-1701) did found a "Philosophical Society" at Boston.[53]

The scientific content of Harvard's educational programme derived greatly from the Protestant Peter Ramus.[54] Ramus had formulated an educational curriculum which in contrast to that of the Catholic universities laid great stress on the study of the sciences.[55] His ideas were welcomed in the Protestant universities on the Continent, at Cambridge (which had a greater Puritan and scientific element than Oxford),[56] and later at Harvard, but were firmly denounced in the various Catholic institutions.[57] The Reformation spirit of utilitarianism and "realism" probably accounts largely for the favorable reception of Ramus' views.

---

49. Stimson, op. cit., 332.

50. Porter G. Perrin, "Possible sources of Technologia at early Harvard," New England Quarterly, 1934, 7, 724.

51. Samuel E. Morison, "Astronomy at colonial Harvard," New England Quarterly, 1934, 7, 3-24; also Clifford K. Shipton, "A plea for Puritanism," The American Historical Review, 1935, 40, 463-4.

52. R. F. Young, Comenius in England, 7-8.

53. Ibid., 95.

54. Perrin, op. cit., 723-4.

55. Theobald Ziegler, Geschichte der Pädagogik (München, 1895), I, 108. Ziegler indicates that while the contemporary French Catholic institutions only devoted one-sixth of the curriculum to science, Ramus dedicated fully one-half to scientific studies.

56. David Masson properly calls Cambridge the alma mater of the Puritans. In listing twenty leading Puritan clergymen in New England, Masson found that seventeen of them were alumni of Cambridge, while only three came from Oxford. See his Life of Milton (London, 1875), II, 563; cited by Stimson, op. cit., 332. See also A History of the University of Oxford, by Charles E. Mallet (London, 1924), II, 147.

57. Heinrich Schreiber, Geschichte der Albert-Ludwigs-Universität zu Freiburg (Freiburg, 1857-68), II, 135. For example, at the Jesuit university of Freiburg, Ramus could only be referred to if he were refuted, and "no copies of his books are to be found in the hands of a student."

VALUE-INTEGRATION OF PIETISM AND SCIENCE

Dr. Parker notes that the Puritan academies in England "may be compared with the schools of the Pietists in Germany, which under Francke and his followers prepared the way for the *Realschulen,* for there can be no doubt that just as the Pietists carried on the work of Comenius in Germany, so the Dissenters put into practice the theories of Comenius' English followers, Hartlib, Milton, and Petty."[58] The significance of this comparison is profound for, as has been frequently observed, the values and principles of Puritanism and Pietism are almost identical. Cotton Mather had recognized the close resemblance of these two Protestant movements, saying that "ye American puritanism is so much of a piece with ye Frederician pietism" that they may be considered as virtually identical.[59] Pietism, except for its greater "enthusiasm," might almost be termed the Continental counterpart of Puritanism. Hence, if our hypothesis of the association between Puritanism and interest in science and technology is warranted, one would expect to find the same correlation among the Pietists. And such was markedly the case.

The Pietists in Germany and elsewhere entered into a close alliance with the "new education": the study of science and technology, of *Realia.*[60] The two movements had in common the realistic and practical point of view, combined with an intense aversion to the speculation of Aristotelian philosophers. Fundamental to the educational views of the Pietists were the same deep-rooted utilitarian and empirical values which actuated the Puritans.[61] It was on the basis of these values that the Pietist leaders, August Hermann Francke, Comenius, and their followers emphasized the new science.

Francke repeatedly noted the desirability of acquainting students with practical scientific knowledge.[62] Both Francke and his colleague,

---

58. Parker, *op. cit.,* 135.

59. Kuno Francke, "Cotton Mather and August Hermann Francke," *Harvard Studies and Notes,* 1896, 5, 63. See also the cogent discussion of this point by Max Weber, *Protestant Ethic,* 132-5.

60. Friedrich Paulsen, *German Education: Past and Present,* trans. by T. Lorenz (London, 1908), 104 ff.

61. Alfred Heubaum, *Geschichte des deutschen Bildungswesens seit der Mitte des siebzehnten Jahrhunderts* (Berlin, 1905), 1, 90. "Ziel der Erziehung [among Pietists] ist praktische Verwendbarkeit des Zöglings im Gemeinwohl. Der starke Einfluss des utilitaristischen Moments . . . vermindert die Gefahr der Uebertreibung des religiösen Moments und sichert der Bewegung für die nächste Zukunft ihre Bedeutung."

62. During walks in the field, says Francke, the instructor should "nützliche und erbauliche Geschichten erzählen oder etwas aus der Physik von den Geschöpfen und Werken Gottes vorsagen." ". . . im Naturalienkabinet diente dazu, die Zöglinge in ihren Freistunden durch den Anstaltarzt mit naturwissenschaftlichen Erscheinungen, mit Mineralien, Bergarten, hier und da mit Experimenten bekannt zu machen." Quoted by Heubaum, *op. cit.,* I, 89, 94.

Christian Thomasius, set themselves in opposition to the strong educational movement developed by Christian Weise, which advocated primarily training in oratory and classics, and sought rather "to introduce the neglected modern disciplines, which served their purposes more adequately; such studies as biology, physics, astronomy, and the like."[63]

Wherever Pietism spread its influence upon the educational system there followed the large-scale introduction of scientific and technical subjects.[64] Thus, Francke and Thomasius built the foundations of the University of Halle, which was the first German university to introduce a thorough training in the sciences.[65] The leading professors, such as Friedrich Hoffman, Ernst Stahl (professor of chemistry and famous for his influential phlogiston theory), Samuel Stryk, and, of course, Francke, all stood in the closest relations with the Pietistic movement. All of them characteristically sought to develop the teaching of science and to ally science with practical applications.

Not only Halle, but other Pietistic universities manifested the same emphases. Königsberg, having come under the Pietistic influence of the University of Halle through the activities of Francke's disciple, Gehr, early adopted the natural and physical sciences in the modern sense of the seventeenth century.[66] The University of Göttingen, an offshoot of Halle, was famous essentially for the great progress which it effected in the cultivation of the sciences.[67] The Calvinistic university of Heidelberg was likewise prominent for instituting a large measure of scientific study.[68] Finally, the University of Altdorf, which was at that time the most conspicuous for its interest in science, was a Protestant University subject to Pietistic influence.[69] Heubaum summarizes these developments by asserting that the essential progress in the teaching of science and technology occurred in Protestant, and more precisely, in Pietistic universities.[70]

RELIGIOUS AFFILIATION OF RECRUITS TO SCIENCE

This association of Pietism and science, which we have been led to anticipate from our hypothesis, did not confine itself to the universities.

---

63. *Ibid.*, I, 136.

64. *Ibid.*, I, 176 ff.

65. Koppel S. Pinson, *Pietism as a Factor in the Rise of German Nationalism* (New York, 1934), 18; Heubaum, *op. cit.*, I, 118. "Halle war die erste deutsche Universität von ganz eigenartigem wissenschaftlichen und nationalen Gepräge . . ."

66. Heubaum, *op. cit.*, I, 153.

67. Paulsen, *op. cit.*, 120-1.

68. Heubaum, *op. cit.*, I, 60.

69. S. Günther, "Die mathematischen Studien und Naturwissenschaften an der nürnbergischen Universität Altdorf," *Mitteilungen des Vereins für Geschichte der Stadt Nürnberg*, Heft. III, 9.

70. Heubaum, *op. cit.*, I, 241; see also Paulsen, *op. cit.*, 122; J. D. Michaelis, *Raisonnement über die protestantischen Universitäten in Deutschland* (Frankfurt, 1768), I, section 36.

The same Pietist predilection for science and technology was evidenced in secondary school education. The *Pädagogium* of Halle introduced the subjects of mathematics and natural science; stress being laid, in all cases on the use of object lessons and on practical applications.[71] Johann Georg Lieb, Johann Bernhard von Rohr, and Johann Peter Ludewig (Chancellor of Halle University), all of whom had come under the direct influence of Francke and Pietism, advocated schools of manufacture, physics, mathematics, and economics, in order to study how "manufacture might be ever more and more improved and excelled."[72] They hoped that the outcome of these suggestions might be a so-called *Collegium physicum-mechanicum* and *Werkschulen.*

It is a significant fact, and one which lends additional weight to our hypothesis, that the *ökonomisch-mathematische Realschule* was completely a Pietist product. This school, which centered on the study of mathematics, the natural sciences, and economics, and which was avowedly utilitarian and realistic in temper, was planned by Francke.[73] Moreover, it was a Pietist and a former student of Francke, Johann Julius Hecker, who first actually organized a *Realschule.*[74] Semler, Silberschlag, and Hähn, the directors and coorganizers of this first school, were all Pietists and former students of Francke.[75]

All available evidence points in the same direction. Protestants, without exception, form a progressively larger proportion of the student body in those schools which emphasize scientific and technologic training,[76] while Catholics concentrate their interests on classical and theological training. For example, in Prussia, the following distribution was found.[77]

---

71. Paulsen, *op. cit.,* 127.

72. Heubaum, *op. cit.,* I, 184.

73. Alfred Heubaum, "Christoph Semlers Realschule und seine Beziehung zu A. H. Francke," *Neue Jahrbücher für Philologie und Pädagogik,* 1893, 2, 65-77; see also Ziegler, *Geschichte der Pädagogik,* I, 197, who observes: ". . . einem inneren Zusammenhang zwischen der auf das Praktische gerichteten Realschule und der auf das Praktische gerichteten Frömmigkeit der Pietisten fehlte es ja auch nicht, nur éine ganz einseitig religiöse und theologische Auffassung des Pietismus kann das verkennen: im Geist der praktischen Nützlichkeit und Gemeinnützigkeit ist dieser dem Rationalismus vorangegangen und mit ihm eins gewesen, und aus diesem Geist heraus ist zu Franckes Zeiten in Halle die Realschule entstanden."

74. Paulsen, *op. cit.,* 133.

75. Upon the basis of this and other facts, Ziegler proceeds to trace a close "Kausalzusammenhang" between Pietism and the study of science. See his *Geschichte,* I, 196 ff.

76. The characteristic feature of the *gymnasien* is the classical basis of their curricula. Demarcated from these schools are the *Realschulen,* where the sciences predominate and where modern languages are substituted for the classical tongues. The *Real-gymnasium* is a compromise between these two types, having less classical instruction than the *gymnasium* with more attention paid to science and mathematics. The *Ober-realschulen* and *höheren Bürgerschulen* are both *Realschulen;* the first with a nine-year course, the second with a six-year course. *Cf.* Paulsen, *German Education,* 46 *et passim.*

77. Alwin Petersilie, "Zur Statistik der höheren Lehranstalten in Preussen," *Zeitschrift des königlich Preussischen Statistischen Bureaus,* 1877, 17, 109.

ATTENDANCE AT SECONDARY SCHOOLS DIFFERENTIATED BY
RELIGIOUS AFFILIATIONS OF THE STUDENTS
PRUSSIA, 1875-6

Religious Affiliation.	Pro-gym-nasium.	Gymna-sium.	Real-schule.	Ober-realsch.	Höheren Bürger.	Total.	General Population.
Protestants	49.1	69.7	79.8	75.8	80.7	73.1	64.9
Catholics	39.1	20.2	11.4	6.7	14.2	17.3	33.6
Jews	11.2	10.1	8.8	17.5	5.1	9.6	1.3

This greater propensity of Protestants for scientific and technical studies accords with the implications of our hypothesis. That this distribution is typical may be gathered from the fact that other investigators have noted the same tendency in other instances.[78] Furthermore, these distributions do not represent a spurious correlation resulting from differences in rural-urban distribution of the two religions, as may be seen from the pertinent data for the Swiss canton, Basel-Stadt. As is well known, the urban population tends to contribute more to the fields of science and technology than the rural. Yet for 1910 and following—the period to which Edouard Borel's study, with results similar to those just presented for Prussia, refers—Protestants constituted 63.4 per cent of the total population of the canton, but only 57.1 per cent of the population of Basel (the city proper) and 84.7 per cent of the rural population.[79]

Martin Offenbacher's careful study includes an analysis of the association between religious affiliation and the allocation of educational interests in Baden, Bavaria, Württemberg, Prussia, Alsace-Lorraine, and Hungary. The statistical results in these various places are of the same nature: Protestants, proportionately to their representation in the population at large, have a much higher attendance at the various secondary schools, with the difference becoming especially marked in the schools primarily devoted to the sciences and technology. In Baden,[80] for example, taking an average of the figures for the years 1885-95:

---

78. Edouard Borel, *Religion und Beruf* (Basel, 1930), 93 ff., who remarks the unusually high proportion of Protestants in the technical professions in Basel; Julius Wolf, "Die deutschen Katholiken in Staat und Wirtschaft," *Zeitschrift für Sozialwissenschaft*, 1913, 4, 199, notes that "die Protestanten ihren 'naturgemässen' Anteil überschreiten gilt für die wissenschaftliche und sonstige intellektuelle Betätigung (mit Ausnahme des geistlichen Berufs) . . ." In 1860, Ad. Frantz had already noted the same fact. See his "Bedeutung der Religionunterschiede für das physische Leben der Bevölkerungen," *Jahrbücher für Nationalökonomie und Statistik*, 1868, 11, 51. *Cf.* also similar results for Berlin in *Statistisches Jahrbuch der Stadt Berlin*, 1897, 22, 468-72. Buckle, *op. cit.*, 482, notes that "Calvinism is favourable to science." *Cf.* also Weber, *Protestant Ethic*, 38, 189; and Troeltsch, *Social Teachings* . . ., II, 894.

79. See "Die Bevölkerung des Kantons Basel-Stadt," *Mitteilungen des Statistischen Amtes des Kantons Basel-Stadt*, 1932, 48-49; and the same publication for the years 1910 and 1921.

80. Martin Offenbacher, *Konfession und soziale Schichtung* (Tübingen, 1900), 16. The slight errors of the original are here unavoidably reproduced.

	Protestants. per cent.	Catholics. per cent.	Jews. per cent.
Gymnasien	43	46	9.5
Realgymnasien	69	31	9
Oberrealschulen	52	41	7
Realschulen	49	40	11
Höheren Bürgerschulen	51	37	12
Average for the five types of schools	48	42	10
Distribution in the general population, 1895.	37	61.5	1.5

However, it must be noted that although the *Realschulen* curricula are primarily characterized by their stress on the sciences and mathematics as contrasted with the relatively little attention paid these studies in the *gymnasien*, yet the latter type of school also prepares for scienific and scholarly careers. But, in general, the attendance of Protestants and Catholics at the *gymnasien* represent different interests. The relatively large number of Catholics at the *gymnasien* is due to the fact that these schools prepare for theology as well, while the Protestants generally use the *gymnasien* as a preparation for the other learned professions. Thus, in the three academic years 1891-4, 226, or over 42 per cent of the 533 Catholic graduates of the Baden *gymnasien* subsequently studied theology, while of the 375 Protestant graduates, only 53 (14 per cent) turned to theology, while 86 per cent went into the other learned professions.[81]

Similarly, the Catholic apologist, Hans Rost, though he wishes to establish the thesis that "the Catholic Church has been at all times a warm friend of science," is forced to admit, on the basis of his data, that the Catholics avoid the *Realschulen*, that they show "eine gewisse Gleichgültigkeit und Abneigung gegen diese Anstalten." The reason for this, he goes on to say, is "das die Oberrealschule und das Realgymnasium nicht zum Studium der Theologie berechtigen: denn diese ist häufig die Triebfeder bei den Katholiken zum höheren Studium überhaupt."[82]

Thus, statistical data point to a marked tendency for Protestants, as contrasted with Catholics, to pursue scientific and technical studies. This can also be seen in the statistics for Württemberg, where an average of the years 1872-9 and 1883-98 gives the following figures:[83]

81. H. Gemss, *Statistik der Gymnasialabiturienten im deutschen Reich* (Berlin, 1895), 14-20.

82. Hans Rost, *Die wirtschaftliche und kulturelle Lage der deutschen Katholiken* (Köln, 1911), 167 ff.

83. Offenbacher, *op. cit.*, 18. These data are corroborated by the study of Ludwig Cron pertaining to Germany for the years 1869-93; *Glaubenbekenntnis und höheres Studium* (Heidelberg, 1900). Ernst Engel also found that in Prussia, Posen, Brandenburg, Pomerania, Saxony, Westphalia, and the Rhine Provinces, there is a higher incidence of Evangelical students in these schools which provide a maximum of natural science and technical subjects. See his "Beiträge zur Geschichte und Statistik des Unterrichts," *Zeitschrift des königlich Preussischen statistischen Bureaus,* 1869, 9, 99-116, 153-212.

	Protestants. per cent.	Catholics. per cent.	Jews. per cent.
Gymnasien	68.2	28.2	3.4
Lateinschulen	73.2	22.3	3.9
Realschulen	79.7	14.8	4.2
Total population, 1880 . . .	69.1	30.0	.7

Nor do the Protestants evidence these foci of interest only in education. Various studies have found an unduly large representation of Protestants among outstanding scientists.[84] If the foregoing data simply provide slight probabilities that the connection we have traced does in fact obtain, Candolle's well known *Histoire des sciences et des savants* increases these probabilities considerably. Candolle finds that although in Europe, excluding France, there were 107 million Catholics and 68 million Protestants, yet on the list of scientists named foreign associates by the Academy of Paris from 1666-1883, there were only eighteen Catholics as against eighty Protestants.[85] But as Candolle himself suggests, this comparison is not conclusive since it omits French scientists who may have been Catholic. To correct this error, he takes the list of foreign members of the Royal Society of London at two periods when there were more French scientists included than at any other time: 1829 and 1869. In the former year, the total number of Protestant and Catholic scientists (who are foreign members of the Society) is about equal, while in 1869, the number of Protestants actually exceeds that of Catholics. But, outside the kingdom of Great Britain and Ireland, there were in Europe 139½ million Catholics and only 44 million Protestants.[86] In other words, though in the general population there were more than three times as many Catholics as Protestants, there were actually more Protestant than Catholic scientists.

However, there are yet more significant data than these which are based on different populations, where influence of economy, political regime, and other non-religious factors may be suspected to prevail over the actual influence of religion. A comparison of closely allied populations serves largely to eliminate these "extraneous" factors, but the results are the same. Thus, on the list of foreign associates of the Academy of Paris, there is not a single Irish or English Catholic, although their proportion in the population of the three kingdoms exceeded a fifth.

84. For example, Havelock Ellis' *Study of British Genius*, 66 ff. finds that Protestant Scotland produced twenty-one of the outstanding scientists on his list as against one for Catholic Ireland. Alfred Odin finds that among the littérateurs on his list, the predominant emphasis of Protestants is on scientific and technical matters, rather than on literature, properly so-called. See his *Genèse des grands hommes* (Paris, 1895, I, 477 ff., II, Tables xx-xxi.

85. Alphonse de Candolle, *Histoire des sciences et des savants* (Geneva-Basel, 1885), 329.

86. *Ibid.*, 330. *Cf.* J. Făcăoaru, *Soziale Auslese* (Klausenberg, 1933), 138-9. "Die Konfession hat einen grossen Einfluss auf die Entwicklung der Wissenschaft gehabt. Die Protestanten wiesen überall eine grössere Zahl hervorragender Männer auf."

Likewise, Catholic Austria is not at all represented, while in general Catholic Germany is similarly lacking in the production of scientists of note relative to Protestant Germany. Finally, in Switzerland, where the two religions are largely differentiated by cantons, or mixed in some of them, and where the Protestants are to the Catholics as three to two there have been fourteen foreign Associates, of whom not one was Catholic. The same differentiation exists for the Swiss and for the English and Irish of the two religions in the lists of the Royal Society of London and the Royal Academy of Berlin.[87]

With the presentation of these data we close the empirical testing of our hypothesis. In every instance, the association of Protestantism with scientific and technologic interests and achievements is pronounced, even when extra-religious influences are as far as possible eliminated. The association is largely understandable in terms of the norms embodied in both systems. The positive estimation by Protestants of a hardly disguised utilitarianism, of intra-mundane interests, of a thorough-going empiricism, of the right and even the duty of *libre examen,* and of the explicit individual questioning of authority were congenial to the same values found in modern science. And perhaps above all is the significance of the active ascetic drive which necessitated the study of Nature that it might be controlled. Hence, these two fields were well integrated and, in essentials, mutually supporting, not only in seventeenth-century England but in other times and places.

BIBLIOGRAPHICAL POSTSCRIPT

Max Weber's hypothesis of the role of ascetic Protestantism in the furtherance of modern capitalism has given rise to a substantial library of scholarly and polemical works on the subject. By the mid-thirties, for example, Amintore Fanfani could draw upon several hundred publications in his appraisal of the evidence; *Catholicism, Protestantism and Capitalism* (New York: Sheed & Ward, 1935). Weber did not himself conduct a similar inquiry into the relations between ascetic Protestantism and the development of science but concluded his classic essay by describing one of "the next tasks" as that of searching out "the significance of ascetic rationalism, which has only been touched in the foregoing sketch, . . . [for] the development of philosophical and scientific empiricism, [and for] . . . technical development." (*The Protestant Ethic,* 182-183). First published in 1936, the preceding chapter was conceived as an effort to follow this mandate to extend the line of inquiry which Weber had opened up.

The books and papers cited in this chapter have since been supplemented by others bearing on one or another part of the hypothesis con-

---

87. Candolle, *op. cit.,* 330 ff.

necting Puritanism, Pietism and science. Numerous works have greatly clarified the varieties and shadings of doctrine and values comprised in Puritanism; among these, I have found the following most useful: John Thomas McNeill, *The History and Character of Calvinism* (New York: Oxford University Press, 1954) which shows Calvinism to have formed the core of English Puritanism and traces its varied consequences for society and thought; William Haller, *The Rise of Puritanism* (New York: Columbia University Press, 1939) which describes in rich and convincing detail how Puritan propaganda in press and pulpit helped prepare the way for the parliamentary rebellion, the radicalism of the Levellers, numerous sectarian fissions, an incipient bourgeois ethic and experimental science; Charles H. George, "A social interpretation of English Puritanism," *The Journal of Modern History*, 1953, 25, 327-342, which tries to identify the major components and the major types of Puritanism; G. R. Cragg, *From Puritanism to the Age of Reason* (Cambridge University Press, 1950), a "study of changes in religious thought within the Church of England, 1660-1700."

These and similar works have shown anew that Puritanism, like most religio-social creeds, was not of a piece. Practically all the scholars who have made intensive studies of the matter are agreed that most of the numerous sects comprising ascetic Protestantism provided a value-orientation encouraging work in science. (See also the note by Jean Pelseneer, "L'origine Protestante de la science moderne," *Lychnos*, 1946-47, 246-248.) But there the near-unanimity ends. Some have concluded that it was the more radical sectarians among the Puritans who did most to develop an enlarged interest in science; see, for example, George Rosen, "Left-wing Puritanism and science," *Bulletin of the Institute of the History of Medicine*, 1944, 15, 375-380. The biochemist and historian of science, Joseph Needham, comments on the close connections between the Diggers, the civilian wing of the Levellers, and the new and growing interest in experimental science, in his collection of essays, *Time: The Refreshing River* (New York: The Macmillan Company, 1943), 84-103. Others hold that the climate of values most conducive to an interest in science was found among the *moderate* Puritans, as exemplified by Robert Boyle. See James B. Conant, "The advancement of learning during the Puritan Commonwealth," *Proceedings of the Massachusetts Historical Society*, 1942, 66, 3-31; and for a more generally accessible though less detailed discussion, the same author's *On Understanding Science* (New Haven: Yale University Press, 1947), 60-62. R. Hooykaas, the distinguished Dutch historian of science, reports that his biography of Boyle's scientific and religious orientations confirms the principal findings set out in the foregoing chapter: R. Hooykaas, *Robert Boyle: een studie over Natuurwetenschap en Christendom* (Loosduinen: Kleijwegt, 1943), Chapters 3-4 which analyze Boyle's convictions that the study of natural philosophy is a religiously-founded moral obligation (especially as these are developed in Boyle's *The Christian Virtuoso, shewing, that by being addicted to experimental philosophy a man is rather assisted than indisposed to be a good Christian,* 1690), that empiricism and not merely rationality is required to comprehend God's works, and that tolerance, not persecution, is the policy appropriately governing relations with even the most fanatic sects.

The evidence in support of both the competing premises—that the chief locus of interest is to be found among the radical or the moderate Puritans—is still insufficient to justify a firm conclusion. Detailed distinctions among the various Puritan sects of course serve to specify the hypothesis more rigorously but the data in hand do not yet allow one to say, with any confidence, which of these were most disposed to advance the science of the day.

A recent group of studies provides substantial documentation of the ways in which the ethos of one of these Puritan sects—the Quakers—helped crystallize a distinct interest in science. In much the same terms set forth in the preceding chapter of this book, Frederick B. Tolles, *Meeting House and Counting House* (Chapel Hill: University of North Carolina Press, 1948), 205-213, derives the marked interest of Quakers in science from their religious ethos. Less analytically and, at times, even tendentiously, Arthur Raistrick, *Quakers in Science and Industry, being an account of the Quaker contributions to science and industry during the 17th and 18th centuries* (London: The Bannisdale Press, 1950) emphasizes the *fact* of the large proportion of Quaker members of the Royal Society and the *fact* of their extensive work in science. But as Professor Hooykaas properly notes, these unanalyzed facts do not themselves indicate that the distinctive participation of Quakers in scientific activity stemmed from their religious ethic; it might well be that it reflected the widespread tendency of well-to-do Englishmen, who included a disproportionately large number of Quakers, to turn their interest to matters of natural philosophy (R. Hooykaas, in *Archives Internationales d'Histoire des Sciences,* January 1951). In a compact and instructive paper, however, Brooke Hindle goes on to show that the religious ethic did play this role among the Quakers of one colonial area; *cf.* his "Quaker background and science in colonial Philadelphia," *Isis,* 1955, 46, 243-250; and his excellent monograph, *The Pursuit of Science in Revolutionary America, 1735-1789* (Chapel Hill: University of North Carolina Press, 1956).

It may be remembered that one of the principal hypotheses of the preceding chapter held that it was the *unintended and largely unforeseen consequences* of the religious ethic formulated by the great Reformist leaders which progressively developed into a system of values favorable to the pursuit of science. (580; *cf.* F. S. Mason, "The scientific revolution and the Protestant Reformation. I. Calvin and Servetus in relation to the new astronomy and the theory of the circulation of the blood. II. Lutheranism in relation to iatrochemistry and German nature philosophy," *Annals of Science*, 1953, 9, 64-87, 154-175.) The historical shaping of this ethic was doubtless partly in response to changing social, cultural and economic contexts but partly, also, it was an immanent development of the religious ideas and values themselves (as Wesley, above all other Protestant leaders, clearly perceived). This is only to say again that the rôle of ascetic Protestantism in encouraging the development of science did not remain fixed and unchanging. What was only implicit in the sixteenth and early seventeenth centuries became explicit and visible to many in the later seventeenth and eighteenth centuries. Several recent studies confirm this interpretation.

Based upon a close scrutiny of primary sources and present-day research, Paul H. Kocher's *Science and Religion in Elizabethan England* (San Marino, California: The Huntington Library, 1953) testifies to the long distance scholars have come since the day when they considered only the sources of conflict between science and religion as though conflict were plainly the *only* relation which could, and historically did, subsist between these social institutions. In contrast, this monograph shows that there was ample room for the science of Elizabethan England to develop within the bounds set by the religious doctrine of the time. Nor was this simply a matter of religion *tolerating* science. For the period before 1610, Kocher can find no convincing evidence "for or against" the hypothesis that Puritanism provided a more "fertile soil for natural science than . . . its rival religions in England." (17) The data for this early period are inadequate to reach a sound conclusion. But, he goes on to say, "we can see from our vantage point in the twentieth century that Puritan worldliness was ultimately to aid science more than Puritan otherworldliness was to inhibit it, in proportion more perhaps (though this is much less certain) than could Anglican doctrine or practice. But the effects of such impetus were to become visible only gradually as Puritanism developed. The Elizabethan age came too early to afford concrete evidence for distinguishing and weighing against each other the contributions of Puritans and Anglicans to science." (19) Considered in terms of the immanent dynamic of the religious ethos, however, Kocher's contrast between the 'worldliness' and 'otherworldliness' of successive generations of Puritans is more seeming than real. For, as Weber was able to show in detail, 'worldliness' was historically generated by the originally 'otherworldly' values of Puritanism, which called for active and sustained effort in this world and so subverted the initial value-orientation (this process being an example of what he called the *Paradoxie der Folgen*). Manifest conformity to these values produced latent consequences which were far removed in character from the values which released them.

By the eighteenth century, this process of change had resulted in what has been described by Basil Willey as "the holy alliance between science and religion." (*The Eighteenth Century Background.* New York: Columbia University Press, 1941.) Just as Robert Boyle in the seventeenth century, so Joseph Priestley, the scientist and apostle of Unitarianism, in the eighteenth, symbolized and actualized this alliance.

The later connections between science and religion in England from the late eighteenth to the mid-nineteenth century have been painstakingly examined in the monograph by Charles C. Gillispie, *Genesis and Geology: a study in the relations of scientific thought, natural theology and social opinion in Great Britain, 1790-1850* (Cambridge: Harvard University Press, 1951). Concerned less with the role of religion in the recruitment and motivation of scientists than with the grounds on which the findings of geology were regarded as consistent with religious teachings, Gillispie traces the process through which these tended to become culturally integrated.

When the paper which forms the present chapter was written in 1936, I relied almost entirely on Irene Parker's pioneering study (1914) of the role of the Dissenting Academies in advancing the new scientific education of the 18th century.* The import of her study is not basically changed but is substantially developed and somewhat modified in the remarkable study by Nicholas Hans, *New Trends in Education in the Eighteenth Century* (London: Routledge & Kegan Paul, 1951). Hans bases part of his study upon a statistical analysis of the social origins, formal education and subsequent careers of some 3,500 individuals who formed the intellectual élite of that century, the basic data having been systematically assembled from the individual biographies in that almost inexhaustible mine of materials for historical sociology, the *Dictionary of National Biography.*† Only a few of his numerous pertinent findings

---

* Should it be asked why I did not make use of the later and amply-documented book, M. McLachlan's *English Education under the Test Acts* (1931), I could only reply, in the words of another 'harmless drudge,' "Ignorance, Madam, pure ignorance." It should be added, however, that McLachlan is in fundamental agreement with the major conclusions of Irene Parker.

† Studies in historical sociology have only begun to quarry the rich ore available in comprehensive collections of biography and other historical evidence. Although statistical analyses of such materials cannot stand in place of detailed qualitative analyses of the historical evidence, they afford a *systematic* basis for new findings and, often, for correction of received assumptions. At least, this has been my own experience in undertaking statistical analyses of some 6,000 biographies (in the D.N.B.) of those who comprised the élite of seventeenth-century England; of the lists of important discoveries and inventions listed in Darmstädter's *Handbuch zur Geschichte der Naturwissenschaften und der Technik;* and of 2,000 articles published in the *Philosophical Transactions* during the last third of the seventeenth century. (*Cf.* Merton, *Science, Technology and Society in Seventeenth-Century England,* 1938, Chapters II-III.) The most extensive use of such statistical analyses is found in P. A. Sorokin, *Social and Cultural Dynamics* (New York: American Book Co., 1937). Of course, the preparation of statistical summaries of this kind have their hazards; routinized compilations unrestrained by knowledge of the historical

will be summarized here. He finds, for example, that the Dissenting Schools and Academies produced about 10 per cent of the élite which, as Hans observes, "was far above their relative strength in the total population of England in the eighteenth century." (20) Nevertheless, he notes, as we have seen to be the case, that religious 'motives' were not alone in making for the emergence of modern education (and specifically, of scientific education) in this period; with religion were joined 'intellectual' and 'utilitarian' motives. Thus, while "the Puritans promoted science as an additional support of Christian faith based on revelation, the deists looked upon science as the foundation of any belief in God." (12) The three types of motivation tended to reinforce one another: "The Dissenters, as well as many Puritans within the Church, represented the religious motive for educational reform. The idea of *propagatio fidei per scientia* found many adherents among the Dissenters. The intellectual and utilitarian reasons were put into full motion by secular bodies and teachers before the Dissenting Academies accepted them wholeheartedly." (54)

It is in this last respect that Hans find it necessary to dissent from the thesis put forward by Irene Parker (which I adopted in my own paper), holding that she attributes almost exclusive influence to the Academies in advancing modern education in the eighteenth century. His corrective modification appears, on the ample evidence, to be thoroughly justified. Furthermore, it serves to clarify a problem which, at least one student of the matter can report, has long been troublesome and unresolved. This is the well-recognized fact that certain extreme forms of Calvinist dissent were for a long time inimical to the advancement of science, rather than conducive to it. As Hans now points out, "although the Calvinist tradition was essentially progressive it easily degenerated into narrow and intolerant dogmatism." (55) The Baptists, for example, were thoroughly "averse to the new learning from conviction and only late in the century joined other Dissenters [particularly the Presbyterians and Independents] in promoting the reform." (55) One wing of nonconformity, in short, adhered literally to certain restrictive tenets of Calvinism and it was this subgroup that manifested the hostility to science which has for so long been found in certain fundamentalist sects of Protestantism. Figuratively, it can be said that "Calvinism contained a seed of modern liberal education but it required a suitable environment to germinate and grow." (57) And, as we have

---

contexts of the data can lead to unfounded conclusions. For a discussion of some of these hazards, see P. A. Sorokin and R. K. Merton, "The course of Arabian intellectual development: a study in method," *Isis*, 1935, 22, 516-524; Merton, *op. cit.*, 367 ff., 398 ff.; and for a more thorough review of the problems of procedure, Bernard Berelson, *Content Analysis* (Glencoe: The Free Press, 1951). Numerous recent studies of the social origins of business élite in the historical past have utilized materials of this sort: see the studies by William Miller, C. W. Mills and Suzanne Keller instructively summarized by Bernard Barber, *Social Stratification* (New York: Harcourt, Brace & Co., 1957).

seen, this social and cultural context was progressively provided in England of the time.

Supplementing these studies of the changing relations between Puritanism and science in England is the remarkable study by Perry Miller of these relations under the special conditions afforded by New England. (*The New England Mind: The Seventeenth Century.* Reissue. *The New England Mind: From Colony to Province.* Cambridge: Harvard University Press, 1954.) This comprehensive work demonstrates the notable receptivity to science among the theocratic leaders of the colony and the ensuing process of secularization, with its emphasis on utilitarianism. For a short but instructive comparison of the interpretation advanced by Perry Miller and that advanced in the preceding chapter, see Leo Marx, *Isis,* 1956, 47, 80-81.

As we have seen from the data assembled by Alphonse de Candolle —see pages 594-595 of this book—the connections of ascetic Protestantism and interest in science evidently persisted to some extent through the nineteenth century. Candolle's data have lately been examined again, with the same conclusion. See Isidor Thorner, "Ascetic Protestantism and the development of science and technology," *American Journal of Sociology,* 1952, 58, 25-33, esp. at 31-32. Thorner has also analyzed the data presented by P. A. Sorokin as a basis for questioning this hypothesis and finds that the data are actually in accord with it; *ibid.,* 28-30. For Sorokin's critique, see his *Social and Cultural Dynamics,* II, 150-152.

In another, searching review of Candolle's materials, Lilley has indicated their limitations as well as their uses. S. Lilley, "Social aspects of the history of science," *Archives Internationales d'Histoire des Sciences,* 1949, 28, 376-443, esp. 333 ff. He observes that the correlations between Protestantism and science may be spurious since "on the average the commercial and industrial classes [who have a greater interest in science] have tended to be Protestant in persuasion and the peasantry and more feudal types of landowners to be Catholic." We have taken note of this limitation (592) and have accordingly compared the interest in scientific subjects of Protestants and Catholics drawn from the same areas (592, 594). Lilley also criticizes Candolle's work for failing to take account of historical change in these relationships by lumping together, "without distinction, the whole period from 1666 to 1868." Presumably, religious affiliations in the latter and more secularized period would represent less by way of doctrinal and value commitments than in the earlier period; purely nominal memberships would tend to become more frequent. This criticism also has force, as we have seen. But as Lilley goes on to observe, further evidence in hand nevertheless confirms the underlying relationship between ascetic Protestantism and science, although this relationship may be masked or accentuated by other interdependent social and economic changes.

That the relationship persists to the present day in the United States is indicated by a recent thorough-going study of the social antecedents of American scientists, from 1880 to 1940. R. H. Knapp and H. B. Goodrich, *Origins of American Scientists* (Chicago: University of Chicago Press, 1952). Their evidence on this point is summarized as follows: "Our data have shown the marked inferiority of Catholic [academic] institutions in the production of scientists [but not of other professionals; for example, lawyers] and, on the other hand, the fact that some of our most productive smaller institutions are closely connected with Protestant denominations and serve a preponderantly Protestant clientele. Moreover, the data presented by Lehman and Visher on the 'starred' scientists [i.e. the scientists listed in *American Men of Science* who are judged to be of outstanding merit], although limited, indicate very clearly that the proportion of Catholics in this group is excessively low—that, indeed, some Protestant denominations are proportionately several hundred times more strongly represented. These statistics, taken together with other evidence, leave little doubt that scientists have been drawn disproportionately from American Protestant stock." (274)

Much the same impression, but without systematic supporting data, has been reported by Catholic scientists. "Father Cooper says he 'would be loath to have to defend the thesis that 5 per cent or even 3 per cent of the leadership in American science and scholarship is Catholic. Yet we Catholics constitute something like 20 per cent of the total population.'" J. M. Cooper, "Catholics and scientific research," *Commonweal*, 1945, 42, 147-149, as quoted by Bernard Barber, *Science and the Social Order*, 136. Barber also cites a similar observation by James A. Reyniers, Director of the Lobund Laboratories of Notre Dame University and by Joseph P. Fitzpatrick, S.J.; *ibid.*, 271.

This review of the more recent literature on the subject rather uniformly confirms the hypothesis of an observable positive relationship between ascetic Protestantism and science. The data provided by any one of these studies are typically far from rigorous. But this is, after all, the condition of most evidence bearing upon historically changing relations between social institutions. Considering not this study or that, but the entire array, based upon materials drawn from varied sources, we would seem to have some reasonable assurance that the empirical relationship, supposed in the foregoing study, does in fact exist.

But, of course, the gross empirical relationship is only the beginning, not the end, of the intellectual problem. As Weber noted, early in his celebrated essay on *The Protestant Ethic*, "a glance at the occupational statistics of any country of mixed religious composition brings to light with remarkable frequency a situation which has several times provoked discussion in the Catholic press and literature, and in Catholic congresses in Germany, namely, the fact that business leaders and owners of capital, as well as the higher grades of skilled labor, and even

more the higher technically and commercially trained personnel of modern enterprises, are overwhelmingly Protestant." (35) The fortuity that
comparable statistics on the religious composition of scientists are not
ready to hand but must be laboriously assembled for the present and
partially pieced together for the past does not make the empirical finding any more significant in itself (though it may commend to our respectful attention the arduous labors of those doing the spadework).
For, as we have seen in examining the status of empirical generalizations
(in Chapter 2), this only sets the problem of analyzing and interpreting
the observed uniformity, and it is to this problem that the foregoing
essay has addressed itself.

The principal components of the interpretation advanced in this essay
presumably do not require repetition. However, a recent critique of the
study provides an occasion for reviewing certain empirical and theoretical elements of the interpretation which can, apparently, be lost to sight.
In this critique—"Merton's thesis on English science," *American Journal
of Economics and Sociology,* 1954, 13, 427-432—James W. Carroll reports
what he takes to be several oversights in the formulation. It is suggested
that the heterogeneity of the beliefs included in Protestantism generally
and in Puritanism specifically has been overlooked or imperfectly recognized. Were the charge true, it would plainly have merit. Yet it should
be observed that the hypothesis in question is introduced by a chapter
which begins by noting "the diversity of theological doctrines among
the Protestant groups of seventeenth-century England" and continues by
considering the values, beliefs and interests which are common to the
numerous sects deriving from Calvinism (Merton, *Science, Technology
and Science in Seventeenth-Century England,* Chapter IV, 415 ff.). And,
as may be seen from this bibliographical postscript, historical scholarship has more thoroughly established the similarities, and not only the
differences, among the Puritan sects stemming from ascetic Calvinism.

Carroll goes on to say that the evidence for the connection between
the norms of Puritanism and of science provides only an empirical similarity between the two (or what is described as a Comtean 'correlation
of assertions'). But this is to ignore the demonstrated fact that English
scientists themselves repeatedly invoked these Puritan values and expressly translated them into practice. (*Cf. ibid.,* Chapter V.)

That the Puritan values were indeed expressed by scientists is in fact
implied in Carroll's next suggestion that no basis is provided in the study
for discriminating between the 'rationalizations' and the 'motives' of
these scientists. This touches upon a theoretical problem of such general import, and widespread misunderstanding, that it is appropriate to
repeat part of what was said about it in the earlier study. "Present-day
discussions of 'rationalization' and 'derivations' have been wont to be-
cloud certain fundamental issues. It is true that the 'reasons' adduced

to justify one's actions often do not account satisfactorily for this behavior. It is also an acceptable hypothesis that ideologies [alone] seldom
give rise to action and that both the ideology and the action are rather
the product of common sentiments and values upon which they in turn
react. But these ideas can not be ignored for two reasons. They provide
clues for detecting the basic values which motivate conduct. Such sign-
posts can not be profitably neglected. Of even greater importance is the
rôle of ideas in directing action into *particular* channels. *It is the
dominating system of ideas which determines the choice between alternative modes of action that are equally compatible with the underlying
sentiments."* (*Ibid.*, 450.)

As for distinguishing between the expression of reasons which are
merely accommodative lip-service and those which express basic orientations, the test is here, as elsewhere, to be found in the behavior which
accords with these reasons, even when there is little or no prospect of
self-interested mundane reward. As the clearest and best-documented
case, Robert Boyle can here represent the other Puritans among his
scientific colleagues who, in varying degree, expressed their religious
sentiments in their private lives as in their lives as scientists. It would
seem unlikely that Boyle was 'merely rationalizing' in saying "that those
who labour to deter men from sedulous Enquiries into Nature do
(though I grant, designlessly) take a course which tends to defeat God.
. . ." (Robert Boyle, *Some Considerations Touching the Usefulness of
Experimental Natural Philosophy,* (Oxford, 1664; 2d edition, 27.) For
this is the same Boyle who had written religious essays by the age of
twenty-one; had, despite his distaste for the study of language, expressed
his veneration for the Scriptures by learning Hebrew, Greek, Chaldee
and Syriac that he might read them in their early versions; had provided a pension for Robert Sanderson to enable him to continue writing
books on casuistry; had largely paid for the costs of printing the Indian,
Irish and Welsh Bibles and, as if this were not enough, for the Turkish
New Testament and the Malayan version of the Gospels and Acts; had
become Governor of the Corporation for the Spread of the Gospel in
New England and as a director of the East India Company had devoted
himself and his resources to the diffusion of Christianity in these areas;
had contributed substantially to the fund for printing Burnet's *History
of the Reformation;* had published his profession of faith in *The Christian Virtuoso* and, quite finally, had provided in his will for endowment
of the 'Boyle lectures' for the purpose of defending Christianity against
unbelievers. (This is the compact record set forth in A. M. Clerke's
biography of Boyle in the *Dictionary of Natural Biography.*) Although
Boyle was foremost in piety among Puritan scientists, he was still only
first among equals, as witness Wilkins, Willughby and Ray among many
others. So far as any historical record of words and action can permit

us to say, it would appear that scientists like Boyle were not simply "rationalizing."

Carroll's final criticism, if intended conscientiously and not frivolously, exhibits a melancholy degree of immunity to commonplace and inconvenient facts of history. He observes that in showing the original membership of the Royal Society to have been preponderantly Protestant, the essay under review does not examine the possibility that the 'invisible college,' from which the Society stemmed, was part of a widespread Protestant movement of reform and that known Catholics were consequently banned from membership. That *Protestants* comprised the original membership of the Royal Society goes, one would suppose, without saying; in that day and age of the 1660's, in spite of the later political traffic of Charles II with the Catholicism of Louis XIV, Catholics would scarcely have been granted the prerogative of founding an association under the auspices of the Crown. The fact which is of more than passing interest is not, of course, that the Society was preponderantly *Protestant*, but that it was preponderantly *Puritan*. As for the observation that avowed Catholics were banned from academic posts, it evidently needs to be recalled that the Test Act of 1673, though later occasionally nullified in particular instances, excluded Nonconformists and not only Catholics and Jews from the universities. Yet, although this remained in force into the nineteenth century, Nonconformists continued to provide a large fraction of the men of science.

This short review of the most recently accumulated evidence suggests that, however contrary this may have been to the intentions of the Great Reformers, the ascetic Protestant sects developed a distinct predilection for working the field of science. In view of the powerful crosscurrents of other historical forces, which might have deflected this early orientation toward science, it is notable that the association between ascetic Protestantism and science has persisted to the present day. Profound commitments to the values of ascetic Protestantism have presumably become less common, yet the orientation, deprived of its theological meanings, evidently remains. As with any hypothesis, particularly in historical sociology, this one must be regarded as provisional, subject to review as more of the evidence comes in. But as the evidence now stands, the fact is reasonably well established and has definite implications for the broader problem of the connections between science and other social institutions.

The first of these implications is that, in this case at least, the emerging connections between science and religion were indirect and unintended. For, as has been repeatedly said, the reformers were not enthusiastic about science. Luther was at best indifferent; at worst, hostile. In his *Institutes* and his *Commentarie upon Genesis*, Calvin was ambivalent, granting some virtue to the practical intellect but far less than that owing to revealed knowledge. Nevertheless, the religious ethic which stemmed from Calvin promoted a state of mind and a value-orientation which invited the pursuit of natural science.

Second, it appears that once a value-orientation of this kind becomes established, it develops some degree of functional autonomy, so that the predilection for science could remain long after it has cut away from its original theological moorings.

Third, this pattern of orientation, which can even now be detected statistically, may be unwitting and below the threshold of awareness of many of those involved in it.

Fourth and finally, the highly visible interaction of the institutions of science and religion—as in the so-called war between the two in the nineteenth century—may obscure the less visible, indirect and perhaps more significant relationship between the two.

XIX SCIENCE AND ECONOMY OF 17th CENTURY ENGLAND

T HE INTERPLAY BETWEEN socio-economic and scientific development is scarcely problematical. To speak of socio-economic influences
upon science in general unanalyzed terms, however, barely poses the
problem. The sociologist of science is specifically concerned with the
types of influence involved (facilitative and obstructive), the *extent* to
which these types prove effective in different social structures and the
processes through which they operate. But these questions cannot be
answered even tentatively without a clarification of the conceptual tools
employed. All too often, the sociologist who repudiates the mythopoeic
or heroic interpretation of the history of science lapses into a vulgar
materialism which seeks to find simple parallels between social and
scientific development. Such misguided efforts invariably result in a
seriously biased and untenable discussion.

FORMULATION OF THE PROBLEM

We begin by noting three common but unsound postulates. The first
and most illusive is the identification of the personal motivation of scientists with the structural determinants of their research. Second is the
belief that socio-economic factors serve to account exhaustively for the
entire complex of scientific activity; and third is the imputation of "social
needs" where these needs are, in any significant sense, absent.

Clark's recent critique[1] of Hessen's essay may be taken to illustrate
the confusion which derives from loose conceptualization concerning the
relations between the motivation and the structural determinants of
scientists' behavior. Clark tends to restrict the role of socio-economic
factors in science to that of utilitarian motives of scientists and, cor-

---

1. G. N. Clark, *Science and Social Welfare in the Age of Newton* (Oxford, 1937).
See B. Hessen, "The social and economic roots of Newton's *Principia*," *Science at
the Cross Roads* (London, 1931).

relatively, to identify "the disinterested desire to know, the impulse of the mind to exercise itself methodically and without any practical purpose" with scientific activity unconditioned by socio-economic elements.[2] Thus, to illustrate Newton's disinterestedness (in this sense of the word), Clark cites a frequently-reported anecdote to the effect that a friend to whom "he had lent a copy of Euclid's *Elements* asked Newton of what 'use or benefit in life' the study of the book could be. That was the only occasion on which it is recorded that Newton laughed."[3] Granting the reliability of this tale, its relevance to the issue in question is negligible, except on the assumption that people are invariably *aware* of the social forces which condition their behavior and that their behavior can be understood only in terms of their conscious motivations.

Motives may range from the desire for personal aggrandisement to a wholly "disinterested desire to know" without necessarily impugning the demonstrable fact that the thematics of science in seventeenth century England were in large part determined by the social structure of the time. Newton's own motives do not alter the fact that astronomical observations, of which he made considerable use,[4] were a product of Flamsteed's work in the Greenwich Observatory, which was constructed at the command of Charles II for the benefit of the Royal Navy.[5] Nor do they negate the striking influence upon Newton's work of such practically-oriented scientists as Halley, Hooke, Wren, Huyghens and Boyle. Even in regard to the question of motivation, Clark's thesis is debatable in view of the explicit awareness of many scientists in seventeenth century England concerning the practical implications of their research in pure science. It is neither an idle nor unguarded generalization that *every English scientist of this time* who was of sufficient distinction to merit mention in general histories of science at one point or another explicitly related at least some of his scientific research to immediate

---

2. *Ibid.*, p. 86; and throughout Ch. 3.

3. *Ibid.*, p. 91. The original, slightly variant, version is in the *Portsmouth Collection.*

4. See the correspondence between Newton and Flamsteed, quoted extensively in L. T. More, *Isaac Newton* (New York, 1934), Ch. 11.

5. It was interest in the improvement of navigation which, according to Flamsteed, the first Astronomer Royal, led directly to the construction of the Greenwich Observatory. (Incidentally, Colbert proposed the Paris Observatory for the same purpose.) A Frenchman, Le Sieur de St. Pierre, visited England and proposed "improved" methods of determining longitude at sea. Flamsteed indicated in an official report that this project was not practicable, since "the lunar tables differed from the heavens." The report being shown to Charles, "he, startled at the assertion of the fixed stars' being false in the catalogue; said with some vehemence, 'he must have them anew observed, examined, and corrected, for the use of his seamen.'" Whereupon it was decided both to erect the Observatory and to appoint Flamsteed the Astronomer Royal. See Francis Baily, *An Account of the Rev'd John Flamsteed, compiled from his own manuscripts* (London, 1935), p. 37. To be sure, Flamsteed's salary was but 100 pounds a year. He was privileged to provide himself with all requisite instruments—at his own expense.

practical problems.[6] But in any case, analysis exclusively in terms of (imputed) motives is seriously misleading and tends to befog the question of the modes of socio-economic influence upon science.[7]

It is important to distinguish the personal attitudes of individual men of science from the social role played by their research. Clearly, some scientists were sufficiently enamored of their subject to pursue it for its own sake, at times with little consideration of its practical bearings. Nor need we assume that *all* individual researches are directly linked to technical tasks. The relation between science and social needs is two-fold: direct, in the sense that some research is advisedly and deliberately pursued for utilitarian purposes and indirect, in so far as certain problems and materials for their solution come to the attention of scientists although they need not be cognizant of the practical exigencies from which they derive.

In this connection, one is led to question Sombart's generalization that seventeenth century technology was almost completely divorced[8] from the contemporary science, that the scientist and inventor had gone their separate ways from the time of Leonardo to the eighteenth century. To be sure, the alliance of the two is not equally secure in all social structures but the assertion of Sombart (and others) that seventeenth century technology was essentially that of the empiric seems exaggerated in view of the many scientists who turned their theoretical knowledge to practical account. Wren, Hooke, Newton, Boyle, Huyghens, Halley, Flamsteed—to mention but an illustrious few—devoted themselves to the prosecution of both theory and practice. What is more important, scientists were uniformly confident of the practical fruits which their continued industry would ensure. It was this conviction, quite apart from the question of its validity, which partly influenced their choice of problems. The grain of truth in Sombart's thesis is reduced to the fact that these men of science were concerned not with advancing the development of industrial machinery for factory use—since this had not developed sufficiently to claim their interest—but with innovations which implemented commerce, mining and military technique.[9]

---

6. Documentation supporting this statement may be found in my *Science, Technology and Society in 17th-Century England* (Bruges, 1938).

7. For a systematic treatment of this problem, see Joseph Needham, "Limiting factors in the advancement of science as observed in the history of embryology," *Yale Journal of Biology and Medicine*, 1935, 8, 1-18.

8. See Werner Sombart, *Der moderne Kapitalismus* (Munich, 1921), I, 466-67. The metaphor is highly appropriate in view of the remark by Oldenburg, the quondam secretary of the Royal Society, that the natural philosophers sought "the Marriage of Nature and Art, [whence] a happy issue may follow for the use and benefit of Humane Life," *Philosophical Transactions*, 1665, 1, 109.

9. Franz Borkenau has perceived this necessary distinction: "Die Naturwissenschaft des 17. Jahrhunderts stand nicht im Dienste der *Industriellen Produktion, obwohl sie das seit Bacons Zeiten gewünscht hätte.*" *Der Uebergang vom feudalen zum bürgerlichen Weltbild* (Paris, 1934), 3. (Italics supplied.)

Within this context, Clark's criticism of Hessen narrows down to a repudiation of the thesis that economic factors are *alone* determinant of the development of science. In company with Hessen I hasten to assent to this judgment. The primitive thesis of exclusively economic determination is no more intrinsic to Hessen's analysis, as he himself indicates (*op. cit.*, p. 177), than to the work of Marx and Engels.

There remains the third problem—of ascertaining social needs—which can best be handled in specific empirical terms. The widely accepted notion that need precipitates appropriate inventions and canalizes scientific interests demands careful restatement. Specific emergencies have often focused attention upon certain fields, but it is equally true that a multitude of human needs have gone unsatisfied throughout the ages. In the technical sphere, needs far from being exceptional, are so general that they explain little. Each invention *de facto* satisfies a need or is an attempt to achieve such satisfaction. It is also necessary to realize that certain needs may not exist for the society under observation, precisely because of its culture and social structure.[10] It is only when the goal is actually part and parcel of the culture in question, only when it is actually experienced as such by some members of the society, that one may properly speak of a need directing scientific and technological interest in certain channels. Moreover, economic needs may be satisfied not only technologically but also by changes in social organization. But given the routine of fulfilling certain types of needs by technologic invention, a pattern which was becoming established in the seventeenth century; given the prerequisite accumulation of technical and scientific knowledge which provides the basic fund for innovation; given (in this case) an *expanding* capitalistic economy; and it may then be said that necessity is the (foster) mother of invention and the grandparent of scientific advance.

TRANSPORT AND SCIENCE

The burgeoning of capitalistic enterprise in seventeenth century England intensified interest in more adequate means of transport and communication. St. Helena, Jamaica, North America were but the beginnings of England's great colonial expansion. This and the relatively low cost of water-transport[11] led to the marked growth of the merchant marine. More than forty per cent of the English production of coal was carried by water. Similarly, internal trade enhanced the need for improved facilities for land and river transport. Proposals for turnpikes and canals were common throughout the century.

---

10. For a lucid discussion of needs, see Lancelot Hogben's introduction to the volume edited by him, *Political Arithmetic* (New York, 1938).

11. The difference in costs of land and water transportation is strikingly, though perhaps exaggeratedly, indicated by Petty. "The water carriage of goods around the Globe of the Earth is but about double of the price of Land Carriage from Chester to London of the like goods," *Phil. Trans.*, 1684, 14, 666.

Foreign trade was assuming world-wide proportions. The best available, though defective, statistics testify to these developments. Imports and exports increased by almost 300 per cent between 1613 and 1700.[12] Wheeler, writing at the very beginning of the century, observed that for approximately sixty years, not four ships of over 120 tons carrying capacity had sailed on the Thames.[13] At Elizabeth's death there were only four merchant ships of 400 tons each in England.[14] The number of ships, particularly those of heavy tonnage, increased rapidly under the Commonwealth, partly in response to the impetus provided by the Dutch War. Ninety-eight ships, with a net tonnage of over 40,000, were built within one decade (1649-59).[15] Adam Anderson notes that the tonnage of English merchant ships in 1688 was double that in 1666,[16] and Sprat claims more than a duplication during the preceding two decades.[17] The official report on the Royal Navy submitted by Samuel Pepys in 1695 comments upon the notable naval expansion during the century. In 1607, the Royal Navy numbered forty ships of 50 tons and upwards; the total tonnage being about 23,600 with 7,800 manning the ships. By 1695, the corresponding figures were over 200 ships, with a tonnage of over 112,400 and with more than 45,000 men.

A substantial element in the heightened tempo of shipbuilding and the increased size of ships was, as Sombart has suggested, military necessity. Though the growth of the merchant marine was considerable, it did not match that of the Royal Navy,[18] as is evidenced by the comparative statistics assembled by Sombart. Military exigencies often prompted increased speed in shipbuilding as well as improvements in naval architecture.

Shipbuilding was furthered by military interests in three ways: more and larger ships were demanded, and above all, they were required within a shorter period. The requirements of the merchant marine could have been satisfied by handicraft methods of shipbuilding for yet another century. But these methods became discountenanced by the growing demands of the war marine; first in the construction of warships themselves, and then, of all ships, as the merchant marine was drawn into the stream of development. . . .[19]

Though Sombart tends to exaggerate the role of military exigencies

---

12. See the actual figures in E. Lipson, *The Economic History of England* (London, 1931), 11, 189.

13. John Wheeler, *Treatise of Commerce* (Middelburgh, 1601), 23.

14. Sir William Monson, *Naval Tracts* (London, 1703), 294.

15. The tonnage figures do not include 17 ships for which the data are not available. Adapted from M. Oppenheim, *A History of the Administration of the Royal Navy and of Merchant Shipping* (London, 1896), 330-37.

16. Adam Anderson, *Origin of Commerce,* (Dublin, 1790), III, 111.

17. Thomas Sprat, *The History of the Royal-Society of London* (London, 1667), 404.

18. Werner Sombart, *Krieg and Kapitalismus* (Munich, 1913), 179 ff.

19. *Ibid.,* 191.

in fostering more efficient methods of shipbuilding, it is clear that this factor combined with the intensified need for a larger merchant marine to accelerate such developments. In any event, available statistical data indicate a marked expansion in both mercantile and military marine beginning with the late sixteenth century.[20]

These developments were accompanied by increased emphasis upon a number of technical problems. Above all, the increase of commercial voyages to distant points—India, North America, Africa, Russia—stressed anew the need for accurate and expedient means of determining position at sea, of finding latitude and longitude.[21] Scientists were profoundly concerned with possible solutions to these problems.[22] Both mathematics and astronomy were signally advanced through research oriented in this direction.

Napier's invention of logarithms, expanded by Henry Briggs, Adrian Vlacq (in Holland), Edmund Gunter and Henry Gellibrand, was of aid to astronomer and mariner alike.[23] Adam Anderson possibly reflects the general attitude toward this achievement when he remarks that "logarithms are of great special utility to mariners at sea in calculations relating to their course, distance, latitude, longitude, etc."[24] Sprat, the genial historiographer of the Royal Society, asserted that the advance-

---

20. "Nos recherches [based on an examination of port-books] montrent à l'evidence que le commerce et la navigation de l'Angleterre faisaient de grands progrès au déclin du XVIᵉ et pendant la premiere moitié du XVIIᵉ siecle. On n'exagère guère en disant que la navigation anglaise a quadruplé, sinon quintuplé de 1580 jusqu'à 1640." A. O. Johnson, "L'acte de navigation anglais du 9 octobre 1651," *Revue d'histoire moderne*, 1934, 9, 13.

21. Hessen, *op. cit.*, 157-58.

22. In a paper read before the Royal Society by Dr. Bainbridge, it was stated: "Nullum est in tota ferè mathesi problema, quod mathematicorum ingenia magis exercet, nullum, quod astronomiae mágis conducit, quam problema inveniendi meridianorum sive longitudinum differentias." From the minutes of the Royal Society as transcribed in Thomas Birch, *History of the Royal Society of London* (London, 1757), IV, 311. Among the aims of the Society as stated by Oldenburg in the preface to the ninth volume (1674) of the Philosophical Transactions are: "spreading of practical mathematiques in all our Trade-towns and ports: making great rivers navigable; aiding the Fishery and Navigation; devising means of fertilizing barren lands, and cultivating waste lands; increasing the Linnen-trade; producing Latton [*sic*] and salt and saltpetre of our own."

23. Published in his *Mirifici logarithmorum canonis descriptio* (Edinburg, 1614). It is to be noted that Briggs, who was the first to make Napier's work appreciated and who in 1616 suggested the base 10 for the system of logarithms, wrote several works on navigation. Likewise, that Gellibrand was probably the first Englishman to correct Gilbert's conclusion that magnetic declination is "constant at a given place," by discovering the secular variation of the declination. See his *Discourse Mathematical on the Variation of the Magneticall Needle* (London, 1635).

24. *Op. cit.*, II, 346. Anderson notes likewise Sir Henry Savile's "noble establishment [in 1630] of two professors of mathematics in the University of Oxford; one of which was for geometry, and the other for astronomy. . . . Both which branches of mathematics are well known to be greatly beneficial to navigation and commerce." *Ibid.*, I, 177.

ment of navigation was one of the chief aims of the group.[25] Hooke, the irascible "curator of experiments" of the Society, who was at once an eminent scientist and probably the most prolific inventor of his time, wrote in this same connection:

First it is earnestly desired that all observations that have been already made of the variation of the magnetical needle in any part of the world, might be communicated, together with all the circumstances remarkable in the making thereof; of the celestiall observations for knowing the true meridian, or by what other means it may be found. . . . But from a considerable collection of such observations, Astronomy might be made available of that admirable effect of the body of the earth toucht by a loadstone, that if it will (as is probable it may) be usefull for the direction of seamen or others for finding the longitude of places, the observations collected, together with good navigation, which they [the Royal Society] engage to doe soe soon as they have a sufficient number of such observations. . . .[26]

A ballad written shortly after the Society began to meet at Gresham College reflects the popular appreciation of this interest, as is manifest in the following excerpt:

> This College will the whole world measure
> Which most impossible conclude,
> And navigation make a pleasure,
> By finding out the longitude:
> Every Tarpaulian shall then with ease
> Saile any ship to the Antipodes.[27]

Meeting officially as the Royal Society or foregathering at coffee-houses and private quarters, the scientific coterie discussed without end technical problems of immediate concern for the profit of the realm. Hooke's recently published diary discloses the varied pressures exerted upon him by the Society, the King and interested nobles to devote his studies to "things of use."[28] He would frequently repair to Garaways or Jonathans, the coffee-houses in Change Alley, where, with Christopher

25. Sprat, *op. cit.*, 150.

26. Robert Hooke, *Papers*, British Museum, Sloan MSS. 1039, f. 112. See also Hooke's *A Description of Helioscopes, and, Some Other Instruments* (London, 1676), postscript.

27. *In praise of the choice company of Philosophers and Witts, who meet on Wednesdays, weekly, at Gresham College*, By W[illiam?] G[lanville]. *Cf.* Dorothy Stimson, "Ballad of Gresham Colledge," *Isis*, 1932, 18, 103-17, who suggests that the author was probably Joseph Glanville.

28. *The Diary of Robert Hooke*, ed. by H. W. Robinson and W. Adams (London, 1935). For example, note the following entries: "At Sir Fr. Chaplains. Lodowick here about Longitude. Affirmed 3000 pound premium and 600 pounds more from the States," p. 160. "To Garaways with Sir Ch: Wren, mett Clark and Seignior, discoursed about watches for pocket and for Longitude. . . . Resolvd to complete [measuring?] degree. New Clepsydra ship, New Theory of sound," 221. "To Sir J. Williamson. He very kindly called me into his chamber. Spoke to me about the . . . Experiment, admonisht me to be diligent for this year to study things of use, to make the Kings Barometer . . .," 337.

Wren and others of their company, he would "discourse about Celestiall Motions" over a pot of tea while at nearby tables more mundane speculations engrossed the attention of stock-jobbers and lottery touts. Problems considered at Garaways were often made the object of special inquiry by the Society. In short, the prevailing picture is not that of a group of "economic men" jointly or severally seeking to improve their economic standing, but one of a band of curious students coöperatively delving into the arcana of nature. The demands of economically-derived needs posed new questions and emphasized old, opening up fresh avenues of research and coupling with this a persistent pressure for the solution of these problems. This proved largely effective since the scientist's sense of achievement was not exclusively in terms of scientific criteria. Scientists were not immune from the interest in social acclaim, and discoveries which promised profitable application were heralded far beyond the immediate circle of virtuosi. Scientific achievement carried with it the seldom-undesired privilege of mingling with persons of rank; it was, to some extent, a channel for social mobility. The case of Graunt is well-known. Similarly, Hooke, the son of a humble curate of Freshwater, found himself the friend of noblemen and could boast of frequent chats with the King. The untutored reactions of the laity to the different orders of scientific research might be represented by the contrasting responses of Charles II to the "weighing of ayre," the fundamental work on atmospheric pressure which to his limited mind seemed nothing but childish diversion and idle amusement, and to directly utilitarian researches on finding the longitude at sea, with which he was "most graciously pleased." Attitudes such as these served to guide a considerable part of scientific work into fields which might bear immediate fruit.[29]

A CASE: PROBLEM OF THE LONGITUDE

This engrossing problem of finding the longitude perhaps illustrates best the way in which practical considerations focused scientific interest upon certain fields. There can be no doubt that the contemporary astronomers were thoroughly impressed with the importance of discovering a satisfactory way of finding the longitude, particularly at sea. Time and time again they evince this predominant interest. Rooke, Wren, Hooke, Huyghens, Henry Bond, Hevelius, William Molineux, Nicolaus Mercator, Leibniz, Newton, Flamsteed, Halley, La Hire, G. D. Cassini, Borelli—

---

29. In this connection, see Adam Anderson's remarks on the Royal Society: ". . . its improvements in astronomy and geography are alone sufficient to exalt its reputation, and to demonstrate its great utility even to the mercantile world, without insisting on its many and great improvements in other arts and sciences, some of which have also a relation to commerce, navigation, manufactures, mines, agriculture, &c.," *Origin of Commerce*, II, 609.

practically all of the leading astronomers and virtuosi of the day repeatedly testify to this fact.

The various methods proposed for finding longitude led to the following investigations:

1. Computation of lunar distances from the sun or from a fixed star. First widely used in the first half of the sixteenth century and again in the latter seventeenth century.

2. Observations of the eclipses of the satellites of Jupiter. First proposed by Galileo in 1610; adopted by Rooke, Halley, G. D. Cassini, Flamsteed and others.

3. Observations of the moon's transit of the meridian. Generally current in the seventeenth century.

4. The use of pendulum clocks and other chronometers at sea, aided by Huyghens, Hooke, Halley, Messy, Sully, and others.

Newton clearly outlined these procedures, as well as the scientific problems which they involved, upon the occasion of Ditton's claim of the reward for an accurate method of determining longitude at sea.[30] The profound interest of English scientists in this subject is marked by an article in the first volume of the *Philosophical Transactions,* describing the use of pendulum clocks at sea.[31] As Sprat put it, the Society had taken the problem "into its peculiar care." Hooke attempted to improve the pendulum clock and, as he says, "the success of these [trials] made me further think of improving it for finding the Longitude, and . . . quickly led me to the use of Springs instead of Gravity for the making a Body vibrate in any posture. . . ."[32] A notorious controversy then raged about Hooke and Huyghens concerning priority in the successful construction of a watch with spiral balance spring. However the question of priority be settled, the very fact that two such eminent men of

---

30. William Whiston, *Longitude Discovered* (London, 1738), historical preface.

31. Major Holmes, "A Narrative concerning the Success of Pendulum Watches at Sea for the Longitude," *Phil. Trans.,* 1665, 1, 52-58.

32. Richard Waller, *The Posthumous Works of Robert Hooke* (London, 1705), Introduction. Galileo had apparently described a pendulum clock in 1641; Huyghens' invention in 1656 was independently conceived. Huyghens went on to invent the watch with a spring mechanism. See his description of the invention in the *Phil. Trans.,* 1675, 11, 272; reprinted from the *Journal des Sçavans,* Feb. 25, 1675. This led to the notorious dispute between Hooke and Oldenburg, who defended Huyghens' priority in actual construction. It is of some interest, in connection with the question of pecuniary motivation, that Hooke, at the meeting of the Society following that at which Huyghens' communication concerning his "new pocket watch" was read, mentioned "that he had an invention for finding the longitude to a minute of time, or fifteen minutes in the heavens, which he would make out and render practical, if a due compensation were to be had for it." Whereupon Sir James Shaen promised "that he would procure for him a thousand pounds sterling in a sum, or a hundred and fifty pounds per annum. Mr. Hooke declaring that he would choose the latter, the council pressed him to draw up articles accordingly, and to put his invention into act." *Cf.* Birch, *op. cit.,* III, 191. For further details, see Waller, *op. cit.,* Introduction.

science, among others, focused their attention upon this sphere of inquiry is itself significant. These simultaneous inventions are a resultant of two forces: the intrinsically scientific one which provided the theoretical materials employed in solving the problem in hand, and the non-scientific, largely economic, concern which served to direct interest toward the general problem. The limited range of practicable possibilities leads to independent duplicate inventions.

This problem continued to fire scientific research in other directions as well. Thus, Borelli, of the Royal Academy of Sciences at Paris (organized at the suggestion of the perspicacious Colbert), published an offer in both the *Journal des Sçavans* and the *Philosophical Transactions* to explain his method of making large glasses for telescopes or even to send glasses to those persons who were not in a position to make them, so that they might "observe the eclipses of the Satellites of Jupiter which happen almost every day, and afford so fair a way for establishing the Longitudes over all the Earth." Moreover, "the Longitudes of places at Sea, Capes, Promontories, and divers Islands being once exactly known by this means, would doubtless be of great help and considerable usefulness to Navigation."[33]

It is precisely these episodes, with their acknowledged practical implications, which clearly illustrate the role of utilitarian elements in furthering scientific advance. For it may be said, upon ample documentary grounds, that Giovanni Domenico Cassini's astronomical discoveries were largely a result of utilitarian interests. In almost all of Cassini's papers in the *Transactions* he emphasizes the value of observing the moons of Jupiter for determining longitude, by means of the method first suggested by Galileo.[34] It is perhaps not too much to say that from

---

33. *Phil. Trans.*, 1676, 11, 691-92.

34. See Leonard Olschki, *Galileo und seine Zeit* (Halle, 1927), 274 and 438, and the chapter on "Die Briefe über geographische Ortbestimmung." This method did not enable sufficient precision to be of much practical use. In the paper discussing his discovery of an unusual spot on Jupiter and fixing the period of the planet's rotation, Cassini observes that "a Travellour . . . may make use of it [the rotation] to find the Longitudes of the most remote places of the earth," *Phil. Trans.*, 1672, 7, 4042. In his discussion of the inequality of the time of rotation of the spots in different latitudes, he indicates the importance of this fact for a more precise determination of the longitude, *ibid.*, 1676, 6, 683. The announcement of his discovery of the third and fourth satellites of Saturn begins thus: "The Variety of wonderful Discoveries, which have been made this Century in the Heavens, since the invention of the Telescope, and the great Utility that may possibly be drawn therefrom, for perfecting natural Knowledg, and the Arts necessary to the Commerce and Society of Mankind, has incited Astronomers more strictly to Examine, if there were not something considerable that had not been hitherto perceived." Translated from the *Journal des Sçavans*, April 22, 1685; reprinted in *Phil. Trans.*, 1696, 16, 79. In the presentation of Cassini's tables for the eclipses of the first satellites of Jupiter, it is remarked that beyond doubt observations of these eclipses best enable the use of portable telescopes for finding the longitude. "And could these satellites be observed at Sea, a Ship at Sea might be enabled to find the Meridian she was in, by help of the tables Monsieur Cassini has given us in this volume [*Recueuil d'observations*

this interest derived his discovery of the rotation of Jupiter, the double ring of Saturn, and the third, fourth, fifth, sixth and eighth satellites of Saturn[35] for, as he suggests, astronomical observations of this sort were "incited" because of their practical implications. Lawrence Rooke, who was one of the original company constituting the Royal Society, often noted the "nautical value" of these observations.[36] Flamsteed frequently noticed the usefulness of observing the satellites of Jupiter, because their eclipses "have been esteemed, and certainly are a much better expedient for the discovery of the Longitude than any yet known."[37]

Newton was likewise deeply interested in the same general problem. Early in his career, he wrote a now famous letter of advice to his friend, Francis Aston, who was planning a trip on the Continent, in which he suggested among other particulars that Aston "inform himself whether pendulum clocks be of any service in finding out the longitude." In a correspondence which we have reason to believe ultimately led Newton to the completion of the *Principia,* both Halley and Hooke urged Newton to continue certain phases of his research because of its utility for navigation.[38]

---

faites en plusieurs Voiages pour perfectionner l'Astronomie & la Geographie], discovering with very great exactness the said Eclipses, beyond what we can yet hope to do by the Moon, tho' she seem to afford us the only means Practicable for the Seaman. However before Saylors can make use of the Art of finding the Longitude, it will be requisite that the Coast of the whole Ocean be first laid down truly, for which this Method by the Satellites is most apposite: And it may be discovered, by the time the Charts are compleeted; or else that some Invention of shorter Telescopes manageable on Ship-board may suffice to shew the Eclipses of the Satellites at Sea. . . .," *Phil. Trans.,* 1694, 17, 237-38. The latter part of this quotation definitely and lucidly illustrates the way in which scientific and technical research was "called forth" by practical needs. Worthy of note is the fact that Halley was commissioned by the Admiralty "to continue the Meridian as often as conveniently may be from side to side of the Channell, in order to lay down both coasts truly against one another" as well as to observe "the Course of the Tides in the Channell of England. . . ." See his letter of June 11, 1701 to Burchett in *Correspondence and Papers of Edmond Halley,* edited by E. F. MacPike (Oxford, 1932). 117-18.

35. The third (Tethys) and fourth (Dione) satellites were discovered in 1684; the fifth (Rhea) in 1672; the sixth (Titan) and eighth (Japetus) in 1671.

36. See "Mr. Rook's Discourse concerning the Observations of the Eclipses of the Satellites of Jupiter," reprinted in Sprat, *op. cit.,* 183-90. Rooke was Gresham professor of astronomy from 1652 to 1657 and Gresham professor of geometry from 1657 until his death in 1662.

37. *Phil. Trans.,* 1683, 12, 322. Flamsteed elaborated this view more pointedly in other papers on the same subject. See *Phil. Trans.,* 1685, 15, 1215; XVI (1686), p. 199; XIII (1683), p. 405-7. In passing it might be noted that Leibniz invented a portable watch "principally designed for the finding of the longitude." See his paper in *Phil. Trans.,* 675, 10, 285-88.

38. This is the type of evidence which G. N. Clark overlooks entirely when he writes that "the one piece of evidence which can be adduced to show that during his great creative period he [Newton] was actuated by an interest in technology is the letter to Francis Aston . . .," *op. cit.,* 67. See Hooke's letter to Newton (Jan. 6, 1680) in which he writes: ". . . the finding out the proprietys of a curve made by two such principles [one of which was the hypothesis of attraction varying inversely

In 1694, Newton sent his well-known letter to Nathanael Hawes outlining a new course of mathematical reading for the neophyte navigators in Christ's Hospital, in which he criticized the current course, saying in part, that "the finding the difference of Longitude, Amplitude, Azimuts, and variation of the compass is also omitted, tho these things are very useful in long voyages, such as are those to the East Indies, and a Mariner who knows them not is an ignorant."[39] In August, 1699, Newton made public an improved form of his sextant (independently invented by Hadley in 1731), which in conjunction with lunar observations might enable the finding of the longitude at sea. He had already presented the initial outlines of his lunar theory in the first edition of the *Principia.* Furthermore, it was upon Newton's recommendation that the Act of 1714 was passed for a reward to those persons who should devise a successful method for ascertaining longitude at sea.[40] In the course of these activities, Newton was demonstrating his awareness of the utilitarian implications not only of much of his own scientific work, but also that of his contemporaries.

Newton's lunar theory was the climactic outcome of scientific concentration on this subject. As Whewell suggests,

The advancement of astronomy would perhaps have been a sufficient motive for this labour; but there were other reasons which would urge it on with a stronger impulse. A perfect Lunar Theory, if the theory could be perfected, promised to supply a method of finding the Longitude of any place on the earth's surface; and thus the verification of a theory which professed to be complete in its foundations, was identified with an object of immediate practical use to navigators and geographers, and of vast acknowledged value.[41]

Halley, who had decided that the various methods of determining

---

as the square of the distance!] will be of great concerne to mankind because the invention of the longitude by the heavens is a necessary consequence of it." See the letter in W. W. Rouse Ball, *An Essay on Newton's Principa* (London, 1893) 147. Likewise, Halley, in his letter of July 5, 1687, writes: "I hope . . . you will attempt the perfection of the Lunar Theory, which will be of prodigious use in navigation, as well as of profound and subtle speculation." Complete letter is quoted *ibid.,* 174.

39. Newton's letters to Hawes are published in J. Edleston, *Correspondence of Sir Isaac Newton and Professor Cotes* (London, 1850), 279-99. An examination of the scientific preparation which Newton deemed necessary for a properly trained mariner finds that it includes a smattering of a substantial part of the physical research most prominently prosecuted during this period. In the list Newton mentions the subjects and problems with which not only he was chiefly concerned in the course of his own scientific career, but also his confreres. He indicates further that he was far from unaware of the practical bearings of the greater part of his abtruse discussions in the *Principia;* for example, his theory of the tides, the determination of the trajectory of projectiles, the lunar theory, his work in hydrostatics and hydrodynamics.

40. Edleston, *op. cit.,* LXXVI. The importance attributed to the solution of this problem may be gauged from the rewards offered by other governments as well. The Dutch had sought to persuade Galileo to apply his talents to its solution; Philip III of Spain also offered a reward and in 1716, the Regent Duke of Orleans established a prize of 100,000 francs for the discovery of a practical method.

41. William Whewell, *History of the Inductive Sciences* (New York, 1858), I, 434.

longitude were all defective and had declared that "it would be scarce possible ever to find the Longitude at sea sufficient for sea uses, till such time as the Lunar Theory be fully perfected," constantly prompted Newton to continue his work.[42] Flamsteed, and (from 1691 to 1739) Halley, also endeavored to rectify the lunar tables sufficiently to attain "the great object, of finding the Longitude with the requisite degree of exactness." Observations of the eclipses of the moon were recommended by the Royal Society for the same purpose.[43]

Another field of investigation which received added attention because of its probable utility is the study of the compass and magnetism in general. Thus, Sprat specifically relates such investigations by Wren to current needs when he states that "in order to Navigation he [Wren] has carefully pursu'd many Magnetical Experiments."[44] Wren himself, in his inaugural address as Gresham professor of astronomy, strikes the same keynote. The study of the magnetic variation is to be pursued diligently for it may prove of great value to the navigator, who may thus be enabled to find the longitude, "than which former Industry hath hardly left any Thing more glorious to be aim'd at in Art."[45] La Hire, remarking that nothing is so troublesome on long sea voyages as the variation of the needle, states that "this put me upon finding out some means independent from Observations to discover the variations at Sea."[46] Henry Bond, Hevelius, Molineux and Mercator were likewise interested in the study of magnetic phenomena with the same general aim in view.[47] Halley, in the famous paper in which he made known his theory of four magnetic poles and of the periodic movement of the magnetic line without declination, emphasized repeatedly the utilitarian desirability of studying the variation of the compass, for this research "is of that great concernment in the Art of Navigation: that the neglect thereof, does little less than render useless one of the noblest Inventions mankind has ever yet attained to." This great utility, he argues, seems a sufficient incitement "to all philosophical and Mathematical heads, to take under serious consideration the several Phenomena. . . ." He presents his new hypothesis in order to stir up the natural philosophers of the age that they might "apply themselves more attentively to this useful speculation."[48] Apparently the currently assiduous work in this field was not sufficient to satisfy his standards. It was for the purpose of enriching this useful speculation that Halley was given the rank of a captain in the

---

42. *Correspondence and Papers of Edmond Halley*, 212.

43. *Phil. Trans.*, 1693, 17, 453-54.

44. *History of the Royal-Society*, 315-16.

45. Christopher Wren, *Parentalia* (London, 1750), 206.

46. *Phil. Trans.*, 1687, 16, 344-50.

47. See *Phil. Trans.*, *passim*; *e.g.*, 1668, 3, 790; 1670, 5, 2059; 1674, 8, 6065.

48. "A Theory of the Variation of the Magnetical Compass," *Phil. Trans.*, XIII 1683, 13, 208-21. See also his addendum, *ibid.*, 1693, 17, 563-78.

navy and the command of the *Paramour Pink* in which he made three voyages. One outcome was Halley's construction of the first isogonic map.

Thus we are led to see that the scientific problems emphasized by the manifest value of a method for finding longitude were manifold. If the scientific study of various possible means of achieving this goal was not invariably dictated by the practical utility of the desired result, it is clear that at least part of the continued diligence exercised in these fields had this aim. In the last analysis it is impossible to determine with exactitude the extent to which practical concern focused scientific attention upon certain problems. What can be conscionably suggested is a certain correspondence between the subjects most intensively investigated by the contemporary men of science and the problems raised or emphasized by economic developments. It is an inference—usually supported by the explicit statements of the scientists themselves—that these economic requirements or, more properly, the technical needs deriving from these requirements, directed research into particular channels. The finding of the longitude was one problem which, engrossing the attention of many scientists, fostered profound developments in astronomy, geography, mathematics, mechanics, and the invention of clocks and watches.

NAVIGATION AND SCIENCE

Another navigational problem of the period was determining the time of the tides. As Flamsteed indicated in a note appended to his first tide-table, the error in the almanacs amounted to about two hours; hence a scientific correction was imperative for the Royal Navy and navigators generally.[49] Accordingly, from time to time, he drew up several tide-tables accommodated to ports not only in England but also in France and Holland. This work was the continuation of an interest in providing a theory of the tides emphasized by the Royal Society from its very inception. The first volume of the *Transactions* included several papers presenting observations of the time of the tides in various ports. Boyle, Samuel Colepresse, Joseph Childrey, Halley, Henry Powle, and most notably, John Wallis made contributions to this subject.

Newton took up the task as a further basis for the verification of the general law of attraction and, as Thomson remarks, "his theory of the tides is not less remarkable either for the sagacity involved, or for its importance to navigation." His theory accounted for the most evident aspects of the tides: the differences between the spring and neap tides and the morning and evening tides, the effect of the moon's and sun's declination and parallax, and the tides at particular places, making use of the observations of Halley, Colepresse and others to check his cal-

---

49. *Phil. Trans.*, 1683, 13, 10-15; for later tables see *ibid.*, 1684, 14, 458 and 821; 1685, 15, 1226; 1686, 16. 232 and 428.

culated results.[50] Halley, seeking as always to minister to the marriage of theory and practice, was not slow to inform the Lord High Admiral of the "generall use to all shipping" to be derived from these researches.[51] It was not, however, until the work of Euler, Bernoulli and D'Alembert, and later of Laplace, Lubbock and Airy, that the theory could be applied with sufficient precision to promise service for practical purposes. Again, one can correlate scientific interests—in this instance, the study of so esoteric a subject as the theory of attraction—with economic exigencies.

Another problem of grave concern for maritime affairs was the depletion of forest preserves to the point that eventually unseasoned wood had to be used in the construction of ships. Timber had become relatively scarce, both because of its use as fuel and its rapid consumption in the naval wars and in the rebuilding of London. The solution to the fuel problem was partially solved by the use of coal for various industries—such as brass and copper casting, brewing, dyeing and ironware, though not for the production of raw iron. The depletion of timber so jeopardized shipbuilding that the commissioners of the Royal Navy appealed to the Society for suggestions concerning the "improvement and planting of timber." Evelyn, Goddard, Merret, Winthrop, Ent and Willughby contributed their botanical knowledge toward the solution of this problem, their individual papers being incorporated in Evelyn's well-known *Sylva*. Not unrelated to such practical urgencies, then, is the fact that one of the "chief activities" of the Society was the "propagating of trees." Furthermore, says Sprat, the members of the Society "have employ'd much time in examining the Fabrick of ships, the forms of their Sails, the shapes of their Keels, the sorts of Timber, the planting of Firr, the bettering of Pitch, and Tarr, and Tackling."[52] This led not only to the study of silviculture and allied botanical studies, but also to investigations in mechanics, hydrostatics and hydrodynamics. For as Newton noted in his letters to Hawes, the solution of such problems as the determination of the stress of ropes and timber, the power of winds and tides and the resistance of fluids to immersed bodies of varying shapes would be of great utility for the mariner.

Moreover, when one compares the requisites of a man-of-war as enumerated by Sir Walter Ralegh in his *Observations on the Navy* at the beginning of the century with the types of research conducted by the Society, it becomes apparent that all the major problems had become the object of scientific study. Ralegh lists six desirable qualities of a fighting ship: strong build, speed, stout scantling, ability to fight the guns in all weathers, ability to lie easily in a gale, and ability to stay well. Contemporary scientists attempted to devise means of satisfying all these

50. *Principia Mathematica* (London, 1713; second edition), Bk. III, Prop. XXIV, XXXVI and XXXVII.

51. *Correspondence*, 116.

52. Sprat, *op. cit.*, 150.

requirements. In many instances they were led to solve derivative problems in "pure science" in the prospect of using their knowledge for these purposes. Thus, Goddard, Petty and Wren investigated methods of shipbuilding with the object of improving existing procedures. Hooke was ordered by the Society to determine the most "stout scantling" by testing the resistance of the "same kinds of wood, of several ages, grown in several places, and cut at different seasons of the year."[53] At times in coöperation with Boyle, Hooke performed numerous experiments to "try the strength of wood," and of twisted and untwisted cords. These experiments were in progress at the time Hooke arrived at the law which bears his name (*ut tensio sic vis.*)

In order to discover ways of increasing the speed of ships, it is necessary to study the movement of bodies in a resistant medium, one of the basic tasks of hydrodynamics.[54] Accordingly, Moray, Goddard, Brouncker, Boyle, Wren and Petty were concerned with this problem.[55] In this instance, the connection between a given technical task and the appropriate "purely scientific" investigation is explicit. Petty, at the time he wrote that "the fitts of the Double-Bottome [ship] do return very fiercely upon mee," experimented in hydrodynamics to determine the velocity of "swimming bodies." The general connection is established by Sprat in his description of the instruments of the Society:

> [There are] several instruments for finding the velocity of swimming Bodies of several Figures, and mov'd with divers strengths, and for trying what Figures are least apt to be overturn'd, in order to the making of a true theory, of the Forms of Ships, and Boats for all uses.[56]

Christopher Wren, who was for Newton one of "the greatest Geometers of our times," also investigated the laws of hydrodynamics precisely because of their possible utility for improving the sailing qualities of ships.[57] And Newton, after stating his theorem on the manner in which the resistance of a fluid medium depends upon the form of the body

---

53. Birch, *op. cit.,* I, 460.

54. *Cf.* Hessen, *op. cit.,* 158-59.

55. *The Petty-Southwell Correspondence,* ed. by the Marquis of Lansdowne (London, 1928), 117; Birch, *op. cit.,* I, 87.

56. Sprat, *op. cit.,* 250. See Hooke's letter to Boyle in the latter's *Works,* V, 537.

57. "It being a Question amongst the Problems of Navigation, very well worth resolving, to what Mechanical powers the Sailing (against the wind especially) was reducible; he [Wren] shew'd it to be a Wedge: And he demonstrated how a transient Force upon an oblique Plane, would cause the motion of the Plane against the first Mover. And he made an Instrument, that Mechanically produc'd the same effect, and shew'd the reason of Sayling to all Winds.

"The Geometrical Mechanics of Rowing, he shew'd to be a Vectis on a moving or cedent Fulcrum. For this end he made Instruments, to find what the expansion of Body was towards the hindrance of Motion in a Liquid Medium; and what degree of impediment was produc'd by what degree of expansion: with other things that are the necessary Elements for laying down the Geometry of Sailing, Swimming, Rowing, Flying, and the Fabricks of Ships." Sprat, *op. cit.,* 316. Once again we see how the immediate technical aim leads to the study of derivative problems in science.

moving in it, adds: "which proposition I conceive may be of use in the building of ships."[58]

The Society maintained a continued interest in under-water contrivances, ranging from diving bells to Hooke's proposal of a full-fledged submarine which would move as fast as a wherry on the Thames. A committee on diving considered leaden "diving boxes" and Halley's "diving bell," which were tested in the Thames and, with more convenience to the spectators than the diver, in a tub set up at one of their weekly meetings. Wilkins laid great stress on the feasibility and advantage of submarine navigation which would be of undoubted use in warfare, would obviate the uncertainty of tides and might be used to recover sunken treasures.[59] Hooke linked many of his experiments on respiration with technical problems deriving from such efforts.

Wilkins introduced the "umbrella anchor" to the Society; a device "to stay a ship in a storm." Wren proposed "a convenient way of using artillery on ship-board," and Halley, pointing out that England "must be masters of the Sea, and superior in navall force to any neighbour," described a method of enabling a ship to carry its guns in bad weather.[60] Petty, fondly hoping "to pursue the improvement of shipping upon new principles," built several of his double-bottomed boats with which the Society was well pleased. Unfortunately, his most ambitious effort, the *St. Michael the Archangel,* failed miserably, which led him to conclude that both the fates and the King were opposed to him.

The Society periodically discussed means of preserving ships "from worms," a problem which proved greatly disturbing both to the commissioners of the Royal Navy and to private shipowners. Newton had evidenced interest in this same vexing problem, asking Aston to determine "whether the Dutch have any tricks to keep their ships from being all worm-eaten." No appreciable progress resulted from these discussions, however.

In general, then, it may be said that the seventeenth century men of science, ranging from the indefatigable virtuoso Petty to the nonpareil Newton, definitely focused their attention upon technical tasks made urgent by problems of navigation and upon derivative scientific research. The latter category is difficult to delimit. Although it is true

---

58. *Principia Mathematica*, Bk. II, Sect. VII, Prop. XXXIV, Scholium. To my knowledge, Newton's remark has not been noticed heretofore in this connection. It reads: "Quam quidem propositionem in construendis Navibus non inutilem futuram esse censeo."

59. John Wilkins, *Mathematical Magick* (London, 1707; 5th edition), Ch. 5. As early as 1551, Tartaglia had suggested a largely effective means for raising sunken ships to the water's surface. Several patents had been granted for "diving engines" since at least 1631. By the help of one of these devices "and good luck," says Anderson, Sir William Phipps "fished up" nearly 200,000 pounds sterling in pieces of eight from a Spanish fleet which had been sunk off the West Indies. See *Origin of Commerce*, III, 73. Hooke and Halley, as well as several others, responded to this success with new devices for recovering treasures from the deep.

60. Wren, *Parentalia*, 240; *Correspondence . . . of Halley*, 165.

that a congeries of scientific research may be immediately traced to technical requirements, it appears equally evident that some of this research is a logical development of foregoing scientific advance. It is indubitable, however, in the light of what the scientists themselves had to say about the practical implications of their work, that practical problems exercised an appreciable directive influence. Even that "purest" of disciplines, mathematics, was of primary interest to Newton when designed for application to physical problems.[61]

Some attention was likewise paid to inland transportation although to a less extent than to maritime transport, possibly because of the greater economic significance of the latter. The growing interior traffic demanded considerable improvement. Such improvements, said Defoe, are "a great help to Negoce, and promote universal Correspondence without which our Inland Trade could not be managed."[62] Travelling merchants, who might carry as much as a thousand pounds of cloth, extended their trade all over England,[63] and required improved facilities. Because of the "great increase of carts, waggons, &c., by the general increase of our commerce," says Adam Anderson, the King (somewhat optimistically, no doubt) ordered in 1662 that all common highways be enlarged to eight yards. Characteristically, contemporary scientists also sought to overcome technical difficulties. Petty, with his keen interest in economic affairs, devised several chariots guaranteed to "passe rocks, precipices, and crooked ways."[64] Wren endeavored to perfect coaches for "ease, strength and lightness" and, as did Hooke, invented a "way-wiser" to register the distance travelled by a carriage.[65] Wilkins, possibly following Stevin's invention of a half century earlier, described a "sailing Chariot, that may without Horses be driven on the Land by the Wind, as ship are on the Sea."[66] Likewise, the Society delegated Hooke, at his own suggestion, to carry on "the experiment of land-carriage, and of a speedy conveying of intelligence."[67] Such efforts indicate the attempts of scientists to contribute technological props to business enterprise; in these particular instances to facilitate the possible extension of markets, one of the primary requirements of a nascent capitalism.

---

61. E. A. Burtt, *The Metaphysical Foundations of Modern Physical Science*, 210.

62. D[aniel] D[efoe], *Essays upon Several Projects* (London, 1702), 73 ff.

63. Daniel Defoe, *Tour of Great Britain*, (London, 1727), III, 119-20.

64. *Petty-Southwell Correspondence*, 41, 51 and 125. "And it seems to me [writes Petty] that this carriage can afford to carry fine goods between Chester and London for lesse than 3*d* in the pound." With all due honesty, Petty admits that this "Toole is not exempt from being overthrowne," but adds comfortingly, "but if it should bee overthrowne (even upon a heape of flints) I cannot see how the Rider can have any harme."

65. *Parentalia*, 199, 217 and 240.

66. Wilkins, *op. cit.*, Bk. II, Ch. 2.

67. Birch, *op. cit.*, I, 379 and 385; Hooke, *Diary*, 418. This subject was discussed at some fifteen meetings of the Society within a three-year period.

THE EXTENT OF ECONOMIC INFLUENCE

In a sense, the foregoing discussion provides materials which only illustrate the connections we have been tracing. We have still to determine the extent to which socio-economic influences were operative. The minutes of the Royal Society as transcribed in Birch's *History of the Royal Society* provide one basis for such a study. A feasible, though in several obvious respects inadequate, procedure consists of a classification and tabulation of the researches discussed at these meetings, together with an examination of the context in which the various problems came to light. This should afford some ground for deciding the *approximate* extent to which extrinsic factors operated.

Meetings during the four years 1661, 1662, 1686 and 1687 will be considered. There is no reason to suppose that these did not witness meetings typical of the general period. The classification employed is empirical rather than logically ordered. Items were classified as "directly related" to socio-economic demands when the individual conducting the research explicitly indicated some such connection or when the immediate discussion of the research evidenced a prior appreciation of such a relation. Items classified as "indirectly related" comprise researches which had a clear-cut connection with current practical needs, intimated in the context, but which were not definitely so related by the investigators. Researches which evidenced no relations of this sort were classified as "pure science." Many items have been classified in this category which have (for the present-day observer) a conceivable relation to practical exigencies but which were not so regarded explicitly in the seventeenth century. Thus, investigations in the field of meteorology could readily be related to the practical desirability of forecasting the weather but when these researches were not explicitly related to specific practical problems they were classified as pure science. Likewise, much of the work in anatomy and physiology was undoubtedly of value for medicine and surgery, but the same criteria were employed in the classification of these items. It is likely, therefore, that if any bias is involved in this classification, it is in the direction of over-estimating the scope of "pure science."

Each research discussed was "counted" as one "unit." It is obvious that this procedure provides only a gross approximation to the extent of extrinsic influences upon the selection of subjects for scientific study, but when greater precision is impossible one must rest temporarily content with less. The results, as summarized in the following tabulation, can merely suggest the relative extent of the influences which we have traced in a large number of concrete instances.[68]

---

68. For a more complete discussion of the procedure used and a detailed classification of the categories, see my *Science, Technology and Society in Seventeenth-Century England*, Ch. 10. Appendix A provides illustrations of the items classified in the various categories.

From this tabulation it appears that less than half (41.3%) of the investigations conducted during the four years in question are classifiable as "pure science." If we add to this the items which were but indirectly related to practical needs, then about seventy per cent of this research had no explicit practical affiliations. Since these figures are but grossly approximate, the results may be summarized by saying that from forty to seventy per cent occurred in the category of pure science and correlatively that from thirty to sixty per cent were influenced by practical requirements.

Again, considering only the research directly related to practical needs, it appears that problems of marine transport attracted the most attention. This is in accord with the impression that the contemporary men of science were well aware of the problems raised by England's insular position—problems both military and commercial in nature—and were eager to rectify them.[69] Of almost equal importance was the influence of military exigencies. Not only were there some fifty years of actual warfare during this century, but also the two great revolutions in English history. Problems of a military nature left their impress upon the culture of the period, including scientific development.

Likewise, mining which developed so markedly during this period, as we may see from the studies of Nef and other economic historians, had an appreciable influence. In this instance, the greater part of scientific, if one may divorce it from technologic, research was in the fields of

APPROXIMATE EXTENT OF SOCIO-ECONOMIC INFLUENCES UPON
THE SELECTION OF SCIENTIFIC PROBLEMS BY MEMBERS OF
THE ROYAL SOCIETY OF LONDON, 1661-62 AND 1686-87

	Number		Total for the four years Per cent	
Pure Science	333		41.3	
Science related to socio-economic needs	473		58.7	
Marine transport		129	16.0	
Directly related			69	8.6
Indirectly related			60	7.4
Mining		166	20.6	
Directly related			25	3.1
Indirectly related			141	17.5
Military technology		87	10.8	
Directly related			58	7.2
Indirectly related			29	3.6
Textile industry		26	3.2	
General technology and husbandry		65	8.1	
TOTAL	806		100.0	

69. See, for example, Edmond Halley's observation: "that the Inhabitants of an Island, or any State that would defend an Island, must be masters of the Sea, and superior in navall force to any neighbor that shall think fitt to attack it, is what I suppose needs no argument to enforce." In his paper read before the Royal Society and reprinted in *Correspondence . . . of Halley*, 164-65.

mineralogy and metallurgy with the aim of discovering new utilizable ores and new methods of extracting metals from the ore.

It is relevant to note that, in the latter years considered in this summary, there was an increasing proportion of investigation in the field of pure science. A conjectural explanation is not far to seek. It is probable that at the outset the members of the Society were anxious to justify their activities (to the Crown and the lay public generally) by obtaining practical results as soon as possible; therefore, the initially marked orientation toward practical problems. Furthermore, many of the problems which were at first advisedly investigated because of their utilitarian importance may later be studied with no awareness of their practical implications. On the basis of the (perhaps biased) criteria adopted in this compilation, some of the later researches would arbitrarily be classified as pure science.

On the grounds afforded by this study it seems justifiable to assert that the range of problems investigated by seventeenth century English scientists was appreciably influenced by the socio-economic structure of the period.

BIBLIOGRAPHICAL NOTE

I am indebted to the following editors and publishers for permission to reprint the papers in this volume:

Editors of the *American Sociological Review*
"The bearing of empirical research upon the development of social theory," 1948, volume 13.

Editors of the *American Journal of Sociology*
"Sociological theory," 1945, volume 50.

Harper and Brothers
"Social structure and anomie," from *The Family: Its Function and Destiny,* Ruth N. Anshen (editor), 1949.

"Patterns of influence: a study of interpersonal influence and of communications behavior in a local community," from *Communications Research 1948-49,* Paul F. Lazarsfeld and Frank Stanton (editors), 1949.

Editors of *Social Forces*
"Bureaucratic structure and personality," 1940, volume 18.
"The role of the intellectual in public bureaucracy," 1945, volume 23.

Editors of the *Antioch Review*
"The self-fulfilling prophecy," Summer 1948.

The Philosophical Library
"The sociology of knowledge," from *Twentieth Century Sociology,* G. Gurvitch and W. E. Moore (editors), 1945.

Editors of the *Journal of Liberal Religion*
"Karl Mannheim and the sociology of knowledge," 1941, volume 2.

New York Academy of Sciences
"Studies in radio and film propaganda," from *Transactions of the New York Academy of Sciences,* 1943, series II, volume 6.

Editors of *Philosophy of Science*
"Science and the social order," 1938, volume 5.

Editors of the *Journal of Legal and Political Sociology*
"Science and technology in a democratic order," 1942, volume 1.

Editors of *Science*

> "The machine, the worker and the engineer," 1947, volume 105.

Editors of the *Sociological Review*

> "Puritanism, Pietism and science," 1936, volume 28.

Editors of *Science and Society*

> "Science and the economy of 17th-century England," 1939, volume 3.

Random House

> For permission to quote from *The Collected Poetry of W. H. Auden,* 1945.

INDEX OF NAMES

SUBJECT INDEX

Academic man, role of, 485
Accidie, 188
Adaptation, individual, 139-141
Aggression, 136, 520
Alienation, 163
Alternative cultural goals, 183, 184
Altruism, 365
Ambiguity, intolerance of, 186-187
Ambivalence, 136
  in ex-member of group, 295-296
American dream, 136, 137
Anarchism, 121
Anhedonia, 189
Anomic factor, 165
Anomic pressures, family influence and, 179-180
Anomics, 162
Anomie, 109, 111, 135, 157-159, 267:
  acute, 63;
  class differentials in, 163;
  distinguished from value—conflict, 190-191;
  indicators of, 164-166;
  innovation as response to, 176-180, 181;
  need for data on, 175-176;
  objective scale of, 165-166, 175;
  as part of social processes, 180;
  psychological concept of, 161-162;
  as result of strains on mobility, 191-192;
  ritualism as adaptation to, 185-187;
  simple, 163;
  sociological concept of, 161, 162, 163;
  subjective scale of, 164-165, 175
Anomy, 161-162
Anticipatory socialization, 265-268; 290, 305, 384, 385;
  in context of mobility, 293;
  processes curbing, 269-270; 271
Anti-intellectualism, 539, 540
Anxiety, in de-grouping process, 274, 275
Apathy, 189-190
Aristocracy, 319
A-socialization, 270
Assimilation, 279
Attitude scales, 116

Audience, 482:
  in communications research, 450-452;
  measurement, 451;
  and social bases of knowledge, 482-483
Authority, in group, 339-340, 341, 342, 346-347, 348, 350, 353
Autism, 359
Autonomy, group, 322

Behavior, deviant,
  See Deviant behavior
Behavior, social, 121, 122, 140
Biological drives, 131, 133
Boomerang effect, in propaganda, 517-521
Boss, political, 72-76
Bourgeoisie, 191-192, 477
Breakage effect, 334
Bureaucracy, 125, 196, 200, 201, 212, 317:
  discipline in, 198-199, 200;
  displacement of goals in, 199-201;
  dysfunctions of, 197-200;
  as formal organization, 204-205;
  norm of impersonality in, 202-203;
  and personality types in, 205-206;
  power in, 195;
  as rationally organized social structure, 195-196;
  secrecy in, 197;
  trained incapacity in, 197-198, 202-203
Bureaucrat, relations with public, 202-204
Bureaucratic dysfunctions, 124
Bureaucratic personality, 123-124
Bureaucratic structure, 123-124
Bureaucratic virtuosos, 185
Bureaucratization, 196-197
Business class culture, 137-138

Categories: 447-480;
  morphological, 495;
  social, definition of, 299-300;
  of thought, social basis of, 472-475, 479-480, 489, 490
Catholics, and science, 593-595, 602